ECONOMICS & POLITICS

DICTIONARY • DICTIONNAIRE
English-French • Français-Anglais

HARRAP

First published in Great Britain in 2003
by Chambers Harrap Publishers Ltd
7 Hopetoun Crescent
Edinburgh EH7 4AY

©Chambers Harrap Publishers Ltd 2003

All rights reserved. No part of this
publication may be reproduced in any
form or by any means without the prior
permission of Chambers Harrap Publishers Ltd.

ISBN 0245 60715 3 (UK)
ISBN 0245 50507 5 (France)

www.harrap.co.uk
www.harrap.com

Dépôt légal : juillet 2003

Designed and typeset by Chambers Harrap Publishers Ltd, Edinburgh
Printed and bound in France by IFC

Editors/Rédactrices
Rachel Skeet
Anna Stevenson

with/avec
Nadia Cornuau
Georges Pilard

Publishing Manager/Direction éditoriale
Patrick White

Specialist Consultants/Consultants spécialistes

Sophie Gherardi
Rédactrice en chef de *Courrier
International*

Donald Rutherford
Department of Economics
University of Edinburgh

Prepress/Prépresse
David Kennedy
David Reid

Contents
Table des Matières

Preface

Developed and expanded from the databases used for **Harrap's French Business Dictionary** and **Harrap's Unabridged**, this book is the latest in the *Vie des Affaires* series. It aims to provide the user with comprehensive coverage of all the key terms relating to the fields of economics and politics.

Economics is a discipline with a rapidly-expanding lexicon; this book covers the vocabulary of microeconomics, macroeconomics and the major economic theories. Established key terms such as **balance of payments**, **diminishing returns** and **leads and lags** all have their place in this book. The field of politics is represented by terms covering fields such as party politics, voting systems and parliamentary procedure, along with newer terms such as **champagne socialism**, **influence peddling** and **New Labour**. Finally, the ongoing expansion of the European Union has led to a corresponding expansion in related vocabulary. Terms such as **codecision procedure**, **convergence criteria** and **pre-accession agreement** are all featured in this book.

As with all the dictionaries in this series, we have sought to help the reader by providing extra information in the form of **practical help** and **context.**

Practical help has been provided in the form of a two-part supplement containing detailed articles on the structures of the UK, US, French, Belgian and Swiss political systems, together with a feature on the institutions of the European Union. In addition, several panels integrated into the dictionary text provide encyclopedic information on world economic unions and the history of the European Union and its member states.

Context is provided for the more interesting terms or for those which are difficult to translate by the inclusion of hundreds of quotations from French and English newspapers, magazines and websites which illustrate the use of the relevant term in the real world.

Préface

Le présent ouvrage est le dernier titre en date de la série *La Vie des affaires*. Il a été conçu à partir des bases de données utilisées lors de l'élaboration du **Harrap's French Business Dictionary** et du **Harrap's Unabridged**. Il propose à l'utilisateur un traitement complet de tous les principaux termes ayant trait à l'économie et à la politique.

Le lexique lié à l'économie n'a cessé de croître au cours de ces dernières années. Cet ouvrage regroupe le vocabulaire se rapportant aussi bien à la micro et à la macro-économie qu'aux principales théories économiques. L'utilisateur y trouvera donc des termes clés tels que **balance commerciale**, **rendements décroissants** et **taux effectif global**. Le domaine politique est quant à lui représenté d'une part par des termes issus de la politique de parti, des systèmes électoraux et des procèdures parlementaires, tels que **jusqu'au-boutiste**, **navette parlementaire** et **panachage** et, d'autre part, par des expressions et des termes plus récents. Enfin, l'élargissement actuel de l'Union européenne génère simultanément une augmentation du vocabulaire lié à ce domaine. Des termes tels que **cours pivot**, **critères de convergence** et **pays pré-in** figurent tous dans ce livre.

Cet ouvrage, comme tous ceux de la collection *La Vie des affaires* de Harrap met l'accent sur **l'aide pratique à l'utilisateur** ainsi que sur **la mise en contexte**.

L'aide pratique à l'utilisateur se présente sous forme d'un supplément en deux parties contenant des informations détaillées sur la structure des systèmes politiques britannique, américain, français, belge et suisse, et d'un article sur les institutions de l'Union européenne. Par ailleurs, plusieurs encadrés intégrés au texte renseigneront l'utilisateur sur les unions économiques mondiales ainsi que sur l'histoire de l'Union européenne et de ses États membres.

La mise en contexte des termes les plus intéressants ou posant des problèmes de traduction est assurée par la présence de nombreuses citations extraites de journaux, de magazines et de sites Internet aussi bien en français qu'en anglais. Ces citations permettent de montrer comment les termes en question sont réellement utilisés.

Labels

Indications d'usage

gloss	=	glose
[introduces an explanation]		[introduit une explication]
cultural equivalent	≃	équivalent culturel
[introduces a translation which has a roughly equivalent status in the target language]		[introduit une traduction dont les connotations dans la langue cible sont comparables]

abbreviation	*abbr, abrév*	abréviation
adjective	*adj*	adjectif
adverb	*adv*	adverbe
North American English	*Am*	anglais américain
British English	*Br*	anglais britannique
Canadian French	*Can*	canadianisme
economics	*Econ, Écon*	économie
feminine	*f*	féminin
familiar	*Fam*	familier
masculine	*m*	masculin
masculine and feminine noun [same form for both genders, eg **libertarian** libertaire *mf*]	*mf*	nom masculin ou féminin [formes identiques]
masculine and feminine noun [different form in the feminine, eg **voter** électeur(trice) *m,f*]	*m,f*	nom masculin ou féminin [formes différentes]
noun	*n*	nom
feminine noun	*nf*	nom féminin
feminine plural noun	*nfpl*	nom féminin pluriel
masculine noun	*nm*	nom masculin
masculine and feminine noun [same form for both genders, eg **activiste** *nmf*]	*nmf*	nom masculin ou féminin [formes identiques]

masculine and feminine noun	*nm,f*	nom masculin ou féminin
[different form in the feminine, eg **militant, -e** *nm,f*]		[formes différentes]
masculine plural noun	*nmpl*	nom masculin pluriel
parliament	*Parl*	parlement
pejorative	*Pej, Péj*	péjoratif
plural	*pl*	pluriel
politics	*Pol*	politique
Swiss French	*Suisse*	helvétisme
verb	*v*	verbe
intransitive verb	*vi*	verbe intransitif
reflexive verb	*vpr*	verbe pronominal
transitive verb	*vt*	verbe transitif
inseparable transitive verb	*vt insep*	verbe transitif à particule inséparable [par exemple : **preside over** (présider): **to preside over a meeting** (présider une réunion)]
[phrasal verb where the verb and the adverb or preposition cannot be separated, eg **preside over**:to **preside** over a meeting]		
separable transitive verb	*vt sep*	verbe transitif à particule séparable [par exemple : **throw out** (rejeter); Parliament **threw out** the bill *ou* Parliament **threw** the bill **out** (le Parlement a rejeté le projet de loi)]
[phrasal verb where the verb and the adverb or preposition can be separated, eg **throw out**: Parliament **threw out** the bill *or* Parliament **threw** the bill **out**]		

English – French
Anglais – Français

AAUP n (abbr **American Association of University Professors**) = syndicat américain des professeurs d'université

abdicate 1 vt **to abdicate the throne** (of monarch) abdiquer
2 vi abdiquer

abdication n (of throne) abdication f

about-face, about-turn n Pol revirement m; **the government has been forced into an about-turn** le gouvernement a été contraint de faire volte-face

<blockquote>
A senior Labour MP has added his voice to health groups' anger at the government's **about-turn** on banning cigarette advertising. David Hinchcliffe, the chairman of the House of Commons select committee on health, joined anti-smoking group ASH in condemning the u-turn. The government's change of heart was confirmed by the omission from this morning's Queen's speech of the tobacco advertising bill. "I am shocked and disappointed that, after what ministers have said about the importance of this legislation, it is now being shelved," said Mr Hinchcliffe.
</blockquote>

absentee n
◇ Pol **absentee ballot** vote m par correspondance; **to vote by absentee ballot** voter par correspondance

◇ Pol **absentee voter** électeur(trice) m,f votant par correspondance

absolute adj
◇ Econ **absolute advantage** avantage m absolu
◇ Econ **absolute efficiency** efficience f absolue, efficacité f parfaite
◇ Econ **absolute income hypothesis** hypothèse f de revenu absolu (hypothèse selon laquelle l'espérance de vie d'un individu est proportionnelle à ses revenus)
◇ Pol **absolute majority** majorité f absolue
◇ Pol **absolute majority vote** scrutin m majoritaire à majorité absolue
◇ **absolute monarch** souverain(e) m,f absolu(e)
◇ **absolute monarchy** monarchie f absolue
◇ Pol **absolute personal power** pouvoir m personnel
◇ Pol **absolute power** pouvoir m absolu
◇ **absolute ruler** autocrate m
◇ Pol **absolute veto** véto m formel

absolutism n Pol absolutisme m

absolutist Pol **1** n absolutiste mf
2 adj absolutiste

absorb vt (company) absorber, incorporer

absorption n (of company) absorption f, incorporation f

abstain vi Pol s'abstenir; **ten members voted for the proposal and three abstained** dix députés ont voté pour le projet et trois se sont abstenus

abstainer n Pol abstentionniste mf

abstention n Pol abstention f

abstentionist n Pol abstentionniste mf

abundance n Econ abondance f

abuse of privilege n Parl abus m de droit

ACAS n (abbr **Advisory, Conciliation and Arbitration Service**) = organisme britannique de conciliation et d'arbitrage des conflits du travail, ≃ conseil m de prud'hommes

accede vi (a) **to accede to the throne** monter sur le trône; **to accede to office** entrer en fonction; **both countries aim to accede to the EU in 2007** les deux pays ont pour objectif de devenir membres de l'UE en 2007 (b) **to accede to a treaty** adhérer à un traité

acceleration principle n Econ principe m d'accélération

accelerator n Econ accélérateur m

◇ **accelerator principle** principe m d'accélération

acceptance speech n (by president, leader) discours m de réception

access barrier n Econ barrière f d'accès

accession n (a) (to office, position, power) accession f (**to** à); **Queen Victoria's accession (to the throne)** l'accession au trône ou l'avènement de la reine Victoria; **Greece's accession to the EU** l'accession de la Grèce au statut de membre de l'UE (b) (to treaty) adhésion f (**to** à)

◇ EU **accession country** pays m en phase d'adhésion

accord n Pol (agreement) accord m; (treaty) traité m; **to reach an accord** parvenir à un accord

accountability n (responsibility) responsabilité f (**to** envers); **the public wants more government accountability** le public attend du gouvernement qu'il réponde davantage de la politique qu'il mène

accountable adj (responsible) responsable (**to** envers); **government ministers are accountable to the legislature** les ministres du gouvernement ont des comptes à rendre au corps législatif

accredit vt (official) accréditer; **the ambassador accredited to Morocco** l'ambassadeur accrédité au Maroc

accredited adj (official) accrédité(e), autorisé(e); **the accredited representative to the United Nations** le représentant accrédité aux Nations unies

ACLU n Pol (abbr **American Civil Liberties Union**) = ligue américaine des droits du citoyen

ACP Group n Pol (abbr **African, Caribbean and Pacific Group of States**) Groupe m ACP

ACPO n (abbr **Association of Chief Police Officers**) = syndicat d'officiers supérieurs de la police britannique

acquis communautaire n EU acquis m communautaire

act n (a) Pol acte m, loi f (b) (deed) acte m

◇ **act of Congress** acte m du Congrès

◇ **act of Parliament** acte m du Parlement

◇ **act of State** acte m du gouvernement

◇ **act of terrorism** acte m de terrorisme

◇ **act of war** acte m de guerre

acting adj (temporary) intérimaire, par intérim

◇ **acting prime minister** Premier ministre m intérimaire, Premier ministre m par intérim

action group n Pol groupe m de pression

active adj actif(ive); **to be politically active** être engagé(e)

◇ Pol **active minority** minorité f agissante

activism n Pol activisme m

activist n Pol militant(e) m,f, activiste mf

activity n (in business, market) activité f
◊ **activity indicator** indicateur m d'activité

additionality n Econ additionnalité f

additional member system n Pol = mode de scrutin en vigueur au pays de Galles et en Écosse selon lequel les électeurs votent deux fois: d'abord pour un candidat représentant leur circonscription locale puis au niveau régional, pour la liste d'un parti ou pour un candidat indépendant

address 1 n (speech) discours m
2 vt (speak to) s'adresser à; **the PM will address the US Congress next week** le Premier ministre s'adressera au Congrès américain la semaine prochaine

adhere vi **to adhere to a political party** adhérer à un parti politique

adherence n (to political party) adhésion f (**to** à)

adherent n (to political party) adhérent(e) m,f; **she was an adherent to the Republican party** elle était membre du parti Républicain

adjourn Pol **1** vt (debate, meeting) (interrupt) suspendre; (defer) ajourner, remettre, reporter; **the president adjourned the meeting** (closed) le président a levé la séance
2 vi (a) (of person, committee) (interrupt) suspendre la séance; (defer) ajourner la séance; (close) lever la séance (b) (of debate, meeting) (be interrupted) être suspendu(e); (be deferred) être ajourné(e); (be closed) être levé(e)

adjournment n Pol (of debate, meeting) (interruption) suspension f; (deferral) ajournement m; (closure) levée f; **to call for an adjournment** (interruption) demander une suspension de séance; (deferral) demander un ajournement; Parl **to move the adjournment** (seek closure) demander la clôture

◊ Br Parl **adjournment debate** = débat de clôture à la Chambre des Communes

adjust vt Econ (prices, salaries, currency, statistics) ajuster

adjustment n Econ (of prices, salaries, currency, statistics) ajustement m

administer vt (manage) (business, institution) diriger, administrer, gérer; (finances, fund) gérer; (country, territory, public institution) administrer

administered adj
◊ Econ **administered price** prix m imposé
◊ Econ **administered pricing** fixation f des prix par le gouvernement

administration n (a) (process) (of business, institution) direction f, administration f, gestion f; (of finances, fund) gestion f; (of country, territory, public institution) administration f
(b) (people) (of business, institution) direction f, administration f; (of country, territory, public institution) administration f
(c) Am Pol **the Administration** le gouvernement; **under the last Administration** sous le dernier gouvernement; **the Bush Administration** le gouvernement Bush

administrative adj administratif(-ive)
◊ **administrative body** corps m administratif
◊ Br **the administrative grade** (in civil service) les fonctionnaires mpl supérieurs
◊ **administrative headquarters** siège m administratif
◊ **administrative structures** structures fpl administratives

administrator n administrateur(-trice) m,f

admission n admission f; **the admission of Turkey into the European Union** l'admission de la Turquie dans l'Union européenne

admit vt admettre; **two more countries will be admitted into the EU next year** deux pays supplémentaires seront admis dans l'Union européenne l'année prochaine

adopt vt Pol (a) (bill, motion) adopter (b) (candidate) sélectionner

adoption n Pol (a) (of bill, motion) adoption f (b) (of candidate) sélection f

ADR n Econ (abbr **American Depositary Receipt**) certificat m américain de dépôt

ad valorem adj Econ (rights, tax) proportionnel(elle)

advanced country n pays m avancé, pays m industrialisé

advance man n Am Pol organisateur m de la publicité (pour une campagne politique)

He won a dark-horse campaign to be senior class president and wrote "an embarrassing letter" to then President Clinton "as one president to another" asking for a summer job. He got it, then interrupted his senior year to accept a full-time job as a White House **advance man** – planning the President's political trips by scouting locations and planning face-to-face meetings with governors, senators, mayors, international dignitaries, and the media.

advantage n Econ avantage m

adviser, Am **advisor** n conseiller(ère) m,f

advisory adj (board, committee) consultatif(ive)

advocate n
◇ EU **advocate general** avocat m général
◇ Pol **Advocate General for Scotland** = conseiller principal du gouvernement pour le droit écossais

AEEU n (abbr **Amalgamated Engineering and Electrical Union**) = syndicat britannique de l'industrie mécanique

affairs of state npl Pol affaires fpl d'État

affirmative action n Am Pol mesures fpl d'embauche anti-discriminatoires (en faveur des minorités); **to take affirmative action** prendre des mesures anti-discriminatoires

"They've essentially ratified **affirmative action**. They're looking high and low for Hispanics they can bring into the administration and the Republican party. The Republicans learned in the 1990s that if you look hostile to blacks, it will hurt you with white women." Bush can hardly look hostile to black people – no administration in history has had two, Powell and Rice, among its five most influential figures.

AFGE n (abbr **American Federation of Government Employees**) = syndicat américain de fonctionnaires

AFL-CIO n (abbr **American Federation of Labor and Congress of Industrial Organizations**) = la plus grande confédération syndicale américaine

African adj
◇ Pol **African, Caribbean and Pacific Group of States** Groupe m des États d'Afrique, des Caraïbes et du Pacifique
◇ Pol **African National Congress** Congrès m national africain, ANC m
◇ Pol **African Union** Union f africaine

AFSA n (abbr **American Federation of School Administrators**) = syndicat américain du personnel administratif des établissements scolaires

AFSCME n (abbr **American Federation of State, County and Municipal Employees**) = syndicat américain des travailleurs du service public et du secteur de la santé

AFSJ n EU (abbr **Area of Freedom, Security and Justice**) ELSJ m

AFT n (abbr **American Federation of Teachers**) = syndicat américain d'enseignants

agency n service m, bureau m
◇ Am **Agency for International Development** = agence américaine pour le développement international

agenda n (of government) programme m; **the problem of the homeless doesn't come very high on the government's agenda** le problème des sans-abri ne figure pas parmi les priorités du gouvernement; **to set the agenda** mener le jeu
◇ EU **Agenda 2000** Agenda m 2000
◇ **agenda setting** = fait d'influencer la direction d'un débat

> **"**
>
> The managers of global institutions also enjoy considerable **agenda setting** power, affecting not just which issues are debated but, more critically, when they are brought forward ... And in international financial institutions like the World Bank and the IMF, leaders can exert heavy influence over the global distribution of enormous financial resources.
>
> **"**

agglomeration economy n Econ économie f d'agglomération

aggregate Econ **1** n agrégat m
2 adj global(e)
◇ **aggregate demand** demande f globale
◇ **aggregate demand curve** courbe f de la demande globale
◇ **aggregate economic activity** ensemble m des activités économiques
◇ **aggregate expenditure** dépenses fpl globales
◇ **aggregate output** production f globale

◇ **aggregate supply** offre f globale
◇ **aggregate supply curve** courbe f de l'offre globale

agitate vi Pol **to agitate for/against sth** faire campagne en faveur de/contre qch; **they are agitating for better working conditions** ils réclament de meilleures conditions de travail

agitation n Pol (unrest) agitation f, troubles mpl; (campaign) campagne f mouvementée; **there was a lot of agitation in favour of nuclear disarmament** il y avait un fort mouvement de contestation pour réclamer le désarmement nucléaire

agitator n Pol agitateur(trice) m,f

agitprop n Pol agit-prop f

agree 1 vt (reach agreement on) convenir de; **the budget has been agreed** le budget a été adopté
2 vi (reach agreement) se mettre d'accord (**about** sur)

agreed statement n (in the media) déclaration f commune

agreement n Pol accord m; **under the (terms of the) agreement** selon les termes de l'accord

agribusiness n agro-industrie f

agricultural adj agricole
◇ **agricultural cooperative** coopérative f agricole
◇ **agricultural economics** agro-économie f
◇ **agricultural economy** économie f du secteur agricole
◇ EU **agricultural levies** prélèvements mpl agricoles
◇ **agricultural minister** ministre m de l'agriculture

agriculture n agriculture f

AID n Am (abbr **Agency for International Development**) = agence américaine pour le développement international

aid Pol **1** n (to developing countries, for disaster relief) aide f; **the government gives aid to depressed areas** le gou-

vernement octroie des aides aux régions en déclin

2 vt (industry, region) aider, soutenir

◇ **aid agency** organisation f humanitaire

◇ **aid organization** organisation f humanitaire

aide n Pol (to president, minister)
conseiller(ère) m,f

alienate vt Pol aliéner; **this tax will
alienate the people** avec cet impôt, ils
vont s'aliéner la population; **no government wishes to alienate voters** aucun gouvernement ne souhaite
s'aliéner les électeurs

alienated adj Pol aliéné(e)

alienation n Pol aliénation f; **this
measure resulted in the alienation of
many of the party's traditional voters**
avec cette mesure, le parti s'est aliéné
une grande partie de son électorat
traditionnel

align Pol **1** vt aligner; **to align oneself
with sb** s'aligner sur qn

2 vi s'aligner; **to align with sb** s'aligner sur qn

alignment n Pol alignement m

allegiance n Pol allégeance f; **to
swear allegiance (to sb)** faire serment
d'allégeance (à qn); **to switch allegiance** changer de bord

❝

Throughout almost 18 years of
Conservative government, the Sun
was the flagship journal for Thatcher's and, to a lesser extent, Major's
political agenda. But once News International **switched allegiance** to
Blair and New Labour in 1997, it
went after the Tories with a ven-
geance, running banner headlines
on every sexual peccadillo it found
among their ranks.

❞

alliance n (agreement) alliance f; **to enter into** or **to form an alliance with sb**
s'allier avec qn, faire alliance avec qn

allied adj **(a)** Pol (unions, nations) al-
lié(e) **(b)** Econ (product, industry) assi-
milé(e)

all-night adj **an all-night sitting of Parliament** une session parlementaire de
nuit

allocative efficiency n Econ efficacité f d'allocation

allowance n (paid to MPs) indemnité
f

all-party adj Pol

◇ **all-party committee** = comité où
tous les partis sont représentés

◇ **all-party talks** = discussions entre
tous les partis

❝

Seeking to end the impasse, Major
and Irish Prime Minister John Bruton
jointly proposed an election as a
prelude to **all-party talks** that
would begin on June 10. Under his
plan, voters in each of the 18 parliamentary constituencies located in
Northern Ireland will cast ballots for
political parties, and the top five
vote-getters in each constituency
will send delegates to the forum ...
Each party represented will then select from its delegates a negotiating
team for the June 10 **all-party
talks**; the forum itself will have no
role in those talks.

❞

ally Pol **1** n allié(e) m,f; **to become allies**
s'allier; **the two countries were allies**
les deux pays étaient alliés

2 vt allier, unir; **to ally oneself with sb**
s'allier avec qn; **we must ally ourselves
with other unions** nous devons nous
allier à ou nous associer avec d'autres
syndicats

alternat n Pol alternat m

alternate Pol **1** vt alterner
2 vi alterner

alternative vote n Pol = mode de
scrutin en vigueur en Australie selon
lequel les électeurs numérotent les

candidats par ordre de préférence sur le bulletin de vote

AM n Pol (abbr **(Welsh) Assembly Member**) membre m de l'assemblée galloise

amalgamate 1 vt (companies, industries, unions) fusionner
2 vi (of companies, industries, unions) fusionner

amalgamated union n fédération f de syndicats

amalgamation n (of companies, industries) fusion f; (of unions) fédération f

ambassador n ambassadeur(drice) m,f; **the Spanish ambassador to Morocco** l'ambassadeur d'Espagne au Maroc
◇ **ambassador extraordinary** ambassadeur(drice) m,f extraordinaire
◇ **ambassador extraordinary and plenipotentiary** ambassadeur(drice) m,f extraordinaire et plénipotentiaire
◇ **ambassador plenipotentiary** ambassadeur(drice) m,f plénipotentiaire

ambassador-at-large n Am ambassadeur(drice) m,f extraordinaire, chargé(e) m,f de mission

ambassadorial adj d'ambassadeur

ambassadorship n fonction f d'ambassadeur

ambassadress n ambassadrice f

amend vt Pol (bill, constitution) amender

amendable adj Pol (bill, constitution) amendable

amendment n Pol (to bill, constitution) amendement m; **an amendment to the law** une révision de la loi; **to move an amendment (to sth)** proposer un amendement (à qch); **the third/fourteenth Amendment** (to the American Constitution) le troisième/quatorzième amendement

American adj

◇ Pol **American Civil Liberties Union** = ligue américaine des droits du citoyen
◇ Econ **American Depositary Receipt** certificat m américain de dépôt

AMICUS n = syndicat industriel britannique né de la fusion de l'AEEU et du MSF

AMS n Pol (abbr **additional member system**) = mode de scrutin en vigueur au pays de Galles et en Écosse selon lequel les électeurs votent deux fois: d'abord pour un candidat représentant leur circonscription locale puis au niveau régional, pour la liste d'un parti ou pour un candidat indépendant

AMU n (abbr **Arab Maghreb Union**) UMA f

ANA n (a) (abbr **American Newspaper Association**) = syndicat américain de la presse écrite (b) (abbr **American Nurses Association**) = syndicat américain d'infirmiers

analysis n Econ & Pol analyse f

analyst n (a) Pol analyste mf politique (b) Econ économiste-statisticien(enne) m,f

anarchic, anarchical adj Pol anarchique

anarchism n Pol anarchisme m

anarchist n Pol anarchiste mf

anarchistic adj Pol anarchiste

anarchize vt Pol anarchiser

anarcho-syndicalism n Pol anarcho-syndicalisme m

anarcho-syndicalist Pol **1** n anarcho-syndicaliste mf
2 adj anarcho-syndicaliste

anarchy n Pol anarchie f

ANC n Pol (abbr **African National Congress**) ANC m

Anglo-Irish agreement n Pol = accord conclu en 1985 entre le Royaume-Uni et la république d'Irlande pour garantir la paix et la stabilité en Irlande du Nord

annex *vt Pol* annexer (**sth to sth** qch à qch); **part of their territory has been annexed** une partie de leur territoire a été annexé

annexation *n Pol* annexion *f*

annexational *adj Pol* annexionniste

annexationism *n Pol* annexionnisme *m*

annexationist *n Pol* annexionniste *mf*

announce 1 *vt* annoncer; **the PM has announced that there will be a general election this year** le Premier ministre a annoncé qu'il y aurait des élections législatives cette année

2 *vi Am Pol* **to announce for the presidency** se déclarer candidat(e) à la présidence

> But Bush never mentioned campaign finance reform when he **announced for the presidency**, didn't talk about it when he first came to Iowa or New Hampshire. Now the Texas Governor, who's raised and spent more money than any presidential candidate ever, is promising wholesale reform.

annual percentage rate, annualized percentage rate *n Econ* taux *m* effectif global

annul *vt Pol (law)* abroger, abolir

annulment *n Pol (of law)* abrogation *f*, abolition *f*

anti-American *adj* antiaméricain(e)

anti-Americanism *n* antiaméricanisme *m*

antiapartheid *adj Pol* antiapartheid

anticapitalism *n Pol* anticapitalisme *m*

anticapitalist *Pol* **1** *n* anticapitaliste *mf*
2 *adj* anticapitaliste

anticlerical *Pol* **1** *n* anticlérical(e) *m,f*
2 *adj* anticlérical(e)

anticlericalism *n Pol* anticléricalisme *m*

anticolonial *adj Pol* anticolonial(e)

anticolonialism *n Pol* anticolonialisme *m*

anticolonialist *adj Pol* **1** *n* anticolonialiste *mf*
2 *adj* anticolonialiste

anticommunism *n Pol* anticommunisme *m*

anticommunist *Pol* **1** *n* anticommuniste *mf*
2 *adj* anticommuniste

anticompetitive *adj Econ* anticoncurrentiel(elle)

anticonstitutional *adj Pol* anticonstitutionnel(elle)

antidemocratic *adj Pol* antidémocratique

antidumping *adj (law, legislation)* antidumping

anti-Establishment *adj Pol* anticonformiste

antifascism *n Pol* antifascisme *m*

antifascist *Pol* **1** *n* antifasciste *mf*
2 *adj* antifasciste

antiglobalization *Pol* **1** *n* antimondialisation *f*
2 *adj* d'antimondialisation

antigovernment *adj Pol* antigouvernemental(e)

anti-imperialism *n Pol* anti-impérialisme *m*

anti-imperialist *Pol* **1** *n* anti-impérialiste *mf*
2 *adj* anti-impérialiste

anti-inflationary *adj Econ* anti-inflationniste

antimarketeer *n Br Pol* adversaire *mf* du Marché commun

antimilitarism *n Pol* antimilitarisme *m*

antimilitarist *Pol* **1** *n* antimilitariste *mf*
  2 *adj* antimilitariste

antimonarchical *adj* antimonarchique

antimonarchist 1 *n* antimonarchiste *mf*
  2 *adj* antimonarchiste

antimonopoly *adj Br Econ (law, legislation)* antitrust

antinational *adj Pol* antinational(e)

antinationalism *n Pol* antinationalisme *m*

antiparliamentarianism, antiparliamentarism *n Pol* antiparlementarisme *m*

antiparliamentary *adj Pol* antiparlementaire

antiparty *adj Pol* antiparti

antiprotectionist *Pol* **1** *n* antiprotectionniste *mf*
  2 *adj* antiprotectionniste

antirepublican *Pol* **1** *n* antirépublicain(e) *m,f*
  2 *adj* antirépublicain(e)

antislavery *adj Pol* antiesclavagiste

antisystem party *n Pol* = parti politique qui s'oppose au système dans lequel il opère

antiterrorist *adj* antiterroriste

antitrust *adj Econ (law, legislation)* antitrust

apartheid *n Pol* apartheid *m*
◇ *apartheid laws* lois *fpl* de l'apartheid

APC *n Econ (abbr* **average propensity to consume)** PmaC

APEC *n (abbr* **Asia-Pacific Economic Co-operation)** APEC *f*

apolitical *adj* apolitique

apparatchik *n Pol* apparatchik *m*

apparent consumption *n Econ* consommation *f* apparente

appease *vt Pol* apaiser

appeasement *n Pol* apaisement *m*

applicant country *n EU* pays *m* candidat

appoint *vt Pol (person)* nommer, désigner; *(committee)* constituer, nommer

appointment *n Pol (of person, committee)* nomination *f*, désignation *f*; *(office filled)* poste *m*; *(posting)* affectation *f*; **his appointment to the office of Lord Chancellor** sa nomination au poste de grand chancelier

apportion *vt Pol (seats)* répartir

apportionment *n Pol (of seats)* répartition *f*

appropriation *n Am Pol* crédit *m* budgétaire
◇ *appropriations bill* projet *m* de loi de finances
◇ *Appropriations Committee* = commission des finances de la Chambre des Représentants qui examine les dépenses

approval *n (of document, treaty, decision)* ratification *f*, homologation *f*
◇ *Pol* **approval rating** *(of politician)* cote *f* de popularité
◇ *Pol* **approval voting** vote *m* par approbation *(mode de scrutin où les électeurs peuvent voter pour autant de candidats qu'ils le désirent mais n'ont pas le droit de donner plus d'une voix à chaque candidat)*

> **"**
>
> President Bush has reversed the slip in his **approval rating** and is turning his attention to new health care, privacy and education proposals. After hitting a low of 52% two weeks ago, Bush's **approval rating** rebounded to 57% in a USA TODAY/CNN/Gallup Poll taken this week. At the same point in Bill Clinton's presidency in 1993, Clinton's **approval rating** was 45%.
>
> **"**

approve vt (document, treaty, decision) ratifier, homologuer; **approved by the government** agréé(e) par l'État

APR n Econ (abbr **annual** or **annualized percentage rate**) TEG m

APS n Econ (abbr **average propensity to save**) PmaE

APWU n (abbr **American Postal Workers Union**) = syndicat américain de postiers

Arab League n Pol **the Arab League** la Ligue arabe

arbitrage n Econ arbitrage m

arbitrate 1 vt arbitrer, juger
2 vi décider en qualité d'arbitre, arbitrer

arbitration n arbitrage m; **to go to arbitration** (of union) soumettre le différend à l'arbitrage; (of dispute) être soumis à l'arbitrage; **they referred the dispute to arbitration** ils ont soumis le conflit à l'arbitrage; **settlement by arbitration** règlement m par arbitrage
◇ **arbitration board** commission f d'arbitrage
◇ **arbitration clause** clause f compromissoire
◇ **arbitration court** instance f chargée d'arbitrer les conflits sociaux, tribunal m arbitral
◇ **arbitration tribunal** instance f chargée d'arbitrer les conflits sociaux, tribunal m arbitral

arbitrator n arbitre m, médiateur(-trice) m,f; **the dispute has been referred to the arbitrator** le litige a été soumis à l'arbitrage

arm 1 n **(a)** Pol (section) section f, branche f; **Sinn Fein is the political arm of the IRA** Sinn Fein est la section politique de l'IRA **(b)** (weapon) arme f
2 vt (country) armer
◇ Pol **arms control** contrôle m des armements
◇ Pol **arms control agreement** accord m de contrôle des armements
◇ Pol **arms embargo** embargo m sur les armes

◇ Pol **arms expenditure** dépenses fpl en armes
◇ Pol **arms limitation** limitation f des armements
◇ Pol **arms limitation talks** négociations fpl pour la limitation des armements
◇ Pol **arms proliferation** prolifération f des armes
◇ Pol **arms race** course f aux armements
◇ Pol **arms sales** ventes fpl d'armes

armed peace n paix f armée

army n armée f
◇ **army of occupation** armée f d'occupation

arrangement n (agreement) arrangement m

ASEAN n (abbr **Association of South East Asian Nations**) ANASE f, ANSEA f

Asia-Pacific Economic Cooperation n Coopération f économique des pays d'Asie-Pacifique

ASLEF n (abbr **Associated Society of Locomotive Engineers and Firemen**) = syndicat des cheminots en Grande-Bretagne

assassin n assassin m

assassinate vt assassiner

assassination n assassinat m
◇ **assassination attempt** attentat m

assembly n Pol assemblée f

assemblyman n Am Pol = homme qui siège à une assemblée législative

assemblywoman n Am Pol = femme qui siège à une assemblée législative

assentor n Br Pol = signataire à l'appui d'un candidat aux élections gouvernementales

assent procedure n EU procédure f de l'avis conforme

assets npl actif m; **the assets amount to £5 million** l'actif s'élève à cinq millions de livres

Assistant Whip n Br Pol = assistant du parlementaire chargé de la discipline de son parti et qui veille à ce que ses députés participent aux votes

association n (organization) association f
◇ **association agreement** accord m d'association
◇ **Association of South East Asian Nations** Association f des nations de l'Asie du Sud-Est

asylum n asile m; **to seek asylum** demander l'asile; **he was granted/refused asylum** on lui a accordé/refusé l'asile; **the right to** or **of asylum** le droit d'asile

asylum-seeker n demandeur(euse) m,f d'asile

asymmetric information n Econ information f asymétrique

ATL n (abbr **Association of Teachers and Lecturers**) = syndicat d'enseignants en Angleterre, au pays de Galles et en Irlande du Nord

Atlanticism n atlantisme m

attaché n Pol attaché(e) m,f

Attorney General n Pol (in England, Wales and Northern Ireland) = principal avocat de la couronne; (in US) ≃ ministre m de la Justice, garde m des Sceaux

attrition n Econ attrition f, départs mpl volontaires

ATU n (abbr **Amalgamated Transit Union**) = syndicat américain et canadien des travailleurs du secteur des transports

auction n (vente f aux) enchères fpl; **to sell sth at** or **by auction** vendre qch aux enchères

austereness = austerity

austerity n Econ austérité f, pratique f austère
◇ **austerity measures** mesures fpl d'austérité
◇ **austerity policy** politique f d'austérité

◇ **austerity programme** plan m d'austérité

AUT n (abbr **Association of University Teachers**) = syndicat britannique d'enseignants universitaires

autarchy n Pol autocratie f

autarkic adj Econ & Pol autarcique

autarky n Econ & Pol (a) (system) autarcie f (b) (country) pays m en autarcie

authoritarian Pol **1** n autoritaire mf **2** adj autoritaire

authoritarianism n Pol autoritarisme m

authority n (a) (power) autorité f, pouvoir m; **those in authority in Haiti** ceux qui gouvernent en Haïti (b) (people in command) autorité f; Pol **the authorities** les autorités fpl, l'administration f; **the proper authorities** qui de droit, les autorités compétentes

autocentric adj Econ autocentré(e)

autocracy n Pol (absolute rule) autocratie f; Pej (dictatorship) dictature f

autocrat n Pol (absolute ruler) autocrate m; Pej (dictator) despote mf

autocratic adj Pol (ruler) absolu(e); (government, policies) autocratique; Pej (dictator) despotique

autocratically adv Pol (rule) autocratiquement; Pej (dictatorially) despotiquement

automatic stabilizer n Econ stabilisateur m automatique

autonomous adj Pol autonome
◇ Econ **autonomous consumption** consommation f autonome
◇ Econ **autonomous investment** investissement m autonome

autonomy n Pol (a) (self-government) autonomie f (b) (country) pays m autonome

Autumn Statement n Br Formerly Parl = document remis au Parlement par le gouvernement britannique, généralement en novembre, traitant des prévisions économiques et des dépenses publiques pour les trois années à venir

AV *n Pol* (*abbr* **alternative vote**) = mode de scrutin en vigueur en Australie selon lequel les électeurs numérotent les candidats par ordre de préférence sur le bulletin de vote

availability *n Am Pej Pol* (*of candidate*) = caractère inoffensif; **they've settled for availability rather than greatness in their candidate** ils ont décidé de présenter un candidat qui inspire la confiance plutôt que l'admiration

available *adj Am Pej Pol* (*candidate*) sûr(e) (*en raison de son caractère inoffensif*)

average 1 *n* moyenne *f*
2 *adj* moyen(enne)
3 *vt* (**a**) (*find the average of*) établir *ou* faire la moyenne de (**b**) (*perform typical number of*) atteindre la moyenne de; **household spending averages £150 per week** les dépenses des ménages sont de *ou* atteignent les 150 livres par semaine en moyenne

◇ *Econ* **average propensity to consume** propension *f* moyenne à consommer

◇ *Econ* **average propensity to save** propension *f* moyenne à épargner

aye *n Parl* (*in voting*) oui *m inv*; **25 ayes and 3 noes** 25 oui et 3 non, 25 pour et 3 contre; **the ayes have it** les oui l'emportent

◇ *Aye Lobby* = salle où se réunissent les partisans d'une motion à la Chambre des communes

◇ *aye vote* vote *m* favorable

back *vt Pol (bill, candidate)* soutenir

backbench *Parl* **1** *n* = banc des membres du Parlement britannique sans fonctions ministérielles ou qui ne font pas partie du cabinet fantôme ; **there is some discontent on the backbenches** il y a du mécontentement parmi les députés de base

2 *adj (opinion, support)* des députés de base ; **she got backbench support** elle a eu le soutien des députés de base

◇ *backbench amendment* = amendement présenté par un député de base

◇ *backbench rebellion* rébellion *f* des députés de base

"

Tony Blair was last night facing a **backbench rebellion** over welfare reform within a month of his re-election after he refused to back down over plans to impose stricter supervision of incapacity benefit payments for the disabled.

"
---

backbencher *n Parl* = parlementaire sans fonction ministérielle ou qui ne fait pas partie du cabinet fantôme

backing *n Pol (of bill, candidate)* soutien *m*

backlash *n* retour *m* de manivelle ; **there has been a backlash of violence against the policy** il y a eu des réactions violentes contre cette mesure

backward *adj*

◇ *Econ* **backward integration** intégration *f* en amont, intégration *f* ascendante

◇ *Econ* **backward pricing** rajustement *m* des prix

backwoodsman *n Br Fam Pol* = membre de la Chambre des lords qui ne fait acte de présence que lorsqu'il s'intéresse à un vote

bad *n Econ* = produit qui ne satisfait pas le consommateur

▸ **bail out** *vt sep Econ* renflouer

balance *n* équilibre *m*, balance *f*
◇ *Econ* **balance of payments** balance *f* des paiements
◇ *Econ* **balance of payments deficit** déficit *m* de la balance des paiements, déficit *m* extérieur
◇ *Pol* **balance of power** *(in government)* équilibre *m* des pouvoirs ; *(between states)* balance *f* des forces, équilibre *m* des forces ; **he holds the balance of power** il peut faire pencher la balance, tout dépend de lui
◇ *balance of terror* équilibre *m* de la terreur
◇ *balance of trade* balance *f* commerciale
◇ *balance of trade surplus* excédent *m* de la balance commerciale

balanced *adj*
◇ *Econ* **balanced budget** budget *m* équilibré, équilibre *m* budgétaire
◇ *Econ* **balanced growth** croissance *f* équilibrée

Balkanization, balkanization *n Pol* balkanisation *f*

Balkanize, balkanize vt Pol balkaniser

> Mr Jospin's Interior Minister, Jean-Pierre Chevènement, resigned over the bill, fearing it would spark separatist demands in other regions of France. "Should the republic remain one and indivisible or should we **balkanize** France?" asked another opponent of the bill, Gaullist former Interior Minister Charles Pasqua.

ballot Pol **1** n (**a**) (process) tour m de scrutin; (vote) scrutin m; **to vote by ballot** voter à bulletin secret; **in the second ballot** au deuxième tour de scrutin; **to take a ballot** procéder à un scrutin ou à un vote (**b**) (voting paper) bulletin m de vote; **to cast one's ballot for sb** voter pour qn; **to return a ballot** voter

2 vt (voters) sonder au moyen d'un vote; **union members will be balloted on Tuesday** les membres du syndicat décideront par voie de scrutin mardi

3 vi (vote) voter par (voie de) scrutin; **to ballot for/against sb** voter pour/contre qn

◇ *ballot box* (for ballot papers) urne f; (method of voting) système m électoral, système m démocratique; **change cannot be achieved by the ballot box alone** le système électoral à lui seul ne suffit pas à faire bouger les choses

◇ Am *ballot box stuffing* fraude f électorale

◇ Am *ballot initiative* référendum m

◇ *ballot paper* bulletin m de vote

◇ *ballot rigging* fraude f électorale

balloting n Pol scrutin m

BALPA n (abbr **British Airline Pilots' Association**) = syndicat britannique des pilotes de ligne

ban 1 n interdiction f; **the government has issued a ban on fox hunting** le gouvernement a interdit la chasse au renard

2 vt interdire

banana republic n Fam république f bananière

> Malaysian Prime Minister Mahathir Mohamad likened global megacompanies Friday to wealthy plantation owners in the so-called **banana republics** in Latin America and warned these firms may expand their control from the economic sphere to politics. In an address to an international meeting on Asia, Mahathir said, "As we all know, the great plantation owners in the **banana republics** practically own the countries they invest in. They determine the politics of the country."

bandwagon n Pol **to jump** or **to climb on the bandwagon** prendre le train en marche, Pej suivre le mouvement

bank n banque f

◇ *Bank of England* Banque f d'Angleterre

◇ *Bank of France* Banque f de France

◇ *Bank for International Settlements* Banque f des règlements internationaux

◇ *bank reserves* réserves fpl bancaires

banking n (activity) opérations fpl bancaires, activités fpl bancaires

banknote n Br billet m de banque

bar n Br Parl = endroit au Parlement où le public peut venir s'adresser aux députés ou aux lords

bargaining theory n Econ théorie f de la négociation

barnstorm vi Am Pol faire une tournée électorale

barnstormer n Am Pol orateur(-trice) m,f électoral(e)

barnstorming n Am Pol tournée f électorale, campagne f électorale

barrier n Econ barrière f, obstacle m
◇ **barriers to entry** barrières fpl à l'entrée

barter Econ **1** n échange m, troc m; **a system of barter** une économie de troc
2 vt échanger
3 vi faire un échange, faire un troc
◇ **barter economy** économie f de troc
◇ **barter society** société f vivant du troc
◇ **barter system** économie f de troc

base n Econ & Pol base f
◇ **base date** date f de base
◇ Econ **base rate** taux m de base (bancaire)
◇ Econ **base year** année f de référence

basic adj
◇ Econ **basic commodity** denrée f de base
◇ Econ **basic industry** industrie f de base
◇ Econ **basic population** population f mère

basing point pricing n Econ = tarification des frais de transport à partir d'un point de base unique

basket of currencies n Econ panier m de devises, panier m de monnaies

BASW n (abbr **British Association of Social Workers**) = syndicat britannique des travailleurs sociaux

battle n Pol bataille f; **a battle for control of the government** un combat pour obtenir le contrôle du gouvernement

BECTU n (abbr **Broadcasting, Entertainment, Cinematograph and Theatre Union**) = syndicat britannique des techniciens du cinéma, du théâtre et de l'audiovisuel

beef mountain n EU montagne f de bœuf

Beige Book n = rapport sur la conjoncture économique publié huit fois par an aux États-Unis par la banque centrale

beltway n Am Pol **inside the beltway** à Washington

> **"**
>
> It appears that President Bush and the U.S. Congress have agreed to cut taxes by $1.35 trillion over 10 years. But beyond the inside-the-**beltway** haggle over the specifics of the tax cut package, one question looms large: Just how much money is $1.35 trillion?
>
> **"**

bench n Br Parl (in Parliament) banc m; **the government benches** les bancs mpl du gouvernement

Benelux n Bénélux m
◇ **Benelux countries** pays mpl du Bénélux; **in the Benelux countries** au Bénélux

Bennism n Pol = politique de nationalisation de l'industrie en Grande-Bretagne (d'après Tony Benn, ministre de l'aile gauche du parti travailliste en 1974)

Bennite Pol **1** n = partisan des idées de Tony Benn (homme politique de l'aile gauche du parti travailliste)
2 adj = partisan des idées de Tony Benn

BFAWU n (abbr **Bakers, Food and Allied Workers Union**) = syndicat britannique des travailleurs de la boulangerie et du secteur alimentaire

bicameral adj Pol bicaméral(e)

bicameralism n Pol bicamérisme m, bicaméralisme m

BIFU n (abbr **The Banking, Insurance and Finance Union**) = syndicat britannique des employés du secteur financier

big adj
◇ Am Pej Pol **Big Government** = gouvernement interventionniste sur le plan social
◇ **big stick diplomacy** diplomatie f musclée

"

This exchange of charge and countercharge has ratcheted up the tension between politicians in Washington and Havana and increased the possibility that the Bush administration will add the Castro regime to the list of countries it will treat as a state supporter of terrorism. Those nations that are branded with this label by U.S. officials and do not abandon their objectionable conduct "can expect to become our targets," Bolton said. Given this looming threat of **big stick diplomacy**, Carter's trip to Cuba couldn't be better timed.

"

bilateral adj bilatéral(e)
◇ **bilateral agreement** accord m bilatéral
◇ **bilateral aid** aide f bilatérale
◇ **bilateral monopoly** monopole m bilatéral
◇ **bilateral talks** pourparlers mpl bilatéraux
◇ **bilateral trade** commerce m bilatéral

bilateralism n bilatéralisme m

bilaterally adv bilatéralement

bill n (a) Pol (draft of law) projet m de loi; **to introduce a bill in Parliament** présenter un projet de loi au Parlement; **to vote on a bill** mettre un projet de loi au vote; **to pass/reject a bill** adopter/repousser un projet de loi (b) Am (banknote) billet m de banque
◇ **bill of exchange** effet m de commerce
◇ Am **Bill of Rights** = les dix premiers amendements à la Constitution américaine garantissant, entre autres droits, la liberté d'expression, de religion et de réunion

biopolitics n biopolitique f

bipartisan adj Pol biparti(e), bipartite

bipartisanship n Pol bipartisme m

bipartism n Pol bipartisme m

bipartite adj Pol biparti(e), bipartite

bipolar adj Pol bipolaire

bipolarity n Pol bipolarité f

bipolarization n Pol bipolarisation f

bipolarized adj Pol bipolarisé(e)

BIS n (abbr Bank for International Settlements) BRI f

black adj
◇ Pol **Black Caucus** = groupe représentant les membres noirs du Congrès américain; **the Black caucus of the Labour Party** = les personnalités noires du parti travailliste
◇ Pol **black consciousness** négritude f
◇ Econ **black economy** économie f noire
◇ Econ **black market** marché m noir; **on the black market** au marché noir
◇ Econ **black marketeer** vendeur(-euse) m,f au marché noir
◇ Econ **black money** (earned on black market) argent m du marché noir; (undeclared) argent m non déclaré au fisc
◇ Pol **Black Nationalism** = mouvement nationaliste noir américain
◇ Am Pol **Black Power** Black Power m (mouvement séparatiste noir né dans les années 60 aux États-Unis)
◇ Parl **Black Rod** = huissier chargé par la Chambre des lords britannique de convoquer les Communes
◇ Pol **the black vote** le vote noir

Blair babe, Blair Babe n Pol = femme député, membre du "New Labour"

"

Despite commitments by every political party to try to increase women's representation in Parliament, fewer than 20 per cent of the candidates standing in the general election are female. Many of the 1997 intake of so-called **Blair Babes**, such as Julia

Drown, who had been the MP for South Swindon, and Angela Smith, the former MP for Basildon who is tipped for promotion after the election, are expected to hold their seats.

"

Blairism n Pol blairisme m (courant politique travailliste incarné par Tony Blair)

Blairite Pol **1** n = partisan des idées de Tony Blair
   2 adj = partisan des idées de Tony Blair

blank ballot paper n Pol bulletin m blanc, vote m blanc

bloc n Pol bloc m

block 1 vt Parl **to block a bill** faire obstruction à un projet de loi
   2 n
◇ Br Pol **block grant** dotation f (aux collectivités locales)
◇ Br Pol **block vote** = mode de scrutin utilisé par les syndicats britanniques par opposition au mode de scrutin "OMOV"

blocking minority n Pol minorité f de blocage

bloodless adj Pol (coup, victory) sans effusion de sang

blue Pol **1** n = membre du parti conservateur britannique
   2 adj conservateur(trice)

BNP n Pol (abbr **British National Party**) = parti d'extrême-droite britannique

body politic n Pol corps m politique

Bolshevik Pol **1** n bolchevik mf
   2 adj bolchevique

Bolshevism n Pol bolchevisme m

Bolshevist Pol **1** n bolchevik mf
   2 adj bolchevique

bolshie, bolshy Br Fam Pol **1** n rouge mf
   2 adj rouge

▸ **bolster up** vt sep (government, regime) appuyer, soutenir

bolt vt Am Pol (break away from) abandonner, laisser tomber; **four prominent Republicans have bolted the party in recent weeks** au cours des dernières semaines quatre Républicains influents ont abondonné leur parti

bond n (certificate of debt) bon m

boom Econ **1** n (period of expansion) (vague f de) prospérité f, boom m, période f d'essor; (of trade) forte hausse f, forte progression f; **boom and bust (cycle)** cycle m expansion-récession
   2 vi (prosper) prospérer, réussir

"

Entering the single currency at the wrong exchange rate would trigger a **boom and bust cycle** in the UK economy which could potentially push up unemployment by nearly a third, forecasters warn today. In a report prepared for the anti-euro campaign, Oxford Economic Forecasters highlight the problem of choosing the right rate to lock sterling against the euro, should the government win a referendum on the single currency.

"

boost 1 n (of productivity) augmentation f, croissance f; (of economy) relance f; **the announcement gave the pound a boost on the foreign exchanges** la nouvelle a fait grimper la livre sur le marché des changes
   2 vt (productivity) développer, accroître; (economy) relancer; **these measures are designed to boost the economy** ces mesures sont destinées à relancer l'économie

border n frontière f
◇ **border area** zone f frontière
◇ **border trade** commerce m frontalier

borough n (a) (British town) = ville représentée à la Chambre des communes par un ou plusieurs députés (b) (in London) = une des 32 subdivisions administratives de Londres (**c**) *(in New York)* = une des cinq subdivisions administratives de New York

◇ *borough council* = conseil municipal d'une ville représentée à la Chambre des communes par un ou plusieurs députés

borrow 1 *vt (money)* emprunter (**from** à)

  2 *vi* emprunter, faire un emprunt (**from** à)

borrowing *n (of money)* emprunt *m*

boss *n Am Fam (politician)* manitou *m* (du parti)

bottleneck 1 *n (in industry)* goulet *m* d'étranglement, goulot *m* d'étranglement

  2 *vt Am* **strikes have bottlenecked production** les grèves ont ralenti la production

▸ **bottom out** *vi Econ (of recession, inflation, unemployment)* atteindre son plus bas niveau

boundary *n* circonscription *f*

◇ *Br Parl* **boundary change** *(of parliamentary constituency)* = modification des limites d'une circonscription

◇ *Br Parl* **Boundary Commission** commission *f* de délimitation des frontières

Bow Group *n Pol* = société influente de jeunes conservateurs britanniques

boycott 1 *n* boycottage *m*, boycott *m*
  2 *vt* boycotter

boycotter *n* boycotteur(euse) *m,f*

boycotting *n* boycottage *m*

brain drain *n* fuite *f* des cerveaux

branch *n (of government, civil service)* service *m*

◇ *branch economy* économie *f* de succursales

brass-collar *adj Am Pol* qui soutient sans faille la ligne du parti, inconditionnel(elle)

breach of privilege *n Parl* atteinte *f* aux privilèges parlementaires

▸ **break off** *vt sep (talks, relations)* rompre, suspendre; **Italy had broken off diplomatic relations with Libya** l'Italie avait rompu ses relations diplomatiques avec la Libye

▸ **break up 1** *vt sep Pol (coalition)* briser, rompre
  2 *vi (of talks, negotiations)* cesser

breakaway *adj Pol* séparatiste, dissident(e); **a breakaway group** un groupe dissident

breakthrough *n Econ* percée *f*

Bretton Woods agreement *n EU* accords *mpl* de Bretton Woods

brief *Pol* **1** *n (job)* mission *f*; *(post)* poste *m*
  2 *vi* **to brief against sb** dire du mal de qn par l'intermédiaire de la presse

briefing *n Pol* (**a**) *(meeting)* réunion *f* d'information, briefing *m* (**b**) **negative briefing** *(by spin doctor, MP)* = fait d'essayer d'influencer l'opinion contre quelqu'un en se servant de la presse

▸ **bring down** *vt sep* (**a**) *(prices)* faire baisser; *(currency)* déprécier, avilir; *(inflation, unemployment)* réduire (**b**) *Pol (government, leader)* faire tomber, renverser

▸ **bring in** *vt sep* (**a**) *(laws, system)* introduire, présenter; **the government has brought in a new tax bill** le gouvernement a présenté *ou* déposé un nouveau projet de loi fiscale (**b**) *Econ (capital)* apporter

brinkmanship, brinksmanship *n Pol* politique *f* de la corde raide; **the country is engaged in a tense game of diplomatic brinkmanship with the West** le pays a entamé un bras de fer diplomatique avec l'Ouest

British National Party *n Pol* = parti d'extrême-droite britannique

broadsheet *n Br (newspaper)* journal *m* plein format; **the broadsheets** les journaux *mpl* de qualité

bubble n Econ bulle f
◇ **bubble economy** économie f de bulle

> One view is that the economy is made up of three parts, the rural subsistence economy, the urban service-oriented economy and a **bubble economy**, created by the presence of well-paid UN staff. "It creates demands for hotels, restaurants, transportation services ... and is a bit of a **bubble economy** that will disappear as the number of internationals winds down," Michael Francino, finance minister in East Timor's transitional cabinet, has said.

budget Econ **1** n (financial plan) budget m ; Br Pol **the Budget** le budget
  2 adj budgétaire
  3 vt budgétiser, inscrire au budget
  4 vi dresser un budget, préparer un budget
◇ Econ **budget allocation** enveloppe f budgétaire
◇ **budget appropriations** affectations fpl budgétaires
◇ Br Pol **budget box** = attaché-case que le chancelier de l'Échiquier brandit devant les photographes de presse lorsqu'il a établi le budget de l'année
◇ Br Pol **budget briefcase** = attaché-case que le chancelier de l'Échiquier brandit devant les photographes de presse lorsqu'il a établi le budget de l'année
◇ **budget committee** commission f du budget
◇ Econ **budget constraint** contrainte f budgétaire
◇ Econ **budget cuts** coupes fpl budgétaires
◇ Br Pol **Budget Day** = jour de la présentation du budget par le chancelier de l'Échiquier
◇ Econ **budget deficit** déficit m budgétaire

◇ Econ **budget forecast** prévision f budgétaire
◇ Econ **budget planning** planification f budgétaire
◇ Pol **budget speech** = discours à l'occasion de la présentation du budget au parlement
◇ Econ **budget surplus** excédent m budgétaire
▸ **budget for** vt insep Econ inscrire au budget, porter au budget, budgétiser

budgetary adj Econ budgétaire
◇ **budgetary control** gestion f budgétaire
◇ **budgetary limit** plafond m des charges budgétaires
◇ **budgetary mechanism** mécanisme m budgétaire
◇ Br **budgetary policy** politique f budgétaire
◇ **budgetary variance** écart m budgétaire
◇ **budgetary year** exercice m budgétaire

budgeting n Econ budgétisation f, planification f budgétaire

buffer n Econ **a buffer against inflation** une mesure de protection contre l'inflation
◇ Pol **buffer state** État m tampon
◇ Econ **buffer stock** stock m tampon
◇ Pol **buffer zone** région f tampon, zone f tampon

building society n Br ≃ société f de crédit immobilier

bureaucracy n bureaucratie f

bureaucrat n bureaucrate mf

bureaucratic adj bureaucratique

bureaucratization n bureaucratisation f

bureaucratize vt bureaucratiser

Bushite Pol **1** n = partisan de la politique menée par George W. Bush
  2 adj = partisan de George W. Bush et de sa politique

"

How do they rationalize putting us smack into a raging civil war against a guerilla movement that poses zero threat to our borders? Easy – by simply declaring that the rebels are "terrorists," thereby automatically making them targets of George W.'s limitless global war on terrorism. As an unnamed senior **Bushite** told the Washington Post, "All we are trying to do is to add the words 'counter-terrorism' to what the U.S. can do in helping Colombia."

"

business n (a) *(trade)* affaires *fpl*; *(commerce)* commerce m; **to do business with sb** faire affaire *ou* des affaires avec qn; **we have lost business to foreign competitors** nous avons perdu une partie de notre clientèle au profit de concurrents étrangers (b) *(company)* affaire *f*, entreprise *f*; **the small business sector** la petite entreprise (c) *(on agenda)* points *mpl* divers

◇ *business cycle* cycle m des affaires, cycle m conjoncturel

◇ *business economics* économie *f* d'entreprise

◇ *business economist* économiste *mf* d'entreprise

◇ *Br Business Expansion Scheme* = système de dégrèvement fiscal visant à encourager les investissements dans les petites entreprises

◇ *business finance* finance *f* d'entreprise

◇ *business indicator* indicateur m d'alerte

◇ *business partner* partenaire *mf*

◇ *business sector* secteur m tertiaire, secteur m d'affaires

◇ *business taxation* imposition *f* des entreprises

butter mountain n *EU* montagne *f* de beurre

buyer n *Econ*

◇ *buyer's market* marché m à la baisse, marché m demandeur

◇ *buyer's monopoly* monopole m d'achat

byelaw = bylaw

by-election, bye-election n *Br Pol* élection *f* (législative) partielle

◇ *by-election result* résultat m partiel

bylaw n *Br (of local authority)* arrêté m municipal

cabinet n Pol cabinet m; **to form a cabinet** former un cabinet ou un ministère; **he was in Major's cabinet** il faisait partie du cabinet ou gouvernement Major; **they took the decision in cabinet** ils ont pris la décision en conseil des ministres

◇ **cabinet meeting** conseil m des ministres

◇ **cabinet minister** ministre m siégeant au cabinet; **he was a cabinet minister under Major** or **in the Major government** il était ministre sous (le gouvernement) Major

◇ **Cabinet Office** = organisme gouvernemental britannique dont le rôle est d'améliorer le fonctionnement de divers services publics

◇ **cabinet reshuffle** remaniement m ministériel

CACM n (abbr **Central American Common Market**) MCAC m, MCCA m

cadre n Pol cadre m

call 1 vt (a) Parl **to call to order** rappeler à l'ordre (b) **to call an election** annoncer des élections; **to call a strike** appeler à la grève

2 n

◇ Parl **call to order** rappel m à l'ordre

camarilla n Pol camarilla f

camp n (group) camp m, parti m; **the Conservative camp** le parti ou camp conservateur, les conservateurs mpl; **to go over to the other camp** changer de camp; **to be in the same camp** être du même bord

◇ **Camp David** Camp David m

◇ **Camp David agreement** accords mpl de Camp David

campaign Pol **1** n campagne f; **to conduct** or **to lead a campaign against drugs** mener une campagne ou faire campagne contre la drogue; **to be on the campaign trail** être en pleine campagne électorale

2 vi mener une campagne, faire campagne; **to campaign against/for sth** mener une campagne contre/en faveur de qch

◇ Br **Campaign Group** = groupe de députés travaillistes de l'aile gauche du parti

◇ **campaign manager** chef m de campagne électorale

◇ Br **Campaign for Nuclear Disarmament** = mouvement pour le désarmement nucléaire

◇ **campaign plan** plan m de campagne

◇ **campaign rally** rassemblement m électoral

◇ **campaign strategy** stratégie f de campagne

candidacy n Pol candidature f

candidate n Pol candidat(e) m,f; **he's a candidate** or **he's standing as candidate for mayor** il est candidat à la mairie

candidature n Pol candidature f

canvass Pol **1** n (a) (of votes) démarchage m électoral (b) Am (of ballots) pointage m

2 vt (a) (person) solliciter la voix de; (area) faire du démarchage électoral dans (b) Am (ballots) pointer

3 vi (of candidate, campaign worker) faire campagne (en faisant du porte-

à-porte); **we're canvassing for the Greens** nous faisons campagne pour les Verts

canvasser n Pol (a) *(of votes)* agent m électoral *(qui sollicite des voix)* (b) Am *(of ballots)* scrutateur(trice) m,f

canvassing n Pol (a) *(of votes)* démarchage m électoral (b) Am *(of ballots)* pointage m

CAP n EU *(abbr* **Common Agricultural Policy)** PAC f

capacity n Econ capacité f
◇ **capacity utilization** utilisation f du potentiel de production

capital n Econ *(funds)* capital m, capitaux mpl, fonds mpl; *(funds and assets)* capital m (en espèces et en nature)
◇ **capital accumulation** accumulation f de capital
◇ **capital asset** actif m immobilisé
◇ **capital asset pricing model** modèle m d'évaluation des actifs
◇ **capital consumption** consommation f de capital
◇ **capital consumption allowance** provision f pour consommation du capital
◇ **capital control** contrôle m des capitaux
◇ **capital deepening** augmentation f de capital
◇ **capital expenditure** mise f de fonds, dépenses fpl d'équipement
◇ **capital flight** fuite f des capitaux
◇ **capital gain** plus-value f
◇ **capital goods** biens mpl capitaux, biens mpl d'équipement
◇ **capital inflow** *(into economy)* entrée f de capitaux; *(into company)* afflux m de capitaux
◇ **capital investment** mise f de fonds
◇ **capital market** marché m des capitaux
◇ **capital stock** capital m social, fonds mpl propres
◇ **capital transfer tax** droits mpl de mutation
◇ **capital widening** élargissement m du capital

capital-intensive adj Econ capitalistique

capitalism n capitalisme m

capitalist 1 n capitaliste mf
2 adj capitaliste
◇ **capitalist economy** économie f capitaliste

capitalistic adj capitaliste

capitalization n Econ *(of interest, revenue)* capitalisation f

capitalize vt Econ *(interest, revenue)* capitaliser

capital-labour ratio n Econ ratio m capital-travail

capital-output ratio n Econ ratio m d'intensité de capital

Capitol n Am **the Capitol** *(national)* le Capitole *(siège du Congrès américain)*; *(state)* le Capitole *(siège du Congrès de l'État)*
◇ **Capitol Hill** = la colline du Capitole, à Washington, où se trouve le congrès américain; **the proposed bill is in danger of being rejected on Capitol Hill** la proposition de loi risque d'être rejetée par le Congrès américain

captive adj Econ *(market)* captif(ive)

card n
◇ **card holder** *(of political party)* membre m, adhérent(e) m,f
◇ Br **card vote** vote m sur carte *(chaque voix représentant le nombre de voix d'adhérents représentés)*

cardinal utility n Econ utilité f cardinale

career adj *(diplomat, politician)* de carrière

caretaker adj *(government, prime minister)* intérimaire; **a caretaker government was appointed until the crisis was resolved** un gouvernement intérimaire a été nommé le temps que la crise soit résolue

CARICOM n *(abbr* **Caribbean Community)** CARICOM f

carpetbagger n Pej candidat(e) m,f étranger(ère) à la circonscription

> **❝**
>
> Clinton's most obvious liability in the Senate race is her **carpetbagger** problem: She's never lived, worked or spent much time in New York. And while the state overwhelmingly supported her husband in 1992 and 1996, it is hard to know how much Clinton scandal fatigue – or general Clinton fatigue – will hurt her candidacy.
>
> **❞**

carriage n Pol (of bill) passage m

▸ **carry off** vt sep Pol (victory) remporter

cartel n Pol cartel m; **oil/steel cartel** cartel m du pétrole/de l'acier

cartelization n Pol cartellisation f

cartelize vt Pol cartelliser

cartellization, cartellize = cartelization, cartelize

cash n (coins and banknotes) espèces fpl, (argent m) liquide m; (money in general) argent m
◊ **cash crop** culture f de rapport, culture f commerciale
◊ **cash deficit** déficit m de trésorerie
◊ **cash flow** cash-flow m, trésorerie f
◊ **cash limits** = système de contrôle des dépenses publiques
◊ **cash ratio** ratio m de trésorerie
◊ **cash reserves** réserves fpl en espèces

cast vt Pol **to cast one's vote (for sb)** voter (pour qn); **the number of votes cast** le nombre de voix ou de suffrages

casting vote n Parl voix f prépondérante; **the Speaker of the House has the casting vote** le représentant de la Chambre a voix prépondérante

castrate vt Pol (political movement) émasculer

castration n Pol (of political movement) émasculation f

Castroism n Pol castrisme m

Castroist Pol **1** n castriste mf
2 adj castriste

casualization of labour n Econ précarisation f de l'emploi

catchword n Pol (slogan) mot m d'ordre, slogan m

CATU n (abbr **Ceramic and Allied Trades Union**) = syndicat britannique des travailleurs de l'industrie de la céramique

caucus n Pol (a) Am (committee) comité m électoral, caucus m; **the Democratic caucus** le groupe ou le lobby démocrate (b) Br (party organization) comité m
◊ Am **caucus meeting** réunion f du comité électoral

CBI n (abbr **Confederation of British Industry**) = association du patronat britannique, ≃ Medef m

CC n (a) (abbr **county council**) ≃ conseil m général (b) (abbr **corps consulaire**) CC m

CCI n (abbr **Chamber of Commerce and Industry**) CCI f

CD n (abbr **certificate of deposit**) certificat m de dépôt

CE n (a) Br (abbr **Chancellor of the Exchequer**) Chancelier m de l'Échiquier, ≃ ministre m des Finances (en Grande-Bretagne) (b) (abbr **Council of Europe**) Conseil m de l'Europe

CEEC n (abbr **Central and Eastern European Countries**) PECO m

ceiling n Econ plafond m; **to reach a ceiling** (of prices, interest rates) plafonner; **prices have reached their ceiling** les prix ont atteint leur plafond; **to have a ceiling of** être plafonné(e) à; **to fix or set a ceiling to sth** fixer un plafond à qch; **the government has set a three percent ceiling on wage rises** le gouvernement a limité à trois pour cent les augmentations de salaire
◊ **ceiling price** prix m plafond

cell n Pol cellule f

CEMAC n (abbr **Central African Economic and Monetary Community**) CEMAC f

censure Pol **1** n censure f
  2 vt censurer

census n recensement m; **to conduct** or **to take a census** faire un recensement
◇ Am **Census Bureau** Bureau m des statistiques
◇ **census return** formulaire m de recensement
◇ **census taker** agent m recenseur, recenseur(euse) m,f

center Am = **centre**

central adj central(e)
◇ **central bank** Banque f centrale
◇ **central banker** membre m du conseil de la Banque centrale
◇ **central committee** comité m central
◇ **Central and East European Countries** pays mpl de l'Europe centrale et orientale
◇ **Central Europe** Europe f centrale
◇ **central government** gouvernement m central
◇ Am **Central Intelligence Agency** CIA f
◇ Br Parl **Central Lobby** = hall principal de la Chambre des communes
◇ Br Pol **Central Office** = siège du parti conservateur britannique
◇ Econ **central rate** cours m pivot

centralism n Pol centralisme m

centralist Pol **1** n centraliste mf
  2 adj centraliste

centralization n centralisation f

centralize 1 vt centraliser
  2 vi se centraliser

centralized adj centralisé(e)

centralizing adj centralisateur(-trice)

centrally adv (organized) de façon centralisée; Econ **a centrally planned economy** une économie dirigée

centre, Am **center** n Pol centre m; **to**

be left/right of centre être du centre gauche/droit

centre-left adj Pol (politician, party, views) du centre gauche

centre-right adj Pol (politician, party, views) du centre droit

centrism n Pol centrisme m

centrist Pol **1** n centriste mf
  2 adj centriste

certificate of deposit n certificat m de dépôt

CET n EU (abbr **common external tariff**) tarif m externe commun

CFP n EU (abbr **Common Fisheries Policy**) PCP f

CFSP n EU (abbr **Common Foreign and Security Policy**) PESC f

chaebol n Econ chaebol m

chairman n (of party) secrétaire mf général(e); (of committee, meeting) président m
◇ Br Parl **Chairman of Ways and Means** = assistant du président de la Chambre des communes

chairperson n (of party) secrétaire mf général(e); (of committee, meeting) président(e) m,f

chairwoman n (of party) secrétaire f générale; (of committee, meeting) présidente f

challenge Pol **1** n (to leadership) défi m; (to policy, authority) mise f en question, contestation f; **to throw down** or **to issue a challenge** lancer un défi; **Jackson's challenge for the leadership of the party** la tentative de Jackson pour s'emparer de la direction du parti; **the new law met with a challenge from the people** la nouvelle loi s'est vue contestée par le peuple
  2 vt (leadership) défier; (policy, authority) mettre en question, contester; **their position was challenged by a group of MPs** leur position a été contestée par un groupe de députés

challenger n Pol challenger m

chamber *n Pol* chambre *f*
◇ *Chamber of Commerce* Chambre *f* de commerce
◇ *Chamber of Commerce and Industry* Chambre *f* de commerce et d'industrie
◇ *Chamber of Deputies* Chambre *f* des députés

champagne *n*
◇ *Pol champagne socialism* la gauche caviar
◇ *Pol champagne socialist* membre *m* de la gauche caviar

> **"**
>
> Communism, as George Orwell pointed out in Animal Farm, is privilege for the few, not the masses. 'Some animals were more equal then others.' Capitalism, in its present guise, is hardly any better. Chief Executives earn million-pound bonuses while shop floor workers are relatively poorly paid and work the longest hours in Europe. And like some sort of bourgeois **champagne socialist**, Tony Blair in his chauffeur-driven Daimler cruises up the M4 bus lane while thousands of other drivers sit, fuming, in traffic jams.
>
> **"**

chancellery = chancery

chancellor *n Pol* chancelier *m*; **the Chancellor** *(Chancellor of the Exchequer)* Chancelier *m* de l'Échiquier, ≃ ministre *m* des Finances *(en Grande-Bretagne)*
◇ *Pol Chancellor of the Exchequer* Chancelier *m* de l'Échiquier, ≃ ministre *m* des Finances *(en Grande-Bretagne)*

chancellorship *n Pol* direction *f* des finances; **the economy had done extremely well under Mr Smith's chancellorship** l'économie avait montré d'excellents résultats lorsque M. Smith était au ministère des Finances

chancery *n Pol* chancellerie *f*

channel *n Econ* canal *m*, circuit *m*

chargé d'affaires *n Pol* chargé(e) *m,f* d'affaires

charter *n* charte *f*
◇ *Charter of Fundamental Rights* charte *f* des droits fondamentaux
◇ *Charter of Human Rights* charte *f* des droits de l'homme

chartist *n Econ* chartiste *mf*

checks and balances *npl Pol* contrepoids *mpl*; *Am* **(system of) checks and balances** (système *m* d')équilibre *m* des pouvoirs

Chequers *n* = résidence secondaire officielle du Premier ministre britannique, située dans la campagne anglaise (comté du Buckinghamshire)

chief *adj*
◇ *Am Pol Chief Diplomat* = le président des États-Unis en sa qualité de chef de la diplomatie
◇ *Am Pol Chief Executive* = le président des États-Unis en sa qualité de chef de l'exécutif
◇ *Br Pol Chief Secretary to the Treasury* ≃ ministre *m* du Budget
◇ *Am Pol Chief of Staff (at White House)* secrétaire *mf* général(e) de la Maison Blanche
◇ *Br Pol Chief Whip* = responsable du maintien de la discipline à l'intérieur d'un parti à la Chambre des communes et à la Chambre des lords

Chiltern Hundreds *n Pol* **to apply for the Chiltern Hundreds** démissionner *(du Parlement britannique)*

> **"**
>
> Neil Kinnock was the last MP to resign from the House in January 1995; when he became a European Commissioner, he applied for the **Chiltern Hundreds**. Mr Merchant therefore had to apply for the Manor of Northstead. The last MP to do that was Labour's Bryan Gould in May 1994.
>
> **"**

> **66**
>
> Technically speaking MPs cannot voluntarily give up their seats during a Parliament. So if a Member wishes to resign they must accept an office of profit under the Crown which legally disqualifies them from continuing as an MP. These offices exist as a purely nominal device for this purpose. The two offices still in use are the **Chiltern Hundred**s – of Stoke, Desborough and Burnham – and the Manor of Northstead.
>
> **99**

Christian Democracy n Pol démocratie f chrétienne

Christian Democrat Pol **1** n démocrate-chrétien(enne) m,f
 2 adj démocrate-chrétien(enne)

Christian Socialism n Pol socialisme m chrétien

Christian Socialist Pol **1** n social(e)-chrétien(enne) m,f
 2 adj social(e)-chrétien(enne)

CIA n Am (abbr **Central Intelligence Agency**) CIA f

circular flow of income n Econ flux m circulaire des revenus

circulate 1 vt (banknotes) mettre en circulation, émettre ; (money, goods) faire circuler
 2 vi (of banknotes, money, goods, services) circuler

circulation n (of banknotes, money, goods, services) circulation f

CIS n (abbr **Commonwealth of Independent States**) CEI f

citizen n (of nation, state) citoyen(-enne) m,f
◇ **Citizens' Charter** = programme lancé par le gouvernement britannique en 1991 et qui vise à améliorer la qualité des services publics
◇ Am Pol **citizen's initiative** initiative f populaire
◇ **citizen rights** droits mpl du citoyen

citizenship n citoyenneté f

City n **the City** la Cité ou City (de Londres) (centre des affaires) ; **he's in the City** il est dans la finance (dans la Cité de Londres)
◇ **the City Companies** les corporations fpl de la Cité de Londres

city n
◇ **city council** ≃ conseil m d'arrondissement
◇ Am **city hall** (building) mairie f, hôtel m de ville ; (municipal government) administration f (municipale) ; **you can't fight city hall** on ne peut rien contre l'administration

civic adj (authority, building) municipal(e) ; (duty) civique
◇ **civic rights** droits mpl civiques

civil adj
◇ Pol **civil disobedience** désobéissance f civile
◇ **civil libertarian** défenseur m des droits du citoyen
◇ **civil liberties** libertés fpl civiques
◇ Br **civil list** liste f civile (allouée à la famille royale britannique)
◇ **Civil and Public Services Association** = syndicat britannique de la fonction publique
◇ **civil rights** droits mpl civils
◇ Am **Civil Rights Commission** = organisme gouvernemental qui veille au respect des droits civiques
◇ **the civil rights movement** la lutte pour les droits civils ou civiques
◇ **civil servant** fonctionnaire mf
◇ **civil service** fonction f publique, administration f ; **to be in the civil service** être fonctionnaire ou dans l'administration ou dans la fonction publique
◇ **Civil Service Commission** = commission de recrutement des fonctionnaires
◇ **civil service exam** concours m administratif
◇ **Civil Service Union** = syndicat britannique de la fonction publique
◇ **civil society** société f civile
◇ **civil war** guerre f civile

CJEC n EU (abbr **Court of Justice of the European Communities**) CJCE f

CJHA n Formerly EU (abbr **Cooperation in Justice and Home Affairs**) CJAI f

class n classe f
◊ *class struggle* lutte f des classes
◊ *class system* système m des classes
◊ *class war* lutte f des classes

classical adj
◊ Econ *classical economics* économie f classique
◊ Pol *classical liberalism* libéralisme m classique
◊ Econ *classical unemployment* chômage m classique

clause n Pol (of treaty, law) clause f, article m
◊ *Clause 4* = article de la constitution du Parti travailliste britannique affirmant son attachement au principe de propriété publique des grands secteurs industriels (abrogé en 1995)
◊ *Clause 28* = disposition juridique en Grande-Bretagne interdisant aux enseignants du secondaire d'aborder le thème de l'homosexualité en classe

clean float n Econ taux m de change libre ou flottant

cleavage n Pol clivage m

clerk n
◊ Parl *Clerk of the House* ≃ secrétaire mf général(e) de l'Assemblée
◊ Parl *Clerk of the Parliaments* ≃ secrétaire mf général(e) du Sénat
◊ Parl *Clerk of the Senate* ≃ secrétaire mf général(e) du Sénat

client n
◊ Pej *client government* gouvernement m à la solde d'un autre
◊ Pej *client state* État m à la solde d'un autre

“

Iran, Russia and Pakistan could cause trouble if they see the Taliban's demise as a chance to impose a **client government** in Kabul. That

can't happen. The world was intent on using Afghanistan as a cold war battlefield for years. Now it has to be intent not on who controls Afghanistan, but on how Afghanistan controls itself.

”

clientelism n Pej Pol clientélisme m

clientelist n Pej Pol clientéliste mf

clientilism, clientilist = clientelism, clientelist

▸ **climb down** vi reculer, faire machine arrière; **the government has been forced to climb down over last week's statement** le gouvernement a dû faire machine arrière après sa déclaration de la semaine dernière

climbdown n reculade f; **a government climbdown over the issue looks likely** il est probable que le gouvernement fera machine arrière à ce sujet

Clintonite Pol **1** n = partisan de Bill Clinton et de sa politique
2 adj = partisan de Bill Clinton et de sa politique

Clintonomics n Pol = politique formulée par le Comité des conseillers économiques du président américain Bill Clinton pour une meilleure répartition des richesses

closed adj (economy) fermé(e)
◊ Am Pol *closed primary* = élection primaire à laquelle ne participent que les membres du parti concerné
◊ Am Pol *closed rule* = règle de la Chambre des représentants qui interdit tout amendement à un projet de loi en cours de discussion
◊ *closed shop* (practice) = système selon lequel une entreprise n'embauche que des travailleurs syndiqués; (establishment) = entreprise qui n'embauche que des travailleurs syndiqués

closure n Parl clôture f; **to move the closure** demander la clôture
◊ *closure motion* = motion présentée par un député à la Chambre des

communes, visant à clore un débat de façon à procéder à un vote

◇ *Am **closure rule*** = règle limitant le temps de parole au Sénat américain

cloture *Parl* **1** *n* clôture *f*
2 *vt* clôturer

◇ *Am **cloture rule*** = règle limitant le temps de parole au Sénat américain

CND *n Br* (*abbr* **Campaign for Nuclear Disarmament**) = mouvement pour le désarmement nucléaire

coalition *n Pol* coalition *f*; **to form a coalition** former une coalition, se coaliser

◇ *coalition government* gouvernement *m* de coalition

coalitionist *Pol* **1** *n* coalitionniste *mf*
2 *adj* coalitionniste

coattail effect *n Am Pol* = effet d'entraînement lorsque des candidats d'un parti sont élus dans le sillage de l'élection de l'un des leurs lors d'un scrutin important

❝

With all the attention on the presidential election, it is natural to wonder if there is some connection between the way people vote in the contest for the White House and how they vote in congressional elections. The short answer is yes. Presidential elections affect congressional elections in at least two ways: increased voter turnout and gains in Congress for the winning candidate's party. The phenomenon of candidates of the same party as the winning presidential candidate being swept into office is generally termed the **coattail effect**.

❞

codecision procedure *n EU* procédure *f* de codécision

code of conduct *n Parl* (*set of rules*) code *m* de conduite

C of E *n* (*abbr* **Council of Europe**) Conseil *m* de l'Europe

cohabitation *n Pol* cohabitation *f*

cohesion policy *n EU* politique *f* de cohésion

COLA *n Am Econ* (*abbr* **cost of living adjustment**) augmentation *f* de salaire indexée sur le coût de la vie

cold *adj*
◇ *Pol **cold war*** guerre *f* froide
◇ *Pol **cold warrior*** partisan(e) *m,f* de la guerre froide

collapse **1** *n* (*of government*) chute *f*; (*of country*) effondrement *m*, débâcle *f*; (*of market, economy, currency*) effondrement *m*; (*of prices*) effondrement *m*, chute *f* subite
2 *vi* (*of government*) tomber, chuter; (*of country, market, economy, currency, prices*) s'effondrer

collective **1** *n* coopérative *f*
2 *adj* collectif(ive)
◇ *collective agreement* convention *f* collective
◇ *collective bargaining* = négociations pour une convention collective
◇ *Econ **collective good*** bien *m* collectif
◇ *Br Pol **collective responsibility*** = principe de responsabilité collective, selon lequel le gouvernement dans son ensemble doit se montrer solidaire des décisions prises par tel ou tel ministre
◇ *collective utility* utilité *f* collective

❝

We support higher wages for public-sector workers whose earnings generally lag significantly behind their west European counterparts. We support higher taxes on the rich and big business profits to fund better public services for all. We believe that, imperfect as it is, **collective bargaining** is the best way in a free society to establish pay levels within companies, industries and public services. We urge the employers to come back to the negotiating table to establish a rate for the job in the

> best interests of the fire service and the communities it serves.

collectivism n Econ collectivisme m

collectivist Econ **1** n collectiviste mf
2 adj collectiviste

collectivity n Econ collectivité f

collectivization n Econ collectivisation f

collectivize vt Econ collectiviser

colonial 1 n colonial(e) m,f
2 adj (power, life) colonial(e); (attitude) colonialiste

colonialism n colonialisme m

colonialist 1 n colonialiste mf
2 adj colonialiste

colonization n colonisation f

colonize vt coloniser

colony n colonie f

combine n Econ trust m, cartel m

Comecon n Formerly Econ (abbr **Council for Mutual Economic Aid**) Comecon m

COMESA n (abbr **Common Market for Eastern and Southern Africa**) COMESA m

comitology n EU comitologie f

command n
◊ Econ **command economy** économie f planifiée
◊ Br Parl **command paper** = document présenté au Parlement par le gouvernement

Commander-In-Chief n Am Pol = le président des États-Unis en sa qualité de commandant en chef des forces armées

commerce n (trade) commerce m, affaires fpl

commercial adj commercial(e)
◊ **commercial bill** effet m de commerce
◊ **commercial policy** politique f commerciale

commission n Pol commission f
◊ **commission of enquiry** commission f d'enquête

commissioner n Pol (member of commission) membre m d'une commission, commissaire m; (of government department) haut fonctionnaire m; EU commissaire m européen

commit vt Pol (bill) renvoyer devant une commission

commitment n Pol (of bill) renvoi m devant une commission

committee n (in government) commission f, comité m; **to be** or **to sit on a committee** faire partie d'une commission ou d'un comité; Br Parl **the House went into committee** la Chambre s'est constituée en commission ou en comité
◊ Br Parl **committee meeting** réunion f de commission d'enquête parlementaire
◊ EU **Committee of Permanent Representatives** Comité m des représentants permanents
◊ EU **Committee of the Regions** Comité m des régions
◊ Br Parl **committee room** = salle où se réunit une commission d'enquête parlementaire
◊ Br Parl **committee stage** = stade de discussion d'un projet de loi par une commission
◊ Br Parl **Committee on Standards in Public Life** = comité chargé de veiller à l'intégrité des députés
◊ Br Parl **Committee of Ways and Means** commission f du budget
◊ Br Parl **Committee of the Whole House** = séance de commission étendue à la chambre entière

commodity n Econ (**a**) (product) marchandise f; (consumer good) produit m, article m; (food item) denrée f; **a basic** or **staple commodity** un produit de base; **rice is the staple commodity of China** le riz est la ressource principale de la Chine (**b**) (raw material) produit m de base, matière f première

◇ *commodity agreements* accords *mpl* sur les produits de base

◇ *commodity exchange* échange *m* des marchandises

◇ *commodity market* marché *m* des matières premières

◇ *commodity tax* impôt *m* sur les denrées

◇ *commodity terms of trade* termes *mpl* de l'échange

common *adj*

◇ EU *Common Agricultural Policy* politique *f* agricole commune

◇ *common currency* monnaie *f* commune

◇ EU *common external tariff* tarif *m* externe commun

◇ EU *Common Fisheries Policy* politique *f* commune de la pêche

◇ EU *Common Foreign and Security Policy* politique *f* étrangère et de sécurité commune

◇ Econ *common good* bien *m* commun

◇ *common manifesto* programme *m* commun

◇ EU *the Common Market* le marché commun

◇ *common ownership* copropriété *f*

◇ *common price fixing* fixation *f* concertée des prix

◇ *common pricing* fixation *f* concertée des prix

◇ *common stance* position *f* commune

commoner *n Br Parl* député(e) *m,f*, membre *m* de la Chambre des communes

Commons *npl Br & Can Parl* the Commons les Communes *fpl*

◇ *Br Commons' Amendment* (to bill) amendement *m* (proposé à la Chambre des communes)

◇ *Br Parl Commons Whip* = responsable du maintien de la discipline à l'intérieur d'un parti à la Chambre des communes

Commonwealth *n* the Commonwealth le Commonwealth

◇ *Commonwealth Development*

Group = organisme gouvernemental dont le rôle est de répartir l'aide aux pays en voie de développement

◇ *Commonwealth of Independent States* Communauté *f* des États indépendants

◇ *the Commonwealth of Nations* le Commonwealth

commonwealth *n* (a) (country) pays *m*; (state) État *m*; (republic) république *f* (b) (body politic) corps *m* politique

commune *n* (district) commune *f*

Communism *n Pol* communisme *m*

Communist *Pol* **1** *n* communiste *mf* **2** *adj* communiste

◇ *Communist International* Komintern *m*

◇ *Communist Party* parti *m* communiste

Community *n EU* the (European) Community la Communauté (européenne)

◇ *Community method* méthode *f* communautaire

◇ *Community preference principle* principe *m* de préférence communautaire

company *n* entreprise *f*, société *f*

comparative *adj*

◇ Econ *comparative advantage* avantage *m* comparé

◇ Econ *comparative cost* loi *f* des avantages comparés

compassionate conservatism *n Pol* = conservatisme à visage humain

> **❝**
>
> Compassionate conservatism, coined by Bush and lifted by Duncan Smith, was for a time a phrase graced with truth and common relevance. Pumped out often enough, the mantra helped Bush defeat the legacy of the Clinton years without entirely disowning their tender side.
>
> **❞**

compassion fatigue n = lassitude du public à l'égard des nécessiteux

compensatory adj
◊ EU **compensatory amount** montant m compensatoire
◊ EU **compensatory levy** prélèvement m compensatoire

competition n Econ concurrence f
◊ **Competition Commission** = commission veillant au respect de la législation antitrust en Grande-Bretagne
◊ Econ **competition policy** politique m de concurrence

competitive adj Econ (product, price) concurrentiel(elle), compétitif(ive); (company, industry) compétitif(ive); **industry must become more competitive** l'industrie doit devenir plus compétitive
◊ **competitive advantage** avantage m concurrentiel
◊ **competitive devaluation** dévaluation f compétitive
◊ **competitive equilibrium price** prix m d'équilibre concurrentiel
◊ **competitive marketplace** marché m de concurrence; **in a competitive marketplace** dans un marché de concurrence
◊ **competitive pricing** fixation f des prix compétitifs

competitiveness n Econ compétitivité f

competitor n Econ concurrent(e) m,f

complementarity n Econ complémentarité f

complementary adj Econ complémentaire
◊ **complementary good** bien m complémentaire

compliance cost n Econ coût m de l'application

composite Pol **1** n = proposition discutée au niveau national
2 vt **to composite proposals** = établir une liste de propositions à discuter au niveau national, à partir des propositions émises au niveau régional

compulsory adj
◊ Pol **compulsory vote** vote m obligatoire
◊ Pol **compulsory voting** vote m obligatoire

comrade n Pol camarade mf

Con Pol (abbr **Conservative**) conservateur(trice)

concentration n Econ concentration f

Conciliation Committee n EU comité m de conciliation

conciliatory adj Pol (procedure) conciliatoire

concurrent adj
◊ Pol **concurrent majority** majorité f simultanée
◊ Am Pol **concurrent powers** = pouvoirs partagés par le gouvernement fédéral et les différents États

conditionality n Econ conditionnalité f

condominium n (government) condominium m

confederacy n (alliance) confédération f

confederal adj confédéral(e)

confederate 1 n (member of confederacy) confédéré(e) m,f
2 adj confédéré(e)
3 vt confédérer
4 vi se confédérer

confederation n confédération f
◊ **Confederation of British Industry** = patronat britannique, ≃ Medef m

conference n Pol congrès m, assemblée f; **the Labour Party conference** le congrès du parti travailliste
◊ Am **Conference Committee** = comité composé de membres du Sénat et de la Chambre des représentants dont le rôle est de trouver des compromis sur les projets de loi

confirm vt Pol (treaty) ratifier; (result) confirmer; (election) valider; (nomination) approuver

confirmation n Pol (of treaty) ratification f; (of result) confirmation f; (of election) validation f; (of nomination) approbation f

◊ Am **confirmation hearing** = entretien à l'issue duquel un comité de sénateurs décide si un haut fonctionnaire nommé par le président est un candidat valable

conflict 1 n (disagreement) conflit m; **to be in conflict (with)** être en conflit (avec); **the parties are often in conflict** les partis sont souvent en désaccord; **the unions are in conflict with the management** les syndicats sont en conflit avec la direction; **there is a conflict**
between the two statements les deux déclarations ne concordent pas
2 vi (of ideas, interests) s'opposer, se heurter; **the policies conflict (with one another)** ces politiques sont incompatibles

◊ **conflict of interests** conflit m d'intérêts

conglomerate n Econ conglomérat m

Congress n Pol Congrès m; (session) = session du Congrès américain

Congressional adj Pol du Congrès américain

◊ **Congressional district** = circonscription d'un représentant du Congrès américain

◊ **Congressional Record** = journal officiel du Congrès américain

congressman n Pol membre m du Congrès américain; **Mr Congressman, do you believe that ... ?** ≃ Monsieur le Député, croyez-vous que ... ?

congressman-at-large n Pol = représentant du Congrès américain non attaché à une circonscription électorale

congresswoman n Pol membre m (féminin) du Congrès américain; **Madame Congresswoman, do you believe that ... ?** ≃ Madame la Députée, croyez-vous que ... ?

Connect n = syndicat britannique des professionnels des télécommunications

Cons Pol (abbr **Conservative**) conservateur(trice)

conscientious objector n Pol objecteur m de conscience

consensus politics n politique f consensuelle

Tony Blair has sought consensus for more honourable reasons. He believes "inclusive politics" is necessary to unite the nation behind the drive to modernisation. But however it is expressed, the call for consensus is wrong. **Consensus politics** is a danger to democracy, a rejection of political principle and an excuse to neglect minorities. It is because of **consensus politics** that today no British political party speaks for the poor.

Conservatism n Pol conservatisme m

Conservative Pol **1** n conservateur (trice) m,f
2 adj conservateur(trice)

◊ Br **Conservative Central Office** = siège du parti conservateur britannique

◊ **the Conservative Party** le parti conservateur

consolidated adj

◊ Br Pol **consolidated fund** = "compte en banque" du gouvernement à la Banque d'Angleterre, qui sert à régler toutes les dépenses publiques

◊ Br Pol **consolidated fund bill** = loi qui autorise le gouvernement à effectuer les dépenses publiques prévues

conspicuous consumption n Econ consommation f ostentatoire

constituency Pol **1** n (area) circonscription f électorale; (people) = habitants d'une circonscription électorale

2 adj (meeting, organization) local(e)

◊ Br **the constituency party** la section locale du parti

constituent Pol **1** n administré(e) m,f

2 adj (assembly, power) constituant(e)

◊ **constituent body** corps m constitué

constituted adj Pol constitué(e)

constitution n Pol (statute) constitution f; **the (United States) Constitution** la Constitution

constitutional adj Pol (a) (regime, reform) constitutionnel(elle); **the president's actions are not constitutional** les actions du président sont anticonstitutionnelles (b) (head, privilege) constitutionnel(elle)

◊ **constitutional amendment** amendement m constitutionnel

◊ **constitutional democracy** démocratie f constitutionnelle

◊ **constitutional law** droit m constitutionnel

◊ **constitutional monarch** souverain(e) m,f constitutionnel(elle)

◊ **constitutional monarchy** monarchie f constitutionnelle

constitutionalism n Pol constitutionnalisme m

constitutionalist n Pol constitutionnel(elle) m,f

constitutionality n Pol constitutionnalité f

constitutionalize vt Pol constitutionnaliser

constitutionally adv Pol (act) constitutionnellement; **constitutionally, the government is within its rights** constitutionnellement, le gouvernement est dans ses droits

constructive abstention n EU abstention f constructive

consultant n conseiller(ère) m,f

consumable goods n Econ produits mpl de consommation

consumer n Econ consommateur(-trice) m,f

◊ **consumer confidence index** indice m de confiance

◊ **consumer credit** crédit m à la consommation

◊ **consumer debt** endettement m des consommateurs

◊ **consumer demand** demande f des consommateurs

◊ **consumer durables** biens mpl de consommation durables

◊ **consumer expenditure** dépenses fpl de consommation

◊ **consumer goods** biens mpl de consommation

◊ **consumer group** groupe m de consommateurs

◊ **consumer industry** industrie f de consommation

◊ **consumer loan** prêt m à la consommation

◊ **consumer market** marché m de la consommation

◊ **consumer non durables** biens mpl de consommation non durables

◊ Am **consumer price index** indice m des prix à la consommation

◊ **consumer products** biens mpl de consommation

◊ **consumer protection** défense f des consommateurs

◊ **consumer purchasing power** richesse f vive

◊ **consumer purchasing power index** indice m de richesse vive

◊ **consumer society** société f de consommation

◊ **consumer sovereignty** souveraineté f du consommateur

◊ **consumer spending** dépenses fpl de consommation ou des ménages

consumerism n Econ (consumer protection) consumérisme m; (consumption) consommation f à outrance

consumption n Econ consommation f

◊ **consumption expenditure** dépenses fpl de consommation

◊ **consumption function** fonction f de consommation

◊ **consumption spending** dépenses *fpl* de consommation

contact group *n Pol* groupe *m* de contact

containment *n Pol* endiguement *m*, freinage *m*, retenue *f*

contender *n Pol (for leadership, presidency)* candidat(e) *m,f*; **he is the main contender in the battle for the leadership** c'est le grand favori dans la lutte pour la position de leader

Contents Lobby *n Br Parl* = à la Chambre des lords, salle où se réunissent les lords en faveur d'une motion lors d'un vote

contest *Pol* **1** *n (for leadership, presidency)* combat *m*, lutte *f* **(for/between** pour/entre)
2 *vt (election, seat)* disputer; *(result, question)* contester, discuter; **a hotly contested seat** un siège très disputé

contestable market *n Econ* marché *m* disputable

contingency tax *n* impôt *m* imprévu

contingent valuation *n Econ* évaluation *f* contingente

Contra *n Pol (Nicaraguan)* contra *mf*

contribute *vt Econ (capital)* apporter

contribution *n Econ (of capital)* apport *m*

contributor *n Econ (of capital)* apporteur *m*

control **1** *n* (a) *(of government, country)* direction *f*; **the rebels have gained control of the capital** les rebelles ont pris le contrôle de la capitale; **the country is no longer under British/government control** le pays n'est plus sous contrôle britannique/gouvernemental
(b) *Econ (of inflation, prices, spending)* contrôle *m*, maîtrise *f*; *(of imports)* limitation *f*; **to impose controls on sth** contrôler qch; **there are to be new government controls on financial practices** il y aura de nouvelles réglementations gouvernementales sur les pratiques financières; **inflation must be kept under**

control il faut maîtriser l'inflation
2 *vt* (a) *(government, country)* diriger (b) *Econ (inflation, prices, spending)* contrôler, maîtriser; *(imports)* limiter

controlled *adj*
◊ *Econ* **controlled economy** économie *f* dirigée *ou* planifiée
◊ *Econ* **controlled market** marché *m* dirigé
◊ *Econ* **controlled price** taxe *f*; **to sell goods at the controlled price** vendre des marchandises à la taxe

convention *n* (a) *(agreement)* convention *f*; **to sign a convention on sth** signer une convention sur qch (b) *(meeting)* convention *f*, congrès *m*; *Am Pol* convention *f*

convergence *n EU* convergence *f*
◊ **convergence criteria** critères *mpl* de convergence
◊ **convergence process** processus *m* de convergence

convertible *adj (money, currency)* convertible

conviction politics *n* politique *f* de conviction

> **❝**
>
> Iain Duncan Smith has brought more clarity than William Hague to Conservative rejection of the single currency forever. There will be a real argument, with no blurring. **Conviction politics** will range two leaders against each other in an existential contest. It could be as benign a galvanising event for Britain as Le Pen's advance has been a corrosive one for France.
>
> **❞**

cooperation *n Econ* coopération *f*
◊ **cooperation agreement** accord *m* de coopération
◊ *EU* **cooperation in justice and home affairs** coopération *f* en justice et affaires intérieures
◊ *EU* **cooperation procedure** procédure *f* de coopération

cooperative 1 n coopérative f
   2 adj coopératif(ive)
◊ Am Pol **cooperative federalism** fédéralisme m coopératif

Coreper n EU (abbr **Committee of Permanent Representatives**) Coreper m

core region n Econ région f centrale

corporate adj d'entreprise
◊ *corporate finance* finance f d'entreprise
◊ *corporate sector* secteur m des grandes entreprises

corporation n (a) (company) société f, compagnie f (b) (municipal authorities) municipalité f
◊ Am *corporation income tax* impôt m sur les sociétés
◊ Br *corporation tax* impôt m sur les sociétés

corporatism n corporatisme m

corrective adj Econ anticonjoncturel(-elle)

correlate 1 vt (in statistics) corréler; **to correlate sth with sth** corréler qch avec qch; **these two trends are closely correlated** ces deux tendances sont en rapport étroit
   2 vi **to correlate (with sth)** (in statistics) être en corrélation (avec qch)

correlation n (in statistics) corrélation f
◊ *correlation coefficient* coefficient m de corrélation

correlational adj (in statistics) corrélationnel(elle)

corrupt 1 adj (official, politician) corrompu(e)
   2 vt (official, politician) corrompre

corruption n (of official, politician) corruption f

cost 1 n (price) coût m, frais mpl
   2 vt (be priced at) coûter
◊ *cost analysis* analyse f des coûts, analyse f du prix de revient
◊ *cost factor* facteur m coût
◊ *cost of living* coût m de la vie
◊ Am *cost of living adjustment* aug-

mentation f de salaire indexée sur le coût de la vie
◊ *cost of living index* indice m du coût de la vie
◊ *cost sharing* participation f aux frais

cost-benefit analysis n analyse f des coûts et rendements

cost-push inflation n Econ inflation f par les coûts

council 1 n **(a)** (group of people) conseil m
   (b) Br (elected local body) (people) conseil m; (government) municipalité f; **she's standing for election to the council** elle se présente aux élections du conseil; **to be on the council** être au conseil; **the council is improving services** la municipalité est en train d'améliorer les services
   (c) (meeting) conseil m
   2 adj Br (election, service, worker) municipal(e); (leader, meeting) du conseil municipal
◊ Am Pol **Council of Economic Advisors** = groupe de conseillers nommés par le président des États-Unis pour formuler la politique économique du pays
◊ Am Pol **Council on Environmental Quality** = organisme fédéral américain pour la qualité de l'environnement
◊ **Council of Europe** Conseil m de l'Europe
◊ **Council of the European Union** Conseil m de l'Union européenne
◊ EU **Council of Ministers** Conseil m des ministres
◊ Formerly Econ **Council for Mutual Economic Aid** Comecon m
◊ EU **Council for Security and Cooperation in Europe** Conférence f sur la sécurité et la coopération en Europe
◊ **Council of States** (in Swiss Parliament) Conseil m des États
◊ *council of war* conseil m de guerre

councillor, Am **councilor** n conseiller(ère) m,f; **Councillor (John) Murray** Monsieur le Conseiller Murray

councillorship, Am **councilorship** n (a) (rank) dignité f de conseiller (b) (period in office) période f d'exercice des fonctions de conseiller; **during his councillorship** pendant la période où il a exercé en tant que conseiller

councilman n Am conseiller m

councilor, councilorship Am = councillor, councillorship

councilwoman n Am conseillère f

count vt **to count the votes** dépouiller le scrutin, compter les voix

countercyclical adj Econ anticyclique
◇ **countercyclical policy** politique f anticyclique

countertrade n Econ commerce m d'échange, troc m

countertrading n Econ commerce m d'échange, troc m

countervail vt Econ contrebalancer, compenser

countervailing adj Econ compensatoire, compensateur(trice)
◇ **countervailing duty** droit m compensateur
◇ **countervailing power** pouvoir m compensateur

country n pays m; Br Pol **to go to the country** appeler le pays aux urnes
◇ Econ **country risk** risque-pays m

county n
◇ Br Pol **county council** conseil m général
◇ Br Pol **county councillor** conseiller(-ère) m,f général(e)

coup n (overthrow of government) coup m d'État
◇ **coup d'état** coup m d'État

court n (institution) cour f, tribunal m
◇ **Court of Appeal** cour f d'appel
◇ EU **Court of Auditors** Cour f des comptes européenne
◇ EU **Court of First Instance** Tribunal m de première instance
◇ EU **Court of Justice of the European Communities** Cour f de Justice des Communautés européennes

CP n Pol (abbr **Communist Party**) PC m

CPI n Am Econ (abbr **Consumer Price Index**) IPC m

CPS n Pol (abbr **Crown Prosecution Service**) ≃ ministère m public

CPSA n (abbr **Civil and Public Services Association**) = syndicat de la fonction publique en Grande-Bretagne

crash 1 n (slump) krach m, débâcle f
2 vi (of business) faire faillite; (of prices, shares, economy) s'effondrer

crawling peg n Econ parité f rampante

credit n crédit m
◇ **credit card** carte f de crédit
◇ **credit ceiling** plafond m de crédit
◇ **credit control** resserrement m du crédit
◇ **credit freeze** gel m des crédits
◇ Am **credit squeeze** restriction f ou encadrement m du crédit
◇ **credit union** société f ou caisse f de crédit

creditor n Econ créancier(ère) m,f
◇ **creditor country** pays m créditeur
◇ **creditor nation** pays m créditeur

creed n Pol credo m

creeping inflation n Econ inflation f galopante

crisis n Pol choc m, crise f

criterion n critère m

crony n Fam Pej Pol pote m, copain(-ine) m,f; **a Labour crony is believed to have got the top advisory job** le principal poste de conseiller aurait été attribué à un membre du parti travailliste proche du pouvoir
◇ **crony capitalism** capitalisme m de copinage

" —

McCain made reference to the scandals involving Enron, Arthur Anderson, Global Crossing, WorldCom, Tyco, and others, and said,

"the first principles of free markets –
transparency and trust – have been
the first victims of **crony capitalism**."
He said the vast majority of honest
businessmen have been hurt by the
actions of a few. .

"

cronyism *n Fam Pej Pol* copinage *m*

crop *n (produce)* produit *m* agricole,
culture *f*

cross *vt Br Parl* **to cross the floor (of
the House)** changer de parti politique

crossbench *n Br Parl* = à la Chambre
des lords, banc où s'assoient les députés non inscrits à un parti; **on the
crossbenches** du côté des non-inscrits

crossbencher *n Br Parl* = à la Chambre des lords, député non inscrit à
un parti, assis sur les bancs transversaux

cross-border *adj* transfrontières,
transfrontalier(ère)
◇ *cross-border talks* négociations *fpl*
transfrontalières
◇ *cross-border trade* commerce *m*
transfrontalier

cross-elasticity of demand *n Econ*
élasticité *f* croisée de la demande

crossholding *n Econ* participation *f*
croisée

crossover voting *n Am Pol* = fait
pour les membres d'un parti politique
de voter pour un autre parti

cross-party *adj Pol*
◇ *cross-party agreement* accord *m*
entre partis
◇ *cross-party support* = soutien audelà des clivages politiques
◇ *cross-party talks* négociations *fpl*
entre partis

cross-subsidization *n Econ* interfinancement *m*

crowding-in *n Econ* attraction *f*, envahissement *m*

crowding-out *n Econ* éviction *f* financière

Crown *n* **the Crown** la Couronne,
l'État *m* (monarchique)
◇ *Pol* **Crown Agent** = fonctionnaire
du ministère britannique du développement outre-mer chargé des
pays étrangers et des organisations
internationales
◇ *Pol* **Crown Prosecution Service** ≃
ministère *m* public

CSC *n (abbr* **Civil Service Commission**) =
commission de recrutement des
fonctionnaires

CSCE *n EU (abbr* **Council for Security
and Cooperation in Europe**) CSCE *f*

CSP *n (abbr* **Chartered Society of Physiotherapy**) = syndicat britannique de
kinésithérapeutes

CSU *n Br (abbr* **Civil Service Union**) =
syndicat britannique de la fonction
publique

Culture Secretary *n Br Pol* ≃ ministre *m* de la Culture

cumulative voting *n* vote *m* plural

currency *n Econ* monnaie *f*, devise *f*;
bad currency drives out good la mauvaise monnaie chasse la bonne
◇ *currency appreciation* appréciation *f* d'une monnaie
◇ *currency basket* panier *m* de devises
◇ *Currency Board* conseil *m* monétaire, Currency Board *m*
◇ *currency depreciation* dépréciation *f* monétaire
◇ *currency devaluation* dévaluation *f*
monétaire
◇ *currency dumping* dumping *m* de
change
◇ *currency expansion* expansion *f*
monétaire
◇ *currency market* marché *m* monétaire, marché *m* des changes
◇ *currency reserves* réserves *fpl* de
devises
◇ *currency revaluation* réévaluation *f*
monétaire
◇ *currency snake* serpent *m* monétaire
◇ *currency supply* offre *f* de devises

◇ *currency swap* échange *m* de devises

◇ *currency unit* unité *f* monétaire

current *adj*

◇ *Econ* **current account** compte *m* courant

◇ *Econ* **current account equilibrium** équilibre *m* du compte courant

◇ *current affairs* actualité *f*

◇ *Econ* **current balance** balance *f* courante

curve *n Econ* courbe *f*

customs *npl (authorities, checkpoint)* douane *f*; *(duty)* droits *mpl* de douane

◇ *customs barriers* barrières *fpl* douanières

◇ *customs drawback* remboursement *m* des droits de douane

◇ *customs duty* droits *mpl* de douane

◇ *Br* **Customs and Excise** ≃ la Régie

◇ *Br* **Customs and Excise officer** ≃ employé(e) *m,f* de la Régie

◇ *customs rate* tarif *m* douanier

◇ *customs service* service *m* des douanes

◇ *customs union* union *f* douanière

cut 1 *n (in price, taxes)* réduction *f*, diminution *f*; **a cut in government spending** une réduction *ou* diminution des dépenses publiques; **the cuts in the Health Service** la réduction *ou* diminution du budget de la santé

2 *vt (price, taxes)* réduire; **they cut taxes in the run-up to the election** ils ont réduit les impôts juste avant les élections

CWA *n (abbr* **Communications Workers of America***)* = syndicat américain des travailleurs des secteurs des télécommunications, de la télédiffusion câblée et du journalisme

CWU *n (abbr* **Communication Workers Union***)* = syndicat britannique des travailleurs des télécommunications

cycle *n Econ* cycle *m*

cyclical *adj Econ* cyclique

◇ *cyclical fluctuations* fluctuations *fpl* cycliques

◇ *cyclical unemployment* chômage *m* conjoncturel

DAC *n* (*abbr* **Development Assistance Committee**) CAD *m*

Dáil (Éireann) *n Parl* = chambre des députés de la république d'Irlande

dark horse *n Am Pol* candidat(e) *m,f* surprise

> Republican candidate Alan Keyes is a **dark horse** candidate in the 2000 presidential election campaign. The former State Department employee has not received as much media attention or political contributions as the front-runners, but he pulled ahead of other candidates in this week's caucuses in Iowa.

day of action *n* journée *f* d'action

DCF *n Econ* (*abbr* **discounted cash flow**) cash-flow *m* actualisé

deal *n Econ* transaction *f*

debate *Parl* **1** *n* débat *m*
   2 *vt* (*question*) débattre, discuter, agiter; (*subject*) mettre en discussion
   3 *vi* discuter (**with sb/on sth** avec qn/sur qch)

debt *n* dette *f*
◇ *debt burden* surendettement *m*, fardeau *m* de la dette
◇ *debt rating* rating *m* de la dette
◇ *debt ratio* ratio *m* d'endettement
◇ *debt rescheduling* rééchelonnement *m* des dettes
◇ *debt restructuring* rééchelonnement *m* des dettes

◇ *debt trap* piège *m* de la dette

debtor *n* débiteur(trice) *m,f*
◇ *Econ debtor country* pays *m* débiteur
◇ *Econ debtor nation* pays *m* débiteur

decentralist *Pol* **1** *n* décentralisateur(trice) *m,f*
   2 *adj* décentralisateur(trice)

decentralization *n Pol* décentralisation *f*

decentralize *vt Pol* décentraliser

decentralizing *adj Pol* décentralisateur(trice)

declaration *n* déclaration *f*
◇ *declaration of independence* déclaration *f* d'indépendance
◇ *declaration of intent* déclaration *f* d'intention
◇ *declaration of war* déclaration *f* de guerre

declare *vt* (**a**) (*announce*) déclarer; **the government has declared that ...** le gouvernement a déclaré que ...; **to declare war** déclarer la guerre; **the two countries have declared war** (*on each other*) les deux pays se sont déclaré la guerre (**b**) *Pol* **to declare oneself** se présenter, présenter sa candidature

decontrol *Econ* **1** *n* (*of prices*) libération *f*
   2 *vt* (*trade*) lever le contrôle gouvernemental sur; (*prices*) libérer

decree *Pol* **1** *n* décret *m*, arrêté *m*
   2 *vt* décréter, arrêter

deduct *vt* (*payment*) prélever

deduction n (payment) prélèvement m

defeat Parl **1** n (of bill) échec m; (of measure) rejet m
2 vt (bill) faire échouer

defect vi Pol (to another country) passer à un pays ennemi; (to another party) quitter son parti pour un autre; **to defect to the West** passer à l'Ouest; **she defected to the Labour Party** elle a rejoint le parti travailliste

defection n Pol (to another country) passage m à un pays ennemi; (to another party) passage m à un parti adverse

defector n Pol transfuge mf

defence, Am **defense** n défense f; **defences** (weapons) moyens mpl de défense; **how much is spent on defence?** combien dépense-t-on pour la défense?
◇ **defence budget** budget f de la défense
◇ **defence capability** capacités fpl de défense
◇ **defence expenditure** dépenses fpl militaires
◇ **defence facility** installation f militaire
◇ **defence forces** forces fpl armées
◇ **defence industry** industrie f de la défense
◇ **defence programme** programme m de défense
◇ **Defence Secretary** ≃ ministre m de la Défense

deferred division n Br Parl = vote remis à plus tard

deficit n Econ déficit m; **the balance of payments shows a deficit of £800 million** la balance des paiements indique un déficit de 800 millions de livres
◇ **deficit spending** dépenses fpl financées par le déficit

> **"**
> According to Keynes, market economies had a proclivity to fall into depression when consumer and business spending declined. Instead of waiting for self-correcting market mechanisms to work, Keynes advocated deliberate **deficit spending** by the government to stimulate aggregate demand. This would immediately create jobs and incomes for otherwise unemployed workers.
> **"**

deflate Econ **1** vt (prices) faire baisser, faire tomber; **to deflate the currency** provoquer la déflation de la monnaie; **the measure is intended to deflate the economy** cette mesure est destinée à faire de la déflation
2 vi provoquer la déflation de la monnaie

deflation n Econ déflation f

deflationary, deflationist adj Econ (measures) déflationniste
◇ **deflationary fiscal policy** politique f budgétaire déflationniste
◇ **deflationary gap** écart m déflationniste
◇ **deflationary policy** politique f de déflation

DEFRA n Br Pol (abbr **Department of the Environment, Food and Rural Affairs**) = ministère de l'Agriculture et de l'Environnement

deindustrialization n désindustrialisation f

deindustrialize vt désindustrialiser

delegate 1 n délégué(e) m,f
2 vt déléguer
3 vi déléguer

delegated legislation n Pol législation f déléguée

delegation n délégation f

deliver Pol **1** vt (a) (speech) prononcer; **Bush has delivered an ultimatum to Baghdad** Bush a présenté un ultimatum à Bagdad
(b) (fulfil) **can the party deliver its election promises?** est-ce que le parti arrivera à tenir ses promesses électorales?

(c) *Am (guarantee)* **can he deliver the Black vote?** est-ce qu'il peut nous assurer les voix des Noirs?

2 *vi (keep promise)* tenir parole, tenir ses promesses; **can Brown deliver on reform?** est-ce que Brown pourra tenir ses promesses en ce qui concerne les réformes?

demagogic *adj* démagogique

demagogue, *Am* **demagog** *n* démagogue *mf*

demagoguery *n* démagogie *f*

demagogy *n* démagogie *f*

demand *n Econ* demande *f*; **supply and demand** l'offre *f* et la demande
◇ *demand curve* courbe *f* (d'évolution) de la demande
◇ *demand factor* facteur *m* de demande
◇ *demand function* fonction *f* de la demande
◇ *demand management* contrôle *m* de la demande

demand-led *adj Econ* tiré(e) par la demande

demand-pull inflation *n Econ* inflation *f* par la demande

demand-side economics *n Econ* économie *f* de la demande

demarcation *n (of types of work)* attributions *fpl*
◇ *demarcation dispute* conflit *m* d'attributions

demilitarize *vt* démilitariser
◇ *demilitarized zone* zone *f* démilitarisée

democracy *n* démocratie *f*

Democrat *n Pol* (a) *(in US)* démocrate *mf* (b) *(in UK)* = membre des "Liberal Democrats"

democrat *n Pol* démocrate *mf*

Democratic *adj Am Pol* démocrate
◇ *Democratic Convention* convention *f* démocrate
◇ *the Democratic Party* le parti démocrate (américain)

democratic *adj (country, organization, principle)* démocratique; *(person)* démocrate
◇ *democratic deficit* déficit *m* démocratique
◇ *democratic government* la démocratie
◇ *democratic socialism* socialisme *m* démocratique

democratically *adv* démocratiquement

democratization *n* démocratisation *f*

democratize 1 *vt* démocratiser
2 *vi* se démocratiser

demographer *n* démographe *mf*

demographic *adj* démographique
◇ *demographic analysis* analyse *f* démographique
◇ *demographic profile* profil *m* démographique
◇ *demographic segment* segment *m* démographique
◇ *demographic segmentation* segmentation *f* démographique

demographics 1 *n (science)* (étude *f* de la) démographie *f*
2 *npl (statistics)* statistiques *fpl* démographiques

demography *n* démographie *f*

demonetarization, demonetarize = **demonetization, demonetize**

demonetization *n* démonétisation *f*

demonetize *vt* démonétiser

demonstrate *vi* manifester; **to demonstrate for/against sth** manifester pour/contre qch

demonstration *n* manifestation *f*; **to hold** *or* **stage a demonstration** faire une manifestation

demonstrator *n* manifestant(e) *m,f*

department *n Pol (division)* département *m*; *(ministry)* ministère *m*
◇ *Am Department of Agriculture* ministère *m* de l'Agriculture
◇ *Am Department of Commerce* ministère *m* du Commerce

◇ Br **Department of Culture, Media and Sport** ministère *m* de la Culture, de la Communication et des Sports

◇ Am **Department of Defense** ministère *m* de la Défense

◇ Am **Department of Education** ≃ ministère *m* de l'Éducation nationale

◇ Br **Department for Education and Skills** ≃ ministère *m* de l'Éducation nationale

◇ Am **Department of Energy** ministère *m* de l'Énergie

◇ Br **Department of the Environment, Food and Rural Affairs** = ministère de l'Agriculture et de l'Environnement

◇ Br **Department of Health** ministère *m* de la Santé

◇ Am **Department of Health and Human Services** ministère *m* de la Santé

◇ Am **Department of Housing and Urban Development** ministère *m* du logement et de la ville

◇ Am **Department of the Interior** = ministère de l'Intérieur

◇ Br **Department for International Development** = secrétariat d'État à la Coopération

◇ Am **Department of Justice** ministère *m* de la Justice

◇ Am **Department of Labor** = ministère de l'Emploi et de la Solidarité

◇ Br **Department of Public Works** ≃ ministère *m* de l'Équipement

◇ Am **Department of State** Département *m* d'État, ≃ ministère *m* des Affaires étrangères

◇ Am **Department of Trade** ministère *m* du Commerce

◇ Br **Department of Trade and Industry** ministère *m* du Commerce et de l'Industrie

◇ Br **Department of Transport** ministère *m* des Transports

◇ Am **Department of Transportation** ministère *m* des Transports

◇ Am **Department of Veterans Affairs** ministère *m* des Anciens combattants

◇ Br **Department of Work and Pensions** ≃ ministère *m* du Travail

departmental *adj Pol (of division)* du département; *(of ministry)* du ministère

departmentalization *n Pol* division *f* en départements

departmentalize *vt Pol* diviser en départements

dependency *n*

◇ **dependency culture** = situation d'une société dont les membres ont une mentalité d'assistés

◇ *Econ* **dependency theory** théorie *f* de la dépendance

❝

"We should be trying to create a high-wage economy, not a **dependency culture** that covers the majority of workers," says Mr Field. "When we started in 1997 we should have been developing policies that raise productivity so Britain can compete in the world economy. By now we would be seeing the benefits. Instead, the majority of family living standards will only rise if the government can afford to increase the benefits they receive."

❞

depose *vt (sovereign)* déposer, destituer

deposit *n Br Parl* cautionnement *m*; **to lose one's deposit** perdre son cautionnement

deposited papers *npl Br Parl* = documents placés à la bibliothèque de la Chambre des communes ou des lords par un ministre, le plus souvent en réponse à des questions posées par des députés lors de débats

deposition *n (of sovereign)* déposition *f*, destitution *f*

depository institution *n* établissement *m* financier

depreciate 1 *vt (currency)* dévaloriser, déprécier

2 *vi (of currency)* se dévaloriser, se déprécier; **the pound has depreciated against the dollar** la livre a reculé par rapport au dollar

depreciated *adj (currency)* dévalorisé(e), déprécié(e)

depreciation *n (of currency)* dévalorisation *f*, dépréciation; *(amount)* moins-value *f*

depress *vt Econ (trade)* faire languir; *(economy, market)* affaiblir; *(prices, profits, wages)* (faire) baisser; *(area, industry)* toucher

depressed *adj Econ (trade)* languissant(e); *(economy, market)* affaibli(e), déprimé(e), en crise; *(prices, profits, wages)* en baisse; *(area, industry)* touché(e) par la crise, déprimé(e); **one of the most depressed sectors of the economy** un des secteurs économiques les plus touchés par la crise; **the economy has been in a depressed state for nearly three years** l'économie est dans un état de marasme depuis bientôt trois ans

depression *n Econ (slump)* dépression *f*, crise *f* économique; *(fall in output)* ralentissement *m*; **the country's economy is in a state of depression** l'économie du pays est en crise

deputation *n (representatives, action)* députation *f*, délégation *f*

deputize 1 *vt* députer
2 *vi* **to deputize for sb** représenter qn; **the First Secretary deputized for the Ambassador at the reception** le premier secrétaire représentait l'ambassadeur à la réception

deputy *Pol* **1** *n* **(a)** *(elected representative)* député(e) *m,f* **(b)** *(assistant)* adjoint(e) *m,f*
2 *adj*
◇ *Br Pol* **Deputy Chief Whip** = adjoint du responsable du maintien de la discipline à l'intérieur d'un parti à la Chambre des communes et à la Chambre des lords
◇ **Deputy First Minister** = adjoint du

Premier ministre du Parlement d'Écosse ou de l'Assemblée du pays de Galles ou de l'Assemblée législative d'Irlande du Nord
◇ **Deputy Leader** adjoint(e) *m,f* du chef; **he is the former Deputy Leader of the Labour/Conservative Party** c'est l'ancien adjoint du leader du parti travailliste/conservateur
◇ **Deputy Leader of the House** = adjoint du parlementaire de la majorité chargé de certaines fonctions dans la mise en place du programme gouvernemental
◇ **deputy mayor** adjoint(e) *m,f* au maire, maire *m* adjoint
◇ **Deputy Minister** Sous-Ministre *m*
◇ **deputy presiding officer** vice-président(e) *m,f*
◇ **Deputy Prime Minister** vice-Premier-ministre *m*
◇ **Deputy Speaker** = adjoint du président de l'Assemblée

deregister *vt (person, party, organization)* radier

deregistration *n (of person, party, organization)* radiation *f*

deregulate *vt Econ* **(a)** *(prices, wages)* libérer, déréguler **(b)** *(relax restrictions on)* assouplir les règlements de, déréglementer; **he's in favour of deregulating the economy** il est partisan de la déréglementation de l'économie

deregulated price *n Econ* prix *m* libre

deregulation *n Econ* **(a)** *(of prices, wages)* libération *f*, dérégulation *f* **(b)** *(relaxation of restrictions)* assouplissement *m* des règlements, déréglementation *f*
◇ **Deregulation Order** = loi de déréglementation

derivative *n* instrument *m* dérivé

derogatory clause *n* clause *f* dérogatoire

deselect *vt Br Pol (candidate)* ne pas resélectionner

> 〟
>
> It estimates that "around half" the 411 Labour Party members in Hartlepool are so disaffected with their MP, who resigned as Northern Ireland Secretary last year after the Hinduja cash-for-passport scandal, that they would back moves to **deselect** him.
>
> 〞

deselection n Br Pol (of candidate) = fait de ne pas sélectionner

desirability n Econ désidérabilité f

despot n Pol despote m

despotic adj Pol despotique

despotically adv Pol despotiquement; **to govern/rule despotically** gouverner/régner en despote

despotism n Pol despotisme m

destabilization n (of country, regime) déstabilisation f

destabilize vt (country, regime) déstabiliser

destabilizing adj (for country, regime) déstabilisant(e)
◇ **destabilizing factor** facteur m de déséquilibre

de-Stalinization n Pol déstalinisation f

de-Stalinize vt Pol déstaliniser

détente n Pol détente f

deterrence n force f de dissuasion; **nuclear deterrence is indispensable to national security** une force de dissuasion nucléaire est indispensable pour la sécurité nationale

deterrent n (a) (force) agent m de dissuasion; **to act as** or **be a deterrent (to)** exercer un effet dissuasif (contre); **nuclear weapons act as a deterrent** les armes nucléaires ont un rôle dissuasif (b) (weapon) arme f de dissuasion

devaluation n Econ dévaluation f

devalue vt Econ dévaluer; **the pound has been devalued by three percent** le livre a été dévalué de trois pour cent

develop Econ 1 vt (market, region) développer
2 vi (of country, region) se développer

developed adj Econ (market) développé(e); (country, region) développé(e), industrialisé(e)

developer n Econ promoteur(trice) m,f

developing n
◇ Econ **developing country** pays m en voie de développement
◇ Econ **developing nation** nation f en voie de développement

development n Econ (of market, country, region) développement m
◇ **development aid** = aide aux pays en voie de développement
◇ Br **development area** = zone économiquement sinistrée bénéficiant d'aides publiques en vue de sa conversion
◇ **Development Assistance Committee** Comité m d'aide au développement
◇ **development capital** capital-développement m
◇ **development economics** économie f du développement
◇ **development site** terrain m à lotir

deviationist Pol 1 n déviationniste mf
2 adj déviationniste

devolution n (a) (of power) délégation f (b) Pol décentralisation f

devolutionary adj Pol décentralisateur(trice)

devolutionist Pol 1 n partisan(e) m,f de la décentralisation
2 adj décentralisateur(trice)

devolve vt (powers) déléguer
◇ Pol **devolved parliament** ≃ parlement m régional

DfES n Br Pol (abbr **Department for Education and Skills**) ≃ ministère m de l'Éducation nationale

DfID n Br Pol (abbr **Department for International Development**) = secrétariat d'État à la Coopération

dictator n dictateur m

dictatorial adj dictatorial(e)

dictatorship n dictature f

diehard Pol **1** n conservateur(trice) m,f, réactionnaire mf; **the party diehards** les durs du parti
   2 adj réactionnaire; **a diehard liberal** un libéral pur et dur

> **❝**
>
> In the dying days of Major's Government, about five million voters were so keen to see the end of the Tories that they told friends, relatives, neighbours, or workmates that they were not going to vote for them, encouraging others to follow suit. About four million encouraged others to vote Labour, compared with a core of about a million **diehard** Tories who were prepared to stand up and say they were sticking by the stricken Government.
>
> **❞**

differential n Econ différentiel m

digital adj
◇ **digital divide** fracture f numérique
◇ **digital economy** netéconomie f

dignitary n dignitaire m

dignity n (rank) dignité f, haut rang m; (title) titre m, dignité f

diktat n Pol diktat m

diminish 1 vt (price, quality, value) diminuer, réduire
   2 vi diminuer, se réduire; **their profits have diminished** leurs bénéfices ont diminué

diminishing 1 n diminution f, baisse f
   2 adj (price, quality, value) qui baisse, en baisse
◇ Econ **diminishing marginal product** produit m marginal décroissant
◇ Econ **diminishing marginal utility** utilité f marginale décroissante

◇ Econ **diminishing returns** rendements mpl décroissants; **the law of diminishing returns** la loi des rendements décroissants

diplomacy n Pol diplomatie f

diplomat n Pol diplomate mf

diplomatic adj Pol diplomatique
◇ Br **diplomatic bag** valise f diplomatique
◇ **diplomatic corps** corps m diplomatique
◇ **diplomatic crisis** crise f diplomatique
◇ **diplomatic immunity** immunité f diplomatique, inviolabilité f diplomatique; **to claim diplomatic immunity** faire valoir l'immunité ou l'inviolabilité diplomatique
◇ **diplomatic marathon** marathon m diplomatique
◇ **diplomatic mission** mission f diplomatique
◇ Am **diplomatic pouch** valise f diplomatique
◇ **diplomatic protection** asile m diplomatique
◇ **diplomatic relations** relations fpl diplomatiques
◇ **diplomatic row** querelle f diplomatique
◇ **diplomatic sanctions** sanctions fpl diplomatiques
◇ **the Diplomatic Service** la diplomatie, le service diplomatique; **to enter the Diplomatic Service** entrer dans la diplomatie

diplomatically adv Pol diplomatiquement

diplomatist n Pol diplomate mf

direct adj direct(e)
◇ **direct action** action f directe
◇ **direct aid** aide f directe
◇ **direct democracy** démocratie f directe
◇ **direct election** élection f directe
◇ **direct investment** investissement m direct
◇ **direct labour** main-d'œuvre f directe

◇ *direct labour organization* syndicat *m* ouvrier

◇ *Am Pol* **direct primary** élection *f* primaire directe, primaire *f* directe

◇ *Pol* **direct rule** = contrôle direct du maintien de l'ordre par le gouvernement britannique en Irlande du Nord imposé en 1972

◇ *direct suffrage* suffrage *m* direct

◇ *direct tax* impôt *m* direct

◇ *direct taxation* contributions *fpl* directes

◇ *direct universal suffrage* suffrage *m* universel direct

◇ *direct vote* vote *m* direct

directive *n EU & Pol* directive *f*, instruction *f*

directorate general *n EU* conseil *m* d'administration

dirigisme *n Econ & Pol* dirigisme *m*

dirty *adj*

◇ *Econ* **dirty float** taux *m* de change concerté

◇ *Pol* **dirty tricks campaign** = manœuvres déloyales visant à discréditer un adversaire politique

> **"**
>
> But he also expressed fear that information could be used in inappropriate ways once obtained by authorities. Frank made specific reference to a **dirty tricks campaign** against Martin Luther King by former FBI Director J. Edgar Hoover. Having failed to find criminal evidence to use against King, Frank said, Hoover instead used information gained through surveillance to personally embarrass and publicly humiliate the civil rights leader.
>
> **"**

disarm 1 *vt (country)* désarmer
2 *vi (of country)* désarmer

disarmament 1 *n* désarmement *m*
2 *adj (conference, negotiations, talks)* sur le désarmement

disarticulate *vt Econ* désarticuler

disarticulation *n Econ* désarticulation *f*

discount *vt Econ* actualiser

discounted *adj Econ* actualisé(e)

◇ *discounted cash flow* cash-flow *m* actualisé

discounting *n Econ* actualisation *f*

discretionary spending *n Am Pol* = dépenses susceptibles d'être modifiées par le Congrès américain

discriminate *vi* **to discriminate in favour of** favoriser; **she was discriminated against** elle faisait l'objet *ou* était victime de discriminations; **there are many people being sexually/racially discriminated against** nombreux sont ceux qui sont victimes de discrimination sexuelle/raciale

discrimination *n* discrimination *f*

diseconomy *n Econ* déséconomie *f*

◇ *diseconomy of scale* déséconomie *f* d'échelle

disenfranchise *vt Pol (person)* déchoir du droit de vote *ou* de ses droits civiques; *(borough)* déchoir de ses droits de représentation

disenfranchisement *n Pol (of person)* déchéance *f* du droit de vote *ou* de ses droits civiques; *(of borough)* déchéance *f* de ses droits de représentation

disengage *vi Pol* se désengager

disengagement *n Pol* désengagement *m*

disequilibrium *n Econ* déséquilibre *m*

◇ *disequilibrium price* prix *m* de déséquilibre

disincentive *n Econ* facteur *m* décourageant; **to act as a disincentive to sth** avoir un effet dissuasif sur qch; **heavy taxation is a disincentive to expansion** les taxes élevées découragent toute expansion

disinflation *n Econ* désinflation *f*

disinflationary *adj Econ* désinflationniste

disintermediation n Econ désintermédiation f

disinvest vi Econ désinvestir; **to disinvest in sth** désinvestir qch

disinvestment n Econ désinvestissement m

dismiss vt (official) destituer, révoquer, relever de ses fonctions

dismissal n (of official) destitution f, révocation f

dispatch n
◇ **dispatch box** (for documents) boîte f à documents
◇ Br Parl **the dispatch box** = tribune d'où parlent les membres du gouvernement et leurs homologues du cabinet fantôme; **the Minister's strong performance at the dispatch box appears to have secured his future** la belle prestation du ministre à la tribune de la Chambre des communes semble avoir rendu sa position beaucoup plus solide
◇ **dispatch case** serviette f, porte-documents m

> **"**
>
> In a relaxed speech, which was punctuated with several self-deprecating remarks about his own future, Mr Hague showed that he was still adept and at ease at the **dispatch box**; at times, his jokes had the House in fits of laughter.
>
> **"**

dispensation n Pol (system) régime m; **under the present dispensation** dans le système actuel

displaced person n Pol personne f déplacée

disposable 1 n Econ **disposables** biens mpl de consommation non durables
2 adj (available) disponible
◇ Econ **disposable goods** biens mpl de consommation non durables
◇ **disposable income** revenu m disponible

dissaving n Econ désépargne f

dissent Pol **1** n désaccord m; **to voice** or **to express one's dissent** exprimer son désaccord; **voices of dissent** voix fpl discordantes
2 vi (of person) différer; (of opinion) diverger; **to dissent from an opinion** être en désaccord avec une opinion

dissenter n Pol dissident(e) m,f

dissidence n Pol dissidence f

dissident Pol **1** n dissident(e) m,f
2 adj dissident(e)

dissolution n (of Parliament) dissolution f

dissolve **1** vt (Parliament) dissoudre
2 vi (of Parliament) être dissout(e)

distribute vt Econ (wealth) répartir, distribuer; (population) répartir

distribution n Econ (of wealth) répartition f, distribution f; (of population) répartition f

district n (of country) région f; (of town) quartier m; (of city) ≃ arrondissement m; (administrative) district m
◇ Br **district council** conseil m municipal
◇ Br **district councillor** conseiller(ère) m,f municipal(e)

disutility n Econ désutilité f

divergence n Econ divergence f

divide **1** vt (a) Pol (territory) diviser; (party) diviser, scinder (b) Br Parl **to divide the House** faire voter la Chambre
2 vi (a) Pol (of party) se diviser; **a policy of divide and rule** une politique consistant à diviser pour régner (b) Br Parl (go to vote) aller aux voix; **the House divided on the question** la Chambre a voté sur la question

divided adj (territory, party) divisé(e); **the party is divided on the issue** le parti est divisé sur ce problème; **a political party divided against itself** un parti divisé

divided-party government n Am

Pol ≃ cohabitation *f (cas de figure où le Congrès est dominé par un parti qui n'est pas celui du Président)*

division *n* (a) *(dissension)* division *f* (b) *(sharing out)* partage *m* (c) *Br Parl* = vote officiel à la Chambre des communes (pour lequel les députés se répartissent dans les deux "division lobbies"); **a division will be necessary** il faudra procéder à un vote; **the amendment was approved on a division** l'amendement a été approuvé lors d'un vote à la Chambre des communes; **the bill was passed without division** le projet de loi a été adopté sans qu'on ait procédé à un vote; **to carry a division** avoir *ou* remporter la majorité des voix; **to come to a division** procéder à un vote; **to call a division** annoncer un vote; **to call for a division on sth** demander que qch soit soumis à un vote

◇ *Br Parl* **division bell** = sonnerie à la Chambre des communes prévenant les députés qu'il faut venir voter

◇ *Econ* **division of labour** division *f* du travail

◇ *Br Parl* **division list** = liste des députés qui ont voté pour ou contre une motion

◇ *Br Parl* **division lobby** = nom des deux salles dans lesquelles les députés britanniques se répartissent pour voter

divisive *adj* fractionnel(elle)

DLO *n (abbr* **direct labour organization)** syndicat *m* ouvrier

DoH *n Br Pol (abbr* **Department of Health)** ministère *m* de la Santé

dollar *n* dollar *m*

◇ *Econ* **dollar area** zone *f* dollar

◇ **dollar balances** balances *fpl* dollars

◇ **dollar diplomacy** diplomatie *f* du dollar

dollarization *n Econ* dollarisation *f*

domestic *adj (affairs)* intérieur(e); *(currency, economy)* national(e)

◇ **domestic market** marché *m* intérieur

◇ **domestic policy** politique *f* intérieure

◇ *Am Pol* **Domestic Policy Council** = ensemble des conseillers du Président des États-Unis en matière de politique intérieure

◇ **domestic products** denrées *fpl* du pays, produits *mpl* d'origine nationale

◇ **domestic sales** ventes *fpl* domestiques

◇ **domestic trade** commerce *m* intérieur

dominance *n (of political party)* prédominance *f*

dominant *adj (political party)* prédominant(e)

◇ *Econ* **dominant firm** leader *m*, chef *m* de file

dominate *vt Pol* dominer

dominating *adj Pol (force, nation)* dominateur(trice)

domination *n Pol* domination *f*

doorstep *vt Br (of politician)* démarcher

doorstepping *Br* **1** *n (by politician)* démarchage *m* électoral; **doorstepping is a valuable way of generating electoral support** le démarchage électoral est une bonne façon de recruter des partisans

2 *adj (politician)* qui fait du démarchage électoral

double taxation *n* double imposition *f*

◇ **double taxation relief** déduction *f* pour double imposition

doughnut *vi Br Parl (surround speaker)* = à la Chambre des communes ou des lords, faire bloc autour d'un orateur lors d'une session filmée, pour créer l'illusion soit d'une solidarité, soit d'une fréquentation assidue

❝

This book scarcely mentions the media at all. I don't necessarily blame the media for anything, but if a book that discusses how politicians have changed for the worse is to make any sense it must look at the changing demands from the media. The invention of the soundbite ... surrounding the leader in the House of Commons with photogenic faces (or **doughnutting**), Labour's merciless imposition of discipline on its back-benchers, the cult of the party leader, and the increasingly presidential style of government have all been responses to television.

77

dove n Pol colombe f; **the doves and the hawks** les colombes fpl et les faucons mpl

dovish adj Pol (person) partisan(e) de la manière douce; (speech) conciliateur(trice)

downfall n (of person, institution) chute f, ruine f; (of government) écroulement m, effondrement m

downgrade vt (civil servant) rétrograder

Downing Street n Br Pol = rue de Londres où se trouve la résidence officielle du Premier ministre; **there has been no confirmation from Downing Street** le Premier ministre n'a pas apporté de confirmation
◇ **Downing Street declaration** = déclaration faite conjointement en 1993 par le Premier ministre britannique John Major et son homologue irlandais Albert Reynolds dans le but de mettre fin aux hostilités entre catholiques et protestants en Irlande du Nord

downside n Econ aval m

downsize 1 vt (company) réduire les effectifs de
2 vi (of company) réduire ses effectifs

downsizing n (of company) réduction f d'effectifs

downstream Econ **1** adj en aval
2 adv en aval

downswing n (trend) tendance f à la baisse, baisse f

downturn n (in inflation, unemployment figures) baisse f; (in economy) ralentissement m

downward adj
◇ **downward mobility** régression f sociale
◇ **downward trend** tendance f à la baisse ou baissière

DPM n (abbr **Deputy Prime Minister**) vice-Premier-ministre m

draconian adj (law, regime) draconien(enne)

draft 1 n (of bill, proposal) avant-projet m; (of speech) premier jet m
2 vt (bill) préparer; (proposal) rédiger; (speech) faire le brouillon de, rédiger
◇ **draft agreement** protocole m d'accord
◇ **draft budget** projet m de budget
◇ **draft legislation** projet m d'acte législatif
◇ **draft treaty** projet m de convention
▸ **draw up** vt sep (manifesto, bill) rédiger

▸ **drive down** vt sep Econ (prices, inflation) faire baisser

▸ **drive up** vt sep Econ (prices, inflation) faire monter

dry Br Fam Pol **1** n (hardliner) = conservateur en faveur de la politique extrémiste du parti
2 adj (hardline) = en faveur de la politique extrémiste du parti conservateur

44

This is the man who, when he was a minister, was notorious for being among the most arid of the Tory **dries**, described by Thatcher as " ... beyond any questioning a passionate supporter of everything we stood for", who abruptly became passionate in the opposite direction when he was looking to get back into parliament.

77

DTI *n Br Pol* (*abbr* **Department of Trade and Industry**) ministère *m* du Commerce et de l'Industrie

DTR *n* (*abbr* **double taxation relief**) déduction *f* pour double taxation

dual *adj* double
◇ *EU* **dual circulation** (*of currencies*) double circulation *f*
◇ *EU* **dual circulation period** période *f* de double circulation
◇ **dual currency** deux monnaies *fpl*
◇ **dual economy** économie *f* duale
◇ *Am Pol* **dual federalism** fédéralisme *m* dual

dualism *n Econ* dualisme *m*

dualist *n Econ* dualiste *mf*

dualistic *adj Econ* dualiste

dump *vt Econ* **to dump goods** faire du dumping

dumping *n Econ* dumping *m*

duopolistic *adj Econ* duopoliste, duopolistique

duopoly *n Econ* duopole *m*

Dutch auction *n* adjudication *f* à la hollandaise

duty-free **1** *n* marchandises *fpl* hors taxe *ou* en franchise
2 *adj* (*goods*) hors taxe, en franchise
3 *adv* hors taxe, en franchise
◇ **duty-free importation** importation *f* hors taxe *ou* en franchise

DWP *n Br Pol* (*abbr* **Department of Work and Pensions**) ≃ ministère *m* du Travail

EAC n (abbr **Environmental Audit Committee**) comité m d'audit environnemental

EAGGF n (abbr **European Agriculture Guidance and Guarantee Fund**) FEOGA m

Early Day Motion n Br Parl = proposition de loi dont la discussion n'est pas à l'ordre du jour, présentée par un député qui recherche l'appui de collègues de façon à attirer l'attention du parlement sur une question

❝

"These permitted development rights have simply been a way to put masts in inappropriate locations without elected representatives and the public being allowed to voice their concerns." Labour's Howard Stoate, who proposed an **Early Day Motion** on planning issues which was signed by 160 MPs, said: "If the health fears turn out to be groundless I'll be delighted but until then we should adopt the precautionary principle and site masts away from schools and residential areas."

❞

eastern adj
◇ **Eastern Bloc** bloc m de l'Est
◇ **Eastern Europe** Europe f de l'Est
◇ **Eastern European countries** pays mpl d'Europe de l'Est

EBRD n (abbr **European Bank for Reconstruction and Development**) BERD f

EC n Pol (abbr **European Community**) CE f

ECB n (abbr **European Central Bank**) BCE f

ECC n EU (abbr **European Community Commission**) CCE f

ECE n (abbr **Economic Commission for Europe**) Commission f économique pour l'Europe

ECHR n (abbr **European Court of Human Rights**) CEDH f

ECI n (abbr **Employer Cost Index**) = rapport trimestriel du ministère de l'Emploi américain, indiquant le niveau des salaires et des prestations sociales, parfois considéré comme un indicateur du niveau d'inflation

ECJ n (abbr **European Court of Justice**) CJCE f

Ecofin n EU (abbr **Economic Council of Finance Ministers**) (Conseil m) Ecofin m

econometric adj Econ économétrique
◇ **econometric model** modèle m économétrique

econometrician n Econ économétricien(enne) m,f

econometrics n Econ économétrie f

econometrist n Econ économétricien(enne) m,f

economic adj Econ économique
◇ **economic activity** activité f économique
◇ **economic adviser** conseiller(ère) m,f économique

Les grandes unions économiques

AMU

Arab Maghreb Union (1989)
Member countries: Algeria, Libya, Mauritania, Morocco, Tunisia

Aims: • ensure regional stability
• introduce free circulation of goods, services and factors of production

APEC

Asia-Pacific Economic Cooperation (1989)
Member countries: Australia, Brunei Darussalam, Canada, Chile, China, Hong Kong, Indonesia, Japan, Korea, Malaysia, Mexico, New Zealand, Papua New Guinea, Peru, Philippines, Russia, Singapore, Chinese Taipei, Thailand, United States, Vietnam

Aim: • promote open trade and practical economic cooperation between member states

ASEAN

Association of South East Asian Nations (1967)
Member countries: Brunei Darussalam, Cambodia, Indonesia, Laos, Malaysia, Myanmar, Philippines, Singapore, Thailand, Vietnam

Aim: • accelerate economic growth and social and cultural development

CACM

Central American Common Market (1960)
Member countries: Costa Rica, El Salvador, Guatemala, Honduras, Nicaragua

Aim: • promote the coordination of monetary, credit and exchange policies

CAEMC

Central African Economic and Monetary Community (1994)
Member countries: Cameroon, Central African Republic, Chad, Democratic Republic of Congo, Equatorial Guinea, Gabon

Aim: • encourage the process of subregional integration within the framework of economic and monetary union

CAN

Andean Community of Nations (1969)
Member countries: Bolivia, Colombia, Ecuador, Peru, Venezuela

Aims: • improve Andean free-trade zone
• harmonize economic policies of member states

CARICOM

Caribbean Community (1973)
Member countries: Antigua and Barbuda, the Bahamas, Barbados, Belize, Dominica, Grenada, Guyana, Haiti, Jamaica, Montserrat, St Kitts and Nevis, St Lucia, St Vincent and the Grenadines, Surinam, Trinidad and Tobago

Associate Members: Anguilla, British Virgin Islands, Cayman Islands, Turks and Caicos Islands

Aims: • promote economic cooperation through the Caribbean Single Market and Economy
• coordinate foreign policy
• develop common services and cooperation in areas such as health, education and culture, communications and industrial relations

CIS

Commonwealth of Independent States (1991)
Member countries: Armenia, Azerbaijan, Belarus, Georgia, Kazakhstan, Kyrgyzstan, Moldova, Russia, Tajikistan, Turkmenistan, Ukraine, Uzbekistan

Aims: • coordinate the foreign and economic policies of member states
• create a free-market rouble zone

COMESA

Common Market for Eastern and Southern Africa (1994)
Member countries: Angola, Burundi, Comoros, Democratic Republic of Congo, Djibouti, Egypt, Eritrea,

Ethiopia, Kenya, Madagascar, Malawi, Mauritius, Namibia, Rwanda, Seychelles, Sudan, Swaziland, Uganda, Zambia, Zimbabwe

Aim: • form a large economic and trading bloc to encourage economic growth in the region

ECOWAS

Economic Community of West African States (1975)

Member countries: Benin, Burkina Faso, Cape Verde, Côte d'Ivoire, The Gambia, Ghana, Guinea, Guinea-Bissau, Liberia, Mali, Niger, Nigeria, Senegal, Sierra Leone, Togo

Aims: • create an economic and monetary union
• free movement of Community citizens

EU

European Union (1993)

Member countries: Austria, Belgium, Denmark, Finland, France, Germany, Greece, Ireland, Italy, Luxembourg, Netherlands, Portugal, Spain, Sweden, United Kingdom

Aims: • develop the single market (and single currency) among member states based on the free circulation of people, goods, services and capital
• develop policy coordination on wide-ranging issues

MERCOSUR

Southern Common Market (1991)

Member countries: Argentina, Brazil, Paraguay, Uruguay

Aims: • establish more productive and dynamic economies through enlargement of the market
• promote harmonious and balanced socio-economic development

NAFTA

North American Free Trade Agreement (1994)

Member countries: Canada, Mexico, United States

Aims: • eliminate trade barriers
• facilitate cross-border movement of goods and services
• promote fair competition in the free-trade area

OECD

Organization for Economic Cooperation and Development (1960)

Member countries: Australia, Austria, Belgium, Canada, Czech Republic, Denmark, Finland, France, Germany, Greece, Hungary, Iceland, Ireland, Italy, Japan, Korea, Luxembourg, Mexico, Netherlands, New Zealand, Norway, Poland, Portugal, Slovak Republic, Spain, Sweden, Switzerland, Turkey, United Kingdom, United States

Aim: • coordinate economic and social policies

OPEC

Organization of Petroleum Exporting Countries (1960)

Member countries: Algeria, Indonesia, Iran, Iraq, Kuwait, Libya, Nigeria, Qatar, Saudi Arabia, United Arab Emirates, Venezuela

Aims: • coordinate and unify members' petroleum policies
• safeguard members' interests

SADC

Southern African Development Community (1992)

Member countries: Angola, Botswana, Democratic Republic of Congo, Lesotho, Malawi, Mauritius, Mozambique, Seychelles, South Africa, Swaziland, Tanzania, Zambia, Zimbabwe

Aims: • coordinate sustainable economic development
• consolidate regional links

WAEMU

West African Economic and Monetary Union (1994)

Member countries: Benin, Burkina Faso, Côte d'Ivoire, Guinea-Bissau, Mali, Niger, Senegal, Togo

Aims: • reinforce economic and financial competition of member states, including establishing a common external tariff and a common commercial policy
• create a common market among member states based on the free circulation of people, goods, services and capital

◇ *economic agent* agent *m* économique, acteur *m* économique

◇ *economic aid* aide *f* économique, aide *f* au développement économique

◇ *economic analysis* analyse *f* économique

◇ *economic analyst* analyste *mf* économique

◇ *economic appraisal* évaluation *f* économique

◇ *economic assumption* hypothèse *f* économique

◇ *economic blockade* blocus *m* économique

◇ *economic climate* climat *m* économique

◇ *EU Economic Commission for Europe* Commission *f* économique pour l'Europe

◇ *economic convergence* convergence *f* économique

◇ *economic cooperation* coopération *f* économique

◇ *economic cost* coût *m* économique

◇ *economic crisis* crise *f* économique

◇ *economic cycle* cycle *m* économique

◇ *economic determinism* déterminisme *m* économique

◇ *economic development* croissance *f* économique

◇ *economic efficiency* efficacité *f* économique

◇ *economic efficiency principle* principe *m* d'efficacité économique

◇ *economic embargo* embargo *m* économique

◇ *economic expansion* expansion *f* économique, essor *m* économique

◇ *economic factor* facteur *m* économique

◇ *EU Economic and Financial Council of Ministers* Conseil *m* Ecofin

◇ *economic forecast* prévision *f* économique *ou* conjoncturelle

◇ *economic geography* géographie *f* économique

◇ *economic goods* biens *mpl* économiques

◇ *economic growth* croissance *f* économique, expansion *f* économique

◇ *economic growth rate* taux *m* de croissance économique, taux *m* d'expansion économique

◇ *economic hub* pôle *m* économique

◇ *economic indicator* indicateur *m* économique, indicateur *m* d'activité économique

◇ *economic integration* intégration *f* économique

◇ *economic interest group* groupement *m* d'intérêt économique

◇ *economic life* durée *f* de vie utile

◇ *economic man* homme *m* économique

◇ *economic migrant* émigrant(e) *m,f* de la faim *ou* pour des raisons économiques

◇ *economic miracle* miracle *m* économique

◇ *economic model* modèle *f* économique

◇ *Pol Economic and Monetary Union* Union *f* économique et monétaire

◇ *economic paradigm* paradigme *m* économique

◇ *economic paralysis* asphyxie *f* économique

◇ *economic performance* (of country) résultats *mpl* économiques

◇ *economic plan* programme *m* économique

◇ *economic planner* conjoncturiste *mf*

◇ *economic planning* planification *f* économique

◇ *economic policy* politique *f* économique *ou* conjoncturelle

◇ *economic power* puissance *f* économique

◇ *economic pressure* pression *f* économique

◇ *economic programme* programme *m* économique

◇ *economic prospects* prévisions *fpl* économiques *ou* conjoncturelles

◇ *economic rate of return* taux *m* de rentabilité économique

◇ *economic recession* récession *f* *ou* crise *f* économique

◇ *economic recovery* reprise *f* économique

◇ *economic refugee* migrant(e) *m,f* économique

◇ *economic regulations* réglementation *f* économique

◇ *economic rent* loyer *m* économique

◇ *economic restructuring* reconversion *f* économique

◇ *economic sanctions* sanctions *fpl* économiques

◇ *Br* **Economic Secretary** secrétaire *mf* à l'économie

◇ *economic sector* secteur *m* économique

◇ *economic situation* conjoncture *f* économique

◇ *EU* **Economic and Social Committee** Comité *m* Économique et Social

◇ *economic surplus* plus-value *f* économique

◇ *economic system* système *m* économique

◇ *economic test* test *m* économique

◇ *economic trend* tendance *f* ou conjoncture *f* économique

◇ *economic weather* conjoncture *f* économique

◇ *economic welfare* bien-être *m* économique

◇ *economic zone* zone *f* économique

❝

In November 1997 Gordon Brown outlined five **economic tests** by which the government would judge whether the UK economy would benefit from joining the euro. They include whether joining a single currency would be good for jobs, for foreign investment, for the City, and whether the UK economy was marching in step with other European countries, and whether it had enough flexibility to adjust if it wasn't. The government has said it will announce whether or not the UK meets the five **economic tests** by June 2003 – and if it does, it would ask the country's voters to decide in a referendum whether to join the euro.

❞

economically *adv Econ* économiquement

◇ *economically developed country* pays *m* développé

economics *n Econ (science)* économie *f* (politique), sciences *fpl* économiques

◇ *economics correspondent* journaliste *mf* économique

◇ *economics journalist* journaliste *mf* économique

economism *n Econ* économisme *m*

economist *n Econ* économiste *mf*

economy *n (system)* économie *f*

◇ *economy drive (of company, government)* politique *f* de réduction des dépenses

◇ *economy of scale* économie *f* d'échelle

◇ *economy of scope* économie *f* de champ

ECOSOC *n (abbr* **Economic and Social Committee***)* CES *m*

ecotax *n* taxe *f* écologique, écotaxe *f*

ECOWAS *n (abbr* **Economic Community of West African States***)* CEDEAO *f*

ECSC *n (abbr* **European Coal and Steel Community***)* CECA *f*

ECU¹, ecu *n Formerly (abbr* **European Currency Unit***)* ECU *m*, écu *m*

ECU² *n (abbr* **European Customs Union***)* Union *f* douanière européenne

EDC *n* (a) *(abbr* **European Defence Community***)* CED *f* (b) *(abbr* **economically developed country***)* pays *m* développé

EDF *n (abbr* **European Development Fund***)* FED *m*

edict *n Pol* décret *m*

Education Secretary *n Br Pol* ≃ ministre *m* de l'éducation

EEA *n Pol (abbr* **European Economic Area***)* EEE *m*

EEB *n EU (abbr* **European Environmental Bureau***)* BEE *m*

EEC *n Formerly Pol (abbr* **European Economic Community***)* CEE *f*

e-economy n économie f en ligne

Our approach is to work in partnership with business, the voluntary sector, trade unions and consumer groups to maximise the benefits of the **e-economy**. The Internet has opened up a world of opportunities for business and communication. The World Wide Web is now accessed by 93 percent of Scottish businesses, one of the highest figures in Europe.

EEIG n EU (abbr **European Economic Interest Grouping**) GEIE m

EEOC n Am (abbr **Equal Employment Opportunities Commission**) = commission pour l'égalité des chances d'emploi aux États-Unis

effective adj Econ (return, yield) effectif(ive); (value) réel(elle)
◇ **effective annual rate** taux m annuel effectif
◇ **effective demand** demande f effective
◇ **effective exchange rate** taux m de change effectif
◇ **effective income** revenu m réel
◇ **effective production** production f effective
◇ **effective tax rate** taux m d'imposition effectif

efficiency n (of organization, method, system) efficacité f; (productivity) productivité f

efficient adj (organization, method, system) efficace; (productive) productif(ive)
◇ **efficient market** marché m efficient

EFTA, Efta n (abbr **European Free Trade Association**) AELE f

egalitarian 1 n égalitariste mf
2 adj égalitaire

egalitarianism n égalitarisme m

EIB n (abbr **European Investment Bank**) BEI f

EIF n (abbr **European Investment Fund**) FEI m

elastic adj Econ (supply, demand) élastique

elasticity n Econ (supply, demand) élasticité f

elder statesman n (politician) vétéran m de la politique

elect vt Pol élire; **to elect sb President** élire qn président; **to get elected** être élu(e); **to elect sb to office** élire qn

elected adj Pol élu(e)
◇ **elected dictatorship** = gouvernement élu qui se comporte comme une dictature
◇ **elected government** gouvernement m élu

Anyone who believed the second New Labour government would be humbled by its massive victory and start behaving less like an **elected dictatorship** after 7 June will have been disappointed by its behaviour so far. Tony Blair has shown no sign that he is about to drop his control freakery or limit the influence of his spin doctors.

election n Pol élection f; **to stand for election** se présenter aux élections; **to hold an election** procéder à une élection; **the elections** les élections fpl
◇ **election campaign** campagne f électorale
◇ **election day** jour m des élections
◇ **election observer** observateur m électoral
◇ **election platform** plate-forme f électorale
◇ **election programme** programme m électoral
◇ **election promise** promesse f électorale

◇ *election results* résultats *mpl* électoraux

◇ *election speech* discours *m* électoral

◇ *election trail* tournée *f* électorale; **on the election trail** en tournée électorale

electioneer *vi Pol* participer à la campagne électorale; *Pej* faire de la propagande électorale, faire de l'électoralisme

electioneering *Pol* **1** *n* campagne *f* électorale; *Pej* propagande *f* électorale, électoralisme *m*

2 *adj (speech, campaign)* électoral(e); *Pej* propagandiste

elective *adj Pol* (a) *(assembly)* électoral(e) (b) *(official, post)* électif(ive)

◇ *elective dictatorship* = gouvernement élu qui se comporte comme une dictature

elector *n Pol (with power to elect)* électeur(trice) *m,f*; *(in US electoral system)* grand électeur(trice) *m,f*, membre *m* du collège électoral

electoral *adj Pol* électoral(e)

◇ *electoral alliance* apparentement *m*, alliance *f* électorale

◇ *electoral balance* balance *f* électorale

◇ *electoral body* corps *m* électoral

◇ *electoral bribery* corruption *f* électorale

◇ *electoral college* collège *m* électoral *(qui élit le président des États-Unis)*

◇ *Br Electoral Commission* commission *f* électorale

◇ *electoral committee* comité *m* électoral

◇ *electoral corruption* corruption *f* électorale

◇ *electoral debate* débat *m* électoral

◇ *electoral district* circonscription *f* électorale

◇ *electoral franchise* capacité *f* électorale

◇ *electoral geography* géographie *f* électorale

◇ *electoral pact* pacte *m* électoral

◇ *electoral platform* plate-forme *f* électorale

◇ *electoral process* processus *m* électoral

◇ *electoral programme* programme *m* électoral

◇ *electoral promise* promesse *f* électorale

◇ *Br electoral reform* réforme *f* électorale

◇ *Br electoral register* liste *f* électorale; **on the electoral register** sur la liste électorale

◇ *electoral returns* résultats *mpl* des élections

◇ *Br electoral roll* liste *f* électorale; **on the electoral roll** sur la liste électorale

◇ *electoral system* système *m* électoral, régime *m* électoral

◇ *Am electoral vote* vote *m* collégial

◇ *electoral writ* acte *m* de convocation du corps électoral

electorate *n Pol* électorat *m*

eligibility *n Pol* éligibilité *f*

eligible *adj Pol* éligible; **these countries are not eligible to join the EU** ces pays ne peuvent pas poser leur candidature pour devenir membres de l'UE

EMA *n (abbr* **European Monetary Agreement)** AME *m*

embargo *Econ & Pol* **1** *n* embargo *m*; **to put** *or* **to place** *or* **to lay an embargo on sth** mettre l'embargo sur qch; **to lift/to break an embargo** lever/enfreindre un embargo; **there is still an embargo on arms, arms are still under an embargo** les armes sont encore sous embargo

2 *vt* mettre l'embargo sur

embassy *n* ambassade *f*; **the British/ French Embassy** l'ambassade *f* de Grande-Bretagne/France

◇ *embassy official* fonctionnaire *mf* d'ambassade

◇ *embassy secretary* secrétaire *mf* d'ambassade

◇ *embassy staff* personnel *m* d'ambassade

EMCF n Formerly (abbr **European Monetary Cooperation Fund**) FECOM m

emergency n
◇ **emergency aid** aide f d'urgence
◇ Br Parl **emergency debate** débat m d'urgence
◇ **emergency food aid** aide f alimentaire d'urgence
◇ **emergency legislation** loi f d'exception, loi f d'urgence
◇ **emergency measure** mesure f d'urgence
◇ **emergency powers** pouvoirs mpl extraordinaires

emerging adj Econ (country, economy) emergent(e)

EMF n (abbr **European Monetary Fund**) FME m

EMI n Formerly (abbr **European Monetary Institute**) IME m

emigrant 1 n émigrant(e) m,f; (when established abroad) émigré(e) m,f
2 adj (worker, population) émigré(e)

emigrate vi émigrer (**to** à)

emigration n émigration f

emirate n émirat m

empire n empire m

employee n employé(e) m,f, salarié(e) m,f; **management and employees** la direction et les employés ou le personnel; (in negotiations) les partenaires mpl sociaux
◇ **employee's contributions** (to benefits) cotisations fpl salariales, charges fpl sociales salariales

employer n employeur(euse) m,f; **employers** (as a body) patronat m
◇ **employers' association** organisation f patronale, syndicat m patronal
◇ **employer's contributions** (to employee benefits) cotisations fpl patronales, charges fpl sociales patronales
◇ **employer cost index** = rapport trimestriel du ministère de l'Emploi américain, indiquant le niveau des salaires et des prestations sociales,

parfois considéré comme un indicateur du niveau d'inflation
◇ **employers' federation** chambre f syndicale, syndicat m patronal
◇ **employers' organization** organisation f patronale, syndicat m patronal

employment n emploi m; **to be in employment** avoir un emploi ou du travail; **to be without employment** être sans emploi ou travail
◇ Br Pol **Employment Act** = loi sur l'égalité des chances pour l'emploi
◇ **employment law** code m du travail
◇ **employment legislation** législation f du travail

EMS n Formerly (abbr **European Monetary System**) SME m

EMU n Pol (abbr **Economic and Monetary Union**) UME f

enact vt Parl (bill, law) promulguer

enactment n Parl (of bill, law) promulgation f

endogenous adj Econ endogène
◇ **endogenous variable** variable f endogène

endorse vt Pol (candidature, policy) appuyer, soutenir

endorsement n Pol (of candidature, policy) appui m

endow vt (person, institution) doter (**with** de)

endowment n (action, money) dotation f

enfranchise vt Pol (person) admettre au suffrage, accorder le droit de vote à; (borough) accorder le droit de représentation à

enfranchisement n Pol (of person) admission f au suffrage, octroi m du droit de vote; (of borough) octroi m du droit de représentation

English auction n vente f aux enchères

enlargement n (of EU) élargissement m
◇ **enlargement criteria** critères mpl d'élargissement

enosis n Pol énosis f

enroll vt Am Pol (prepare) dresser, rédiger; (register) enregistrer
◊ *enrolled bill* projet m de loi enregistré

entente n entente f

enter vt (politics) se lancer dans; **the government should encourage more women to enter politics** le gouvernement devrait davantage encourager les femmes à se lancer dans la politique

enterprise n (business, project) entreprise f
◊ Br *enterprise allowance* aide f à la création d'entreprises
◊ Br *Enterprise Allowance Scheme* fonds m d'aide à la création d'entreprise
◊ Br *enterprise area* = zone d'encouragement à l'implantation d'entreprises dans les régions économiquement défavorisées
◊ *enterprise culture* = attitude favorable à l'essor de l'esprit d'entreprise
◊ *enterprise economy* = type d'économie qui facilite la création d'entreprises
◊ *enterprise society* = type de société où l'entreprise privée est valorisée
◊ Br *enterprise zone* = zone d'encouragement à l'implantation d'entreprises dans les régions économiquement défavorisées

❝

"The **enterprise culture** will only be truly a British **enterprise culture** if no town, no community however depressed is left behind and if we extend its opportunities and benefits to the poorest areas of Britain where we need not more giro cheques being sent but more businesses being created," Mr Brown told the Transport and General Workers' Union's Manufacturing Matters conference in Leeds.

❞

enthrone vt introniser

enthronement n intronisation f

entrepreneur n entrepreneur(euse) m,f

entrepreneurial adj (activities, decision) d'entrepreneur; (person, society) qui a l'esprit d'entreprise

entrepreneurship n entreprenariat m

entry n (of goods into country) entrée f
◊ *entry barrier* barrière f à l'entrée
◊ *entry permit* permis m d'entrée
◊ *entry talks* pourparlers mpl d'adhésion
◊ *entry visa* visa m d'entrée

entryism n Pol entrisme m, noyautage m

entryist Pol **1** n personne f qui pratique l'entrisme ou le noyautage
2 adj d'entrisme, de noyautage

environment n Econ & Pol environnement m
◊ *Environment Secretary* ≃ ministre m de l'Équipement

environmental adj Econ & Pol écologique
◊ *Environmental Audit Committee* comité m d'audit environnemental
◊ *environmental economics* économie f de l'environnement
◊ Am *Environmental Protection Agency* = agence américaine pour la protection de l'environnement

envoy n (emissary) envoyé(e) m,f, représentant(e) m,f
◊ Pol *envoy extraordinary* ministre m plénipotentiaire

EOC n (abbr **Equal Opportunities Commission**) = commission pour l'égalité des chances en matière d'emploi, en Grande-Bretagne

EP n (abbr **European Parliament**) Parlement m européen

EPC n EU (abbr **European Political Cooperation**) coopération f en matière de politique étrangère

EPP n Pol (abbr **European People's Party**) PPE m

equal adj
◇ Econ **equal distribution** proportionnalité f
◇ Am **Equal Employment Opportunities Commission** = commission pour l'égalité des chances en matière d'emploi, aux États-Unis
◇ **equal opportunities** chances fpl égales, égalité f des chances
◇ Br **Equal Opportunities Commission** = commission pour l'égalité des chances en matière d'emploi, en Grande-Bretagne
◇ **equal opportunity employer** = entreprise s'engageant à respecter la législation sur la non-discrimination dans l'emploi
◇ **equal rights** égalité f des droits

equality n égalité f; **equality of opportunity** égalité f des chances

equalization n (of taxes, wealth) péréquation f

equalize vt (taxes, wealth) faire la péréquation de

equilibrium n Econ équilibre m
◇ **equilibrium price** prix m d'équilibre
◇ **equilibrium quantity** quantité f d'équilibre

Equity n = principal syndicat britannique des gens du spectacle

equity n (of company) capital m actions; (of shareholders) capitaux mpl ou fonds mpl propres; **equities** actions fpl ordinaires

ERDF n (abbr **European Regional Development Fund**) FEDER m

ergonomic adj ergonomique

ergonomics n ergonomie f

ERM n Formerly (abbr **Exchange Rate Mechanism**) mécanisme m de change

ESCB n (abbr **European System of Central Banks**) SEBC m

ESF n (abbr **European Social Fund**) FSE m

establish vt (government) constituer, établir; (political party) implanter

established adj (government) établi(e), au pouvoir; (political party) établi(e)

Establishment n (ruling powers) **the Establishment** les pouvoirs mpl établis, l'ordre m établi, l'establishment m; **to be against the Establishment, to be anti-Establishment** être anticonformiste; **to revolt against the Establishment** se révolter contre l'ordre établi

> **"**
>
> But a dispersed electorate presents more of a challenge for Mr Jospin than it does for the main conservative contender, Jacques Chirac. While Mr Chirac's centre-right rivals are marginal, Mr Jospin finds it much harder to ignore the left-wing candidates snapping at his heels. The main ones are not official members of the "plural left", but **anti-Establishment** candidates who could attract many protest votes.
>
> **"**

establishment n (of government) constitution f; (of political party) implantation f

ethnic adj ethnique
◇ **ethnic cleansing** nettoyage m ethnique
◇ **ethnic group** groupe m ethnique
◇ **ethnic minority** minorité f ethnique

ethnicity n Pol ethnicité f

ethnicize vt Pol ethniciser

ethnocentric adj ethnocentrique

ethnocentrism n ethnocentrisme m

ethnocide n ethnocide f

ETU n (abbr **Electrical Trades Union**) = syndicat britannique d'électriciens

ETUC n (abbr **European Trade Union Confederation**) CES f

EU n (abbr **European Union**) UE f; **the EU member states** les États membres de l'UE; **imports to the EU** les importations vers l'UE

◇ **EU legislation** législation f européenne

◇ **EU policy** politique f communautaire

Eur. (*abbr* **Europe**) l'Europe f

Euratom n (*abbr* **European Atomic En-**
ergy Community) CEEA f, Euratom m

euro n EU (currency) euro m

◇ EU **Euro area** zone f euro

◇ EU **Euro zone** zone f euro, eurozone f

Eurobabble n Fam jargon m de Bruxelles

❝

In a speech at the London School of
Economics today Mr Hain will avoid
dangerous talk about timetables
when he attacks Eurosceptics for
misusing the opaque language
known as **Eurobabble** to promote
what he regards as "Euromyths". But
he will admit that "to normal well-
adjusted people the [treaties] are
completely unreadable" – not because of a Brussels plot, but because politicians from each country
want to "protect everyone's interest"
by being precise.

❞

Eurobank n eurobanque f

Eurobarometer n Eurobaromètre m

Eurocentric adj eurocentrique

Eurocentrism n eurocentrisme m

Eurocommunism n Pol eurocommunisme m

Eurocommunist Pol **1** n eurocommuniste mf
  2 adj eurocommuniste

Eurocorps n Eurocorps m

Eurocracy n eurocratie f

Eurocrat n eurocrate mf

Eurocratic adj eurocratique

eurocurrency n eurodevise f, euromonnaie f

◇ **eurocurrency market** marché m
des eurodevises, euromarché m

eurodollar n eurodollar m

euro-dollar parity n parité f euro-
dollar

Euro-elections n élections fpl européennes

Euroland n Pol Eurolande f

Euromarket, Euromart n marché
m des eurodevises, euromarché m

Euro-MP n (*abbr* **European Member of**
Parliament) député(e) m,f europée-
n(enne), parlementaire mf europée-
n(enne)

Europe n Europe f; **in Europe** en Europe; **in Britain, Europe has become a**
sensitive political subject en Grande-
Bretagne, la question de l'Union européenne est un sujet très délicat;
some MPs want Britain to get out of
Europe certains députés britanniques
veulent que la Grande-Bretagne se
retire de l'Union européenne; **when**
Britain went into Europe in 1973 quand
la Grande-Bretagne est devenue
membre de la CEE en 1973

◇ **Europe agreement** accord m européen

◇ Br Pol **Europe Minister** ministre m
pour l'Europe

European 1 n (inhabitant of Europe)
Européen(enne) m,f; (pro-Europe
person) partisan(e) m,f de l'Europe
unie, Européen(enne) m,f
  2 adj (of Europe) européen(enne);
(pro-Europe) en faveur de l'Europe
unie, européen(enne); **we must adopt**
a more European outlook nous devons
adopter un point de vue plus européen ou plus ouvert sur l'Europe

◇ **European Agriculture Guidance**
and Guarantee Fund Fonds m européen d'orientation et de garantie
agricole

◇ **European amendment** amendement m européen

◇ **European Atomic Energy Commu-**
nity Communauté f européenne de
l'énergie atomique

History of the European Union

Historique de l'Union européenne

Apr 1951	Treaty of Paris establishes the European Coal and Steel Community (ECSC) between France, Germany, Italy, Belgium, the Netherlands and Luxembourg
Oct 1954	The Six and the United Kingdom found the Western European Union (WEU) to strengthen security cooperation between European countries
Mar 1957	Rome Treaties establish the European Economic Community (EEC) and the European Atomic Energy Community (Euratom)
May 1960	European Free Trade Association (Efta) established by Austria, Denmark, Norway, Portugal, Sweden, Switzerland and the United Kingdom
Jan 1962	Common Agricultural Policy agreed by the Six
1963	Turkey signs an association agreement
Jul 1968	European Customs Union established
Oct 1970	European Council creates 'EPC' procedures for foreign policy cooperation
1971	The Werner Report sets out a three-stage process for achieving EMU
Jan 1973	United Kingdom, Ireland and Denmark join the EEC
Mar 1975	European Regional Development Fund established
Mar 1979	Creation of the EMS (European Monetary System): the ERM (Exchange Rate Mechanism) is established with eight member currencies and the Ecu is introduced as the weighted average of all European currencies
Jan 1981	Greece joins the EEC
Feb 1984	Draft Treaty on European Union passed by a large majority in European Parliament
Jun 1985	Schengen Agreement eliminating border controls ratified by Belgium, France, Germany, Luxembourg and the Netherlands
1986	Portugal and Spain join the EEC
1987	Turkey applies for EEC membership
1986-87	The Single European Act formalizes the programme for the European Single Market
1989	Publication of the Delors Report on economic and monetary union: this outlines concrete stages by which EMU is to be implemented
May 1990	Agreement signed to establish the European Bank for Reconstruction and Development
Jun 1990	Second Schengen Agreement signed; all member states now covered except Ireland, the United Kingdom and, to some extent, Denmark
Jul 1990	Stage 1 of EMU: removal of exchange controls across Europe and abolition of capital controls. Cyprus and Malta apply to join the EEC
Dec 1991	Europe Agreements signed with Poland and Hungary; other countries of Central Europe follow at intervals
Feb 1992	Maastricht Treaty establishes the European Union, enshrines principle of monetary union and prescribes convergence criteria for member states signing up to join the single currency; also increases power of European Parliament, introduces European

	citizenship, and sets up two new pillars, for Common Foreign and Security Policy and Cooperation in Justice and Home Affairs
May 1992	The Efta countries sign a pact with the EEC countries to institute the European Economic Area (EEA)
Jan 1993	The EEC becomes the European Union (EU)
Nov 1993	Maastricht Treaty enters into force when composition of the EU currency basket is frozen
Jan 1994	Stage 2 of EMU: the European Monetary Institute (EMI) is founded as a precursor to the European Central Bank
1995	Austria, Finland and Sweden join the EU
Dec 1995	The new currency is officially christened the euro at European Council meeting in Madrid. EU-Turkey Customs Union comes into play
Mar 1996	Start of the Intergovernmental Conference (IGC) in Turin: EU institutional reforms discussed and preparations made for EU enlargement
Dec 1996	The Stability and Growth Pact ensures that economic discipline is maintained within EU countries
1997	Draft Amsterdam Treaty signed: resolution on ERM II links currencies of non-participating member states to the euro; it also increases the scope of co-decision and reforms the pillars on foreign policy and on justice and home affairs
Mar 1998	Accession negotiations with Cyprus, the Czech Republic, Estonia, Hungary, Poland and Slovenia; European strategy for Turkey introduced
May 1998	EMU commences formally: EU heads of state decide which countries qualify for membership of the single currency, fix bilateral currency conversion rate and agree to keep their national economies in line with convergence criteria
Jun 1998	European Central Bank (ECB) inaugurated
Oct 1998	European Council agrees measures of defence cooperation
Jan 1999	The euro becomes the official currency of the EMU participating states: conversion rates of the currencies of these states are locked to the euro
Mar 1999	Agenda 2000 proposals to modify EU policies for enlargement concluded
Jan 2000	Accession negotiations open with Bulgaria, Latvia, Lithuania, Malta, Romania and the Slovak Republic
Dec 2000	Treaty of Nice seeks to prepare the EU institutions for enlargement and facilitates enhanced cooperation between nations. The Charter of Fundamental Rights established
Feb 2001	Treaty of Nice ratified
Jan 2002	Euro banknotes and coins introduced
Jul 2002	Stage 3 of EMU: national coins and notes withdrawn from circulation in EMU-partici-pating countries
Dec 2002	Copenhagen Summit: ten new countries (Cyprus, Czech Republic, Estonia, Hungary, Latvia, Lithuania, Malta, Poland, Slovenia and the Slovak Republic) will accede to the EU in 2004

◇ *European Bank for Reconstruction and Development* Banque *f* européenne pour la reconstruction et le développement

◇ *European Central Bank* Banque *f* centrale européenne

◇ *European Central Securities Depositories Association* Association *f* européenne des dépositaires centraux de titres

◇ *Pol European Coal and Steel Community* Communauté *f* européenne de charbon et de l'acier

◇ *European cohesion fund* Fonds *mpl* européens de cohésion

◇ *European Commission* Commission *f* européenne

◇ *European Commissioner* Commissaire *m* européen

◇ *European Common Market* Marché *m* commun européen

◇ *Pol European Community* Communauté *f* européenne

◇ *European Community Commission* Commission *f* des communautés européennes

◇ *European Convention on the Future of Europe* Convention *f* européenne sur l'avenir de l'Europe

◇ *European Convention for the Protection of Human Rights and Fundamental Freedoms* Convention *f* de sauvegarde des droits de l'homme et des libertés fondamentales

◇ *European Council* Conseil *m* européen

◇ *European Court of Auditors* Cour *f* des comptes européenne

◇ *European Court of First Instance* Tribunal *m* de première instance

◇ *European Court of Human Rights* Cour *f* européenne des droits de l'homme

◇ *European Court of Justice* Cour *f* de justice des communautés européennes

◇ *European currency snake* serpent *m* monétaire européen

◇ *Formerly European Currency Unit* Unité *f* monétaire européenne

◇ *European Customs Union* Union *f* douanière européenne

◇ *European Defence Community* Communauté *f* européenne de défense

◇ *European Development Fund* Fonds *m* européen de développement

◇ *European Economic Area* Espace *m* économique européen

◇ *Formerly European Economic Community* Communauté *f* économique européenne

◇ *European Economic Interest Grouping* Groupement *m* européen d'intérêt économique

◇ *European elections* élections *fpl* européennes

◇ *European Environmental Bureau* Bureau *m* européen de l'environnement

◇ *Formerly European Exchange Rate Mechanism* mécanisme *m* de change européen

◇ *European Free Trade Association* Association *f* européenne de libre-échange

◇ *European integration* intégration *f* européenne

◇ *EU European Investment Bank* Banque *f* européenne d'investissement

◇ *European Investment Fund* Fonds *m* européen d'investissement

◇ *European Monetary Agreement* Accord *m* monétaire européen

◇ *Formerly European Monetary Cooperation Fund* Fonds *m* européen de coopération monétaire

◇ *European Monetary Fund* Fonds *m* monétaire européen

◇ *Formerly European Monetary Institute* Institut *m* monétaire européen

◇ *Formerly European Monetary System* Système *m* monétaire européen

◇ *European Monetary Union* Union *f* monétaire européenne

◇ *European Ombudsman* Médiateur *m* européen

◊ *European Parliament* Parlement *m* européen

◊ *European Political Cooperation* coopération *f* en matière de politique étrangère

◊ *European Regional Development Fund* Fonds *m* européen de développement régional

◊ *European Single Market* Marché *m* unique européen

◊ *European Social Fund* Fonds *m* social européen

◊ *European Standards Commission* Comité *m* européen de normalisation

◊ *European System of Central Banks* Système *m* européen de banques centrales

◊ *European Trade Union Confederation* Confédération *f* européenne des syndicats

◊ *European troika* troïka *f* européenne

◊ *European Union* Union *f* européenne

◊ *Econ* *European unit of account* unité *f* de compte européenne

Europeanism *n* européanisme *m*

Europeanist 1 *n* européaniste *mf*
2 *adj* européaniste

Europeanization *n* européanisation *f*, européisation *f*

Europeanize *vt* européaniser; **to become Europeanized** s'européaniser

Europhile *n* europhile *mf*, partisan(e) *m,f* de l'Europe unie

Europhobe *n* europhobe *mf*

Europhobic *adj* europhobique

Euro-rebel *n* = politicien qui s'oppose à la ligne pro-européenne de son parti

> **"**
>
> At the risk of muddying things, however, let's go back to October 1995, when IDS, then one of Major's **Euro-rebels**, met privately with leaders of the French National Front and later drank with them in a Westminster bar. Bruno Gollnisch, Jean Marie Le Pen's NF deputy and an MEP, was at this meeting of minds to discuss the EU. "I came to meet members of the Conservative party sympathetic to our views," Gollnisch later told the Sunday Mirror. "I met Duncan Smith and others in their offices and later we got together for less formal talks in a bar."
>
> **"**

Eurosceptic 1 *n* eurosceptique *mf*
2 *adj* eurosceptique

Euroscepticism *n* euroscepticisme *m*

Euroseat *n* = siège de député européen

Eurospeak *n* jargon *m* communautaire

Eurostat *n* Eurostat *m*

Eurosterling *n* eurosterling *m*

ex ante *adj* *Econ* ex ante

excess *n* (*in expenditure*) excédent *m*; **there has been an excess of expenditure over revenue** les dépenses ont excédé les recettes

◊ *excess capacity* surcapacité *f*, capacité *f* excédentaire

◊ *excess demand* demande *f* excédentaire

◊ *excess supply* offre *f* excédentaire

excessive taxation *n* fiscalité *f* excessive

exchange *Econ* **1** *n* (*of currency*) change *m*; (*of goods, shares, commodities*) échange *m*
2 *vt* (*currency, goods, shares, commodities*) échanger; **to exchange sterling for dollars** changer des livres contre des dollars

◊ *Br* *exchange control* contrôle *m* des changes

◊ *exchange cross rate* taux *m* de change entre devises tierces

◊ *exchange gain* gain *m* de change

◊ *exchange index* indice *m* boursier

◊ *exchange loss* perte *f* de change

◊ *exchange market* marché *m* des changes

◇ **exchange rate** taux *m* de change, cours *m* de change ; **at the current exchange rate** au cours du jour

◇ Formerly **Exchange Rate Mechanism** mécanisme *m* (des taux) de change (du SME)

◇ **exchange rate parity** parité *f* du change

◇ **exchange rate regime** système *m* de changes

◇ **exchange rate risk** risque *m* de change

◇ **exchange rate stability** stabilité *f* des changes

◇ **exchange transaction** opération *f* de change

◇ **exchange value** contre-valeur *f*, valeur *f* d'échange

Exchequer *n Br* **the Exchequer** *(government department)* l'Échiquier *m*, le Ministère des Finances ; *(money)* le Trésor public

excise *n* (a) *(tax)* taxe *f*, contribution *f* indirecte (b) *Br (government office)* ≃ Régie *f*, service *m* des contributions indirectes

exclude *vt (bar)* exclure ; **to exclude sb from sth** exclure qn de qch ; **women were excluded from power** les femmes étaient exclues du pouvoir

exclusion *n (barring)* exclusion *f* ; **the exclusion of sb from sth** l'exclusion de qn de qch ; **the exclusion of women from voting** le fait que les femmes n'aient pas le droit de vote

exclusionist *Pol* **1** *n* partisan(e) *m,f* d'une politique d'exclusion

2 *adj (person)* partisan(e) d'une politique d'exclusion ; *(action, measure)* qui relève d'une politique d'exclusion

executive 1 *n* (a) *(body)* corps *m* exécutif ; *Pol (branch of government)* exécutif *m* ; *Am Pol* **the executive** l'exécutif *m*, le pouvoir exécutif (b) *(of political party, union)* bureau *m*, comité *m* central ; **the union's national executive** le bureau national du syndicat

2 *adj (function, role)* exécutif(ive) ;

an executive officer in the civil service un cadre de l'administration

◇ *Am Pol* **executive agreement** accord *m* en forme simplifiée *(qui ne nécessite pas l'approbation du Sénat)*

◇ *Am Pol* **the executive branch** l'exécutif *m*

◇ **executive committee** comité *m* exécutif

◇ **executive power** pouvoir *m* exécutif

◇ *Am Pol* **executive privilege** privilège *m* de l'exécutif *(droit dont bénéficie l'exécutif de limiter l'accès du Congrès, des tribunaux et du public à l'information, pour des raisons d'intérêt national)*

◇ *Am Parl* **executive session** *(of Congress)* séance *f* à huis clos

exhaustive ballot *n Pol* scrutin *m* par élimination progressive

exile *n* exil *m* ; **government in exile** gouvernement *m* en exil

exiled *adj* exilé(e) ; **the exiled government** le gouvernement en exil

exit *n*

◇ **exit permit** permis *m* de sortie

◇ *Pol* **exit poll** = sondage réalisé auprès des votants à la sortie du bureau de vote

◇ *Am Pol* **exit survey** = sondage réalisé auprès des votants à la sortie du bureau de vote

> **"**
>
> The Detroit Free Press/WXYZ-TV **exit poll** interviewed a sample of 2,048 voters Tuesday as they left 60 polling places across Michigan. Precincts were randomly selected based on the pattern of turnout in past statewide general elections. Results based on the entire sample have an estimated error margin of plus or minus 3 percentage points. The error margins are slightly higher for subgroups, such as women or people with college degrees.
>
> **"**

exogenous *adj Econ* exogène

◇ *exogenous variable* variable *f* exogène

expand *vt Econ* agrandir, élargir

expansion *n Econ* agrandissement *m*, élargissement *m*

expectations *npl Econ* anticipations *fpl*

expediency *n* (a) *(of measure, policy)* opportunité *f*; **on grounds of expediency** pour des raisons de convenance (b) *(self-interest)* opportunisme *m*; **a measure that smacks of political expediency** une mesure politique opportuniste

expel *vt Pol (from party, country)* expulser

expenditure *n* (a) *(act of spending) (of money)* dépense *f*; *(of resources)* consommation *f* (b) *(money spent)* dépenses *fpl* (**on** en)

◇ *expenditure switching* = actions d'un gouvernement pour encourager la consommation de produits nationaux

◇ *expenditure tax* impôt *m* sur les dépenses

exploit *vt (workers, natural resources)* exploiter

exploitable *adj (resource)* exploitable

exploitation *n (of workers, natural resources)* exploitation *f*

exploitative *adj (practices)* relevant de l'exploitation; **the company's exploitative attitude towards the workforce** la manière dont l'entreprise exploite la main-d'œuvre

export 1 *n* (a) *(product)* exportation *f*; **exports** *(of country)* exportations *fpl* (b) *(activity)* exportation *f*; **for export only** réservé(e) à l'exportation

2 *vt (goods)* exporter; **to export goods to other countries** exporter des marchandises vers d'autres pays

3 *vi* exporter; **the firm exports all over the world** l'entreprise exporte dans le monde entier

◇ *export aid* aide *f* à l'exportation

◇ *export ban* interdiction *f* d'exportation; **to impose an export ban on sth** interdire qch d'exportation

◇ *export bid* offre *f* export

◇ *export company* société *f* d'exportation, entreprise *f* exportatrice

◇ *export credit* crédit *m* à l'exportation

◇ *export credit guarantee* garantie *f* de crédit à l'exportation

◇ *Export Credits Guarantee Department* = organisme d'assurance pour le commerce extérieur, ≃ COFACE *f*

◇ *export credit rate* taux *m* de crédit export

◇ *export drive* campagne *f* visant à stimuler l'exportation

◇ *export duty* droit *m* de sortie *ou* à l'exportation

◇ *export earnings* revenus *mpl ou* recettes *fpl* de l'exportation

◇ *export goods* marchandises *fpl* à l'export

◇ *export incentive* prime *f* à l'exportation

◇ *export levy* prélèvement *m* à l'exportation

◇ *export licence* licence *f* d'exportation

◇ *export list* liste *f* des exportations, tarif *m* de sortie

◇ *export market* marché *m* à l'export

◇ *export permit* permis *m* d'exportation

◇ *export potential* capacité *f* d'exportation

◇ *export price* prix *m* à l'export

◇ *export quotas* contingents *mpl* d'exportation

◇ *export restrictions* restrictions *fpl* à l'exportation

◇ *export revenue* revenus *mpl* de l'exportation

◇ *export sales* ventes *fpl* export *ou* à l'exportation

◇ *export subsidy* prime *f ou* subvention *f* à l'exportation

◇ *export tariff* tarif *m* export

◇ *export tax* taxe *f* à l'exportation

◇ *export trade* commerce *m* d'exportation

exportable *adj* exportable

exportation n (a) *(activity)* exportation f (b) *Am (product)* exportation f, article m d'exportation

export-driven adj *(expansion, recovery)* basé(e) *ou* centré(e) sur les exportations

exporter n (a) *(person)* exportateur(trice) m,f (b) *(country)* (pays m) exportateur m; **Britain is now one of the world's biggest exporters of aircraft** la Grande-Bretagne est maintenant l'un des plus grands exportateurs d'avions du monde

exporting 1 n exportation f
2 adj exportateur(trice)
◇ *exporting company* société f exportatrice
◇ *exporting country* pays m exportateur

export-led growth n croissance f générée par les exportations

ex post adj Econ ex post

expulsion n Pol *(from party, country)* expulsion f

extensification n EU extensification f

extensify vt EU extensifier

external adj *(trade)* extérieur(e)
◇ *external balance* balance f extérieure
◇ *external constraint* contrainte f extérieure
◇ *external debt* dette f extérieure
◇ *external deficit* déficit m extérieur
◇ *external diseconomy* déséconomie f externe
◇ *external foreign debt* dette f extérieure
◇ *external growth* croissance f externe
◇ *external labour market* marché m du travail externe

externality n Econ externalité f

extraparliamentary adj extraparlementaire

extremism n Pol extrémisme m

extremist Pol 1 n extrémiste mf
2 adj extrémiste

Fabian *Pol* **1** *n* Fabien(enne) *m,f*
2 *adj* Fabien(enne)
◊ **Fabian Society** = groupe socialiste de la fin du XIXᵉ siècle en Grande-Bretagne

Fabianism *n Pol* fabianisme *m*

Fabianist *Pol* **1** *n* = partisan des Fabiens
2 *adj* = qui est partisan des Fabiens

faction *n Pol* (**a**) *(group)* faction *f* (**b**) *(strife)* dissension *f*, discorde *f*

factional *adj Pol* de faction

factionalism *n Pol* esprit *m* de dissension *ou* de discorde, fractionnisme *m*

factionalist *Pol* **1** *n* fractionniste *mf*
2 *adj* fractionniste

factor *n Econ* (**a**) *(element)* facteur *m* (**b**) *(factoring company)* société *f* d'affacturage
◊ **factor market** marché *m* des facteurs de production
◊ **factor of production** facteur *m* de production

factorial terms of trade *npl* termes *mpl* factoriels de l'échange

factoring *n Econ* affacturage *m*
◊ **factoring agent** agent *m* d'affacturage
◊ **factoring charges** commission *f* d'affacturage
◊ **factoring company** société *f* d'affacturage

Falangist *Pol* **1** *n* phalangiste *mf*
2 *adj* phalangiste

fall 1 *n (of government, regime)* chute *f*, renversement *m*
2 *vi (of government, regime)* tomber, être renversé(e)

fanatic *Pol* **1** *n* fanatique *mf*
2 *adj* fanatique

fanatical *adj Pol* fanatique

fanaticism *n Pol* fanatisme *m*

FAO *n (abbr* **Food and Agriculture Organization of the United Nations**) FAO *f*

fascism *n Pol* fascisme *m*

fascist *Pol* **1** *n* fasciste *mf*
2 *adj* fasciste

fascistic *adj Pol* fasciste

fast-track 1 *adj (procedure, method)* accéléré(e)
2 *vt (procedure, method)* accélérer

Father of the House *n Parl* **the Father of the House** = titre traditionnel donné au doyen (par l'ancienneté) des parlementaires britanniques

favorite son *n Am Pol* = candidat favorisé par les électeurs du même État que lui

> ❝
> Democrats say the Volunteer State's failure to elect **favorite son** Al Gore to the presidency two years ago has fired up their base like nowhere else in the country. Gore lost the state's 11 electoral votes by a three-point margin in 2000, a surprise defeat that not only cost him the state, but also, ultimately, the White House.
> ❞

FBI n Am (abbr **Federal Bureau of Investigation**) **the FBI** le FBI
◇ **FBI agent** agent m du FBI

FBU n Br (abbr **Fire Brigades Union**) = syndicat britannique de pompiers

FCO n Br Pol (abbr **Foreign and Commonwealth Office**) **the FCO** le Foreign Office, le ministère britannique des Affaires étrangères

FDA n = syndicat britannique de hauts fonctionnaires

FDI n Econ (abbr **foreign direct investment**) IED m

featherbed vt Econ (industry, business) subventionner excessivement

featherbedding n Econ (of industry, business) subventionnement m excessif

Fed n Am (a) (abbr **Federal Reserve Board**) banque f centrale (des États-Unis) (b) (abbr **Federal Reserve (System)**) (système m de) Réserve f fédérale (c) (abbr **Federal Reserve Bank**) banque f membre de la Réserve fédérale
◇ **Fed bias** = rapport de la banque centrale américaine sur le niveau d'inflation de l'économie nationale, considéré comme un indicateur de sa politique à venir en matière de taux d'intérêt

❝
The sudden mid-day drop came because investors were hoping for a shift in the official **Fed bias** from inflationary to neutral and that didn't happen, according to Charles Payne ... "At this point in the game it would be great if the **Fed** would acknowledge that we are no longer in an inflationary climate, and that the **Fed** was ready to lower rates, not raise rates, so that was a psychological blow that hit the market," he said.
❞

federal adj (a) (republic, system) fédéral(e) (b) (responsibility, funding) du gouvernement fédéral
◇ **federal assembly** assemblée f fédérale
◇ Am **the Federal Bureau of Investigation** le FBI
◇ Am **Federal Debt** dette f publique ou de l'État
◇ Am **Federal funds** fonds mpl fédéraux
◇ **federal government** gouvernement m fédéral
◇ **federal legislature** législature f fédérale
◇ Am **Federal Open Market Committee** Comité m fédéral de l'open market (sorte de comité américain des opérations de Bourse)
◇ **federal republic** république f fédérale
◇ Am **Federal Reserve** Réserve f fédérale
◇ Am **Federal Reserve Bank** banque f membre de la Réserve fédérale
◇ Am **Federal Reserve Board** banque f centrale (des États-Unis)
◇ Am **Federal Reserve System** système m de Réserve fédérale
◇ **federal state** État m fédéral
◇ Am **Federal Surplus** surplus m du budget fédéral
◇ **federal tax** impôt m fédéral
◇ **federal taxation** imposition f fédérale
◇ Am **Federal Trade Commission** = commission fédérale chargée de veiller au respect de la concurrence sur le marché

federalese n Am Fam = jargon utilisé par les bureaucrates du gouvernement fédéral

federalism n fédéralisme m

federalist 1 n fédéraliste mf 2 adj fédéraliste

federalistic adj fédéraliste

federalization n union f en fédération, fédération f

federalize 1 vt (a) (unite in a federal union) fédéraliser (b) (subject to fed-

eral control) soumettre à l'autorité d'un gouvernement fédéral
  2 *vi* se fédéraliser

federally *adv* **to be federally funded** être financé(e) par le gouvernement fédéral

federate 1 *adj* fédéré(e)
  2 *vt* fédérer
  3 *vi* se fédérer

federation *n* fédération *f*

feudal *adj (society, system)* féodal(e)

feudalism *n* féodalisme *m*

Fianna Fáil *n Pol* le Fianna Fáil *(parti politique irlandais de centre-droit)*

fiat *n (decree)* décret *m*
  ◇ **fiat money** monnaie *f* fiduciaire

FIFG *n EU (abbr* **Financial Instrument for Fisheries Guidance)** IFOP *m*

fifth *adj*
  ◇ *Am* **Fifth Amendment** Cinquième Amendement *m (de la Constitution des États-Unis, permettant à un accusé de ne pas répondre à une question risquant de jouer en sa défaveur)*
  ◇ *Pol* **fifth column** cinquième colonne *f*
  ◇ *Pol* **fifth columnist** membre *m* de la cinquième colonne
  ◇ **the Fifth Republic** la Cinquième *ou* Ve République

fight 1 *n* lutte *f*; **the fight for the leadership of the party** la lutte pour la tête du parti
  2 *vt (person)* se battre contre; **to fight an election** *(of politician)* se présenter à une élection; *Br* **to fight an election campaign** mener une campagne électorale; *Br* **John Brown is fighting Amersham for the Tories** John Brown se présente à Amersham pour les conservateurs

filibuster *Pol* **1** *n* obstruction *f* (parlementaire)
  2 *vt (legislation)* faire obstruction à
  3 *vi* faire de l'obstruction

filibusterer *n Pol* obstructionniste *mf*

filibustering *n Pol* obstructionnisme *m*

final consumer goods *npl Econ* biens *mpl* de consommation finale

finance 1 *n* finance *f*
  2 *vt* financer
  ◇ *Pol* **Finance Act** loi *f* de Finances
  ◇ *Pol* **finance bill** projet *m* de loi de finances
  ◇ **finance capital** capital *m* financier
  ◇ *Pol* **Finance Minister** ≃ ministre *m* de l'Économie et des Finances

financial *adj* financier(ère)
  ◇ **financial capital** capital *m* financier
  ◇ **financial centre** centre *m* financier
  ◇ **financial imbalance** déséquilibre *m* financier
  ◇ **financial institution** institution *f* financière
  ◇ **financial instrument** instrument *m* financier
  ◇ *EU* **Financial Instrument for Fisheries Guidance** instrument *m* financier d'orientation de la pêche
  ◇ **financial integration** intégration *f* financière
  ◇ **Financial Services Authority** = organisme gouvernemental britannique chargé de contrôler les activités du secteur financier
  ◇ *Br* **financial year** *(in business)* exercice *m* financier; *(in politics)* année *f* budgétaire

financing *n* financement *m*
  ◇ **financing capacity** capacité *f* de financement
  ◇ **financing gap** déficit *m* de financement

Fine Gael *n Pol* le Fine Gael *m (parti politique irlandais de centre-droit)*

Finlandization *n Pol* finlandisation *f*

fireside chat *n (by politician)* causerie *f* au coin du feu

❝

"He's a really, really charismatic politician," Mr. Yago said ... He recalled his first interview with the Texas governor, a **fireside chat** during a New

Hampshire snowstorm. He figured he'd get two or three questions off and that would be it. But Mr. Bush sat and answered all three sheets' worth of questions that MTV had prepared.

"

firm n (company) firme f, entreprise f

first adj

◇ Am **the First Amendment** le Premier Amendement (de la Constitution des États-Unis, garantissant les libertés individuelles du citoyen américain, notamment la liberté d'expression)

◇ Econ **first best** optimum m de premier rang

◇ Am **First Family** (presidential family) famille f présidentielle; (in a State) famille f du gouverneur

◇ Am **First Lady** = femme du président des États-Unis

◇ Pol **First Minister** (of Scottish Parliament, Welsh Assembly, Northern Ireland Assembly) Premier ministre m

◇ Br Parl **first reading** (of bill) première lecture f

◇ Pol **First Secretary** premier secrétaire m

◇ **First World** pays mpl industrialisés

"

The plight of women under the the Taleban is set to be highlighted in a new campaign fronted by Cherie Blair and US **First Lady** Laura Bush. The prime minister's wife will join female cabinet ministers at an event at Downing Street next week in order to "lift the veil" on the treatment of women under the regime that banned their education and forced them to wear burqas. Meanwhile Mrs Bush will make a radio broadcast in the US on the issue.

"

first-best theory n Econ théorie f de l'optimum de premier rang

first-past-the-post n Br Pol (system) scrutin m majoritaire à un tour; **first-past-the-post does not favour smaller parties** le scrutin majoritaire à un tour défavorise les petits partis

fiscal adj fiscal(e)

◇ **fiscal austerity** austérité f fiscale

◇ **fiscal balance** équilibre m fiscal

◇ **fiscal drag** frein m fiscal, érosion f fiscale

◇ **fiscal effect** incidence f fiscale

◇ **fiscal measure** mesure f fiscale

◇ **fiscal policy** politique f budgétaire ou fiscale

◇ **fiscal stance** politique f budgétaire

◇ Am **fiscal year** exercice m (financier), année f fiscale ou d'exercice

five o'clock shuffle n Parl = vote des députés de la Chambre des communes destiné à établir la liste des questions qui seront posées lors de la session hebdomadaire avec le Premier ministre

Five-Year Plan n Econ Plan m quinquennal

fix vt Econ (price, quota, rate) fixer

fixed adj Econ fixe

◇ Econ **fixed capital** capital m fixe

◇ Econ **fixed exchange rate** taux m de change fixe

◇ Econ **fixed rate** taux m fixe

flexibility n Econ (of workforce) flexibilité f

flexible adj Econ (workforce) flexible

flight of capital n évasion f de capitaux, fuite f de capitaux

float Econ 1 n flottant m
2 vt (currency) faire flotter, laisser flotter
3 vi (of currency) flotter

floating adj

◇ Econ **floating capital** capital m circulant ou flottant

◇ Econ **floating debt** dette f flottante

◇ Econ **floating exchange rate** taux m de change flottant

◇ Econ **floating rate** taux m flottant

◇ Econ **floating rate note** obligation f à taux flottant

◇ Pol **floating vote** indécis *mpl*, électorat *m* flottant

◇ Pol **floating voter** (électeur(trice) *m,f*) indécis(e) *m,f*

floor *n* (in parliament, assembly) enceinte *f*; **the floor of the House** ≃ l'Hémicycle *m*; **to have/to take the floor** (of speaker) avoir/prendre la parole; **Mr Taylor has the floor** la parole est à M. Taylor; **he had the floor for twenty minutes** il a parlé *ou* a gardé la parole pendant vingt minutes

◇ Am Parl **floor leader** = chef de file d'un parti siégeant au Sénat ou à la Chambre des représentants aux États-Unis

◇ Econ **floor price** prix *m* seuil

flow of funds account *n* compte *m* des flux financiers

fluctuate *vi* Econ fluctuer

fluctuating *n* Econ fluctuant(e)

fluctuation *n* Econ fluctuation *f*

◇ **fluctuation band** bande *f* de fluctuation

◇ **fluctuation margin** marge *f* de fluctuation

fluid *adj* Econ (workforce) fluide

fluidity *n* Econ (of workforce) fluidité *f*

flying picket *n* piquet *m* de grève volant

focus group *n* Pol groupe *m* témoin

follower *n* Pol adepte *mf*

FOMC *n* Am (abbr **Federal Open Market Committee**) Comité *m* fédéral de l'open market (sorte de comité américain des opérations de Bourse)

food *n*

◇ **Food and Agriculture Organization of the United Nations** Organisation *f* des Nations Unies pour l'alimentation et l'agriculture

◇ **food aid** aide *f* alimentaire

forced *adj* Econ

◇ **forced currency** cours *m* forcé

◇ **forced loan** emprunt *m* forcé

◇ **forced saving** épargne *f* forcée

forecast 1 *n* prévision *f*
2 *vt* prévoir

◇ **forecast of demand** prévision *f* de la demande

forecaster *n* prévisionniste *mf*, expert *m*

forecasting *n* prévision *f*

foreign *adj* (country) étranger(ère); (visit) (to country) à l'étranger; (from country) de l'étranger; (goods) de l'étranger; (politics) extérieur(e)

◇ Pol **foreign affairs** affaires *fpl* étrangères, relations *fpl* extérieures

◇ **foreign aid** (to foreign country) aide *f* aux pays étrangers; (from foreign country) aide *f* de l'étranger

◇ Br Pol **Foreign and Commonwealth Office** Foreign Office *m*, ministère *m* britannique des Affaires étrangères

◇ Pol **Foreign and Commonwealth Secretary** = ministre britannique des Affaires étrangères

◇ Econ **foreign competition** concurrence *f* étrangère

◇ Econ **foreign currency** devises *fpl* étrangères; **to buy foreign currency** acheter des devises étrangères

◇ Econ **foreign currency assets** avoirs *mpl* en devises étrangères

◇ Econ **foreign currency earnings** apport *m* de devises étrangères

◇ Econ **foreign currency holding** avoir *m* en devises étrangères

◇ Econ **foreign currency loan** prêt *m* en devises étrangères

◇ Econ **foreign currency option** option *f* de change

◇ Econ **foreign currency reserves** réserves *fpl* de change, réserves *fpl* en devises

◇ **foreign debt** endettement *m* extérieur

◇ Econ **foreign direct investment** investissement *m* étranger direct

◇ **foreign exchange** devises *fpl* étrangères

◇ **foreign exchange market** marché *m* des devises étrangères

◇ Econ **foreign investment** investissement *m* à l'étranger

◇ Pol **foreign market** marché m extérieur
◇ Pol **foreign minister** ministre m des affaires étrangères
◇ Br Pol **Foreign Office** Foreign Office m, ministère m britannique des Affaires étrangères
◇ Pol **foreign policy** politique f étrangère ou extérieure
◇ Pol **foreign relations** relations fpl avec l'étranger
◇ Pol **Foreign Secretary** = ministre britannique des Affaires étrangères
◇ Am Pol **Foreign Service** service m diplomatique
◇ Econ **foreign trade** commerce m extérieur
◇ Econ **foreign trade multiplier** multiplicateur m du commerce extérieur

form vt (government) former; **the Prime Minister has been asked to form a new government** après la réélection de son parti, le Premier ministre va former un nouveau gouvernement; **the Liberal Party is confident of forming the next government** le parti libéral est sûr de former le prochain gouvernement

formation n (of government) formation f

forward adj
◇ Econ **forward exchange market** marché m des changes à terme
◇ Econ **forward integration** intégration f en aval, intégration f descendante
◇ Econ **forward market** marché m à terme

fraction n Pol (of communist party) fraction f, groupe m fractionnaire

fractional adj
◇ **fractional interest** fraction f d'intérêt
◇ **fractional money** monnaie f divisionnaire

franchise n Pol suffrage m, droit m de vote

free adj libre
◇ Econ **free banking** banque f libre

◇ Econ **free enterprise** libre entreprise f
◇ Econ **free market** marché m libre
◇ Econ **free marketeer** libéral(e) m,f
◇ EU **free movement** (of goods, people) libre circulation f
◇ Pol **free rider** = ouvrier non-syndiqué qui profite des avantages gagnés par les syndicats
◇ Econ **free trade** libre-échange m
◇ **free vote** vote m libre
◇ Pol **the Free World** le monde libre
◇ **free zone** zone f franche

freedom n liberté f
◇ **freedom of association** liberté f de réunion
◇ **freedom of conscience** liberté f de conscience
◇ **freedom of enterprise** liberté f d'entreprise
◇ **freedom of entry** liberté f d'entrée
◇ **freedom of exit** liberté f de sortie
◇ **freedom fighter** guérillero m, révolutionnaire mf
◇ **freedom of information** liberté f d'information
◇ **Freedom of Information Act** = loi sur la communication aux citoyens des informations de source gouvernementale
◇ **freedom of religion** liberté f de culte
◇ **freedom of speech** liberté f d'expression
◇ **freedom of trade** liberté f du commerce
◇ **freedom of worship** liberté f du culte

free-enterprise adj Econ libéral(e)
◇ **free-enterprise economy** économie f de libre entreprise

free-market adj Econ libéral(e)
◇ **free-market economics** libéralisme m
◇ **free-market economy** économie f libérale ou de marché

free-trade adj Econ libre-échangiste
◇ **free-trade agreement** accord m ou association f de libre-échange
◇ **free-trade area** zone f de libre-échange

◇ **Free-Trade Area of the Americas** Zone *f* de libre-échange des Amériques

◇ **free-trade association** association *f* de libre-échange

◇ **free-trade policy** politique *f* anti-protectionniste, politique *f* de libre-échange

◇ **free-trade zone** zone *f* de libre-échange

freeze Econ **1** *n* (of credit, wages) gel *m*, blocage *m*; (of currency, prices, assets) gel *m*

2 *vt* (credit, wages) geler, bloquer; (currency, prices, assets) geler

freezing *n* Econ (of credit, wages) gel *m*, blocage *m*; (of currency, prices, assets) gel *m*

frictional unemployment *n* Econ chômage *m* frictionnel

fringe *n*

◇ Econ **fringe benefit** avantage *m* accessoire

◇ Pol **fringe group** frange *f*, groupe *m* marginal

◇ Econ **fringe market** marché *m* marginal

FRN *n* Econ (abbr **floating rate note**) OTV *f*, obligation *f* à taux variable

front *n* Pol (group) front *m*

frontbench *n* Br Pol (members of the government) ministres *mpl*; (members of the opposition) ministres *mpl* du cabinet fantôme; **he's never been on the frontbench** (in government) il n'a jamais été ministre; (in opposition) il n'a jamais été membre du cabinet fantôme; **the frontbenches** = à la Chambre des communes, bancs situés à droite et à gauche du Président et occupés respectivement par les ministres du gouvernement en exercice et ceux du gouvernement fantôme

◇ **frontbench spokesman** (of cabinet) porte-parole *m* du gouvernement; (of shadow cabinet) porte-parole *m* du cabinet fantôme

◇ **frontbench team** (cabinet) équipe *f*

ministérielle; (shadow cabinet) cabinet *m* fantôme

> **❝**
>
> In an interview in today's Independent, Lord Heseltine says that unless the Tory leader is toppled there is "not any prospect" of the party having "a ghost of a chance of winning the next election. We've got a better shadow cabinet on the backbenches than we have in the actual shadow cabinet on the **frontbench**," he says.
>
> **❞**

frontbencher *n* Br Pol (member of the government) ministre *m*; (member of the opposition) membre *m* du cabinet fantôme

frozen adj Econ (credit, wages) gelé(e), bloqué(e); (currency, prices, assets) gelé(e)

FSA *n* (abbr **Financial Services Authority**) = organisme gouvernemental britannique chargé de contrôler les activités du secteur financier

FTA *n* Econ (a) (abbr **free-trade association**) ALE *f* (b) (abbr **free-trade area**) zone *f* de libre-échange

FTAA *n* (abbr **Free-Trade Area of the Americas**) ZLEA *f*

full employment *n* Econ plein emploi *m*

function *n* Econ fonction *f*

functionalism *n* Econ fonctionnalisme *m*

functionalist Econ **1** *n* fonctionnaliste *mf*

2 adj fonctionnaliste

functionary *n* (civil servant) fonctionnaire *mf*

fund 1 *n* (reserve of money) fonds *m*, caisse *f*; **funds** (cash resources) fonds *mpl*; (of government) fonds *mpl* publics; Br **the Funds** les bons *mpl* du Trésor

2 *vt* (project) financer; (company) pourvoir de fonds; (public debt) consolider; **to fund money** placer de l'argent dans les fonds publics

fundamentalism *n* fondamentalisme *m*

fundamentalist 1 *n* fondamentaliste *mf*

2 *adj* fondamentaliste

fundamental law *n* loi *f* fondamentale

FY *n* *Am* (*abbr* **fiscal year**) exercice *m* (financier), année *f* fiscale *ou* d'exercice

G7 n Econ & Pol le G7, le groupe des 7

G8 n Econ & Pol le G8, le groupe des 8

G25 n Econ & Pol le G25, le groupe des 25

gag n
◊ Am **gag resolution** règle f du bâillon (procédure parlementaire permettant de limiter le temps de parole et d'éviter l'obstruction systématique)
◊ Am **gag rule** règle f du bâillon (procédure parlementaire permettant de limiter le temps de parole et d'éviter l'obstruction systématique)

galloping inflation n Econ inflation f galopante

Gallup Poll n sondage m Gallup (réalisé par l'institut Gallup, institut américain de sondages d'opinion)

game theory n Econ théorie f des jeux

gangway n Parl = escaliers qui relient les bancs occupés par les députés de la majorité à ceux occupés par le principal parti de l'opposition; **below the gangway** = partie de la Chambre des communes où siègent les députés des partis minoritaires

"

It is not simply the fact that the Conservative party is no longer plausible as a party of government. It is no longer plausible even as a party of opposition. If things carry on as they are for much longer, it is very easy to imagine a small group of Tory MPs occupying the Commons benches **below the gangway** where Charles Kennedy and his Liberal Democrats sit now.

"

GAO n Am (abbr **General Accounting Office**) = bureau de comptabilité générale du Congrès (chargé entre autres choses de surveiller l'usage des fonds publics)

GATS n Econ (abbr **General Agreement on Trade in Services**) AGCS m

GATT n Econ (abbr **General Agreement on Tariffs and Trade**) GATT m

Gaullism n Pol gaullisme m

Gaullist Pol **1** n gaulliste mf
2 adj gaulliste

GCHQ n (abbr **Government Communications Headquarters**) = centre d'interception des télécommunications étrangères en Grande-Bretagne

GCIU n (abbr **Graphic Communications International Union**) = syndicat américain des imprimeurs et des métiers du livre

GDP n Econ (abbr **gross domestic product**) PIB m
◊ **GDP per capita** PIB m par habitant

GE n Econ (abbr **general equilibrium**) équilibre m général

general adj général(e)
◊ Am **General Accounting Office** = bureau de comptabilité générale du Congrès (chargé entre autres choses de surveiller l'usage des fonds publics)
◊ Econ **General Agreement on Tariffs and Trade** Accord m Général sur les

Tarifs Douaniers et le Commerce
◇ *Econ* **General Agreement on Trade in Services** Accord *m* Général sur le Commerce des Services
◇ **General Assembly** *(of UN)* Assemblée *f* générale
◇ *Pol* **general election** élections *fpl* législatives
◇ *Econ* **general equilibrium** équilibre *m* général
◇ **general government** administrations *fpl* publiques
◇ **general policy document** document *m* de politique générale

Generalized System of Preferences *n* système *m* généralisé de préférences

genocidal *adj* génocide, génocidaire

genocide *n* génocide *m*

geopolitical *adj* géopolitique

geopolitics *n* géopolitique *f*

gerrymander *Pol* **1** *n* charcutage *m* électoral
2 *vt* redécouper (à des fins électorales)
3 *vi* faire du charcutage électoral, redécouper des circonscriptions

gerrymandering *n* *Pol* charcutage *m* électoral

> **"**
>
> The Chicago City Council may have given local lawyers a Christmas present in the form of a recently passed ward redistricting ordinance that will likely encourage numerous lawsuits. The new map, required because of newly released 2000 U.S. census figures, was approved by the Council by a 48-1 vote just before the holidays. And once again, the re-map process has raised the issue of racial **gerrymandering** ... Under the remap ... predominantly Hispanic wards increase from the present 7 to 11. Hispanic interest groups, however, had actually been hoping that the remap would give them 12 or 13 wards.
>
> **"**

▸ **get through** **1** *vt sep* *(bill, motion, legislation)* faire adopter, faire passer; **the party got the bill through the Senate** le parti a fait voter *or* adopter le projet de loi par le Sénat
2 *vt insep* *(of bill, motion, legislation)* passer; **the bill got through both Houses** le projet de loi a été voté *ou* adopté par les deux Chambres
3 *vi* *(of bill, motion, legislation)* passer, être adopté(e) *ou* voté(e)

Giffen good *n* *Econ* bien *m* de Giffen

GLA *n* *(abbr* **Greater London Authority***)* = conseil municipal de Londres

gladiatorial politics *n* = politique qui fait de la confrontation son moyen d'action

glasnost *n* *Pol* glasnost *f*

global *adj* **(a)** *(worldwide)* mondial(e), planétaire **(b)** *(system, view)* global(e)
◇ **global corporation** multinationale *f*
◇ **global economy** économie *f* mondiale
◇ **global finance** finance *f* internationale
◇ **global governance** gouvernance *f* mondiale
◇ **global market** marché *m* global *ou* international
◇ **global marketplace** marché *m* global *ou* international
◇ **global village** village *m* planétaire

globalism *n* mondialisme *m*

globalist *n* mondialiste *mf*

globalization *n* mondialisation *f*

globalize *vt* rendre mondial(e), mondialiser; **a globalized conflict** un conflit mondial; **to become globalized** se mondialiser

GMB *n* *(abbr* **General, Municipal, Boilermakers and Allied Trades Union***)* = important syndicat britannique

GMWU *n* *(abbr* **General and Municipal Workers' Union***)* = syndicat britannique des employés des collectivités locales

GNE *n Econ* (*abbr* **gross national expenditure**) DNP *f*

GNP *n Econ* (*abbr* **gross national product**) PNB *m*

◇ *GNP per capita* PNB *m* par habitant

▸ **go through** **1** *vt insep* (*of bill, law*) être voté(e); **the bill went through Parliament last week** le projet de loi a été voté la semaine dernière au Parlement

2 *vi* (*of bill, law*) passer, être voté(e)

gold *n* or *m*

◇ *gold bullion* lingots *mpl* d'or

◇ *gold bullion standard* étalon *m* or-lingot

◇ *gold currency* monnaie *f* d'or

◇ *gold exchange standard* étalon *m* de change-or

◇ *gold export point* point *m* de sortie de l'or

◇ *gold fix* cotation *f* de l'or

◇ *gold fixing* cotation *f* de l'or

◇ *gold import point* point *m* d'entrée de l'or

◇ *gold loan* emprunt *m* or

◇ *gold market* marché *m* de l'or

◇ *gold money* monnaie *f* d'or

◇ *gold point* point *m* d'or

◇ *gold pool* pool *m* de l'or

◇ *gold reserve* réserve *f* d'or

◇ *gold share* valeur *f* aurifère

◇ *gold standard* étalon-or *m*

good *n Econ* (**a**) = produit qui satisfait le consommateur (**b**) **goods** marchandises *fpl*, biens *mpl*

◇ Can *goods and services tax* taxe *f* sur les produits et services

Good Friday Agreement *n Pol* accord *m* du vendredi saint (*accord de paix signé à Belfast en avril 1998 qui a mis en place la "Northern Ireland Assembly", un parlement quasi-autonome avec un partage démocratique du pouvoir entre les communautés protestante et catholique*)

goodwill mission *n Pol* mission *f* de bons offices

GOP *n Am Pol* (*abbr* **Grand Old Party**) parti *m* républicain

"

As much as Bush deserves credit for the **GOP** [Grand Old Party] now controlling Congress, he should be careful of what he wished for. To the victor belong both the spoils and toils of controlling both ends of Pennsylvania Avenue.

"

Gov *n* (**a**) (*abbr* **government**) gouvernement *m* (**b**) (*abbr* **governor**) gouverneur *m*

govern **1** *vt* (*country*) gouverner, régner sur; (*city, region*) gouverner; (*affairs*) administrer, gérer; (*company, organization*) diriger, gérer; **the politicians who govern Britain** les politiciens qui gouvernent la Grande-Bretagne

2 *vi* gouverner, commander, diriger

governable *adj* gouvernable

governing **1** *n* gouvernement *m*

2 *adj* gouvernant(e), dirigeant(e); *Pol* **the governing party** le parti au pouvoir

government *n* (**a**) *Pol* (*governing authority*) gouvernement *m*; (*type of authority*) gouvernement *m*, régime *m*; (*the State*) gouvernement *m*, État *m*; **the Conservative government** le gouvernement conservateur; **to form a government** constituer *ou* former un gouvernement; **the government has fallen** le gouvernement est tombé; **the socialists have joined the coalition government** les socialistes sont entrés dans le gouvernement de coalition; **the project is financed by the government** le projet est financé par l'État *ou* le gouvernement

(**b**) (*process of governing*) (*of country*) gouvernement *m*, direction *f*; (*of city, region*) gouvernement *m*; (*of affairs*) conduite *f*; (*of company, organization*) administration *f*, gestion *f*

◇ *government action* action *f* gouvernementale

◇ **government advertising** publicité f d'intérêt général

◇ **government adviser** conseiller m du gouvernement

◇ **government agency** agence f gouvernementale

◇ **government aid** aide f gouvernementale ou de l'État

◇ **government auditor** commissaire m aux comptes

◇ **government bonds** obligations fpl d'État, bons mpl du Trésor

◇ **government borrowings** emprunts mpl de l'État

◇ Br **government broker** agent m du trésor

◇ Br Pol **government chief whip** = responsable du maintien de la discipline à l'intérieur du parti de la majorité à la Chambre des communes

◇ **government circular** circulaire f gouvernementale

◇ **government commissioner** commissaire m du gouvernement

◇ **Government Communications Headquarters** = centre d'interception des télécommunications étrangères en Grande-Bretagne

◇ **government deficit** déficit m public

◇ **government developmental grant** prime f de développement

◇ **government developmental subsidy** prime f de développement

◇ **government employee** employé(e) m,f d'administration

◇ **government expenditure** dépenses fpl publiques

◇ **government finance** financement m par l'État

◇ **government grant** subvention f de l'État

◇ **government handouts** subventions fpl gouvernementales

◇ Br **Government House** bureaux mpl des autorités locales

◇ **government intervention** intervention f gouvernementale

◇ **government loan** emprunt m public ou d'État

◇ **government manifesto** programme m de gouvernement

◇ **government market** marché m de l'État

◇ **government monopoly** monopole m d'État

◇ **government offices** bureaux mpl du gouvernement

◇ **government organization** collectivité f publique, organisation f publique

◇ Am **the Government Printing Office** = maison d'édition publiant les ouvrages ou documents émanant du gouvernement, ≃ l'Imprimerie f nationale

◇ **government property** propriété f de l'État

◇ **government representative** représentant m du gouvernement

◇ **government restrictions** restrictions fpl gouvernementales

◇ **government revenue** recettes fpl publiques

◇ **government securities** effets mpl publics, fonds mpl publics ou d'État

◇ **government spending** dépenses fpl publiques

◇ **government spending review** examen m des dépenses publiques

◇ **government stock** effets mpl publics, fonds mpl publics ou d'État

◇ **government subsidy** subvention f d'État

◇ **government targets** objectifs mpl du gouvernement

governmental adj gouvernemental(e), du gouvernement

◇ **governmental organization** organisation f gouvernementale

government-funded adj subventionné(e) par l'État

government-sponsored adj parrainé(e) par le gouvernement

◇ **government-sponsored terrorism** terrorisme m d'État

governor n gouverneur m

govt (abbr **government**) gvt

GPMU n Br (abbr **Graphical, Paper and Media Union**) = syndicat britannique des ouvriers du livre

GPO n Am (abbr **Government Printing Office**) = maison d'édition publiant les ouvrages ou documents émanant du gouvernement, ≃ Imprimerie f nationale

gradualism n Pol réformisme m

gradualist Pol **1** n réformiste mf
2 adj réformiste

graduate tax n = frais de scolarité prélevés sur les revenus des anciens étudiants sous forme d'impôt

Grand Old Party n Am Pol parti m républicain

grass roots n Pol base f; **the feeling at the grass roots is that ...** le sentiment à la base est que ... ; **at (the) grass roots level** au niveau de la base

◇ **grass roots opposition** résistance f de la base

◇ **grass roots support** soutien m de la base

> Conservative leader Iain Duncan Smith's dramatic "unite or die" warning has succeeded in gaining **grass roots** party backing, according to a BBC survey. More than half of the party's constituency chairmen questioned by Radio 4's Today programme thought Tory MPs were to blame for the current leadership crisis.

Greater London Authority n = conseil municipal de Londres

Green n Br Pol **the Greens** les Verts mpl, les écologistes mpl; **he used to vote Labour but he's a Green now** avant il votait travailliste mais maintenant il est pour les écologistes

◇ **the Green party** les Verts mpl, le parti écologiste

green adj Econ & Pol (ecological) vert(e)

◇ EU **green currency** monnaie f verte

◇ EU **green dollar** dollar m vert

◇ Pol **green paper** = document for-mulant des propositions destinées à orienter la politique gouvernementale

◇ Br EU **green pound** livre f verte

◇ EU **green rate** taux m vert

◇ **green revolution** révolution f verte

◇ **green taxation** fiscalité f écologique

gross 1 n (total amount) **the gross** la quantité totale
2 adj (overall, total) brut(e)
3 vt (of company, person) faire ou obtenir une recette brute de

◇ **gross domestic product** produit m intérieur brut

◇ **gross national debt** dette f nationale brute

◇ **gross national expenditure** dépense f nationale brute

◇ **gross national income** revenu m national brut

◇ **gross national product** produit m national brut

group n Pol (party) groupement m

grow 1 vt **to grow the business** augmenter le chiffre d'affaires; **to grow a company** développer une entreprise
2 vi (increase) augmenter, s'accroître; **our market share has grown by five percent in the last year** notre part du marché a augmenté de cinq pour cent au cours de l'année dernière

growth n (in numbers, amount) augmentation f, croissance f; (of market, industry) croissance f, expansion f

◇ **growth area** secteur m en expansion

◇ **growth company** société f en expansion

◇ **growth curve** courbe f de croissance

◇ **growth factor** facteur m de croissance

◇ **growth index** indice m de croissance

◇ **growth industry** industrie f en plein essor ou de pointe

◇ **growth market** marché m porteur

◇ **growth rate** taux m de croissance

◇ **growth sector** secteur m en expansion ou de croissance

◇ *EU* **Growth and Stability Pact** pacte *m* de stabilité et croissance
◇ **growth theory** théorie *f* de la croissance
◇ **growth trend** tendance *f* de croissance

GSP *n* (**a**) (*abbr* **Generalized System of Preferences**) SGP *m* (**b**) *EU* (*abbr* **Growth and Stability Pact**) PSC *m*

gubernatorial *adj Am* de/du gouverneur
◇ **gubernatorial elections** élections *fpl* des gouverneurs

guerrilla *n Pol* guérillero *m*
◇ **guerrilla attacks** attaques *fpl* de guérilleros
◇ **guerrilla group** guérilla *f*, groupe *m* de guérilleros
◇ **guerrilla warfare** guérilla *f (combat)*

guillotine *Parl* **1** *n* = procédure parlementaire consistant à fixer des délais stricts pour l'examen de chaque partie d'un projet de loi
2 *vt* **to guillotine a debate** limiter la durée d'un débat

> **"**
>
> All governments occasionally use the **guillotine**, by which bills are timetabled to finish at a certain time, but only this government has used them as a matter of course, regardless of how well the bill is progressing, regardless of whether it is even opposed in principle and only this government has routinely cut short the committee stage of bills, which is, of course, where all the serious examination takes place.
>
> **"**

► **hand over 1** *vt sep (power, authority)* transmettre (**to** à); **should Britain hand over Gibraltar to Spain?** est-ce que la Grande-Bretagne devrait rétrocéder Gibraltar à l'Espagne?

2 *vi* **to hand over to sb** *(transfer power)* passer le pouvoir à qn

Hansard *n Br Parl* = compte rendu quotidien des débats de la Chambre des communes

hard *adj*

◇ **hard core** *(of people)* noyau *m* dur; **there is a hard core of resistance to the reforms** il y a un noyau de résistance à ces réformes

◇ **hard currency** monnaie *f* ou devise *f* forte; **a hard currency shop** un magasin où on paye en devises

◇ **hard landing** *(during economic crisis)* atterrissage *m* brutal

◇ *Pol* **the hard left** l'extrême gauche *f*

◇ *Pol* **hard line** ligne *f* de conduite dure; **to take a hard line on sb/sth** adopter une ligne de conduite dure avec qn/sur qch

◇ *Econ* **hard loan** prêt *m* aux conditions du marché

◇ **hard money** argent *m* liquide

◇ *Pol* **the hard right** l'extrême droite *f*

◇ *Econ* **hard terms** conditions *fpl* du marché

hard-core *adj (reactionary, supporter)* dur(e)

hardline *adj Pol (policy, doctrine)* dur(e); *(politician)* intransigeant(e), endurci(e), intraitable

hardliner *n Pol* partisan(e) *m,f* de la manière forte, dur(e) *m,f*

harmonization *n* harmonisation *f*

harmonize *vt* harmoniser

hatchet man *n Pol* = personne dont le rôle est de restructurer une entreprise ou une organisation, le plus souvent à l'aide de mesures impopulaires

hawk *n Pol* faucon *m*

> US Vice-President Dick Cheney has given one of the clearest signals yet that the Bush administration intends to depose Saddam Hussein. Mr Cheney, a leading **hawk**, said a policy of containment was no longer an option because doing nothing was riskier than acting against the Iraqi leader.

hawkish *adj Pol* belliciste

HCSA *n (abbr* **Hospital Consultants and Specialists Association***)* = syndicat de médecins spécialistes employés par le NHS

HDI *n (abbr* **Human Development Index***)* IDH *m*

head 1 *n (leader)* chef *m*; **the crowned heads of Europe** les têtes *fpl* couronnées de l'Europe

2 *vt (project, revolt)* diriger, être à la tête de; **she headed the attack on the Government's economic policy** elle menait l'attaque contre la politique économique du gouvernement

◇ **head of government** chef *m* de gouvernement; **the European heads of government** les chefs *mpl* de gouvernement européens

◇ **head of state** chef *m* d'État

headquarter *Am* **1** *vt* **to be headquartered in Chicago** avoir son siège à Chicago

2 *vi* **to headquarter in Chicago** établir son siège à Chicago

headquarters *npl (of organization, government office)* bureau *m* principal, siège *m* social; *(of UN)* siège *m*; **they have their headquarters in Geneva** leur siège est à Genève

health *n (of economy)* santé *f*

◇ **health expenditure** dépenses *fpl* de santé

◇ *Br* **Health Secretary** ≃ ministre *m* de la Santé

◇ **health sector** secteur *m* sanitaire

◇ *Br* **health service** = système créé en 1946 en Grande-Bretagne et financé par l'État, assurant la gratuité des soins et des services médicaux, ≃ Sécurité *f* sociale

◇ **health services** services *mpl* de santé

healthy *adj (economy)* sain(e)

heartland *n* cœur *m*, centre *m*; **the Socialist heartland** le fief des socialistes

heavy industry *n* industrie *f* lourde

hegemony *n* hégémonie *f*

HERE *n (abbr* Hotel Employees and Restaurant Employees International Union) = syndicat américain et canadien des employés des secteurs de l'hôtellerie et de la restauration

hereditary *adj* héréditaire

◇ **hereditary monarchy** monarchie *f* héréditaire

◇ *Br Pol* **hereditary peer** = membre de la Chambre des lords dont le titre est héréditaire

hidden *adj*

◇ **hidden economy** économie *f* noire

◇ **hidden tax** impôt *m* indirect *ou* déguisé

◇ **hidden unemployment** chômage *m* déguisé

high *adj* **(a)** *(cost, price, rate)* élevé(e); *(salary)* élevé(e), gros (grosse); **areas of high unemployment** des régions à fort taux de chômage **(b)** *(in rank, importance)* haut(e), important(e); **to hold a high position in the government** occuper un poste important au gouvernement; **a high official** un haut fonctionnaire

◇ **High Court** Haute cour *f*

◇ **high treason** haute trahison *f*

highest average system *n Pol* méthode *f* de la plus forte moyenne

high-income *adj* à haut revenu

◇ **high-income group** groupe *m* des gros salaires, groupe *m* des salaires élevés

high-tech industry *n* industrie *f* de pointe

hijack *vt Pol (movement)* récupérer

hijacking *n Pol (of movement)* récupération *f*

HMG *n Br (abbr* His/Her Majesty's Government) = expression utilisée sur des documents officiels en Grande-Bretagne

HMSO *n Br (abbr* His/Her Majesty's Stationery Office) = maison d'édition publiant les ouvrages ou documents approuvés par le Parlement, les ministères et autres organismes officiels, ≃ l'Imprimerie *f* nationale

HMT *n Br (abbr* His/Her Majesty's Treasury) la Trésorerie, ≃ le ministère des Finances

HO *n Br Pol (abbr* Home Office) ≃ Ministère *m* de l'Intérieur

hoard *vt Econ* thésauriser

hoarding *n Econ* thésaurisation *f*

home *n*

◇ *Econ* **home consumption** consommation *f* intérieure

◇ **home market** marché *m* intérieur

◇ *Br Pol* **Home Office** ≃ Ministère *m* de l'Intérieur

◇ *Econ* **home produce** produits *mpl* nationaux *ou* domestiques

◇ *Pol* **home rule** *(devolution)* décentralisation *f*

◇ *Econ* **home sales** ventes *fpl* sur le marché intérieur

◇ *Br Pol* **Home Secretary** ≃ ministre *m* de l'Intérieur

◇ *Econ* **home trade** commerce *m* intérieur

honeymoon period *n (of prime minister, president)* lune *f* de miel, état *m* de grâce

But [Mr Blair] decided against an early euro referendum in his **honeymoon period** and the tight spending controls of Labour's first two years made later public disappointment about the state of railways and hospitals almost inevitable.

Honourable *adj Br Parl* **the Honourable** = titre donné aux membres du Parlement britannique; **my Honourable Friend** *(to member of same party)* mon honorable collègue; **the Honourable Lady will be aware that ...** *(to member of another party)* mon honorable collègue n'est pas sans savoir que ...; **the Honourable Gentleman should know that ...** *(to member of another party)* mon honorable collègue devrait savoir que ...; **the Honourable Member for Suffolk South** le député de la circonscription Suffolk South; **the Honourable Member will no doubt recall ...** mon honorable collègue se rappellera sans doute ...

horizontal *adj Econ*

◇ *horizontal concentration* concentration *f* horizontale

◇ *horizontal discrimination* discrimination *f* horizontale

◇ *horizontal equity* équité *f* horizontale

◇ *horizontal integration* intégration *f* horizontale

◇ *horizontal merger* fusion *f* horizontale

hostile 1 *adj* hostile

2 *n Am* ennemi *m*

◇ *hostile act* acte *m* d'hostilité

hot *adj*

◇ *Pol* **hot line** ligne *f* directe; **he has a hot line to the president** il a une ligne directe avec le président

◇ *Fam* **hot potato** sujet *m* brûlant et délicat; **a political hot potato** une question *ou* un sujet politique brûlant(e)

In political campaigns across the country this year, some Democratic candidates who traditionally support gay civil rights balked when it came to embracing what many still view as a **political hot potato**: marriage rights for same-sex couples.

House *n Parl* **the House** *(in Britain and Canada)* la Chambre; *(in USA)* la Chambre des représentants; **the House overwhelmingly approved two military spending measures** la Chambre a approuvé les dépenses militaires proposées à une très grande majorité; **the GOP has taken over the House majority** le parti républicain est maintenant majoritaire à la Chambre des représentants

◇ *the House of Commons* la Chambre des communes

◇ *the House of Commons Chamber* = salle des débats de la Chambre des communes

◇ *the House of Commons Commission* = organe régulateur de la Chambre des communes

◇ *House of Commons Papers* = documents de travail de la Chambre des communes

◇ *the House of Lords* la Chambre des lords *ou* des pairs

◇ *the House of Lords Appointments Commission* = commission effectuant des recommandations pour la nomination de nouveaux membres non affiliés à un parti politique à la Chambre des lords

◇ **the House of Lords Chamber** = salle des débats de la Chambre des lords

◇ **the Houses of Parliament** le Parlement (britannique)

◇ **the House of Representatives** la Chambre des représentants *(aux États-Unis)*

house arrest *n* assignation *f* à domicile *ou* à résidence; **to place sb under house arrest** assigner qn à domicile *ou* à résidence; **he is under house arrest** il est assigné à domicile, il est en résidence surveillée

household *Econ* **1** *n (in economics, statistics)* ménage *m*; *(for tax purposes)* foyer *m* fiscal
   2 *adj (in economics, statistics)* des ménages

◇ **household consumption** consommation *f* des ménages

◇ **household expenditure** dépenses *fpl* des ménages

housing starts *npl Am Econ* = mise en chantier de logements

human *adj*

◇ **human capital** capital *m* humain

◇ **Human Development Index** indice *m* de développement humain

◇ **human rights** droits *mpl* de l'homme; **a human rights organization** une organisation pour les droits de l'homme

hung parliament *n Pol* parlement *m* sans majorité

hybrid bill *n Br Pol* = loi dont certaines dispositions sont d'application générale et d'autres d'application restreinte

hyperinflation *n Econ* hyperinflation *f*

IAFF n (abbr **International Association of Fire Fighters**) = syndicat de pompiers américains et canadiens

IBEW n (abbr **International Brotherhood of Electrical Workers**) = syndicat américain et canadien d'électriciens

IBRD n (abbr **International Bank for Reconstruction and Development**) BIRD f

IBT n (abbr **International Brotherhood of Teamsters**) = syndicat de travailleurs américains et canadiens

ICC n (abbr **International Criminal Court**) CPI f

ICFTU n (abbr **International Confederation of Free Trade Unions**) CISL f

ICJ n (abbr **International Court of Justice**) CIJ f

IDA n (abbr **International Development Association**) AID f

ideology n idéologie f

IGC n (abbr **Intergovernmental Conference**) CIG f

IGO n (abbr **Intergovernmental Organization**) OIG f

ILA n (abbr **International Longshoremen's Association**) = syndicat international de dockers

illegal immigrant n immigré(e) m,f clandestin(e)

illiberal adj Pol (regime) intolérant(e); (legislation) restrictif(ive)

illiberality n Pol (of regime) intolérance f; (of legislation) caractère m restrictif

illiquid adj Econ non liquide

◇ **illiquid assets** actif m non-disponible ou immobilisé

illiquidity n Econ illiquidité f

ILO n (a) (abbr **International Labour Office**) BIT m (b) (abbr **International Labour Organization**) OIT f

ILWU n (abbr **International Longshoremen's and Warehousemen's Union**) = syndicat international de dockers et de magasiniers

imbalanced growth n Econ croissance f déséquilibrée

IMF n (abbr **International Monetary Fund**) FMI m

immigrant 1 n immigré(e) m,f
2 adj immigré(e)
◇ **immigrant worker** travailleur(-euse) m,f immigré(e)

immigrate vi immigrer

immigration n immigration f; **the government wants to reduce immigration** le gouvernement veut restreindre l'immigration
◇ **Immigration Control Act** = loi de 1986 permettant aux immigrés illégaux résidant aux États-Unis depuis 1982 de recevoir un visa
◇ **immigration laws** lois fpl sur l'immigration
◇ Br **Immigration and Nationality Directorate** = organisme gouvernemental traitant des questions d'immigration et de citoyenneté

immobilism n Pol immobilisme m

immobilist Pol 1 n immobiliste mf
2 adj immobiliste

immune adj (exempt) **immune from** exempt(e) de, exonéré(e) de; **immune from taxation** exonéré(e) ou exempt(e) d'impôts

immunity n (a) (exemption) exemption f, exonération f (**from** de); **immunity from taxation** exemption f ou exonération f d'impôts (b) Pol (diplomatic, parliamentary) immunité f

impeach vt Am Pol entamer une procédure d'"impeachment" contre

impeachable adj Am Pol = qui peut donner lieu à une procédure d'"impeachment"

impeachment n Am Pol = mise en accusation d'un élu devant le Congrès

> **"**
>
> Just talking about invading Iraq has a very useful effect for President Bush. It stops a public debate about his catastrophic record as President. Indeed, had President Clinton or any Democrat a similar record, **impeachment** would already be underway.
>
> **"**

imperfect adj Econ imparfait(e)
◇ **imperfect competition** concurrence f imparfaite
◇ **imperfect market** marché m imparfait

imperialism n impérialisme m

imperialist 1 n impérialiste mf
2 adj impérialiste

implicit contract theory n Econ théorie f du contrat implicite

import 1 n (a) (product) article m ou produit m d'importation; **imports** (of country) importations fpl; **the government has put a tax on imports** le gouvernement a instauré une taxe sur les produits d'importation ou les produits importés (b) (activity) importation f; **import and export** l'importation f et l'exportation f

2 vt (goods) importer; **lamb imported from New Zealand into Britain** agneau de Nouvelle-Zélande importé en Grande-Bretagne
◇ **import ban** interdiction f d'importation; **to impose an import ban on sth** interdire qch d'importation
◇ **import controls** contrôles mpl à l'importation
◇ **import credit** crédit m à l'importation
◇ **import duty** droit m de douane à l'importation
◇ **import firm** maison f d'importation
◇ **import goods** marchandises fpl à l'import
◇ **import licence** licence f d'importation
◇ **import list** liste f des importations; (of prices) tarif m d'entrée
◇ **import penetration** pénétration f des importations
◇ **import permit** permis m d'importer ou d'importation
◇ **import potential** capacité f d'importation
◇ **import price** prix m à l'importation, prix m (à l')import
◇ **import quotas** contingents mpl d'importation
◇ **import restrictions** restrictions fpl à l'importation
◇ **import substitution** substitution f d'importation
◇ **import surcharge** surtaxe f à l'importation
◇ **import surplus** surplus m d'importation
◇ **import tariff** tarif m import
◇ **import tax** taxe f à l'importation
◇ **import trade** commerce m d'importation

importable adj importable

importation n (a) (activity) importation f (b) Am (product) importation f, article m d'importation

importer n (a) (person) importateur(trice) m,f (b) (country) pays m importateur; **an oil importer** un pays importateur de pétrole; **this country**

is a big importer of luxury goods ce pays est un gros importateur de produits de luxe ; **Japan is still a net importer of technology** le Japon est toujours un importateur net de technologie

import-export n import-export m
◇ **import-export company** société f d'import-export

importing 1 n importation f
2 adj importateur(trice)
◇ **importing country** pays m importateur

IMS n Econ (abbr **International Monetary System**) SMI m

inaugural 1 n Am discours m inaugural (d'un président des États-Unis)
2 adj inaugural(e), d'inauguration
◇ **inaugural address** discours m inaugural
◇ **inaugural speech** discours m inaugural

> **"**
> Properly, the president's **inaugural address** did not allude to the bitterly disputed election. He also avoided mistakes made by his two predecessors, who sounded **inaugural** themes that were foreign to their campaigns ... George W. Bush's address was fully consistent with his conservative campaign.
> **"**

inaugurate vt (a) (policy) inaugurer, instaurer (b) (official) investir, installer (dans ses fonctions)

inauguration n (a) (of policy) inauguration f (b) (of official) investiture f
◇ **Inauguration Day** = jour de l'investiture du président des États-Unis (le 20 janvier)

incendiarism n Pol sédition f

incendiary Pol **1** n fauteur m de troubles
2 adj incendiaire, séditieux(euse)

income n (of person) revenu m ; (of company) recettes fpl, revenus mpl, rentrées fpl
◇ **income bracket** tranche f de salaire ou de revenu ; **most people in this area belong to the lower/higher income bracket** la plupart des habitants de ce quartier sont des économiquement faibles/ont des revenus élevés
◇ Econ **income distribution** répartition f des revenus
◇ Econ **income elasticity** élasticité f par rapport au revenu
◇ Econ **income elasticity of demand** élasticité f de la demande par rapport au revenu
◇ **income group** tranche f de salaire ou de revenu
◇ Br Pol **incomes policy** politique f des revenus
◇ **income redistribution** redistribution f des revenus
◇ **income tax** impôt m sur le revenu
◇ Econ **income velocity of capital** vitesse f de transformation des capitaux
◇ Econ **income velocity of money** vitesse-revenu f de la monnaie

incoming adj (president, leader) entrant(e)

increasing returns npl Econ rendements mpl croissants

incumbency n Pol (office) office m, fonction f

incumbent Pol **1** n (office holder) titulaire mf
2 adj (in office) en fonction, en exercice ; **the incumbent president** (current) le président en exercice ; (during election campaign) le président sortant

independence n Pol indépendance f ; **the country has recently gained its independence** le pays vient d'accéder à l'indépendance
◇ **independence movement** mouvement m indépendantiste

independent Pol **1** n indépendant(e) m,f, non-inscrit(e) m,f
2 adj indépendant(e)

index *Econ* **1** *n* indice *m*
2 *vt* indexer
◇ *index of growth* indice *m* de croissance
◇ *index number* indice *m*

indexation *n Econ* indexation *f*
◇ *indexation clause* clause *f* d'indexation

index-based *adj Econ* indiciaire

indexed *adj Econ* indexé(e); **indexed to inflation** indexé(e) sur l'inflation

index-link *vt Econ* indexer

index-linked *adj Econ* indexé(e); **this pension is index-linked to the cost of living** cette retraite est indexée sur le coût de la vie

indicator *n Econ* indicateur *m*

indifference curve *n Econ* courbe *f* d'indifférence

indirect *adj* indirect(e)
◇ *Pol* **indirect election** élection *f* indirecte
◇ *Econ* **indirect investment** investissement *m* indirect
◇ *Econ* **indirect labour** main-d'œuvre *f* indirecte
◇ *Pol* **indirect suffrage** suffrage *m* indirect
◇ *Econ* **indirect tax** impôt *m* indirect
◇ *Econ* **indirect taxation** contributions *fpl* indirectes, fiscalité *f* indirecte
◇ *Pol* **indirect universal suffrage** suffrage *m* universel indirect
◇ *Pol* **indirect vote** vote *m* indirect

individualism *n Pol* individualisme *m*

individualist *Pol* **1** *n* individualiste *mf*
2 *adj* individualiste

industrial *adj* industriel(elle)
◇ *industrial action* grève *f*, action *f* syndicale *ou* revendicative
◇ *industrial activity* activité *f* industrielle
◇ *industrial activity index* indice *m* d'activité industrielle
◇ *industrial democracy* démocratie *f* industrielle
◇ *industrial dispute* conflit *m* social, conflit *m* du travail

◇ *industrial earnings* produit *m* industriel
◇ *industrial economics* économie *f* industrielle
◇ *industrial group* groupe *m* industriel
◇ *industrial monopoly* trust *m* industriel
◇ *industrial organization* économie *f* industrielle
◇ *industrial policy* politique *f* industrielle
◇ *industrial power* puissance *f* industrielle
◇ *industrial production* production *f* industrielle
◇ *industrial redeployment* reconversion *f* industrielle
◇ *industrial relations* relations *fpl* industrielles
◇ *industrial revolution* révolution *f* industrielle
◇ *industrial society* société *f* industrielle
◇ *industrial trade* échanges *mpl* industriels
◇ *industrial union* syndicat *m* d'industrie
◇ *industrial unit* atelier *m*
◇ *industrial unrest* agitation *f* syndicale

industrialism *n* industrialisme *m*

industrialist *n* industriel *m*

industrialization *n* industrialisation *f*

industrialize **1** *vt* industrialiser
2 *vi* s'industrialiser

industrialized *adj* industrialisé(e)
◇ *industrialized countries* pays *mpl* industrialisés

━━ 44 ━━

National income, or its rate of growth, has most often been used in the West to indicate success. To many poorer countries, however, the idea of turning into a replica of one of the **industrialized countries**, pursuing high money incomes and high growth rates as goals in their own right, appears neither feasible nor desirable.

"

industry n industrie f
◇ *industry forecast* prévision f de l'industrie

inelastic adj Econ (market, supply, demand) fixe

inequality n inégalité f

infant industry n Econ industrie f naissante

"

Just two years ago, the lobbyists for America Online could persuade Congress that the access fees of this **infant industry** should be exempt from state and local taxes. In January 2000, AOL proposed a $165 billion merger with Time Warner, a global media powerhouse.

"

infiltrate Pol **1** vt infiltrer, noyauter; **the police had infiltrated the terrorist group** la police avait infiltré ou noyauté le groupe terroriste
2 vi s'infiltrer

infiltration n Pol noyautage m

inflammatory adj Pol provocateur(-trice)

inflate Econ **1** vt (prices, money) faire monter, augmenter; (economy) provoquer l'inflation de; **to inflate the currency** accroître la circulation monétaire
2 vi (of prices, money) subir une inflation; **the government decided to inflate** le gouvernement a décidé d'avoir recours à des mesures inflationnistes

inflated adj Econ (price) exagéré(e)
◇ *inflated currency* inflation f monétaire

inflation n Econ inflation f; **inflation is down/up on last year** l'inflation est en baisse/en hausse par rapport à l'an-

née dernière; **inflation now stands at five percent** l'inflation est maintenant à cinq pour cent
◇ *inflation accounting* comptabilité f d'inflation
◇ *inflation differential* différentiel m d'inflation
◇ *inflation targeting* ciblage m de l'inflation
◇ *inflation tax* taxe f d'inflation

inflationary adj Econ inflationniste
◇ *inflationary gap* écart m inflationniste
◇ *inflationary policy* politique f inflationniste
◇ *inflationary pressure* pression f inflationniste
◇ *inflationary spiral* spirale f inflationniste
◇ *inflationary surge* poussée f inflationniste
◇ *inflationary trend* tendance f inflationniste

inflation-busting adj (pay rise, deal) = qui n'a pas d'effets inflationnistes

inflationism n Econ inflationnisme m

inflationist Econ **1** n inflationniste mf
2 adj inflationniste

inflow n Econ (of capital) apport m

influence peddling n Pol trafic m d'influence

"

During Bill Clinton's presidency, Republicans were loud in accusing the White House of being too cozy with campaign contributors and lobbyists and relentlessly looking to shape policy to appeal to this or that group of minority voters. **Influence peddling** seemed rife, as did special treatment and access for corporate bigwigs who shelled out for the Democrats.

"

influx n Econ (of capital) apport m

informal adj (visit, talks) non officiel(-

elle); **they had informal talks with the Russians** ils ont eu des entretiens non officiels avec les Russes

◊ *Econ **informal economy*** économie *f* informelle

infrastate *adj* infraétatique

infrastructure *n* infrastructure *f*

inheritance tax *n* droits *mpl* de succession

initiative *n (idea)* initiative *f*

inject *vt (money)* injecter (**into** dans); **they've injected billions of dollars into the economy** ils ont injecté des milliards de dollars dans l'économie

injection *n (of money)* injection *f* (**into** dans); **an injection of capital** une injection de capitaux

inner circle *n* **in the inner circles of power** dans les milieux proches du pouvoir; **her inner circle of advisers** le cercle de ses conseillers les plus proches

> **"**
> The resignation will add to the perception that blacks, who vote overwhelmingly for the Democrats, have no place in the Republican party – despite the presence of Colin Powell and Condoleezza Rice in the president's **inner circle**.
> **"**

input *n Econ (of production)* input *m*, intrant *m*

input-output analysis *n Econ* analyse *f* d'entrée-sortie

insolvency *n Econ* insolvabilité *f*

insolvent *Econ* **1** *n* insolvable *mf*
2 *adj* insolvable

instability *n (of regime, market, prices)* instabilité *f*

instant runoff voting *n Pol* = mode de scrutin par élimination

institute *n (organization)* institut *m*; *(governmental)* organisme *m*

institution *n (organization)* organisme *m*, établissement *m*; *(governmental)* institution *f*

institutional savings *npl* épargne *f* institutionnelle

insurgency, insurgence *n* insurrection *f*

insurgent 1 *n* insurgé(e) *m,f*
2 *adj* insurgé(e)

integrate 1 *vt (combine)* intégrer; **the law was intended to integrate racial minorities** cette loi visait à l'intégration des minorités raciales
2 *vi (end segregation)* ne plus pratiquer la ségrégation raciale

integration *n* **(a)** *(process of integrating)* intégration *f* **(b)** *Econ* intégration *f*

integrative growth *n Econ* croissance *f* par intégration

intelligence *n Pol (information)* renseignements *mpl*; *(department)* services *mpl* de renseignements; **intelligence is** *or* **are working on it** les services de renseignements y travaillent; **he used to work in intelligence** il travaillait pour les services de renseignements

◊ *Am **intelligence agency*** services *mpl* de renseignements

◊ ***intelligence gathering*** renseignement *m*, espionnage *m*

◊ ***intelligence officer*** officier *m* de renseignements

◊ *Br **intelligence service*** services *mpl* de renseignements

intensive *adj Econ* intensif(ive)

interdepartmental *adj (in ministry)* interdépartemental(e)

interdependence *n Pol* interdépendance *f*

interdependent *adj Pol* interdépendant(e)

interest *n* **(a)** *(group with common aim)* intérêt *m*; **the oil/steel interests in the country** l'industrie *f* pétrolière/sidérurgique du pays; **big business in-**

terests de gros intérêts commerciaux (**b**) *(on loan, investment)* intérêts *mpl*
◇ *interest group* groupe *m* d'intérêt
◇ *interest rate* taux *m* d'intérêt; **the interest rate is four percent** le taux d'intérêt est de quatre pour cent
◇ *interest rate differential* différentiel *m* de taux d'intérêt
◇ *interest rate swap* échange *m* de taux d'intérêt
◇ *interest relief* bonification *f* d'intérêts

interference *n Pol* ingérence *f*

intergovernmental *adj Pol* intergouvernemental(e)
◇ *Intergovernmental Conference* Conférence *f* Intergouvernementale
◇ *Intergovernmental Organization* Organisation *f* Intergouvernementale
◇ *Intergovernmental Panel on Climate Change* Groupement *m* Intergouvernemental de l'Étude du climat

interim 1 *n* intérim *m*
2 *adj (government, measure, report)* provisoire; *(post, function)* intérimaire; **the interim minister** le ministre par intérim *ou* intérimaire

intermediary *n* médiateur(trice) *m,f*

intermediate consumer goods *npl* biens *mpl* de consommation intermédiaire

intern *Pol* **1** *n* interné(e) *m,f* (politique)
2 *vt* interner

internal *adj (trade)* intérieur(e)
◇ *internal affairs* affaires *fpl* intérieures
◇ *internal balance* équilibre *m* interne
◇ *internal debt* endettement *m* intérieur
◇ *internal growth* croissance *f* interne
◇ *internal labour market* marché *m* interne du travail
◇ *Econ internal rate of return* taux *m* de rentabilité interne

internalization *n Econ* internalisation *f*

internalize *vt Econ* internaliser

international *adj* international(e); **the international community** la communauté internationale
◇ *international affairs* affaires *fpl* internationales
◇ *international agency* organisation *f* internationale
◇ *International Bank for Reconstruction and Development* Banque *f* internationale pour la reconstruction et le développement
◇ *international bureaux* bureaux *mpl* internationaux
◇ *International Chamber of Commerce* Chambre *f* de commerce internationale
◇ *international commodity agreements* accords *mpl* internationaux sur les produits de base
◇ *international company* multinationale *f*
◇ *International Court of Justice* Cour *f* internationale de justice
◇ *International Criminal Court* Cour *f* internationale pénale
◇ *international currency* devise *f* internationale
◇ *International Finance Corporation* Société *f* financière internationale
◇ *International Labour Office* Bureau *m* international du travail
◇ *International Labour Organization* Organisation *f* internationale du travail
◇ *international mandate* mandat *m* international
◇ *International Monetary Fund* Fonds *m* monétaire international
◇ *international monetary reserves* réserves *fpl* monétaires internationales
◇ *Econ International Monetary System* système *m* monétaire international
◇ *international money market* marché *m* monétaire international
◇ *international organization* organisation *f* internationale

◇ *international peace conference* conférence *f* internationale sur la paix

◇ *international relations* relations *fpl* internationales

◇ *international socialism* socialisme *m* international

◇ *international society* communauté *f* internationale

◇ *International Standards Organization* Organisation *f* internationale de normalisation

◇ *international trade* commerce *m* international, échanges *mpl* internationaux

◇ *Am International Trade Commission* = organisme fédéral américain traitant de questions de commerce international

◇ *International Trade Organization* Organisation *f* internationale du commerce

◇ *international trading corporation* société *f* de commerce international

internationalism *n* internationalisme *m*

internationalist 1 *n* internationaliste *mf*
  2 *adj* internationaliste

internationality *n* internationalité *f*

internationalization *n* internationalisation *f*

internationalize *vt* internationaliser

interparliamentary *adj Pol* interparlementaire

interparty *adj Pol (talks, negotiations)* entre différents partis politiques

interpellate *vt Parl* interpeller

interstate *adj* interétatique

intervene *vi* intervenir; **the government intervened to save the dollar from falling** le gouvernement est intervenu pour arrêter la chute du dollar

intervention *n Econ & Pol* intervention *f*

◇ *Econ intervention price* prix *m* d'intervention

◇ *Econ intervention rate* taux *m* d'intervention

interventionism *n Econ* interventionnisme *m*

interventionist *Econ* 1 *n* interventionniste *mf*
  2 *adj* interventionniste

intifada *n* intifada *f*

intra-Community *adj EU* intracommunautaire

◇ *intra-Community acquisition* acquisition *f* intracommunautaire

◇ *intra-Community trade* échange *m* intracommunautaire

introduce *vt (bill, law, legislation)* déposer, présenter; *(government)* constituer, établir; *(reform, new methods)* introduire; **the government hopes to introduce the new bill next week** le gouvernement espère déposer son nouveau projet de loi la semaine prochaine

introduction *n (of bill, law, legislation)* introduction *f*, présentation *f*; *(of government)* constitution *f*; *(of reform, new methods)* introduction *f*

invest 1 *vt* (a) *Econ (money)* investir, placer; *(capital)* investir; **to invest money in a business** mettre de l'argent *ou* placer des fonds dans un commerce; **the government will invest a billion pounds in the National Health Service** le gouvernement va investir un milliard de livres dans les services de santé (b) *Pol (president)* installer
  2 *vi* investir, faire des placements; **to invest in the oil industry** investir dans l'industrie pétrolière; **to invest in property** faire des placements dans l'immobilier; **the company has invested heavily in its Asian subsidiary companies** la société a beaucoup investi dans ses filiales asiatiques

investment *n* investissement *m*, placement *m*; *(money invested)* investissement *m*, mise *f* de fonds; **the**

company has investments all over the world la société a des capitaux investis dans le monde entier

◇ *investment appraisal* appréciation *f* des investissements

◇ *investment bank* banque *f* d'affaires

◇ *investment banking* banque *f* d'affaires

◇ *investment borrowing* = emprunts destinés à l'investissement

◇ *investment grant* subvention *f* d'investissement

◇ *investment house* société *f* financière

◇ *investment incentives* encouragements *mpl* à l'investissement

◇ *investment market* marché *m* des capitaux

◇ *investment policy* politique *f* d'investissement

◇ *investment spending* dépenses *fpl* d'investissement

◇ *investment subsidy* prime *f* à l'investissement

◇ *investment trust* société *f* de placement

invisible *Econ* **1** *n* invisibles invisibles *mpl*
2 *adj*

◇ *invisible asset* actif *m* incorporel, immobilisation *f* (incorporelle)

◇ *invisible earnings* gains *mpl* invisibles

◇ *invisible exports* exportations *fpl* invisibles

◇ *invisible hand* main *f* invisible

◇ *invisible imports* importations *fpl* invisibles

◇ *invisible trade* transactions *fpl* invisibles

invocation *n Pol* invocation *f*

invoke *vt* invoquer; **they invoked the non-intervention treaty** ils ont invoqué le traité de non-intervention; **she invoked the principle of free speech** elle a invoqué le principe de la liberté d'expression

involuntary unemployment *n Econ* chômage *m* involontaire

inward investment *n Econ* investissement *m* de l'étranger

Scotland's share of **inward investment** soared by 30% last year as the UK once again won the largest share within Europe. According to Ernst and Young's European Investment Monitor, Scotland attracted 55 projects last year compared with 42 in 1999. Much of Scotland's success last year came from the US which provided 31 direct investment projects.

IRA *n* (*abbr* **Irish Republican Army**) IRA *f*

Irish Republican Army *n* IRA *f*

Iron *adj*
◇ *Pol **Iron Curtain*** rideau *m* de fer
◇ *Br Pol **Iron Lady*** Dame *f* de Fer (*surnom donné à Margaret Thatcher*)

IRR *n Econ* (*abbr* **internal rate of return**) taux *m* de rentabilité interne

irredentism *n Pol* irrédentisme *m*

irredentist *Pol* **1** *n* irrédentiste *mf*
2 *adj* irrédentiste

IRV *n Pol* (*abbr* **Instant Runoff Voting**) = mode de scrutin par élimination

Islam *n* Islam *m*

Islamic *adj* islamique

Islamism *n* islamisme *m*

Islamist *n* islamite *mf*

isocracy *n Pol* isocratie *f*

isolated *adj Pol* isolé(e)

isolation *n Pol* isolement *m*

isolationism *n Pol* isolationnisme *m*

isolationist *Pol* **1** *n* isolationniste *mf*
2 *adj* isolationniste

ISPA *n EU* (*abbr* **Instrument for Structural Policies for Pre-Accession**) ISPA *m*

issue voting *n Pol* = notion selon laquelle les électeurs se prononcent en fonction des enjeux en présence, plus que par loyauté envers tel ou tel parti

ISTC *n* (*abbr* **Iron and Steel Confederation**) = syndicat britannique des ouvriers de la sidérurgie

ITC *n* (**a**) *Am* (*abbr* **International Trade Commission**) = organisme fédéral américain traitant de questions de commerce international (**b**) (*abbr* **international trading corporation**) société *f* de commerce international

item veto *n Pol* veto *m* partiel

ITO *n* (*abbr* **International Trade Organization**) OMC *f*

ITS *npl* (*abbr* **International Trade Secretariats**) SPI *mpl*

IUOE *n* (*abbr* **International Union of Operating Engineers**) = syndicat industriel américain et canadien

IUPA *n* (*abbr* **International Union of Police Associations**) = syndicat de policiers américains et canadiens

J-Curve n Econ courbe f en J

jingoism n chauvinisme m

jingoist 1 n chauvin(e) m,f, cocardier(-ère) m,f
  2 adj chauvin(e), cocardier(ère)

jingoistic adj chauvin(e), cocardier(-ère)

join 1 vt (become member of) adhérer à; **he joined the Conservative party in 1979** il est devenu membre du parti conservateur en 1979
  2 vi (become member) devenir membre

joint adj
◇ **joint agreement** accord m commun
◇ **joint commission** commission f mixte ou paritaire
◇ **joint committee** commission f mixte ou paritaire
◇ **joint demand** demande f conjointe
◇ **joint manifesto** programme m commun
◇ **joint negotiations** négociations fpl collectives
◇ Am Pol **joint resolution** ≃ projet m de loi
◇ **joint statement** déclaration f commune
◇ **joint venture** (undertaking) entreprise f commune
◇ **joint venture agreement** accord m de partenariat
◇ **joint venture company** société f d'exploitation en commun

journalist n journaliste mf

judge n juge m

judicial adj
◇ Am Pol **judicial branch** branche f judiciaire
◇ **judicial review** (of ruling) examen m d'une décision de justice (par une juridiction supérieure); (of law) examen m de la constitutionnalité d'une loi

judiciary n pouvoir m judiciaire

junior adj
◇ **junior defence minister** sous-secrétaire mf d'État à la Défense
◇ **junior foreign office minister** sous-secrétaire mf d'État aux Affaires étrangères
◇ **junior minister** sous-secrétaire mf d'État
◇ **junior trade minister** sous-secrétaire mf d'État au Commerce
◇ **junior transport minister** sous-secrétaire mf d'État aux Transports

junta n junte f

Justice Department n Am ≃ ministère m de la Justice

just war n guerre f juste

❝
There is no such thing as a **just war**, it is argued, because modern weapons are so horrific. All wars, therefore, are unjust, and the only alternative for Christians is passive resistance to those who attack them. Insofar as this position would deny humans the right of self-defense, it seems to lack common sense. If it were followed in the early 1940s, either Hitler or Stalin would have ruled the world and most of us would be either dead or unborn.
❞

keiretsu n Econ keiretsu m

key adj (important) clé

Keynesian Econ **1** n keynésien(enne) m,f
    2 adj keynésien(enne)
◇ **Keynesian economics** économie f keynésienne
◇ **Keynesian unemployment** chômage m keynésien

Keynesianism n Econ keynésianisme m

keynote n (of policy) point m capital ou principal; **industrial recovery is the keynote of government policy** le redressement industriel constitue l'axe central de la politique gouvernementale
◇ **keynote address** discours-programme m
◇ **keynote speaker** intervenant(e) m,f principal(e)
◇ **keynote speech** discours-programme m

keynoter n Am orateur(trice) m,f qui prononce le discours d'ouverture

king n roi m; **the King of Spain** le roi d'Espagne

◇ **King's Speech** (in UK) = allocution prononcée par le roi (mais préparée par le gouvernement) lors de la rentrée parlementaire et dans laquelle il définit les grands axes de la politique gouvernementale

kingdom n royaume m

kitchen cabinet n Br Pol cabinet m restreint (conseillers proches du chef du gouvernement)

❝

Ed Balls, 35 – also known as the chancellor's brain – is at the centre of Gordon Brown's **kitchen cabinet**. He has been Brown's confidant, adviser, and head policy wonk since the dark days of opposition, and the chancellor rarely makes a decision without consulting him.

❞

knee-jerk support n Pol soutien m systématique ou inconditionnel

know-how n Econ know-how m

Labour *Pol* **1** *n* le parti travailliste britannique ; **to vote Labour** voter travailliste

  2 *adj (government, victory)* travailliste

◊ *Labour leader* dirigeant(e) *m,f* (du parti) travailliste

◊ *Labour Member (of Parliament)* député(e) *m,f* travailliste

◊ *Labour Party* parti *m* travailliste

◊ *Labour Party chairman* leader *m* du parti travailliste

◊ *Labour voter* = personne qui vote travailliste

labour, *Am* **labor** *n Econ* **(a)** *(work)* travail *m* **(b)** *(manpower)* main-d'œuvre *f* ; *(workers)* ouvriers *mpl* ; **capital and labour** le capital et la main-d'œuvre

◊ *labour dispute* conflit *m* social, conflit *m* du travail

◊ *labour force* effectifs *mpl* ; *(of country)* population *f* active

◊ *labour law* droit *m* du travail

◊ *labour laws* législation *f* du travail

◊ *labour legislation* législation *f* du travail

◊ *labour market* marché *m* du travail

◊ *labour movement* mouvement *m* ouvrier

◊ *labour regulations* réglementation *f* du travail

◊ *labour relations* relations *fpl* sociales

◊ *labour shortage* pénurie *f* de main-d'œuvre

◊ *labour turnover* rotation *f* du personnel

◊ *Am* *labor union* syndicat *m*

Labourite *Pol* **1** *n* travailliste *mf*

  2 *adj* travailliste

Laffer curve *n Econ* courbe *f* de Laffer

lagging indicator *n* indicateur *m* retardé

laisser-faire, laissez-faire *n Econ* laisser-faire *m*

◊ *laisser-faire policy* politique *f* de laisser-faire

lame duck *n Am Pol* = candidat sortant non réélu qui attend l'arrivée de son successeur

lame-duck president *n Am Pol* = président sortant non réélu

> In some respects, President Clinton is following the classic profile of a **lame-duck president**. He's focused heavily on foreign affairs, as his triumphal tour in Europe this week shows in the wake of the Kosovo conflict. But he's finding less success at home, as he's epitomized by his stinging defeat on gun control in Congress.

land *n* terre(s) *f(pl)*

land-based *adj Econ* basé(e) sur la propriété terrienne

landslide 1 *n (majority, victory)* victoire *f* écrasante ; **to win the elections by a landslide** gagner les élections avec une majorité écrasante

  2 *adj (majority, victory)* écrasant(e)

> **"**
>
> Jacques Chirac made a grab for France's middle ground yesterday after his **landslide** victory over the far-right leader Jean-Marie Le Pen, setting out a centrist stall ahead of June's general elections by naming an inoffensive moderate as prime minister.
>
> **"**

lateral integration n Econ intégration f latérale

law n (a) (legal provision) loi f; **a law against gambling** une loi qui interdit les jeux d'argent
(b) (legislation) loi f; **by law** selon la loi; **in** or **under British law** selon la loi britannique; **the bill became law** le projet de loi a été voté ou adopté
(c) (legal system) droit m
(d) (justice) justice f, système m juridique; Br **to go to law** aller en justice
(e) (principle) loi f; Econ **the law of supply and demand** la loi de l'offre et de la demande
◇ **law court** tribunal m, cour f de justice
◇ Br **Law Lords** = membres de la Chambre des lords siégeant en tant que cour d'appel de dernière instance

lawful adj légitime

lawmaker n législateur(trice) m,f

lawmaking adj législateur(trice)

▸ **lay off** vt sep Econ (employees) licencier; (temporarily) mettre en chômage technique

layoff n Econ (sacking) licenciement m; (inactivity) chômage m technique

LCD n Br Pol (abbr Lord Chancellor's Department) ≃ ministre m de la Justice (en Grande-Bretagne)

LDC n (abbr less developed country) PMA m

leader n Pol chef m, leader m, dirigeant(e) m,f

◇ Br **Leader of the House** (in the Commons) = parlementaire de la majorité chargé de certaines fonctions dans la mise en place du programme gouvernemental; (in the Lords) = porte-parole du gouvernement
◇ Br **Leader of the Opposition** chef m de l'opposition

leadership n (a) (direction) direction f; **during** or **under her leadership** sous sa direction; **he was offered the party leadership** on lui a offert la direction du parti (b) (leaders) direction f, dirigeants mpl; **the leadership of the movement is divided on this issue** les chefs ou les dirigeants du mouvement sont divisés sur cette question
◇ **leadership battle** lutte f pour la position de leader
◇ **leadership contest** lutte f pour la position de leader
◇ **leadership election** élections fpl pour la position de leader
◇ **leadership selection** sélection f du leader (d'un parti politique)

leading adj
◇ Pol **leading candidate** tête f de liste
◇ Econ **leading indicators** principaux indicateurs mpl économiques
◇ Am Econ **leading price indicator** indice m composite des principaux indicateurs

leads and lags npl Econ termaillage m

leaflet n (political) tract m

League of Nations n the League of Nations la Société des Nations

leak 1 n (of information, secret) fuite f
2 vt (information, secret) divulguer; **to leak sth to the press** divulguer qch à la presse; **the budget details were leaked** il y a eu des fuites sur le budget; **the documents had been leaked to a local councillor** quelqu'un avait communiqué ou avait fait parvenir les documents à un conseiller municipal

leakage n Econ fuite f

least-developed country n pays m parmi les moins avancés

lebensraum n Pol espace m vital

left Pol 1 n **the left** la gauche; **to be on the left** être à gauche; **to be to the left** être à gauche; **the parties of the left** les partis de (la) gauche; **the far** or **extreme left** l'extrême gauche; **she is further to the left than he is** elle est (politiquement) plus à gauche que lui
  2 adv à gauche; **to vote left** voter à gauche
  ◊ **left wing** gauche f; **the left wing of the party** l'aile f gauche du parti

leftism n Pol idées fpl de gauche; (extreme left) gauchisme m

leftist Pol 1 n (man) homme m de gauche; (woman) femme f de gauche; (extreme left-winger) gauchiste mf
  2 adj de gauche; (extremely left-wing) gauchiste

left-of-centre adj Pol de centre-gauche; **his views are slightly left-of-centre** ses opinions sont plutôt de centre-gauche

left-wing adj Pol de gauche; **a left-wing publication** une publication de gauche; **she's very left-wing** elle est très à gauche; **he has slightly left-wing ideas** il a des idées gauchisantes

left-winger n Pol (man) homme m de gauche; (woman) femme f de gauche; **she's a left-winger** elle est de gauche; **the policy is popular with left-wingers** les gens de gauche approuvent cette mesure

lefty n Br Fam Pej Pol (man) homme m de gauche; (woman) femme f de gauche

❝

Next month's Labour Party annual conference is reportedly going to be a showcase for the British **lefties'** opposition to a war against Saddam's regime. Blair can fight against those resolutions in his own party conference, but the ballgame may be over by the time that conference begins.

❞

legalism n légalisme m

legalist n légaliste mf

legalistic adj légaliste

legislate vi légiférer; **to legislate in favour of/against sth** légiférer en faveur de/contre qch

legislation n législation f; **a piece of legislation** une loi; **to bring in legislation in favour of/against sth** légiférer en faveur de/contre qch; **the legislation on immigration** la législation sur l'immigration

legislative adj législatif(ive)
  ◊ **legislative assembly** assemblée f législative
  ◊ **the Legislative Assembly** (in Ireland, Australia, India, Canada) l'Assemblée f législative
  ◊ **legislative body** corps m législatif
  ◊ Am Pol **legislative branch** branche f législative
  ◊ **legislative council** conseil m législatif
  ◊ **the Legislative Council** (in Australia, India) le Conseil législatif
  ◊ **legislative majority** majorité f parlementaire
  ◊ **legislative power** pouvoir m législatif
  ◊ **legislative programme** programme m législatif
  ◊ **legislative session** session f législative

legislatively adj législativement

legislator n législateur(trice) m,f

legislature n (corps m) législatif m

legitimacy n légitimité f

legitimate adj légitime
  ◊ **legitimate government** gouvernement m légitime
  ◊ **legitimate state** État m légitime

lend 1 vt (money) prêter (**to** à)
  2 vi prêter; **to lend at 12 percent** prêter à 12 pour cent

lender n (person) prêteur(euse) m,f; (institution) organisme m de crédit
◇ **lender of last resort** prêteur m en dernier ressort

lending n prêt m; **bank lending has increased** le volume des prêts bancaires a augmenté
◇ **lending bank** banque f de crédit
◇ **lending country** pays m créancier
◇ **lending policy** (of bank, country) politique f de prêt
◇ **lending rate** taux m de prêt

lend-lease n Econ prêt-bail m

less developed country n pays m moins avancé

lethargic adj (economy) somnolent(e)

lethargy n (of economy) somnolence f

leveller, Am **leveler** n Pol égalitariste mf

leverage n Am Econ (gearing) effet m de levier; (as percentage) ratio m d'endettement, ratio m de levier

liaison committee n Br Pol = comité composé des présidents des différentes commissions d'enquête parlementaires de la Chambre des communes

Lib Dem n Pol (abbr Liberal Democrat)
1 n = membre du parti libéral démocrate; **the Lib Dems** le parti libéral démocrate
2 adj libéral démocrate

Liberal Pol **1** n (party member) membre m du parti libéral; (voter, supporter) partisan m du parti libéral; **to vote Liberal** voter pour le parti libéral
2 adj du parti libéral
◇ **the Liberal Party** le parti Libéral

liberal Pol **1** n centriste mf
2 adj centriste
◇ **liberal globalization** mondialisation f libérale

Liberal Democrat Pol **1** n = membre du parti libéral démocrate; **to vote Liberal Democrat** voter pour le parti libéral démocrate; **the Liberal Demo-**crats parti m libéral démocrate (parti politique britannique de tendance centriste)
2 adj libéral démocrate
◇ **Liberal Democrat leader** leader m du parti libéral démocrate
◇ **Liberal Democrat Member (of Parliament)** député(e) m,f affilié(e) au parti libéral démocrate
◇ **Liberal Democrat Party** parti m libéral démocrate (parti politique britannique de tendance centriste)
◇ **Liberal Democrat voter** = personne qui vote pour le parti libéral démocrate

liberalism n Pol libéralisme m

liberalization n Pol libéralisation f

liberalize vt Pol libéraliser

liberating adj Pol libérateur(trice)

liberator n Pol libérateur(trice)

libertarian Pol **1** n libertaire mf
2 adj libertaire

libertarianism n Pol (doctrine) doctrine f libertaire; (political ideas) convictions fpl libertaires

life adj
◇ Econ **life cycle** cycle m de vie
◇ Br Parl **life peer** pair m à vie
◇ Br Parl **life peerage** pairie f à vie
◇ **life president** président(e) m,f à vie

life-cycle hypothesis n Econ hypothèse f du cycle de vie

lift vt (sanctions, embargo) lever

lifting n (of sanctions, embargo) levée f

light industry n industrie f légère

line-item veto n Am Pol veto m sélectif (qui offre au président la possibilité de s'opposer à certaines dispositions d'une loi)

liquid adj liquide
◇ **liquid assets** actif m liquide, liquidités fpl
◇ **liquid capital** actif m liquide, liquidités fpl
◇ **liquid debt** dette f liquide

◇ *liquid resources* moyens *mpl* liquides

◇ *liquid securities* valeurs *fpl* liquides

liquidity *n Econ* liquidité *f*

◇ *liquidity preference* préférence *f* pour la liquidité, coefficient *m* de liquidité

list *n Pol (of candidates)* liste *f*

◇ *list system* scrutin *m* de liste

LIUNA *n (abbr* **Laborers' International Union of North America)** = syndicat de travailleurs américains et canadiens

LLDC *n (abbr* **least-developed country)** PMD *m*

loan *n (money borrowed)* emprunt *m*; *(money lent)* prêt *m*

lobby *Pol* **1** *n* **(a)** *(pressure group)* groupe *m* de pression, lobby *m*; *(action)* pression *f*; **the ecology lobby** le lobby écologiste; **yesterday's lobby of parliament** la pression exercée hier sur le parlement; **the nurses' lobby for increased pay** la pression exercée par les infirmières pour obtenir une augmentation de salaire **(b)** *Br (hall)* salle *f* des pas perdus

2 *vt (person, parliament)* faire pression sur; **a group of teachers came to lobby the minister** un groupe d'enseignants est venu faire pression sur le ministre

3 *vi* faire campagne; **he has been lobbying hard in recent weeks** il a mené une campagne intensive ces dernières semaines; **ecologists are lobbying for the closure of the plant** les écologistes font pression pour obtenir la fermeture de la centrale; **he's being paid to lobby on behalf of the dairy farmers** il est payé par les producteurs laitiers pour défendre leurs intérêts

◇ *Br Pol* **lobby correspondent** journaliste *mf* parlementaire

◇ *Br Pol* **lobby reporter** journaliste *mf* parlementaire

◇ *Br Pol* **lobby system** système *m* de conférence de presse où seuls certains journalistes sont conviés

A delegation of students from Bradford will **lobby** MPs on Wednesday, over the 'financial crisis' facing those studying at the city's university. Students' Union officers will tackle MPs from the city and other constituencies about controversial funding changes planned by the government.

lobbying *n Pol* pressions *fpl*; **there has been intense lobbying against the bill** il y a eu de fortes pressions pour que le projet de loi soit retiré

lobbyist *n Pol* lobbyiste *mf*, membre *m* d'un groupe de pression

local *adj Pol* local(e), communal(e), municipal(e)

◇ *local authority* administration *f* locale; *(in town)* municipalité *f*

◇ *local council* conseil *m* municipal, *Belg* conseil *m* communal

◇ *local councillor* conseiller(ère) *m,f* municipal(e), *Belg* conseiller(ère) *m,f* communal(e)

◇ *local government* administration *f* municipale

◇ *local government elections* élections *fpl* municipales

◇ *local government finance* finances *fpl* des collectivités locales

◇ *local government minister* = ministre responsable des collectivités locales

◇ *local government official* fonctionnaire *mf* de l'administration municipale

◇ *local labour market* marché *m* du travail régional

◇ *local politics* politique *f* locale

◇ *local tax* impôt *m* local

◇ *local taxation* impôts *mpl* locaux

logroll *Am Pol* **1** *vt (bill, legislation)* = faire voter grâce à des échanges de faveurs

2 *vi* user d'échanges de faveurs

logrolling *n Am Pol* échange *m* de faveurs *(accord entre hommes politiques selon lequel on se rend mutuellement des services)*

❝

The author describes how the system is skewed toward expansion of the government. With benefits concentrated in a small group of citizens and costs dispersed among all taxpayers, an interest group has an incentive to invest money to create and protect programs. Then there is **logrolling** (or vote trading) in which a representative votes for another's program in return for the other voting for his program. The result is a government looked upon as the benevolent provider of all things.

❞

Lomé Convention *n EU* convention *f* de Lomé

London *n* Londres *m*
◇ *London School of Economics* = grande école de sciences économiques et politiques à Londres
◇ *London Stock Exchange* = la Bourse de Londres

long-term *adj (forecast, loan)* à long terme
◇ *Econ long-term planner* prospectiviste *mf*
◇ *Econ long-term planning* planification *f* à long terme
◇ *long-term policy* politique *f* à long terme
◇ *Econ long-term unemployment* chômage *m* structurel

loophole *n (in law, regulations)* point *m* faible

Lord *n Br Pol (in House of Lords)* lord *m*
◇ *Lords' Amendment (to bill)* = amendement proposé par la Chambre des lords
◇ *Lord Chamberlain* grand chambellan *m*
◇ *Lord Chancellor* lord *m* Chancelier, ≃ ministre *m* de la Justice, ≃ garde *m* des Sceaux

◇ *Lord Chancellor's Department* ≃ ministère *m* de la Justice
◇ *Lord Chief Justice* ≃ président *m* de la Haute Cour
◇ *Lord High Chancellor* lord *m* Chancelier; ≃ ministre *m* de la Justice, ≃ garde *m* des Sceaux
◇ *Lord Mayor* lord-maire *m*, maire *m*
◇ *Lord Privy Seal* = titre du doyen du gouvernement britannique
◇ *Lords Spiritual* = membres ecclésiastiques de la Chambre des lords
◇ *Lords Temporal* = membres laïques de la Chambre des lords
◇ *Lords Whip* = membre de la Chambre des lords chargé de la discipline de son parti

loss *n* déficit *m*; **to make a loss** perdre de l'argent; **the company announced losses of** *or* **a loss of a million pounds** la société a annoncé un déficit d'un million de livres

loss-making *adj* déficitaire

low *adj* (a) *(cost, price, rate)* bas (basse), faible; *(profit)* faible, maigre; **there has been low economic growth** la croissance économique a été faible (b) *(in rank)* bas (basse), inférieur(e); **low ranking officials** petits fonctionnaires *mpl*, fonctionnaires *mpl* subalternes

lower *vt (price, rate, tax)* abaisser

Lower Chamber, Lower House *n Pol* Chambre *f* basse

lowering *n (of price, rate, tax)* abaissement *m*

low-income *adj* à faible revenu
◇ *low-income group* groupe *m* de contribuables à faibles revenus

Loyalism, loyalism *n Pol* loyalisme *m*

Loyalist, loyalist *Pol* **1** *n* loyaliste *mf* **2** *adj* loyaliste

LSE *n* (a) *(abbr London School of Economics)* = grande école de sciences économiques et politiques à Londres (b) *(abbr London Stock Exchange)* = la Bourse de Londres

Maastricht treaty *n* traité *m* de Maastricht

machinery of state *n Pol* appareil *m* étatique

macroeconomic *adj* macroéconomique

macroeconomics *n* macroéconomie *f*

macroeconomy *n* macroéconomie *f*

MAI *n Econ (abbr* **Multilateral Agreement on Investment)** AMI *m*

maiden speech *n Br Parl* = premier discours prononcé par un parlementaire nouvellement élu

"

Andrew Duff, Lib Dem MEP for Eastern England has been the first of the new Liberal Democrat MEP's to make his **maiden speech** in the European Parliament. Speaking only 24 hours after taking his seat at Strasbourg Mr Duff used his **maiden speech** to send a clear message from the Liberal Group to the Commission that it has to clean up its act.

"

main product *n Econ* produit *m* principal

mainstream *n* courant *m*; **he is in the mainstream of politics** en politique, il suit la plus forte pente *ou* la tendance générale; **mainstream French politics** le courant dominant de la politique française

mainstreeting *n Can Pol* bains *mpl*

de foule; **to go mainstreeting** prendre un bain de foule

majesty *n*
◊ *His/Her Majesty's Government* = expression utilisée sur des documents officiels en Grande-Bretagne
◊ *His/Her Majesty's Stationery Office* = maison d'édition publiant les ouvrages ou documents approuvés par le Parlement, les ministères et autres organismes officiels, ≃ l'Imprimerie *f* nationale
◊ *His/Her Majesty's Treasury (government department)* la Trésorerie, ≃ le ministère des Finances

majority 1 *n* majorité *f*; **to be in a majority** être majoritaire; **a two-thirds majority** une majorité des deux tiers; **the proposition had an overwhelming majority** la proposition a recueilli une écrasante majorité; **she was elected by a majority of six** elle a été élue avec une majorité de six voix *ou* par six voix de majorité
2 *adj* majoritaire
◊ *majority decision* décision *f* prise à la majorité *(à la Chambre des représentants et au Sénat)*
◊ *majority party* parti *m* majoritaire
◊ *majority rule* gouvernement *m* à la majorité absolue, système *m* majoritaire
◊ *Am majority runoff* = second tour d'un scrutin majoritaire
◊ *majority vote* vote *m* majoritaire, majorité *f*
◊ *majority voting* scrutin *m* majoritaire

maladministration n *(of country, economy)* mauvaise administration f

malcontent n *Pol* mécontent(e) m,f

malpractice n *(political)* fraude f

Malthusian 1 n malthusien(enne) m,f
2 adj malthusien(enne)

Malthusianism n malthusianisme m

manage vt **(a)** *(company, factory, project)* diriger **(b)** *(economy, money, resources)* gérer

managed adj
◇ Econ **managed currency** devise f contrôlée *ou* dirigée
◇ Econ **managed float** flottement m dirigé

management n **(a)** *(of company, factory, project)* gestion f, direction f **(b)** *(of economy, money, resources)* gestion f
◇ **management control** contrôle m de gestion

M&A n *(abbr* **mergers and acquisitions***)* fusions-acquisitions fpl

mandarin n *Pej Pol* mandarin m

> **"**
>
> While a Herald System Three poll of more than a thousand voters across 40 Scottish constituencies in March 2000 found a majority in favour of PR running at a ratio of almost six-to-one, many of Labour's **mandarins** are fighting to keep the corrupt first past the post electoral system which ensures a job for life for the party hacks who would be incapable of running raffle, let a full-blown council.
>
> **"**

mandate *Pol* **1** n **(a)** *(authority)* mandat m; **the government receives its mandate from the electorate** c'est l'électorat qui mandate les membres du gouvernement; **the government has no mandate to introduce the new tax** le gouvernement n'a pas été mandaté pour mettre en place ce nouvel impôt

(b) *(country)* (territoire m sous) mandat m; **under British mandate** sous mandat britannique
2 vt **(a)** *(give authority to)* mandater; **to mandate sb to do sth** donner mandat à qn de faire qch
(b) *(country)* mettre sous mandat, administrer par mandat

manifesto n manifeste m

manufacture 1 n fabrication f; *(of machinery, cars)* construction f
2 vt fabriquer; *(machinery, cars)* construire
◇ **manufactured goods** biens mpl manufacturés
◇ **manufactured products** produits mpl manufacturés

manufacturing n fabrication f; **the decline of manufacturing** le déclin de l'industrie manufacturière
◇ **manufacturing capacity** capacité f de production
◇ **manufacturing industry** industrie f manufacturière
◇ **manufacturing monopoly** monopole m de fabrication
◇ **manufacturing output** production f manufacturière

Maoism n *Pol* maoïsme m

Maoist *Pol* **1** n maoïste mf
2 adj maoïste

marginal 1 n *Pol* = en Grande-Bretagne, circonscription dont le député ne dispose que d'une majorité très faible
2 adj Econ marginal(e)
◇ Econ **marginal analysis** analyse f marginale
◇ Econ **marginal cost** coût m marginal
◇ Econ **marginal cost pricing** méthode f des coûts marginaux
◇ Econ **marginal costing** méthode f des coûts marginaux
◇ Econ **marginal disinvestment** désinvestissement m marginal
◇ Econ **marginal efficiency of capital** efficacité f marginale du capital
◇ Econ **marginal productivity** productivité f marginale

- ◇ Econ **marginal propensity to consume** propension *f* marginale à consommer
- ◇ Econ **marginal propensity to save** propension *f* marginale à épargner
- ◇ Econ **marginal revenue** revenu *m* marginal
- ◇ Pol **marginal seat** = en Grande-Bretagne, circonscription dont le député ne dispose que d'une majorité très faible
- ◇ Econ **marginal utility** utilité *f* marginale
- ◇ Econ **marginal value** valeur *f* marginale

> A few councils changed hands but Labour's success in keeping hold of both Trafford (a middle class area south of Manchester) and Croydon (which the Conservatives believed they were certain to gain) will give comfort to many Labour MPs in **marginal seats**.

marginalism *n* Econ marginalisme *m*

marginalist Econ **1** *n* marginaliste *mf*
  2 *adj* marginaliste

marker barrel *n* Econ prix *m* du baril de pétrole

market *n* Econ marché *m*; **home and foreign market** marché *m* intérieur et extérieur; **to withhold goods from the market** accaparer des marchandises
- ◇ **market capitalization** capitalisation *f* boursière
- ◇ **market demand** demande *f* du marché
- ◇ **market demand function** fonction *f* de la demande du marché
- ◇ **market division** division *f* du marché
- ◇ **market economy** économie *f* de marché
- ◇ **market failure** défaillance *f* du marché
- ◇ **market forces** forces *fpl* du marché
- ◇ **market forecasting** prévision *f* du marché

- ◇ **market growth** croissance *f* du marché
- ◇ **market indicator** indicateur *m* de marché, signal *m* du marché
- ◇ **market maker** teneur *m* de marché
- ◇ **market mechanism** mécanisme *m* du marché
- ◇ **market power** pouvoir *m* d'un acheteur sur le marché
- ◇ **market share** part *f* de marché
- ◇ **market society** société *f* de marché
- ◇ **market structure** structure *f* du marché
- ◇ **market trend** tendance *f* du marché

market-driven *adj* déterminé(e) par les contraintes du marché
- ◇ **market-driven economy** économie *f* de marché

marketization *n* Econ marchéisation *f*

marketize *vt* Econ convertir à l'économie de marché

market-orientated economy *n* économie *f* de marché

marketplace *n* Econ marché *m*; **the international/European marketplace** le marché international/européen; **the products in the marketplace** les produits sur le marché

martial *adj* martial(e)
- ◇ **martial law** loi *f* martiale; **to declare martial law** proclamer l'état de siège

Marxian *adj* marxien(enne)

Marxism *n* marxisme *m*

Marxism-Leninism *n* marxisme-léninisme *m*

Marxist 1 *n* marxiste *mf*
  2 *adj* marxiste

Marxist-Leninist 1 *n* marxiste-léniniste *mf*
  2 *adj* marxiste-léniniste

mass *adj*
- ◇ Econ **mass consumption** consommation *f* de masse
- ◇ Econ **mass production** fabrication *f* ou production *f* en série
- ◇ Econ **mass unemployment** chômage *m* sur une grande échelle

mature economy n économie f en pleine maturité

maverick 1 n (politician) franc-tireur m, indépendant(e) m,f

2 adj non conformiste, indépendant(e); **a maverick Marxist** un franc-tireur du marxisme; **a maverick MP** un député non conformiste

> ❝
>
> Maverick Labour MP George Galloway is to travel overland to Iraq on a double-decker bus. The Glasgow MP, a staunch opponent of last year's air strikes against Iraq, is using the trip as part of his ongoing campaign against the sanctions imposed on the country.
>
> ❞

mayor n (man) maire m; (woman) maire m ou f, mairesse f

mayoral adj de/du maire

mayoralty n mandat m de maire

mayoress n (woman mayor) maire m ou f, mairesse f

McCarthyism n Pol maccartisme m, maccarthysme m

McCarthyist, McCarthyite Pol **1** n partisan(e) m,f du maccartisme
2 adj maccartiste

mean 1 n (average) moyenne f
2 adj (average) moyen(enne)

means 1 n (method) moyen m
2 npl (income, wealth) moyens mpl, ressources fpl

◇ **means of production** moyen m de production

◇ **means test** (for state benefit) enquête f sur les revenus (d'une personne désirant bénéficier d'une allocation d'État)

measure n (step, legislation) mesure f; **to take measures** prendre des mesures; **parliament must draft measures to halt this trade** le parlement doit élaborer des mesures pour mettre fin à ce trafic

mechanism n (process) mécanisme m

median 1 n (average) médiane f
2 adj (average) médian(e)

mediate 1 vt (agreement, peace) obtenir par médiation; (dispute) servir de médiateur dans, se faire le médiateur de; **the United States mediated an agreement between the two countries** les États-Unis ont servi de médiateur pour qu'un accord soit conclu entre les deux pays

2 vi (act as peacemaker) servir de médiateur; **to mediate in a dispute** servir de médiateur dans un conflit; **to mediate between** servir d'intermédiaire entre

mediating adj médiateur(trice)

mediation n médiation f

mediatization n Pol médiatisation f

mediatize vt Pol médiatiser

mediator n médiateur(trice) m,f

mediatory adj médiateur(trice)

medium of exchange n Econ moyen m d'échange

medium-term adj (forecast, loan) à moyen terme

◇ EU **medium-term financial assistance** aide f financière à moyen terme

meeting n Pol assemblée f, meeting m

Member n (of legislative body) ≃ député(e) m,f; **the Member for Oxford** le député d'Oxford

◇ Am **Member of Congress** membre m du Congrès

◇ EU **Member of the European Parliament** député(e) m,f européen(enne)

◇ Am **Member of the House of Representatives** membre m de la Chambre des représentants

◇ Br **Members' Lobby** = salle adjacente à la salle des débats de la Chambre des communes, où se retrouvent les députés

◇ **Member of the National Assembly**

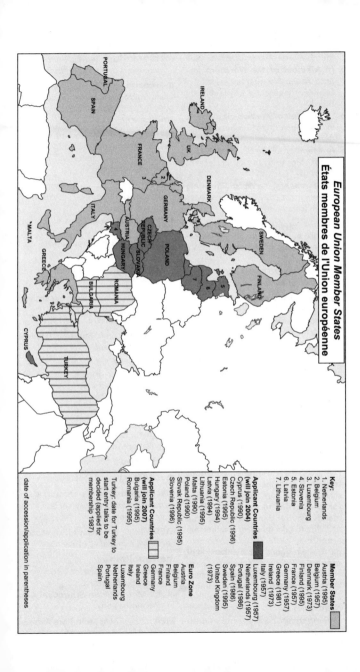

European Union Member States
États membres de l'Union européenne

Key:
1. Netherlands
2. Belgium
3. Luxembourg
4. Slovenia
5. Estonia
6. Latvia
7. Lithuania

Applicant Countries (will join 2004)
Cyprus (1990)
Czech Republic (1996)
Estonia (1995)
Hungary (1994)
Latvia (1995)
Lithuania (1995)
Malta (1990)
Poland (1990)
Slovak Republic (1995)
Slovenia (1996)

Applicant Countries (will join 2007)
Bulgaria (1995)
Romania (1995)

Turkey: date for Turkey to
start entry talks to be
decided (applied for
membership 1987)

date of accession/application in parentheses

Member States
Austria (1995)
Belgium (1957)
Denmark (1973)
Finland (1995)
France (1957)
Germany (1957)
Greece (1981)
Ireland (1973)
Italy (1957)
Luxembourg (1957)
Netherlands (1957)
Portugal (1986)
Spain (1986)
Sweden (1995)
United Kingdom (1973)

Euro Zone
Austria
Belgium
Finland
France
Germany
Greece
Ireland
Italy
Luxembourg
Netherlands
Portugal
Spain

membre *m* de l'Assemblée nationale
◊ *Br* **Member of the Northern Ireland Assembly** membre *m* de l'Assemblée législative d'Irlande du Nord
◊ *Br* **Member of Parliament** membre *m* de la Chambre des communes, ≃ député(e) *m,f*
◊ *Br* **Member of the Scottish Parliament** député(e) *m,f* du parlement écossais
◊ *Br* **Member of the Welsh Assembly** membre *m* de l'Assemblée du pays de Galles

member *n (of union, political party)* membre *m*, adhérent(e) *m,f*; **he became a member of the party in 1995** il a adhéré au parti en 1995
◊ *member country* pays *m* membre
◊ *member state* État *m* membre

member-at-large *n Am Pol* = membre de la Chambre des représentants pour tout un État *(les États les moins peuplés – l'Alaska, le Delaware, le Montana, le Dakota du nord, le Dakota du sud, le Vermont et le Wyoming – ne disposent que d'un membre à la Chambre des représentants)*

membership *n* (a) *(condition)* adhésion *f*; **membership of the union will entitle you to vote in meetings** l'adhésion au syndicat vous donne le droit de voter lors des réunions; **his country's membership of UNESCO is in question** l'adhésion de son pays à l'UNESCO est remise en question; **to apply for membership** faire une demande d'adhésion; **they have applied for membership to the EU** ils ont demandé à entrer dans *ou* à faire partie de l'UE; **to take up party membership** prendre sa carte du *ou* adhérer au parti; **she resigned her membership of the party** elle a rendu sa carte du parti
(b) *(body of members)* **the party membership increased last year** le nombre d'adhérents au parti a augmenté l'année dernière
◊ *membership treaty* traité *m* d'adhésion

memorandum *n (diplomatic communication)* mémorandum *m*

memorial *n (diplomatic memorandum)* mémorandum *m*; *(petition)* pétition *f*; *(official request)* requête *f*, mémoire *m*

MEP *n EU (abbr* **Member of the European Parliament**) député(e) *m,f* à l'Assemblée européenne, membre *m* du Parlement européen

mercantile *adj Econ* mercantile
◊ *mercantile nation* nation *f* commerçante
◊ *mercantile operations* opérations *fpl* mercantiles
◊ *mercantile system* système *m* marchand

mercantilism *n Econ* mercantilisme *m*

mercantilist *Econ* **1** *n* mercantiliste *mf*
2 *adj* mercantiliste

Mercosur *n (abbr* **Southern Common Market**) Mercosur *m*

merge **1** *vt* (a) *Pol (countries, political parties)* unifier (b) *Econ (companies)* amalgamer, fusionner
2 *vi* (a) *Pol (of countries, political parties)* s'unir (b) *Econ (of companies)* s'amalgamer, fusionner

merger *n Econ* fusion *f*; **mergers and acquisitions** fusions-rachats *fpl*

merit good *n Econ* bien *f* tutélaire

meritocracy *n* méritocratie *f*

meritocratic *adj* méritocratique
◊ *meritocratic society* société *f* méritocratique

MES *n (abbr* **minimum efficient scale**) échelle *f* minimale d'efficience

metropolitan *adj*
◊ *metropolitan district* circonscription *f* administrative
◊ *Am* **Metropolitan Statistical Area** ≃ conurbation *f*

MFA *n Econ (abbr* **Multi-fibre Arrangement**) AMF *m*

MFN n (abbr **most-favoured nation**) NPF f

MI5 n Br (abbr **Military Intelligence 5**) = service de contre-espionnage britannique

MI6 n Br (abbr **Military Intelligence 6**) = service de renseignements britannique

microeconomic adj microéconomique

microeconomics n microéconomie f

microeconomy n microéconomie f

microfinance n microfinance f

microstate n micro-État m

middle adj
◇ **middle class** classes fpl moyennes
◇ **middle classes** classes fpl moyennes

middle-roader n Am Pol modéré(e) m,f

midterm elections, midterms npl Pol = aux États-Unis, élections législatives qui ont lieu au milieu du mandat présidentiel

migrant n (worker) (seasonal) (travailleur(euse)) m,f saisonnier(ère) m,f; (foreign) travailleur(euse) m,f immigré(e)

migrate vi (of person, family) (from region) migrer, se déplacer; (from country) émigrer; **the people migrated to the cities** les gens ont migré vers les villes

migration n (of people) émigration f

militant Pol 1 n militant(e) m,f
2 adj militant(e); **she's a militant feminist** c'est une féministe militante
◇ **Militant Tendency** = groupe d'extrême gauche à l'intérieur du parti travailliste britannique

militarization n militarisation f

militarize vt militariser

military 1 npl **the military** les militaires mpl, l'armée f; **the military were called in** on a fait venir l'armée
2 adj militaire; **a strong military presence** une forte présence militaire
◇ **military attaché** attaché m militaire
◇ **military dictatorship** dictature f militaire
◇ **military government** gouvernement m militaire
◇ **military regime** régime m militaire
◇ **military rule** régime m militaire

minibudget n Br Pol budget m auxiliaire

minimal state n État m minimal

minimum 1 n minimum m
2 adj minimum, minimal(e)
◇ **minimum efficient scale** échelle f minimale d'efficience
◇ Br Formerly **minimum lending rate** taux m de base
◇ **minimum living wage** minimum m vital
◇ **minimum wage** salaire m minimum, ≃ SMIC m

minister n (a) Pol ministre m (b) (diplomat) ministre m
◇ **Minister for Agriculture** ministre m de l'Agriculture
◇ **Minister of Defence** ministre m de la Défense
◇ **Minister of Finance** ministre m des Finances
◇ **Minister Plenipotentiary** ministre m plénipotentiaire
◇ **Minister without portfolio** ministre m sans portefeuille
◇ **Minister of State** secrétaire mf d'État

ministerial adj Pol (post) de ministre; (crisis, project) ministériel(elle); (function) exécutive; **to hold ministerial office** être ministre
◇ **ministerial adviser** conseiller(ère) m,f ministériel(elle)
◇ **ministerial bench** banc m des ministres
◇ **ministerial conference** conférence f ministérielle

ministry n Pol (department) ministère m; (government) gouvernement m
◇ Br **Ministry of Defence** ministère m de la Défense

◇ *Ministry of Finance* ministère *m* des Finances

minority 1 *n* minorité *f*; **to be in a minority** être en minorité
2 *adj* minoritaire

◇ *minority government* gouvernement *m* minoritaire

◇ *minority group* minorité *f*, groupe *m* minoritaire

◇ *minority holding* participation *f* minoritaire

◇ *minority interest* participation *f* minoritaire

◇ *Am minority leader* = leader de la minorité *(à la Chambre des représentants et au Sénat)*

◇ *minority party* parti *m* minoritaire

◇ *minority politics* politique *f* minoritaire

◇ *Parl minority report* rapport *m* exprimant l'opinion d'une minorité

miscount *Pol* **1** *n (of votes)* erreur *f* dans le dépouillement du scrutin
2 *vt (votes)* mal compter, faire une erreur en comptant
3 *vi (count votes wrongly)* se tromper dans le compte

misery index *n Econ* = indice qui prend en compte les taux de chômage et d'inflation, censé donner un aperçu de l'état de l'économie et du niveau de confiance des consommateurs

❝
One, admittedly artificial, indicator of financial conditions is the **misery index**, which is an average of the depreciation of the currency, the change in the stock market index, and the change in domestic interest rates (in basis points). This index shows that the major developing countries have seen substantial declines in interest rates, exchange rate appreciation, and stock market increases since December 1998.
❞

mission *n Pol* mission *f*

misuse 1 *n* (a) *(of privilege, one's position)* abus *m* (b) *(of funds)* détournement *m*
2 *vt* (a) *(privilege, position)* abuser de; *(money)* mal employer; **the government is misusing our natural resources** le gouvernement fait un mauvais usage de nos ressources naturelles (b) *(funds)* détourner

mixed *adj*

◇ *mixed economy* économie *f* mixte

◇ *Pol mixed system (of voting)* scrutin *m* mixte

MLA *n (abbr* **Member of the Legislative Assembly)** *(in Australia, India, Canada, Northern Ireland)* membre *m* de l'Assemblée législative

mobility *n Econ (of capital, labour)* mobilité *f*

mobilization *n Econ (of capital, labour)* mobilisation *f*

mobilize *Econ* **1** *vt (capital, labour)* mobiliser
2 *vi (of capital, labour)* mobiliser

MOD, MoD *n Br Pol (abbr* **Ministry of Defence)** ministère *m* de la Défense

mode *n (average)* mode *m*

model *n Econ* modèle *m*

moderate *Pol* **1** *n* modéré(e) *m,f*
2 *adj* modéré(e)

◇ *moderate left* centre gauche *m*

◇ *moderate right* centre droit *m*

Modernisation Committee *n Br Pol* = comité de la Chambre des communes dont le rôle est de réfléchir aux moyens d'en moderniser les procédures

modernize *Pol* **1** *vt* moderniser
2 *vi* se moderniser; **the party must modernize if it is to win the next election** le parti doit se moderniser s'il veut remporter les prochaines élections

modernizer *n Pol* modernisateur(-trice) *m,f*

modulation *n EU* modulation *f*

monarch *n* monarque *m*

monarchism n monarchisme m

monarchist 1 n monarchiste mf
2 adj monarchiste

monarchy n monarchie f

Monday Club n Br Pol = club conservateur britannique

monetarism n Econ monétarisme m

monetarist Econ **1** n monétariste mf
2 adj monétariste

monetary adj Econ monétaire
◇ **monetary adjustment** alignement m monétaire
◇ **monetary aggregate** agrégat m monétaire
◇ **monetary alignment** alignement m monétaire
◇ **monetary area** zone f monétaire
◇ **monetary base** base f monétaire
◇ **monetary base control** contrôle m de la base monétaire
◇ **monetary bloc** bloc m monétaire
◇ **monetary compensatory amounts** montants mpl compensatoires monétaires
◇ **monetary control** contrôle m monétaire
◇ **monetary inflation** inflation f monétaire
◇ **monetary parity** parité f des monnaies
◇ **monetary policy** politique f monétaire
◇ Br **Monetary Policy Committee** = comité formé de quatre membres de la Banque d'Angleterre et de quatre économistes nommés par le gouvernement, dont l'un des rôles est de fixer les taux d'intérêt
◇ **monetary reform** réforme f monétaire
◇ **monetary reserves** réserves fpl de change ou monétaires
◇ **monetary system** système m monétaire
◇ **monetary unit** unité f monétaire

monetization n Econ monétisation f

monetize vt Econ monétiser

money n argent m; (currency) monnaie f, devise f
◇ **money of account** unité f de compte monétaire
◇ **money market** marché m monétaire ou financier
◇ **money market fund** fonds m commun de placement, ≃ sicav f monétaire
◇ **money supply** masse f monétaire

monolithic adj (government, state) monolithique

monometallic adj Econ monométalliste

monometallism n Econ monométallisme m

monopolist n monopoleur(euse) m,f

monopolistic adj monopoliste, monopolistique
◇ **monopolistic competition** concurrence f monopolistique

monopolization n monopolisation f

monopolize vt monopoliser

monopoly n monopole m; **to have a monopoly of sth** or **on sth** avoir ou détenir le monopole de qch, monopoliser qch; **to form a monopoly** constituer un monopole
◇ **monopoly control** contrôle m monopolistique
◇ **monopoly market** marché m monopolistique
◇ Formerly **Monopolies and Mergers Commission** = commission veillant au respect de la législation antitrust en Grande-Bretagne

monopsonist n Econ = partisan du monopsone

monopsonistic adj Econ monopsoniste

monopsony n Econ monopsone m

Monster Raving Loony Party n Br Pol = parti politique fantaisiste qui attire souvent les votes des déçus de la politique

moral hazard n Econ risque m moral

❝

The US Congress is reluctant to fund President Clinton's promise of $210m ... for the initiative, and Japan fears that a write off of its $10bn share will create a **moral hazard**. An added condition for indebted countries to fulfil, linking debt relief to poverty reduction, has also caused delays as poor countries struggle to prepare "poverty reduction strategy papers" to the satisfaction of their creditors. The result is that most of the neediest countries are getting nothing from the process.

❞

moratorium n (a) *(suspension of activity)* moratoire m; **they are calling for a moratorium on arms sales** ils appellent à un moratoire sur les ventes d'armes (b) *Econ (of debt, tax)* moratoire m, suspension f; **to declare a moratorium** décréter un moratoire

mossback *Am Pol* **1** n ultraconservateur(trice) m,f, réactionnaire mf
2 adj ultraconservateur(trice), réactionnaire

most-favoured nation n nation f la plus favorisée; **this country has most-favoured nation status** ce pays bénéficie de la clause de la nation la plus favorisée
◊ **most-favoured nation clause** clause f de la nation la plus favorisée

motion n *Parl (in debate)* motion f, résolution f; **to carry a motion** faire adopter une motion; **to propose** or **to bring a motion** présenter une motion, soumettre une proposition; **to table a motion of no confidence** déposer une motion de censure

move vt *Parl (propose)* proposer; **to move an amendment** proposer un amendement; **I move that we vote on it** je propose que nous procédions au vote

▸ **move over** vi *Pol (stand down)* se désister

movement n (a) *Pol (group)* mouvement m (b) *Econ (trend)* mouvement m, tendance f; *(of capital)* circulation f; *(of share prices)* mouvement m; *(of market)* activité f

MP n *Br & Can Pol (abbr* **Member of Parliament***)* ≃ député(e) m,f; **the MP for Finchley** le député de Finchley

MPC n *Econ* (a) *(abbr* **marginal propensity to consume***)* PmoC (b) *Br (abbr* **Monetary Policy Committee***)* = comité formé de quatre membres de la Banque d'Angleterre et de quatre économistes nommés par le gouvernement, dont l'un des rôles est de fixer les taux d'intérêt

MPS n *Econ (abbr* **marginal propensity to save***)* PmoE

MSA n *Am (abbr* **Metropolitan Statistical Area***)* ≃ conurbation f

MSP n *Pol (abbr* **Member of the Scottish Parliament***)* député(e) m,f du parlement écossais

MTFA n *EU (abbr* **medium-term financial assistance***)* aide f financière à moyen terme

mugwump n *Am Pej Pol* indépendant(e) m,f

Multi-fibre Arrangement n *Econ* Accord m multifibres

multilateral adj multilatéral(e)
◊ **Multilateral Agreement on Investment** accord m multilatéral sur l'investissement
◊ **multilateral aid** aide f multilatérale
◊ **multilateral diplomacy** diplomatie f multilatérale
◊ **multilateral trade agreement** accord m commercial multilatéral
◊ **multilateral trade negotiations** négociations fpl commerciales multilatérales

multilateralism n multilatéralisme m

multinational 1 n multinationale f
2 adj multinational(e)
◊ **multinational company** société f ou firme f multinationale

◇ *multinational corporation* société *f* multinationale

◇ *multinational enterprise* entreprise *f* multinationale

multipartite *adj (talks)* multipartite, multilatéral(e)

multiparty *adj* multipartite, pluripartite

◇ *multiparty system* multipartisme *m*, pluripartisme *m*

multiplier *n Econ* multiplicateur *m*

NACODS *n* (*abbr* **National Association of Colliery Overmen, Deputies and Shotfirers**) = syndicat britannique de mineurs

NAFTA *n* (*abbr* **North American Free Trade Agreement**) ALENA *m*

NAIRU *n Econ* (*abbr* **non-accelerating inflation rate of unemployment**) taux *m* naturel de chômage

NALC *n* (*abbr* **National Association of Letter Carriers**) = syndicat américain de postiers

name *vt Br Parl* **to name an MP** ≃ suspendre un député

nanny state *n* État *m* paternaliste

"

The return of the **nanny state** with the return of a Labour government should surprise nobody, since the socialist idea – whether incarnated as New Labour, Old Labour, Social Democracy or a "Third Way" – is that government is parental and the citizenry dependent: in contrast to British conservatism, for which ideally – if not always in practice – the government is a watchman and the citizens free and responsible.

"

NAO *n Br* (*abbr* **National Audit Office**) ≃ Cour *f* des comptes

NAS/UWT *n* (*abbr* **National Association of Schoolmasters/Union of Women Teachers**) = syndicat d'enseignants et de chefs d'établissement en Grande-Bretagne

NATCA *n* (*abbr* **National Air Traffic Controllers Association**) = syndicat américain des aiguilleurs du ciel

NATFHE *n* (*abbr* **National Association of Teachers in Further and Higher Education**) = syndicat d'enseignants et de chefs d'établissement en Grande-Bretagne

nation *n* (**a**) *(country)* pays *m*, nation *f*; **the British nation** la nation britannique (**b**) *(people)* nation *f*; *Br Pol* **to go to the nation** en appeler au peuple

national 1 *n (person)* ressortissant(e) *m,f*; **all EU nationals** tous les ressortissants des pays de la UE
2 *adj* national(e)
◇ *National Assembly (in Quebec, France)* Assemblée *f* nationale
◇ *national auditing* comptabilité *f* nationale
◇ *Br National Audit Office* ≃ Cour *f* des comptes
◇ *national bank* = banque agréée par le gouvernement américain et qui doit faire partie du système bancaire fédéral
◇ *national coalition* union *f* nationale
◇ *Am Pol National Convention* = grande réunion du parti démocrate ou républicain pour choisir le "ticket" (candidats à la présidence et à la vice-présidence)
◇ *national debt* dette *f* publique, dette *f* de l'État, dette *f* intérieure
◇ *national demand* demande *f* intérieure

◇ *Am Pol* **National Economic Council** Conseil *m* économique national *(groupe créé pour coordonner l'élaboration de la politique commerciale nationale et internationale du gouvernement)*

◇ *Br Pol* **National Executive Committee** = comité chargé de définir la ligne d'action du parti travailliste

◇ **national expenditure** dépense *f* nationale

◇ **National Front** = parti d'extrême-droite britannique, ≃ Front *m* national

◇ **National Health Service** ≃ Sécurité *f* sociale

◇ **national income** revenu *m* national

◇ *Br* **National Insurance** = système britannique de sécurité sociale (maladie, retraite) et d'assurance chômage

◇ *Br* **national insurance contributions** charges *fpl* sociales, cotisations *fpl* à la Sécurité sociale

◇ **national interest** intérêt *m* national

◇ **national market** marché *m* national

◇ **national minority** minorité *f* nationale

◇ *Pol* **national populism** national-populisme *m*

◇ **national product** produit *m* national

◇ **national security** sécurité *f* nationale, sécurité *f* intérieure

◇ *Am Pol* **National Security Adviser** = conseiller du président américain sur les questions de sécurité nationale

◇ *Am Pol* **National Security Council** Conseil *m* de sécurité nationale

◇ **national treatment** traitement *m* national

◇ **national unity** unité *f* nationale

◇ **national wealth** richesse *f* nationale

nationalism *n Pol* nationalisme *m*

nationalist *Pol* **1** *n* nationaliste *mf*
2 *adj* nationaliste

nationalistic *adj Pol* nationaliste

nationalization *n* nationalisation *f*

nationalize *vt* nationaliser

nationalized *adj* nationalisé(e)
◇ **nationalized industry** industrie *f* nationalisée

National Socialism *n Pol* national-socialisme *m*

National Socialist *Pol* **1** *n* national-socialiste *mf*
2 *adj* national-socialiste

nationhood *n* statut *m* de nation; **to attain nationhood** être reconnu(e) en tant que nation

nation-state *n* État-nation *m*

nativism *n Pol* exclusivisme *m* en faveur des autochtones

nativist *Pol* **1** *n* partisan(e) *m,f* de l'exclusivisme en faveur des autochtones
2 *adj* qui favorise les autochtones

❝

A century ago, Europe was in the throes of economic and social turmoil which has many parallels with today. Then it was industrialisation, with drastic social change fed by railways, steamships and telegraphs. Now it's globalisation, the information revolution and hi-tech (which means low-employment) industries. Then as now there were great migrations of peoples, which produced **nativist** reactions.

❞

NATO *n Pol* (*abbr* **North Atlantic Treaty Organization**) l'OTAN *f*

natural *adj Econ*
◇ **natural monopoly** monopole *m* naturel

◇ **natural rate of unemployment** taux *m* de chômage naturel

◇ **natural resources** ressources *fpl* naturelles

◇ **natural wastage** départs *mpl* volontaires et en retraite

nay *n Parl* vote *m* défavorable; **the nays have it** les non l'emportent

NCU *n* (*abbr* **National Communications**

Union) = syndicat des salariés qui travaillent dans les télécommunications en Grande-Bretagne

NDP n Econ (abbr **net domestic product**) PIN m

NDPB n Br Pol (abbr **non-departmental public body**) = organisme semi-public

near money n Econ quasi-monnaie f

need n Econ besoin m

negative income tax n impôt m négatif sur le revenu

negotiate Pol **1** vt (bill) négocier
2 vi négocier, parlementer; **the unions will have to negotiate with the management for higher pay** il faudra que les syndicats négocient une augmentation de salaire auprès de la direction; **we should negotiate instead of preparing for war** nous ferions mieux de négocier au lieu de nous préparer à la guerre; **to negotiate for peace** entreprendre des pourparlers de paix

negotiating table n Pol table f des négociations; **to sit round the negotiating table** s'asseoir à la table des négociations

"
As Fire Brigades Union leaders return to the **negotiating table** today, their straightforward claim for more money for a very dangerous job has been escalated by the government into a major social confrontation. They now find themselves not merely dealing with a posse of hapless local authority worthies anxious to scrimp on the pay bill, but a united establishment baying for their blood.
"

negotiation n Pol (discussion) négociation f, pourparlers mpl; **to be in negotiation with sb** être en pourparler(s) avec qn; **to enter into negotiation** or **negotiations with sb** entamer des négociations avec qn; **to break off/resume negotiations**

rompre/reprendre les négociations; **the pay deal is subject to negotiation** l'accord salarial est sujet à négociation

negotiator n Pol négociateur(trice) m,f

neocapitalism n néocapitalisme m

neocapitalist 1 n néocapitaliste mf
2 adj néocapitaliste

neoclassical economics n économie f néoclassique

neocolonial adj néocolonial(e)

neocolonialism n néocolonialisme m

neocolonialist 1 n néocolonialiste mf
2 adj néocolonialiste

neofascism n Pol néofascisme m

neofascist Pol **1** n néofasciste mf
2 adj néofasciste

neoliberal 1 n néolibéral(e) m,f
2 adj néolibéral(e)

neoliberalism n néolibéralisme m

neo-Malthusian 1 n néomalthusien(-enne) m,f
2 adj néomalthusien(enne)

neo-Malthusianism n néomalthusianisme m

neo-Marxism n néomarxisme m

neo-Marxist 1 n néomarxiste mf
2 adj néomarxiste

neomercantilism n Econ néomercantilisme m

neomercantilist Econ **1** n néomercantiliste mf
2 adj néomercantiliste

neo-Nazi Pol **1** n néonazi(e) m,f
2 adj néonazi(e)

neo-Nazism n Pol néonazisme m

neo-Ricardian Econ **1** n néoricardien(-enne) m,f
2 adj néoricardien(enne)

neo-Ricardianism Econ n néoricardisme m

net 1 adj (overall, total) net (nette)
2 vt (of company, person) faire ou obtenir une recette nette de; (of sale) produire net
◇ EU **net contributor** contributeur m net
◇ Econ **net domestic product** produit m intérieur net
◇ Econ **net investment** investissement m net
◇ Econ **net national income** revenu m national net
◇ Econ **net national product** produit m national net
◇ Econ **net present value** valeur f actuelle nette

neutral Pol **1** n (person) ressortissant(e) m,f d'un État neutre; (country) État m ou pays m neutre
2 adj (country) neutre; (policy) de neutralité; **to remain neutral** garder la neutralité, rester neutre

neutralism n Pol neutralisme m

neutralist Pol **1** n neutraliste mf
2 adj neutraliste

neutrality n Pol neutralité f

neutralize vt Pol neutraliser

new adj
◇ **new classical economics** nouvelle économie f classique
◇ Pol **the New Deal** (in US) le New Deal (programme de réformes sociales mises en place aux États-Unis par le président Roosevelt au lendemain de la grande dépression des années 30); (in UK) = programme du gouvernement Blair destiné à aider les jeunes à trouver un emploi
◇ Can Pol **New Democratic Party** Nouveau Parti m démocratique
◇ **new economy** nouvelle économie f
◇ Br Pol **New Labour** = nouveau nom donné au parti travailliste vers le milieu des années 90 dans le souci d'en moderniser l'image
◇ Br Pol **the New Left** la nouvelle gauche
◇ Br Pol **the New Right** la nouvelle droite

❝
"But I've been a member of the Labour Party since I was 15. And for people like me and others on the left it has always been more than a party – it's about the ideas and the principles. **New Labour** may have ditched some of those principles and Old Labour may be much weakened – but Old Labour does still exist in the party, somewhere."
❞

newly adv
◇ **newly independent state** nouvel État m indépendant
◇ **newly industrialized country** nouveau pays m industrialisé
◇ **newly industrialized economy** économie f nouvellement industrialisée

newspaper n journal m; **a full copy of the statement will appear in the evening newspapers** une version complète de la déclaration sera publiée dans les journaux du soir

NFU n (abbr **National Farmers' Union**) = syndicat britannique d'exploitants agricoles

NGA n (abbr **National Graphical Association**) = syndicat britannique d'imprimeurs

NGO n (abbr **non-governmental organization**) ONG f

NHS n Br (abbr **National Health Service**) ≃ Sécurité f sociale

NIC n (a) (abbr **newly industrialized country**) pays m en voie d'industrialisation (b) Br (abbr **national insurance contributions**) charges fpl sociales, cotisations fpl à la Sécurité sociale

niche n Econ créneau m

NIDL n (abbr **new international division of labour**) nouvelle division f internationale du travail

1922 Committee n Pol = comité rassemblant les députés de base du parti conservateur

NIO n (abbr **Northern Ireland Office**) = ministère des affaires d'Irlande du Nord

NIS n (abbr **newly independent state**) NEI m

NNP n Econ (abbr **net national product**) PNN m

no n Parl (in voting) non m inv; **123 noes and 56 ayes** 123 contre and 56 pour; **the noes have it** les non l'emportent
◇ **No Lobby** = salle où se réunissent les opposants d'une motion à la Chambre des communes
◇ **'no' vote** vote m défavorable

nomenklatura n Pol nomenklatura f

nominal adj Econ
◇ **nominal GDP** PIB m nominal
◇ **nominal income** revenu m nominal
◇ **nominal tax rate** taux m nominal d'imposition

nominate vt (a) (propose) proposer (la candidature de) (b) (appoint) nommer, désigner; (president, judge) investir; **she was nominated to replace Mr Sheridan as minister** elle a été nommée ministre en remplacement de M. Sheridan

nomination n (a) (proposal) proposition f; **who will get the Democratic nomination (for president)?** qui obtiendra l'investiture démocrate (à l'élection présidentielle)? (b) (appointment) nomination f; (of president, judge) investiture f

nominee n (a) (proposed) candidat(e) m,f (b) (appointed) personne f désignée ou nommée; **the government nominees on the commission** les membres de la commission nommés par le gouvernement

non-accountability n (of head of state) irresponsabilité f

non-accountable adj (head of state) qui n'a de comptes à rendre à personne; **to be non-accountable to sb** ne pas avoir à répondre devant qn, ne pas avoir de comptes à rendre à qn

non-aggression n non-agression f
◇ **non-aggression pact** pacte m de non-agression

nonaligned adj Pol non-aligné(e)
◇ **nonaligned countries** pays mpl non alignés

nonalignment n Pol non-alignement m

non-departmental public body n Pol = organisme semi-public

non-EU country n EU pays m tiers

non-floating exchange rate n Econ taux m de change fixe

non-governmental organization n organisation f non gouvernementale

nonintervention n non-intervention f

noninterventionist 1 n non-interventionniste mf
2 adj de non-intervention; **a noninterventionist policy** une politique de non-intervention

non-market adj Econ non-marchand(e)

non-nuclear adj (country) non nucléarisé(e); (war, defence, policy) non nucléaire

nonpolitical adj apolitique

non-productive adj Econ improductif(ive)

non-profit adj Am à but non lucratif
◇ **non-profit organization** société f à but non lucratif

non-profit-making adj Br à but non lucratif
◇ **non-profit-making organization** société f à but non lucratif

non-proliferation n non-prolifération f
◇ **non-proliferation treaty** traité m de non-prolifération

non-racial adj (society, democracy, government) qui ne pratique pas la discrimination raciale

non-seasonally adjusted adj Econ

non-corrigé(e) des variations saisonnières

non-tariff barrier n barrière f non
tarifaire

nontradable Econ **1** n bien m non
marchand
   2 adj non marchand(e)

non-violence n non-violence f

non-violent adj non-violent(e)

non-voter n (not eligible to vote) personne f qui n'a pas le droit de vote ;
(not exercising the right to vote) abstentionniste mf

non-voting adj (not eligible to vote)
qui n'a pas le droit de vote ; (not exercising the right to vote) abstentionniste

non-working adj Econ (population)
inactif(ive)

normal profit n Econ profit m normal

normative economics n économie
f normative

north adj
◊ Econ **North American Free Trade
Agreement** Accord m de libre-
échange nord-américain
◊ Econ **North Atlantic Treaty Organization** Organisation f du traité de
l'Atlantique du Nord

northern adj
◊ **Northern Europe** l'Europe f du
Nord
◊ **Northern Ireland** Irlande f du Nord
◊ **Northern Ireland Assembly** As-
semblée f législative d'Irlande du
Nord
◊ **Northern Ireland Executive** = gou-
vernement de l'Irlande du Nord
◊ **Northern Ireland Office** ministère
m des affaires d'Irlande du Nord
◊ **Northern Ireland Secretary** minis-
tre m des affaires d'Irlande du Nord

not-for-profit adj à but non lucratif
◊ **not-for-profit organization** société
f à but non lucratif

NPV n Econ (abbr **net present value**)
VAN f

NTB n (abbr **non-tariff barrier**) BNT f

NUAAW n (abbr **National Union of
Agricultural and Allied Workers**) =
syndicat britannique des employés
du secteur agricole

nuclear adj nucléaire
◊ **nuclear bomb** bombe f atomique
◊ **nuclear capability** puissance f ou
potentiel m nucléaire
◊ **nuclear capacity** puissance f nucléaire
◊ **nuclear deterrent** force f de dissuasion nucléaire
◊ **nuclear disarmament** désarmement m nucléaire
◊ **Nuclear Non-Proliferation Treaty**
traité m de non-prolifération nucléaire
◊ **nuclear power** puissance f nucléaire
◊ **nuclear testing** essais mpl nucléaires
◊ **nuclear umbrella** parapluie m atomique ou nucléaire
◊ **nuclear war** guerre f atomique
◊ **nuclear warhead** ogive f ou tête f
nucléaire
◊ **nuclear weapons** armes fpl nucléaires

NUCPS n (abbr **National Union of Civil
and Public Servants**) = syndicat britannique des employés de la fonction
publique

NUDAGO n (abbr **National Union of
Domestic Appliances and General Op-
eratives**) = syndicat britannique des
travailleurs de l'électroménager

NUJ n (abbr **National Union of Journalists**) = syndicat britannique des journalistes

NUM n (abbr **National Union of Mineworkers**) = syndicat britannique de
mineurs

NUMAST n (abbr **National Union of
Marine, Aviation and Shipping Transport Officers**) = syndicat britannique
des travailleurs de la marine marchande

Number n
◊ Br Pol **Number Eleven (Downing**

Street) = résidence officielle du Chancelier de l'Échiquier
◇ *Br Pol* **Number Ten (Downing Street)** = résidence officielle du Premier ministre britannique; **Number Ten denied the rumour** le gouvernement a démenti la rumeur
◇ ***Number Ten Policy Unit*** = groupe de conseillers du Premier ministre

"

The Blair approach differs from Bush only in that the Prime Minister displays more sensitivity to international opinion than the hawks of the White House. Downing Street has more use for the United Nations than the Oval Office. **Number 10** would also like to see more emphasis from the Americans on the Israeli-Palestinian crisis.

"

NURMTW *n* (*abbr* **National Union of Rail, Maritime and Transport Workers**) = syndicat britannique des cheminots, gens de mer et routiers

NUS *n Br* (*abbr* **National Union of Students**) ≃ UNEF *f*

NUT *n* (*abbr* **National Union of Teachers**) = syndicat britannique d'enseignants

oath n serment m; **to take the oath of allegiance** faire (le) serment d'allégeance

observer n (commentator) spécialiste mf, expert m; **political observers have commented that...** de nombreux spécialistes ont remarqué que...

obstruct vt Parl (bill) faire obstruction à

obstruction n Pol obstruction f

obstructionism n Pol obstructionnisme m

obstructionist Pol 1 n obstructionniste mf
   2 adj obstructionniste

obstructive adj Pol **to use obstructive tactics** user de tactiques obstructionnistes

Occident n the Occident l'Occident m

Occidental 1 n Occidental(e) m,f
   2 adj occidental(e)

occupation n Pol (of country, territory) occupation f; **under French occupation** sous occupation française; **they organized an occupation of the Embassy** ils ont organisé l'occupation de l'Ambassade

occupied adj Pol (country) occupé(e)
◇ *occupied territories* territoires mpl occupés

occupy vt Pol (country, territory) occuper

occupying army n Pol armée f d'occupation

ochlocracy n Pol ochlocratie f

ochlocrat n Pol ochlocrate mf

ochlocratic adj Pol ochlocratique

ODA n (abbr **Official Development Assistance**) aide f publique au développement

OECD n (abbr **Organization for Economic Cooperation and Development**) OCDE f

OEEC n (abbr **Organization for European Economic Cooperation**) OECE f

office n (a) (government department) bureau m, département m
   (b) (position, power) fonction f; **to run for** or **to seek office** se présenter aux élections; **he's one of the candidates seeking office** c'est l'un des candidats qui se présentent aux élections; **to be in** or **to hold office** (of political party) être au pouvoir; (of mayor, minister, official) être en fonction(s); **to take office** (of political party) arriver au pouvoir; (of mayor, minister, official) entrer en fonctions; **elected to the office of president** élu(e) à la présidence; **to resign/leave office** se démettre de/quitter ses fonctions; **to be out of office** avoir quitté ses fonctions; **to hold high office** détenir un poste élevé; **to rise to high office** être promu(e) à un poste élevé
◇ Br **Office of the Deputy Prime Minister** = service du vice-Premier-ministre
◇ **Office of Fair Trading** = organisme britannique de défense des consommateurs et de régulation des pratiques commerciales

◇ Am **Office of Homeland Security** = département chargé de la sécurité du territoire

◇ Am **Office of Management and Budget** = service administratif américain dont le rôle principal est d'aider le président à préparer le budget

◇ Am **Office of National Drug Control Policy** = agence gouvernementale américaine chargée d'élaborer une stratégie anti-drogues

◇ Br **Office for National Statistics** ≃ INSEE *m*

◇ Am **Office of the United States Trade Representative** = département traitant des questions de commerce

officeholder *n Pol* titulaire *mf* d'une fonction

officer *n (in local government)* fonctionnaire *mf*; *(of trade union)* représentant(e) *m,f* permanent(e); *(of association, institution)* membre *m* du bureau

official 1 *n (representative)* officiel *m*; *(civil servant)* fonctionnaire *mf*; **a government official** un haut fonctionnaire

2 *adj (formal)* officiel(elle); **she's here on official business** elle est ici en visite officielle; **she was speaking in her official capacity as General Secretary** elle parlait en sa qualité de Secrétaire général

◇ *Econ* **official financing** financement *m* officiel

◇ Br **official opposition** = le principal parti de l'opposition

◇ **Official Secrets Act** = loi britannique sur les secrets d'État

> 〝
> Charles Kennedy, the Liberal Democrat leader, has asked the prime minister to abolish the role of an **official opposition**, placing his party on equal footing in the Commons with the Conservatives. In a leaked policy document, Mr Kennedy brands the two-party system an "anachronism" and attacked the £500,000 of taxpayers' money that the **official opposition** currently enjoys.
> 〟

officialdom *n (officials)* administration *f*; *(bureaucracy)* bureaucratie *f*, fonctionnarisme *m*

officialese *n Pej* jargon *m* administratif

officialism *n (of civil service)* bureaucratie *f*, fonctionnarisme *m*

off-message *Pol* **1** *adj* = qui ne respecte pas scrupuleusement la ligne du parti

2 *adv* **to go/stay off-message** cesser de/continuer à ne pas respecter la ligne du parti

> 〝
> A Labour MP has **gone off-message** to expose the truth behind the party's great conference pager-messaging scandal. Ealing North MP Stephen Pound admitted that Labour MPs received a message instructing them all to stand up and shout "More! More!" at the end of Home Secretary Jack Straw's law and order address to the party's conference ... Straying even further **off-message**, Mr Pound went on to impersonate the prime minister on air.
> 〟

offshoot *n (of organization, political party, movement)* ramification *f*

off-year *n Pol* = année présidentielle sans élection aux États-Unis

oil 1 *n (petroleum)* pétrole *m*

2 *adj (industry, production, corporation)* pétrolier(ère); *(deposit, reserves)* de pétrole; *(magnate, sheikh)* du pétrole

◇ **oil crisis** choc *m* pétrolier

◇ **oil kingdom** pétromonarchie *f*

◇ *oil prices* prix *mpl* pétroliers

oil-producing country *n* pays *m* pétrolier

Oireachtas *n Pol* = parlement irlandais

old *adj*
◇ *old economy* vieille économie *f*
◇ *Pol old guard* vieille garde *f*; **Powell criticized the Republican old guard for their failure to modernize** Powell a reproché à la vieille garde du parti Républicain de ne pas avoir su se moderniser
◇ *Br Pol Old Labour* = parti travailliste traditionnel, attaché aux valeurs de la gauche

oligarch *n Pol* oligarque *m*

oligarchical *adj Pol* oligarchique

oligarchy *n Pol* oligarchie *f*

oligopolist *n Econ* oligopoliste *mf*

oligopolistic *adj Econ* oligopoliste

oligopoly *n Econ* oligopole *m*

oligopsonist *n Econ* = partisan d'une situation oligopsoniste

oligopsonistic *adj Econ* oligopsoniste

oligopsony *n Econ* oligopsone *m*

OMB *n* (*abbr* **Office of Management and Budget**) = service administratif américain dont le rôle principal est d'aider le président à préparer le budget

ombudsman *n* ombudsman *m*, médiateur(trice) *m,f* (*entre individus et instances gouvernementales*)

Omov, OMOV *n Pol* (*abbr* **one member one vote**) = système de scrutin "un homme, une voix"

one member one vote *n Pol* = système de scrutin "un homme, une voix"

one-party *adj Pol* à parti unique
◇ *one-party rule* = régime à parti unique
◇ *one-party state* État *m* à parti unique

◇ *one-party system* (*of government*) système *m* du parti unique

on-message *Pol* **1** *adj* = qui respecte scrupuleusement la ligne du parti
2 *adv* **to go/stay on-message** se mettre à/continuer à respecter scrupuleusement la ligne du parti

> When pressed, on the PM programme, to justify her claim, she went so far as to say that this was new money for tackling heart disease but adamantly refused to accept that since it came from resources already allocated, it could only have been found by taking money away from some other service. She simply read and re-read her brief and stayed **on-message**, despite the fact that even she must have realised that the message was flawed.

ONS *n Br* (*abbr* **Office for National Statistics**) ≃ INSEE *m*

OPEC *n* (*abbr* **Organization of Petroleum Exporting Countries**) OPEP *f*
◇ *OPEC countries* pays *mpl* membres de l'OPEP

open 1 *adj* ouvert(e); (*administration, policy*) transparent(e)
2 *vt* (*campaign*) ouvrir, commencer; (*negotiations*) ouvrir, engager; **to open Parliament** ouvrir la session du Parlement
◇ *Pol open city* ville *f* ouverte
◇ *Econ open economy* économie *f* ouverte
◇ *Pol open government* administration *f* transparente
◇ *Econ open market* marché *m* libre
◇ *Econ open market policy* politique *f* d'open market, politique *f* de marché ouvert
◇ *Econ open money market* marché *m* libre des capitaux
◇ *Am Pol open primary* = élection primaire américaine ouverte aux non-inscrits d'un parti

◊ **open shop** Br (open to non-union members) = entreprise ne pratiquant pas le monopole d'embauche; Am (with no union) établissement m sans syndicat

open-door policy n Econ (for importing goods) politique f de la porte ouverte

opening n (action) ouverture f; **the opening of Parliament** l'ouverture f du Parlement

opinion n opinion f

◊ **opinion poll** sondage m (d'opinion); **the PM is faring well in the opinion polls** le Premier ministre est bien placé dans les sondages

opponent n Pol opposant(e) m,f

opportunity cost n Econ coût m d'opportunité ou de renoncement

opposing adj Pol opposant(e)

opposition Pol 1 n **the Opposition** l'opposition f; **Labour spent the 1980s in opposition** les travaillistes furent dans l'opposition pendant toutes les années 80; **the Opposition was** or **were unable to decide** l'opposition fut incapable de prendre une décision
2 adj (committee, spokesperson) de l'opposition

◊ **Opposition benches** bancs mpl de l'opposition

oppositional adj Pol oppositionnel(-elle)

oppositionist Pol 1 n oppositionnel(-elle) m,f
2 adj oppositionnel(elle)

oppress vt Pol (tyrannize) opprimer

oppressive adj (a) Pol (regime, government) oppressif(ive) (b) (tax, debt) accablant(e)

oppressiveness n (a) Pol (of regime, government) caractère m oppressif (b) (of tax, debt) caractère m accablant

optimal adj optimal(e), optimum

◊ Econ **optimal resource allocation** répartition f optimale des ressources

optimum 1 n optimum m
2 adj optimum, optimal(e)

◊ **optimum conditions** conditions fpl optimales

◊ Econ **optimum employment of resources** emploi m optimum des ressources

◊ Econ **optimum population** population f optimale

▸ **opt out** vi Pol (of school, hospital) = choisir l'autonomie vis-à-vis des pouvoirs publics

opt-out n Pol (of school, hospital) = décision de choisir l'autonomie vis-à-vis des pouvoirs publics; **Britain's opt-out from the Social Chapter** la décision de la Grande-Bretagne de ne pas souscrire à la chapitre social européen

◊ **opt-out clause** clause f d'exemption

oral question n Parl question f orale

Orange adj Pol orange

◊ **Orange Lodge** association f d'orangistes

◊ **Orange Order** Ordre m des orangistes

◊ **Orange Walk** = défilé des orangistes (le 12 juillet)

Orangeism n Pol orangisme m

Orangeman n Pol (in Ireland) orangiste m (Protestant)

◊ **Orangeman's Day** = fête annuelle des orangistes (le 12 juillet)

Orangewoman n Pol (in Ireland) orangiste f (Protestante)

order n Parl order(, order)! de l'ordre!

◊ **order of business** ordre m du jour

◊ Br **Order in Council** décret m du gouvernement, arrêté m ministériel

◊ **order of the day** ordre m du jour

◊ **order paper** (feuille f de l')ordre m du jour

ordinal utility n Econ utilité f ordinale

ordinary adj Pol (session) ordinaire

organ n (institution, publication) organe m; **the official organ of the Party** le porte-parole officiel du Parti

organic law n loi f organique

organization n (association) organisation f, association f; (official body) organisme m, organisation f

◇ **Organization for Economic Co-operation and Development** Organisation f de Coopération et de Développement économique

◇ **Organization for European Economic Cooperation** Organisation f européenne de coopération économique

◇ **Organization of Petroleum Exporting Countries** Organisation f des pays exportateurs de pétrole

◇ **Organization for Security and Co-operation in Europe** Organisation f sur la sécurité et la coopération en Europe

organizational behaviour n Econ comportement m de l'individu au sein d'une organisation

organize 1 vt (into union) syndiquer
2 vi se syndiquer

organized adj (unionized) syndiqué(e)
◇ **organized labour** main-d'œuvre f syndiquée

OSCE n (abbr **Organization for Security and Cooperation in Europe**) OSCE f

oust vt (opponent, rival) évincer, chasser; **the president was ousted from power** le président a été évincé du pouvoir

outgoing adj (president, leader, minister) sortant(e); (following resignation) démissionnaire

outlook n Econ (prospect) horizon m, perspectives fpl (d'avenir)

output Econ 1 n (a) (production) production f (b) (productivity) productivité f, rendement m
2 vt (of factory) produire
◇ **output gap** écart m de production

outsource vt Econ externaliser

outsourcing n Econ externalisation f

outvote vt (a) (bill, reform) rejeter (à la majorité des voix); **the bill was outvoted** une majorité a voté contre le projet de loi (b) (government) mettre en minorité

outward investment n Econ investissement m à l'étranger

Oval Office n Am bureau m ovale (bureau du président des États-Unis à la Maison-Blanche); **he has decided to make a bid for the Oval Office** il a décidé de se présenter à la Maison-Blanche

"

The Blair approach differs from Bush only in that the Prime Minister displays more sensitivity to international opinion than the hawks of the White House. Downing Street has more use for the United Nations than the **Oval Office**.

"

overall adj
◇ Econ **overall budget** budget m global, demande f globale
◇ Pol **overall majority** majorité f absolue

overcapacity n Econ surcapacité f

overconsume vt Econ consommer trop de

overconsumption n Econ surconsommation f

overdemand n Econ demande f excédentaire

overheat Econ 1 vt surchauffer
2 vi entrer en surchauffe

overheating n Econ surchauffe f

overindebted adj Econ surendetté(e)

overinvest Econ 1 vt trop investir
2 vi surinvestir (**in** dans)

overinvestment n Econ surinvestissement m

overproduce vt Econ surproduire

overproduction n Econ surproduction f

oversaturate *vt Econ* sursaturer

oversaturation *n Econ* sursaturation *f*

overseas *adj (market)* étranger(ère); *(trade)* extérieur(e); *(colony)* d'outre-mer

◇ *overseas aid* aide *f* au tiers-monde

◇ *overseas investment* investissement *m* extérieur

◇ *overseas territories (French)* territoires *mpl* d'outre-mer

overshooting *n Econ* surréaction *f*

oversupply *n Econ* suroffre *f*

overthrow 1 *n (of regime, government)* renversement *m*, chute *f*
2 *vt (regime, government)* renverser

overtime *n* (**a**) *(work)* heures *fpl* supplémentaires; **to do** *or* **work overtime** faire des heures supplémentaires; **an hour's overtime** une heure supplémentaire (**b**) *(pay)* rémunération *f* des heures supplémentaires; **to be**

paid overtime être payé(e) en heures supplémentaires

◇ *overtime ban* refus *m* de faire des heures supplémentaires

◇ *overtime rate* tarif *m* des heures supplémentaires

"

National long distance services were hit earlier this week as Indian Telecom Service workers took action because of concern about the Indian Telecom Department's corporatization on October 1. According to local media reports, officials agreed on Thursday to cancel an **overtime ban** – that had seen workers leave their jobs each day at 5pm – and put in extra hours.

"

overturn *vt (regime, government)* renverser; *(bill)* rejeter

PAC n (**a**) Am (abbr **political action committee**) = aux États-Unis, comité qui réunit des fonds pour soutenir une cause politique (**b**) Br (abbr **Public Accounts Committee**) = comité chargé de veiller au bon usage des fonds publics

PACE n (abbr **Paper, Allied-Industrial, Chemical and Energy Workers International Union**) = syndicat industriel américain et canadien

pacification n Pol pacification f

pacify vt Pol pacifier

pact n pacte m

paid political broadcast n Am émission f d'un parti politique

pair n Br Parl = deux membres de partis adverses qui se sont entendus pour ne pas participer à un vote ou pour s'abstenir de voter durant une période déterminée

Palace of Westminster n palais m de Westminster (siège du parlement britannique)

pamphlet n Pol pamphlet m

pamphleteer n Pol pamphlétaire mf

panachage n Pol panachage m

Pan-African 1 n partisan(e) m,f du panafricanisme
2 adj panafricain(e)

Pan-Africanism n panafricanisme m

Pan-American adj panaméricain(e)

Pan-Americanism n panaméricanisme m

Pan-Arab 1 n panarabe mf
2 adj panarabe

Pan-Arabism n panarabisme m

Pan-Arabist n partisan(e) m,f du panarabisme

Pan-European adj paneuropéen(enne)

parachuted candidate n Can Pol candidat(e) m,f parachuté(e)

"

"I'm surprised there were 3,000 (3,053) voters out there prepared to consider a candidate with strong ties to the NDP who put nothing into his campaign. I thought he'd get less than 500," Harris said. Crist, who topped the polls by a substantial margin, says Schreck came across as a **parachuted candidate** with a reputation for "establishment arrogance" rather than a local spokesman.

"

paradox of thrift n Econ paradoxe m de l'épargne

parallel adj parallèle
◊ **parallel importing** importations fpl parallèles
◊ **parallel imports** importations fpl parallèles
◊ **parallel market** marché m parallèle

paralyse, Am **paralyze** vt (industry, business) immobiliser; (government) paralyser

paralysed, Am **paralyzed** adj (industry, business) immobilisé(e); (government) paralysé(e)

paralysis n (of industry, business) immobilisation f; (of government) paralysie f

paralyze, paralyzed Am = **paralyse, paralysed**

paramilitary 1 n (group) formation f paramilitaire; (person) membre m d'une formation paramilitaire
2 adj paramilitaire

Pareto n Econ
◇ **Pareto's law** loi f de Pareto
◇ **Pareto optimality** optimalité f de Pareto, optimalité f parétienne
◇ **Pareto's rule** règle f 80/20

Paris Club n Club m de Paris

parish n Pol ≃ commune f (en Angleterre)
◇ **parish council** ≃ conseil m municipal (d'une petite commune en Angleterre)

parity n Econ parité f; the two currencies were at parity les deux monnaies étaient à parité f de change
◇ **parity ratio** rapport m de parités
◇ **parity value** valeur f au pair

parliament n parlement m; Parliament has decided that... le Parlement a décidé que...; in Parliament au Parlement; she was elected to Parliament in 2001 elle a été élue député en 2001; the French Parliament l'Assemblée f nationale (française)

parliamentarian 1 n parlementaire mf
2 adj parlementaire

parliamentarianism n parlementarisme m

parliamentary adj parlementaire
◇ Br **Parliamentary agent** = juriste qui tente de promouvoir ou d'empêcher le passage de lois pour le compte d'organisations
◇ **parliamentary candidate** candidat(e) m,f aux (élections) législatives
◇ Br **Parliamentary committee** commission f parlementaire
◇ **parliamentary correspondent** journaliste mf parlementaire
◇ **parliamentary counsel** = juristes qui aident à la préparation des projets de loi
◇ **parliamentary draftsman** = juriste qui aide à la préparation des projets de loi
◇ **parliamentary elections** élections fpl législatives
◇ **parliamentary group** groupe m parlementaire
◇ Br **Parliamentary Labour Party** députés mpl du Parti travailliste britannique
◇ **parliamentary majority** majorité f parlementaire
◇ **parliamentary minority** minorité f parlementaire
◇ **parliamentary monarchy** monarchie f parlementaire
◇ **parliamentary party** parti m parlementaire
◇ **Parliamentary Private Secretary** = en Grande-Bretagne, député qui assure la liaison entre un ministre et la Chambre des communes
◇ **parliamentary privilege** immunité f parlementaire
◇ **parliamentary procedure** procédure f parlementaire
◇ Br **parliamentary question** = question posée au cours d'un débat parlementaire
◇ **Parliamentary recess** vacances fpl parlementaires
◇ **parliamentary regime** régime m parlementaire
◇ **parliamentary rules** règles fpl parlementaires
◇ Br **Parliamentary Secretary of State** ≃ sous-secrétaire m d'État
◇ Br **parliamentary sovereignty** souveraineté f parlementaire
◇ Br **Parliamentary Under-Secretary of State** ≃ sous-secrétaire mf d'État

participation rate n Econ taux m d'activité

participatory democracy n démocratie f participative

partisan 1 n (supporter) partisan(e) m,f

   2 adj partisan(e); **to act in a partisan spirit** (of politician) faire preuve d'esprit de parti

◊ **partisan politics** politique f partisane

partisanship n partialité f; (of politician) esprit m de parti

partition Pol **1** n (of country) partition f

   2 vt (country) diviser, démembrer

partner n partenaire mf; **our European partners** nos partenaires européens

partnership n association f; **to work in partnership with sb/sth** travailler en association avec qn/qch

◊ **partnership agreement** accord m de partenariat, accord m de coopération

◊ EU **Partnership and Cooperation Agreements** Accords mpl de partenariat et de coopération

party n Pol parti m; **the Conservative/Democratic Party** le parti conservateur/démocrate; **he joined the Socialist Party in 1936** il est entré au parti socialiste en 1936

◊ **party chairman** premier secrétaire m du parti

◊ **Party Conference** Congrès m du parti

◊ **party convention** Congrès m du parti

◊ **party executive** bureau m politique

◊ **party faithful** fidèles mfpl du parti

◊ **party leader** leader m du parti

◊ **party leadership** direction f du parti

◊ **party line** ligne f du parti; **to toe or follow the party line** suivre la ligne du parti

◊ **party machine** machine f du parti

◊ **party member** membre m du parti

◊ **party platform** = annonce du programme d'un parti politique

◊ **party political broadcast** émission f reservée à un parti politique

◊ **party politics** politique f de parti; Pej politique f politicienne

◊ **party quarrels** querelles fpl partisanes

◊ **party spirit** esprit m de parti

◊ **party system** système m des partis

> **"**
>
> The address to the RNC's winter meeting came as Bush began his first full day in Washington in a countdown to his inauguration Saturday. He has scheduled a flurry of speaking engagements over the next two days. In his speech to the **party faithful**, in a downtown Washington hotel ballroom, Bush reiterated his intention to move quickly on one of his central campaign promises – for an across-the-board income tax cut.
>
> **"**

party-list system n Pol (of voting) scrutin m de liste

pass Parl **1** vt (bill, law) voter; (motion, resolution) adopter; **to pass a bill through Parliament** faire adopter une loi par le Parlement

   2 vi (of bill, law) être voté(e); (motion, resolution) être adopté(e); **to pass through Parliament** être adopté par le Parlement

passage n Parl (of bill) procédures fpl d'adoption d'une loi; **the bill had an uninterrupted passage through Parliament** la loi a été adoptée sans encombre par le Parlement

passing n Parl (of bill, law, motion, resolution) adoption f

paternalism n Pol paternalisme m

paternalist, paternalistic adj Pol paternaliste

patronage n Pol pouvoir m de nomination; **he got the promotion through the Minister's patronage** il a obtenu de l'avancement grâce à l'influence du ministre

pauperization n Econ paupérisation f

pauperize *vt Econ* paupériser; **to become pauperized** se paupériser

PAYE *n Br (abbr* **pay-as-you-earn***)* prélèvement *m* de l'impôt à la source

Paymaster General *n* Trésorier-payeur-général *m* britannique

payroll *n (money paid)* masse *f* salariale

◇ *payroll tax* impôt *m* sur la masse salariale

PCA *n EU (abbr* **Partnership and Co-operation Agreements***)* Accords *mpl* de partenariat et de coopération

PCE *n Am Econ (abbr* **Personal Consumption Expenditures***)* consommation *f* des ménages

PCS *n (abbr* **Public and Commercial Services Union***)* = syndicat britannique des travailleurs du tertiaire des secteurs public et privé

peace *n* **(a)** *(absence of war, conflict)* paix *f*; **in time of peace** en temps de paix; **the country is at peace now** la paix est maintenant rétablie dans le pays; **to win the peace** réussir à maintenir la paix **(b)** *(treaty)* (traité *m* de) paix *f*; **they wanted to sign a separate peace with the invaders** ils voulaient conclure *ou* signer une paix séparée avec les envahisseurs

◇ *peace activist* activiste *mf* en faveur de la paix

◇ *peace agreement* accord *m* de paix

◇ *peace camp* = camp installé près d'une base militaire en signe de protestation contre les activités qui s'y déroulent

◇ *peace campaigner* militant(e) *m,f* pour la paix

◇ *Peace Corps* = organisation américaine de coopération avec les pays en voie de développement

◇ *peace dividend* dividende *m* de paix

◇ *peace formula* formule *f* de paix

◇ *peace initiative* initiative *f* de paix

◇ *peace movement* mouvement *m* pour la paix *ou* pacifiste

◇ *peace negotiations* négociations *fpl* pour la paix

◇ *peace offensive* offensive *f* de paix

◇ *peace overture* initiative *f* de paix

◇ *peace process* processus *m* de paix

◇ *peace proposal* proposition *f* de paix

◇ *peace rally* rassemblement *m* pour la paix

◇ *peace talks* pourparlers *mpl* de paix

◇ *peace treaty* traité *m* de paix

peacekeeper *n (of United Nations)* Casque *m* bleu

peacekeeping 1 *n* maintien *m* de la paix
2 *adj* de maintien de la paix; **a United Nations peacekeeping force** des forces des Nations unies pour le maintien de la paix, des Casques bleus

peace-loving *adj* pacifique

peacemaker *n* pacificateur(trice) *m,f*

peacemaking *adj* pacificateur(trice)

peer *n Pol* pair *m*; **the Conservative Peers** les pairs *mpl* conservateurs *(en Grande-Bretagne)*

◇ *peer of the realm* pair *m* du royaume

peg *vt Econ (set) (price, increase)* fixer; *(tie) (currency)* indexer **(to** sur**)**; **oil was pegged at $20 a barrel** le prix du pétrole était fixé à 20 dollars le baril; **to peg sth to the rate of inflation** indexer qch sur le taux de l'inflation; **countries which have pegged their currencies to the euro** les pays qui ont indexé leur monnaie sur l'euro; **export earnings are pegged to the exchange rate** le revenu des exportations varie en fonction du taux de change

pension *n* pension *f*; *(after retirement)* (pension *f* de) retraite *f*

◇ *pension fund* caisse *f* de retraite

◇ *pension plan* plan *m* de retraite

◇ *pension point* point *m* de retraite

◇ *pension scheme* régime *m* de retraite

Pentagon *n Pol* **the Pentagon** le Pentagone; **the Pentagon has issued a**

statement le Pentagone a fait une déclaration

◊ *the Pentagon papers* = documents secrets détenus par le Pentagone, portant sur l'intervention des États-Unis au Vietnam, publiés par le New York Times en 1971 et objet d'un procès qui établit le droit du public américain à l'information

people *npl Pol* **the people** le peuple ; **the people are behind her** le peuple la soutient *ou* est avec elle ; **to go to the people** en appeler au peuple ; **a people's government/democracy** un gouvernement/une démocratie populaire

per capita *adv Econ* par personne, par tête

◊ *per capita consumption* consommation *f* par tête

◊ *per capita growth* croissance *f* par tête

◊ *per capita income* revenu *m* par habitant ; **per capita income is higher in the south** le revenu par habitant est plus élevé dans le sud

perestroika *n* perestroïka *f*

perfect *adj Econ*

◊ *perfect capital market* marché *m* des capitaux parfait

◊ *perfect competition* concurrence *f* parfaite

perform *vi (of economy, investment, currency)* se comporter

performance *n (of economy)* résultats *mpl*, performances *fpl* ; *(of investment, currency)* performance *f* ; **the country's poor economic performance** les mauvais résultats économiques du pays

periodic unemployment *n Econ* chômage *m* récurrent

peripheral *adj*

◊ *peripheral economy* économie *f* périphérique

◊ *Econ peripheral region* région *f* périphérique

permanent *adj*

◊ *permanent arrangement* arrangement *m* permanent

◊ *permanent post (in public service)* poste *m* de titulaire

◊ *permanent representation* représentation *f* permanente

◊ *permanent representative* représentant *m* permanent

◊ *Br Permanent Secretary* ≃ secrétaire *m* général

◊ *permanent staff (in public service)* personnel *m* titulaire

◊ *Br Permanent Undersecretary* ≃ secrétaire *mf* général(e) *(dans la fonction publique)*

personal *adj*

◊ *Am Econ Personal Consumption Expenditures* consommation *f* des ménages

◊ *Pol personal power* pouvoir *m* personnel

persuasion *n Pol* tendance *f*

petition **1** *n (with signatures)* pétition *f* ; **to hand in/sign a petition** remettre/signer une pétition ; **they got up a petition against the council's plans** ils ont préparé une pétition pour protester contre les projets de la municipalité
   2 *vt (government, MP)* adresser une pétition à ; **they petitioned the government for the release of** *or* **to release the political prisoners** ils ont adressé une pétition au gouvernement pour demander la libération des prisonniers politiques

petticoat *adj Pol (government, politics)* de femmes

PFI *n (abbr private finance initiative)* partenariat *m* public-privé

PHARE *n (abbr Poland and Hungary: aid for economic reconstruction)* programme *m* PHARE

physiocracy *n Econ* physiocratie *f*

physiocrat *n Econ* physiocrate *m*

picket **1** *n* **(a)** *(group)* piquet *m* de grève ; *(individual)* gréviste *mf* (en faction) ; **there was a picket outside the factory** il y avait un piquet de grève devant l'usine ; **to be on picket duty** faire partie d'un piquet de grève ; **20 pickets stood in front of the factory** 20 grévistes se tenaient devant l'usine **(b)** *(outside embassy, ministry)* *(group)* groupe *m* de manifestants ; *(individual)* manifestant(e) *m,f*

2 *vt (workplace, embassy, ministry)* **the strikers picketed the factory** les grévistes ont mis en place un piquet de grève devant l'usine ; **demonstrators picketed the consulate at the weekend** des manifestants ont bloqué le consulat ce week-end

3 *vi* mettre en place un piquet de grève

◇ *picket duty* piquet *m*

◇ *picket line* piquet *m* de grève ; **to be** *or* **to stand on a picket line** faire partie d'un piquet de grève ; **to cross a picket line** franchir un piquet de grève

picketing *n* **(a)** *(of workplace)* piquets *mpl* de grève ; **there is heavy picketing at the factory gates** les piquets de grève sont très nombreux aux portes de l'usine **(b)** *(of ministry, embassy)* **there was picketing outside the embassy today** aujourd'hui, il y a eu des manifestations devant l'ambassade

pillar *n EU* pilier *m*

pilot *vt Parl* **she piloted the bill through Parliament** elle s'est assurée que le projet de loi serait voté

pink *adj Fam Pol* de gauche, gauchisant(e)

◇ *pink economy* = activités économiques générées par le pouvoir d'achat des homosexuels

◇ *pink pound* = pouvoir d'achat des homosexuels

pinkish *adj Fam Pol* gauchisant(e)

pinko *Fam Pol* **1** *n* gaucho *mf*
2 *adj* gaucho

place *n Br Parl* **the other place, another place** *(in House of Commons)* la Chambre des lords ; *(in House of Lords)* la Chambre des communes

“

Mr Blair responded: "It certainly will be a free vote because there are hugely different views right across this house and I think it would be foolish for anyone to say that [in] any political party in this house, either here or in **the other place**, there was unanimity."

”

Plaid Cymru *n* = parti nationaliste gallois

plan *Econ* **1** *n* plan *m*
2 *vt (economy)* planifier

plank *n Pol* article *m* ; **the main plank of their policy** la pièce maîtresse de leur politique

plannable *adj Econ (economy)* planifiable

planned economy *n Econ* économie *f* dirigée *ou* planifiée

planner *n Econ (of economy)* planificateur(trice) *m,f*

planning *n Econ (of economy)* planification *f*

platform *n Pol (programme)* plateforme *f* ; **he's running on a platform of traditional values** il fait campagne autour de valeurs traditionnelles

plebiscite *n* plébiscite *f* ; **to elect sb by a plebiscite** plébisciter qn

plenary *Pol* **1** *n* séance *f* plénière
2 *adj* plénier(ère)

◇ *plenary assembly* assemblée *f* plénière

◇ *plenary powers* pleins pouvoirs *mpl*

plenum *n Pol (assembly)* plénum *m*

plural *adj*

◇ *Pol plural majority* majorité *f* plurielle

◇ *plural society* société *f* plurielle

◇ *Pol plural vote* vote *m* plural

◇ *Pol plural voting* vote *m* plural

pluralism *n Pol* **(a)** *(in industrial relations)* pluralisme *m* **(b)** *(holding of sev-*

eral offices) cumul *m* des fonctions *ou* des mandats

pluralist *Pol* **1** *n* (**a**) *(in industrial relations)* pluraliste *mf* (**b**) *(who holds several offices)* = personne qui cumule plusieurs fonctions
2 *adj* (**a**) *(in industrial relations)* pluraliste (**b**) *(holding several offices)* = qui a trait au cumul des fonctions

plurality *n Pol* (**a**) *Am (relative majority)* majorité *f* relative (**b**) *(holding of several offices)* cumul *m* des fonctions *ou* des mandats

PMQs *n Parl (abbr* **prime minister's question time**) = session hebdomadaire du Parlement britannique réservée aux questions des députés au Premier ministre

Isn't **PMQs** just a relic from the old political days, about as relevant now as soapbox meetings on the street corner and tin mugs of tea for the canvassers? ... When has a prime minister ever been put on the spot at prime minister's questions? When has he or she ever given an interesting answer, that wasn't just reading out statistics and hurling back abuse, tinged with a little sarcasm, at the other side?

POA *n (abbr* **Prison Officers' Association**) = syndicat des agents pénitentiaires en Grande-Bretagne

pocket *Am Pol* **1** *vt* **to pocket a bill** = garder un projet de loi sous le coude pour l'empêcher d'être adopté
2 *adj*
◇ **pocket veto** = refus par le Président (ou par le gouverneur d'un État) de signer une proposition de loi, pour l'empêcher d'être adoptée à temps par les députés; **the President used the pocket veto to kill the abortion bill** le Président a refusé de signer le projet de loi sur l'avortement pour

qu'il n'ait aucune chance d'être adopté à temps par le Congrès

Clinton had until midnight Tuesday to sign the H-1B legislation to prevent a **pocket veto** – wherein congressionally approved legislation dies because the President fails to sign it within 10 days of receiving the bill. Absorbed in Middle East peace negotiations, Clinton had delayed signing the bill, which he strongly supported.

pointer *n Econ* indicateur *m*

point of order *n Parl* point *m* de procédure; **he rose on a point of order** il a demandé la parole pour soulever un point de procédure

Police Federation *n* = syndicat de la police britannique

policy *n Pol* politique *f*; **the government's economic policies** la politique économique du gouvernement
◇ **policy adviser** conseiller(ère) *m,f* politique
◇ **policy of appeasement** politique *f* d'apaisement
◇ **policy of austerity** politique *f* d'austérité
◇ **policy of containment** politique *f* d'endiguement
◇ **policy document** document *m* de politique
◇ **policy machine** machine *f* politique
◇ **policy meeting** séance *f* de concertation
◇ **policy paper** = document énonçant une position de principe
◇ **policy position** position *f* de principe
◇ **policy statement** déclaration *f* de principe
◇ **policy unit** comité *m* politique
◇ *Am* **policy wonk** conseiller(ère) *m,f* politique

policymaker *n Pol* responsable *mf* politique

Politburo n Politburo m

political adj (a) (relating to politics) politique (b) (interested in politics) **he's always been very political** il s'est toujours intéressé à la politique

◇ **political action committee** = aux États-Unis, comité qui réunit des fonds pour soutenir une cause politique

◇ **political activity** activité f politique

◇ **political affiliations** attaches fpl politiques

◇ **political agenda** agenda m politique

◇ **political allegiance** allégeance f politique

◇ **political analyst** analyste mf politique

◇ **political asylum** asile m politique ; **to request/be granted political asylum** demander/se voir accorder l'asile politique

◇ **political awareness** politisation f

◇ **political beliefs** opinions fpl politiques

◇ **political brinkmanship** politique f de la corde raide

◇ **political commentator** journaliste mf politique

◇ **political correspondent** journaliste mf politique

◇ **political credo** credo m politique

◇ **political creed** credo m politique

◇ **political crisis** crise f politique

◇ **political economy** économie f politique

◇ **political editor** rédacteur(trice) m,f en chef politique

◇ **political élite** élite f politique

◇ **political establishment** classe f politique dirigeante

◇ **political geography** géographie f politique

◇ **political group** formation f politique

◇ **political huckster** politicard(e) m,f

◇ **political huckstering** politicailleries fpl, trafics mpl

◇ **political institution** institution f politique

◇ **political journalist** journaliste mf politique

◇ **political leader** responsable mf politique

◇ **political leanings** orientation f politique

◇ **political leverage** moyens mpl de pression politiques

◇ **political map** carte f politique

◇ **political observer** expert m ou spécialiste mf en politique

◇ **political offence** délit m politique

◇ **political opponent** (democratic) adversaire mf politique ; (of regime) opposant(e) m,f politique

◇ **political organization** organisation f politique

◇ **political party** parti m politique

◇ **political pragmatism** réalisme m politique

◇ **political prisoner** prisonnier(ère) m,f ou détenu(e) m,f politique

◇ **political realism** réalisme m politique

◇ **political reform** réforme f politique

◇ **political rival** rival(e) m,f politique

◇ **political science** sciences fpl politiques

◇ **political scientist** spécialiste mf en sciences politiques

◇ **political structure** structure f politique

◇ **political struggle** lutte f politique

◇ **political suicide** suicide f politique

◇ **political tendency** tendance f politique

◇ **political theory** théorie f politique

◇ **political unrest** agitation f politique

44

We must create a coherent democratic framework that links the concerns people feel over war, Europe, sleaze, the media, local government, and the power of multi-national companies. These links have not yet been made. It is up to reforming groups and individuals to create this agenda, and act together to serve notice on the **political establishment** that people throughout the country demand to be listened to.

77

politically adv politiquement ; **politic-**

ally informed au courant des choses de la politique; **to be politically aware** avoir une conscience politique, être politisé(e)

politician n (a) *(man)* homme m politique, politique m; *(woman)* femme f politique, politique f (b) Am *(self-interested)* politicien(enne) m,f

politicization n politisation f

politicize 1 vt politiser; **the whole issue has become highly politicized** on a beaucoup politisé toute cette question
    2 vi faire de la politique

politicking n = activité politique visant uniquement à obtenir des suffrages; **the issue has been bogged down by last-minute politicking** des tractations de politique politicienne ont fait s'enliser la discussion

politico n Fam politicien(enne) m,f

politico-economic adj politico-économique

politics 1 n *(as a profession)* politique f; **to go into politics** faire de la politique; **politics has never attracted her** la politique ne l'a jamais intéressée
    2 npl *(opinions)* idées fpl ou opinions fpl politiques; **what exactly are her politics?** quelles sont ses opinions politiques au juste?; **his politics are right of centre** politiquement parlant il se situe à droite

polity n *(state)* État m; *(administration)* organisation f politique ou administrative; *(political unit)* entité f politique

poll Pol 1 n (a) *(elections)* élections fpl, scrutin m; **the poll took place in June** les élections ont eu lieu en juin; **to go to the polls** voter, se rendre aux urnes; **the country will go to the polls in September** la population se rendra aux urnes en septembre, le pays votera en septembre; **the party is likely to be defeated at the polls** le parti sera probablement battu aux élections
    (b) *(vote)* vote m; *(votes cast)* suffra-

ges mpl (exprimés), nombre m de voix; **there was an unexpectedly heavy poll** contrairement aux prévisions, il y a eu un fort taux de participation au scrutin; **the ecology candidate got three percent of the poll** le candidat écologiste a obtenu ou recueilli trois pour cent des suffrages ou des voix
    (c) *(of opinion, intentions)* sondage m (d'opinion); **the latest poll puts the Socialists in the lead** le dernier sondage donne les socialistes en tête
    (d) *(count, census)* recensement m
    (e) *(list)* *(of electors)* liste f électorale; *(of taxpayers)* rôle m nominatif
    2 vt (a) *(votes)* recueillir, obtenir; **the Greens polled 14 percent of the vote** les verts ont obtenu 14 pour cent des voix
    (b) *(person)* sonder, recueillir l'opinion de; **most of those polled supported the government's actions** la plupart des sondés sont favorables à l'action du gouvernement
    (c) Am *(assembly)* inscrire le vote de
    3 vi (a) *(cast one's vote)* voter
    (b) *(receive votes)* **the party polled well** le parti a remporté une bonne proportion des suffrages ou des voix
◇ **poll tax** *(in UK)* = appellation courante de l'impôt aboli en 1993, regroupant taxe d'habitation et impôts locaux, payable par chaque occupant adulte d'une même habitation, ≃ impôts mpl locaux; *(in US)* = impôt, aboli en 1964, donnant droit à être inscrit sur les listes électorales

polling n Pol (a) *(elections)* élections fpl, scrutin m; *(voting)* vote m, suffrage m; **the result of the polling** le résultat du scrutin ou des élections; **polling takes place every five years** le scrutin a lieu tous les cinq ans; **the first round of polling** le premier tour de scrutin ou des élections; **polling is up on last year** la participation au vote est plus élevée que l'année dernière
    (b) *(of opinion, intentions)* sondage m
◇ **polling booth** isoloir m
◇ Br **polling card** carte f d'électeur

◇ **polling company** institut *m* de sondage

◇ **polling day** jour *m* des élections *ou* du scrutin

◇ **polling guru** = stratège politique fondant son action sur les sondages d'opinion

◇ **polling station** bureau *m* de vote

> **"**
>
> Polling wasn't really a player politically until the 1930s, historians agree. A botched poll predicted Franklin Delano Roosevelt would lose to Alf Landon. FDR won and went on to become the first president to regularly use polls to gauge public opinion. In the 1960s, John F. Kennedy used a pollster to help shape his campaign. By the 1980s, no presidential campaign staff was complete without a **polling guru**. President Clinton and his handlers read overnight polls every morning during his bid for re-election.
>
> **"**

pollster *n Fam* enquêteur(euse) *m,f*, sondeur(euse) *m,f*; **the pollsters are predicting a high turnout** les sondages prévoient un fort taux de participation

polycentrism *n Pol* polycentrisme *m*

polycentrist *Pol* **1** *n* polycentriste *mf*
2 *adj* polycentriste

pool *n Econ* pool *m*

poor 1 *npl* **the poor** les pauvres *mpl*
2 *adj* pauvre

popular *adj* populaire

◇ *Pol* **popular front** front *m* populaire

◇ **popular sovereignty** souveraineté *f* populaire

◇ **popular support** soutien *m* populaire

◇ **popular unrest** mécontentement *m* populaire

◇ **popular vote** vote *m* populaire

popularity *n* popularité *f*; **the prime minister's popularity has risen in re**cent months la cote de popularité du Premier ministre a augmenté au cours des derniers mois

population 1 *n* population *f*
2 *adj* démographique, de la population

◇ **population census** recensement *m* démographique *ou* de la population

◇ **population explosion** explosion *f* démographique

◇ **population growth** croissance *f* démographique

◇ **population statistics** statistiques *fpl* démographiques

populism *n Pol* populisme *m*

populist *Pol* **1** *n* populiste *mf*
2 *adj* populiste

◇ **populist support** support *m* populaire

pork, pork barrel *n Am Pol* = fait pour un politicien d'entreprendre des projets uniquement à des fins électorales

pork-barrel *adj Am Pol* (*politics, legislation, spending*) électoraliste

> **"**
>
> Almost no bill of any kind ever makes it through Congress without a chunk of what Democrats are now calling "special interest provisions." It's more commonly known as **pork-barrel** spending, or just plain pork ... Members of congress routinely, and shamelessly, stuff funding for special projects into every bill they can. A bill on sex discrimination may well have subsidies for blueberry research, money for stoplights in small-town Idaho, and computers for libraries in San Jose; a bill on gun safety might well contain money to build a monument in Kansas City, and a special waiver for an auto insurance company in Nevada.
>
> **"**

portfolio *n* (**a**) *Pol* portefeuille *m* (**b**) *Econ* (*of shares*) portefeuille *m*

◇ **portfolio analysis** analyse *f* de portefeuille

⬦ **portfolio diversification** diversification *f* de portefeuille
⬦ **portfolio insurance** assurance *f* de portefeuille
⬦ **portfolio management** gestion *f* de portefeuille
⬦ **portfolio manager** gestionnaire *mf* de portefeuille

position paper *n Pol* déclaration *f* de principe

positive *adj Am Pol (progressive)* progressiste
⬦ **positive discrimination** discrimination *f* positive *(mesures favorisant les membres de groupes minoritaires)*
⬦ **positive vetting** contrôle *m* ou enquête *f* de sécurité *(sur un candidat à un poste touchant à la sécurité nationale)*

post 1 *n (job)* poste *m*, emploi *m*; **he got a post as an economist** il a obtenu un poste d'économiste; **a diplomatic post** un poste de diplomate; **a government post** un poste au gouvernement **2** *vt (assign)* muter, affecter; **to be posted to a different branch** être muté(e) dans une autre succursale; **to be posted overseas** être en poste à l'étranger

postal *adj*
⬦ *Br Pol* **postal ballot** vote *m* par correspondance
⬦ *Br Pol* **postal vote** vote *m* par correspondance

post-colonial *adj* post-colonial(e)

post-colonialism *n* post-colonialisme *m*

post-colonialist 1 *n* post-colonialiste *m,f*
2 *adj* post-colonialiste

post-industrial *adj* postindustriel(-elle)
⬦ **post-industrial society** société *f* postindustrielle

potentate *n Pol* potentat *m*

potential GDP *n Econ* PIB *m* potentiel

pound *n (unit of currency)* livre *f*

poverty *n* pauvreté *f*

⬦ **poverty line** seuil *m* de pauvreté; **to live above/on/below the poverty line** vivre en dessus/à la limite/en dessous du seuil de pauvreté
⬦ **Poverty Reduction Strategy Paper** Document *m* stratégique de réduction de la pauvreté *(situation inextricable de ceux qui dépendent de prestations sociales qu'ils perdent pour peu qu'ils trouvent une activité, même peu rémunérée)*

> ❝
> Mr Brown's approach has been to concentrate resources on the poor by means of greater selectivity and means-testing. But more support for the poorest, which is then rapidly withdrawn as they earn higher sums from work, serves to extend the **poverty trap** – even if its extremes are smoothed out.
> ❞

power *n Pol* **(a)** *(influence, control)* pouvoir *m*; *(authority)* autorité *f*, pouvoir *m*; **to be in power** être au pouvoir; **to come (in)to/to take power** arriver au/prendre le pouvoir; **to lose power** perdre le pouvoir
(b) *(influential group or person)* puissance *f*; **the President is the real power in the land** c'est le président qui détient le véritable pouvoir dans le pays
(c) *(state)* puissance *f*; **the great Western powers** les grandes puissances occidentales
⬦ **power politics** politique *f* du plus fort
⬦ **power sharing** partage *m* du pouvoir
⬦ **power struggle** lutte *f* pour le pouvoir

power-sharing *adj (deal, coalition, talks)* de partage du pouvoir
⬦ **power-sharing arrangement** accord *m* de partage du pouvoir

PPI *n (abbr* **Producer Price Index***)* IPP *m*

PPP *n (abbr* **Public-Private Partnership***)* partenariat *m* public-privé

PR n Pol (abbr **proportional representation**) RP f

pragmatic adj Pol pragmatique

pragmatism n Pol pragmatisme m

pragmatist Pol **1** n pragmatiste mf **2** adj pragmatiste

prayers npl Parl prière f

pre-accession n EU préadhésion f
◊ *pre-accession agreement* accord m de préadhésion
◊ *pre-accession funding* financement m de préadhésion

pre-budget n Br Parl avant-projet m de budget
◊ *pre-budget report* rapport m pré-budgétaire
◊ *pre-budget statement* = déclaration pré-budgétaire ayant lieu en novembre

precautionary principle adj Pol principe m de précaution

precinct n Am Pol circonscription f électorale

preemption n préemption f

preemptive adj
◊ *preemptive strike* attaque f préventive
◊ *preemptive war* guerre f préventive

prefect n (in France) préfet(ète) m,f

prefecture n préfecture f

preference n Econ tarif m ou régime m de faveur; **imports entitled to preference** importations fpl bénéficiant d'un régime de faveur

preferential adj
◊ Econ *preferential duty* préférence f douanière
◊ Econ *preferential price* prix m préférentiel
◊ Pol *preferential vote* vote m préférentiel
◊ Pol *preferential voting* vote m préférentiel

pre-industrial adj préindustriel(-elle)

◊ *pre-industrial society* société f préindustrielle

premier n Premier ministre m

premiership n poste m de Premier ministre; **to be elected to the premiership** être élu(e) Premier ministre; **during her premiership** alors qu'elle était Premier ministre; **he had a successful premiership** il a rempli son mandat de Premier ministre avec succès

prerogative powers npl Pol = pouvoir de décision d'un chef d'État ne nécessitant pas l'approbation du pouvoir législatif

present vt **to present a bill in Parliament** présenter ou introduire un projet de loi au parlement

preside vi présider

▸ **preside over** vt insep présider

presidency n présidence f; **during his presidency** durant sa présidence; **the Clinton presidency** la présidence de Clinton; **to assume the presidency** assumer la présidence

president n (a) (of state) président(e) m,f; **President Jackson** le président Jackson; **Mr President** Monsieur le Président (b) (of organization) président(e) m,f
◊ Br Pol *President of the Board of Trade* ministre mf du Commerce et de l'Industrie
◊ EU *President of the Commission* président(e) m,f de la Commission
◊ Am *President's Day* = jour férié en l'honneur des anniversaires des présidents Washington et Lincoln
◊ *President of the European Parliament* président(e) m,f du Parlement européen
◊ Am *President's Foreign Intelligence Advisory Board* = comité conseillant le président des États-Unis, chargé d'évaluer l'efficacité des services de renseignement américains à l'étranger
◊ *President of the Senate* président m du Sénat

president-elect n = titre donné à un président entre son élection et son investiture

presidential adj (candidate) présidentiel(elle); (aeroplane, suite) présidentiel(elle), du président; **to nurse presidential ambitions** or **aspirations** aspirer à ou ambitionner la présidence; **it's a presidential year** c'est l'année des élections présidentielles

◇ **presidential appointment** = poste à pourvoir sur nomination présidentielle

◇ **presidential ballot** élections fpl présidentielles, scrutin m présidentiel

◇ **presidential contest** élection f présidentielle

◇ **presidential elections** (élections fpl) présidentielles fpl

◇ **presidential hopeful** présidentiable mf

◇ **presidential pardon** grâce f présidentielle

◇ **presidential term of office** mandat m présidentiel

◇ **presidential veto** veto présidentiel

> The Senate hopeful's personal style will require skillful handling by a top-notch campaign team, including a strong advance operation. Even so, a Senate candidate isn't put under the media microscope as much as a **presidential hopeful** is, and it should be easier for aides to assure more comfortable settings for Dole in North Carolina. Just as important, she's already been through one high-profile race.

presiding adj qui préside

◇ **presiding officer** (of polling station) président(e) m,f (de bureau de vote); (of assembly) président(e) m,f

press n presse f

◇ **press conference** conférence f de presse

◇ **press corps** journalistes mpl; **the White House press corps** les journalistes accrédités à la Maison-Blanche

◇ **press gallery** (in Houses of Parliament) tribune f de la presse

◇ **press office** service m de presse

◇ **press officer** responsable mf des relations avec la presse

◇ **press release** communiqué m de presse

◇ Pol **press secretary** ≃ porte-parole m du gouvernement

pressure group n groupe m de pression

pressurize vt (person, government) faire pression sur; **the government was accused of pressurizing the unions** on a accusé le gouvernement de faire pression sur les syndicats

preventive war n guerre f préventive

price 1 n prix m; (of shares) cours m, cote f
2 vt Econ (quantity) valoriser

◇ **price cartel** cartel m de prix

◇ **price ceiling** plafond m de prix

◇ **price control** contrôle m des prix

◇ **price differential** écart m ou différentiel m de prix

◇ **price discrimination** tarif m discriminatoire

◇ **price effect** effet m de prix

◇ **price elasticity** élasticité f des prix

◇ **price fluctuation** fluctuation f des prix

◇ **price freeze** blocage m des prix

◇ **prices and incomes policy** politique f des prix et des salaires

◇ **price index** indice m des prix

◇ **price indicator** indicateur m de prix

◇ **price inflation** inflation f des prix

◇ **price instability** instabilité f des prix

◇ **price leadership** = position dominante en matière de fixation des prix

◇ **price level** niveau m de prix

◇ **price mechanism** mécanisme m des prix

◇ **price monopoly** monopole m des prix

◇ *price pegging* soutien *m* des prix

◇ *price policy* politique *f* des prix

◇ *price regulation* réglementation *f* des prix

◇ *price ring* monopole *m* des prix

◇ *price support* soutien *m* des prix

◇ *price theory* théorie *f* des prix

◇ *price war* guerre *f* des prix

price-earnings ratio *n* ratio *m* cours-bénéfices, rapport *m* cours-bénéfices

primary 1 *n Am Pol* (élection *f*) primaire *f*

2 *adj Econ* primaire

◇ *Econ* **primary dealer** spécialiste *mf* en valeurs du Trésor

◇ *Am Pol* **primary election** (élection *f*) primaire *f*

◇ *Econ* **primary employment** activité *f* primaire

◇ *Econ* **primary industry** industrie *f* primaire

◇ *Econ* **primary market** marché *m* primaire

◇ *Econ* **primary product** produit *m* primaire

◇ *Econ* **primary sector** secteur *m* primaire

prime *adj*

◇ *Pol* **prime minister** Premier ministre *m*

◇ *Pol* **Prime Minister's Question Time** = session hebdomadaire du Parlement britannique réservée aux questions des députés au Premier ministre

◇ *Pol* **prime ministership** poste *m* de Premier ministre; **during her prime ministership** pendant qu'elle était Premier ministre

◇ *Pol* **prime ministry** fonctions *fpl* de Premier ministre

principal 1 *n Econ* **(a)** *(capital)* capital *m*; *(of debt)* principal *m*; **principal and interest** capital *m* et intérêts *mpl* **(b)** *(employer of agent)* mandant *m*, commettant *m*; **principal and agent** mandant *m* et mandataire *m*

2 *adj*

◇ *Br Pol* **principal private secretary** ≃ directeur(trice) *m,f* de cabinet

principality *n* principauté *f*

prisoner *n* prisonnier(ère) *m,f*

◇ *prisoner of conscience* prisonnier(-ère) *m,f* d'opinion

◇ *Econ* **prisoner's dilemma** dilemme *m* du prisonnier

◇ *prisoner of war* prisonnier(ère) *m,f* de guerre

private *adj (not state-run)* privé(e)

◇ *private company* société *f* privée

◇ *private debt* dette *f* privée

◇ *private enterprise (company)* entreprise *f* privée; *(principle)* libre entreprise *f*

◇ *private finance* finances *fpl* privées

◇ *private finance initiative* partenariat *m* public-privé

◇ *Econ* **private good** bien *m* privé

◇ *private investment* investissement *m ou* placement *m* privé

◇ *private investor* investisseur *m* privé

◇ *Parl* **private member** = simple député

◇ *Parl* **private member's bill** = proposition de loi faite par un simple député

◇ *Br Pol* **private secretary** = haut fonctionnaire dont le rôle est d'assister un ministre

◇ *private sector* secteur *m* privé

◇ *private sector investment* investissements *mpl* du secteur privé

◇ *private sector salaries* salaires *mpl* du secteur privé

◇ *private session* = débat parlementaire auquel seuls les députés sont autorisés à assister

◇ *private sitting* = débat parlementaire auquel seuls les députés sont autorisés à assister

privatization *n* privatisation *f*

privatize *vt* privatiser

privy *adj*

◇ *Privy Council* = le Conseil privé du souverain en Grande-Bretagne *(il se compose de tous les ministres présents et passés du gouvernement ainsi*

que d'autres personnalités du Commonwealth et compte environ 400 membres)
◊ *Privy Councillor* = membre du Conseil privé

"

The UK is set for a diplomatic row with Trinidad and Tobago after stepping in to block the execution of nine convicted killers. Drugs baron Dole Chadee and eight members of his gang had been scheduled to die by hanging in groups of three on Tuesday, Wednesday and Thursday. But on Monday Britain's **Privy Council** stayed the executions of the nine, sparking anger among some Trinidadians. Although Trinidad and Tobago became independent in 1976, the **Privy Council** in London remains its court of last resort.

"

probability n probabilité f
◊ *probability method* (of sampling) méthode f probabiliste
◊ *probability sample* échantillon m probabiliste
◊ *probability sampling* échantillonnage m probabiliste

process n processus m; **the democratic process** le processus démocratique

produce vt produire, fabriquer

producer n Econ (of raw materials, goods) producteur(trice) m,f; **this region is Europe's biggest wine producer** cette région est la plus grande productrice de vin d'Europe
◊ *producers' association* syndicat m de producteurs
◊ *producers' cooperative* coopérative f de production
◊ *producer goods* biens mpl de production
◊ *producer price index* indice m des prix à la production

product n Econ produit m

◊ *product market* marché m de produit

production n Econ (process) production f, fabrication f; (amount produced) production f; **an increase/a fall in production** une hausse/une baisse de la production
◊ *production factor* facteur m de production
◊ *production function* fonction f de production

productive adj Econ productif(ive)
◊ *productive forces* forces fpl productives
◊ *productive labour* main-d'œuvre f productive

productively adv Econ d'une manière productive

productivity n Econ productivité f, rendement m
◊ *productivity bargaining* = négociations entre les partenaires sociaux en vue d'améliorer la productivité

professional association n association f professionnelle

profit 1 n (financial gain) profit m, bénéfice m; **to make a profit** faire un bénéfice; **to be in profit** être bénéficiaire
2 vi profiter
◊ *profit indicator* indice m de profit
◊ *profit and loss account* compte m de résultat
◊ *profit maximization* maximisation f des profits
◊ *profit tax* impôt m sur les bénéfices

profitability n rentabilité f

profitable adj rentable, lucratif(ive)

profitably adv avec profit, d'une manière rentable

profit-making adj (a) (aiming to make profit) à but lucratif (b) (profitable) rentable
◊ *profit-making organization* association f à but lucratif

profit-related pay n Econ salaire m lié aux bénéfices

profit-sharing n participation f ou intéressement m aux bénéfices; **we have a profit-sharing agreement/ scheme** nous avons un accord/un système de participation (aux bénéfices)

profit-taking n prise f de bénéfices

programme, Am **program** n Pol (for election) programme m

programming n Econ programmation f

progressive 1 n Pol (politician) progressiste mf
  2 adj (**a**) Pol (idea, party, outlook) progressiste (**b**) Econ (movement) progressif(ive)
◇ Econ **progressive tax** impôt m progressif
◇ Econ **progressive taxation** imposition f progressive

progressively adv Pol d'une manière progressiste; **to think progressively** avoir des idées progressistes

proliferation n (of arms) prolifération f

pro-marketeer n Br Pol partisan(e) m,f du Marché commun

propaganda n propagande f

propagandist 1 n propagandiste mf
  2 adj propagandiste

propagandize 1 vt (ideas, views) faire de la propagande pour ou en faveur de; (person, masses) faire de la propagande auprès de
  2 vi faire de la propagande

▸ **prop up** vt sep (regime, business, currency) soutenir; **the government stepped in to prop up the dollar** le gouvernement est intervenu pour soutenir le dollar

propensity n Econ propension f
◇ **propensity to consume** propension f à consommer
◇ **propensity to import** propension f à importer
◇ **propensity to save** propension f à épargner

property tax n impôt m foncier

proportional adj
◇ Pol **proportional representation** représentation f proportionnelle, scrutin m proportionnel
◇ **proportional tax** impôt m proportionnel

proportionally adj proportionnellement

propose vt Pol (candidate, applicant) parrainer

proposer n Pol (of candidate, applicant) parrain m, parraineur m

prorogation n Pol prorogation f

prorogue vt Pol proroger

> Sri Lankan President Chandrika Kumaratunga's surprise move on Tuesday to **prorogue** Parliament which was poised to topple her ruling People's Alliance government through a joint opposition no-confidence motion and her call for a referendum on a new constitution has drawn criticism from political parties in the war-torn country.

Prospect n = syndicat britannique interprofessionnel

protect vt Econ (industry) protéger

protectionism n Econ protectionnisme m

protectionist Econ **1** n protectionniste mf
  2 adj protectionniste
◇ **protectionist measures** mesures fpl protectionnistes

protective adj Econ protecteur(-trice)
◇ **protective measures** mesures fpl protectrices
◇ **protective tariff** tarif m protecteur

protectorate n protectorat m

protest 1 n protestation f, contestation f; **to make a protest against** or about sth élever une protestation contre qch, protester contre qch; **in protest against** *or* **at sth** en signe de protestation contre qch; **to stage a protest** *(complaint)* organiser une protestation; *(demonstration)* organiser une manifestation

2 *adj* de protestation, de contestation

3 *vt* protester contre, contester

4 *vi* protester **(against/about** contre/à propos de)

◇ **protest demonstration** manifestation *f*

◇ **protest march** manifestation *f*

◇ **protest marcher** manifestant(e) *m,f*

◇ **protest movement** mouvement *m* de contestation *ou* de protestation

◇ **protest rally** mouvement *m* de protestation

◇ **protest vote** vote *m* de protestation

protocol *n Pol* protocole *m*

province *n (region, district)* province *f*

Provisional *Pol* **1** *n* membre *m* de l'IRA provisoire

2 *adj* provisoire

◇ **the Provisional IRA** l'IRA *f* provisoire *(branche de l'IRA favorable à la lutte armée)*

provisional *adj* provisoire

◇ *Econ* **provisional budget** budget *m* prévisionnel

◇ *Pol* **provisional government** gouvernement *m* provisoire

proximity talks *n Pol* négociations *fpl* rapprochées

proxy *n (person)* mandataire *mf*, fondé(e) *m,f* de pouvoir; *(authorization)* procuration *f*, mandat *m*; **to vote by proxy** voter par procuration

PRSP *n (abbr* **Poverty Reduction Strategy Paper)** DSRP *m*

PSBR *n Br Econ (abbr* **public sector borrowing requirement)** = besoins d'emprunt du secteur public non couverts par les rentrées fiscales

PSCR *n Br Econ (abbr* **public sector cash requirement)** = besoins d'emprunt du secteur public non couverts par les rentrées fiscales

public *adj* **(a)** *(of, by the state)* public(-ique); **to hold public office** avoir des fonctions officielles **(b)** *(publicly known, open)* public(ique); **to go into public life** se lancer dans les affaires publiques; **she's active in public life** elle prend une part active aux affaires publiques; **his first public statement** sa première déclaration publique

◇ **public accountability** transparence *f*; **the minister must not try to avoid public accountability** le ministre doit jouer la transparence sans se dérober

◇ *Br* **Public Accounts Committee** = comité chargé d'examiner les comptes publics

◇ **public affairs** affaires *fpl* publiques

◇ **public authorities** pouvoirs *mpl* publics

◇ *Br Pol* **public bill** ≃ projet *m* de loi d'intérêt général

◇ **public body** corporation *f* de droit public

◇ **public company** entreprise *f* publique

◇ *Br* **public corporation** entreprise *f* publique

◇ **public debate** débat *m* public

◇ **public debt** dette *f* publique *ou* de l'État

◇ **public deposits** = avoirs des différents services du gouvernement britannique à la Banque d'Angleterre

◇ **public enterprise** entreprise *f* publique

◇ **public expenditure** dépenses *fpl ou* charges *fpl* publiques

◇ **public finance** finances *fpl* publiques

◇ **public foreign debt** dette *f* publique extérieure

◇ **public funds** fonds *mpl ou* finances *fpl* publiques

◇ **public gallery** *(in Houses of Parliament)* tribune *f* du public

◇ *public good* bien *m* public

◇ *public interest* intérêt *m* public; **in the public interest** dans l'intérêt du public

◇ *public office* fonction *f* publique

◇ *public official* fonctionnaire *mf*

◇ *public opinion* opinion *f* publique

◇ *public opinion poll* sondage *m* (d'opinion)

◇ *public ownership* nationalisation *f*, étatisation *f*

◇ *public revenue* revenu *m* public *ou* de l'État

◇ *public sector* secteur *m* publique

◇ *public sector borrowing requirement* = besoins d'emprunt du secteur public non couverts par les rentrées fiscales

◇ *public sector cash requirement* = besoins d'emprunt du secteur public non couverts par les rentrées fiscales

◇ *public sector deficit* déficit *m* du secteur public

◇ *public sector earnings* revenus *mpl* du secteur public

◇ *public servant* fonctionnaire *mf*

◇ *public service (amenity)* service *m* public; *Br (civil service)* fonction *f* publique; **she's in public service** elle est fonctionnaire

◇ *public spending* dépenses *fpl* publiques *ou* de l'État

◇ *public utility Br (amenity)* service *m* public; *Am (company)* = société privée assurant un service public et réglementée par une commission d'État

◇ *Br public utility company* société *f* d'utilité publique

◇ *public works* travaux *mpl* publics

publicity campaign *n* campagne *f* d'information

publicly *adv* publiquement, en public; *Econ* **publicly owned** nationalisé(e); **the company is 51 percent publicly controlled** la société est contrôlée à 51 pour cent par des capitaux publics

Public-Private Partnership *n* partenariat *m* public-privé

pump priming *n Econ* = relance de l'économie par injection de fonds publics

pump-priming *adj Econ (plan, measure)* = de relance par injection de fonds publics

“

House Minority Leader Richard A. Gephardt ... and Senate Majority Leader Tom Daschle ... once again charged that Mr. Bush's across-the-board tax cuts had led to a weakened economy, increased unemployment and a declining stock market. Both offered five-point, **pump-priming** economic plans that called for hundreds of billions of dollars in new spending for school construction and health care, a higher $6.65 minimum wage, extended unemployment benefits, and short-term, targeted tax cuts for low- and middle-income workers – whether they pay income taxes or not.

”

puppet *adj*

◇ *Pol puppet government* gouvernement *m* fantoche

◇ *puppet monarch* souverain(e) *m,f* fantoche

◇ *Pol puppet president* président(e) *m,f* fantoche

purchase 1 *n* achat *m*; *(of company)* rachat *m*

2 *vt* acheter, acquérir

3 *vi* acheter

◇ *purchase tax* taxe *f* à l'achat

purchasing *n* achat *m*; *(of company)* rachat *m*

◇ *Econ purchasing power* capacité *f* d'achat, pouvoir *m* d'achat

◇ *Econ purchasing power parity* parité *f* du pouvoir d'achat

pure competition *n Econ* concurrence *f* pure

purge *Pol* **1** *n (of party, organization)* purge *f*, épuration *f*

2 *vt (party, organization)* purger,

épurer; **the extreme right was purged from the party** le parti s'est débarrassé de son extrême droite

purging n Pol (of party, organization) épuration f

▸ **put up 1** vt sep (**a**) (candidate) présenter; **we are not putting up any candidates** nous ne présentons aucun candidat

(**b**) (increase) faire monter, augmenter, hausser; **this will put up the price of oil** ça va faire augmenter ou monter le prix du pétrole

2 vi (in election) se présenter, se porter candidat; **she put up as a Labour candidate** elle s'est présentée comme candidate du parti travailliste

pyramid n Econ pyramide f

pyramidal adj Econ pyramidal(e)

q

QMV *n EU* (*abbr* **qualified majority voting**) vote *m* à la majorité qualifiée

qualified majority voting *n EU* vote *m* à la majorité qualifiée

quality circle *n Econ* cercle *m* de qualité

quango *n Br* (*abbr* **quasi-autonomous non-governmental organization**) = organisme semi-public

quantity theory of money *n Econ* théorie *f* quantitative de la monnaie

quartile *n Econ* quartile *m*

queen *n* reine *f*; **the Queen of Spain** la reine d'Espagne

◇ *Queen's Speech (in UK)* = allocution prononcée par la reine (mais préparée par le gouvernement) lors de la rentrée parlementaire et dans laquelle elle définit les grands axes de la politique gouvernementale

question *n* question *f*; *Parl* **to put down a question for sb** adresser une interpellation à qn

◇ *Question Time* = session hebdomadaire du Parlement britannique réservée aux questions des députés aux membres du gouvernement

> **"**
>
> The chancellor, Gordon Brown, and his chief policy adviser, Ed Balls, yesterday sent an unmistakable Treasury olive branch to Tony Blair when they both stated publicly that the promised euro referendum could be won – provided the economic terms were right. On a day when the prime minister endured opposition taunts in the Commons at **Question Time** over another significant policy difference between No 10 and No 11 – student top-up fees – Mr Brown was seen on the government frontbench chatting with his leader.
>
> **"**

questioner *n Parl* interpellateur(-trice) *m,f*

quit rate *n Econ* taux *m* de départs

quorum *n Parl* quorum *m*; **to have a quorum** être en nombre

quota *n* quota *m*, contingent *m*; **to apportion** *or* **fix quotas for import** déterminer les quotas d'importation

race 1 *n* **the race for the presidency** la course à la présidence
2 *vt* **to race a bill through Parliament** faire adopter un projet de loi en toute hâte

radical *Pol* **1** *n* radical(e) *m,f*
2 *adj* radical(e)
◇ *radical chic* ≃ socialisme *m* de salon
◇ *Radical Party* parti *m* Radical

radicalism *n Pol* radicalisme *m*

radicalization *n Pol* radicalisation *f*

radicalize *vt Pol* radicaliser

radical-socialism *n Pol* radical-socialisme *m*

radical-socialist *Pol* **1** *n* radical-socialiste *mf*
2 *adj* radical-socialiste

raft *n (of measures, policies)* ensemble *m* ; **a raft of new tax-cutting proposals has been announced by the government** le gouvernement a annoncé tout un ensemble de projets de réduction des impôts

railroad *vt Fam (force acceptance of)* **to railroad a bill through parliament** imposer un projet de loi au parlement

raise *vt (increase) (price, cost of living)* hausser, augmenter

raison d'état *n* raison *f* d'État

rally *Pol* **1** *n (gathering)* rassemblement *m*, (grand) meeting *m*
2 *vt (gather)* rallier, rassembler ; **she's trying to rally support for her bill** elle essaie de rallier des gens pour soutenir son projet de loi

3 *vi (gather)* se rassembler ; *(of supporters)* se rallier ; **they rallied to the party/to the defence of their leader** ils se sont ralliés au parti/pour défendre leur chef

rank and file *n (in political party, union)* base *f* ; **we'll have to consult the rank and file** il faudra que nous consultions la base

rank-and-filer *n (in political party, union)* membre *m* de la base

ratchet effect *n Econ* **this had a ratchet effect on prices** cela a entraîné une augmentation irréversible des prix

❝

Two additional points need to be raised in relation to the economic impact of a minimum wage. The first has to do with the possibility of a **ratchet effect** on the structure of wages when the minimum rises. The argument has been made that there are traditional "differentials" between various job classifications and when the minimum wage rises, this upsets these differentials and will set in motion a whole series of adjustments up the entire structure of wages. In other words, hourly workers may wish to preserve the gaps between themselves and the minimum wage.

❞

rate *n (of tax, interest)* taux *m* ; **the rate is 20p in the pound** le taux est de 20 pence par livre

◇ *rate of exchange* cours *m* ou taux *m* du change

◇ *rate of growth* taux *m* d'accroissement ou de croissance

◇ *rate of inflation* taux *m* d'inflation

◇ *rate of interest* taux *m* d'intérêt

◇ *rate of return* (on investment) taux *m* de rendement

◇ *rate of return analysis* analyse *f* du rendement

◇ *rate of return pricing* fixation *f* de prix au taux de rendement établi

◇ *rate of taxation* taux *m* d'imposition

ratification *n* (of treaty) ratification *f*

ratify *vt* (treaty) ratifier

rating *n* Econ rating *m*

ratio *n* Econ ratio *m*

ration Econ **1** *n* ration *f*; **rations** (food) vivres *mpl*

2 *vt* (**a**) (food) rationner (**b**) (funds) limiter; **arts subsidies are being rationed because of the recession** les subventions à la culture sont limitées du fait de la récession

rationality *n* Econ rationalité *f*

rationalization *n* Econ (of company, production, industry) rationalisation *f*

rationalize *vt* Econ (company, production, industry) rationaliser

rationing *n* Econ (**a**) (of food) rationnement *m* (**b**) (of funds) limitation *f*; **banks are warning of mortgage rationing** les banques annoncent qu'elles vont limiter le nombre de prêts immobiliers

reaction *n* Pol réaction *f*; **the forces of reaction** les forces *fpl* réactionnaires

reactionary Pol **1** *n* réactionnaire *mf*

2 *adj* réactionnaire

◇ *reactionary government* gouvernement *m* réactionnaire

◇ *reactionary vote* vote *m* réactionnaire

read *vt* Pol (bill, speech) lire

reading *n* Pol (of bill, speech) lecture *f*; **to give a bill its first/second reading**

examiner un projet de loi en première/deuxième lecture

readmission *n* (to political party) réintégration *f*

readmit *vt* (to political party) réintégrer

Reaganite Pol **1** *n* reaganien(enne) *m,f*

2 *adj* reaganien(enne)

Reaganomics *n* = politique reaganienne selon laquelle l'argent des riches finit par profiter aux pauvres

real *adj*

◇ Econ *real GDP* PIB *m* réel

◇ Econ *real growth* croissance *f* réelle

◇ Econ *real income* revenu *m* réel

◇ Econ *real interest rate* taux *m* d'intérêt réel

◇ Econ *real purchasing power* pouvoir *m* d'achat réel

◇ Econ *real rate of return* taux *m* de rendement réel

realign **1** *vt* (**a**) Pol regrouper (**b**) Econ réaligner

2 *vi* (**a**) Pol se regrouper (**b**) Econ se réaligner

realignment *n* (**a**) Pol regroupement *m* (**b**) Econ réalignement *m*

◇ Econ *realignment of currencies* réalignement *m* monétaire

realpolitik *n* Pol realpolitik *f*

rearm **1** *vt* (nation) réarmer

2 *vi* réarmer

rearmament *n* Pol réarmement *m*

reasons of State *npl* raison *f* d'État

reassemble *vi* Pol se rassembler; **Parliament reassembles in September** la rentrée parlementaire a lieu en septembre

reassembly *n* Pol rentrée *f*

rebate *n* (on tax) dégrèvement *m*

rebel **1** *n* rebelle *mf*

2 *adj* rebelle

3 *vi* se rebeller; **to rebel against sb/sth** se révolter contre qn/qch

◇ *rebel MP* parlementaire *mf* rebelle

"

Privately, Kinnock has his criticisms of New Labour, but he is in many ways its founding father. [He] had to change not only the Labour Party, but also himself. In the 1970s, he was an anti-marketeer, a unilateralist and a **rebel MP** who attacked the Labour government for cutting public expenditure. But this book makes clear that the stereotype of a leftwing firebrand who became a vote-seeking pragmatist is simplistic. Kinnock always was a pragmatic streak, one that led to a breach with the Bennite left in dramatic circumstances in 1981, two years before he became leader.

"

rebellion n (by MPs) rébellion f, révolte f; **a rebellion by 52 Labour MPs saw the government defeated on the asylum bill** le projet de loi du gouvernement sur l'asile politique a échoué car 52 députés travaillistes ont refusé de le soutenir

recall 1 n (of Parliament) rappel m, reconvocation f

2 vt (Parliament) rappeler (en session extraordinaire); (ambassador) rappeler

recess 1 n (of Parliament) vacances fpl parlementaires, intersession f parlementaire; **Parliament is in recess for the summer** le Parlement est en vacances pour l'été

2 vi **Parliament will recess next week** les vacances parlementaires commenceront la semaine prochaine

recession n Econ récession f; **the economy is in recession** l'économie est en récession

recessional adj Econ de récession

recessionary adj Econ de récession; **to have a recessionary effect** (of policy) entraîner une récession

◊ **recessionary gap** écart m déflationniste

reciprocal adj (bilateral) réciproque, bilatéral(e)

◊ **reciprocal agreement** accord m réciproque

◊ **reciprocal demand** demande f réciproque

◊ **reciprocal trading** commerce m réciproque

reciprocity n réciprocité f

recognition n Pol (of state, organization, trade union) reconnaissance f; **to withhold recognition from** refuser de reconnaître

recognize vt Pol (state, organization, trade union) reconnaître

recommend vt (a) (speak in favour of) recommander (**to/for** à/pour); **I'll recommend you to the Minister** j'appuyerai votre candidature auprès du ministre (b) (advise) recommander, conseiller

recommendation n (a) (personal) recommandation f; **on his recommendation** sur sa recommandation (b) (of committee, advisory body) recommandation f; **to make a recommendation** faire une recommandation

recommit vt Am Pol (bill) renvoyer devant une commission

recommittal n Am Pol (of bill) renvoi m devant une commission

reconstitute vt Pol (government) reconstituer

reconstitution n Pol (of government) reconstitution f

reconstruct vt (government) reconstituer; (economy) restaurer

reconstruction n (of government) reconstitution f; (of economy) restauration f

record 1 n (of proceedings, debate) procès-verbal m, compte rendu m; **records** (of government, organization) archives fpl

2 vt Parl **to record a vote** (of MP) voter; **how many votes were recorded?** combien de voix ont été exprimées?

recount Pol **1** n nouveau décompte m ; **to demand a recount** exiger un nouveau décompte ; **there were four recounts** on a compté le nombre de bulletins de vote à quatre reprises **2** vt recompter, compter de nouveau

recover vi (of currency, economy) se redresser, rebondir ; (of market, business) reprendre, se redresser ; (of prices, shares) se redresser, remonter

recovery n (of currency, economy) relance f, redressement m, rebond m ; (of market, business) reprise f, redressement m ; (of prices, shares) redressement m, remontée f
◇ **recovery plan** plan m de redressement

recurrent unemployment n Econ chômage m récurrent

red Fam **1** n (a) Pol (communist) rouge mf, coco mf ; **the reds-under-the-bed syndrome** la phobie anti-communiste (b) Econ **to be in the red** être dans le rouge ; **to get out of the red** sortir du rouge
2 adj Pol (communist) rouge

redistribute vt Econ & Pol (income, wealth, land) redistribuer ; Pol **to redistribute seats** redécouper les circonscriptions électorales

redistribution n Econ & Pol (of income, wealth, land) redistribution f ; Pol **the redistribution of seats** le nouveau découpage des circonscriptions

reduce vt (price) baisser, réduire ; (rate, expenses, cost, investment) réduire ; (tax) alléger, réduire

reduction n (of price) baisse f, diminution f ; (of rate, expenses, cost, investment) réduction f ; (of taxes) allègement m

redundancy n Br Econ (layoff) licenciement m ; (unemployment) chômage m ; **5,000 redundancies have been announced** on a annoncé 5000 licenciements ; **there is a high level of redundancy here** il y a un fort taux de chômage ici

redundant adj Br Econ (worker) licencié(e), au chômage ; **to make sb redundant** (of employer) licencier qn, mettre qn au chômage ; **to be made redundant** être licencié(e), être mis(e) au chômage

re-elect vt (candidate) réélire ; (group, assembly) renouveler ; **she is sure to be re-elected** sa réélection est assurée

re-election n réélection f ; **to stand** or **to run for re-election** se représenter aux élections

re-enact vt Pol (legislation) remettre en vigueur

re-enactment n Pol (of legislation) remise f en vigueur

re-examination n (of policy) réexamen m

re-examine vt (policy) réexaminer

re-export 1 n (activity) réexportation f ; (product) article m de réexportation ; **re-exports** réexportations fpl **2** vt réexporter
◇ **re-export trade** commerce m de réexportation

re-exportation n réexportation f

referendum n référendum m ; **to hold a referendum** organiser un référendum

reflate vt Econ relancer

reflation n Econ relance f (économique)

reflationary adj Econ (policy) de relance
◇ **reflationary pressure** pression f pour une relance (économique) ·

reform 1 n (of law, system, institution) réforme f
2 vt (law, system, institution) réformer
◇ **reform proposal** proposition f de réforme

reformism n Pol réformisme m

reformist Pol **1** n réformiste mf
2 adj réformiste

refugee n réfugié(e) m,f

regent n régent(e) m,f

regime, régime n Pol régime m; **under the present regime** sous le régime actuel

region n région f

regional adj régional(e)
◇ **regional council** conseil m régional
◇ **regional councillor** conseiller(ère) m,f régional(e)
◇ Br **regional development** (of land, buildings) aménagement m du territoire; (for jobs) action f régionale
◇ Br **regional development corporation** = organisme pour l'aménagement du territoire
◇ **regional policy** politique f régionale

regionalism n Pol régionalisme m

regionalist Pol 1 n régionaliste mf
2 adj régionaliste

regionalization n Pol régionalisation f

regionalize vt Pol régionaliser

register 1 n (of members, voters) liste f
2 vt (name) (faire) enregistrer, (faire) inscrire; (on list) inscrire; **to register one's vote** exprimer son vote; **to register a protest** protester; Br Pol **to register an interest** = déclarer une activité (tel qu'un poste de consultant pour qu'une société privée) ou un don qui risque d'affecter ses prises de position à la Chambre des communes
3 vi (on electoral list) se faire inscrire sur la liste électorale
◇ **Register of Members' Interests** = registre où figurent les divers intérêts des députés (postes de consultants, appartenance à telle ou telle organisation etc) risquant d'influencer leur action à la Chambre des communes

"
However, he also pointed out that they could award only a nominal sum if they found Mr Hamilton's conduct in relation to the stay at Mr

Fayed's Ritz hotel in Paris, and his attempt to conceal moving an amendment to finance legislation shortly before being paid a £10,000 consultancy fee by the Mobil oil company, was so "reprehensible and discreditable" that his reputation suffered. But, he added: "You may well think that there is a world of difference between failing to **register an interest** and lack of candour on the one hand and the grave accusation of corruption."
"

regrade vt (civil servant) reclasser

regrading n (of civil servant) reclassement m

regressive adj régressif(ive)
◇ Pol **regressive legislation** législation f régressive
◇ Econ **regressive tax** impôt m régressif
◇ Econ **regressive taxation** imposition f régressive

regular Am Pol 1 n membre m fidèle (du parti)
2 adj fidèle au parti

regulate vt réglementer

regulation n (a) (ruling) règlement m; **it complies with EU regulations** c'est conforme aux dispositions communautaires (b) (by law) réglementation f

regulative adj régulateur(trice)

regulator n (person) régulateur(trice) m,f

regulatory adj (framework) réglementaire; (authority) de contrôle
◇ **regulatory body** instance f de contrôle

reign 1 n règne m
2 vi régner (**over** sur)

reinstate vt (civil servant) réintégrer, rétablir

reinstatement n (of civil servant) réintégration f, rétablissement m

rejoin vt Pol (political party) rejoindre; **to rejoin the majority** rallier la majorité

relations npl (between leaders, countries) relation f

relative adj
◇ Pol **relative majority** majorité f relative ou simple
◇ Econ **relative poverty** pauvreté f relative

relax vt (controls, regulations) assouplir

relaxing n (of controls, regulations) assouplissement m

removal n (of politician, civil servant) révocation f, renvoi m, destitution f

remove vt (politician, civil servant) révoquer, destituer; **his opponents had him removed from office** ses opposants l'ont fait révoquer

renegade n (traitor) transfuge mf

renew vt (mandate) reconduire

renewable adj reconductible, renouvelable
◇ **renewable energy** énergie f renouvelable
◇ **renewable resource** ressource f renouvelable

renewal n (of mandate) reconduction f

rent n Econ rente f

reorganization n (of company, resources) redéploiement m

reorganize vt (company, resources) redéployer

reorientate vt Pol réorienter

reorientation n Pol réorientation f

Rep. Am Pol (a) (abbr **Representative**) ≃ député(e) m,f (b) (abbr **Republican**) républicain

repeal 1 n (of law) abrogation f; (of decree) révocation f
2 vt (law) abroger, annuler; (decree) rapporter, révoquer

repeat vi Am Pol voter plus d'une fois (à une même élection)

repeater n Am Pol électeur(trice) m,f qui vote plus d'une fois (à une même élection)

report 1 n rapport m; **the government plans to publish a report on its recommandations** le gouvernement a l'intention de publier un rapport sur ses recommandations
2 vt (announce) annoncer, déclarer, signaler
3 vi (make a report) (of committee) faire son rapport, présenter ses conclusions
◇ Br Pol **report stage** = étape du processus législatif lors de laquelle une commission rend compte de ses travaux à la Chambre des communes entre la deuxième et la troisième lecture d'un projet de loi

▸ **report out** vt sep Am Pol (bill, legislation) renvoyer après examen

reporter n (spokesperson) rapporteur(-euse) m,f; (in Parliament) sténographe mf

reposition vt Pol (political party) repositionner

repositioning n Pol (of political party) repositionnement m

represent vt (a) Pol (voters, members) représenter; **she represents Tooting** elle est députée de ou elle représente la circonscription de Tooting (b) (be delegate for) représenter; **the President was represented by the ambassador** le Président était représenté par l'ambassadeur

representation n Pol représentation f; **they have increased their representation to six** le nombre de leurs délégués est passé à six; **they still lacked representation in Parliament** ils n'étaient toujours pas représentés au parlement

Representative Am Pol **1** n = membre de la Chambre des représentants
2 adj de la Chambre des représentants

representative *Pol* **1** *n* représentant(e) *m,f*
2 *adj* représentatif(ive)
◇ *representative democracy* démocratie *f* représentative
◇ *representative government* gouvernement *m* représentatif

reprisal *n* représailles *fpl*, mesure *f* de rétorsion; **there have been threats of reprisal** il y a eu des menaces de représailles

republic *n Pol* république *f*

Republican *Am Pol* **1** *n* républicain(e) *m,f*
2 *adj* républicain(e)
◇ *the Republican party* le Parti républicain

republican *Pol* **1** *n* républicain(e) *m,f*
2 *adj* républicain(e)

republicanism *n Pol* républicanisme *m*

resale price maintenance *n Econ* prix *m* de vente imposé

reselect *vt Pol (candidate)* sélectionner de nouveau

reselection *n Pol (of candidate)* = fait d'être à nouveau choisi par son parti en tant que candidat pour des élections

reserve *n (of money)* réserve *f*
◇ *reserve assets* réserve *f* légale
◇ *reserve capital* capital *m* de réserve
◇ *reserve currency* monnaie *f* de réserve
◇ *reserve fund* volant *m* de sécurité

reshape *vt (policy)* réaménager

reshaping *n (of policy)* réaménagement *m*

reshuffle *Pol* **1** *n* remaniement *m*
2 *vt (cabinet)* remanier

"

David Blunkett today arrived at the Home Office as Tony Blair **reshuffled** his cabinet team following yesterday's election triumph. There were also reports that Chris Smith has been sacked as culture secretary. Mr Blunkett has spent four years as education secretary. Earlier today, Mr Blair proclaimed he had a "mandate for reform and investment" in his victory address from Downing Street. Announcing that he had an "instruction to deliver", he said the government would deal with issues such as economic stability, public services and the criminal justice system.

"

resolution *n Pol (formal motion)* résolution *f*; **they passed/adopted/rejected a resolution to limit the budget** ils ont voté/adopté/rejeté une résolution pour limiter le budget; **to put a resolution to the meeting** soumettre *ou* proposer une résolution à l'assemblée; **the statutes can only be changed by resolution** les statuts ne peuvent être modifiés que par l'adoption d'une résolution

restore *vt* restaurer, rétablir; **to restore sb to power** remettre quelqu'un au pouvoir; **if the left-wing government is restored to power** si le gouvernement de gauche revient au pouvoir

restrict *vt Econ (production)* restreindre, limiter

restricted suffrage *n Pol* suffrage *m* restreint

restriction *n Econ (of production)* restriction *f*, limitation *f*; **to place restrictions on sth** imposer des restrictions *ou* des limitations sur qch

restrictive *adj* restrictif(ive)
◇ *restrictive clause* clause *f* restrictive
◇ *restrictive practices* pratiques *fpl* restrictives

restructure *vt (company, resources)* restructurer, redéployer

restructuring *n (of company, resources)* restructuration *f*, redéploiement *m*

result *n (of election)* résultat *m*; **the**

by-election results will be announced live tonight les résultats des élections partielles seront annoncés ce soir en direct

retail *n*
◇ *Br Econ* ***Retail Price Index*** indice *m* des prix de détail

retaliate *vi* se venger, riposter; **the government retaliated by banning all foreign coal imports** le gouvernement a riposté en interdisant toutes les importations de charbon

retaliation *n* représailles *fpl*

retaliatory *adj* de représailles, de rétorsion; **to take retaliatory measures** exercer des représailles, riposter
◇ *retaliatory attack* riposte *f*
◇ *retaliatory bombing* des représailles *fpl* sous forme de bombardements

return *Pol* **1** *n* **on his return to office** quand il a été réélu
2 *vt Br (elect)* élire; **she was returned as member for Tottenham** elle a été élue députée de Tottenham
3 *vi* **to return to office** être réélu

returning officer *n Pol* président(e) *m,f* du bureau de vote

returns *npl (results)* résultats *mpl*; *(statistics)* statistiques *fpl*, chiffres *mpl*; **the election returns** les résultats des élections; **first returns indicate a swing to the left** les premiers résultats du scrutin indiquent un glissement à gauche

reunification *n Pol* réunification *f*

reunify *vt Pol* réunifier

revaluation *n Econ (of currency)* réévaluation *f*

revalue *vt Econ (currency)* réévaluer

revenue *n* revenu *m*
◇ *revenue sharing* partage *m* des recettes fiscales
◇ *revenue tariff* tarif *m* douanier fiscal

revise *vt (bill, plan)* remanier

revision *n (of bill, plan)* remaniement *m*

revisionism *n* révisionnisme *m*

revisionist **1** *n* révisionniste *mf*
2 *adj* révisionniste

revitalization *n (of economy, region)* revitalisation *f*

revitalize *vt (economy, region)* revitaliser

revival *n (in business, economy)* relance *f*

revive **1** *vt (business, economy)* relancer
2 *vi (of business, economy)* reprendre

revolt *Pol* **1** *n* révolte *f*, rébellion *f*
2 *vi* se révolter, se rebeller, se soulever

revolution *n* révolution *f*

revolutionary **1** *n* révolutionnaire *mf*
2 *adj* révolutionnaire

revolutionism *n* révolutionnarisme *m*

revolutionist **1** *n* révolutionnaire *mf*
2 *adj* révolutionnaire

revolutionize *vt (country)* faire une révolution dans; *(people)* insuffler des idées révolutionnaires à

rhetoric *n* rhétorique *f*; **his speech consisted of nothing but rhetoric** son discours ne consistait qu'en de belles phrases vides de sens; **it's just empty rhetoric** ce ne sont que des mots

Ricardian *Econ* **1** *n* ricardien(enne) *m,f*
2 *adj* ricardien(enne)

Ricardianism *n Econ* ricardisme *m*

rich **1** *npl* **the rich** les riches *mpl*
2 *adj* riche

riding *n Pol (in Canada, New Zealand)* circonscription *f* électorale

rift *Pol* **1** *n* scission *f*; **a rift in the opposition** une scission au sein de l'opposition
2 *vt* scinder
3 *vi* se scinder

right *Pol* **1** *n* **(a) the right** la droite; **to**

be on the right être à droite; **to be to the right** être à droite; **the right is** or **are divided** la droite est divisée; **he's to the right of the party leadership** il est plus à droite que les dirigeants du parti; **the far** or **extreme right** l'extrême droite

(b) *(entitlement)* droit *m*

2 *adv* à droite; **to vote right** voter à droite

◇ *right of association* liberté *f* d'association

◇ *right of asylum* droit *m* d'asile

◇ *Br Right Honourable* = titre donné aux membres du Parlement britannique qui sont également des membres du "Privy Council"; **my Right Honourable Friend** *(form of address in Parliament)* mon honorable collègue; **the Right Honourable Member for Edinburgh West** le député de la circonscription "Edinburgh West"; **the Right Honourable Nicholas Johns has the floor** la parole est à Nicholas Johns

◇ *right to vote* droit *m* de vote

◇ *right wing* droite *f*; **the right wing of the party** l'aile *f* droite du parti

◇ *right to work* liberté *f* du travail

rightism *n Pol* idées *fpl* de droite; *(extreme right)* extrême droite *f*

rightist *Pol* **1** *n (man)* homme *m* de droite; *(woman)* femme *f* de droite

2 *adj* de droite; *(extremely right-wing)* d'extrême droite

right-of-centre *adj Pol* de centre-droite; **her political beliefs are slightly right-of-centre** politiquement, elle se situe plutôt au centre-droit

right-wing *adj Pol* de droite; **a right-wing newspaper** un journal de droite; **she's more right-wing than the others** elle est plus à droite que les autres

right-winger *n Pol (man)* homme *m* de droite, droitiste *mf*; *(woman)* femme *f* de droite, droitiste *mf*; **he's a right-winger** il est de droite; **these measures are unpopular with right-wingers** ces mesures sont peu appréciées par la droite

ring-fence *vt Br (money, funds)* allouer *(à des fins pré-établies par le gouvernement)*

> **❝**
>
> The government has put some money into pay for colleges. Since 2001, £142m of **ring-fenced** funding has supported lecturer pay levels, but staff have to meet certain criteria to receive this award, and the money has not been available to support them. In addition, colleges do not know if such funds will be available to them in years to come.
>
> **❞**

rise 1 *n (increase) (in price, cost of living)* hausse *f*, augmentation *f*; *(of affluence, wealth)* augmentation *f*; **there has been a steep rise in the cost of living** il y a eu une forte augmentation du coût de la vie

2 *vi* **(a)** *(increase) (of price, cost of living)* monter, augmenter; *(of affluence, wealth)* augmenter

(b) *(of Parliament, an assembly) (at end of day)* lever *ou* clore la session; *(at end of session)* entrer en vacances; **Parliament rose for the summer recess** la session parlementaire est close pour les vacances d'été

rising 1 *n* **(a)** *(revolt)* insurrection *f*, soulèvement *m* **(b)** *(of prices, cost of living)* augmentation *f*, hausse *f* **(c)** *(of Parliament, an assembly)* ajournement *m*, clôture *f* de séance

2 *adj (prices, cost of living)* en hausse

risk *n (possibility)* risque *m*

◇ *risk aversion* aversion *f* pour le risque

◇ *risk pooling* mise *f* en commun des risques

◇ *risk premium* prime *f* de risque de marché

rival 1 *n* rival(e) *m,f*

2 *adj* rival(e)

RMT *n Br (abbr* National Union of Rail, Maritime and Transport Workers*)* = syndicat britannique des cheminots et des gens de mer

rogue state n État m voyou, État m paria

roorback n Am Pol pamphlet m diffamatoire

round n (of discussions, negotiations) série f; (of elections) tour m; **the next round of talks will be held in Moscow** les prochains pourparlers auront lieu à Moscou; **he came out on top in the first round of voting** il est arrivé en tête du premier tour des élections

ROW n Econ (abbr **rest of the world**) reste m du monde

royal adj
◇ **royal assent** = signature royale qui officialise une loi
◇ **royal charter** acte m du souverain
◇ **royal commission** = commission nommée par le monarque sur recommandation du premier ministre

RPI n Br Econ (abbr **retail price index**) indice m des prix de détail

RPM n Econ (abbr **resale price maintenance**) prix m de vente imposé

RRR n Econ (abbr **real rate of return**) taux m de rendement réel

RTGS n (abbr **Real-Time Gross Settlement**) RTGS m
◇ **RTGS system** système m RTGS

rubber n
◇ Am Fam Pol **rubber chicken circuit** = série de visites dans de petites villes au cours d'une campagne électorale
◇ Fam **rubber stamp parliament** = parlement qui ne fait qu'entériner les lois

“

In the six-month run up to the election they have accused the president of pulling together a so-called "King's Party," designed to ensure a parliament supportive of the military. "He wants to make his party win a majority of seats by hook or by crook so that that party creates a **rubber stamp parliament** that supports all steps he has taken so far," says Siddique-ul-Farooque of the opposition branch of the Pakistan Muslim League.

”

rule 1 n (government) gouvernement m, autorité f; (reign) règne m; **a return to majority/mob rule** un retour à la démocratie/à l'anarchie; **the territories under French rule** les territoires sous autorité française
2 vt (country, people) gouverner; **to rule a nation** régner sur une nation
3 vi (of monarch, dictator) régner; (of elected government) gouverner

ruler n (sovereign) souverain(e) m,f; (president, prime minister) dirigeant(e) m,f, gouvernant(e) m,f

ruling adj (monarch) régnant(e); (party) au pouvoir; (class) dirigeant(e)
◇ **ruling body** instances fpl (dirigeantes)

rump n (of political party) restant m; **the rump Yugoslavia** ce qui reste de la Yougoslavie
◇ **rump party** parti m croupion
◇ **rump state** état m croupion

run 1 n (a) Am Pol (in election) candidature f; **his run for the presidency** sa candidature à la présidence
(b) Econ (on currency) ruée f (**on** sur); **a run on the banks** un retrait massif des dépôts bancaires
2 vt Am Pol (enter for election) présenter; **they're running a candidate in every constituency** ils présentent un candidat dans chaque circonscription
3 vi Am Pol (be candidate, stand) se présenter; **to run for president** or **the presidency** se présenter aux élections présidentielles, être candidat(e) aux élections présidentielles ou à la présidence; **to run for office** se porter candidat(e); **she's running on a law-and-**

order ticket elle se présente aux élections avec un programme basé sur la lutte contre l'insécurité; **he ran against Bush in 2000** il s'est présenté contre Bush en 2000

running mate n Am Pol candidat(e) m,f à la vice-présidence

"

Joseph Lieberman's nomination as Al Gore's **running mate** in 2000 made him the first Jew to run on a US presidential ticket. Since then, the 60-year-old senator for Connecticut has left no-one in any doubt that he has presidential ambitions of his own.

"

run-off election n Pol élection f pour départager deux candidats

S

SADC n (abbr **Southern African Development Community**) SADC f

safe seat n Br Pol = siège de député qui traditionnellement va toujours au même parti

Boris Johnson, the colourful editor of the Spectator, took the **safe seat** of Henley – the former seat of the former deputy prime minister, Michael Heseltine – for the Conservatives by a huge majority. Mr Johnson took the seat as expected with a majority of over 11,000, taking 46.1% of the vote, although the majority was lower than in 1997.

salary n Econ salaire m
◇ **salary grade** échelon m des salaires
◇ **salary grading** indice m de rémunération, indice m de traitement
◇ **salary scale** grille f des salaires, échelle f des salaires
◇ **salary structure** structure f des salaires

sale n (act, event) vente f; **sales** (turnover) chiffre m d'affaires; (sector) la vente
◇ **sales monopoly** monopole m de vente

sample 1 n échantillon m; **a representative sample of the population** un échantillon représentatif de la population
2 vt (public opinion) sonder

sampling n échantillonnage m

sanction 1 n **(a)** (approval) sanction f, accord m, consentement m; **with the sanction of the government** avec l'accord du gouvernement; **it hasn't yet been given official sanction** ceci n'a pas encore été officiellement approuvé ou sanctionné, ceci n'a pas encore eu l'approbation ou sanction officielle
(b) (punitive measure) sanction f; **to impose (economic) sanctions on a country** prendre des sanctions (économiques) à l'encontre d'un pays
2 vt (authorize) sanctionner, entériner; **to sanction a plan** donner son accord ou son aval à un plan
◇ **sanctions busting** violation f des sanctions

Sapard n EU (abbr **Special Accession Programme for Agriculture and Rural Development**) SAPARD m

satellite 1 n (country) satellite m
2 adj
◇ **satellite country** pays m satellite
◇ **satellite nation** nation f satellite

save 1 vt (money) (keep for future) mettre de côté; (not waste) économiser
2 vi (put money aside) économiser, faire des économies; **to save on sth** économiser sur qch

saving n épargne f; Econ **savings** dépôts mpl d'épargne
◇ Am **savings and loan association** ≃ société f de crédit immobilier
◇ Econ **savings rate** taux m d'épargne
◇ Econ **savings ratio** taux m d'épargne

Say's Law n Econ loi f de Say

scale n Econ échelle f

scarce adj Econ rare

scarcity n Econ rareté f

scheme n (plan) plan m, projet m; **the unions would not agree to the new productivity scheme** les syndicats ont refusé d'accepter ou ont rejeté le nouveau plan de productivité; **a scheme for new investment** un plan ou projet pour de nouveaux investissements; **government unemployment schemes** plans mpl antichômage du gouvernement

Schengen agreement n accord m de Schengen

scission n Pol scission f

Scotland n
◇ **Scotland Office** = ministère des affaires écossaises
◇ **Scotland Secretary** = ministre des affaires écossaises à Westminster

Scottish adj
◇ **Scottish Executive** = gouvernement semi-autonome de l'Écosse
◇ **Scottish National Party** = parti indépendantiste écossais fondé en 1934
◇ **Scottish Office** = ministère des affaires écossaises
◇ **Scottish Parliament** parlement m écossais

scratch vt Am Pol (candidate) rayer de la liste

scrutineer n Br Pol scrutateur(trice) m,f

scrutinize vt Br Pol scruter, pointer

scrutiny n Br Pol dépouillement m (d'un scrutin)

SDLP n (abbr **Social Democratic and Labour Party**) = parti travailliste d'Irlande du Nord

SDR n Econ (abbr **Special Drawing Rights**) droits mpl de tirage spéciaux

SEA n (abbr **Single European Act**) AUE m

search unemployment n Econ chômage m frictionnel

seasonal adj Econ saisonnier(ère)
◇ **seasonal adjustment** correction f des variations saisonnières
◇ **seasonal fluctuation** fluctuation f saisonnière
◇ **seasonal index** coefficient m saisonnier
◇ **seasonal swings** fluctuations fpl saisonnières
◇ **seasonal unemployment** chômage m saisonnier
◇ **seasonal variations** variations fpl saisonnières

seasonality n Econ caractère m saisonnier

seasonally adv Econ de façon saisonnière
◇ **seasonally adjusted index** indice m corrigé des variations saisonnières
◇ **seasonally adjusted statistics** statistiques fpl corrigées des variations saisonnières, statistiques fpl désaisonnalisées

seat n Pol siège m; **he kept/lost his seat** il a été/n'a pas été réélu; **she has a seat in Parliament** elle est députée; **he was elected to a seat on the council** il a été élu conseiller municipal; **the government has a 30-seat majority** le gouvernement a une majorité de 30 sièges

secede vi Pol faire sécession, se séparer; **they voted to secede from the federation** ils ont voté en faveur de leur sécession de la fédération

seceder n Pol sécessionniste mf, séparatiste mf

seceding adj Pol sécessionniste

secession n Pol sécession f, scission f

secessionism n Pol sécessionnisme m

secessionist Pol **1** n sécessionniste mf, séparatiste mf
2 adj sécessionniste

second adj
◇ Pol **second ballot** deuxième tour m
◇ Econ **second best** optimum m second
◇ Pol **second chamber** deuxième

chambre *f*; *(in UK)* Chambre *f* des lords; *(in US)* Sénat *m*

◇ *Br Parl* **second reading** *(of bill)* deuxième lecture *f*

secondary *adj Econ* secondaire

◇ **secondary employment** activité *f* secondaire

◇ **secondary industry** industrie *f* secondaire

◇ **secondary legislation** législation *f* secondaire

◇ **secondary market** marché *m* secondaire

◇ **secondary sector** secteur *m* secondaire

second-best theory *n Econ* théorie *f* de l'optimum de second rang

secret *adj*

◇ **secret ballot** vote *m* à bulletin secret

◇ **secret service** *(government organization)* services *mpl* secrets *ou* spéciaux

◇ **the Secret Service** *(in US)* = service de protection des hauts fonctionnaires américains et de leurs familles

secretariat *n* secrétariat *m*

secretary *n* (a) *Pol (minister)* ministre *m*; *(non-elected official)* secrétaire *mf* d'État (b) *(diplomat)* secrétaire *mf* d'ambassade

◇ *Am* **Secretary of Agriculture** ministre *m* de l'Agriculture

◇ *Am* **Secretary of Commerce** ministre *m* du Commerce

◇ *Am* **Secretary of Defense** ministre *m* de la Défense

◇ *Am* **Secretary of Education** ≃ ministre *m* de l'Éducation nationale

◇ *Am* **Secretary of Energy** = ministre de l'énergie

◇ *Am* **Secretary of Health and Human Services** ≃ ministre *m* de la Santé et de la Sécurité sociale

◇ *Am* **Secretary of Housing and Urban Development** = ministre du logement et du développement urbain

◇ *Am* **Secretary of (the) Interior** ministre *m* de l'Intérieur

◇ *Am* **Secretary of Labor** ministre *m* du Travail

◇ *Am* **Secretary of the Senate** secrétaire *mf* du Sénat

◇ **Secretary of State** *(in UK)* ministre *m*; *(in US)* secrétaire *mf* d'État, ministre *m* des Affaires étrangères

◇ *Br* **Secretary of State for Environment, Food and Rural Affairs** = ministre de l'environnement, de l'alimentation et des affaires rurales

◇ *Br* **Secretary of State for Transport** ministre *m* des Transports

◇ *Br* **Secretary of State for Work and Pensions** = ministre du travail et des retraites

◇ *Am* **Secretary of Transportation** ministre *m* des Transports

◇ *Am* **Secretary of (the) Treasury** ≃ ministre *m* de l'Économie et des Finances

◇ *Am* **Secretary of Veterans' Affairs** = ministre des anciens combattants

secretary-general *n* secrétaire *mf* général(e)

◇ **Secretary-General of the UN** secrétaire *mf* général(e) de l'ONU

secretaryship *n* secrétariat *m*

Section 28 *n Pol* = disposition juridique en Grande-Bretagne interdisant aux enseignants du secondaire d'aborder le thème de l'homosexualité en classe

"

Scottish Education Minister Sam Galbraith has repeated his pledge that parents will continue to be consulted over the repeal of **Section 28** ... Mr Galbraith sets out the reasons – personal and on behalf of the Scottish Executive – for the law being abolished. **Section 28** prevents local authorities from promoting homosexuality in state-maintained schools. Mr Galbraith says: "There have been fears that removing **Section 28** will allow our schools to be overrun with pornography. As a parent myself, I can reassure everyone in Scotland that this will not happen."

꡷꡷

sector n Econ secteur m

secure vt Pol (seat) obtenir; **to secure a majority** emporter la majorité

securities npl titres mpl, actions fpl, valeurs fpl

segregate vt Pol soumettre à la ségrégation

segregated adj Pol où l'on pratique la ségrégation

segregation n Pol ségrégation f

segregationist Pol **1** n ségrégationniste mf
2 adj ségrégationniste

seignorage n Econ seigneurage m

SEIU n (abbr **Service Employees International Union**) = syndicat nord-américain regroupant principalement des employés des services publics et de la santé

seize vt (power) accaparer

select committee n Parl commission f d'enquête parlementaire

selective distribution n Econ distribution f sélective

self-determination n Pol autodétermination f

self-determined adj Pol autodéterminé(e)

self-employed **1** adj indépendant(e), qui travaille à son compte
2 npl **the self-employed** les travailleurs mpl indépendants

self-employment n travail m en indépendant, travail m à son propre compte

self-governing adj Pol autonome

self-government n Pol autonomie f

self-interest n Econ intérêt m personnel

self-management n autogestion f

self-managing adj d'autogestion

self-regulating adj autorégulateur(trice)

self-regulation n autorégulation f

self-rule n Pol autonomie f

self-ruling adj Pol autonome

self-sufficiency n (of nation, resources) autosuffisance f, autosubsistance f; Econ autarcie f

self-sufficient adj (nation, resources) autosuffisant(e), autosubsistant(e); Econ autarcique; **self-sufficient in oil** autosuffisant(e) en pétrole

sell vt vendre

seller n Econ offreur(euse) m,f, vendeur(euse) m,f
◊ **seller's market** marché m à la hausse, marché m vendeur

semi-presidential adj Pol semi-présidentiel(elle)

semi-public company n société f d'économie mixte

Senate n Pol Sénat m; **the United States Senate** le Sénat américain; **the French Senate** le Sénat
◊ **Senate majority** majorité f sénatoriale

senator n Pol sénateur m

senatorial adj Pol sénatorial(e)

▶ **send forth** vt sep Am Pol **the senate has sent forth the bill to the president** le sénat a transmis le projet de loi au président

senior adj
◊ **senior civil servant** administrateur(trice) m,f civil(e)
◊ **senior government official** haut(e) fonctionnaire m,f

separate **1** vi Pol (of party) se scinder; **the party separated into various factions** le parti s'est scindé en diverses factions
2 adj
◊ **separate peace** paix f séparée

separation n (a) (division) séparation f; **the separation of Church and State** la séparation de l'Église et de l'État (b) Pol (in party) scission f

◇ Pol **separation of powers** séparation f des pouvoirs

separatism n Pol séparatisme m

separatist Pol **1** n séparatiste mf
2 adj séparatiste, indépendantiste
◇ **separatist movement** mouvement m séparatiste ou indépendantiste

serjeant-at-arms, Am **sergeant-at-arms** n Parl ≃ huissier m d'armes

serve vt (monarch, country) servir

service n Econ service m; **goods and services** biens mpl et services mpl; **more and more people will be working in services** de plus en plus de gens travailleront dans le tertiaire
◇ **service industry** industrie f de services
◇ **service sector** secteur m tertiaire, tertiaire m, secteur m des services

session n Pol séance f, session f; **the House is not in session during the summer months** la Chambre ne siège pas pendant les mois d'été

setaside n EU gel m des terres

setback n revers m, échec m; **the government has suffered a setback in its plans to change the legislation** le gouvernement a vu son projet de réforme compromis; **this has been a severe setback for the government** cela a constitué un grave revers ou échec pour le gouvernement

shadow adj Br Pol **the Shadow Education Secretary/Defence Secretary** le porte-parole de l'opposition pour l'éducation/pour la défense nationale
◇ Br Pol **shadow cabinet** cabinet m fantôme

shake-out n Econ dégraissage m

shared powers npl Pol pouvoirs mpl partagés

share economy n économie f d'actionnariat populaire

shift Pol **1** n (change) changement m; **a shift to the right/left** un glissement à droite/gauche
2 vi (change) changer; **their policy** has shifted over the last week leur politique a changé ou s'est modifiée au cours de la semaine

shop steward n Br délégué(e) m,f syndical(e)

short-term adj (forecast, loan) à court terme
◇ EU **short-term monetary support** soutien m monétaire à court terme
◇ **short-term planning** planification f à court terme
◇ **short-term unemployment** chômage m à court terme

short-termism n politique f à court terme, court terme m

short-time (working) n Econ chômage m partiel; **to be on short-time (working)** être en chômage partiel

shuttle diplomacy n Pol = pratique diplomatique de certains hommes politiques qui consiste à voyager dans le monde pour résoudre les problèmes

> 44
>
> UK Prime Minister Tony Blair is set to renew his efforts to cement a coalition against global terrorism with a new round of **shuttle diplomacy**. Russia and Pakistan are both reportedly expecting Mr Blair at some point after he sets off on Thursday afternoon, although Downing Street will only go as far as confirming a trip is planned.
>
> 77

shyster n Fam (politician) politicien(enne) m,f véreux(euse)

> 44
>
> The former cabinet minister Mo Mowlam yesterday accused Tony Blair of neglecting Britain's problems, throwing away the British constitution, and shaping himself as a president ... "Even the cabinet has noticed," she added. "As one of them at the Chequers away-day said:

'People think we are a load of **shy-sters**'.' Dr Mowlam's comments came as Labour's longest-serving MP, Tam Dalyell, suggested it might be time for a leadership challenge.

"

sign vt (document) signer

signatory country n Pol pays m signataire

signature n (on document) signature f; Am Pol **the bill is awaiting signature** le projet de loi attend la signature du président

silent majority n majorité f silencieuse

simple majority vote n Pol (system) scrutin m majoritaire à un tour

single adj
◇ **single currency** monnaie f unique
◇ **Single European Act** Acte m unique européen
◇ **Single European Market** Marché m unique européen
◇ **Single Market** Marché m unique
◇ Pol **single transferable vote** scrutin m uninominal préférentiel avec report de voix

single-chamber adj Pol monocaméral

Sinn Féin n le Sinn Féin (action politique de l'IRA)

sin tax n (on alcohol, tobacco) = appellation humoristique de la taxe sur l'alcool et le tabac

"

Mr Brown said he would raise the price of cigarettes 5% above the rate of inflation - roughly equal to another 25p a pack - and he promised this would mean an additional £300m going directly to the health service. On the other "**sin tax**" – alcohol duty – Mr Brown secured a more even reception with most of the drinks industry remaining unfazed by his decision to freeze duty on a

bottle of spirits, to increase the price of a pint of beer by 1p and a bottle of wine by 4p.

"

sit vi Br Pol (a) (be a member) **to sit in Parliament** ≃ être député(e); **he sat for Swansea** il était député de Swansea (b) (be in session) être en séance, siéger; **the council was still sitting at midnight** à minuit, le conseil siégeait toujours ou était toujours en séance; **the House sits for another two months** la session de la Chambre doit durer encore deux mois

sitting n Pol (of parliament, committee) séance f, session f

SIU n (abbr **Seafarers International Union of North America**) = syndicat nord-américain de la marine marchande

slate Am Pol **1** n liste f provisoire de candidats; **the Republicans have a full slate** les Républicains présentent des candidats dans toutes les circonscriptions
2 vt proposer (un candidat); **Magee is slated for President** Magee a été choisi comme candidat aux élections présidentielles

sleaze n Fam (corruption) corruption f; **it's the sleaze factor that led to the government's downfall** ce sont les affaires de corruption dans lesquelles le gouvernement a été impliqué qui en ont provoqué la chute

"

The Conservatives have renewed their attack on the government over its links with collapsed US energy giant Enron. Ministers have continued to deny allegations of **sleaze** after it emerged Enron handed over £38,000 to Labour party funds, money which the Tories say gave it access to ministers – a claim denied by Labour.

"

sleeping economy n économie f à ressources sous-exploitées

slide Econ **1** n glissement m; **a yearly four percent slide** une progression annuelle de quatre pour cent en glissement; **the alarming slide of the economy** le dérapage alarmant de l'économie
2 vi glisser

sliding scale n Econ échelle f mobile

slow adj (business, market) calme

► **slow down 1** vt sep ralentir; **production is slowed down during the winter** pendant l'hiver, la production tourne au ralenti
2 vi ralentir; **growth slowed down in the second quarter** il y a eu un ralentissement de la croissance au cours du deuxième trimestre

slowdown n (economic) ralentissement m (**in** de)

sluggish adj Econ (market) inactif(-ive)

sluggishness n Econ (of market) inactivité f

slump 1 n **(a)** (in prices, market) chute f, forte baisse f, effondrement m; **there has been a slump in investment** les investissements sont en forte baisse; **a slump in demand** une forte baisse de la demande **(b)** Econ (economic depression) crise f économique; (recession) récession f
2 vi (of prices, market) s'effondrer

slumpflation n Econ = forte récession accompagnée d'une inflation des prix et des salaires

❝

Prior to the Soviet transition to a market economy, there had been several notable conquests of severe inflation elsewhere – for example, in 1985–86 in Bolivia, a developing economy, and in Israel, a developed one. Developed countries had experienced deflation and depression (as in the 1930s) as well as stagflation (inflation without growth), but **slumpflation** (high inflation and seriously negative growth) was unprecedented.

❞

slush fund n Pol caisse f noire

small adj
◊ **small business** (firm) petite entreprise f, PME f; (shop) petit commerce m
◊ **small businessman** petit entrepreneur m ou patron m
◊ Br **Small Business Service** = service du ministère britannique du Commerce et de l'Industrie qui défend les intérêts des petites entreprises

SME n (abbr **small and medium-sized enterprise**) PME f

smear 1 n (defamation) diffamation f; (verbal) calomnie f; **to use smear tactics** avoir recours à la calomnie
2 vt (defame) diffamer; (verbally) calomnier; (person's reputation) salir; **an attempt to smear the prime minister** une tentative de diffamation du Premier ministre
◊ **smear campaign** campagne f de diffamation ou dénigrement

SMI n (abbr **small and medium-sized industry**) PMI f

smokestack industry n industrie f lourde

snake n Econ serpent m (monétaire)

snap election n Pol élection f surprise; **the PM has called a snap election** le Premier ministre a annoncé une élection surprise

SNP n (abbr **Scottish National Party**) = parti indépendantiste écossais fondé en 1934

social adj social(e)
◊ **social benefits** acquis mpl sociaux
◊ **the Social Chapter** le volet social (du traité de Maastricht)
◊ **Social Charter** Charte f sociale
◊ **social class** classe f sociale

⋄ *social contract* contrat *m* social, convention *f* sociale
⋄ *social cost* coût *m* social
⋄ *Econ* *social credit* = doctrine selon laquelle le gouvernement doit exercer un contrôle sur les prix afin de remédier aux inégalités de pouvoir d'achat
⋄ *social democracy (system)* social-démocratie *f*; *(country)* démocratie *f* socialiste; **we live in a social democracy** nous vivons dans une démocratie socialiste
⋄ *social democrat* social(e)-démocrate *m,f*
⋄ *Social Democratic and Labour Party* = parti travailliste d'Irlande du Nord
⋄ *Social Democratic Party* Parti *m* social-démocrate
⋄ *social dumping* dumping *m* social
⋄ *social economy* économie *f* sociale
⋄ *social Europe* l'Europe *f* sociale
⋄ *social integration* insertion *f ou* intégration *f* sociale
⋄ *social justice* justice *f* sociale
⋄ *social mobility* mobilité *f* sociale
⋄ *social movement* mouvement *m* social
⋄ *social ownership* propriété *f* collective
⋄ *social rights* droits *mpl* sociaux
⋄ *social security* prestations *fpl* sociales; *Br (money paid to unemployed)* ≃ allocations *fpl* de chômage; **to be on social security** toucher une aide sociale
⋄ *social security benefits* prestations *fpl* sociales
⋄ *social security contribution* prélèvement *m* social
⋄ *social security system* régime *m* de Sécurité sociale
⋄ *social stratification* stratification *f* sociale
⋄ *social unrest (discontent)* malaise *m* social; *(disorder)* troubles *mpl* sociaux
⋄ *social welfare* protection *f* sociale
⋄ *social welfare system* système *m ou* régime *m* de protection sociale

social-democratic *adj* social(e)-démocrate

socialism *n Pol* socialisme *m*

socialist *Pol* **1** *n* socialiste *mf*
2 *adj* socialiste
⋄ *socialist economy* économie *f* socialiste

socialistic *adj Pol* socialiste, de nature socialiste

socialization *n Pol* socialisation *f*

socialize *vt Pol* socialiser

social-revolutionary **1** *n* social(e)-révolutionnaire *m,f*
2 *adj* social(e)-révolutionnaire

society *n* société *f*

socio-economic *adj* socio-économique
⋄ *socio-economic classification* classification *f* socio-professionnelle
⋄ *socio-economic group* groupe *m* socio-économique

soft *adj*
⋄ *soft currency* monnaie *f ou* devise *f* faible
⋄ *soft landing* atterrisage *m* en douceur
⋄ *Pol* **the soft left** la gauche modérée
⋄ *Am Pol* *soft line* ligne *f* de conduite modérée; **to take a soft line on sth** adopter une ligne modérée sur qch; *(compromise)* adopter une politique de compromis sur qch
⋄ *Econ* *soft loan* prêt *m* avantageux *ou* à des conditions avantageuses
⋄ *Am Pol* *soft money* = sommes employées pour le financement d'une campagne électorale en employant divers stratagèmes afin de rester dans la légalité
⋄ *Pol* **the soft right** la droite modérée
⋄ *Econ* *soft terms* conditions *fpl* favorables

SOGAT *n* (*abbr* **Society of Graphical and Allied Trades**) = syndicat britannique des métiers du graphisme

Solicitor General *n* **(a)** *(in England and Wales)* conseil *m* juridique de la

Couronne **(b)** *(in US)* représentant(e) *m,f* du gouvernement *(auprès de la Cour suprême)*

solid *adj* Pol *(firm)* massif(ive); *(unanimous)* unanime; **we have the solid support of the electorate** nous avons le soutien massif des électeurs; **the south is solid for the Christian Democrats** le sud soutient massivement les démocrates-chrétiens

solidarity *n* solidarité *f*; **they went on strike in solidarity with the miners** ils ont fait grève par solidarité avec les mineurs

◇ **solidarity organization** organisation *f* de solidarité

◇ **solidarity principle** principe *m* de solidarité

◇ **solidarity strike** grève *f* de solidarité

Southern Europe *n* l'Europe *f* méridionale, l'Europe *f* du Sud

soundbite *n* petite phrase *f (prononcée par un homme politique à la radio ou à la télévision pour frapper les esprits)*

┌─ **"** ──────────────

Deputy Prime Minister John Prescott has said Labour needs more than just **soundbites** and spin to win over voters. Mr Prescott demanded an end to the ceaseless repetition of approved phrases like "for the many, not the few" and "boom and bust" in favour of an effort to enthuse Labour supporters into spreading the government's message personally.

────────────── **"** ─┘

sovereign Pol **1** *n* souverain(e) *m,f*
2 *adj (state, territory)* souverain(e); *(powers)* souverain(e), suprême; *(rights)* de souveraineté; **Parliament remains sovereign** le parlement reste souverain

◇ **sovereign loan** prêt *m* garanti par l'État

sovereignty *n* Pol souveraineté *f*; **with no loss of sovereignty** sans perte de souveraineté

Soviet 1 *n (inhabitant)* Soviétique *mf*
2 *adj* soviétique

◇ **the Soviet Bloc** le bloc soviétique

◇ **Soviet Russia** la Russie soviétique

◇ **Soviet Union** l'Union *f* soviétique; **in the Soviet Union** en Union soviétique

soviet *n (council)* soviet *m*

sovietism *n* soviétisme *m*

sovietization *n* soviétisation *f*

sovietize *vt* soviétiser

Speaker *n* Parl speaker *m*, président(e) *m,f* de l'assemblée; Br **Mr/ Madam Speaker** = formule utilisée pour s'adresser à la personne qui préside la Chambre des communes; **to catch the Speaker's eye** attirer l'attention du/de la président(e)

◇ Am **the Speaker of the House** = le président de la Chambre des représentants américaine

◇ Br **the Speaker of the House of Commons** = le président de la Chambre des communes

spearhead 1 *n* fer *m* de lance
2 *vt (campaign, movement)* mener, être à la tête de

special *adj*

◇ Econ **special arrangements** régime *m* préférentiel

◇ Econ **special drawing rights** droits *mpl* de tirage spéciaux

◇ Econ **special economic zone** pôle *m* de conversion

◇ Pol **special powers** pouvoirs *mpl* extraordinaires *ou* exceptionnels

◇ Pol **special relationship** = relations d'amitié entre les USA et la Grande-Bretagne

◇ Pol **special session** *(of assembly, committee)* assemblée *f* extraordinaire

┌─ **"** ──────────────

From Winston Churchill to Tony Blair, Hotline to the President makes clear that the man in the Oval Office always calls the shots. The Anglo-American **special relationship** may grant unrivalled access to prime ministers who can occasionally restrain or goad the president, but key military decisions are invariably taken well above a prime minister's head.

"

spectrum n the political spectrum l'éventail m politique; **people across the political spectrum** des représentants de toutes les tendances politiques

speech n discours m; **to make a speech on** or **about sth** faire ou prononcer un discours sur qch

speechify vi Pej discourir, faire de beaux discours

speechifying n Pej beaux discours mpl, laïus m

speechwriter n personne f qui écrit des discours; **she's the president's speechwriter** c'est elle qui écrit les discours du président

spend 1 n dépenses fpl; **this year's spend has exceeded the budget by ten percent** nous avons dépassé de dix pour cent les dépenses prévues au budget de l'année écoulée
2 vt (money) dépenser

spending n dépenses fpl; **a cut in defence spending** une réduction du budget de la défense
◇ **spending bill** projet m de loi sur les dépenses
◇ **spending cuts** réductions fpl des dépenses
◇ Econ **spending power** pouvoir m d'achat
◇ **spending review** examen m des dépenses

spillover n Econ retombées fpl (économiques)

spin Fam Pej Pol **1** n (on information) **to put the right spin on a story** présenter une affaire sous un angle favorable; **the government put its own spin on the situation** le gouvernement a présenté la situation sous un angle qui lui convenait; **the government has**

been criticized for indulging in too much spin** on a reproché au gouvernement de trop manipuler les informations fournies au public; **this government is all spin and no substance** ce gouvernement est très fort pour le bavardage mais n'a aucun programme réel
2 vi (of spin doctor) présenter les choses sous un angle favorable
◇ **spin doctor** = chargé des relations publiques d'un parti politique

"

The much discredited new Scottish Parliament building is to have its own **spin doctor**. Sources at Holyrood confirmed yesterday that they are on the brink of appointing the man or woman who will be set the task of rescuing the project from its present place in the demonology of devolution. The parliament authorities believe apparently that "there is a positive story to be told", despite the ever-increasing cost of the building, which has risen eight-fold from the original £40 million to more than £300 million in four years.

"

spiral Econ **1** n spirale f; **an inflationary spiral** une spirale inflationniste
2 vi (of prices, inflation) s'envoler, monter en flèche; **to spiral downwards** chuter

splinter 1 vi (of political party) se scinder, se fractionner
2 n
◇ **splinter group** groupe m dissident ou scissionniste

split Pol **1** n (in party) scission f, schisme m
2 vt (party) diviser, créer ou provoquer une scission dans; **this split the party three ways** ceci a divisé ou scindé le parti en trois; **to split the vote** disperser les voix; **the vote was split down the middle** les deux camps avaient obtenu exactement le même nombre de voix; Am **to split one's ticket**

panacher son bulletin de vote

3 vi (of party) se scinder; **the party split over the question of pollution** le parti s'est scindé ou divisé sur la question de la pollution

4 adj

◇ Am **split ticket** panachage m

▸ **split up** vi Pol (of party) se diviser, se scinder

splitting up n Pol (of party) scission f

split-up n Pol (of party) scission f

spoil Pol **1** vt (ballot paper) rendre nul (nulle)

2 n

◇ Am **spoils system** système m des dépouilles

spoiler n Pol (candidate) = candidat qui se présente dans le but pur et simple de compromettre les chances d'un autre candidat

spoilsman n Am Pol = personne qui bénéficie d'un piston politique

spoilt adj Pol (ballot paper) nul (nulle)

spokesman n porte-parole m inv; **a government spokesman, a spokesman for the government** un porte-parole du gouvernement

spokesperson n porte-parole m inv

spokeswoman n porte-parole m inv (femme)

sponsor vt Pol (**a**) (bill) présenter (**b**) (candidate) parrainer

sponsorship n Pol (**a**) (of bill) proposition f, présentation f (**b**) (of candidate) parrainage m

Sports Minister n Br Pol ministre m des Sports

squeeze Econ **1** n (on profits, wages) baisse f (**on** de); **a squeeze on jobs** des suppressions fpl d'emploi

2 vt (profits, budget) réduire; (taxpayer, workers) pressurer; **the British car industry has been squeezed by foreign competition** l'industrie automobile britannique subit la pression de la concurrence étrangère

stability n (of prices, economy, political situation) stabilité f; **a period of political stability** une période de stabilité politique

◇ EU **stability pact** pacte m de stabilité et de croissance

stabilization n (of prices, economy, political situation) stabilisation f

◇ **stabilization fund** fonds m de stabilisation

◇ **stabilization plan** plan m d'assainissement

stabilize **1** vt (prices, economy, political situation) stabiliser

2 vi (of prices, economy, political situation) se stabiliser

stabilizer n Econ stabilisateur m

stabilizing adj stabilisateur(trice); **to have a stabilizing influence on prices** exercer une influence stabilisatrice sur les prix

◇ **stabilizing policy** politique f de stabilité

stable adj (prices, economy, political situation) stable

staff n Pol état-major m; **she was asked to join the President's campaign staff** on lui a demandé de faire partie de l'état-major de campagne du Président

stagflation n Econ stagflation f

“

The Government's main fear for the coming year is that the economy will enter a period of **stagflation**, with minimal growth combined with stubborn inflationary pressures.

”

stagnant adj (economy, prices, trade) stagnant(e)

stagnate vi (of economy, prices, trade) stagner

stagnation n (of economy, prices, trade) stagnation f

Stalinism n Pol stalinisme m

Stalinist *Pol* **1** *n* stalinien(enne) *m,f*
 2 *adj* stalinien(enne)

stalking horse *n Pol* **we'll use him as
a stalking horse** on va s'en servir
comme d'un candidat bidon

> **"**
>
> It is true that Labour has never over-
> thrown a leader while in office, but Mr
> Blair himself has changed the party
> in all sorts of unthinkable ways ... The
> atmosphere indeed is reminiscent of
> the late 1980s, right down to the
> whispers that the Prime Minister has
> gone slightly mad. Is it time for a La-
> bour version of Sir Anthony Meyer,
> the **stalking horse** who first stood
> against Lady Thatcher to test the ex-
> tent of serious opposition to her? And
> should anybody on the left support
> such an idea?
>
> **"**

stand *vi Br (in election)* se présenter,
être candidat(e); **she stood for Waltham** elle a été candidate à la circonscription de Waltham; **will he stand
for re-election?** va-t-il se représenter
aux élections?; **she's standing as an independent** elle se présente en tant
que candidate indépendante

▸ **stand down** *vi Br Pol (withdraw)* se
désister; *(resign)* démissionner; **will
he stand down in favour of a younger
candidate?** va-t-il se désister en faveur d'un candidat plus jeune?

standard **1** *n (official specification,
norm)* norme *f*
 2 *adj (ordinary, regular)* normal(e)
◇ **standard bearer** *(of cause)* porte-
drapeau *m*; *(of political party)* chef
m de file
◇ **standards committee** organisme *m*
de normalisation
◇ **standard deviation** *(in statistics)*
écart-type *m*
◇ **standard error** *(in statistics)* écart-
type *m*
◇ *Econ* **standard of living** standard *m*
de vie

◇ **standard rate** *(of tax)* taux *m* standard

standardization *n* standardisation *f*

standardize *vt* standardiser

standing **1** *n (position) (of country)*
rang *m*, place *f*; *(of party, politician)*
popularité *f*; **her standing in the opinion polls is at its lowest yet** sa cote de
popularité dans les sondages est au
plus bas; **the standings in the Senate
are Liberals 62 seats and Conservatives
30** la répartition des sièges au Sénat
est de 62 sièges pour les libéraux et
30 pour les conservateurs
 2 *adj*
◇ *Pol* **standing committee** comité *m*
permanent
◇ *Br Pol* **standing order** règlement *m*
intérieur *(d'une assemblée délibérative)*

standoff *n Pol (inconclusive clash)* af-
frontement *m* indécis; *(deadlock)* impasse *f*; **their debate ended in a
standoff** leur débat n'a rien donné;
**the standoff over the budget is making
Wall Street nervous** l'impasse dans laquelle se trouve le budget inquiète
Wall Street

staple *n Econ (item)* article *m* de base;
(raw material) matière *f* première

state **1** *n* **(a)** *Pol (nation, body politic)*
État *m*; **a state within a state** un État
dans l'État **(b)** *(in US, Australia,
India)* État *m* **(c)** *(condition)* état *m*
 2 *adj* **(a)** *(of, relating to the state) (security, pension, law)* de l'État; *(business, documents)* d'État **(b)** *(public)
(sector)* public(ique) **(c)** *(nationalized)
(airline, railway)* national(e) **(d)** *Am
(not federal) (law, legislature, policy)*
de l'État **(e)** *(official, ceremonious)
(dinner)* officiel(elle)
◇ **state budget** budget *m* de l'État
◇ **state capitalism** capitalisme *m*
d'État
◇ **state control** contrôle *m* étatique;
(doctrine) étatisme *m*; **to be put** or
placed under state control être na-
tionalisé(e)

◇ Am **State Department** ≃ ministère m des Affaires étrangères

◇ **state of emergency** état m d'urgence; **a state of emergency has been declared** l'état d'urgence a été déclaré

◇ **state government** gouvernement m d'État

◇ **state intervention** intervention f de l'État

◇ **States of Jersey** États mpl de Jersey

◇ **state monopoly** monopole m d'État

◇ **state monopoly capitalism** capitalisme m monopolistique d'État

◇ **state occasion** cérémonie f officielle

◇ **the State Opening of Parliament** = ouverture officielle du Parlement britannique en présence du souverain

◇ **state paper** imprimé m officiel

◇ **state planning** planification f nationale

◇ **state revenue** recettes fpl publiques

◇ **state secret** secret m d'État

◇ Br **state sector** secteur m public

◇ **state of siege** état m de siège

◇ **State socialism** socialisme m d'État

◇ **state subsidy** subvention f d'État

◇ **State Supreme Court** = la plus haute instance judiciaire dans chaque État américain

◇ Am **State of the Union message** discours m sur l'état de l'Union

◇ **state visit** visite f officielle; **he's on a state visit to Japan** il est en voyage officiel au Japon

state-controlled adj étatisé(e), étatique

statecraft n (in politics) habileté f politique; (in diplomacy) (art m de la) diplomatie f; **he is a master of statecraft** c'est un maître confirmé de la diplomatie

statehood n **the struggle for statehood** la lutte pour l'indépendance; **to achieve statehood** devenir un État

stateless adj apatride

◇ **stateless person** apatride mf

◇ **stateless society** société f sans État

statelessness n apatridie f

statelet n Pol micro-État m

statement n déclaration f, affirmation f; (to the press) communiqué m; **to put out** or **to issue** or **to make a statement about sth** émettre un communiqué concernant qch; **the minister was asked to withdraw his statement** le ministre a été prié de retirer sa déclaration; **a statement to the effect that...** une déclaration selon laquelle...

state-owned adj nationalisé(e)

◇ **state-owned company** société f d'État, entreprise f publique

statesman n homme m d'État

statesmanlike adj digne d'un homme d'État

statesmanship n qualités fpl d'homme d'État; **he showed great statesmanship in dealing with the crisis** il a traité cette crise avec toute l'habileté d'un grand chef d'État

stateswoman n femme f politique

Stationery Office n = maison d'édition britannique publiant les documents approuvés par le Parlement, les ministères et autres organismes officiels, ≃ Imprimerie f nationale

statism n étatisme m

statist 1 n étatiste mf
2 adj étatiste

statistic n chiffre m, statistique f; **that particular statistic is certain to embarrass the government** ces chiffres ou statistiques vont sûrement embarrasser le gouvernement

statistical adj (analysis, data, technique) statistique; (error) de statistique

◇ **statistical indicator** indicateur m statistique

◇ **statistical inference** inférence f statistique

statistically adv statistiquement

statistician n statisticien(enne) m,f

statistics 1 n (science) statistique f
2 npl (figures) statistiques fpl, chiffres mpl

status n (standing) statut m; **to have executive/civil servant status** avoir le statut de cadre/de fonctionnaire; **he is asking for political refugee status** il réclame le statut de réfugié politique

statute n loi f; Br Pol (act) acte m du Parlement
◇ Br **statute book** code m (des lois), recueil m de lois; **the new law is not yet on the statute book** la nouvelle loi n'est pas encore entrée en vigueur
◇ **statute law** droit m écrit
◇ **statute of limitations** loi f de prescription, prescription f légale; **the statute of limitations in this country is ten years** dans ce pays, il y a prescription de dix ans

steady 1 adj (growth, increase, decline) régulier(ère), progressif(ive); (price, rate) stable; **inflation remains at a steady five percent** l'inflation s'est stabilisée à cinq pour cent
2 vi (of growth, increase, decline) devenir régulier(ère); (of price, rate) se stabiliser

stealth tax n = mesure visant à augmenter les recettes du gouvernement par un moyen détourné, afin d'éviter une hausse directe et visible des impôts qui mécontenterait les citoyens

> ❝
> The chancellor was accused of introducing a **stealth tax** last night when accountants spotted a £600m increase in national insurance hidden in the post-speech documents.
> ❞

steamroller vt (force) **to steamroller a bill through Parliament** = faire passer une loi à la Chambre sans tenir compte de l'opposition

> ❝
> MPs had been given a free vote on the issue but the outcome will widely be seen as a major humiliation for Mr Blair's re-elected government ... Conservative deputy chairman Nigel Evans said the vote was "a lesson" for the government and "they better think very carefully and make sure that they fully consult with their backbenchers before they try to **steamroller** anything through that is counter to the wishes of parliament".
> ❞

steer vt Pol **to steer a bill through Parliament** réussir à faire voter un projet de loi par le Parlement

steering committee n Pol comité m directeur

sterling n (livre f) sterling m; **in sterling** en livres sterling; **five thousand pounds sterling** cinq mille livres sterling
◇ **sterling area** zone f sterling
◇ **sterling balances** soldes mpl ou balances fpl en sterling
◇ **sterling bloc** bloc m sterling

STMS n EU (abbr **short-term monetary support**) SMCT m

stock n (a) (supply) réserve f, provision f, stock m (b) (shares) (in Britain) valeurs fpl, actions fpl; (in US) actions fpl ordinaires; **stocks and shares** valeurs fpl boursières ou mobilières, titres mpl
◇ **stock exchange** bourse f des valeurs
◇ **the Stock Exchange** la Bourse
◇ **stock market** marché m boursier
◇ **the Stock Market** la Bourse
◇ **stock market boom** envolée f du marché boursier
◇ **stock market bubble** bulle f boursière
◇ **stock market crash** krach m boursier
◇ **stock market forecast** prévision f boursière

stonewall *Parl vt* bloquer, faire barrage à

stonewaller *n Parl* obstructionniste *mf*

stonewalling *n Parl* obstructionnisme *m*

stop-and-go policy *n Br Econ* politique *f* économique en dents de scie *(alternant arrêt de la croissance et mesures de relance)*, politique *f* du stop-and-go

Stormont *n Pol* = château de la banlieue de Belfast qui a abrité le parlement d'Irlande du Nord entre 1921 et 1972

◇ *Stormont Executive* = gouvernement d'Irlande du Nord

straight-line *adj Econ* constant(e)

straight ticket *n Am Pol* liste *f* non panachée

straight-ticket *adj Am Pol (voting, option)* sans panachage

stranger *n Br Formerly Parl* **I spy strangers!** *(in House of Commons)* je demande le huis clos!

◇ *Br Parl* **Strangers' Gallery** = la tribune du public à la Chambre des communes et à la Chambre des lords

strategic *adj* stratégique

◇ *strategic planning* planification *f* stratégique

◇ *strategic withdrawal* repli *m* stratégique

strategist *n* stratège *m*

strategy *n* stratégie *f*

straw *adj*

◇ *Am* **straw poll** *(vote)* vote *m* blanc; *(opinion poll)* sondage *m* d'opinion

◇ *Am* **straw vote** *(vote)* vote *m* blanc; *(opinion poll)* sondage *m* d'opinion

streamline *vt Econ (company, production, industry)* rationaliser

streamlining *n Econ (of company, production, industry)* rationalisation *f*

strength *n* (a) *(of government, country)* puissance *f* (b) *(of currency, economy, prices)* solidité *f*; *(of market)* fermeté *f*

strike 1 *n* (a) *(refusal to work)* grève *f*; **to go on strike** se mettre en *ou* faire grève; **the nurses went on strike over the minister's decision to freeze wages** les infirmières ont fait grève suite à la décision du ministre de bloquer les salaires; **to be (out) on strike** être en grève; **to threaten strike action** menacer de faire *ou* de se mettre en grève

(b) *(military)* raid *m*, attaque *f*

2 *adj* (a) *(committee, movement)* de grève

(b) *(mission)* d'intervention, d'attaque; *(aircraft)* d'assaut

3 *vt* (a) *(deal, treaty, agreement)* conclure

(b) *Am (go on strike at)* **the union is striking four of the company's plants** le syndicat a déclenché des grèves dans quatre usines de la société

4 *vi (of workers)* faire grève; **they're striking for more pay** ils font grève pour obtenir une augmentation de salaire

◇ *strike ballot* = vote avant que les syndicats ne décident d'une grève

◇ *strike force (nuclear capacity)* force *f* de frappe

◇ *strike fund* = caisse de prévoyance permettant d'aider les grévistes

◇ *strike pay* salaire *m* de gréviste *(versé par le syndicat ou par un fonds de solidarité)*

stringency *n Econ (of market)* reserrement *m*; **in times of stringency** en période d'austérité

stringent *adj Econ (market)* serré(e), tendu(e); **stringent economic measures** des mesures d'austérité

strong *adj* (a) *(government, country)* puissant(e) (b) *(currency, economy, prices)* solide; *(market)* ferme; **the dollar has got stronger** le dollar s'est raffermi

strongarm *Fam* **1** *adj (methods)* brutal(e), violent(e); **to use strongarm tactics** employer la manière forte

2 *vt* **Labour strongarmed the union leaders into calling off the strike** le parti travailliste a forcé la main aux dirigeants syndicaux pour qu'ils mettent fin à la grève

stronghold *n* bastion *m*, fief *m*; **a Conservative Party stronghold** un bastion *ou* fief du parti conservateur

structural *adj* structurel(elle)
◇ *Econ* **structural adjustment** ajustement *m* structurel
◇ *Econ* **structural change** changement *m* stucturel
◇ *Econ* **structural and cohesion funds** fonds *mpl* structurel et de cohésion
◇ *Econ* **structural fund** fonds *m* structurel
◇ *Econ* **structural unemployment** chômage *m* structurel

structure *n* *(of department, company)* structure *f*

struggle *n Pol* lutte *f*; **the struggle for independence/for freedom** la lutte pour l'indépendance/pour la liberté

stuff *vt Am Pol* **to stuff the ballot box** *(fill with false ballot papers)* remplir les urnes de faux bulletins de vote; *(rig election)* truquer les élections; **the only way he'll win is if they stuff the ballot box** sa seule chance de gagner, c'est la fraude électorale

stump *Am Pol* **1** *n* estrade *f* *(d'un orateur politique)*; **to be/go on the stump** faire une tournée électorale
2 *vt (constituency, state)* faire une tournée électorale dans
3 *vi* faire une tournée électorale

❝ ————————

Bush was devoting his public appearances Monday to politics, looking to add to the Republican majority in the House and to put the Senate back in control of the GOP. Most of the remaining eight days before the Nov. 5 elections will be spent **on the stump**, with the focus on tight races. Bush has been on the road since Thursday morning, starting with campaign stops in North Carolina, South Carolina and Alabama.

                                    ❞

STV *n Pol* *(abbr* **single transferable vote**) scrutin *m* uninominal préférentiel avec report de voix

subcommittee *n* sous-comité *m*, sous-commission *f*

subject *Pol* **1** *n (of monarch)* sujet(-ette) *m,f*; **she is a British subject** c'est une ressortissante britannique
2 *adj (subordinate) (people, country)* soumis(e), assujetti(e); **they are subject to my authority** ils sont placés sous mon autorité, ils dépendent de moi; **we are all subject to the rule of law** nous sommes tous soumis à la loi
3 *vt (people, country)* soumettre, assujettir
◇ **subject states** États *mpl* dépendants

subjection *n* (a) *(act of subjecting)* assujettissement *m* (b) *(state of being subjected)* sujétion *f*, assujettissement *m*

subsidiarity *n EU* subsidiarité *f*

subsidization *n* fait *m* de subventionner

subsidize *vt* subventionner; **to be subsidized by the State** recevoir une subvention de *ou* être subventionné par l'État

subsidized *adj* subventionné(e)
◇ **subsidized industry** industrie *f* subventionnée

subsidy *n* subvention *f*; **the EU plans to slash subsidies** l'UE prévoit une réduction considérable des subventions

subsistence *n Econ* subsistance *f*
◇ **subsistence economy** économie *f* de subsistance

suffrage *n Pol* (a) *(right to vote)* droit *m* de suffrage *ou* de vote; **women's suffrage** le droit de vote pour les femmes (b) *(vote)* suffrage *m*, vote *m*

suffragette *n Pol* suffragette *f*

summit *Pol* **1** *n (meeting)* sommet *m*
2 *adj (talks, agreement)* au sommet
◇ *summit conference* réunion *f* au sommet

summiteer *n Pol* participant(e) *m,f* à un sommet

supernormal profit *n Econ* profit *m* supérieur à la normale, surprofit *m*

superpower *n Pol* superpuissance *f*
◇ *superpower talks* négociations *fpl* entre les superpuissances

supply *n* **(a)** *Econ* offre *f*; **supply and demand** l'offre *f* et la demande **(b)** *Pol (money)* crédits *mpl*
◇ *Econ* **supply curve** courbe *f* de l'offre
◇ *Econ* **supply and demand mechanism** mécanisme *m* de l'offre et de la demande

supply-side economics *n Econ* économie *f* de l'offre

support **1** *n (backing)* soutien *m*, appui *m*; **support for the Socialist Party is declining** le parti socialiste est en baisse *ou* en perte de vitesse; **there is widespread support for the government** le gouvernement bénéficie d'un très large soutien
2 *vt (back) (action, campaign, person)* soutenir, appuyer; *(cause, idea)* être pour, soutenir; **she supports the Labour Party** elle est pour *ou* elle soutient le parti travailliste; **to support a candidate** appuyer *ou* soutenir un candidat; **the Democrats will support the bill** les Démocrates seront pour *ou* appuieront le projet de loi
◇ *support price* prix *m* de soutien

supporter *n (of political party)* partisan(e) *m,f*

suprastate *adj* superétatique

surgery *n Br Pol* permanence *f*; **our MP holds a surgery on Saturdays** notre député tient une permanence le samedi

surplus *Econ* **1** *n (overabundance)* surplus *m*, excédent *m*; **a labour surplus** un surplus de main-d'œuvre; **Japan's trade surplus** l'excédent

commercial du Japon
2 *adj (items)* en surplus, excédentaire; **they export their surplus agricultural produce** ils exportent leurs surplus agricoles
◇ *surplus population* population *f* excédentaire
◇ *surplus production* production *f* excédentaire
◇ *surplus stock* stocks *mpl* excédentaires, surplus *m*

suspend *vt (official, member, talks)* suspendre

suspension *n (of official, member, talks)* suspension *f*

sustainable *adj (agriculture, politics)* viable, durable
◇ *sustainable development* développement *m* durable

suzerain *Pol* **1** *n (state)* État *m* dominant
2 *adj (state, power)* dominant(e)
◇ *suzerain lord* suzerain *m*

▸ **swear in** *vt sep Pol (president, MP)* faire prêter serment à, assermenter

swing **1** *n* **(a)** *(in public opinion, voting)* revirement *m*; *(in prices, market)* fluctuation *f*; **the party needs a ten percent swing to win the election** le parti a besoin d'un revirement d'opinion de dix pour cent pour gagner les élections
(b) *Am Pol (tour)* tournée *f*; **on his swing around the circle, the President visited 35 States** pendant sa tournée électorale, le Président a visité 35 États
2 *vt (cause to change)* **to swing the voters** faire changer les électeurs d'opinion; **that swung the decision our way/against us** cela a influencé la décision finale en notre faveur/en notre défaveur; **to swing the voting in favour of sb** faire pencher la balance en faveur de qn
3 *vi (change opinion)* virer; **the country has swung to the left** le pays a viré à gauche
◇ *swing voter* électeur(trice) *m,f* indécis(e)

❝

To rally the troops, Bush has prepared an itinerary leading up to the Nov. 5 elections packed with get-out-the-vote campaign appearances. He has hit Minnesota, Maine, Pennsylvania and Missouri, with a stop in Charlotte kicking off his Southern **swing**.

❞

swinging voter n Austr électeur(-trice) m,f indécis(e)

Swiss Confederation n Confédération f helvétique

sympathizer n sympathisant(e) m,f

syndicalism n (doctrine) syndicalisme m

syndicalist 1 n syndicaliste mf
2 adj de syndicalisme

synergy n Econ synergie f

system n système m; **they live in a totalitarian system** ils vivent dans un système totalitaire

table 1 *n (diagram)* tableau *m*
  2 *vt Parl* (a) *Br (submit) (bill, motion)* présenter (b) *Am (postpone) (bill, motion)* ajourner, reporter; **the bill has been tabled** la discussion du projet de loi a été reportée

tabloid *n (newspaper)* tabloïde *m*; **it's front-page news in all the tabloids** c'est à la une de tous les journaux à sensation

tactical *adj*
◇ *tactical nuclear weapons* armes *fpl* nucléaires tactiques
◇ *tactical vote* vote *m* utile
◇ *tactical voter* = personne qui fait un vote utile
◇ *tactical voting* vote *m* utile; **there has been a lot of tactical voting** beaucoup de gens ont voté utile

take-off *n Econ* décollage *m* (économique)

▸ **take over** 1 *vt sep* s'emparer de; **the military took over the country** l'armée a pris le pouvoir
  2 *vi* prendre le pouvoir

takeover *n (of power, government)* prise *f* de pouvoir; *(of company)* prise *f* de contrôle, absorption *f*, rachat *m*

talk 1 *n* (a) *(formal)* entretien *m*; **during his talk with the ambassador** pendant son entretien avec l'ambassadeur (b) **talks** *(negotiations)* négociations *fpl*, pourparlers *mpl*; *(conference)* conférence *f*; **official peace talks** des pourparlers officiels sur la paix; **the Madrid talks on European integration** les négociations de Madrid concernant l'intégration eu-

ropéenne; **so far there have only been talks about talks** jusqu'ici il n'y a eu que des négociations préliminaires
  2 *vt* **to talk business/politics** parler affaires/politique
  3 *vi (formally)* s'entretenir (**to/with** avec)

▸ **talk out** *vt sep Pol* **to talk out a bill** = prolonger la discussion d'un projet de loi jusqu'à ce qu'il soit trop tard pour le voter avant la clôture de la séance

tariff *n (tax)* tarif *m* douanier
◇ *tariff agreement* accord *m* tarifaire
◇ *tariff barrier* barrière *f* douanière *ou* tarifaire
◇ *tariff laws* lois *fpl* tarifaires
◇ *tariff level indices* taux *mpl* indices des tarifs
◇ *tariff reform* réforme *f* des tarifs douaniers
◇ *tariff wall* barrière *f* douanière *ou* tarifaire

task force *n Pol* groupe *m* d'intervention

tax 1 *n* (a) *(on income)* contributions *fpl*, impôt *m* (b) *(on goods, services, imports)* taxe *f*; **there is a high tax on whisky** le whisky est fortement taxé; **to put a ten percent tax on sth** imposer *ou* taxer qch à dix pour cent; **to levy a tax on sth** frapper qch d'une taxe; **to be liable to tax** être assujetti(e) à l'impôt; **before tax** avant impôt; *(income)* avant impôt; **after tax** après impôt; **exclusive of tax** hors taxe
  2 *vt (person, company)* imposer, frapper d'un impôt; *(goods, services, imports)* taxer, frapper d'une taxe;

the rich will be more heavily taxed les riches seront plus lourdement imposés; **luxury goods are taxed at 28 per cent** les articles de luxe sont taxés à 28 pour cent; **small businesses are being taxed out of existence** accablées d'impôts, les petites entreprises disparaissent

◇ *tax avoidance* = moyen (légal) pour payer moins d'impôts

◇ *tax base* assiette *f* fiscale

◇ *tax break* réduction *f* d'impôt, allègement *m* fiscal

◇ *tax burden* charge *f* fiscale, fardeau *m* fiscal, pression *f* fiscale, poids *m* de la fiscalité

◇ *tax ceiling* plafond *m* de l'impôt

◇ *tax credit* aide *f* fiscale, avoir *m* fiscal

◇ *tax dollars* impôts *mpl* (payés par la population)

◇ *tax evasion* fraude *f* fiscale, évasion *f* fiscale

◇ *tax expenditure* dépenses *fpl* fiscales

◇ *EU tax harmonization* harmonisation *f* fiscale

◇ *tax haven* paradis *m* fiscal

◇ *tax impact* incidence *f* fiscale

◇ *tax incentive* incitation *f* fiscale, avantage *m* fiscal

◇ *tax incidence* incidence *f* fiscale

◇ *tax law* droit *m* fiscal

◇ *tax package* paquet *m* fiscal

◇ *tax relief* allègement *m* fiscal

◇ *tax revenue* recettes *fpl* fiscales, rentrées *fpl* fiscales

◇ *tax and spend* = financement des grandes dépenses budgétaires par des taux d'imposition élevés; **the Chancellor has resorted to a policy of tax and spend** le ministre des Finances a recours à une politique d'imposition pour financer les grandes dépenses

◇ *tax system* régime *m* fiscal, régime *m* d'imposition

◇ *tax take* ponction *f* fiscale

◇ *tax year* année *f* fiscale, année *f* d'imposition

"

In past budgets, Mr Brown was careful not to make too much of his tax hikes, fearing he would be accused of returning to the "bad old days" of **tax and spend**. The difference now is that he and the prime minister are almost boasting about it. It may be that they believe the public mood has changed and that voters now mean it when they say they are prepared to pay a bit extra to fund the public services.

"

---

taxable *adj (goods, land)* imposable

◇ *taxable base* base *f* d'imposition

◇ *taxable income* revenu *m* imposable, assiette *f* fiscale *ou* de l'impôt

taxation *n* (a) *(of person, company)* imposition *f*, prélèvement *m* fiscal; *(of goods)* taxation *f*; **taxation at source** prélèvement *m* de l'impôt à la source, imposition *f* à la source (b) *(taxes)* impôts *mpl*, contributions *fpl*

◇ *taxation authorities* administration *f* fiscale, fisc *m*

◇ *taxation year* année *f* fiscale, année *f* d'imposition

tax-deductible *adj* déductible des impôts

tax-exempt *adj (income)* exonéré(e) d'impôts; *(goods)* exonéré(e) de taxes

tax-free *adj (income)* exonéré(e) d'impôts; *(goods)* exonéré(e) de taxes

taxman *n Br Fam* **the taxman** le fisc

taxpayer *n* contribuable *mf*

Taylorism *n* taylorisme *m*

TCU *n (abbr* **Transportation Communications International Union)** = syndicat nord-américain des transports et des communications

TD *n Pol* (a) *(abbr* **Treasury Department)** ministère *m* des Finances (b) *Pol (abbr* **Teachta Dála)** ≃ député(e) *m,f (du Parlement irlandais)*

Teachta Dála n Pol ≃ député(e) m,f (du Parlement irlandais)

telegraph vt Can Pol **to telegraph votes** voter frauduleusement

televised debate n (during election campaign) débat m télévisé

teller n Pol (of votes) scrutateur(trice) m,f

temporary adj (work, employee) intérimaire, temporaire; (measures) temporaire, provisoire
◊ **temporary entry** admission f temporaire
◊ **temporary importation** importation f temporaire

tendency n Pol tendance f, groupe m

term n (a) Pol (of parliament) session f; (of elected official) mandat m; **the president is elected for a five-year term** le président est élu pour (une période ou une durée de) cinq ans (b) **terms** (conditions) (of agreement, contract) termes mpl; **under the terms of the agreement** selon les termes de l'accord
◊ Pol **term of office** mandat m; **during my term of office** pendant mon mandat
◊ Econ **terms of trade** termes mpl de l'échange

territorial adj territorial(e)
◊ **territorial dispute** contentieux m territorial

territory n territoire m

terrorism n terrorisme m

terrorist 1 n terroriste mf
2 adj (bomb) de terroriste; (campaign, attack, group) terroriste

tertiarization n Econ tertiairisation f, tertiarisation f

tertiary adj Econ tertiaire
◊ **tertiary employment** activité f tertiaire
◊ **tertiary sector** secteur m tertiaire

TEU n (abbr Treaty on European Union) TUE m

TGWU n Br (abbr Transport and General

Workers' Union) = le plus grand syndicat interprofessionnel britannique

Thatcherism n Pol thatchérisme m

Thatcherite Pol 1 n thatchérien(-enne) m,f
2 adj thatchérien(enne)

thaw 1 n (in relations) détente f, dégel m (in de)
2 vi (of relations) se dégeler, être plus détendu(e)

theory n théorie f
◊ Econ **theory of first best** théorie f de l'optimum de premier rang
◊ Econ **theory of second best** théorie f de l'optimum de second rang

think tank n Pol cellule f ou groupe m de réflexion

third adj
◊ EU **third country** pays m tiers
◊ Pol **third reading** (of bill) dernière lecture f
◊ Br Pol **the Third Way** la troisième voie (politique consensuelle prêchée par le parti travailliste réformé de Tony Blair, censée dépasser les clivages traditionnels droite-gauche de façon à rassembler toutes les classes sociales)
◊ **the Third World** le Tiers-monde

"

In Britain, the **Third Way** has given Labour an unprecedented second full term in power. In Germany, soon after Tony Blair spoon-fed it to the reluctant Gerhard Schröder, the **Third Way** (or "new middle") brought another previously failing left party to power; now the SPD seems poised for an even stronger second term.

"

thirty-year rule n Br Pol règle f des trente ans

1000 Club n Br Pol = club du parti travailliste pour les hommes d'affaires, les membres du parti, etc, permettant de recueillir des fonds

three-line whip *n Br Pol* = convocation urgente d'un député par un
"whip" à un vote lors d'une séance
parlementaire

❝

Within minutes of his statement, Mr
Clarke showed his contempt for Mr
Duncan Smith by declaring: "It
would be much easier to unite as a
party if Iain Duncan Smith would re-
frain from imposing **three-line
whips** on subjects which have always been left to the judgment of individual MPs."

❞

three-way marginal *n Br Pol* = circonscription où trois candidats ont
d'égales chances de succès

threshold *n Econ* limite *f*, seuil *m*; **the
government has raised tax thresholds
in line with inflation** le gouvernement
a relevé les tranches de l'impôt pour
tenir compte de l'inflation

◊ *Br Econ* **threshold agreement** accord *m* d'indexation des salaires sur
les prix

◊ *Br Econ* **threshold policy** politique *f*
d'indexation des salaires sur les prix

◊ *Br Econ* **threshold wage agreement** accord *m* d'indexation des salaires sur les prix

◊ *Br Econ* **threshold wage policy** politique *f* d'indexation des salaires sur
les prix

▸ **throw out** *vt sep (bill, proposal)* rejeter, repousser

ticket *n Am Pol (platform)* programme
m; *(list)* liste *f*; **he fought the election
on a Democratic ticket** il a basé son
programme électoral sur les principes du Parti démocrate; **to run on a
presidential ticket** être candidat à la
vice-présidence

◊ *ticket splitting* panachage *m*

tied aid *n* aide *f* liée

tight money *adj Econ* argent *m* rare

▸ **tighten up** *vt sep (control, regula-*

tion, blockade) renforcer; **the law on
drug peddling has been tightened up**
la loi sur le trafic de drogue a été ren-
forcée

▸ **tighten up on** *vt insep* **the government is tightening up on drug
pushers/tax evasion** le gouvernement
renforce la lutte contre les reven-
deurs de drogue/la fraude fiscale

topple 1 *vt (cause to fall)* faire tomber; **the scandal almost toppled the
government** ce scandale a failli faire
tomber *ou* renverser le gouvernement

2 *vi (fall)* tomber

Tory *Pol* **1** *n (party member)* tory *m*,
membre *m* du parti conservateur;
(voter, supporter) = partisan du parti
conservateur; **to vote Tory** voter
conservateur

2 *adj* tory, conservateur(trice)

Toryism *n Pol* torysme *m*

totalitarian *Pol* **1** *n* totalitaire *mf*
2 *adj* totalitaire

◊ *totalitarian regime* régime *m* totalitaire

totalitarianism *n Pol* totalitarisme *m*

totter *vi (of government)* chanceler,
être dans une mauvaise passe

touchstone issue *n* pierre *f* de touche

❝

But as Mr Bercow waited in the
Commons to make a speech Mr
Portillo struck. In a brief intervention,
which electrified the sleepy Tory
benches, Mr Portillo asked the
frontbench how it could reconcile Mr
Duncan Smith's pledge to modern-
ise with his determination to understand the **touchstone issue** of gay
adoption.

❞

town *n* ville *f*

◊ *town council* conseil *m* municipal

◊ *town councillor* conseiller(ère) *m,f*
municipal(e)

◇ ***town and country planning*** aménagement *m* urbain et rural

◇ ***town hall*** hôtel *m* de ville, mairie *f*

◇ ***town planning*** aménagement *m* urbain

tradable *adj Econ* négociable, commercialisable

trade **1** *n* commerce *m*, affaires *fpl*
2 *vi (of country)* faire du commerce, commercer; **to trade with sb** avoir *ou* entretenir des relations commerciales avec qn; **they stopped trading with Iran** ils ont arrêté toute relation commerciale avec l'Iran

◇ ***trade agreement*** accord *m* commercial

◇ ***trade association*** association *f* professionnelle, syndicat *m* professionnel

◇ ***trade ban*** interdiction *f* de commerce

◇ ***trade barriers*** barrières *fpl* douanières *ou* commerciales

◇ ***trade body*** syndicat *m* professionnel

◇ ***trade credit*** crédit *m* commercial

◇ ***trade cycle*** cycle *m* de commercialisation

◇ ***trade deficit*** déficit *m* de la balance commerciale

◇ ***trade embargo*** embargo *m* commercial

◇ ***trade gap*** déficit *m* commercial

◇ *Br* ***Trade and Industry Secretary*** ≃ ministre *m* du Commerce

◇ ***trade mission*** mission *f* commerciale

◇ ***trade policy*** politique *f* commerciale

◇ ***trade register*** Registre *m* du Commerce

◇ ***trade route*** route *f* commerciale

◇ ***trade surplus*** excédent *m* commercial

◇ *Br* ***trade(s) union*** syndicat *m*; **to join a trade(s) union** se syndiquer; **the workers formed a trade(s) union** les ouvriers ont formé un syndicat; **I am in the trade(s) union** je suis syndiqué, j'appartiens au syndicat

◇ *Br* ***Trades Union Congress*** = Confé-

dération des syndicats britanniques

◇ ***trade unionism*** syndicalisme *m*

◇ ***trade(s) unionist*** syndicaliste *mf*

◇ ***trade union tariff*** tarif *m* syndical

◇ ***trade war*** guerre *f* commerciale

trade-weighted index *n Econ* indice *m* pondéré par le commerce extérieur

trading *n* commerce *m*, négoce *m*

◇ *Econ* ***trading partner*** partenaire *m* commercial

◇ *Econ* ***trading syndicate*** comptoir *m*

traditionalist *Pol* **1** *n* traditionaliste *mf*
2 *adj* traditionaliste

transaction *n Econ* transaction *f*

◇ ***transaction cost*** coût *m* de transaction

transfer **1** *n (of employee, civil servant)* mutation *f*
2 *vt (employee, civil servant)* transférer, muter

◇ *Econ* ***transfer income*** revenu *m* de transfert

◇ *Pol* ***transfer of power*** passation *f* des pouvoirs

◇ *Econ* ***transfer pricing*** établissement *m* des prix de transfert

transferable vote *n* = voix pouvant se reporter sur un autre candidat

transference *n (of employee, civil servant)* mutation *f*

transition economy *n* économie *f* de transition

transitional *adj (government, administration)* provisoire

transparency *n (of government, policy)* transparence *f*

transparent *adj (government, policy)* transparent(e)

transport *n*

◇ ***Transport and General Workers' Union*** = le plus grand syndicat interprofessionnel britannique

◇ ***Transport House*** = bâtiment à Londres abritant le siège de la "TGWU" et, jusqu'en 1980, le parti travailliste

treason n Pol trahison f

treasury n (funds) trésor m (public); Br **the Treasury** (government department) la Trésorerie, ≃ le ministère des Finances
◇ **Treasury bench** banc m des ministres (au Parlement britannique)
◇ **Treasury bill** bon m du Trésor
◇ Am **Treasury Department** ≃ ministère m des Finances
◇ Br **Treasury Minister** ≃ ministre m des Finances
◇ Am **Treasury Secretary** ≃ ministre m des Finances

treaty n Pol traité m; **to sign a treaty (with sb)** signer ou conclure un traité (avec qn); **there is a treaty between the two countries** les deux pays sont liés par traité m d'alliance
◇ **Treaty on European Union** traité m sur l'Union européenne

trend n (tendency) tendance f; **political/electoral trends** tendances fpl politiques/électorales

Tribune group n Pol = groupe des députés de gauche du parti travailliste britannique

trickle-down economics, trickle-down theory n Econ = théorie selon laquelle les richesses accumulées par un petit nombre bénéficieront à tous les membres de la société

❝

And on Sunday, the Archbishop of Canterbury, George Carey (at a service of dedication to mark – of all things – the advent of the single European market), inveighed against the **"trickle-down" theory** of wealth distribution, whereby ever-higher incomes for the wealthy are somehow supposed "naturally" to find their way through to the poor.

❞

troika n troïka f

Trot n Fam Pej Pol (abbr **Trotskyist**) trotskiste mf

Trotskyism n Pol trotskisme m

Trotskyist, Trotskyite Pol **1** n trotskiste mf
2 adj trotskiste

troubleshooter n Pol (in conflict) médiateur(trice) m,f

troubleshooting n Pol (in conflict) médiation f

truce n trève f; **to call a truce** conclure ou établir une trève

true-blue Br Pol **1** n conservateur(trice) m,f
2 adj conservateur(trice), tory; **a true-blue Tory** un fidèle du parti conservateur

trust n (cartel) trust m, cartel m

trustbuster n Am = fonctionnaire chargé de veiller à l'application des lois anti-trust

❝

Critics like former U.S. Circuit Court judge Robert Bork pan Pitofsky for assuming **trustbusters** can forecast market share and other changes in an economy well enough to remove emerging monopolies ... Bork and other "Chicago School" theorists also say Pitofsky mistakenly rejects the notion that **trustbusters** should curb a company only when there's evidence it has illegally hampered competition through schemes like price collusion. "The fact is, Pitofsky ... is pushing forward with cases that shouldn't be brought," says Bork.

❞

trustbusting Am **1** n démantèlement m des trusts
2 adj qui a trait au démantèlement des trusts

trusteeship n Pol (of territory) tutelle f

TSO n (abbr **The Stationery Office**) = maison d'édition publiant les ouvrages ou documents approuvés par le

Parlement, les ministères et autres organismes officiels, ≃ l'Imprimerie *f* nationale

TSSA *n* (*abbr* **Transport Salaried Staffs' Association**) = syndicat britannique des salariés du secteur des transports

TU *n Br* (*abbr* **trade(s) union**) syndicat *m*

TUC *n Br* (*abbr* **Trades Union Congress**) = Confédération des syndicats britanniques; **the TUC annual conference** le congrès annuel des syndicats

turnout *n Pol* (*at election*) (taux *m* de) participation *f*; **there was a good turnout at the elections** il y avait un fort taux de participation aux élections

two-chamber *adj Pol* bicaméral(e)

two-line whip *n Br Parl* = convocation d'un député par un "whip" à un débat ou à un vote lors d'une séance parlementaire

two-party system *n Pol* (*of government*) système *m* bipartite *ou* biparti

two-speed *adj* à deux vitesses

◇ **two-speed economy** économie *f* à deux vitesses

◇ **two-speed Europe** Europe *f* à deux vitesses

◇ **two-speed monetary union** union *f* monétaire à deux vitesses

TWU *n* (*abbr* **Transport Workers Union of America**) = syndicat américain des employés des transports

turnover *n Br* (*of company*) chiffre *m* d'affaires; (*of capital*) rotation *f*; **his turnover is £100,000 per annum** il fait 100 000 livres d'affaires par an

◇ **turnover tax** impôt *m ou* taxe *f* sur le chiffre d'affaires

Tynwald *n Parl* **the Tynwald** = le Parlement de l'île de Man

UAN *n* (*abbr* **United American Nurses**) = syndicat américain des infirmières

UAW *n* (*abbr* **United Automobile, Aerospace and Agricultural Implement Workers**) = syndicat américain regroupant des employés de divers secteurs, dont les principaux sont l'industrie automobile, l'aérospatial et le matériel agricole

UCATT *n* (*abbr* **Union of Construction, Allied Trades and Technicians**) = syndicat britannique des employés du bâtiment

UCW *n* (*abbr* **Union of Communication Workers**) = syndicat britannique des communications

UDM *n* (*abbr* **Union of Democratic Mineworkers**) = syndicat britannique de mineurs

UFCW *n* (*abbr* **United Food and Commercial Workers International Union**) = syndicat nord-américain d'employés issus de différents secteurs, et tout particulièrement de l'industrie alimentaire

UFW *n* (*abbr* **United Farm Workers of America**) = syndicat américain des ouvriers agricoles

UK Unionist Party *n* = parti politique britannique pour le maintien, la protection et la défense de l'Union de la Grande-Bretagne et de l'Irlande du Nord

UKUP *n* (*abbr* **UK Unionist Party**) = parti politique britannique pour le maintien, la protection et la défense de l'Union de la Grande-Bretagne et de l'Irlande du Nord

Ulster *n* (**a**) *(province)* Ulster *m* (**b**) *(Northern Ireland)* Irlande *f* du Nord, Ulster *m*

◇ *Ulster Democratic Unionist Party* = parti politique essentiellement protestant exigeant le maintien de l'Irlande du Nord au sein du Royaume-Uni

◇ *Ulster Unionists* = parti politique essentiellement protestant, favorable au maintien de l'Irlande du Nord au sein du Royaume-Uni

◇ *Ulster Volunteer Force* = organisation paramilitaire déclarée hors la loi, favorable au maintien de l'Irlande du Nord au sein du Royaume-Uni

ultraleft *Pol* **1** *n* extrême gauche *f* **2** *adj* d'extrême gauche

ultraright *Pol* **1** *n* extrême droite *f* **2** *adj* d'extrême droite

UMWA *n* (*abbr* **United Mineworkers of America**) = syndicat américain de mineurs

UN *n* (*abbr* **United Nations**) the UN l'ONU *f*, l'Onu *f*

◇ *UN peacekeeping forces* les Casques *mpl* bleus

◇ *UN resolution* résolution *f* de l'ONU

◇ *UN Secretary-General* secrétaire *mf* général(e) de l'ONU

◇ *UN Secretary-Generalship* secrétariat *m* général de l'ONU

◇ *UN Security Council* Conseil *m* de sécurité de l'ONU

unaligned *adj Pol* non-aligné(e)

unamended *adj Parl* sans amendement

unanimity n unanimité f; **there must be unanimity on the issue** il faut qu'il y ait unanimité à ce sujet

unanimous adj unanime; **passed by a unanimous vote** voté à l'unanimité; **we must give him our unanimous support** il faut que nous soyons unanimes à le soutenir; **to reach a unanimous decision** se prononcer à l'unanimité

unanimously adv (decide, agree) à l'unanimité, unanimement; (vote) à l'unanimité

unbalanced growth n Econ croissance f déséquilibrée

unchallengeable adj **to be in an unchallengeable position** (of politician) être hors d'atteinte

Uncle Sam n l'Oncle m Sam (gouvernement des USA)

uncontested adj (position, authority) non disputé(e), incontesté(e); Pol **the seat was uncontested** il n'y avait qu'un candidat pour le siège

UNCTAD n (abbr **United Nations Conference on Trade and Development**) CNUCED f

undercapitalization n Econ sous-capitalisation f

undercapitalized adj Econ sous-capitalisé(e)

underconsumption n Econ sous-consommation f

underdeveloped adj Econ (country, society) sous-développé(e), arriéré(-e)

underdevelopment n Econ (of country, society) sous-développement m

underemployed adj Econ sous-employé(e)

underemployment n Econ sous-emploi m
◇ **underemployment economy** économie f de sous-emploi

underequipment n Econ (of country) sous-équipement m

underequipped adj Econ (country) sous-équipé(e)

underfunded adj Econ sous-capitalisé(e)

underfunding n Econ sous-capitalisation f

underground 1 n Pol (resistance) résistance f
2 adj Pol (secret) secret(ète), clandestin(e)
◇ **underground economy** économie f souterraine ou immergée
◇ Pol **underground movement** (clandestine) mouvement m clandestin; (resistance) mouvement m de résistance

underlying adj (rate, figure) sous-jacent(e)

underproduce 1 vt produire insuffisamment de
2 vi produire insuffisamment

underproduction n sous-production f

under-representation n Pol sous-représentation f

under-represented adj Pol sous-représenté(e)

undersecretary n Pol (a) Br (in department) chef m de cabinet (b) (politician) sous-secrétaire mf
◇ **undersecretary of state** sous-secrétaire mf d'État

UNDP n (abbr **United Nations Development Programme**) PNUD m

unearned adj Econ non gagné(e) en travaillant ou par le travail
◇ **unearned income** revenus mpl non professionnels, rentes fpl
◇ Econ **unearned increment** plus-value f

unease n Pol (unrest) troubles mpl; (tension) tension f

uneconomic n Br (unprofitable) peu rentable

unemployed 1 npl **the unemployed** les chômeurs mpl, les demandeurs mpl d'emploi

2 adj (person) en ou au chômage ; **she was unemployed for months** elle est restée au chômage pendant des mois

unemployment n chômage m

◇ Br Formerly **unemployment benefit** allocation f (de) chômage

◇ Am **unemployment compensation** allocation f (de) chômage

◇ **unemployment figures** chiffres mpl du chômage

◇ **unemployment fund** caisse f de chômage

◇ **unemployment level** taux m de chômage

◇ **unemployment rate** taux m de chômage

◇ **unemployment trap** cercle m vicieux du chômage

unequal exchange n échange m inégal

unicameral adj Pol monocaméral(e)

unicameralism n Pol monocamérisme m

UNIDO n (abbr United Nations Industrial Development Organization) ONUDI f, Onudi f

UNIFI n = syndicat britannique des employés du domaine financier

unification n unification f ; **the unification of Germany** l'unification f de l'Allemagne

unified adj unifié(e)

unify vt (a) (country) unifier (b) (legislation, prices) uniformiser

unilateral adj (action, decision) unilatéral(e) ; **a unilateral declaration of independence** une déclaration unilatérale d'indépendance

◇ **unilateral disarmament** désarmement m unilatéral

unilateralism n unilatéralisme m, doctrine f du désarmement unilatéral

unilateralist n partisan(e) m,f du désarmement unilatéral

union n (a) (trade union) syndicat m ; **to join a union** se syndiquer ; **to form a union** créer un syndicat ; **unions and**

management les syndicats mpl et la direction, les partenaires mpl sociaux (b) (between countries, people) association f, union f

◇ **union agreement** convention f collective

◇ **union leader** dirigeant(e) m,f syndical(e)

◇ **union member** (in general) membre m d'un syndicat, syndiqué(e) m,f ; (of particular union) membre m du syndicat, syndiqué(e) m,f

◇ **union official** responsable mf syndical(e)

◇ **union representative** délégué(e) m,f ou représentant(e) m,f syndical(e)

◇ **union rights** liberté f syndicale

◇ **union shop** atelier m d'ouvriers syndiqués

union-bashing n Br Fam antisyndicalisme m

> **"**
>
> Plaid Cymru leader Ieuan Wyn Jones also applauded the cancellation of the second eight-day strike, which would again leave Wales with military cover. "I congratulate Andy Gilchrist and the FBU for making this decision," Mr Jones said. "It is a brave and mature decision compared to the government's determination to demonise the firefighters. New Labour must stop this Thatcherite **union-bashing**."
>
> **"**

Unionism n Pol (in Northern Ireland) unionisme m

unionism n (a) (trade union system) syndicalisme m (b) Pol (in Northern Ireland) unionisme m

Unionist Pol **1** n (in Northern Ireland) unioniste mf

　2 adj (in Northern Ireland) unioniste

unionist 1 n (a) (supporter of trade union) syndicaliste mf (b) Pol (in Northern Ireland) unioniste mf

2 *adj* (a) *(supportive of trade union)* syndicaliste (b) *Pol (in Northern Ireland)* unioniste

unionization *n* syndicalisation *f*

unionize 1 *vt* syndicaliser, syndiquer **2** *vi* se syndiquer

unionized *adj* syndiqué(e)

unipolar coalition *n Pol* coalition *f* unipolaire

UNISON *n* = "super-syndicat" de la fonction publique en Grande-Bretagne

unitary *adj* (a) *(united, single)* unitaire (b) *(government)* centralisé(e)

unit cost *n* coût *m* unitaire

unite 1 *vt (country, party)* unifier, unir; **common interests that unite two countries** intérêts communs qui unissent deux pays
2 *vi* s'unir; **the two countries united in opposing** *or* **to oppose oppression** les deux pays se sont unis pour s'opposer à l'oppression

united *adj (country, party)* uni(e), unifié(e); **to present a united front** montrer un front uni; **to be united against sb/sth** être uni contre qn/qch
◇ **the United Nations** les Nations *fpl* unies
◇ **United Nations Conference on Trade and Development** Conférence *f* des Nations unies pour le commerce et le développement
◇ **United Nations Industrial Development Organization** Organisation *f* des Nations unies pour le développement industriel
◇ **United Nations Organization** Organisation *f* des Nations Unies
◇ **United States Trade Representative** représentant(e) *m,f* des États-Unis pour le commerce extérieur

unit of account *n Econ* unité *f* de compte

unity *n* unité *f*, union *f*; **national/political unity** unité *f* nationale/politique

universal suffrage *n* suffrage *m* universel

UNO *n (abbr* United Nations Organization) ONU *f*

unopposed *adj Parl (reading)* = qui ne rencontre aucune opposition; *(candidate)* élu(e) par acclamation

unparliamentary *adj (action)* contraire au règles du parlement
◇ *Br Parl* **unparliamentary language** langage *m* grossier

unperson *n Pol* non-personne *f*

unpolitical *adj* (a) *(not relating to politics)* non politique (b) *(not interested in politics)* apolitique

unrepresented *adj Pol* qui n'est pas représenté(e)

unrest *n Pol* agitation *f*

unseat *vt (government)* faire tomber; *(MP)* faire perdre son siège à

unstable *adj (government, price)* instable
◇ *Econ* **unstable equilibrium** équilibre *m* instable

unweighted *adj Econ (index)* non pondéré(e)
◇ **unweighted figures** chiffres *mpl* bruts

upheaval *n (political)* bouleversement *m*; *(social unrest)* agitation *f*, perturbations *fpl*; **the great political upheavals of the twentieth century** les grands bouleversements politiques du vingtième siècle

Upper Chamber, Upper House *n Parl* Chambre *f* haute

uprate *vt (benefit, pension, salary)* augmenter

uprating *n (of benefit, pension, salary)* augmentation *f*

upset *n (of government)* renversement *m*; **the result caused a major political upset** le résultat a entraîné de grands bouleversements politiques

upside *n (trend)* **prices have been on the upside** les prix ont été à la hausse

upstream *Econ* **1** *adj* en amont
2 *adv* en amont

upswing n *Econ* tendance f à la hausse, hausse f

upward *adj*
◇ **upward mobility** mobilité f sociale
◇ **upward trend** tendance f à la hausse *ou* haussière

USA Freedom Corps n *Pol* = programme national lancé par le président Bush en 2002, permettant aux Américains de servir volontairement leur communauté, leur pays ou le monde

USDAW n (*abbr* **Union of Shop, Distributive and Allied Workers**) = syndicat britannique des personnels de la distribution

usury n (*system, interest*) usure f

USWA n (*abbr* **United Steelworkers of America**) = syndicat américain des employés de la sidérurgie

utilitarian 1 n utilitariste mf
   2 *adj* utilitariste

utilitarianism n utilitarisme m

utility n (*service*) service m ; **they plan to improve utilities** ils ont l'intention d'améliorer les services publics

utopia, Utopia n utopie f

utopian, Utopian 1 n utopiste mf
   2 *adj* utopique
◇ **utopian socialism** socialisme m utopique

utopianism, Utopianism n utopisme m

U-turn n volte-face f, revirement m ; **the government were accused of making a U-turn on health policy** le gouvernement a été accusé de faire volte-face en matière de politique de santé

UWUA n (*abbr* **Utility Workers Union of America**) = syndicat américain des employés des services publics

vacant seat *n Pol* siège *m* à pourvoir *ou* vacant

value *n (monetary worth)* valeur *f*

value-added *adj (product, service)* à valeur ajoutée
◇ *Br* **value-added tax** taxe *f* sur la valeur ajoutée

variable **1** *n* variable *f*
2 *adj* variable
◇ **variable capital** capital *m* variable
◇ **variable cost** coût *m* variable
◇ *EU* **variable import levy** prélèvement *m* à l'importation

variance *n (in statistics)* variance *f*

variate *n (in statistics)* variable *f* aléatoire

variation *n* variation *f*; **the level of demand is subject to considerable variation** le niveau de la demande peut varier considérablement

VAT *n Br (abbr* **value-added tax)** TVA *f*

velocity *n Econ* vélocité *f*, vitesse *f*
◇ **velocity of circulation** vitesse *f* de circulation de la monnaie
◇ **velocity of circulation of money** vitesse *f* de circulation de la monnaie
◇ **velocity of money** vitesse *f* de circulation de la monnaie

VER *n Econ (abbr* **voluntary export restraint)** RVE

vertical *adj Econ*
◇ **vertical concentration** concentration *f* verticale
◇ **vertical integration** intégration *f* verticale
◇ **vertical merger** fusion *f* verticale

vest *vt* investir; **to vest sb with power/authority** investir qn de pouvoir/d'autorité; **the power vested in the government** le pouvoir dont le gouvernement est investi; **the president is vested with the power to veto the government** le président est doté du pouvoir d'opposer son veto aux projets du gouvernement; **legislative authority is vested in Parliament** le Parlement est investi du pouvoir législatif

veteran *n* ancien combattant *m*, vétéran *m*
◇ *Br* **Veterans Agency** ≃ Office *m* national des anciens combattants et victimes de guerre
◇ **Veterans Association** association *f* d'anciens combattants

veto *Pol* **1** *n* **(a)** *(power)* droit *m* de veto; **to use one's veto** exercer son droit de veto **(b)** *(refusal)* veto *m*; **to put a veto on sth** mettre *ou* opposer son veto à qch
2 *vt* mettre *ou* opposer son veto à; **he vetoed it** il y a mis *ou* opposé son veto

viability *n Econ (of company, economy, state)* viabilité *f*

viable *adj Econ (company, economy, state)* viable

vice-premier *n* vice-premier ministre *m*

vice-presidency *n* vice-présidence *f*

vice-president *n* vice-président(e) *m,f*

vice-presidential *adj* vice-présidentiel(elle)

◇ *vice-presidential candidate* candidat(e) *m,f* à la vice-présidence

◇ *vice-presidential hopeful* prétendant(e) *m,f* à la vice-présidence

victory *n Pol* victoire *f*; **a Labour victory seems inevitable** la victoire du Parti travailliste semble inévitable

visible *Econ* **1** *n* **visibles** biens *mpl* visibles

2 *adj*

◇ *visible assets* actif *m* corporel

◇ *visible earnings* gains *mpl* visibles

◇ *visible exports* exportations *fpl* visibles

◇ *visible imports* importations *fpl* visibles

◇ *visible trade* commerce *m* de biens

> **"**
>
> The Treasury has stuck to its earlier forecast of a £15 billion current-account deficit this year. It expects a smaller invisibles surplus than before, but the forecasters are a lot more optimistic about **visible trade**: exports ignore booming.
>
> **"**

voice vote *n Am Pol* vote *m* par acclamation

volte-face *n* volte-face *f inv*; **the speech represents a complete volte-face** ce discours marque un revirement complet *ou* représente une véritable volte-face

voluntary export restraint *n Econ* restriction *f ou* limitation *f* volontaire des exportations

voodoo economics *n Am* = politique économique qui tient de l'illusionnisme

> **"**
>
> Back in 1980, Ronald Reagan campaigned for the Republican presidential nomination with promises to slash corporate and personal in-

come taxes for the rich, overturn environmental and other regulations, and spend tens of billions on new weapons of war. Cutting taxes on "society's most productive members," his economic advisers claimed, would promote investment, job creation, and economic growth. Reagan's then-opponent, George Bush, derided the plan as "**voodoo economics**." But Reagan's economic fantasies have become the guiding ideology of the Republican Party.
>
> **"**

vote 1 *n* **(a)** *(ballot)* vote *m*; **to have a vote on sth** voter sur qch, mettre qch aux voix; **to put a question to the vote** mettre une question aux voix; **to take a vote on sth** procéder au vote de qch

(b) *(in parliament)* vote *m*, scrutin *m*; **70 MPs were present for the vote** 70 députés étaient présents pour le vote; **the vote went in the government's favour/against the government** les députés se sont prononcés en faveur du/contre le gouvernement

(c) *(individual choice)* vote *m*, voix *f*; **to give one's vote to sb** voter pour qn; **they've got my vote** je vote pour eux; **to cast one's vote for sb** voter pour qn; **to count the votes** dépouiller le scrutin; **the candidate got 15,000 votes** le candidat a recueilli 15 000 voix; **to be elected by one vote** être élu à une voix de majorité; **one member, one vote** = système de scrutin "un homme, une voix"

(d) *(ballot paper)* bulletin *m* de vote

(e) *(suffrage)* droit *m* de vote; **to have the vote** avoir le droit de vote; **to give the vote to sb** accorder le droit de vote à qn; **the suffragettes campaigned for votes for women** les suffragettes ont fait campagne pour qu'on accorde le droit de vote aux femmes

(f) *(collectively)* *(voters)* vote *m*, voix *fpl*; *(votes cast)* voix *fpl* exprimées; **they hope to win the working-class**

vote ils espèrent gagner les voix des ouvriers; **the Scottish vote went against the government** le vote écossais a été défavorable au gouvernement; **they won 40 percent of the vote** ils ont remporté 40 pour cent des voix *ou* des suffrages; **they increased their vote by 12 percent** ils ont amélioré leurs résultats de 12 pour cent

(g) *Br* (grant) vote *m* de crédits; **a vote of £100,000** un vote de crédits de 100 000 livres

2 *vt* (a) *(in election)* voter; **vote Ford!** votez Ford!; **to vote Labour/Republican** voter travailliste/républicain; **our family have always voted Conservative** notre famille a toujours voté conservateur *ou* pour le parti conservateur

(b) *(in parliament, assembly) (motion, law)* voter; **they voted that the sitting (should) be suspended** ils ont voté la suspension de la séance

(c) *(elect)* élire; *(appoint)* nommer; **she was voted president** elle a été élue présidente

3 *vi* voter; **France is voting this weekend** la France va aux urnes ce weekend; **how did the country vote?** comment est-ce que le pays a voté?; **to vote for/against sb** voter pour/contre qn; **I'm going to vote for Ford** je vais voter (pour) Ford *ou* donner ma voix à Ford; **to vote in favour of/against sth** voter pour/contre qch; **the party conference voted on the question of fox hunting** le congrès du parti a voté sur la question de la chasse au renard; **to vote by a show of hands** voter à main levée; **to vote with one's feet** *(by leaving)* manifester *ou* signifier son mécontentement en partant; *(by not turning up)* manifester *ou* signifier son mécontentement par le boycott

◇ **vote bundle** = ensemble des documents distribués quotidiennement aux députés de la Chambre des communes les informant des débats et des votes de la journée

◇ **vote of confidence** vote *m* de confiance

◇ **vote of no confidence** motion *f* de censure, vote *m* de défiance

◇ **Vote Office** = bureau responsable de la distribution des documents parlementaires

▸ **vote down** *vt sep* (bill, proposal) rejeter *(par le vote)*

▸ **vote in** *vt sep* (bill, proposal) voter, adopter; *(person, government)* élire

▸ **vote out** *vt sep* (bill, proposal) rejeter; *(person, government)* relever de ses fonctions

▸ **vote through** *vt sep* (bill, reform) voter, ratifier

vote-buying *n* achat *m* de voix *ou* de votes; **the Japanese government was accused of vote-buying to secure an agreement** on a accusé le gouvernement japonais d'avoir acheté des voix afin d'obtenir un accord

vote-catcher *n* politique *f* électoraliste; **the government believes its new policy will be a vote-catcher** le gouvernement pense que sa nouvelle politique va lui rapporter des voix

vote-catching *adj* électoraliste

vote-loser *n* = politique peu populaire qui risque de faire perdre des voix; **his proposal to raise income tax is certain to be a vote-loser** sa proposition d'augmenter l'impôt sur le revenu va très certainement lui faire perdre des voix

vote-losing *adj* = peu populaire, qui risque de faire perdre des voix

voter *n* électeur(trice) *m,f*, mandant(e) *m,f*; **the voters** l'électorat *m*; **French voters go to the polls tomorrow** les Français vont aux urnes demain

◇ **voter apathy** apathie *f* électorale *ou* des électeurs

◇ **voter registration** inscription *f* sur les listes électorales

◇ *Am* **voter registration card** carte *f* d'électeur

◇ **voter turnout** taux m de participation électorale

> A range of measures designed to lure voters back to the polls is being proposed by the Electoral Commission. The commission has investigated why turnout was an all-time low of 59% at the 7 June general election. In the first official report into the poll, published on Tuesday, it maintains that responsibility for reversing **voter apathy** rests primarily with politicians. Only 59% of voters went to the polls this year. But it also accepts that making voting easier would help.

vote-rigging n manipulations fpl électorales

vote-selling n vente f de voix ou de votes

vote-trading n échange m de voix ou de votes

vote-winner n = politique populaire permettant de remporter une victoire électorale; **Labour believes its plans to cut taxes were a vote-winner at last year's elections** le Parti travailliste pense que c'est son intention de réduire les impôts qui lui a valu la victoire aux élections de l'année dernière

vote-winning adj = qui permet de remporter une victoire électorale

voting n vote m, scrutin m; **voting takes place on Sunday** le scrutin a lieu dimanche, les électeurs vont aux urnes dimanche; **I don't know how the voting will go** je ne sais pas comment les gens vont voter

◇ **voting assembly** assemblée f électorale

◇ **voting behaviour** comportement m électoral

◇ **voting booth** isoloir m

◇ **voting card** carte f d'électeur

◇ Am **voting machine** machine f pour enregistrer les votes

◇ **voting method** méthode f électorale

◇ **voting paper** bulletin m de vote

◇ **voting pattern** répartition f des votes

◇ Am **voting precinct** circonscription f électorale

WAEMU n (abbr **West African Economic and Monetary Union**) UEMOA f

wage n wage(s) salaire m, paie f
◇ *wage adjustment* ajustement m des salaires
◇ *wage differential* écart m salarial ou de salaire
◇ *wage dispute* conflit m salarial
◇ *wage drift* dérive f salariale
◇ *wage economy* économie f salariale
◇ *wage freeze* gel m ou blocage m des salaires
◇ *wage inflation* inflation f des salaires
◇ *wage and price index* indice m des prix et des salaires
◇ *wage rate* taux m des salaires
◇ *wage restraint* restriction f salariale
◇ *wage round* cycle m ou série f de négociations salariales

wage-price spiral n spirale f des prix et des salaires

Wales n
◇ *Wales Office* = ministère des affaires galloises
◇ *Wales Secretary* = ministre des affaires galloises

walkabout n to go on a walkabout (of politician) prendre un bain de foule

Wall Street n Wall Street (quartier de la Bourse de New York)

ward n Pol (district) circonscription f ou sélection f électorale
◇ Am *ward heeler* agent m électoral (qui sollicite des voix)

warhead n ogive f

warmonger n belliciste mf

warmongering 1 n (a) (activities) activités fpl bellicistes (b) (attitude) bellicisme m (c) (propaganda) propagande f belliciste
2 adj belliciste, va-t-en-guerre

watchdog n organisme m de surveillance ou de contrôle; **the committee acts as a watchdog on environmental issues** le comité veille aux problèmes d'environnement

> **"**
>
> The Parliamentary Commission for Standards, the only independent **watchdog** investigating allegations of sleaze and corruption against MPs, is to be downgraded next year. Elizabeth Filkin, its head, will be replaced by a commissioner working a reduced schedule for a lower salary.
>
> **"**

WCL n (abbr **World Confederation of Labour**) CMT f

weak adj (a) (government, country) faible, impuissant(e) (b) (currency, economy) faible; (market, prices) en baisse, baissier(ère)

weaken 1 vt (a) (government, country) affaiblir (b) (currency, economy) affaiblir, faire baisser; (market, prices) faire fléchir
2 vi (a) (of influence, power) diminuer, baisser (b) (of currency, economy) s'affaiblir, baisser; (of market, prices) fléchir; **the pound has weak-**

ened against the dollar la livre est en baisse par rapport au dollar

weakness n (a) (of government, country) faiblesse f, fragilité f (b) (of currency, economy) faiblesse f; (of market, prices) fléchissement m

wealth n richesse f, prospérité f
◇ **wealth distribution** répartition f des richesses

wealthy adj riche

weapon n arme f
◇ **weapons inspector** inspecteur m du désarmement
◇ **weapons of mass destruction** armes fpl de destruction massive

weight vt Econ (index, average) pondérer

weighted adj Econ (index, average) pondéré(e)
◇ **weighted average** moyenne f pondérée

weighting n Econ (of index, average) pondération f, coefficient m

welfare n
◇ Am **welfare benefits** avantages mpl sociaux
◇ **welfare economics** économie f du bien-être
◇ **welfare economy** économie f du bien-être
◇ **welfare payments** prestations fpl sociales
◇ **Welfare State** (concept) État m providence; **the government wants to cut back on the Welfare State** le gouvernement veut réduire les dépenses de sécurité sociale

welfare-to-work n Pol = principe selon lequel les bénéficiaires de l'allocation de chômage doivent fournir un travail en échange

well-being n Econ bien-être m inv

Welsh adj
◇ **Welsh Assembly** Assemblée f galloise ou du pays de Galles
◇ **Welsh Assembly Executive** = gouvernement semi-autonome du pays de Galles

◇ **Welsh Office** = ministère des affaires galloises

western adj Pol (powers, world) occidental(e)
◇ **Western Alliance** bloc m des pays occidentaux ou de l'Ouest
◇ **Western European Union** Union f de l'Europe occidentale

Westerner n Pol Occidental(e) m,f

Westminster n = nom du quartier du centre de Londres où se trouvent le Parlement et le palais de Buckingham, que l'on utilise souvent pour parler du Parlement lui-même ; **Westminster will vote on the bill tomorrow** un vote du Parlement décidera du sort du projet de loi demain

wet Br Pol **1** n modéré(e) m,f, mou (molle) m,f (du parti conservateur)
2 adj modéré(e), mou (molle) (du parti conservateur)

WEU n Pol (abbr **Western European Union**) UEO f

WFP n (abbr **World Food Programme**) PAM m

WFTU n (abbr **World Federation of Trade Unions**) FSM f

whip n Parl (a) (MP) = parlementaire chargé de la discipline de son parti et qui veille à ce que ses députés participent aux votes (b) Br (summons) convocation f (c) Br (paper) = calendrier des travaux parlementaires envoyé par le "whip" aux députés de son parti
▸ **whip in** vt sep Br Parl battre le rappel de (pour voter)

whispering campaign n campagne f de diffamation

❝❝

Gwyneth Dunwoody, veteran chairwoman of the House of Commons transport select committee, yesterday accused ministers of attempting to smear her after she lambasted the government's 10 year transport plan. To the irritation of ministers, who had hoped to draw a line under recent rows about spin, Mrs Dunwoody said the government's "deep insecurity" has prompted ministers to start a fresh **whispering campaign** against her.

99

whistle-stop *vi Am Pol* = faire une tournée électorale en passant par des petites villes

white *adj*
◇ *Am* **the White House** la Maison-Blanche
◇ *Am Pol* **White House Military Office** cabinet *m* militaire de la Maison-Blanche
◇ *Br* **white paper** *(government report)* livre *m* blanc

Whitehall *n* = nom d'une rue du centre de Londres qui réunit de nombreux services gouvernementaux et que l'on utilise souvent pour parler du gouvernement lui-même; **a secret Whitehall memo reveals that the government is considering accepting the deal** un document secret émanant de services gouvernementaux révèle que le gouvernement envisage d'accepter l'accord

wholesale price index *n* indice *m* des prix de gros

win *Pol* **1** *vt (election)* gagner; **the Greens have won ten seats** les Verts ont gagné dix sièges; **they won the seat from Labour** ils ont enlevé le siège aux Travaillistes
2 *vi (in election)* gagner

▸ **win back** *vt sep Pol (votes, voters, seats)* récupérer, recouvrer

windfall *n*
◇ *windfall dividends* dividendes *mpl* exceptionnels
◇ *windfall profit* bénéfice *m* exceptionnel
◇ *windfall revenues* revenus *mpl* inespérés *ou* exceptionnels
◇ *windfall tax* impôt *m* sur les bénéfices exceptionnels

wing *n Pol* aile *f*; **the radical wing of the party** l'aile *ou* la fraction radicale du parti

withdraw **1** *vt (diplomat, envoy)* rappeler; *Parl* **to withdraw the whip from an MP** exclure temporairement un député de son parti *(le député continue de siéger à la Chambre des communes mais ne représente plus son parti)*
2 *vi (of candidate)* se retirer, se désister

withdrawal *n (of diplomat, envoy)* rappel *m*; *(of candidate)* retrait *m*, désistement *m*

withholding tax *n* impôt *m* retenu à la source, retenue *f* fiscale

women's suffrage *n Pol* le droit de vote pour les femmes

Woolsack *n Br Parl* **the Woolsack** *(seat)* = coussin rouge sur lequel s'assoit le Lord Chancellor (à la Chambre des lords); *(office)* = le siège du Lord Chancellor (à la Chambre des lords)

66

In the meantime, "we are engaged in a peace process, and many will wish to support that process". Whether this means that Gerry Adams should be allowed to gaze at Lord Irvine, as he sat majestically and scarlet-faced on the **Woolsack**, she did not say.

99

work **1** *n* **(a)** *(labour)* travail *m* **(b)** *(employment)* travail *m*, emploi *m*; **to be out of work** être sans travail *ou* sans emploi
2 *vt (employee)* faire travailler
3 *vi (of person)* travailler
◇ *works council* comité *m* d'entreprise

worker *n* travailleur(euse) *m,f*; *(in industry)* ouvrier(ère) *m,f*
◇ *worker control* ouvriérisme *m*
◇ *workers' cooperative* coopérative *f* ouvrière
◇ *workers' organization* organisation *f* de travailleurs

◇ *worker participation* participation *f* ouvrière

workfare *n Pol* = principe selon lequel les bénéficiaires de l'allocation de chômage doivent fournir un travail en échange

workforce *n* main-d'œuvre *f*, effectifs *mpl*

working *adj*
◇ *working capital* capital *m* d'exploitation
◇ *working class* classe *f* ouvrière, classe *f* populaire
◇ *working group* groupe *m* de travail
◇ *working party* groupe *m* de travail
◇ *working poor* travailleurs *mpl* pauvres
◇ *working population* population *f* active

work-to-rule *n Br* grève *f* du zèle

world 1 *n* monde *m*
  2 *adj* mondial(e), du monde
◇ *World Bank* Banque *f* mondiale
◇ *world economy* économie *f* mondiale
◇ *World Federation of Trade Unions* Fédération *f* syndicale mondiale
◇ *World Food Programme* programme *m* alimentaire mondial
◇ *world market* marché *m* mondial
◇ *world power* puissance *f* mondiale
◇ *world reserves* réserves *fpl* mondiales
◇ *World Social Forum* Forum *m* social mondial
◇ *world trade* commerce *m* international
◇ *World Trade Organization* Organi-

sation *f* mondiale du commerce

worldwide *adj* (depression, famine) mondial(e), global(e)
◇ *worldwide rights* droits *mpl* d'exploitation pour le monde entier

wrecking amendment *n Parl* = amendement proposé dans le but de faire échouer un projet de loi ou de faire en sorte qu'il ne soit pas adopté en temps voulu

> **"**
>
> Even the Conservative front bench admits the current working hours are indefensible, proposing a **wrecking amendment** calling for a 9.30am start against Mr Cook's suggested 11.30am, rather than attempting to put the case for the status quo.
>
> **"**

writ *n Pol* (for elections) ordonnance *f* (émanant du président de la Chambre des communes et convoquant les députés pour un vote)

▸ **write in** *vt sep Am Pol* (a) (name) ajouter, inscrire (sur un bulletin de vote) (b) (vote for) voter pour (en ajoutant le nom sur le bulletin de vote)

write-in *n Am Pol* (addition of name) inscription *f*, rajout *m*; (name added) nom *m* rajouté

written question *n Pol* question *f* écrite

WTO *n* (abbr **World Trade Organization**) OMC *f*

yea n Parl (in vote) oui m; **the yeas and nays** les oui et les non, les voix pour et contre

year-on-year, year-over-year 1 adj (growth, decline) d'une année à l'autre
  2 adv (grow, decline) d'une année à l'autre

yes vote n Parl vote m pour; **to give a yes vote** voter pour

young adj
◇ Br Pol **Young Conservatives** = organisation de jeunes conservateurs
◇ Pol **Young Turk** jeune-turc (jeune-turque) m,f

zealot n fanatique mf, zélateur(trice) m,f

zealotry n fanatisme m

zero n zéro m
◇ Econ **zero growth** croissance f zéro, croissance f économique nulle
◇ Pol **zero option** option f zéro
◇ Pol **zero tolerance** tolérance f zéro

> ❝
> The right wing coalition parties, RPR and UDF, are expected to triumph at the French legislative elections due to take place at the end of this month but, regardless of who wins, the French economy is set to go into recession in the first half of this year with even the most optimistic forecasters predicting **zero growth**.
> ❞

zone n (area) zone f

THE POLITICAL SYSTEMS OF FRANCE, BELGIUM AND SWITZERLAND

FRANCE

CENTRAL GOVERNMENT

Executive (Head of State)

The French Head of State is the President (*Président de la République*)

Composition:

- five-year term of office

- minimum age for presidential candidate: 23

- can sit for more than one term of office

- elected by direct universal suffrage

- electors vote for a single candidate

- two rounds of voting: first round by absolute majority vote; second round by simple majority vote

Functions :

- guarantees the proper functioning of the State

- appoints the Prime Minister (*Premier ministre*)

- appoints the Cabinet (on the advice of the Prime Minister) and acts as chairperson

- has the right to dissolve the *Assemblée nationale*

- has the right to address the *Assemblée nationale* and the *Sénat*

- appoints individuals to civil and military posts of State

- can deliver referenda to the people on the advice of the government or of the two Chambers acting jointly

- can implement special powers in cases of national emergency

- is Commander-in-Chief of the Armed Forces

Legislature

National Assembly (*Assemblée nationale*) (Lower House)

Composition:

- 577 members (*députés*) serving a five-year term of office

- minimum age for *député*: 23

- can sit for more than one term of office

- elected by direct universal suffrage

- electors vote for a single candidate

- two rounds of voting: first round by absolute majority vote; second round by simple majority vote

- the *Président de l'Assemblée Nationale* presides over the *Assemblée*. He or she chairs debates and ensures that the House rules and regulations are observed

Functions:

- adopts legislation along with the *Sénat*

- has the right to initiate and modify bills

- supervises government policy

- has the right to pass a vote of no confidence in the government

Senate (*Sénat*) (Upper House)

Composition:

- 321 senators (*sénateurs*) serving a nine-year term of office, with one third of senators elected every three years

- minimum age for senator: 35

- elected by indirect universal suffrage by an electoral college in each *département*

- electoral college composed of *députés*, *conseillers généraux*, regional councillors and local council representatives

- the *Président du Sénat* presides over the Senate. He or she chairs debates and ensures that the House rules and regulations are observed. The *Président du Sénat* ranks second in the State hierarchy. The President must consult him or her on constitutional affairs and he or she replaces the President in case of death or resignation

Functions:

- adopts legislation along with the *Assemblée Nationale*

- has the right to initiate and modify bills

- supervises government policy

- represents local authority interests in Parliament

- nominates individuals to senior institutional positions

- *sénateurs* have the same powers as *députés*, except the right to take a vote of no confidence

LOCAL GOVERNMENT

There are three types of local authority in France, responsible for the commune (*commune*), the canton (*canton*) and the region (*région*).

Local Council (*Conseil municipal*)

The *conseil municipal* is responsible for a *commune* (the smallest administrative division in France).

- local councillors (*conseillers municipaux*) serve a six-year term of office

- minimum age for *conseiller municipal*: 18

- elected by direct universal suffrage

- two rounds of majority voting

- in communes with fewer than 3,500 inhabitants, electors vote for as many candidates as there are seats, and can vote for candidates from more than one list

- in communes with more than 3,500 inhabitants, electors vote for as many candidates as there are seats, with some seats allocated proportionally

Departmental Council (*Conseil général*)

The *conseil général* is responsible for a *canton* (an administrative subdivision of a department (*département*)).

- departmental councillors (*conseillers généraux*) serve a six-year term of office, with half of the departmental council elected every three years

- minimum age for *conseiller général*: 18

- elected by direct universal suffrage

- two rounds of voting: first round by absolute majority vote; second round by simple majority vote

- electors vote for a single candidate

Departmental Council (*Conseil régional*)

The *conseil régional* is responsible for a *région* (an administrative division made up of several *départements*).

- regional councillors (*conseillers régionaux*) serve a six-year term of office

- minimum age for *conseiller régional*: 21

- elected by direct universal suffrage

- one round of voting

- electors vote from a list of candidates covering a *département*

- remaining seats are allocated using highest average system: seats are divided among parties in proportion to the results achieved

MAJOR FRENCH POLITICAL PARTIES

PARTY NAME	POLITICAL LEANING	DATE FOUNDED
Chasse, Pêche, Nature et Tradition (CPNT)	promotes rural life, hunting, fishing and environmental protection	1989
Front National (FN)	extreme right	1972
Ligue Communiste Révolutionnaire (LCR)	militant Trotskyist	1938, French branch of the IVe Internationale de Trotski
Lutte Ouvrière (LO)	militant Trotskyist	1968, replaced the Voix Ouvrière
Parti Communiste Français (PCF)	communist	1943, replaced the French branch of the Internationale Communiste (SFIC), which was founded in 1920
Parti Socialiste (PS)	socialist	1969, replaced the French branch of the Internationale Ouvrière (SFIO), which was founded in 1905
Pôle Républicain (PR)	socialist splinter group, formed in opposition to certain aspects of European integration	2002, replaced the Mouvement des Citoyens (MDC) which was founded in 1992
Union pour la Démocratie Française (UDF)	right-of-centre	1978
Union pour la Majorité Présidentielle (UMP)	right	2002, formed largely from a union between Démocratie Libérale and Rassemblement pour la République
Les Verts	green; forms a coalition with the main left-wing political groups	1984

BELGIUM

The federal state is made up of ten provinces (*provinces*) and 589 communes (*communes*). Communes are the smallest unit of administration. Depending on the powers exercised, they are supervised by the federal government, the Community (*Communauté*) or the Region (*Région*) (see below).

As well as the federal government and the legislature, there are also three *Régions* – Brussels (*Bruxelles*), Flanders (*Flandre*) and Wallonia (*Wallonie*) – based on local economies and three *Communautés* (Dutch, French and German) based on linguistic and cultural ties. (The protection of linguistic and cultural rights is a very important issue in Belgium.) The Flemish *Communauté* exercises its powers in the Flemish provinces and in Brussels, the French *Communauté* in the Walloon provinces, with the exception of German-speaking communes, and in Brussels and the German-speaking *Communauté* in the communes of the province of Liège that forms the German language area. These institutions have equal status but have powers and responsibilities for different fields.

Executive

Head of State

The Belgian Head of State is the reigning monarch.

Composition:

- the Belgian monarchy is hereditary and constitutional

- the Crown passes to the eldest male heir of the monarch (or to the eldest female if the monarch has no sons)

Functions:

The monarch has limited, mainly ceremonial powers. He or she does not exercise any personal authority: the government ministers bear full responsibility by jointly signing the draft laws that are enacted by Parliament and Royal Decrees.

- appoints and dismisses Cabinet ministers

- opens and dissolves Parliament

- nominates *ministres d'État* (with the approval of the Prime Minister)

Federal government (*Gouvernement fédéral*)

Composition:

- there are a maximum of 15 ministers in the Cabinet (*Conseil des ministres*)

- the *Conseil des ministres* consists of the Prime Minister, who is head of the government, seven French-speaking ministers, seven Dutch-speaking ministers and the secretaries of state (*ministres d'État*)

- the title of *ministre d'État* is honorary and the *ministres d'État* are usually leading figures from society. They are not part of the government and may not attend the *Chambre des représentants* or the *Sénat*

Functions:

- has the right to initiate and amend bills

- ratifies legislation

- is responsible for national issues such as defence, foreign policy and monetary policy

Legislature

Chamber of Representatives (*Chambre des représentants*) (Lower House)

Composition:

- 150 members (*députés*) serving four-year term of office

- minimum age for a *député*: 21

- elected by direct universal suffrage using a system of proportional representation (party list system)

Functions:

- initiates and debates bills

- is responsible for budgets and other financial matters

- acts as a check on the government

- questions government and sets up committees of enquiry

- shares certain responsibilities with the *Sénat*, such as amendments to the Constitution, ratifying international treaties and approving appointments made by the monarch

- can submit private member's bills and examine government bills

Senate (*Sénat*) (Upper House)

Composition:

- divided into two linguistic groups, Dutch and French

- 71 senators (*sénateurs*) serving four-year term of office

- minimum age for a *sénateur*: 21

- 40 *sénateurs* elected by direct universal suffrage (25 by Dutch-speaking electoral college and 15 by French-speaking electoral college)

-21 *sénateurs* nominated by the Community councils (*conseils de Communauté*): ten nominated by the Flemish Community Council (*Vlaams Parlement*), ten by the French Community Council (*Parlement de la Communauté française*) and one by the German Community Council (*Rat der Deutschsprachigen Gemeinschaft*). These *sénateurs* are known as "Community senators" (*sénateurs de communauté*)

- ten *sénateurs* (six Dutch-speaking and four French-speaking) nominated by co-option by the other groups of *sénateurs*

Functions:

- acts as a check on the government

- mediates conflicts of interest between the different federal institutions; *sénateurs de communauté* act as a bridge between the federal parliament and the other federal institutions as they are both senators and members of community councils

- nominates key senior officials and approves appointments made by the monarch

- can submit private member's bills and examine government bills

- must defer to the *Chambre des représentants*

Régions and Communautés

Each *Région* and *Communauté* has its own directly-elected council and its own government: they make their own laws regarding a number of specific matters and ensure their implementation. *Conseils de Communauté* look after issues such as education, culture and health care. *Conseils régionaux* look after issues relating to geographical areas, such as the economy, transport, the environment and agriculture. Members are elected by direct universal suffrage and the minimum age for a member is 21.

The *Régions* and *Communautés* are structured as follows:

Flemish Region and Flemish Commmunity (*Région flamande/ Communauté flamande*): 124 members in council (joint councils)

Wallon Region (*Région Wallone*): 75 members in council

Brussels-Capital Region (*Région de Bruxelle-Capitale*): 75 members in council (64 French-speaking and 11 Dutch-speaking)

French-speaking Community (*Communauté française*): 94 members in council

German-speaking Community (*Communauté germanophone*): 25 members in council

BELGIAN POLITICAL GROUPINGS

Belgian *députés* and *sénateurs* are organized into political groupings based on political orientation. The major groups are:

GROUP NAME	POLITICAL LEANING	LANGUAGE GROUP
Anders gaan leven (Agalev)	green	Dutch-speaking
Centre Démocrate Humaniste (CDH)	christian democrat	French-speaking
Christen-Democratisch & Vlaams (CD&V)	christian democrat	Dutch-speaking
Écologistes confédérés pour l'organisation de luttes originales (Écolo)	green	French-speaking
Mouvement Réformateur (MR)	liberal	French-speaking
Parti Socialiste (PS)	socialist	French-speaking
Socialistische Partij Anders (SP)	socialist	Dutch-speaking
Vlaams Blok (VB)	right-wing	Dutch-speaking
Vlaamse Liberalen en Democraten (VLD)	liberal	Dutch-speaking
Volksunie (VU)	Flemish nationalist	Dutch-speaking

SWITZERLAND

The Swiss Confederation is made up of administrative states known as cantons (*cantons*). There are 20 *cantons* and 6 half-cantons (*demi-cantons*). Each canton is a semi-autonomous region; it has internal sovereignty as well as a constitution. Half-cantons were formed when two former cantons split; they have the same level of autonomy as cantons.

Executive

Federal Council (*Conseil fédéral*)

Composition:

- the highest authority in the country

- seven equal members (elected by the *Assemblée fédérale*) serving a four-year term of office

- can sit for more than one term of office

- President of the Confederation (*Président de la Confédération*) is elected from among their number and serves a one-year term of office. He or she acts as both Head of State and Head of Government and presides over the *Conseil fédéral*. The *Président de la Confédération* must be impartial but has the casting vote if necessary

Functions:

- responsible for government activities; plans and implements government policy

- supervises the *Assemblée fédérale*

- has legislative role; can submit federal laws to the *Assemblée fédérale*

- appoints civil servants

- enforces federal law

- safeguards national security

- ratifies treaties

Legislature

National Council (*Conseil national*)

Composition:

- 200 members serving a four-year term of office

- elected by universal suffrage

- each canton constitutes an electoral constituency and elects at least one member, whatever its population

- cantons and half-cantons with a single seat use a first-past-the-post electoral system

- the remaining cantons use a system of proportional representation whereby seats are allotted in proportion to the population of each constituency

- President of the Council (*Président du Conseil*) serves a one-year term of office. He or she represents and speaks on behalf of the *Conseil national*, enforces its rules and regulations and chairs debates

Council of States (*Conseil des États*)

Composition:

- 46 members serving a four-year term of office

- members elected according to the constitutions of individual cantons

- two members elected per canton, one per half-canton

- majoritarian system used, usually absolute majority vote (with the exception of the Jura canton which uses a system of proportional representation)

- President of the Council (*Président du Conseil*) serves a one-year term of office. He or she represents and speaks on behalf of the *Conseil des États*, enforces its rules and regulations and chairs debates

Functions:

The two houses have equal powers:

- have legislative authority

- ratify treaties

- determine the budget and other financial issues

- act as a check on the *Conseil fédéral* and the government

The *Conseil national* and the *Conseil des États* are collectively known as the Federal Assembly (*Assemblée fédérale*). The *Assemblée fédérale* is not made up of professional parliamentary members; the members of both Councils exercise their mandates in addition to other professional activities. They participate in four annual three-week-long sessions of the *Assemblée fédérale*, as well as any extraordinary or special sessions. The federal constitution also allows for considerable direct democracy. For example, bills passed by parliament have to be approved by the electorate by referendum if 50,000 signatures against the bill are collected. Note that the *Assemblée fédérale* is not made up of political parties, but is divided into groups or factions. The factions comprise members of the same party or of parties with a similar political orientation.

MAJOR SWISS POLITICAL PARTIES

PARTY NAME	POLITICAL LEANING
Démocrates Suisses (DS)	extreme right
Evangelische Volkspartei (EVP)	Protestant party to the right of the political spectrum
Grünes Bündnis (GB)	green
Lega dei Ticinesi	regionalist party, to the right of the political spectrum
Parti Chrétien-Social (PCS)	progressive christian democrat
Parti Démocrate-Chrétien (PDC)	christian-democrat, Centrist
Parti Libéral Suisse (PLS)	liberal
Parti Radical-démocratique Suisse (PRD)	liberal
Parti Socialiste Suisse (PSS)	to the left of the political spectrum
Parti Suisse du Travail (PST)	communist
Union Démocratique du Centre (UDC)	extreme right
Union Démocratique Fédérale (UDF)	to the right of the political spectrum
Les Verts (Parti écologiste suisse) (PES)	green

LE ROYAUME UNI

LE GOUVERNEMENT CENTRAL

Le chef d'État

Le chef d'État du Royaume-Uni est le souverain régnant.

Composition :

- la monarchie britannique est héréditaire et constitutionnelle

- la Couronne est transmise au fils aîné du monarque (ou à la fille aînée si le monarque n'a pas de fils)

Fonctions :

Les pouvoirs du monarque sont limités, ses fonctions étant principalement cérémonielles.

- il donne son assentiment (*Royal Assent*) à chaque nouvelle loi

- il nomme le Premier ministre (*Prime Minister*) (par convention, le Premier ministre est toujours le leader du parti majoritaire aux élections législatives)

- il nomme les pairs à vie (sur l'avis du Premier ministre)

- il ouvre et dissout le Parlement

Le pouvoir exécutif

Le pouvoir exécutif est détenu par le *cabinet*, sous la houlette du Premier ministre.

Composition :

- le Premier ministre est le chef du gouvernement, c'est-à-dire le leader du parti majoritaire aux élections législatives

- le cabinet se compose d'environ 20 ministres choisis par le Premier ministre

Fonctions :

- le cabinet décide de la politique gouvernementale et coordonne le travail des différents ministères

Le pouvoir législatif

Le Parlement de Westminster, organe législatif britannique, se compose de la Chambre des communes (*House of Commons*) et de la Chambre des lords (*House of Lords*).

La Chambre des communes (Chambre basse)

Composition :

- 659 députés élus pour cinq ans ; un député ou *MP* (*Member of Parliament*) par circonscription électorale (*constituency*)

- âge minimum requis : 21 ans

- leur mandat est renouvelable

- ils sont élus au suffrage universel direct

- scrutin majoritaire à un tour (*first-past-the-post electoral system*). Le candidat qui obtient le plus grand nombre de voix remporte les élections, sans qu'il ait besoin de passer la barre des 50%. Une fois les députés élus, le parti qui détient le plus grand nombre de sièges au Parlement forme normalement le nouveau gouvernement

- le/la président(e) de la Chambre des communes s'appelle le *Speaker*, député impartial qui préside les séances et les débats parlementaires et veille à ce que le règlement de la Chambre des communes soit respecté

Fonctions :

- elle joue un rôle majeur dans le processus législatif ; les députés débattent et examinent en détail les propositions de nouvelles lois

- elle se doit de surveiller le travail du gouvernement

- elle examine en particulier le travail du gouvernement en matière de finances et doit approuver les mesures fiscales et budgétaires du gouvernement

La Chambre des lords (Chambre haute)

Composition :

- 693 pairs comprenant les membres laïques ou *Lords Temporal* (91 pairs héréditaires, 578 pairs à vie) et les membres ecclésiastiques ou *Lords Spiritual* (24 évêques et archevêques)

- âge minimum requis : 21 ans

- les pairs ne sont pas élus et conservent leur siège à vie, à l'exception des évêques, qui eux prennent leur retraite

- le/la président(e) de la Chambre des lords est le *Lord Chancellor* qui est nommé(e) par le Premier ministre et fait partie du cabinet, et qui est à la tête du ministère responsable entre autres de l'administration des cours de justice. Le *Lord Chancellor* a le droit de parler au nom du gouvernement lors des débats, et de voter

Fonctions :

- elle revoit les projets de loi votés par la Chambre des communes

- elle sert de contrepoids au pouvoir du gouvernement

- elle constitue la plus haute cour d'appel (et fait donc partie du pouvoir judiciaire)

À l'heure actuelle, l'électorat ne pouvant donner son avis sur la nomination des pairs, la Chambre des lords est en train de subir petit à petit une série de réformes visant à la rendre plus démocratique et plus représentative de la population. Une première réforme de 1999 a permis de réduire énormément le nombre de pairs héréditaires et des discussions sont en cours pour savoir comment procéder à une autre vague de réformes.

LES COLLECTIVITÉS LOCALES

En Écosse, au pays de Galles et dans certaines régions d'Angleterre, ce sont des conseils uniques qui sont responsables de toutes les fonctions des collectivités locales. Ces conseils qui exercent tous les pouvoirs locaux sont appelés différemment selon les régions. Les *Metropolitan authorities* ("collectivités métropolitaines") couvrent les régions d'Angleterre à forte densité de population, et les *London Borough authorities*, la région de Londres. Au pays de Galles, en Écosse et dans les parties non métropolitaines d'Angleterre, on trouve les *Unitary authorities* ("collectivités unitaires").

Dans le reste de l'Angleterre (principalement dans les zones rurales), on a un système à deux niveaux territoriaux : deux conseils (*County Council* et *District Council*) se partagent les responsabilités et s'occupent de différents services au sein des collectivités locales :

- *County Council* (≃ conseil général) : la plus grande division administrative du gouvernement local

- *District Council* (≃ conseil municipal) : subdivision administrative d'un comté (*county*). Selon les régions, on les appelle aussi les *Borough Councils* ou *City Councils*.

Les comtés d'Angleterre et du pays de Galles sont aussi divisés en circonscriptions administratives plus petites. Dans les zones rurales, les conseils municipaux de ces petites communes s'appellent les *parish councils* (ou *community councils* au pays de Galles). Les *parish councils* situés dans des zones urbaines peuvent décider, par le biais d'une résolution, de s'appeler *town councils*.

Composition :

- le nombre de membres varie d'un conseil à l'autre, mais tous les conseillers sont élus pour quatre ans

- âge minimum requis : 21 ans

- ils sont élus au suffrage universel direct

- les collectivités locales ont à leur tête un(e) président(e) ou *Chairperson* (*District Councils*) ou un maire ou *Mayor* (*Borough Councils* ou *City Councils*). Certaines zones urbaines plus grandes, comme Londres, ont des lords-maires (*Lord Mayors*)

- les conseillers doivent avoir suffisamment d'attaches au niveau local pour pouvoir se présenter aux élections

LES PARLEMENTS RÉGIONAUX

Les parlements régionaux (ou *devolved Parliaments*) du Royaume-Uni détiennent certains pouvoirs législatifs et exécutifs.

L'ÉCOSSE

Le Parlement écossais

Composition :

- 129 députés ou *MSPs* (*Members of the Scottish Parliament*) élus pour cinq ans

- âge minimum requis : 21 ans

- ils sont élus au suffrage universel direct

- *additional member electoral system* : mode de scrutin selon lequel les électeurs votent une première fois, au scrutin majoritaire à un tour, pour un candidat représentant leur circonscription locale (73 *constituencies*), et une deuxième fois pour la liste d'un parti ou pour un candidat indépendant au niveau des régions, appelées *Scottish Parliament Regions* (au nombre de huit). Chaque région détient sept sièges supplémentaires au Parlement. À l'intérieur de chaque région, les partis ont droit à des sièges supplémentaires en fonction du nombre de sièges obtenus au niveau local. On désigne les membres choisis pour occuper ces 56 sièges supplémentaires sous le nom de *regional members*

- le/la président(e) du Parlement écossais s'appelle le *Presiding Officer*

Fonctions :

- il vote les lois

- il examine le travail et les politiques de l'exécutif écossais

- il débat des questions d'actualité

- il fait des enquêtes et publie des rapports

Le pouvoir exécutif écossais

Composition :

- le pouvoir exécutif écossais est détenu par le gouvernement d'Écosse auquel le gouvernement britannique a transféré certains pouvoirs, notamment en matière de fiscalité, de santé, d'environnement, d'agriculture, etc. ; le gouvernement écossais est formé par le(s) parti(s) majoritaire(s) au Parlement

- le chef de l'exécutif s'appelle le *First Minister* (et non *Prime Minister*), qui est en général le leader du parti qui compte le plus de députés

- le *First Minister* nomme, avec l'accord du Parlement, les membres de l'exécutif (les *Scottish Ministers*) qui formeront son cabinet

Fonctions :

- la plupart des ministres sont responsables d'un domaine politique particulier choisi par le *First Minister*

- les ministres écossais sont responsables envers le Parlement écossais

LE PAYS DE GALLES

L'Assemblée nationale du pays de Galles

La *National Assembly for Wales* est communément appelée la *Welsh Assembly*, l'Assemblée galloise.

Composition :

- 60 membres ou *AMs* (*Welsh Assembly Members*) élus pour quatre ans

- âge minimum requis : 21 ans

- ils sont élus au suffrage universel direct

- *additional member electoral system* : mode de scrutin selon lequel les électeurs votent une première fois, au scrutin majoritaire à un tour, pour un candidat représentant leur circonscription locale (40 *constituencies*), et une deuxième fois pour la liste d'un parti ou pour un candidat indépendant au niveau régional (cinq *electoral regions*). Chaque région détient quatre sièges supplémentaires à l'Assemblée. À l'intérieur de chaque région, les partis ont droit à des sièges supplémentaires en fonction du nombre de sièges obtenus au niveau local

- le/la président(e) de l'Assemblée galloise s'appelle le *Presiding Officer*

Fonctions :

- elle vote les lois

- elle examine le travail et les politiques de l'exécutif gallois

- elle débat des questions d'actualité

- elle fait des enquêtes et publie des rapports

Le pouvoir exécutif gallois

Composition :

- le pouvoir exécutif gallois est détenu par le gouvernement du pays de Galles auquel le gouvernement britannique a transféré certains pouvoirs ; il est formé par le(s) parti(s) majoritaire(s) au parlement

- le chef de l'exécutif s'appelle le *First Minister* ; il est en général le leader du parti qui compte le plus de députés

- le *First Minister* nomme, avec l'accord de l'Assemblée, les ministres qui formeront son cabinet

Fonctions :

- la plupart des ministres sont responsables d'un domaine politique particulier choisi par le *First Minister*

- les ministres gallois sont responsables envers l'Assemblée galloise

L'IRLANDE DU NORD

L'Assemblée législative d'Irlande du Nord

Composition :

- 108 membres, six pour chacune des 18 *constituencies* d'Irlande du Nord

- âge minimum requis : 21 ans

- ils sont élus au suffrage universel direct

- scrutin proportionnel : scrutin uninominal préférentiel avec report de voix

- l'Assemblée est présidée par le *Speaker*

Fonctions :

- elle examine et vote les lois

- elle examine le travail et les politiques de l'exécutif

- elle débat des questions d'actualité

- elle fait des enquêtes et publie des rapports

Le pouvoir exécutif d'Irlande du Nord

Composition :

- le pouvoir exécutif d'Irlande du Nord est détenu par le gouvernement d'Irlande du Nord auquel le gouvernement britannique a transféré certains pouvoirs

- le chef de l'exécutif s'appelle le *First Minister* ; il dirige, avec le *Deputy First Minister* (vice-Premier ministre), un comité exécutif de ministres. Le *First Minister* et le *Deputy First Minister* doivent se présenter ensemble aux élections et obtenir le soutien des communautés catholiques et protestantes d'Irlande du Nord.

- le partage du pouvoir prévaut en Irlande du Nord : c'est un gouvernement mixte dans lequel les partis protestants et catholiques sont représentés. Les postes ministériels sont attribués proportionnellement au nombre de députés que compte chaque parti à l'Assemblée

Fonctions :

- chaque ministre est responsable de la formulation de la politique de son ministère et reçoit les conseils et l'aide des comités ministériels

En 1998, le *Good Friday Agreement*, accord de paix qui permit d'établir l'exécutif d'Irlande du Nord, autorisa l'inclusion du *Sinn Fein* (l'aile politique de l'IRA) à condition qu'il suive les objectifs républicains par des moyens pacifiques et démocratiques. Depuis sa création, l'Assemblée d'Irlande du Nord a été suspendue trois fois par le ministre britannique d'Irlande du Nord, avec retour du contrôle direct de l'Irlande du Nord par Westminster. La cause de telles suspensions réside dans l'échec des tentatives visant à sortir l'Irlande du Nord de l'impasse politique dans laquelle elle se trouve enlisée, échec en partie dû aux problèmes que pose le désarmement de l'IRA.

<u>LES PRINCIPAUX PARTIS POLITIQUES REPRÉSENTÉS À WESTMINSTER</u>

NOM DU PARTI	TENDANCE POLITIQUE	DATE DE CRÉATION
Conservative (Parti conservateur)	à droite de l'éventail politique	formé à partir du *Tory Party* (crée au 18ème siècle), le nom *Conservative party* a été progressivement introduite vers le milieu du 19ème siècle
Democratic Unionist	il cherche à maintenir l'union politique entre la Grande-Bretagne et l'Irlande	1971
Labour (Parti travailliste)	à gauche de l'éventail politique	1900
Liberal Democrats	tendance centriste	1988
Scottish National Party/Plaid Cymru (ils forment un groupement politique à la Chambre des communes)	SNP : à gauche de l'éventail politique, en faveur de l'indépendance de l'Écosse Plaid Cymru : à gauche de l'éventail politique, en faveur de l'indépendance du pays de Galles	SNP : 1934 Plaid Cymru : 1925
Sinn Fein	parti républicain irlandais : il cherche à obtenir l'autodétermination de l'Irlande	1905
Social Democratic and Labour Party (SDLP)	à gauche de l'éventail politique, en Irlande du Nord	1970
Ulster Unionist	il cherche à maintenir l'union politique entre la Grande-Bretagne et l'Irlande	1905

LES ÉTATS-UNIS

Le mode de scrutin en vigueur aux États-Unis est le scrutin majoritaire à un tour (*first-past-the-post electoral system*). Les électeurs votent directement pour les candidats de leur choix lors des législatives (pour élire les membres du Congrès fédéral et ceux du Congrès de chaque État) et lors des élections des gouverneurs. Le candidat qui obtient le plus grand nombre de voix remporte les élections, sans qu'il ait besoin de passer la barre des 50%.

LE GOUVERNEMENT FÉDÉRAL

Le pouvoir exécutif (le chef d'État et le gouvernement)

Le chef d'État des États-Unis est le Président.

Composition :

- le candidat à la présidence est élu par un collège électoral de 538 membres élus au suffrage universel

- âge minimum requis : 35 ans

- mandat présidentiel de quatre ans, renouvelable une fois

Fonctions :

- il nomme et dirige le gouvernement fédéral (il y a environ 20 ministères)

- il est responsable des différents ministères et agences du gouvernement fédéral

- il mène les politiques étrangère et intérieure

- il est Commandant en chef des forces armées

Le pouvoir législatif

Le Congrès, organe législatif américain, se compose de la Chambre des représentants (*House of Representatives*) et du Sénat (*Senate*).

La Chambre des représentants (Chambre basse)

Composition :

- 435 membres élus pour deux ans (le nombre de sièges d'un État est fonction de la taille de sa population, chaque État ayant au moins droit à un membre)

- âge minimum requis : 25 ans

- leur mandat est renouvelable

- ils sont élus au suffrage universel direct

- le *Speaker*, élu parmi les membres du parti majoritaire, préside les séances et les débats de la Chambre des représentants

Fonctions :

- de manière générale, elle a le même statut que le Sénat

- elle détient le pouvoir législatif ; les membres débattent et examinent en détail les propositions de nouvelles lois

- elle exerce un pouvoir législatif plus important que le Sénat en matière de fiscalité et des dépenses

- elle se doit de surveiller le travail de l'exécutif

Le Sénat (Chambre haute)

Composition :

- 100 sénateurs, deux par État, élus pour six ans avec un tiers renouvelable tous les deux ans

- âge minimun pour être sénateur : 30 ans

- ils sont élus au suffrage universel direct

- le Sénat est présidé par un sénateur du parti majoritaire qui interprète le règlement et la jurisprudence du Sénat

Fonctions :

- il détient le pouvoir législatif, peut revoir les projets de loi votés par la Chambre des représentants

- il peut amender ou rejeter les projets de loi financiers

- il confirme ou rejette les nominations présidentielles, y compris celles des membres du cabinet

- il ratifie les traités

- il sert de contrepoids au pouvoir exécutif ; il peut, par exemple, annuler les véto présidentiels

LE GOUVERNEMENT D'ÉTAT

Chacun des 50 États américains, à l'exception du Nebraska (qui a un système monocaméral), a un système législatif bicaméral qui suit le modèle du pouvoir législatif fédéral. Chacun des États est autonome en matière de législation et de fiscalité. Dans chaque État, le pouvoir exécutif est détenu par un gouverneur.

LES PRINCIPAUX PARTIS POLITIQUES REPRÉSENTÉS AU CONGRÈS

NOM DU PARTI	TENDANCE POLITIQUE	DATE DE CRÉATION
Parti démocrate	tendance libérale	1828
Parti républicain	à droite de l'éventail politique	1854

COMMITTEE OF THE REGIONS

- comprises 222 members (the number reflects the population of the Member States)

- members nominated by European Council members for a four-year renewable term

- composed of representatives from local and regional authorities

- advises on and promotes local and regional policies such as culture, education, employment, the environment and transport

COUNCIL OF THE EUROPEAN UNION

- comprises one representative of each Member State at ministerial level

- composition varies according to the subject under discussion

- Presidency of the Council held in turn by each Member State for six months

- draws up and implements legislation in co-decision with European Parliament

- coordinates the economic policies of Member States

- coordinates the activities of Member States

- concludes international agreements on behalf of the European Union

- frames and implements the common foreign and security policy

ECONOMIC AND SOCIAL COMMITTEE

- comprises 222 members appointed by the European Council for a four-year renewable term (the number reflects the population of the Member States)

- composed of representatives from economic and social interest groups who are nominated by Member State governments

- advises on economic and social policies such as consumer protection, social affairs and trade

- fosters links with international community

EUROPEAN CENTRAL BANK

- comprises staff from all Member States

- finances and implements European monetary policy

- conducts foreign exchange operations and ensures the smooth functioning of payment systems

EUROPEAN COMMISSION

- comprises 20 members, including a President and two Vice-Presidents

- members appointed by national governments for a five-year term

- embodies and upholds the general interests of the European Union

- drafts legislation and presents initiatives to the European Parliament and European Council

- implements legislation, budget and programmes adopted by the European Parliament and European Council

- enforces Community law

- represents the Community's interests at an international level

EUROPEAN COUNCIL

- brings together the President of the European Commission and the Head of State/Government of each of the Member States

- takes place in and is hosted by Member State holding the Presidency of the Council of the European Union

- defines European Union political guidelines

- responsible for the development of the European Union

- mediates and resolves problem issues

EUROPEAN COURT OF AUDITORS

- comprises 15 members, one per Member State

- members appointed by the European Commission for a renewable six-year term

- audits all revenue and expenditure of the European Union

- assists the European Parliament in monitoring the implementation of the Community budget

EUROPEAN COURT OF FIRST INSTANCE

- comprises 15 judges appointed by governments of Member States for a renewable six-year term

- deals with all actions brought by companies and individuals against decisions of Community institutions and agencies

EUROPEAN COURT OF JUSTICE

- comprises 15 judges and nine advocates general appointed by Member State governments

- appointed for a six-year term with partial reappointment every three years

- enforces Community law

- has jurisdiction in disputes involving Member States, EU institutions, businesses and individuals

EUROPEAN INVESTMENT BANK

- comprises staff from all Member States

- finances investment projects which contribute to the development of the European Union

EUROPEAN OMBUDSMAN

- elected by the European Parliament for the duration of its term

- investigates complaints about maladministration by institutions and bodies of the European Union

EUROPEAN PARLIAMENT

- comprises 626 members elected every five years by direct universal suffrage

- members belong to pan-European political groupings

- shares power to legislate with the European Council

- shares budgetary authority with the European Council

- exercises control over the European Commission and European Council

BANQUE CENTRALE EUROPÉENNE

- son personnel provient de tous les États membres de l'Union européenne

- elle finance et met en œuvre la politique monétaire européenne

- elle conduit les opérations de change et assure le bon fonctionnement des systèmes de paiement

BANQUE EUROPÉENNE D'INVESTISSEMENT

- son personnel provient de tous les États membres de l'Union européenne

- elle finance des projets d'investissement qui contribuent au développement de l'Union européenne

COMITÉ ÉCONOMIQUE ET SOCIAL

- il comprend 222 membres nommés par le Conseil pour un mandat de quatre ans renouvelable (le nombre est fonction de la population des États membres)

- il est composé de représentants des différentes catégories de la vie économique et sociale, nommés par les gouvernements des États membres

- il est consulté pour les questions de politique économique et sociale, telles que la protection des consommateurs, les affaires sociales et le commerce

- il favorise les relations avec la communauté internationale

COMITÉ DES RÉGIONS

- il comprend 222 membres (le nombre est fonction de la population des États membres)

- les membres sont nommés par les membres du Conseil européen pour un mandat de quatre ans renouvelable

- il est composé de représentants des collectivités locales et régionales

- il favorise les politiques locales et régionales et il est consulté dans des domaines tels que la culture, l'éducation, l'emploi, l'environnement et le transport

COMMISSION EUROPÉENNE

- elle comprend 20 membres, dont le président et deux vice-présidents

- les membres sont nommés pour cinq ans par les gouvernements des États membres

- elle incarne et défend l'intérêt général de l'Union européenne

- elle détient le droit d'initiative législative et propose des textes de loi soumis au Parlement européen et au Conseil européen

- elle assure l'exécution des lois, du budget et des programmes adoptés par le Parlement européen et le Conseil européen

- elle veille au respect du droit communautaire

- elle représente les intérêts de l'Union européenne sur la scène internationale

CONSEIL EUROPÉEN

- il réunit le Président de la Commission européenne et le chef d'État/ de gouvernement de chaque État membre

- il est organisé par et se déroule dans l'État membre assumant la présidence du Conseil de l'Union européenne

- il définit les orientations politiques de l'Union européenne

- il est responsable du développement de l'Union européenne

- il sert de médiateur et résout les problèmes

CONSEIL DE L'UNION EUROPÉENNE

- il comprend un représentant de chaque État membre au niveau ministériel

- sa composition varie en fonction des questions à l'ordre du jour

- la présidence du Conseil est assumée à tour de rôle par chaque État membre pour une durée de six mois

- il établit et fait appliquer les lois en codécision avec le Parlement européen

- il assure la coordination des politiques économiques des États membres

- il assure la coordination de l'action des États membres

- il conclut, au nom de l'Union européenne, les accords internationaux

- il définit et met en œuvre la politique étrangère et de sécurité commune

COUR DES COMPTES EUROPÉENNE

- elle comprend 15 membres, un par État membre

- les membres sont nommés par la Commission européenne pour un mandat de six ans renouvelable

- elle vérifie toutes les recettes et les dépenses de l'Union européenne

- elle aide le Parlement européen à veiller à la bonne exécution du budget communautaire

COUR DE JUSTICE EUROPÉENNE

- elle comprend 15 juges et neuf avocats généraux nommés par les gouvernements des États membres

- ils sont nommés pour un mandat de six ans avec renouvellement partiel tous les trois ans

- elle veille au respect du droit communautaire

- elle est compétente en matière de litiges impliquant les États membres, les institutions communautaires, les entreprises et les particuliers

MÉDIATEUR EUROPÉEN

- il est élu par le Parlement européen pour la durée de sa législature

- il enquête sur les plaintes de mauvaise administration dans le cadre des institutions ou des organes de l'Union européenne

PARLEMENT EUROPÉEN

- il comprend 626 membres élus tous les cinq ans au suffrage universel direct

- les membres appartiennent à des formations politiques paneuropéennes

- il partage le pouvoir législatif avec le Conseil européen

- il partage la fonction budgétaire avec le Conseil européen

- il exerce un contrôle sur la Commission européenne et le Conseil européen

TRIBUNAL DE PREMIÈRE INSTANCE

- il comprend 15 juges nommés par les gouvernements des États membres pour six ans renouvelables

- elle se prononce sur les recours déposés par des entreprises ou des particuliers contre les décisions des institutions ou des agences communautaires

Français – Anglais
French – English

abaissement *nm Écon (des prix, des taux, d'un impôt)* lowering, reduction; *(d'une monnaie)* weakening

abaisser *vt Écon (prix, taux, impôt)* to lower, to reduce; *(monnaie)* to weaken

abdication *nf* abdication

abdiquer 1 *vt (pouvoir)* to abdicate
2 *vi* to abdicate, to give in; **elle n'abdiquera jamais devant les syndicats** she'll never give in to the unions

abolir *vt Parl (loi)* to annul

abolition *nf Parl (d'une loi)* annulment

abondance *nf Écon* abundance

abrogation *nf Parl (d'une loi)* annulment, repeal

abroger *vt Parl (loi)* to annul, to repeal

absolu, -e *adj Pol (pouvoir, monarque, majorité)* absolute

absolutisme *nm Pol* absolutism

absolutiste *Pol* 1 *adj* absolutist
2 *nmf* absolutist

absorber *vt Écon (entreprise)* to take over, to absorb; **la multinationale va absorber cette entreprise** the multinational is going to take over *or* absorb this company

absorption *nf Écon (d'une entreprise)* takeover, absorption; **l'absorption d'une petite société par une grosse** the takeover *or* absorption of a small company by a large one

abstenir s'abstenir *vpr Pol* to abstain

abstention *nf Pol* abstention
◇ *UE* ***abstention constructive*** constructive abstention

abstentionnisme *nm Pol* abstention

abstentionniste *Pol* 1 *adj* abstentionist
2 *nmf* abstainer

abus *nm (de pouvoir, privilège)* abuse
◇ ***abus de droit*** abuse of privilege

> **"**
>
> Le président de la FCSQ, M. André Caron, déplore cette façon de faire du gouvernement du Québec qui change les règles du jeu en apportant des modifications législatives rétroactives pour s'harmoniser avec une loi fédérale qu'on n'a pas encore modifiée. "Il s'agit d'un **abus de droit** et de pouvoir. En agissant ainsi le gouvernement du Québec privera les commissions scolaires du Québec de ressources financières importantes pour l'organisation du transport scolaire de 650 000 élèves quotidiennement."
>
> **"**

abuser abuser de *vt ind (pouvoir, privilège)* to abuse

accaparement *nm* (a) *Pol (du pouvoir)* seizing (b) *Écon (du marché)* cornering

accaparer *vt* (a) *Pol (pouvoir)* to seize (b) *Écon (marché)* to corner; **accaparer des marchandises** *(pour contrôler le marché)* to withhold goods from the market

accéder accéder à *vt ind (trône)* to accede to; *(indépendance)* to gain, to attain; **faire accéder qn au pouvoir** to bring sb to power; **la résolution de l'ONU vise à les faire accéder à l'indépendance** the UN resolution is aimed at allowing them to become independent

accélérateur *nm Écon* accelerator

accession *nf (arrivée)* accession au trône accession to the throne; **le pays fête son accession à l'indépendance** the country's celebrating becoming independent *or* achieving independence; **l'accession de la Grèce au statut de membre de l'Union européenne** Greece's entry into the European Union

accommoder s'accommoder *vpr* **s'accommoder avec qn** to come to an agreement with sb

accord *nm* (a) *(entente)* agreement, accord (b) *(convention)* agreement; *(pour résoudre un conflit)* settlement; **signer un accord** to sign an agreement; **arriver** *ou* **parvenir à un accord** to come to an agreement, to reach (an) agreement
◇ *accord d'association* partnership agreement
◇ *accord bilatéral* bilateral agreement
◇ *UE accords de Bretton Woods* Bretton Woods Agreement
◇ *accords de Camp David* Camp David Agreement
◇ *accord commercial* trade agreement
◇ *accord commercial multilatéral* multilateral trade agreement
◇ *accord commun* joint agreement
◇ *accord de contrôle des armements* arms control agreement
◇ *Pol accords conventionnels* = agreements resulting from collective bargaining
◇ *accord de coopération* cooperation agreement
◇ *accord européen* Europe agreement

◇ *Écon Accord général sur le commerce des services* General Agreement on Trade and Services
◇ *Écon Accord Général sur les Tarifs Douaniers et le Commerce* General Agreement on Tariffs and Trade
◇ *accords internationaux sur les produits de base* international commodity agreements
◇ *Accord de libre-échange* Free Trade Agreement
◇ *Accord de libre-échange nord-américain* North American Free Trade Agreement
◇ *UE Accord monétaire européen* European Monetary Agreement
◇ *Accord multifibres* Multi-fibre Arrangement
◇ *accord multilatéral sur l'investissement* multilateral agreement on investment
◇ *accord de paix* peace agreement
◇ *accord de partenariat* partnership agreement
◇ *UE accord de préadhésion* pre-accession agreement
◇ *accords sur les produits de base* commodity agreements
◇ *accord réciproque* reciprocal agreement
◇ *accord de Schengen* Schengen Agreement
◇ *accord tarifaire* tariff agreement

accrédité, -e *adj (personne, représentant)* accredited

accréditer *vt (personne, représentant)* to accredit

accroissement *nm* rise, increase (de in); *(du capital)* accumulation; **l'accroissement de la population** population growth; **avec l'accroissement de leur pouvoir d'achat** with their increased purchasing power

accroître s'accroître *vpr* to rise, to increase, to grow

achat *nm (fait d'acheter)* purchase, purchasing; *(chose achetée)* purchase
◇ *Pol achat de voix* vote-buying

acheter *vt* to purchase, to buy

à-coup *nm (de l'économie)* upheaval

ACP *nm (abrév* **Groupe des États d'Afrique, des Caraïbes et du Pacifique)** ACP Group

acquis *nm*
◊ *UE* **acquis communautaire** acquis communautaire *(entire body of legislation ratified by the EU since its inception, to which all new member states must adhere)*
◊ **acquis sociaux** social benefits

acquisition intracommunautaire *nf UE* intra-Community acquisition

acte *nm* (a) *(action)* action, act (b) *Pol (action légale, politique)* act
◊ **acte de gouvernement** *(en France)* act of State
◊ **acte de guerre** act of war
◊ **acte d'hostilité** hostile act
◊ **Acte du Parlement** *(en Grande-Bretagne)* Act of Parliament; **c'est maintenant un Acte du Parlement** it has now become law
◊ **acte du souverain** ≃ royal charter
◊ **acte de terrorisme** terrorist action, act of terrorism
◊ **Acte unique européen** Single European Act

acteur économique *nm* economic agent *or* player

> La Scandinavie apparaît comme un **acteur économique** mondial de taille moyenne qui prend son envergure en tant que nation maritime importante. Enfin, à puissance commerciale égale, les pays asiatiques contrôlent en général des flottes plus importantes que les pays européens. A noter le grand absent de cette carte, la Grèce, première puissance maritime mondiale mais **acteur économique** mineur sur la scène internationale.

actif, -ive 1 *adj* (a) *Pol (membre, supporter)* active; **être actif sur le plan politique** to be politically active (b) *Écon (marché)* active (c) *Écon (population)* working, active
    2 *nm* (a) *Écon (travailleur)* member of the active *or* working population; **les actifs** the active *or* working population (b) *(patrimoine)* assets
◊ **actif immobilisé** capital asset

action *nf* (a) *(intervention)* action (b) *(mesures)* measures; *(campagne)* campaign (c) *(titre, valeur)* share; **actions** shares, *Am* stock
◊ **action directe** direct action
◊ **action gouvernementale** government action; **l'action gouvernementale en faveur des sans-abri** the government's measures to help the homeless
◊ **action revendicative** *(des travailleurs)* industrial action; *(des étudiants, des citoyens)* protests
◊ **action syndicale** industrial action; **une action syndicale est à prévoir** some industrial action is expected

activisme *nm Pol* activism

activiste *Pol* 1 *adj* activist
    2 *nmf* activist

activité *nf Écon* **être sans activité** to be unemployed; **avoir une activité professionnelle** to be actively employed; **avoir une activité non rémunérée** to be in unpaid work
◊ **activité économique** economic activity
◊ **activité industrielle** industrial activity
◊ **activité politique** political activity
◊ **activité primaire** primary-sector employment
◊ **activité secondaire** secondary-sector employment
◊ **activité tertiaire** tertiary-sector employment

actualisation *nf Écon* discounting

actualisé, -e *adj Écon* discounted

actualiser *vt Écon* to discount

actualité *nf (événements récents)* current affairs

adepte *nmf Pol* follower

adhérent, -e *nm,f* member, adherent

adhérer *vi* **adhérer à** to join, to become a member of; **ils promettent n'importe quoi pour faire adhérer les gens à leur parti** they make all sorts of promises to get people to join their party

adhésion *nf* membership, accession; **après leur adhésion à l'Union européenne** after joining the European Union

> A moitié satisfaits des résultats du sommet européen de Bruxelles, qui s'est félicité en fin de semaine dernière des progrès réalisés par la Turquie, mais n'a pas évoqué de date pour commencer des négociations sur son **adhésion** à l'Union, les dirigeants turcs affichent leur détermination, à une semaine des élections du 3 novembre, d'obtenir davantage d'ici au prochain rendez-vous des Quinze en décembre.

adjoint, -e 1 *adj* assistant, deputy 2 *nm,f* assistant, deputy
◇ **adjoint au maire** deputy mayor

admettre *vt (pays)* to admit

administrateur, -trice *nm,f (dans les affaires publiques)* administrator
◇ **administrateur civil** senior civil servant

administratif, -ive *adj* administrative

administration *nf* **(a)** *(d'un pays)* government, running; *(d'une commune)* running; *(d'affaires)* administration; **la mauvaise administration d'un pays** the mismanagement of a country
(b) *(fonction publique)* **l'Administration** the Civil Service; **entrer dans l'Administration** to become a civil servant, to enter the Civil Service
(c) *(service public)* government ser-

vice; *(fonctionnaires)* civil servants, authorities
(d) *(équipe présidentielle)* **l'Administration Clinton** the Clinton administration
◇ **administration communale** local government
◇ **administration fiscale** tax authorities
◇ **administration locale** local authority
◇ **administration municipale** local government
◇ **administration privée** private administration
◇ **administration publique** public administration; *(fonction)* ≃ Civil Service

administré, -e *nm,f Pol* constituent

administrer *vt (pays)* to govern, to run; *(commune)* to run

admission *nf* admission, entry; **l'admission des pays de l'Est dans l'Union européenne** the entry *or* admission of Eastern European countries into the European Union

adopter *vt (politique)* to adopt, to take up; *(loi, projet)* to adopt, to pass; **le projet de loi a été adopté** the bill went through; **ils ont fait adopter le projet de loi par l'Assemblée** they managed to get the bill through Parliament; **adopté à l'unanimité** carried unanimously

adoption *nf (d'une politique)* adoption; *(d'une loi, d'un projet)* adoption, passing

adversaire *nmf Pol* opponent

AELE *nf (abrév* **Association européenne de libre-échange)** EFTA, Efta

affacturage *nm Écon* factoring

affaiblir *vt* **(a)** *(institution)* to weaken, to undermine; **un pays affaibli par la guerre** a country weakened by war **(b)** *(monnaie)* to weaken

affaire *nf* **(a)** *(entreprise)* business, firm, company **(b)** *(transaction)* deal, transaction **(c)** *(scandale)* **affaire (po-**

litique) (political) scandal *or* affair; **l'affaire des pots-de-vin** the bribery scandal

affaires *nfpl* (a) *Écon (activités commerciales)* business (b) *Pol (ensemble de dossiers)* affairs; **être aux affaires** to run the country, to be the head of state; **depuis qu'il est revenu aux affaires** since he's been back in power; **les Affaires** = financial scandals involving members of government
◇ *Pol* **affaires de l'État** affairs of state
◇ **affaires étrangères** foreign affairs
◇ **affaires intérieures** internal *or* domestic affairs
◇ **affaires internationales** international affairs
◇ **affaires publiques** public affairs
◇ **Affaires sociales** Social Affairs (department)

affaissement *nm Écon (d'une monnaie, d'un marché)* collapse, slump

affaisser s'**affaisser** *vpr Écon (monnaie, marché)* to collapse, to slump

affectation *nf* (a) *(de fonds, de crédits)* allocation (b) *(d'une personne)* appointment, nomination; *(à une ville, un pays)* posting
◇ *Écon* **affectations budgétaires** budget appropriations

affecter *vt* (a) *(fonds, crédits)* to allocate (b) *(personne)* to appoint, to nominate; *(à une ville, un pays)* to post; **être affecté à un poste** to be appointed to a post

afropessimisme *nm* compassion fatigue *(towards underdeveloped African countries)*, Africa fatigue

"

L'**afropessimisme** européen a fait beaucoup de dégâts depuis une douzaine d'années. Le désintérêt à l'égard des problèmes d'un continent si proche n'a pas peu pesé dans la décomposition de l'Afrique noire. La cause est entendue : c'est d'abord à l'Afrique de prendre son

destin en mains. Mais cela ne se décrète pas, et ne peut pas se réaliser à court terme.

"

AGCS *nm Écon (abrév* **Accord général sur le commerce des services)** GATS

agenda *nm*
◇ *UE* **Agenda 2000** Agenda 2000
◇ **agenda politique** political agenda

agent *nm*
◇ *Écon* **agent d'affacturage** factoring agent
◇ **agent de dissuasion** deterrent
◇ **agent économique** economic agent *or* player
◇ *Pol* **agent électoral** canvasser, *Am* ward heeler
◇ **agent de l'État** civil servant
◇ **agent du gouvernement** government official
◇ **agent recenseur** census taker
◇ *Pol* **agent de renseignements** intelligence agent
◇ **agent du trésor** government broker

Agétac *nm Écon (abrév* **Accord Général sur les Tarifs Douaniers et le Commerce)** GATT

agitateur, -trice *nm,f Pol* agitator

agitation *nf Pol* unrest, agitation; **agitation parmi la population** civil unrest
◇ **agitation syndicale** industrial unrest

agiter *Pol* **1** *vt (troubler)* to trouble, to upset; **agiter le peuple contre le gouvernement** to incite the people to rise up against the government
  2 s'**agiter** *vpr (se révolter)* to be in a state of unrest

agit-prop *nf inv Pol* agitprop

agrandir s'**agrandir** *vpr Écon* to expand; **le marché des logiciels s'agrandit** the software market is expanding

agrandissement *nm Écon* expansion

agrégat *nm Écon* aggregate

◇ *agrégat monétaire* monetary aggregate

agricole *adj (économie, pays)* agricultural; *(population)* farming

agriculture *nf* agriculture

agro-économie *nf* agricultural economics

agro-industrie *nf* agribusiness

AID *nf (abrév Association Internationale de Développement)* IDA

aide *nf Pol (don d'argent)* aid
◇ *aide alimentaire* food aid
◇ *aide au développement* foreign aid (to developing countries)
◇ *aides directes* direct aid
◇ *aide économique* economic aid
◇ *aide de l'État* government aid
◇ *aide à l'exportation* export aid
◇ *aide financière* financial aid
◇ *UE aide financière à moyen terme* medium-term financial assistance, MTFA
◇ *Écon aide fiscale* tax credit
◇ *aide liée* tied aid
◇ *UE aide de préadhésion* pre-accession aid
◇ *aide au tiers-monde* overseas aid

aider *vt Pol (industrie, région, pays)* to aid

aile *nf Pol* wing; **l'aile gauche du parti** the left wing of the party

ajournement *nm (après le début de la séance)* adjournment

ajourner *vt (après le début de la séance)* to adjourn

ajustement *nm Écon (des prix, des salaires, d'une monnaie, des statistiques)* adjusting, adjustment
◇ *ajustement structurel* structural adjustment

ajuster *vt Écon (prix, salaires, monnaie, statistiques)* to adjust

ALE *nf (abrév Association de libre-échange)* FTA

ALENA *nm Écon (abrév Accord de libre-échange nord-américain)* NAFTA

aliénation *nf Pol* alienation

aliéné, -e *adj Pol* alienated

aliéner *vt Pol* to alienate; **les dirigeants ont aliéné la base** the leadership has alienated the rank and file

alignement *nm Écon* **(a)** *(d'un prix, d'une monnaie, d'une économie)* alignment; **l'alignement des salaires sur le coût de la vie** bringing salaries into line with the cost of living **(b)** *(d'une nation, d'un gouvernement)* alignment; **leur alignement sur la politique des socialistes** their coming into line with the socialists' policy
◇ *alignement monétaire* monetary alignment *or* adjustment

aligner 1 *vt Écon (prix, monnaie, économie)* to align, to bring into line (**sur** with)
2 s'aligner *vpr* **s'aligner sur** *(nation, gouvernement)* to fall into line *or* to align oneself with; **la Corée du Sud sera obligée de s'aligner sur les prises de position nipponnes** South Korea will be forced to fall into line with the Japanese position

allégeance *nf Pol* allegiance; **il a perdu son emploi à cause de son allégeance au parti** he lost his job because of his allegiance to the party
◇ *allégeance politique* political allegiance

allégement, allègement *nm Écon (d'impôts, de charges, de dépenses)* reduction; **ils sont en faveur de l'allégement des charges sociales pour les entreprises** they are in favour of reducing employers' social security contributions
◇ *allégement fiscal* tax relief

alléger *vt Écon (impôts, charges, dépenses)* to reduce; **alléger les impôts de dix pour cent** to reduce tax by ten percent, to take ten percent off tax

alliance *nf (pacte)* alliance, pact, union; **l'alliance entre socialistes et communistes** *ou* **les socialistes et les communistes** the alliance between *or* of Socialists and Communists;

conclure une alliance avec un pays to enter into or to forge an alliance with a country

allié, -e Pol **1** adj (pays, gouvernements, chefs) allied

2 nm,f (pays, gouvernement, chef) ally

allier Pol **1** vt (pays, gouvernements, chefs) to unite, to ally (together)

2 s'allier vpr (pays) to become allied; **s'allier avec un pays** to ally oneself to a country, to form an alliance with a country; **s'allier contre** to unite against

allocation nf (prestation financière) allowance, Br benefit, Am welfare

◊ **allocation (de) chômage** Br unemployment benefit, Am unemployment compensation

◊ **allocations familiales** family allowance, child benefit

◊ **allocation (de) logement** Br housing benefit, Am rent subsidy or allowance

◊ **allocation (de) maternité** maternity benefit

◊ **allocation de parent isolé** = single-parent allowance

◊ **allocation de rentrée scolaire** = allowance paid to parents to help cover costs incurred at the start of the school year

◊ **allocation de solidarité spécifique** = allowance paid to long-term unemployed people who are no longer entitled to unemployment benefit

◊ **allocation unique dégressive** = unemployment allowance that gradually decreases over time, the sum depending on age, previous salary and amount of national insurance paid

◊ **allocation vieillesse** old-age pension

altermondialisation nf ethical globalization

alternance nf Pol alternance (du pouvoir) changeover of political power; **pratiquer l'alternance** to take turns running a country

❝

Il y a deux "facteurs de classe", deux principes de domination, étroitement imbriqués et pourtant distincts, et pour une part antagoniques. C'est pourquoi il y a, de façon si régulière, dans les sociétés capitalistes développées, une **alternance** si caractéristique entre deux partis dominants et dominateurs. Deux partis, au sens large, de l'**alternance**.

❞

alternatif, -ive 1 adj Pol alternative

2 nf Écon **alternative** alternative

◊ **alternatives économiques** economic alternatives

alterner Pol **1** vt to alternate

2 vi to alternate

ambassade nf (a) (bâtiment) embassy; **l'ambassade du Canada** the Canadian embassy (b) (fonction) ambassadorship (c) (personnel) embassy (staff) (d) (mission) mission; **être envoyé en ambassade auprès de qn** to be sent on a mission to sb

ambassadeur, -drice nm,f ambassador (**auprès de** to); **c'est l'ambassadeur du Canada** he's the Canadian Ambassador

◊ **ambassadeur extraordinaire** ambassador extraordinary, Am ambassador-at-large

AME nm Écon (abrév **Accord monétaire européen**) EMA

aménagement nm Écon planning, development

◊ **aménagement du territoire** regional development, town and country planning

◊ **aménagement urbain** town planning

◊ **aménagement urbain et rural** town and country planning

aménager vt Écon to plan, to develop

amendable adj Pol amendable

amendement nm Pol amendment;

proposer un amendement (à qch) to move an amendment (to sth)

◇ *amendement constitutionnel* constitutional amendment

◇ *amendement européen* European amendment

amender *vt Pol* to amend

AMF *nf* (*abrév* **Association des maires de France**) = French association of mayors

AMI *nm Écon* (*abrév* **Accord multilatéral sur l'investissement**) MAI

amont *nm Écon* upside; **d'amont** (*activités*) upstream; **en amont** (*société*) upstream

analyse *nf Écon* analysis

◇ *analyse des coûts* cost analysis

◇ *analyse des coûts et rendements* cost-benefit analysis

◇ *analyse démographique* demographic analysis

◇ *analyse économique* economic analysis

◇ *analyse de portefeuille* portfolio analysis

◇ *analyse du prix de revient* cost analysis

◇ *analyse du rendement* rate of return analysis

anarchie *nf Pol* anarchy

anarchique *adj Pol* anarchic, anarchical

anarchiser *vt Pol* to anarchize

anarchisme *nm Pol* anarchism

anarchiste *Pol* **1** *adj* anarchistic
2 *nmf* anarchist

anarcho-syndicalisme *nm Pol* anarcho-syndicalism

anarcho-syndicaliste *Pol* **1** *adj* anarcho-syndicalist
2 *nmf* anarcho-syndicalist

ANASE *nf* (*abrév* **Association des nations de l'Asie du Sud-Est**) ASEAN

ANC *nm Pol* (*abrév* **African National Congress**) ANC

année *nf* year

◇ *année fiscale Br* financial year, *Am* fiscal year

◇ *année d'imposition* tax year

◇ *Écon année de référence* base year

annexe *nf* (*à un traité, un projet de loi*) annexe

annexer *vt Pol* to annex

annexion *nf Pol* annexation

ANSEA *nf* (*abrév* **Association des nations du Sud-Est asiatique**) ASEAN

antiaméricain, -e *adj* anti-American

antiaméricanisme *nm* anti-Americanism

antiapartheid *adj Pol* anti-apartheid

anticapitalisme *nm Pol* anticapitalism

anticapitaliste *Pol* **1** *adj* anticapitalist
2 *nmf* anticapitalist

antichômage *adj* (*politique, mesure*) that aims to reduce unemployment

anticipations *nfpl Écon* expectations

anticlérical, -e *Pol* **1** *adj* anticlerical
2 *nm,f* anticlerical

anticléricalisme *nm Pol* anticlericalism

anticolonialisme *nm Pol* anticolonialism

anticolonialiste *Pol* **1** *adj* anticolonialist
2 *nmf* anticolonialist

anticommunisme *nm Pol* anticommunism

anticommuniste *Pol* **1** *adj* anticommunist
2 *nmf* anticommunist

anticoncurrentiel, -elle *adj Écon* anticompetitive

anticonformiste **1** *adj* nonconformist
2 *nmf* nonconformist

anticonjoncturel, -elle *adj Écon* corrective

anticonstitutionnel, -elle *adj* anticonstitutional

anticyclique *adj Écon* countercyclical

antidémocratique *adj Pol* antidemocratic

antidumping *adj inv (loi, législation)* antidumping

antiesclavagisme *nm Pol* opposition to slavery

antiesclavagiste *Pol* **1** *adj* antislavery
    2 *nmf* opponent of slavery

antiétatique *adj Pol* opposed to state intervention, noninterventionist

antifascisme *nm Pol* antifascism

antifasciste *Pol* **1** *adj* antifascist
    2 *nmf* antifascist

antigouvernemental, -e *adj Pol* antigovernment

antihausse *adj Écon* regulating price increases, anti-inflationary

anti-impérialisme *nm Pol* anti-imperialism

anti-impérialiste *Pol* **1** *adj* anti-imperialist
    2 *nmf* anti-imperialist

anti-inflationniste *adj Écon* anti-inflationary

antimilitarisme *nm Pol* antimilitarism

antimilitariste *Pol* **1** *adj* antimilitarist
    2 *nmf* antimilitarist

antimonarchique *adj* antimonarchical

antimonarchiste **1** *adj* antimonarchist
    2 *nmf* antimonarchist

antimondialisation *nf Pol* antiglobalization

antinational, -e *adj Pol* antinational

antinationalisme *nm Pol* antinationalism

antiparlementaire *adj Pol* antiparliamentary

antiparlementarisme *nm Pol* antiparliamentarism

antiparti *adj inv Pol* antiparty

antiprotectionniste *Écon* **1** *adj* antiprotectionist, free trade
    2 *nmf* antiprotectionist, free-trader

antirépublicain, -e *Pol* **1** *adj* antirepublican
    2 *nm,f* antirepublican

antisyndical, -e *adj* anti-union

antisyndicalisme *nm* union-bashing

antiterroriste *adj* antiterrorist

antitrust *adj inv (loi, législation)* antitrust, *Br* antimonopoly

apaisement *nm Pol (d'opposants, de mécontents)* appeasement

apaiser *vt Pol (opposants, mécontents)* to appease, to pacify

apartheid *nm Pol* apartheid

apatride **1** *adj* stateless
    2 *nmf* stateless person

apatridie *nf* statelessness

APEC **1** *nm (abrév* **Asia-Pacific Economic Cooperation)** APEC
    2 *nf (abrév* **Association pour l'emploi des cadres)** = agency providing information and employment and training opportunities for professionals

apolitique **1** *adj (sans convictions politiques)* apolitical; *(non affilié)* nonpolitical
    2 *nmf* apolitical person

apolitisme *nm (refus de s'engager)* apolitical stance; *(engagement sans affiliation)* nonpolitical stance

apparatchik *nm Pol* apparatchik

appareil étatique *nm Pol* machinery of state, state apparatus

> **44**
>
> Toutes les pratiques sociales qui favorisent l'exclusion de certaines catégories de personnes alimentent la

violence. De nombreux comportements et décisions à un niveau supérieur de l'**appareil étatique** ou de divers "lobbies", qui sont autant de lieux de concentration de pouvoir, sont porteurs d'une violence potentielle. Tous les individus qui ne peuvent s'épanouir dans notre société d'excellence et de gagnants veulent pourtant être reconnus à leur juste valeur.

"

apparenté, -e *Pol* **1** *adj (allié)* allied; **candidat apparenté à un parti** = candidate who, though not a member of a party, can count on its support in an election; **des listes apparentées** grouped electoral lists *(in proportional elections)*
2 *nm,f* **les socialistes et apparentés** the socialists and their allies

"

es députés UDF et **apparentés** militent en faveur de la baisse des prélèvements obligatoires, de manière à atteindre au moins la moyenne de nos partenaires européens. Ils rappellent leur attachement à l'équilibre des finances publiques et insistent sur le respect des engagements de la France dans ce domaine, en particulier européens.

"

appel *nm* **(a)** *Écon* call **(b)** *Pol* **lancer un appel au peuple** to make a public appeal
◇ *appel de fonds* call for funds; **faire un appel de fonds** to call up capital

apport *nm Écon (de capitaux)* inflow, influx

apporter *vt Écon (capitaux)* to bring in, to contribute

apporteur *nm Écon (de capitaux)* contributor

appréciation *nf Écon* **(a)** *(estimation)* appraisal **(b)** *(augmentation)* appreciation

◇ *appréciation des investissements* investment appraisal
◇ *appréciation monétaire* currency appreciation

apprécier *Écon* **1** *vt (estimer)* to appraise
2 *s'apprécier* *vpr (augmenter)* to appreciate

appui *nm (soutien)* support, backing; **apporter son appui à une initiative** to back or to support an initiative

appuyer *vt (candidat, réforme)* to back, to support; *(gouvernement, régime)* to support, to bolster up

arbitrage *nm* **(a)** *Écon* arbitrage **(b)** *Pol* arbitration; **recourir à l'arbitrage** to go to arbitration; **soumettre un différend à un arbitrage** to refer a dispute to arbitration; **trancher par arbitrage** to settle by arbitration

arbitre *nm Pol* arbitrator; **exercer un rôle d'arbitre** to act as arbitrator, to arbitrate

arbitrer *Pol* **1** *vt* to arbitrate
2 *vi* to arbitrate

argent *nm (richesse)* money
◇ *Écon* **argent rare** tight money

arme *nf (objet)* arm, weapon; *(arsenal)* weapons; **armes** arms, weapons, weaponry
◇ *arme biologique* biological weapon
◇ *arme chimique* chemical weapon
◇ *armes conventionnelles* conventional weapons
◇ *armes de destruction massive* weapons of mass destruction
◇ *armes de dissuasion* deterrent
◇ *arme nucléaire* nuclear weapon
◇ *armes nucléaires tactiques* tactical nuclear weapons

armée *nf* army
◇ *armée d'occupation* army of occupation

arrangement *nm* arrangement, settlement
◇ *arrangement permanent* permanent arrangement

arrêté *nm Pol (décret)* order, decree

◇ *arrêté ministériel* ministerial order
◇ *arrêté municipal* ≃ bylaw
◇ *arrêté préfectoral* bylaw *(issued by a "préfecture")*

arriéré, -e *adj Écon (pays)* underdeveloped, backward

article *nm*
◇ *Écon article de base* staple
◇ *articles d'exportation* export goods, exports
◇ *articles de grande consommation* consumables, consumer goods
◇ *articles d'importation* import goods, imports
◇ *articles de réexportation* re-export goods, re-exports

ASI *nf* (*abrév* **association de solidarité internationale**) international aid organization

asile *nm Pol* asylum
◇ *asile diplomatique* diplomatic protection; **demander l'asile diplomatique** to seek diplomatic protection
◇ *asile politique* political asylum; **demander l'asile politique** to seek political asylum

asphyxie *nf (d'un pays, de l'économie)* paralysis
◇ *asphyxie économique* economic paralysis

❝

Tandis que l'armée israélienne multiplie les incursions meurtrières dans les villes "autonomes", les autorités d'occupation imposent de nouvelles mesures restrictives à la circulation des biens et des personnes : la Cisjordanie est divisée en huit "cantons", entre lesquels il faudra des permis spéciaux pour se déplacer. Ces décisions, qui accentuent l'**asphyxie économique**, enterrent les accords d'Oslo.

❞

asphyxié, -e *adj (pays, économie)* paralysed

asphyxier 1 *vt (pays, économie)* to paralyse

2 s'asphyxier *vpr (pays, économie)* to become paralysed

assassin *nm* assassin

assassinat *nm* assassination

assassiner *vt* to assassinate

assemblée *nf Pol* (**a**) *(élus)* **l'Assemblée** the National Assembly (**b**) *(bâtiment)* **l'Assemblée** ≃ the House (**c**) *(réunion)* meeting, assembly
◇ *assemblée constituante* constituent assembly
◇ *assemblée électorale* voting assembly
◇ *assemblée extraordinaire* special session, extraordinary meeting
◇ *assemblée fédérale (en Suisse)* (Swiss) federal assembly
◇ *assemblée législative* legislative assembly
◇ *l'Assemblée nationale* the National Assembly
◇ *Assemblée parlementaire européenne* European Parliament
◇ *assemblée plénière* plenary assembly

assermentation *nf Can & Suisse (d'un fonctionnaire, d'un président)* swearing in

assermenter *vt (fonctionnaire, président)* to swear in

assiette *nf Écon (d'un impôt, d'un taux)* base
◇ *assiette fiscale* taxable income
◇ *assiette de l'impôt* taxable income

assignation à domicile, assignation à résidence *nf Pol* house arrest

assigner *vt Pol* **assigner qn à domicile** *ou* **à résidence** to place sb under house arrest

association *nf (organisation)* association; *(collaboration)* partnership
◇ *association à but lucratif* profit-making organization
◇ *association à but non lucratif* not-for-profit *or Br* non-profit-making organization
◇ *association sans but lucratif* not-

for-profit *or Br* non-profit-making organization

◇ *association de consommateurs* consumer organization

◇ *Association pour l'emploi des cadres* = agency providing information and employment and training opportunities for professionals

◇ *Association européenne des dépositaires centraux de titres* European Central Securities Depositories Association

◇ *Association européenne de libre-échange* European Free Trade Association

◇ *Association de libre-échange* free-trade association

◇ *Association des maires de France* = French association of mayors

◇ *association professionnelle* professional association, trade association

◇ *association de solidarité internationale* international aid organization

assouplir *Écon* **1** *vt (règlement, contrôle)* to relax

2 s'assouplir *vpr (règlement, contrôle)* to become more relaxed

assouplissement *nm Écon (du règlement, du contrôle)* relaxing

atlantisme *nm Pol* Atlanticism

attaché, -e *nm,f Pol* attaché

◇ *attaché d'ambassade* embassy attaché

◇ *attaché commercial (d'une ambassade)* commercial attaché

◇ *attaché militaire* military attaché

◇ *attaché de presse* press officer; *(du corps diplomatique)* press attaché

atteinte *nf (attaque)* attack; **atteinte aux droits de l'homme** violation of human rights; *Parl* **atteinte aux privilèges parlementaires** breach of privilege

attentat *nm* **(a)** *(assassinat)* assassination attempt; **commettre un attentat contre qn** to make an attempt on sb's life

(b) *(explosion)* attack; **attentat à la bombe** bomb attack, bombing; **l'ambassade a été hier la cible d'un attentat** the Embassy was bombed yesterday

(c) *(atteinte)* **attentat aux libertés constitutionnelles** violation of constitutional liberties; **attentat contre la sécurité de l'État** acts harmful to State security

atterrissage *nm Écon*

◇ *atterrissage brutal* hard landing

◇ *atterrissage en douceur* soft landing

attraction *nf Écon* crowding-in

attributions *nfpl Pol* demarcation

attrition *nf Écon* attrition

audit environnemental *nm* environmental audit

AUE *nm (abrév* **Acte unique européen**) SEA

augmentation *nf* increase **(de** in)

augmenter **1** *vt (impôts, taux d'intérêt, prix)* to increase, to put up, to raise; *(dépenses)* to increase

2 *vi (impôts, taux d'intérêt, prix)* to increase, to go up, to rise; *(dépenses)* to increase

austérité *nf Écon* austerity

autarcie *nf Écon* self-sufficiency, autarky

autarcique *adj Écon* autarkic

autocentré, -e *adj Écon* autocentric

autocrate *nm Pol* autocrat

autocratie *nf Pol* autocracy, autarchy

autocratique *adj Pol* autocratic, autarchic

autocratiquement *adv Pol* autocratically

autodétermination *nf* self-determination

autodéterminé, -e *adj* self-determined

autogérer **1** *vt (entreprise, usine)* to self-manage

2 s'autogérer *vpr (entreprise, usine)* to be self-managing

autogestion *nf* self-management; **une entreprise en autogestion** a self-managed company

autogestionnaire *adj* based on workers' self-management

autonome *adj Pol (État, pays)* autonomous, self-governing; *(gouvernement)* autonomous

autonomie *nf Pol (d'un État, d'un pays)* autonomy, self-government; *(d'un gouvernement)* autonomy

autonomiste *Pol* **1** *adj* separatist **2** *nmf* separatist

autorégulateur, -trice *adj* self-regulating

autorégulation *nf* self-regulation

autoritaire *adj Pol* authoritarian

autoritarisme *nm Pol* authoritarianism

autorité *nf* **(a)** *(pouvoir)* authority, power; **l'autorité de la loi** the authority *or* power of the law; **un territoire soumis à l'autorité de...** an area within the jurisdiction of... **(b)** *(pouvoir établi)* authority; **l'autorité, les autorités** *(personnel)* the authorities; **les autorités françaises** the French authorities
◊ *autorités locales* local authorities
◊ *autorités militaires* military authorities
◊ *autorités régionales* local authorities
◊ *autorités de tutelle* supervisory bodies

autosubsistance *nf Écon* (economic) self-sufficiency

autosuffisance *nf Écon* self-sufficiency

autosuffisant, -e *adj Écon* self-sufficient

aval *nm* **(a)** *(soutien)* support; **donner son aval à qn** to give sb one's backing **(b)** *Écon* downside; **d'aval** *(activités)* downstream; **en aval** *(société)* downstream

avaliser *vt* to back, to support

> Elles ont dénoncé le refus par le conseil des ministres des transports réunis le 17 juin à Luxembourg d'**avaliser** le projet de traversée ferroviaire à grande capacité au centre des Pyrénées.

avantage *nm Écon* advantage
◊ *avantage absolu* absolute advantage
◊ *avantages acquis* long-service benefits
◊ *avantage comparé* comparative advantage
◊ *avantage concurrentiel* competitive advantage
◊ *avantages et coûts comparatifs* comparative advantages and costs
◊ *avantage fiscal* tax incentive
◊ *avantages sociaux* welfare benefits

avant-projet *nm (d'un traité, d'un projet de loi)* draft

avoir *nm Écon (capital)* capital; **avoirs** assets, holdings
◊ *avoir en devises* foreign currency holding
◊ *avoir en devises étrangères* foreign currency holding
◊ *avoir fiscal* tax credit

bain de foule *nm* *Pol* walkabout; **prendre un bain de foule** to go on a walkabout

baisse *nf* drop, fall (**de** in); **une baisse du coût de la vie** a fall in the cost of living; **les prix ont subi une forte baisse** prices have gone down *or* decreased sharply; **une baisse de quatre pour cent** a four percent drop *or* fall; **une baisse des prix** a fall in prices; **pousser qch à la baisse** to have a deflationary effect on sth

baisser **1** *vt* to lower, to reduce, to bring down; **baisser le coût de la vie** to lower *or* reduce *or* bring down the cost of living; **la concurrence fait baisser les prix** competition brings prices down
  2 *vi* to fall; **le dollar a baissé** the dollar has weakened

balance *nf* *Écon* balance; **la balance est en excédent** there is a surplus
◊ *balance commerciale* balance of trade
◊ *balance commerciale déficitaire* trade deficit
◊ *balance courante* current balance
◊ *balances dollars* dollar balances *or* holdings
◊ *Pol* *balance électorale* electoral balance
◊ *balance des paiements* balance of payments
◊ *Pol* *balance des pouvoirs* balance of power
◊ *balances sterling* sterling balances *or* holdings

> Bastion électoral de la social-démocratie allemande, Duisbourg et le Land de Rhénanie du Nord-Westphalie vont peser lourd dans la **balance électorale** : en 1998, ce bassin industriel avait fourni plus d'un quart des voix recueillies par le vainqueur de Helmut Kohl (CDU).

balkanisation *nf* *Pol* Balkanization, balkanization

balkaniser *vt* *Pol* to Balkanize, to balkanize

ballottage *nm* *Pol* **il y a ballottage à Tours** there will be a second ballot in Tours; **être en ballottage** to have *Br* to stand *or Am* to run again in a second round

banc *nm* *Parl* bench
◊ *banc des ministres* government bench, ministerial bench

bande de fluctuation *nf* *Écon* fluctuation band

banque *nf* (établissement, organisation) bank; (activité) banking
◊ *banque d'affaires* investment bank
◊ *Banque centrale* Central Bank
◊ *Banque centrale européenne* European Central Bank
◊ *Banque européenne d'investissement* European Investment Bank
◊ *Banque européenne pour la reconstruction et le développement* European Bank for Reconstruction and Development

◇ *Banque de France* Bank of France

◇ *Banque internationale pour la reconstruction et le développement* International Bank for Reconstruction and Development

◇ *Banque mondiale* World Bank

◇ *Banque des règlements internationaux* Bank for International Settlements

barrière *nf Écon* barrier

◇ *barrière commerciale* trade barrier

◇ *barrière douanière* trade barrier

◇ *barrière à l'entrée* entry barrier

◇ *barrière non tarifaire* non-tariff barrier

◇ *barrière tarifaire* tariff barrier

bas, basse 1 *adj (prix, taux de change, taux d'intérêt)* low

2 *nm (du marché)* low end

base *nf* (a) *Pol* la base the grass roots, the rank and file (b) *Écon* base

◇ *Écon* *base d'imposition* taxable base

◇ *Écon* *base monétaire* monetary base

bastion *nm (d'une doctrine, d'un mouvement)* bastion, stronghold; **un bastion du socialisme** a socialist stronghold, a bastion of socialism

bataille *nf* battle, fight; **une bataille politique/électorale** a political/an electoral contest

battre 1 *vt* battre en brèche *(gouvernement)* to topple; *(politique)* to demolish

2 se battre *vpr* to fight; **se battre contre qn** to fight against sb

BCE *nf (abrév* **Banque centrale européenne)** ECB

BEE *nm UE (abrév* **Bureau européen de l'environnement)** EEB

BEI *nf (abrév* **Banque européenne d'investissement)** EIB

bellicisme *nm* warmongering

belliciste 1 *adj* warmongering, hawkish

2 *nmf* warmonger, hawk

bénef *nm Fam* profit; **faire du bénef** to make a profit

bénéfice *nm* profit; **faire du bénéfice** to make a profit; **faire** *ou* **enregistrer un bénéfice brut/net de 20 000 euros** to gross/to net 20,000 euro; **donner un bénéfice** to show a profit; **réaliser** *ou* **dégager un bénéfice** to make a profit; **bénéfice de** *ou* **pour l'exercice 2003** profits for the year 2003; **rapporter des bénéfices** to yield a profit

◇ *bénéfice exceptionnel* windfall profit

Benelux *nm* le Benelux Benelux; **au Benelux** in the Benelux countries

BERD *nf (abrév* **Banque européenne pour la reconstruction et le développement)** EBRD

besoin *nm Écon* need

bicaméral, -e *adj Pol* bicameral, two-chamber

bicamérisme, bicaméralisme *nm Pol* two-chamber (political) system, bicameralism

bien *nm Écon* possession, good; **biens** possessions, goods, property; **biens et services** goods and services

◇ *biens capitaux* capital goods

◇ *bien collectif* collective good

◇ *bien commun* common good

◇ *bien complémentaire* complementary good

◇ *biens de consommation* consumer products, consumer goods

◇ *biens de consommation durables* consumer durables

◇ *biens de consommation finale* final consumer goods

◇ *biens de consommation intermédiaire* intermediate consumer goods

◇ *biens de consommation non durables* disposable goods, non-durable consumer goods

◇ *biens durables* consumer durables, durable goods

◇ *biens d'équipement* capital goods

◇ *biens d'équipement ménager* consumer durables

◇ *biens intermédiaires* intermediate goods

◇ *bien privé* private good

◇ *biens de production* producer or capital goods

◇ *bien public* public good

◇ *bien tutélaire* merit good

bien-être *nm inv Écon* (material) well-being

bilan *nm* (a) *(d'une entreprise)* balance sheet; *(d'un compte)* balance (b) *(appréciation)* appraisal, assessment; *(résultats)* results; **faire le bilan de qch** to take stock of or to assess sth; **quel est le bilan de ces discussions?** what is the end result of these talks?, what have these talks amounted to?; **un bilan économique positif** positive economic results; **le bilan du gouvernement de gauche en matière d'emploi** the socialist government's record on employment

bilatéral, -e *adj* bilateral

bilatéralement *adv* bilaterally

bilatéralisme *nm* bilateralism

billet *nm Br* banknote, *Am* bill

◇ *billet de banque Br* banknote, *Am* bill

◇ *billet vert* US dollar

biparti, -e *adj Pol* bipartite, two-party, bipartisan

bipartisme *nm Pol* bipartism, two-party system, bipartisanship

bipartite *adj Pol* bipartite, two-party, bipartisan

bipolaire *adj Pol* bipolar

bipolarisation *nf Pol* bipolarization

bipolarisé, -e *adj Pol* bipolarized

bipolarité *nf Pol* bipolarity

BIRD *nf (abrév* **Banque internationale pour la reconstruction et le développement)** IBRD

BIT *nm (abrév* **Bureau international du travail)** ILO

blairisme *nm Pol* Blairism

bleu *nm Can Pol* Conservative

bloc *nm Écon (zone)* bloc

◇ *bloc monétaire* monetary bloc

◇ *bloc des pays occidentaux* Western Alliance

◇ *bloc des pays de l'Ouest* Western Alliance

◇ *bloc sterling* sterling bloc

blocage *nm Écon* freeze

◇ *blocage des prix* price freeze

◇ *blocage des salaires* wage freeze

blocus économique *nm* economic blockade

bloquer *vt Écon (loyers, prix, salaires)* to freeze; *Pol (mesure, vote)* to block; **le ministre a fait bloquer les crédits** the minister imposed a restriction on funding

BM *nf (abrév* **Banque mondiale)** World Bank

BNT *nf (abrév* **barrière non tarifaire)** NTB

bolchevik, bolchevique *Pol* **1** *adj* Bolshevik, Bolshevist
2 *nmf* Bolshevik, Bolshevist

bolchevisme *nm Pol* Bolshevism

bombe *nf* bomb

◇ *bombe atomique* nuclear bomb

bon *nm* bond

◇ *bon du Trésor* Treasury bill; *(obligation à long terme)* Treasury bond

bonapartisme *nm Pol* Bonapartism

bonapartiste *Pol* **1** *adj* Bonapartist
2 *nmf* Bonapartist

bonification d'intérêts *nf Écon* interest relief

bonifier *vt Écon* to credit

boom *nm Écon* boom

bouleversement *nm (changements radicaux)* upheaval, upset; **des bouleversements politiques** political upheavals

bourse *nf* **la Bourse (des valeurs)** the Stock Exchange, the Stock Market; **la Bourse de Londres** the London Stock Exchange; **en** *ou* **à la Bourse** on the Stock Exchange *or* Stock Market

◊ *bourse du travail (réunion)* = meeting of local trade unions for the purpose of reaching agreement on how best to defend their interests and provide community services; *(endroit)* = local trade union centre

boycott *nm* boycott

boycottage *nm* boycotting

boycotter *vt* to boycott; **les syndicats veulent faire boycotter les élections** the unions want people to boycott the elections; **se faire boycotter** to be boycotted

boycotteur, -euse *nm,f* boycotter

BRI *nf* (*abrév* **Banque des règlements internationaux**) BIS

brut, -e 1 *adj* (a) *(bénéfice, marge, valeur, salaire)* gross (b) *(pétrole)* crude
2 *adv* gross; **gagner 10 000 euros brut** to earn 10,000 euro gross
3 *nm* (a) *(salaire)* gross income (b) *(pétrole)* crude oil

budget *nm* budget; *Pol* **le Budget** ≃ the Budget; **le budget de l'éducation** the education budget
◊ *UE* **budget communautaire européen** European Community budget
◊ *budget équilibré* balanced budget
◊ *Écon* **budget de l'État** state budget
◊ *budget global* overall budget
◊ *budget prévisionnel* provisional budget
◊ *budget social de la nation* national welfare budget

budgétaire *adj (dépenses, contrôle)* budgetary; *(déficit, excédent)* budget; *(année) Br* financial, *Am* fiscal

budgétisation *nf* budgeting

budgétiser *vt* to budget for

budgétivore *Fam* 1 *adj* wasteful of State resources
2 *nmf* big spender (of State resources)

> «
>
> Le premier investissement **budgétivore** est le corps professoral, qui coûte de plus en plus cher à toutes les écoles, parce que la règle du jeu aujourd'hui est d'avoir un corps professoral permanent de taille significative.
>
> »

bulle boursière *nf* stock market bubble

bulletin *nm Pol* ballot paper
◊ *bulletin blanc* blank ballot paper
◊ *bulletin nul* spoiled ballot paper
◊ *bulletin secret* secret ballot
◊ *bulletin de vote* ballot paper

bureau *nm* (a) *(commission)* committee (b) **bureaux** *(locaux)* office, offices; **les bureaux du ministère** the Ministry offices
◊ *Pol* **Bureau européen de l'environnement** European Environmental Bureau
◊ *Bureau international du travail* International Labour Office
◊ *Bureau ovale* Oval Office
◊ *bureau politique (d'un parti)* party executives; *(du parti communiste)* Politburo
◊ *bureau principal* headquarters
◊ *bureau de vote* polling station

bureaucrate *nmf* bureaucrat

bureaucratie *nf* (a) *(système)* bureaucracy, officialism (b) *(fonctionnaires)* officials, bureaucrats

bureaucratique *adj* bureaucratic, administrative

bureaucratisation *nf* bureaucratization

bureaucratiser *vt* to bureaucratize

cabaler *vi Can Fam Pol* to campaign

cabinet *nm Pol (gouvernement)* cabinet; *(d'un ministre)* departmental staff; **faire partie du cabinet** to be in *or* a member of the Cabinet; **le cabinet du Premier ministre** the Prime Minister's departmental staff
◇ *cabinet fantôme* shadow cabinet
◇ *cabinet ministériel* minister's advisers, departmental staff
◇ *cabinet restreint* kitchen cabinet

caisse *nf*
◇ *caisse de chômage* unemployment fund
◇ *caisse de compensation* = equalization fund for payments such as child benefit, sickness benefit, pensions
◇ *caisse de crédit* credit union
◇ *Écon caisses de l'État* State coffers
◇ *Caisse nationale d'assurance vieillesse* = French Social Security office dealing with benefit payments relating to old age
◇ *Pol caisse noire* slush fund
◇ *Caisse primaire d'assurance maladie* = French Social Security office in charge of medical insurance
◇ *caisse de retraite* pension fund
◇ *caisse de Sécurité sociale* Social Security office

camarade *nmf Pol* comrade

camarilla *nf Pol* camarilla

camp *nm (faction)* camp, party; **passer dans l'autre camp, changer de camp** to change camps, to go over to the other camp
◇ *Camp David* Camp David

campagne *nf Pol* campaign; **faire campagne pour/contre** to campaign *or* to lobby for/against; **mener une campagne en faveur de/contre qch** to campaign for/against sth; **lancer une campagne pour/contre** to launch a campaign for/against
◇ *campagne de dénigrement* smear campaign
◇ *campagne de diffamation* smear campaign
◇ *campagne électorale* election campaign
◇ *campagne d'information* publicity campaign

CAN *nf (abrév* **Communauté andine***)* CAN

canal *nm Écon* channel

candidat, -e *nm,f Pol* candidate; **être candidat aux élections** to be a candidate in the elections, *Br* to stand *or* *Am* to run in the elections; **être candidat à la présidence** *Br* to stand *or* *Am* to run for president
◇ *Can candidat parachuté* parachuted candidate

candidature *nf Pol* candidature, candidacy; **poser sa candidature** to declare oneself a candidate, *Br* to stand; **proposer la candidature de qn** to nominate sb; **retirer sa candidature** to stand down; **il a retiré sa candidature à la présidence** he has stood down as a presidential candidate
◇ *candidature multiple* *Br* standing *or* *Am* running for election in several constituencies
◇ *candidature officielle* *Br* standing

or Am running as an official candidate

canton *nm (en France)* division of an "arrondissement", canton; *(en Suisse)* canton; *(au Luxembourg)* administrative division, canton; *(au Canada)* township

cantonal, -e *Pol* **1** *adj* ≃ local
2 *nf* **cantonales** = election held every six years for the "conseil général", ≃ local elections

> 🙶
>
> Ca y est, le RPR met ses principes en pratique. Ainsi, Jean-François Mancel, candidat aux **cantonales** dans l'Oise vient de se faire exclure de son parti. Le président du Conseil Général de l'Oise, Jean-François Mancel, s'est fait remarquer avant le scrutin du 15 mars dernier par ses déclarations on ne peut plus accueillantes à l'égard du FN. Car si les élections régionales ne comportent qu'un seul tour, les élections **cantonales** – les veinardes – en ont deux. D'où l'intérêt de faire savoir, dixit Jean-François Mancel, que "si certains représentants du Front National sont prêts à soutenir l'action (de la droite) il n'y a pas de raison que nous refusions leur concours."
>
> 🙷

capacité *nf Écon* capacity
◇ *Écon* **capacité d'achat** purchasing power
◇ *Pol* **capacité électorale** (electoral) franchise
◇ *Écon* **capacité d'exportation** export potential
◇ *Écon* **capacité d'importation** import potential
◇ *Écon* **capacité de production** manufacturing capacity

capital *nm Écon* **(a)** *(avoir) (personnel, d'une société)* capital, assets; **une société au capital de 500 000 euros** a firm with assets of 500,000 euro; **il détient cinq pour cent du capital de la**

société he has a five percent shareholding in the company, he holds five percent of the company's shares
(b) *(monde de l'argent, des capitalistes)* **le capital** capital; **le grand capital** big business
(c) **capitaux** *(valeurs disponibles)* capital
◇ *capital circulant* working *or* floating capital
◇ *capital d'exploitation Br* working capital, *Am* operating capital
◇ *capital financier* finance capital
◇ *capital fixe* fixed *or* capital assets
◇ *capitaux flottants* floating capital
◇ *capital foncier* land
◇ *capitaux gelés* frozen assets
◇ *capital humain* human capital
◇ *capitaux permanents* capital employed, long-term capital
◇ *capital de réserve* reserve capital
◇ *capital social* capital stock
◇ *capital variable* variable capital

capital-développement *nm* development capital

capitalisation *nf Écon (des intérêts, des revenus)* capitalization
◇ *capitalisation boursière* market capitalization

> 🙶
>
> Air France, qui joue pourtant dans une autre catégorie (42 millions de voyageurs par an), prend très au sérieux ce petit concurrent. Le géant français n'a pas tort : la **capitalisation boursière** du trublion irlandais dépasse la sienne ! En France, il est déjà numéro 1 sur les vols Paris-Dublin et ne compte pas en rester là.
>
> 🙷

capitaliser *vt Écon (intérêts, revenus)* to capitalize

capitalisme *nm Écon* capitalism
◇ *capitalisme de copinage* crony capitalism
◇ *capitalisme d'État* state capitalism
◇ *capitalisme monopolistique d'État* state monopoly capitalism

◊ *capitalisme sauvage* ruthless capitalism

❝

L'avènement de l'informatique a accéléré la tendance vers un **capitalisme sauvage**. Oui, l'informatique a libéré l'homme de tâches souvent trop lourdes pour lui. Oui, l'informatique a élevé l'être humain vers les plus hautes sphères du savoir et de la technologie. Mais en même temps elle a semé la misère chez des milliers d'individus qui ont été jetés à la rue, partout en Occident, aux Etats-Unis, au Canada et au Québec, leurs bras n'étant plus nécessaires pour produire.

❞

capitaliste *Écon* **1** *adj* capitalist, capitalistic
2 *nmf* capitalist

capitalistique *adj Écon* capital-intensive

capital-risque *nm* risk capital

caporalisme *nm Pol* military rule

captif, -ive *adj Écon (marché)* captive

carence *nf Écon* insolvency

CARICOM *nf (abrév* **Communauté des Caraïbes**) CARICOM

carte d'électeur *nf* voting *or Br* polling card, *Am* voter registration card

cartel *nm* (a) *Écon (d'entreprises)* cartel; **un cartel de l'acier** a steel cartel; **se rassembler en cartel** to form a cartel (b) *Pol* coalition, cartel
◊ *cartel de prix* price cartel

cartellisation *nf Écon (d'entreprises)* cartelization

cartelliser *vt Écon (entreprises)* to cartelize

cash-flow *nm* cash flow
◊ *Écon cash-flow actualisé* discounted cash flow

casque bleu *nm* member of the UN peacekeeping force; **les casques bleus** the UN peacekeeping force

castrisme *nm Pol* Castroism

castriste *Pol* **1** *adj* Castroist
2 *nmf* Castroist, Castro supporter

CAT *nf (abrév* **Confédération autonome du travail**) = French trade union

caucus *nm Belg Pol* caucus

causerie *nf* (a) *(discussion)* chat, talk (b) *(conférence)* informal talk *(in front of an audience)*

cautionnement *nm Pol* deposit

CC *Pol (abrév* **corps consulaire**) CC

CCE *nf (abrév* **Commission des communautés européennes**) ECC

CCI *nf (abrév* **Chambre de commerce et d'industrie**) CCI

CDS *nm Anciennement Pol (abrév* **Centre des démocrates sociaux**) = French political party

CE 1 *nm* (a) *(abrév* **comité d'entreprise**) works council (b) *UE (abrév* **conseil de l'Europe**) Council of Europe
2 *nf (abrév* **Communauté européenne**) EC

CEC *nm (abrév* **Confédération européenne des cadres**) CEC, European Confederation of Executives and Managerial Staff

CECA, Ceca *nf UE (abrév* **Communauté européenne du charbon et de l'acier**) ECSC

CEDEAO *nf (abrév* **Communauté économique des États d'Afrique de l'Ouest**) ECOWAS

cédétiste 1 *adj* CFDT
2 *nmf* member of the CFDT

CEDH *nf (abrév* **Cour européenne des droits de l'homme**) ECHR

CEE *nf UE (abrév* **Communauté économique européenne**) EEC

CEEA *nf UE (abrév* **Communauté européenne de l'Énergie Atomique**) Euratom

cégétiste 1 *adj* CGT

2 *nmf* member of the CGT

CEI *nf* (*abrév* **Communauté des États Indépendants**) CIS

CEJ *nf* (*abrév* **Cour européenne de justice**) ECJ

cellule *nf Pol* cell
◇ *cellule de réflexion* think tank

CEMAC *nf* (*abrév* **Communauté économique et monétaire de l'Afrique centrale**) CEMAC

censure *nf Pol* censure

censurer *vt Pol* **censurer le gouvernement** to pass a vote of censure *or* of no confidence in the government

central, -e 1 *adj Pol* central, national
2 *nf* **centrale** confederation
◇ *centrale ouvrière* Br trade *or* Am labor union confederation
◇ *centrale syndicale* Br trade *or* Am labor union confederation

centralisateur, -trice *adj Pol* centralizing

centralisation *nf Pol* centralization

centralisé, -e *adj Pol* centralized

centraliser *Pol* **1** *vt* to centralize
2 se centraliser *vpr* to centralize

centralisme *nm Pol* centralism

centraliste *Pol* **1** *adj* centralist
2 *nmf* centralist

centre *nm Pol* middle ground, centre; **il est du centre** he's middle-of-the-road
◇ *centre droit* moderate right; **il est (de) centre droit** he's right-of-centre
◇ *centre gauche* moderate left; **il est (de) centre gauche** he's left-of-centre

centrisme *nm Pol* centrism

centriste *Pol* **1** *adj* centrist
2 *nmf* centrist; **les centristes** the centre

cercle de qualité *nm Écon* quality circle

CES *nf* (*abrév* **Confédération européenne des syndicats**) ETUC

CESP *nm* (*abrév* **Conseil européen des syndicats de police**) CESP, European Council of Police Trade Unions

CFDT *nf* (*abrév* **Confédération française démocratique du travail**) = large French trade union formed from the CFTC in 1964

CFE–CGC *nf* (*abrév* **Confédération française de l'encadrement–Confédération générale des cadres**) = French trade union for engineers and middle and lower management staff

CFTC *nf* (*abrév* **Confédération française des travailleurs chrétiens**) = French trade union with a broadly Christian ethos

CGPME *nf* (*abrév* **Confédération générale des petites et moyennes entreprises**) = French organization of SME employers

CGT *nf* (*abrév* **Confédération générale du travail**) = major association of French trade unions (affiliated to the Communist Party)

chaebol *nm Écon* chaebol

> **❝**
>
> Le sommet pourrait être l'occasion d'engager avec le Sud une coopération économique que souhaitent Séoul et ses milieux d'affaires. La délégation accompagnant Kim Dae-jung à Pyongyang compte dans ses rangs les hauts responsables des quatre **chaebols** (conglomérats industriels) les plus importants de Corée du Sud.
>
> **❞**

challenger *nm Pol* challenger

chambre *nf Pol* House, Chamber; **la Chambre** the House; **siéger à la Chambre** to sit in the House
◇ *Chambre d'agriculture* Chamber of Agriculture
◇ *Chambre basse* Lower Chamber
◇ *Chambre de commerce* Chamber of Commerce
◇ *Chambre de commerce et d'in-*

dustrie Chamber of Commerce and Industry
◇ *Chambre de commerce internationale* International Chamber of Commerce
◇ *Chambre des communes (en Grande-Bretagne)* House of Commons
◇ *Anciennement Chambre des députés (en France)* Chamber of Deputies
◇ *Chambre haute* Upper Chamber
◇ *Chambre des lords (en Grande-Bretagne)* House of Lords
◇ *Chambre de métiers* Guild Chamber
◇ *Chambre des pairs (en Grande-Bretagne)* House of Lords
◇ *Chambre des représentants (aux États-Unis, en Belgique)* House of Representatives
◇ *chambre syndicale* employers' federation

chanceler *vi (pouvoir, institution, autorité)* to falter, to totter; **les émeutes ont fait chanceler le pouvoir** the riots rocked the government

chancelier *nm* **(a)** *(d'ambassade)* (embassy) chief secretary, *Br* chancellor; *(de consulat)* first secretary **(b)** *Pol (en Allemagne, en Autriche)* chancellor
◇ *Pol chancelier de l'Échiquier* ≃ Chancellor of the Exchequer

chancellerie *nf Pol* chancery, chancellery

change *nm (transaction)* exchange; *(taux)* exchange rate; **faire le change** to deal in foreign exchange
◇ *change du dollar* dollar exchange

changement structurel *nm Écon* structural change

charcutage électoral *nm Fam Péj* gerrymandering; **faire du charcutage électoral** to gerrymander

❝
Les personnes les plus à l'aise pourront s'intéresser au problème du **charcutage électoral** qui consiste, en connaissant les opinions politiques de chaque canton (i.e. le pourcentage de personnes votant pour chaque parti politique) de trouver un découpage admissible (populations pas trop déséquilibrées, circonscriptions pas trop "tordues") le plus avantageux possible pour un parti politique donné.
❞

charge *nf (obligation financière)* charge, expense; *(impôt)* tax
◇ *charge fiscale* tax (burden)
◇ *charges patronales* employer's contributions
◇ *charges publiques* public expenditure
◇ *charges sociales* *Br* ≃ national insurance contributions *(paid by the employer)*, *Am* ≃ social security charges *(paid by the employer)*
◇ *charges sociales salariales* *Br* ≃ national insurance contributions *(paid by the employee)*, *Am* ≃ social security charges *(paid by the employee)*

chargé, -e *nm,f*
◇ *chargé d'affaires* chargé d'affaires
◇ *chargé de mission* ≃ (official) representative

charte *nf (document)* charter
◇ *charte des droits fondamentaux* Charter of Fundamental Rights
◇ *charte des droits de l'homme* Charter of Human Rights
◇ *Charte sociale* Social Charter
◇ *charte des valeurs* statement of principles

chartiste *nmf Écon* chartist

chasser *vt (expulser)* to drive out, to expel; **chasser qn du pays** to drive sb from the country

chauvin, -e **1** *adj* jingoist, jingoistic **2** *nm,f* jingoist

chauvinisme *nm* jingoism

chef *nm (d'un parti politique)* leader
◇ *chef de cabinet* ≃ *Br* minister's or

Am secretary of state's principal private secretary
◇ **chef de la diplomatie** foreign minister, *Br* ≃ Foreign Secretary, *Am* ≃ Secretary of State
◇ **chef d'État** head of state
◇ **chef du gouvernement** head of government

chefferie *nf Can Pol* party leadership

chiffre *nm Écon* (a) *(nombre)* figure, number; **inflation à deux chiffres** double-digit inflation (b) *(montant)* amount, sum; **le chiffre des dépenses s'élève à 2000 euros** total expenditure amounts to 2,000 euro (c) *(taux)* figures, rate; **les chiffres du chômage** the unemployment figures
◇ **chiffres bruts** unweighted figures

chiraquien, -enne 1 *adj* (a) *(de Jacques Chirac)* Chirac; **le QG chiraquien** the Chirac HQ (b) *(partisan de Jacques Chirac)* pro-Chirac
2 *nm,f* Chirac supporter

❝

Le président Jacques Chirac a nommé son gouvernement de 27 membres. Il est composé essentiellement de **chiraquiens**, deux membres de la société civile, l'industriel Francis Mer et le philosophe Luc Ferry, et beaucoup de novices. Seul poids lourd non **chiraquien**, le député et maire UDF d'Amiens Gilles de Robien, fidèle de François Bayrou, s'installe aux commandes du ministère de l'Equipement, des Transports, du Logement, du Tourisme et de la Mer.

❞

choc *nm* crisis
◇ **choc pétrolier** oil crisis

chômage *nm* unemployment; **au chômage** out of work, unemployed
◇ *Écon* **chômage conjoncturel** cyclical unemployment
◇ *Écon* **chômage déguisé** hidden unemployment
◇ *Écon* **chômage frictionnel** frictional unemployment

◇ *Écon* **chômage keynésien** Keynesian unemployment
◇ *Écon* **chômage partiel** short-time working
◇ *Écon* **chômage récurrent** periodic *or* recurrent unemployment
◇ *Écon* **chômage saisonnier** seasonal unemployment
◇ *Écon* **chômage structurel** structural *or* long-term unemployment

chômer *vi* to be unemployed

chômeur, -euse *nm,f* unemployed person; **les chômeurs** the unemployed; **le nombre des chômeurs est très important** the unemployment figures are very high; **les chômeurs de longue durée** the long-term unemployed

chrétien-démocrate, chrétienne-démocrate *Pol* **1** *adj* Christian Democrat
2 *nm,f* Christian Democrat

chute *nf* (a) *(d'une monnaie, des exportations, des prix)* drop, fall (**de** in) (b) *(d'un gouvernement, d'une institution)* collapse, fall

CIA *nf* (*abrév* **Central Intelligence Agency**) CIA

CIC *nf* (*abrév* **Confédération internationale des cadres**) CIC, International Confederation of Executives and Managerial Staff

Cidunati *nm* (*abrév* **Comité interprofessionnel d'information et de défense de l'union nationale des travailleurs indépendants**) = union of self-employed craftsmen

CIG *nf* (*abrév* **Conférence Intergouvernementale**) IGC

CIJ *nf* (*abrév* **Cour internationale de justice**) ICJ

cinquième colonne *nf Pol* fifth column

circonscription *nf Pol* area, district
◇ **circonscription administrative** constituency
◇ **circonscription consulaire** consular district

◇ *circonscription électorale (aux municipales)* ward; *(aux législatives)* constituency

circuit *nm Écon* channel

circulation *nf Écon (déplacement)* movement, circulation; **la libre circulation des personnes/des biens/des capitaux** the free movement of people/goods/capital

◇ *circulation monétaire* circulation of money, money in circulation

CISL *nf (abrév* **Confédération internationale des syndicats libres)** ICFTU

citoyen, -enne *nm,f* citizen; **accomplir son devoir de citoyen** *(voter)* to do one's civic duty, to vote

◇ *citoyen d'honneur* ≃ freeman

citoyenneté *nf* citizenship; **prendre la citoyenneté française** to acquire French citizenship

CJAI *nf UE (abrév* **Coopération concernant la justice et les affaires intérieures)** CJHA

CJCE *nf UE (abrév* **Cour de justice des communautés européennes)** CJEC

classe *nf Pol* class; **l'ensemble de la classe politique** the whole of the political establishment *or* class; **une société sans classe** a classless society

◇ *classes dirigeantes* ruling classes

◇ *classes laborieuses* working classes

◇ *classes moyennes* middle classes

◇ *classe ouvrière* working class

◇ *classes populaires* working classes

◇ *classe sociale* social class

classification *nf (répartition)* classification

◇ *classification socio-économique* socio-economic classification

◇ *classification socio-professionnelle* socio-economic classification

classique *adj Écon* classical

clause *nf Pol (d'un traité)* clause

◇ *clause compromissoire* arbitration clause

◇ *clause dérogatoire* derogatory clause

◇ *clause d'exemption* opt-out clause

◇ *clause de la nation la plus favorisée* most-favoured-nation clause

◇ *clause restrictive* restrictive clause

◇ *clause de sauvegarde* safety clause

clientèle électorale *nf Pol* electorate, voters

clientélisme *nm Pol* clientelism

Lorsque quelqu'un comme lui est élu au premier tour (avec 52,8% des suffrages), en rompant avec toute une tradition colombienne de **clientélisme**, il est impossible de dire qu'il est le candidat des paramilitaires.

clientéliste *adj Pol* clientelist; **des pratiques clientélistes** vote-catching practices

clignotant *nm Écon (indice)* (key) indicator; **le clignotant de la hausse des prix** the warning light *or* signal that prices are rising

climat économique *nm* economic climate

clivage *nm Pol (séparation)* split, divide; **il y a un net clivage entre la droite et la gauche** there's a sharp divide between right and left

◇ *clivages partisans* ideological divides, sectarianism; **dépasser les clivages partisans** to bridge the ideological divide

clore *vt* **clore les débats** *(s'arrêter)* to end the discussion, to bring the discussion to a close

clôture *nf Parl (d'un débat, d'une séance)* closure, cloture

clôturer *vt Parl (débat, séance)* to close

CMT *nm (abrév* **Confédération mondiale du travail)** WCL

CNJA *nm (abrév* **Centre national des jeunes agriculteurs)** = French farmers' union

CNPF *nm Anciennement* (*abrév* **Conseil national du patronat français**) = national council of French employers, *Br* ≃ CBI

CNSF–FNCR *nf* (*abrév* **Confédération nationale des salariés de France–Fédération nationale des chauffeurs routiers**) = French trade union representing lorry drivers and workers from other sectors

CNUCED, Cnuced *nf* (*abrév* **Conférence des Nations unies pour le commerce et le développement**) UNCTAD

coalisé, -e *Pol* **1** *adj* allied
   2 *nm,f* allied nation, ally

coaliser *Pol* **1** *vt* to make into a coalition
   2 se coaliser *vpr* to form a coalition

coalition *nf Pol* coalition

cocardier, -ère *Péj* **1** *adj* jingoistic
   2 *nm,f* jingoist

code *nm* statute book
   ◊ *code des lois* statute book

codécision *nf UE* codecision (procedure)

codéveloppement *nm* cooperative development

coefficient *nm Écon* index, ratio
   ◊ *coefficient de corrélation* correlation coefficient
   ◊ *coefficient saisonnier* seasonal index

cœur *nm* (a) *(centre)* heartland; **cette région est véritablement le cœur de l'Allemagne industrielle** this region is really the heartland of industrial Germany (b) *(partie la plus importante)* **la question de la sécurité est au cœur des préoccupations de notre parti** the issue of security is at the heart of our party's interests

cohabitation *nf Pol* = coexistence of an elected head of state and an opposition parliamentary majority
   ◊ *cohabitation monétaire européenne* European monetary cohabitation

❝

Les **cohabitations** à répétition – neuf ans au cours des seize dernières années – ont approfondi le trouble. A l'immunité personnelle du président s'est ajoutée son irresponsabilité politique, dès lors qu'il ne tirait pas d'autre conséquence de l'échec de son camp aux législatives que son pur et simple maintien en fonction pour mieux préparer sa revanche.

❞

cohabitationniste *Pol* **1** *adj* = relating to the coexistence of an elected head of state and an opposition parliamentary majority
   2 *nmf* = advocate of a system where the elected head of state and an opposition party with a parliamentary majority coexist

collectif, -ive *adj* (*en commun*) collective, common; **une démarche collective serait plus efficace** collective representations would have more impact

collectivisation *nf Écon* collectivization, collectivizing

collectiviser *vt Écon* to collectivize

collectivisme *nm Écon* collectivism

collectiviste *Écon* **1** *adj* collectivist
   2 *nmf* collectivist

collectivité *nf* (*société*) community, collectivity
   ◊ *collectivités locales* (*dans un État*) local authorities; (*dans une fédération*) federal authorities
   ◊ *la collectivité nationale* the nation, the country
   ◊ *collectivité publique* government organization
   ◊ *collectivité territoriale* = administrative division with a higher degree of autonomy than a département

collège électoral *nm Pol* body of electors, electoral college

colombe *nf Pol* dove

colonial, -e 1 *adj* colonial
2 *nm,f (habitant)* colonial

colonialisme *nm* colonialism

colonialiste 1 *adj* colonialist
2 *nmf* colonialist

colonie *nf (pays)* colony

colonisation *nf (d'un pays)* colonization; **après la colonisation de l'Afrique**
after the colonization of Africa

coloniser *vt (pays)* to colonize

coloration politique *nf* political
colour *or* tendency

combat *nm (lutte politique)* struggle,
fight

combinaison ministérielle *nf Pol*
composition of a cabinet

❝

... le débat sur la forme du Cabinet
n'est pas encore tranché. De quoi
s'agit-il? On a pu dire que le président de la République, en soutenant
la nécessité d'une **combinaison ministérielle** représentative de toutes
les sensibilités politiques contre la formule du président du Conseil désigné
d'un Cabinet homogène ne cher-
chait, en définitive, qu'à consolider
son rôle d'arbitre. C'est possible et
c'est légitime.

❞

Comecon *nm Anciennement Écon*
(*abrév* **Conseil d'Assistance Économique Mutuelle**) Comecon

COMESA *nm* (*abrév* **Common Market
for Eastern and Southern Africa**) CO-
MESA

comité *nm* committee, board; **faire
partie d'un comité** to sit on a committee

◇ **comité d'action** action committee
◇ **Comité d'aide au développement**
Development Assistance Committee
◇ **comité central** central committee
◇ *UE* **comité de conciliation** Conciliation Committee

◇ **comité de défense** defence
committee
◇ **comité directeur** steering committee
◇ *UE* **Comité Économique et Social**
Economic and Social Committee
◇ *Pol* **comité électoral** electoral
committee, caucus
◇ *UE* **Comité européen de normalisation** European Standards Commission
◇ *Pol* **comité exécutif** executive
committee *or* board
◇ *Pol* **comité permanent** standing
committee
◇ *Pol* **comité de quartier** local
committee
◇ *UE* **Comité des Régions** Committee of the Regions
◇ *UE* **Comité des représentants permanents** Committee of Permanent
Representatives

commerce *nm* **(a)** *(activité)* trade,
commerce **(b)** *(affaires)* business;
faire du commerce avec qn/un pays to
trade with sb/a country; **faire le
commerce de qch** to trade in sth
◇ **commerce bilatéral** bilateral trade
◇ **commerce dirigé** managed trade
◇ **commerce extérieur** foreign trade
◇ **commerce frontalier** border trade
◇ **commerce intérieur** domestic
trade, home trade
◇ **commerce international** international trade
◇ **commerce réciproque** reciprocal
trade *or* trading
◇ **commerce de réexportation** re-
export trade
◇ **commerce de services** invisible
trade
◇ **commerce triangulaire** triangular
trade

commercer *vi* to trade, to deal;
commercer avec un pays to trade with
a country

commercial, -e *adj (activité, attaché)* commercial; *(délégué, direction,
service)* sales; *(relation, embargo, tribunal)* trade

commissaire *nm Pol (membre d'une commission)* commissioner
◇ **commissaire aux comptes** government auditor
◇ **commissaire européen** European commissioner
◇ **commissaire du gouvernement** government commissioner
◇ **commissaire de la République** commissioner of the Republic

commission *nf Pol (groupe)* commission, committee ; **être en commission** to be in committee ; *Pol* **renvoyer un projet de loi en commission** to commit a bill
◇ **commission d'arbitrage** arbitration board
◇ **Commission de Bruxelles** European Commission
◇ **commission du budget** budget committee
◇ **Commission des communautés européennes** European Community Commission
◇ **Commission économique pour l'Europe** Economic Commission for Europe
◇ **commission électorale** electoral commission
◇ **commission d'enquête parlementaire** select committee
◇ **Commission européenne** European Commission
◇ **commission interparlementaire** interparliamentary committee
◇ **commission mixte** joint commission *or* committee
◇ **commission paritaire** joint commission
◇ **commission parlementaire** parliamentary committee *or* commission
◇ **commission permanente** standing committee
◇ *Pol* **commission de sages** advisory committee

Commonwealth *nm* **le Commonwealth** the Commonwealth

communal, -e *adj (équipements, services, projets) (en ville)* ≃ of the urban district; *(à la campagne)* ≃ of the rural district

communautariser *vt* **communautariser la santé/la défense/le droit des travailleurs** to handle the issue of health/defence/workers' rights at an EU level

communautarisme *nm* = emphasis on issues relating to minorities and ethnic communities within society

communautariste *adj (démarche, politique)* = that takes into account issues relating to minorities and ethnic communities within society

❝

A gauche ... une approche **communautariste** à visée électorale s'est depuis longtemps développée. Ainsi dès son arrivée à la tête de la ville de Marseille G. Deferre a largement mis en place une politique **communautariste** intégrée au fonctionnement même des sections de la SFIO puis du P.S. Mais surtout cette démarche que l'on ne retrouvait pas dans d'autres grandes fédérations comme celles du Nord a été, dès 1981, en partie étendue au plan national par F. Mitterrand qui a voulu créer un lien politique avec toutes les populations étrangères à partir d'une conception **communautariste** de l'intégration.

❞

communauté *nf* community
◇ **Communauté andine** Andean Community of Nations
◇ **Communauté économique européenne** European Economic Community
◇ **Communauté des États Indépendants** Commonwealth of Independent States
◇ **Communauté européenne** European Community
◇ **Communauté européenne du charbon et de l'acier** European Coal and Steel Community
◇ **Communauté européenne de défense** European Defence Community

◇ *Communauté européenne de l'énergie atomique* European Atomic Energy Community

◇ *communauté internationale* international community

commune *nf* (a) *(agglomération)* commune (b) **les Communes** *(en Grande-Bretagne)* the House of Commons

communiqué de presse *nm* press release

communisme *nm Pol* Communism

communiste *Pol* **1** *adj* Communist **2** *nmf* Communist

compensateur, -trice *adj Écon* compensating, compensatory

compensatoire *adj Écon* compensatory, compensating

compétitif, -ive *adj Écon* competitive

compétition *nf Écon* competition; **il existe une compétition féroce sur le marché de l'informatique** there is fierce competition within the IT market

compétitivité *nf Écon* competitiveness

complémentaire *adj Écon* complementary

complémentarité *nf Écon* complementarity

comptabilité *nf*
◇ *Écon* **comptabilité nationale** national auditing
◇ *comptabilité publique* public finance

compte *nm* account
◇ *Écon* **compte courant** current account
◇ *Écon* **compte des flux financiers** flow of funds account
◇ *compte rendu* (d'une séance, d'un débat) report

compte-rendu *nm* (d'une séance, d'un débat) report

comptoir *nm Écon* trading syndicate

comté *nm Can Pol* riding

concentration *nf Écon* concentration
◇ *concentration horizontale* horizontal concentration
◇ *concentration verticale* vertical concentration

concert des nations *nm* entente; **le concert des nations africaines** the entente between African nations

conciliatoire *adj Pol* conciliatory

concours *nm* (a) *(épreuve)* competitive examination (b) *(aide)* aid; *(soutien)* support; **prêter son concours à qn/qch** to lend one's support to sb/sth; **grâce au concours du maire** thanks to the mayor's help *or* support
◇ *concours administratif* = examination for entry into government or civil service jobs
◇ *concours financier* financial aid
◇ *concours de la fonction publique* = examination for entry into government or civil service jobs

concurrence *nf Écon* *(concept)* competition
◇ *concurrence étrangère* foreign competition
◇ *concurrence imparfaite* imperfect competition
◇ *concurrence parfaite* perfect competition
◇ *concurrence pure* pure competition

concurrent, -e *Écon* **1** *adj* (entreprises, produits) competing, rival **2** *nm,f* competitor, rival

concurrentiel, -elle *adj Écon* competitive

condition *nf* (préalable) condition; **conditions** terms; **les conditions de l'accord** the terms of the agreement
◇ *Écon* **conditions favorables** soft terms
◇ *Écon* **conditions optimales** optimum conditions

conditionnalité *nf Écon* conditionality

confédéral, -e *adj* confederal

confédération *nf (nation)* confederation, confederacy
◇ *Pol* **Confédération européenne des syndicats** European Trade Union Confederation
◇ **Confédération générale du travail** = major association of French trade unions (affiliated to the Communist Party)
◇ **Confédération helvétique** Swiss Confederation
◇ **Confédération paysanne** = militant French association that defends the rights of farmers and campaigns on rural and environmental issues

confédéré, -e 1 *adj* confederate
2 *nm,f* **(a)** *(membre d'une confédération)* confederate **(b)** *Suisse* = person from another canton

confédérer 1 *vt* to confederate
2 se confédérer *vpr* to confederate

conférence *nf (réunion)* conference
◇ **conférence intergouvernementale** intergovernmental conference
◇ **conférence internationale sur la paix** international peace conference
◇ **conférence ministérielle** ministerial conference
◇ **Conférence des Nations unies pour le commerce et le développement** United Nations Conference on Trade and Development
◇ **conférence de presse** press conference
◇ *UE* **Conférence sur la sécurité et la coopération en Europe** Council for Security and Cooperation in Europe
◇ **conférence au sommet** summit conference

confiance *nf Pol* **voter la confiance au gouvernement** to pass a vote of confidence in the government

conflit *nm* conflict
◇ **conflit d'attributions** demarcation dispute
◇ **conflit frontalier** border conflict
◇ **conflit salarial** wage dispute

◇ **conflit social** labour *or* industrial dispute
◇ **conflit du travail** labour *or* industrial dispute

confusion des pouvoirs *nf Pol* = non-separation of legislative, executive and judiciary powers

> **"**
>
> Quant à la coresponsabilité, même partielle, des affaires publiques entre les deux responsables de l'exécutif, elle a conduit à la **confusion des pouvoirs** et nourri la frustration des Français d'être, en quelque sorte, privés de réelle alternance démocratique.
>
> **"**

conglomérat *nm Écon* conglomerate

congrès *nm Pol* congress, conference
◇ **Congrès américain** Congress
◇ **Congrès national africain** African National Congress
◇ **Congrès du parti** party conference

congressiste *nmf Pol* = participant at a congress

conjoncture *nf Écon* economic situation, economic conditions; **attendre une amélioration de la conjoncture** to wait for economic conditions to improve
◇ **conjoncture économique** economic situation, economic conditions; **on assiste à une dégradation de la conjoncture économique** the economic situation is deteriorating

conjoncturel, -elle *adj Écon (chômage)* cyclical; *(prévisions, stratégie, politique)* economic

conjoncturiste *nmf Écon* economic analyst

conseil *nm (assemblée)* council, committee; *(d'une entreprise)* board; *(réunion)* meeting
◇ **conseil d'administration** *(d'une organisation internationale)* governing body; *(de l'Union européenne)* directorate general

◇ *conseil d'arrondissement* ≃ city council

◇ *Anciennement* **Conseil d'Assistance Économique Mutuelle** Comecon

◇ *conseil de cabinet* cabinet council, council of ministers

◇ *Belg* **conseil communal** ≃ local council

◇ *Conseil constitutionnel* = French government body ensuring that laws, elections and referenda are constitutional

◇ *UE* **Conseil Ecofin** ECOFIN

◇ *Conseil économique et social* = consultative body advising the government on economic and social matters

◇ *Conseil d'État* (French) Council of State

◇ *Suisse* **Conseil des États** Council of States

◇ *Conseil de l'Europe* Council of Europe

◇ *Conseil européen* European Council

◇ *Can* **Conseil exécutif** ≃ Cabinet

◇ *Suisse* **Conseil fédéral** Federal Council, = highest executive body

◇ *conseil général* ≃ departmental council

◇ *conseil de guerre* council of war

◇ *conseil interministériel* interministerial council

◇ *conseil législatif* legislative council

◇ *Conseil des ministres* ≃ cabinet meeting

◇ *conseil monétaire* Currency Board

◇ *conseil municipal (en ville)* ≃ town council, ≃ local (urban) council; *(à la campagne)* ≃ local (rural) council, *Br* ≃ parish council

◇ *Suisse* **Conseil national** National Council

◇ *Conseil national du crédit* National Credit Council

◇ *Conseil de la politique monétaire* Monetary Policy Committee

◇ *conseil de prud'hommes* industrial arbitration court, *Br* ≃ ACAS

◇ *conseil régional* regional council

◇ *Conseil de sécurité* Security Council

◇ *Conseil de sécurité nationale* National Security Council

◇ *Conseil de sécurité de l'ONU* UN Security Council

◇ *Conseil de l'Union européenne* Council of the European Union

conseiller, -ère *nm,f* (a) *(spécialiste)* adviser, aide, consultant (b) *(membre d'un conseil)* council member, councillor

◇ *conseiller économique* economic adviser

◇ *conseiller d'État* member of the "Conseil d'État"

◇ *conseiller général* ≃ departmental county councillor

◇ *conseiller municipal (en ville)* ≃ local *or* town councillor; *(à la campagne)* ≃ local councillor

◇ *conseiller régional* regional councillor

conservateur, -trice *Pol* **1** *adj* conservative

2 *nm,f* conservative; *(en Grande-Bretagne)* Conservative, Tory

conservatisme *nm Pol* conservatism; *(en Grande-Bretagne)* Conservatism

consommateur, -trice *nm,f Écon* consumer; **producteurs et consommateurs** producers and consumers

consommation *nf Écon* consumption

◇ *consommation de capital* capital consumption

◇ *consommation intérieure* domestic consumption

◇ *consommation de masse* mass consumption

◇ *consommation des ménages* household consumption

◇ *consommation par tête* per capita consumption

constant, -e *adj Écon* constant

constituant, -e *Pol* **1** *adj* constituent **2** *nm* constituent

constitué, -e *adj Pol (autorité)* constituted; *(corps)* constituent

constituer *vt Pol (gouvernement)* to form, to set up; *(cabinet)* to form, to select (the members of)

constitution *nf Pol* (a) *(d'un gouvernement)* formation; *(d'un cabinet)* selection (b) *(lois)* constitution
◊ *constitution monarchique* monarchy
◊ *constitution républicaine* republic

constitutionnaliser *vt Pol* to constitutionalize, to make constitutional

constitutionnalisme *nm Pol* constitutionalism

constitutionnalité *nf Pol* constitutionality

constitutionnel, -elle *Pol* 1 *adj* constitutional
2 *nm,f* constitutionalist

constitutionnellement *adv Pol* constitutionally

construction européenne *nf* European integration

❝

L'Europe devra et saura se ressaisir. Pour ce faire, il faut deux conditions supplémentaires : d'abord faire en sorte que les citoyens européens se sentent partie prenante de ce projet … Ensuite veiller à ce que les jeunes soient le fer de lance de la **construction européenne**.

❞

consultatif, -ive *adj (comité, rôle)* advisory

consultation *nf*
◊ *Pol consultation électorale* election
◊ *consultation populaire* consultation of the people

consumérisme *nm Écon* **le consumérisme** consumerism

contentieux, -euse 1 *adj* contentious
2 *nm (conflit)* dispute, disagreement
◊ *contentieux électoral* procedure in contentious electoral matters
◊ *contentieux territorial* territorial dispute

contestation *nf Pol* **la contestation** protest

contester *Pol* 1 *vt* to protest (against), to rebel against
2 *vi* to protest

contingent *nm (quota)* quota
◊ *contingents d'exportation* export quotas
◊ *contingents d'importation* import quotas

contingentement *nm Écon* fixing of quotas, restriction; **le contingentement des importations** the fixing of import quotas

contingenter *vt Écon (importations)* to limit, to fix a quota on; *(produits de distribution)* to restrict the distribution of; **des produits contingentés** fixed-quota products

contra *nm Pol (au Nicaragua)* Contra

contraction *nf Écon (de l'activité, du crédit)* reduction (**de** in); *(de la demande)* fall (**de** in)

contrainte *nf* constraint
◊ *contrainte budgétaire* budget constraint
◊ *Écon contrainte extérieure* external constraint

contrat social *nm* social contract

contre-pouvoir *nm* = challenge to established authority

❝

Les mécanismes nationaux de participation et de représentation citoyenne ne sont, en effet, que de peu d'utilité pour permettre aux populations d'influer sur le cours du monde. En s'efforçant de porter "la voix des sans voix" à l'échelle planétaire, beaucoup d'associations de la société civile tentent de combler ce déficit démocratique … En obtenant l'abandon du projet d'Accord multilatéral sur l'investissement en 1998, elles ont prouvé leur capacité à s'ériger en **contre-pouvoir**.

❞

contre-valeur *nf* exchange value

contribuable *nmf* taxpayer

contributeur net *nm UE* net contributor

contribution *nf (impôt)* tax; **contributions** *(à l'État)* taxes; *(à la collectivité locale) Br* ≃ council tax, *Am* ≃ local taxes

◇ **contributions directes** direct taxation

◇ **contributions indirectes** indirect taxation

◇ **contributions sociales** social security contributions

contrôle *nm* control; **avoir le contrôle de** *(d'un secteur, de sociétés)* to have (owning) control of; *(d'un pays, d'un territoire)* to be in control of

◇ *Pol* **contrôle des armements** arms control

◇ **contrôle de la base monétaire** monetary base control

◇ *Écon* **contrôle budgétaire** budgetary control

◇ *Écon* **contrôle des capitaux** capital control

◇ *Écon* **contrôle des changes** exchange control

◇ *Écon* **contrôle de la demande** demand management

◇ *Écon* **contrôle économique** price control

◇ **contrôle étatique** state control

◇ **contrôles à l'exportation** export controls

◇ *Écon* **contrôle de gestion** management control

◇ **contrôles à l'importation** import controls

◇ *Écon* **contrôle monétaire** monetary control

◇ *Écon* **contrôle monopolistique** monopoly control

◇ *Écon* **contrôle des prix** price control

convenir convenir de *vt ind (se mettre d'accord sur)* to agree upon

convention *nf* **(a)** *(accord) (officiel)* agreement; *(diplomatique)* convention **(b)** *(clause)* article, clause **(c)** *Pol (assemblée) (aux États-Unis)* convention; *(en France)* assembly

◇ **convention collective** collective agreement

◇ **Convention européenne sur l'avenir de l'Europe** European Convention on the Future of Europe

◇ *UE* **convention de Lomé** Lomé Convention

◇ **convention réciproque** reciprocal agreement

◇ *UE* **Convention de sauvegarde des droits de l'homme et des libertés fondamentales** European Convention for the Protection of Human Rights and Fundamental Freedoms

◇ **convention sociale** social contract

convention-cadre *nf* framework convention

conventionnel *nm (membre)* member *(of a convention)*

convergence économique *nf UE* economic convergence

convertible *adj Écon (devise, monnaie)* convertible

convertir *vt Écon (devise, monnaie)* to convert

convocation *nf (d'une assemblée)* convening; *(des ministres)* convening, calling together; *(des journalistes, de la presse)* invitation

convoquer *vt (assemblée)* to convene; *(ministres)* to convene, to call together; *(journalistes, presse)* to invite

coopératif, -ive *Écon* **1** *adj (société, banque)* cooperative

2 *nf* **coopérative** *(association)* cooperative, co-op, collective

◇ **coopérative agricole** agricultural cooperative

◇ **coopérative ouvrière** workers' cooperative

coopération *nf* **(a)** *Écon & Pol (fait de coopérer)* economic cooperation **(b)** *Écon (opération spécifique)* cooperation, cooperative action

copinage *nm Fam Péj Pol* cronyism;
  par copinage through cronyism *or*
  one's connections

copropriété *nf* common ownership

corporation *nf* corporate body
  ◇ *corporation de droit public* public
  body

corporatisme *nm Pol* corporatism

corps *nm*
  ◇ *corps administratif* administrative
  body
  ◇ *corps constitué* constituent body
  ◇ *corps consulaire* corps consulaire
  ◇ *corps diplomatique* diplomatic
  corps
  ◇ *corps électoral* electorate, body of
  voters
  ◇ *corps exécutif* executive
  ◇ *corps législatif* legislative body, legislature
  ◇ *corps politique* body politic

correction *nf Écon (rectificatif)* correction
  ◇ *correction des variations saisonnières* seasonal adjustment

corrélation *nf (en statistique)* correlation; **il y a (une) corrélation entre A
  et B** A and B are correlated; **mettre
  en corrélation** to correlate; **être en
  corrélation étroite** to be closely correlated

corrélationnel, -elle *adj (en statistique)* correlational

corréler *vt (en statistique)* to correlate; **corréler A et B** to correlate A
  and B

corrompre *vt* (a) *(pervertir)* to corrupt (b) *(soudoyer)* to bribe

corrompu, -e *adj* corrupt

corruption *nf* (a) *(vénalité)* corruption (b) *(fait de soudoyer)* corruption,
  bribing

cotation de l'or *nf* gold fixing

cote *nf* (a) *(valeur)* quotation; *(liste)*
  share (price) index (b) *(estime)* *(d'un
  homme politique)* standing
  ◇ *cote d'amour (d'un homme poli-*

tique) standing with the electorate,
(popular) rating *or* popularity
  ◇ *cote de popularité (d'un homme politique)* standing with the electorate, approval rating, popularity

> **❝**
>
> Après une très légère embellie qui
> avait permis en mai et juin au camp
> de Schröder de regagner quelques
> mètres du terrain perdu, l'opposition
> consolide l'avance qu'elle a acquise
> depuis janvier. Non moins grave est
> la baisse de la **cote d'amour** per-
> sonnelle de Gerhard Schröder de
> 54 à 48 % tandis que l'estime que
> les Allemands vouent à Edmund
> Stoiber grimpe de 38 % à 41 %.
>
> **❞**

coup *nm*
  ◇ *coup d'État* coup (d'état)
  ◇ *coup de force* takeover by force

coupe *nf* cut
  ◇ *coupes budgétaires* budget cuts
  ◇ *coupe sombre* drastic cut; **faire des
  coupes sombres dans un budget** to
  drastically cut a budget

cour *nf* court
  ◇ *Cour des comptes européenne*
  Court of Auditors
  ◇ *Cour européenne des droits de
  l'homme* European Court of Human Rights
  ◇ *Cour européenne de justice* European Court of Justice
  ◇ *Cour internationale de justice* International Court of Justice
  ◇ *Cour de justice des communautés
  européennes* Court of Justice of
  the European Communities
  ◇ *Cour pénale internationale* International Criminal Court

courant *nm (tendance)* current,
  trend; **les courants de l'opinion** trends
  in public opinion; **les courants du PS** =
  the different ideological tendencies
  which have traditionally existed
  within the Socialist party

courbe *nf Écon* curve

◇ *courbe de croissance* growth curve

◇ *courbe de la demande* demand curve

◇ *courbe de la demande globale* aggregate demand curve

◇ *courbe en J* J-Curve

◇ *courbe de l'offre* supply curve

◇ *courbe de l'offre globale* aggregate supply curve

◇ *courbe des taux* yield curve

couronne *nf Pol* Crown; **la Couronne d'Angleterre/de Belgique** the English/Belgian Crown

cours *nm* (a) *(de devises)* rate (b) *(d'actions)* price, trading rate

◇ *cours du change* exchange rate

◇ *cours des devises* foreign exchange rate

◇ *cours étranger* foreign exchange

◇ *cours forcé* forced currency

◇ *UE cours pivot* central rate

course *nf*

◇ *course aux armements* arms race

◇ *course au pouvoir* race for power

◇ *course à la présidence* presidential race

coût *nm* cost

◇ *Écon coût économique* economic cost

◇ *Écon coût de main-d'œuvre* labour cost

◇ *Écon coût marginal* marginal cost

◇ *Écon coût d'opportunité* opportunity cost

◇ *Écon coût salarial* labour cost

◇ *Écon coût social* social cost

◇ *Écon coût de transaction* transaction cost

◇ *Écon coût variable* variable cost

◇ *Écon coût de la vie* cost of living

coûter *vi* to cost

CPI *nf* (abrév **Cour pénale internationale**) ICC

CPM *nm* (abrév **Conseil de la politique monétaire**) MPC

CPNT *nf* (abrév **Chasse, Pêche, Nature et Traditions**) = French political movement that promotes rural life, hunting, fishing and environmental protection

créancier, -ère *nm,f Écon* creditor

créateur d'entreprise *nm* entrepreneur

crédit *nm* credit

◇ *crédit commercial* trade credit

◇ *crédit à l'exportation* export credit

◇ *crédit à l'importation* import credit

credo politique *nm* political creed or credo

créneau, -x *nm Écon* niche, gap; **trouver un bon créneau** to find a niche in the market; **exploiter un nouveau créneau** to fill a new gap in the market

◇ *créneau porteur* potentially lucrative market

crise *nf Écon & Pol* crisis

◇ *crise de conjoncture* economic crisis *(due to cyclical and not structural factors)*

◇ *crise conjoncturelle* economic crisis *(due to cyclical and not structural factors)*

◇ *crise diplomatique* diplomatic crisis

◇ *crise économique* economic crisis or slump, recession

◇ *crise du pétrole* oil crisis

◇ *crise politique* political crisis

critère *nm* *(principe)* criterion

◇ *UE critères d'adhésion* membership criteria

◇ *UE critères de convergence* convergence criteria

◇ *UE critères d'élargissement* enlargement criteria

croissance *nf* *(d'un pays)* development, growth; *(d'une entreprise)* growth, expansion

◇ *croissance déséquilibrée* imbalanced or unbalanced growth

◇ *croissance économique* economic growth or development

◇ *croissance économique nulle* zero growth

◇ *croissance équilibrée* balanced growth

◇ *croissance externe* external growth

◇ *croissance par intégration* integrative growth

◇ *croissance interne* internal growth

◇ *croissance du marché* market growth

◇ *croissance par tête* per capita growth

◇ *croissance zéro* zero growth

croître *vi (pays)* to develop, to grow; *(entreprise)* to grow, to expand

CSCE *nf (abrév* **Conférence sur la sécurité et la coopération en Europe**) CSCE

CTI *nf (abrév* **Confédération des travailleurs intellectuels de France**) = French trade union representing intellectual workers

CUE *nm (abrév* **Conseil de l'Union européenne**) CEU

cuisine *nf Fam Pol*

◇ *cuisine électorale* electoral dirty tricks

◇ *cuisine parlementaire* parliamentary dirty tricks

> **"**
>
> Mais la patience de la population palestinienne avait dépassé ses limites. L'étincelle qui mit le feu aux poudres relevait de la **cuisine élec-** torale israélienne. Le 28 septembre 2000, M. Ariel Sharon s'imposait de manière provocatrice sur l'esplanade des Mosquées à Jérusalem. En autorisant cette excursion, M. Ehoud Barak espérait renforcer la position du dirigeant du Likoud face ... à son rival de parti, M. Benyamin Nétanyahou.
>
> **"**

culture *nf* crop

◇ *culture commerciale* cash crop

◇ *culture de rapport* cash crop

cumul *nm Pol*

◇ *cumul des fonctions* plurality of offices, pluralism

◇ *cumul des mandats* plurality of offices, pluralism

cumulard, -e *nm,f Fam Péj Pol* politician with several mandates

CVS *adj Écon (abrév* **corrigé des variations saisonnières**) seasonally adjusted

cycle *nm Écon* cycle

◇ *cycle des affaires* business cycle

◇ *cycle conjoncturel* business cycle

◇ *cycle économique* economic cycle

cyclique *adj Écon* cyclical

date *nf* date
◇ **date de base** base date

débâcle *nf (d'une institution, d'un système)* collapse

débat *nm Parl* debate; **débats** proceedings
◇ **débat électoral** electoral debate
◇ **débat public** public debate
◇ **débat télévisé** televised debate

débattre *vt Parl* to debate

déblocage *nm Écon (des salaires, des prix, de crédits)* unfreezing; *(de fonds)* releasing, making available

débloquer *vt Écon (salaires, prix, crédits)* to unfreeze; *(fonds)* to release, to make available

débrayage *nm (grève)* stoppage, walkout

débrayer *vi (faire grève)* to stop work, to come out *or* to go on strike

décélération *nf Écon* slowing down
◇ **décélération économique** economic slowdown

décélérer *vi Écon* to slow down

décentralisateur, -trice *Pol* **1** *adj* decentralization, decentralist
2 *nm,f* decentralist, supporter of decentralization

décentralisation *nf Pol (de l'administration)* decentralization *(from Paris to regional bodies)*; *(des entreprises, des écoles)* moving away from the capital

décentraliser *vt Pol (administration)* to decentralize *(from Paris to regional bodies)*; *(entreprises, écoles)* to move away from the capital

déchéance *nf Pol (d'un monarque)* deposition, deposing; *(d'un président)* removal *(after impeachment)*

déclaration *nf* **(a)** *(communication)* declaration, statement; **faire une déclaration à la presse** to issue a declaration *or* statement to the press **(b)** *(proclamation)* declaration, proclamation
◇ **déclaration commune** agreed statement, joint statement
◇ **déclaration de guerre** declaration of war
◇ **déclaration d'indépendance** declaration of independence
◇ **déclaration d'intention** declaration of intent
◇ **déclaration de politique générale** statement of general policy
◇ **déclaration de principe** statement *or* declaration of principle

déclarer *vt (proclamer)* to declare, to announce; **le gouvernement a déclaré que...** the government announced *or* declared that...; **déclarer la guerre (à)** to declare war (on)

décollage *nm Écon* take-off

décompter *vt (dénombrer)* to count

déconcentration *nf* **(a)** *Pol (de pouvoir)* devolution, decentralization **(b)** *Écon (d'industries)* dispersion

déconcentrer *vt* **(a)** *Pol (pouvoir)* to devolve, to decentralize **(b)** *Écon (industries)* to disperse

découpage électoral *nm Pol* division into electoral districts, *Am* apportionment; **refaire le découpage**

électoral *Br* to review constituency boundaries, *Am* to redistrict

> Or, la chambre sortante était loin d'être aussi monocolore que celle qui devrait émerger des urnes le 16 juin. A cela, une raison simple : le poids du **découpage électoral**, qui proportionnellement survalorise les circonscriptions rurales, traditionnellement plus ancrées à droite. Voilà pourquoi la nouvelle Assemblée devrait comporter près de 400 députés du camp vainqueur et non 300.

décret *nm* decree; **promulguer un décret** to issue a decree
◊ *décret d'application* = presidential decree affecting the application of a law
◊ *décret ministériel* = order to carry out legislation given by the Prime Minister
◊ *décret présidentiel* *Br* ≃ Order in Council, *Am* ≃ executive order

décréter *vt* to decree

décret-loi *nm* *Br* *Pol* = Order in Council, *Am* ≃ executive order

déductible *adj* (dépense) deductible; **déductible de l'impôt** tax-deductible

déduction *nf* (d'une dépense, d'un frais) deduction; **entrer en déduction de qch** to be deductible from sth; **déduction faite de** after deduction of, after deducting

déduire *vt* (dépense, frais) to deduct

défaite *nf Pol* defeat; **connaître une défaite** to suffer a defeat

défense *nf* defence; **combien dépense-t-on pour la défense?** how much is spent on defence?
◊ *défense nationale* national defence; **un problème concernant la défense nationale** a problem of national defence

défi *nm Pol* challenge; **jeter** *ou* **lancer un défi à qn** to challenge sb

déficit *nm Écon* deficit; **être en déficit** to be in deficit; **accuser un déficit** to show a deficit; **combler un déficit** to make up a deficit
◊ *déficit de la balance commerciale* trade deficit
◊ *déficit budgétaire* budget deficit
◊ *déficit commercial* trade deficit
◊ *déficit démocratique* democratic deficit
◊ *déficit extérieur* external deficit, balance of payments deficit
◊ *déficit de financement* financing gap
◊ *déficit public* government deficit
◊ *déficit du secteur public* public sector deficit
◊ *déficit social* public spending deficit
◊ *déficit de trésorerie* cash deficit

déficitaire *adj Écon* (entreprise) loss-making; (budget) in deficit, adverse; **être déficitaire** to be in deficit

déflation *nf Écon* deflation

déflationniste *adj Écon* deflationary

dégagement *nm Pol* disengagement

dégel *nm Pol* (après un conflit) thaw; **une période de dégel** a period of détente

dégeler *Pol* **1** *vt* (relations diplomatiques) to thaw
2 se dégeler *vpr* (relations diplomatiques) to thaw; **les relations entre les deux pays se dégèlent** there is a thaw in relations between the two countries

dégraissage *nm Écon* downsizing

dégraisser *vt Écon* to downsize

délégation *nf* (a) (groupe envoyé) delegation; **envoyé en délégation (auprès de qn)** sent as a delegation (to sb) (b) (commission) commission (c) (fait de mandater) delegation; **agir par délégation pour qn** to act on the authority of *or* as a proxy for sb
◊ *délégation de pouvoirs* delegation of powers

◇ *délégation de vote* proxy voting

délégué, -e *nm,f* delegate, representative

◇ *délégué syndical* union representative, *Br* shop steward

déléguer *vt* (a) *(groupe, personne)* to delegate (b) *(pouvoir)* to delegate, to devolve

délit politique *nm* political offence

démago *Fam* **1** *adj* demagogic, demagogical
2 *nmf* demagogue

démagogie *nf* demagogy, demagoguery

démagogique *adj* demagogic, demagogical

démagogue **1** *adj* demagogic, demagogical
2 *nmf* demagogue

demande *nf Écon* demand; **l'offre et la demande** supply and demand; **tiré par la demande** demand-led

◇ *demande des consommateurs* consumer demand

◇ *demande effective* effective demand

◇ *demande excédentaire* overdemand, excess demand

◇ *demande globale* global demand, aggregate demand

◇ *demande du marché* market demand

demandeur, -euse d'asile *nm,f* asylum-seeker

démarchage électoral *nm Pol* canvassing, *Br* doorstepping; **faire du démarchage électoral** to canvass, *Br* to doorstep

démarcher *vt Pol* to canvass, *Br* to doorstep

demi-canton *nm Suisse Pol* half-canton

démilitarisation *nf* demilitarization

démilitariser *vt* to demilitarize

démission *nf* resignation; **donner sa démission** to resign, to hand in one's resignation

démissionnaire **1** *adj (qui quitte son poste)* resigning, outgoing
2 *nmf* person resigning; **les démissionnaires** those who have resigned

démissionner **1** *vt Fam (renvoyer)* **démissionner qn** to talk sb into resigning; **ils l'ont démissionné?** did he resign or was he fired?
2 *vi* to resign, to hand in one's resignation

démocrate **1** *adj* democratic; *(aux États-Unis)* Democratic
2 *nmf* democrat; *(aux États-Unis)* Democrat

démocrate-chrétien, -enne **1** *adj* Christian Democrat
2 *nm,f* Christian Democrat

démocratie *nf* (a) *(système)* democracy (b) *(pays)* democracy, democratic country; **vivre en démocratie** to live in a democracy

◇ *démocratie chrétienne* Christian Democracy

◇ *démocratie directe* direct democracy

◇ *Démocratie Libérale* = French political party

◇ *démocratie participative* participatory democracy

◇ *démocratie populaire* people's democracy

◇ *démocratie représentative* representative democracy

démocratique *adj Pol* democratic

démocratiquement *adv Pol* democratically

démocratisation *nf Pol* democratization, making more democratic

démocratiser *Pol* **1** *vt* to democratize, to make more democratic
2 **se démocratiser** *vpr* to become more democratic

démographe *nmf* demographer

démographie *nf (science)* demography, demographics; *(croissance de la population)* population growth

démographique *adj* demographic

démonétisation *nf Écon* demonetization, demonetarization

démonétiser *vt Écon* to demonetize, to demonetarize

denrée *nf Écon* commodity
◇ *denrées de base* basic commodities
◇ *denrées de consommation courante* basic consumer goods
◇ *denrées du pays* domestic products
◇ *denrées de première nécessité* staple commodities
◇ *denrée témoin* basic commodities

départager *vt Pol* départager les votes to settle the voting, to give the casting vote

département *nm* (a) *(du territoire français)* département, department (b) *(ministère)* department, ministry (c) *Suisse* = administrative authority in a Swiss canton
◇ *Département d'État* State Department, Department of State
◇ *département ministériel* ministry
◇ *départements d'outre-mer* French overseas departments

départ volontaire *nm Écon* attrition, voluntary redundancy

dépense *nf (frais)* expense, expenditure; **dépenses** spending, expenditure; *Écon* **dépenses et recettes** expenditure and income
◇ *Écon dépenses de consommation* consumer expenditure, consumer spending
◇ *Écon dépenses d'équipement* capital expenditure
◇ *dépenses de l'État* public spending, government spending
◇ *dépenses fiscales* tax expenditure
◇ *Écon dépenses globales* aggregate expenditure, aggregate spending
◇ *Écon dépenses des ménages* household expenditure
◇ *Écon dépense nationale* national expenditure, government spending
◇ *dépenses publiques* public spending, government spending

◇ *dépenses de santé* health spending, health expenditure
◇ *dépenses sociales* spending on social services

dépenser *vt (argent)* to spend

déplacement *nm Écon* le déplacement de l'offre et de la demande the shift *or* swing in supply and demand

déplacer *vt Pol* déplacer des voix (en faveur de) to shift votes (towards)

déposer *vt* (a) *(projet de loi)* to introduce, *Br* to table (b) *(monarque)* to depose

dépositaire *nmf*
◇ *dépositaire de l'autorité publique* = officer of the State
◇ *dépositaire public* = government official with responsibility for the management of public funds

déposition *nf (d'un monarque)* deposition

dépouillement *nf Pol (d'un scrutin)* counting, scrutiny

dépouiller *vt Pol* dépouiller le scrutin to count the votes

dépréciation *nf (d'une monnaie)* depreciation

déprécié, -e *adj (monnaie)* depreciated

déprécier 1 *vt (monnaie)* to depreciate, to cause to fall in value
2 se déprécier *vpr (monnaie)* to depreciate, to fall in value

dépression *nf Écon* depression, slump

dépressionnaire *adj Écon* slump; le marché a des tendances dépressionnaires the market is heading towards a slump

déprimé, -e *adj Écon* depressed

députation *nf* (a) *(envoi)* deputation, mandating (b) *(groupe)* delegation, deputation (c) *Pol (rôle)* office of deputy, membership of the "Assemblée nationale"; se présenter à la députation to stand for the position of deputy

député, -e *nm,f* (**a**) *(représentant)* delegate, representative (**b**) *Pol (en France)* deputy; *(en Grande-Bretagne)* member of Parliament; *(aux États-Unis)* Congressman, *f* Congresswoman

◇ **député européen** Member of the European Parliament, Euro-MP, MEP

député-maire *nm* = deputy who also holds the post of mayor

députer *vt* to send, to delegate; **députer qn auprès du ministre** to send sb (as a delegate) *or* to delegate sb to speak to the Minister

déréglementation *nf* deregulation

déréglementer *vt* to deregulate

dérégulation *nf* deregulation

déréguler *vt* to deregulate

désaccord *nm Pol* dissent

désarmement *nm Pol* disarmament

◇ **désarmement nucléaire** nuclear disarmament

◇ **désarmement unilatéral** unilateral disarmament

désarmer *vt Pol* to disarm

désarticuler *vt Écon* to disarticulate

déséconomie *nf Écon* diseconomy

◇ **déséconomie d'échelle** diseconomy of scale

◇ **déséconomie externe** external diseconomy

désencadrement *nm Écon (des crédits)* unblocking

désencadrer *vt Écon* **désencadrer les crédits** to unblock credit, to ease credit restrictions

désengorger *vt Écon* **désengorger le marché** to reduce the overload on the market

désépargne *nf Écon* dissaving

déséquilibre *nm Écon (du système, de l'économie)* disequilibrium, imbalance

◇ **déséquilibre de la balance commerciale** unfavourable trade balance

◇ **déséquilibre financier** financial imbalance

déséquilibrer *vt Écon (système, économie)* to throw off balance, to destabilize

désignation *nf* (**a**) *(nomination) (d'un président)* appointment; *(d'un représentant)* nomination (**b**) *(élection)* to elect

désigner *vt* (**a**) *(nommer) (président)* to appoint; *(représentant)* to nominate; **désigner qn pour un poste** to appoint sb to a post (**b**) *(élire)* to elect

désindustrialisation *nf* deindustrialization

désindustrialiser *vt* to deindustrialize

désinflation *nf Écon* disinflation

désinflationniste *adj Écon* deflationary

désintermédiation *nf Écon* disintermediation

désinvestir *vt Écon* to disinvest in

désinvestissement *nm Écon* disinvestment

◇ **désinvestissement marginal** marginal disinvestment

désistement *nm Pol* withdrawal, standing down

désister se désister *vpr Pol* to withdraw, to stand down

désobéissance civile *nf Pol* civil disobedience

despote *nm Pol* despot

despotique *adj Pol* despotic

despotiquement *adv Pol* despotically

despotisme *nm Pol* despotism

déstabilisant, -e *adj (pour un pays, pour un régime)* destabilizing

déstabilisation *nf (d'un pays, d'un régime)* destabilization

déstabiliser *vt (pays, régime)* to destabilize

déstalinisation *nf Pol* de-Stalinization

déstaliniser *vt Pol* to de-Stalinize

destituable *adj (fonctionnaire)* dismissible; **il n'est pas destituable** he cannot be dismissed (from his post)

destituer *vt (fonctionnaire)* to relieve from his/her duties, to dismiss

destitution *nf (d'un fonctionnaire)* dismissal

désutilité *nf Écon* disutility

détente *nf* (a) *Pol* **la détente** détente (b) *Écon (des taux d'intérêt)* lowering, easing

détention croisée *nf Écon* cross-holding

dette *nf (d'argent)* debt
◇ **dette caduque** = debt barred by the Statute of Limitations
◇ *Écon* **dette consolidée** consolidated *or* funded debt
◇ **dette de l'État** national debt
◇ **dette extérieure** external *or* foreign debt
◇ **dette flottante** floating debt
◇ **dette intérieure** national debt
◇ **dette publique** national debt
◇ **dette sociale** social debt

Deuxième Bureau *nm Anciennement Pol* **le Deuxième Bureau** the intelligence service

dévalorisation *nf Écon (de la monnaie)* devaluation

dévaloriser *Écon* **1** *vt (monnaie)* to devalue
2 se dévaloriser *vpr (monnaie)* to become devalued

dévaluation *nf Écon (de la monnaie)* devaluation
◇ **dévaluation compétitive** competitive devaluation

dévaluer *Écon* **1** *vt (monnaie)* to devalue
2 se dévaluer *vpr (monnaie)* to become devalued

développé, -e *adj Écon (pays, économie)* developed

développement *nm Écon (d'un pays, de l'économie)* development; **une région/entreprise en plein développement** a fast-developing area/business
◇ **développement durable** sustainable development

développer *Écon* **1** *vt (pays, économie)* to develop
2 se développer *vpr (pays, économie)* to develop, to become developed; **une région qui se développe** a developing area; **ça se développe beaucoup dans la région** the region is developing quickly

déviationnisme *nm Pol* deviationism

déviationniste *Pol* **1** *adj* deviationist
2 *nmf* deviationist

devise *nf* currency
◇ **devise contrôlée** managed currency
◇ **devise(s) étrangère(s)** foreign currency
◇ **devise faible** soft *or* weak currency
◇ **devise forte** hard *or* strong currency
◇ **devise internationale** international currency
◇ **devise solide** strong currency

devoir d'ingérence *nm Pol* duty to intervene

> ❝
>
> C'est plus généralement le combat en faveur d'un nouvel ordre mondial, réducteur des inégalités de développement économique, social et politique (dont l'Europe serait l'un des instruments face à la puissance américaine) qui est en cause. Le combat contre la faim dans le monde, contre les pandémies qui dévastent l'Afrique, contre l'exploitation des enfants, contre les conflits interethniques ..., bref, le **devoir d'ingérence** systématisé cher à Bernard Kouchner doit revenir au centre des préoccupations. En cela, la gauche est internationaliste.
>
> ❞

DGSE nf (abrév **Direction générale de la sécurité extérieure**) = arm of the Defence Ministry in charge of international intelligence, Br ≃ MI6, Am ≃ CIA

dictateur nm dictator

dictatorial, -e adj dictatorial

dictature nf dictatorship
◇ **dictature militaire** military dictatorship

différentiel nm Écon differential
◇ **différentiel d'inflation** inflation differential
◇ **différentiel de prix** price differential
◇ **différentiel de taux d'intérêt** interest rate differential

dignitaire nm dignitary

dignité nf (fonction) dignity

diktat nm Pol diktat

dilemme du prisonnier nm Écon prisoner's dilemma

diminuer 1 vt (prix, impôts) to reduce, to cut; (consommation, effectif, chômage) to reduce; **diminuer les impôts de cinq pour cent** to reduce tax by five percent
2 vi (prix, impôts) to fall, to come down; (consommation, chômage) to decrease; (effectif) to reduce

diminution nf (de prix, d'impôts) reduction, cutting; (de consommation, de chômage) decrease; (d'effectif) reduction

diplomate Pol 1 adj diplomatic
2 nmf diplomat

diplomatie nf Pol (relations, représentation) diplomacy; **la diplomatie (corps)** the diplomatic corps or service
◇ **diplomatie du dollar** dollar diplomacy

diplomatique Pol adj diplomatic

diplomatiquement adv Pol diplomatically

directeur, -trice nm,f Pol director

◇ **directeur de cabinet** Br ≃ principal private secretary, PPS, Am ≃ chief of staff

direction nf (a) (d'un pays, d'un parti, d'un mouvement) leadership (b) (service) department
◇ **Direction générale de la sécurité extérieure** = arm of the Defence Ministry in charge of international intelligence, Br ≃ MI6, Am ≃ CIA
◇ **Direction de la surveillance du territoire** = internal state security department, Br ≃ MI5, Am ≃ CIA

directive nf Pol directive

directivité nf Pol (d'une politique) authoritative nature

dirigeant, -e nm,f (d'un pays, d'un parti, d'un mouvement) leader
◇ **dirigeant syndical** union leader

diriger vt (pays) to run; (parti, mouvement) to lead

dirigisme nm Écon state control, dirigisme

"

Par rapport aux autres continents, notamment américain, l'Europe se caractérise par la recherche d'un équilibre entre l'individu et le collectif, entre la performance économique et le développement des normes sociales, par la mise en place d'une régulation qui évite l'ultra-libéralisme destructeur et le **dirigisme** étouffant.

"

dirigiste Écon 1 adj dirigist, state-control
2 nmf advocate of state control

discours nm (allocution) speech, address; **faire un discours** to make a speech
◇ **discours sur l'état de l'Union** State of the Union Speech
◇ **discours de réception** acceptance speech
◇ Pol **discours du trône** inaugural speech (of a sovereign before a Par-

liamentary session), *Br* ≃ King's/Queen's Speech

discours-programme *nm* keynote speech

discrimination *nf* discrimination
◇ *discrimination positive* *Br* positive discrimination, *Am* affirmative action

dispersion des votes *nf* voting pattern

> **❝**
>
> Le dernier scrutin présidentiel a déjà mis en évidence à quel point le socle électoral des formations institutionnelles avait été ébréché. La **dispersion des votes** traduit une aspiration à une plus grande diversité de la représentation politique.
>
> **❞**

dispositif *nm (mesure)* plan, measure; **il s'agit d'un dispositif gouvernemental pour favoriser l'emploi des jeunes** it's a government plan to stimulate youth employment

dissidence *nf* (a) *(rébellion)* dissidence; **un mouvement de dissidence** a rebel movement (b) *(dissidents)* dissidents, rebels (c) *(scission)* scission

dissident, -e 1 *adj (rebelle)* dissident, rebel
2 *nm,f (rebelle)* dissident, rebel

dissolution *nf Pol (d'une assemblée, d'un parlement)* dissolution; *(d'un parti)* break-up, dissolution

dissoudre *vt Pol (assemblée, parlement)* to dissolve; *(parti)* to break up, to dissolve

distribution *nf Écon* distribution
◇ *distribution des richesses* distribution of wealth
◇ *distribution sélective* selective distribution

district *nm* (a) *(région)* district, region (b) *Suisse* = administrative subdivision of a canton

DIT *nf (abrév* **division internationale du travail)** international division of labour

divergence *nf Écon* divergence

dividende de paix *nm* peace dividend

divisé, -e *adj* (a) *(opposition, parti)* divided, split; **le parti est divisé sur l'UE** the party is divided on (the question of) the EU (b) *(territoire)* divided

diviser 1 *vt* (a) *(opposition, parti)* to divide; **les dissensions qui divisent le parti** the disagreements that divide the party (b) *(territoire)* to divide up, to partition
2 **se diviser** *vpr (opposition, parti)* to split

division *nf* (a) *(dans l'opposition, dans un parti)* division, rift; **le problème de la défense nationale crée des divisions au sein du parti** the party is divided over the defence issue (b) *(d'un territoire)* division, partition
◇ *division internationale du travail* international division of labour
◇ *Écon division du marché* market division
◇ *Écon division du travail* division of labour

DL *nf (abrév* **Démocratie Libérale)** = French Liberal Democratic Party

doctrine *nf* doctrine

document *nm* document
◇ *document de politique* policy document
◇ *document de politique générale* general policy document
◇ *Document stratégique de réduction de la pauvreté* Poverty Reduction Strategy Paper

dollar *nm* dollar
◇ *dollar américain* US dollar

dollarisation *nf Écon* dollarization

DOM *nm (abrév* **département d'outre-mer)** = French overseas "département"

domestique *adj Écon (consommation, marché)* domestic, home

dominateur, -trice *Pol* **1** *adj (force, nation)* dominating
2 *nm,f* ruler

domination *nf* (a) *Pol (d'une nation, d'un peuple)* domination (**sur** of), domination, rule (**sur** over); **maintenir une île sous sa domination** to have control over an island; **ces territoires sont sous domination allemande** these territories are under German rule (b) *Écon (d'un marché)* control, domination

dominer *vt* (a) *Pol (nation, peuple)* to dominate, to rule (b) *Écon (marché)* to control, to dominate

DOM-TOM *nmpl (abrév* **départements et territoires d'outre-mer***)* = French overseas "départements" and territories

donnée *nf* piece of data; **données** data; *Écon* **en données corrigées des variations saisonnières** with adjustments for seasonal variations, seasonally adjusted

dopage *nm (de l'économie, des ventes)* boosting, artificial stimulation

doper *vt (économie, ventes)* to boost; **la dépréciation de la livre a dopé les ventes à l'étranger** the depreciation in the value of the pound has boosted export sales

dotation *nf* (a) *(fonds versés) (à un particulier, une collectivité)* endowment; *(à un service public)* grant, funds (b) *(revenus) (du président)* (personal) allowance, emolument; *(d'un souverain)* civil list

doter *vt (financer) (particulier, collectivité)* to endow; *(service public)* to fund

douane *nf* (a) *(à la frontière)* **(poste de) douane** customs; **passer à la douane** to go through customs (b) *(administration)* **la Douane** *Br* ≃ Customs and Excise, *Am* ≃ the Customs Service

douanier, -ère **1** *adj (tarif, visite)* customs
2 *nm,f* customs officer

double *adj* double; *Écon* **à double revenu** *(foyer, ménage)* two-income
◇ *UE* **double circulation** *(de monnaies)* dual circulation

draconien, -enne *adj (loi, régime)* draconian

drapeau rouge *nm Pol* red flag

droit *nm* (a) *(lois)* law (b) *(prérogative)* right (c) *(imposition)* duty; *(taxe)* tax
◇ **droits du citoyen** citizen rights
◇ **droits civils** civil rights
◇ **droits civiques** civic rights
◇ **droit compensateur** countervailing duty
◇ **droit constitutionnel** constitutional law
◇ **droit de douane** import duty, customs duty
◇ **droit écrit** statute law
◇ **droit d'entrée** import duty
◇ **droit à l'exportation** export duty
◇ **droit fiscal** tax law
◇ *Écon* **droit fixe** fixed duty
◇ **droits de l'homme** human rights
◇ **droit à l'importation** import duty
◇ *Suisse* **droit d'initiative** = citizens' right to initiate legislation
◇ **droits de mutation** capital transfer tax
◇ **droits sociaux** social rights
◇ **droit de sortie** export duty
◇ **droits de succession** inheritance tax
◇ **droit de suffrage** right to vote, suffrage
◇ **droit du travail** labour law
◇ **droit de veto** veto; **exercer son droit de veto** to use one's power of veto
◇ **droit de vote** right to vote, suffrage; **accorder le droit de vote à qn** to enfranchise sb

droite *nf Pol* (a) **la droite** the right (wing); **être à droite** to be right-wing *or* on the right; **être très à droite** to be very right-wing *or* on the far right; **voter à droite** to vote for the right
(b) **de droite** right-wing; **être de droite** to be right-wing; **les gens de droite** right-wingers, people on the right; **l'électorat de droite** the right-wing electorate

◇ *droite dure* hard right

◇ *droite modérée* soft right

droitier, -ère *adj Pol* right-wing

droitisme *nm Pol* right-wing tendency, rightism

droitiste *Pol* **1** *adj* right-wing
  2 *nmf* right-winger, rightist

DSRP *nm* (*abrév* **Document stratégique de réduction de la pauvreté**) PRSP

DST *nf* (*abrév* **Direction de la surveillance du territoire**) = internal state security department, *Br* ≃ MI5, *Am* ≃ CIA

dualisme *nm Écon* dualism

dualiste *Écon* **1** *adj* dualistic
  2 *nmf* dualist

dumping *nm Écon* dumping; **faire du dumping** to dump goods

◇ *dumping de change* currency dumping

◇ *dumping commercial* dumping

◇ *dumping social* social dumping

On les accuse aussi de se livrer à un **dumping social** en confiant leur fabrication à des imprimeries de labeur qui crachent brochures et magazines à des coûts 35% inférieurs à ceux des presses des quotidiens payants, peuplées d'ouvriers du Livre au statut en béton.

duopole *nm Écon* duopoly

duopoliste *adj Écon* duopolistic

duopolistique *adj Écon* duopolistic

duopsone *nm Écon* duopsony

dur, -e *Pol* **1** *adj* (*intransigeant*) hard, hardline
  2 *nm,f* hardliner; **les durs du parti** the hard core of the party

écart *nm Écon (variation)* differential
◇ *écart budgétaire* budgetary variance
◇ *écart déflationniste* deflationary gap
◇ *écart inflationniste* inflationary gap
◇ *écart de prix* price differential
◇ *écart de salaire* wage differential
◇ *écart salarial* wage differential

écart-type *nm (en statistique)* standard deviation, standard error

échange *nm Écon* **échanges** trade; **les échanges entre la France et l'Allemagne** trade between France and Germany; **le volume des échanges entre les deux pays** the volume of trade between the two countries
◇ *échanges commerciaux* trade
◇ *échange de devises* currency swap
◇ *échanges industriels* industrial trade
◇ *échange inégal* unequal exchange
◇ *échanges internationaux* international trade
◇ *échange intracommunautaire* intra-Community trade
◇ *échange des marchandises* commodity exchange
◇ *échange de taux d'intérêt* interest rate swap
◇ *Pol échange de voix* vote-trading

échantillon *nm (en statistique)* sample
◇ *échantillon non-probabiliste* non-probability sample
◇ *échantillon probabiliste* probability sample

échantillonnage *nm (en statistique)* sampling

◇ *échantillonnage non-probabiliste* non-probability sampling
◇ *échantillonnage probabiliste* probability sampling

échantillonner *vt (en statistique)* to sample

échéance électorale *nf Pol* election day, the elections; **nous sommes à trois mois de l'échéance électorale** there are three months to go before the date set for the election

échec *nm Pol* (a) *(revers)* failure; **l'échec des discussions** the failure *or* breakdown of the negotiations; **après l'échec de la conférence au sommet** after the failure of the summit conference; **faire échec à un coup d'État** to foil *or* to defeat a coup

(b) *(défaite)* defeat; **l'échec du candidat socialiste aux élections a surpris tout le monde** the Socialist candidate's defeat in the elections came as a surprise to everyone

échelle *nf Écon (des prix, des salaires)* scale
◇ *échelle minimale d'efficience* minimum efficient scale
◇ *échelle mobile* sliding scale

Échiquier *nm Pol* l'Échiquier *(en Grande-Bretagne)* the Exchequer

échiquier *nm* arena; **sur l'échiquier européen/mondial** on the European/world scene *or* arena

> Le sommet constitutif de l'Union africaine, à Durban, du 8 au 10 juillet dernier, a une fois de plus illustré

l'ambivalence de la position de la Lybie sur l'**échiquier** du continent africain.

"

échouer *vi Pol (rater) (projet, tentative)* to fail; *(personne)* to fail; **ils ont échoué dans leur tentative de coup d'État** their attempted coup failed

écobilan *nm Écon* lifecycle analysis

Ecofin *nm UE (abrév* **Economic Council of Finance Ministers)** Ecofin

École nationale d'administration *nf* = prestigious university level college preparing students for senior posts in the civil service and public management

écologique *adj Pol* green

écologiste *Pol* **1** *adj* green
2 *nmf* green

économètre *nmf* econometrist, econometrician

économétricien, -enne *nm,f* econometrist, econometrician

économétrie *nf* econometrics

économétrique *adj* econometric

économie *nf* (a) *(discipline)* economics (b) *(système)* economy (c) **économies** savings
◊ *économie du bien-être* welfare economy
◊ *économie capitaliste* capitalist economy
◊ *économie de champ* economy of scope
◊ *économie classique* classical economics
◊ *économie de la demande* demand-side economics
◊ *économie à deux vitesses* two-speed economy
◊ *économie du développement* development economics
◊ *économie dirigée* planned economy
◊ *économie duale* dual economy
◊ *économie d'échelle* economy of scale

◊ *économie d'entreprise* business *or* managerial economics
◊ *économie de l'environnement* environmental economics
◊ *économie éthique* caring economy
◊ *économie illégale* illegal economy
◊ *économie immergée* underground economy
◊ *économie industrielle* industrial organization
◊ *économie informelle* informal economy
◊ *économie keynésienne* Keynesian economics
◊ *économie libérale* free-market economy
◊ *économie de libre entreprise* free-enterprise economy
◊ *économie de marché* market economy
◊ *économie mixte* mixed economy
◊ *économie mondiale* world economy
◊ *économie néoclassique* neoclassical economics
◊ *économie noire* black economy
◊ *économie non monétaire* natural economy
◊ *économie normative* normative economics
◊ *économie nouvellement industrialisée* newly industrialized economy
◊ *économie de l'offre* supply-side economics
◊ *économie ouverte* open economy
◊ *économie parallèle* black economy
◊ *économie planifiée* planned economy
◊ *économie en pleine maturité* mature economy
◊ *économie politique* political economy
◊ *économie de rente* rent economy
◊ *économie salariale* wage economy
◊ *économie sociale* social economy
◊ *économie socialiste* socialist economy
◊ *économie solidaire* economy of solidarity, socially responsible economy
◊ *économie de sous-emploi* underemployment economy

Les grandes unions économiques

Economic Unions

ALENA

Accord de libre-échange nord-américain (1994)

Pays membres : Canada, Mexique, États-Unis

Objectifs : • éliminer les barrières douanières
• faciliter les mouvements transfrontaliers des biens et des services
• promouvoir la concurrence loyale dans la zone de libre-échange

ANSEA

Association des nations du Sud-Est asiatique, ou ANASE : Association des nations de l'Asie du Sud-Est (1967)

Pays membres : Birmanie, Brunei, Cambodge, Indonésie, Laos, Malaisie, Philippines, Singapour, Thaïlande, Viêt Nam

Objectif : • accélérer la croissance économique, ainsi que le développement social et culturel

APEC

Asia-Pacific Economic Cooperation (Coopération économique Asie-Pacifique) (1989)

Pays membres : Australie, Brunei, Canada, Chili, Chine, Corée, États-Unis, Hong Kong, Indonésie, Japon, Malaisie, Mexique, Nouvelle-Zélande, Papouasie-Nouvelle-Guinée, Pérou, Philippines, Russie, Singapour, Taipei chinois, Thaïlande, Viêt Nam

Objectif : • promouvoir le libre-échange, ainsi qu'une coopération économique pratique entre les pays membres

CAN

Communauté andine (1969)

Pays membres : Bolivie, Colombie, Équateur, Pérou, Venezuela

Objectifs : • améliorer la zone de libre-échange andine
• harmoniser les politiques économiques des pays membres

CARICOM

Communauté des Caraïbes (1973)

Pays membres : Antigua-et-Barbuda, Bahamas, Barbade, Belize, Dominique, Grenade, Guyana, Haïti, Jamaïque, Montserrat, Sainte-Lucie, Saint-Kitts-et-Nevis, Saint-Vincent-et-les-Grenadines, Suriname, Trinité-et-Tobago

Membres associés : Anguilla, les îles Vierges britanniques, les îles Caïmans, les îles Turks et Caicos

Objectifs : • promouvoir la coopération économique par le biais du CSME (Caribbean Single Market and Economy, marché et économie uniques)
• coordonner la politique étrangère
• développer la coopération et les services communs dans les domaines de la santé, de l'éducation et de la culture, des communications et des relations industrielles

CEDEAO

Communauté économique des États d'Afrique de l'Ouest (1975)

Pays membres : Bénin, Burkina Faso, Cap-Vert, Côte d'Ivoire, Gambie, Ghana, Guinée, Guinée-Bissau, Liberia, Mali, Niger, Nigeria, Sénégal, Sierra Leone, Togo

Objectifs : • créer une union économique et monétaire
• établir la libre circulation des citoyens de la Communauté

CEI

Communauté des États indépendants (1991)

Pays membres : Arménie, Azerbaïdjan, Biélorussie, Géorgie, Kazakhstan, Kirghizstan, Moldavie, Ouzbékistan, Russie, Tadjikistan, Turkménistan, Ukraine

Objectifs : • coordonner les politiques étrangères et économiques de ses États membres
• créer une zone rouble de libre-échange

CEMAC

Communauté économique et monétaire de l'Afrique centrale (1994)

Pays membres : Cameroun, République centrafricaine, République démocratique du Congo, Guinée équatoriale, Gabon, Tchad

Objectif : • encourager le processus d'intégration subrégionale dans le cadre d'une union économique et monétaire

COMESA

Common Market for Eastern and Southern Africa (Marché commun de l'Afrique orientale et australe) (1994)

Pays membres : Angola, Burundi, Comores, République démocratique du Congo, Djibouti, Égypte, Érythrée, Éthiopie, Kenya, Madagascar, Malawi, Maurice, Namibie, Ouganda, Rwanda, Seychelles, Soudan, Swaziland, Zambie, Zimbabwe

Objectif : • former un grand bloc économique et commercial afin de favoriser la croissance économique dans la région

MCCA

Marché commun centraméricain, ou MCAC : Marché commun d'Amérique centrale (1960)

Pays membres : Costa Rica, Guatemala, Honduras, Nicaragua, Salvador

Objectif : • promouvoir la coordination des politiques monétaires, de crédit et de change

MERCOSUR

Marché commun du cône Sud (1991)

Pays membres : Argentine, Brésil, Paraguay, Uruguay

Objectifs : • établir des économies plus productives et plus dynamiques grâce à l'élargissement du marché
• promouvoir un développement socio-économique équilibré et harmonieux

OCDE

Organisation de coopération et de développement économiques (1960)

Pays membres : Allemagne, Australie, Autriche, Belgique, Canada, Corée, Danemark, Espagne, États-Unis, Finlande, France, Grèce, Hongrie, Irlande, Islande, Italie, Japon, Luxembourg, Mexique, Norvège, Nouvelle-Zélande, Pays-Bas, Pologne, Portugal, Royaume-Uni, Slovaquie, Suède, Suisse, République tchèque, Turquie

Objectif : • coordonner les politiques économiques et sociales

OPEP

Organisation des pays exportateurs de pétrole (1960)

Pays membres : Algérie, Arabie Saoudite, Émirats arabes unis, Indonésie, Irak, Iran, Koweït, Libye, Nigeria, Qatar, Venezuela

Objectifs : • coordonner et unifier les politiques des membres en matière de pétrole
• sauvegarder les intérêts des membres

SADC

Southern Africa Development Community (Communauté de développement de l'Afrique australe) (1992)

Pays membres : Afrique du Sud, Angola, Botswana, République démocratique du Congo, Lesotho, Malawi, Maurice, Mozambique, Seychelles, Swaziland, Tanzanie, Zambie, Zimbabwe

Objectifs : • coordonner un développement économique durable
• consolider les liens régionaux

UE

Union européenne (1992)

Pays membres : Allemagne, Autriche, Belgique, Danemark, Espagne, Finlande, France, Grèce, Irlande, Italie, Luxembourg, Pays-Bas, Portugal, Royaume-Uni, Suède

Objectifs : • développer le marché unique (et la monnaie unique) entre les États membres fondé sur la libre circulation des personnes, des biens, des services et des capitaux;
• développer la coordination politique pour les questions importantes

UEMOA

Union économique et monétaire ouest-africaine (1994)

Pays membres : Bénin, Burkina Faso, Côte d'Ivoire, Guinée-Bissau, Mali, Niger, Sénégal, Togo

Objectifs : • renforcer la concurrence économique et financière des États membres, en établissant notamment un tarif extérieur commun et une politique commerciale commune
• créer un marché commun entre les États membres fondé sur la libre circulation des personnes, des biens, des services et des capitaux

UMA

Union du Maghreb arabe (1989)

Pays membres : Algérie, Libye, Maroc, Mauritanie, Tunisie

Objectifs : • assurer la stabilité régionale
• introduire la libre circulation des biens, des services et des facteurs de production

◇ *économie souterraine* black economy, underground economy

◇ *économie de subsistance* subsistence economy

◇ *économie de succursales* branch economy

◇ *économie de transition* transition economy

◇ *économie de troc* barter economy

❝

Encore ces chiffres ne donnent-ils qu'un état des lieux incomplet : ils ne tiennent pas compte des billets en circulation dans les circuits de l'**économie illégale** ou de l'**économie informelle**, qui représente très souvent plus du tiers du PIB.

❞

économique 1 *adj* economic
2 *nm* **l'économique** the economic situation

économiquement *adv* economically, from an economic point of view; **économiquement viable** economically viable; **les économiquement faibles** the lower-income groups

économiser *vt* (richesse, argent) to economize, to save

économisme *nm* economism

économiste *nmf* economist

◇ *économiste d'entreprise* business economist

écotaxe *nf* ecotax

écrasant, -e *adj* Pol (majorité, victoire) overwhelming, landslide

ÉCU, écu *nm* Anciennement (abrév **European currency unit**) ECU, ecu

EEE *nm* Pol (abrév **Espace économique européen**) EEA

effectif, -ive 1 *adj* Écon (a) (coût, monnaie, taux) effective; (valeur, revenu) real; (circulation) active; (rendement) actual (b) (règlement, mesures) in effect; **cette loi sera effective au 1 janvier** this law will come into effect on 1 January; **l'armistice est de-**

venu effectif ce matin the armistice took effect or became effective this morning
2 *nm* (a) Écon (employés) manpower, labour force (b) (d'un parti) size, strength

effet *nm* (a) (résultat) effect (b) (financier) bill

◇ *effet de commerce* commercial bill

◇ Écon *effet de levier* leverage, gearing

◇ *effet de prix* price effect

◇ *effets publics* government securities, government stock

efficace *adj* (a) (politique, intervention) effective (b) Écon efficient

efficacité *nf* (a) (d'une politique, d'une intervention) effectiveness (b) Écon efficiency

◇ *efficacité économique* economic efficiency

◇ *efficacité marginale du capital* marginal efficiency of capital

◇ *efficacité parfaite* absolute efficiency

efficience *nf* (d'une entreprise) efficiency

efficient, -e *adj* (entreprise) efficient

effondrement *nm* (d'une monnaie) collapse, slump; (des prix, du marché, de la demande) slump (**de** in); (d'un empire) collapse

effondrer s'effondrer *vpr* (monnaie) to collapse, to slump; (prix, marché, demande) to slump; (empire) to collapse

égalitaire *adj* Pol egalitarian

égalitarisme *nm* Pol egalitarianism

égalitariste Pol **1** *adj* egalitarian
2 *nmf* egalitarian

égalité *nf* equality

◇ *égalité des chances* equality of opportunity

élargir 1 *vt* (groupe) to expand
2 s'élargir *vpr* (groupe) to expand

élargissement *nm* (d'un groupe) expansion; **l'élargissement de l'Union eu-**

ropéenne the enlargement of the European Union

◊ Écon **élargissement du capital** capital widening

"

Economiquement et géostratégiquement, les espaces européens et russe sont imbriqués, et le processus d'**élargissement de l'Union européenne** implique une redéfinition des relations avec la Russie.

"

élasticité nf (de la demande, du marché, des prix) elasticity; **quelle est l'élasticité de la demande par rapport au prix du produit?** how elastic is the demand in relation to the price of the product?

◊ **élasticité croisée de la demande** cross-elasticity of demand

élastique adj (demande, marché, prix) elastic

électeur, -trice nm,f Pol voter, elector; **les électeurs** the voters, the electorate; **mes électeurs** the people who voted for me; **les maires et leurs électeurs** the mayors and those who elected them

◊ **électeur flottant** floating voter

◊ **électeur indécis** floating voter

électif, -ive adj Pol elective

élection nf Pol (a) (procédure) election, polls; **les élections ont lieu aujourd'hui** today is election or polling day; **procéder à une élection** to hold an election; **les résultats de l'élection** the election results; **remporter les élections** to win the election; **se présenter aux élections** Br to stand or Am to run as a candidate

(b) (nomination) election; **son élection à la présidence** his/her election as president or to the presidency

◊ **élection anticipée** = election before the end of a mandate

◊ **élections cantonales** = elections held every three years to elect half the members of the "Conseil général"

◊ **élection directe** direct election

◊ **élections européennes** European elections

◊ **élection indirecte** indirect election

◊ **élections législatives** general elections (held every five years)

◊ **élections municipales** = elections held every six years to elect members of the "Conseil municipal"

◊ **élection partielle** by-election

◊ **élection présidentielle** presidential election

◊ **élection primaire** primary (election)

◊ **élection primaire directe** direct primary (election)

◊ **élections régionales** = elections held every six years to elect members of the "Conseil régional"

◊ **élections sénatoriales** = elections held every three years to elect one third of the members of the "Sénat"

◊ **élection surprise** snap election

électoral, -e adj Pol (liste) electoral; (succès) electoral, election; (campagne, promesse) election; (assemblée) elective; **en période électorale** at election time; **nous avons le soutien électoral des syndicats** we can rely on the union vote

électoralisme nm Péj Pol electioneering

électoraliste adj Péj Pol (promesse, programme) vote-catching

électorat nm Pol (a) (électeurs) electorate; **l'importance de l'électorat féminin/noir** the importance of the women's/the black vote (b) Pol (droit de vote) franchise

◊ **électorat flottant** floating voters

◊ **électorat indécis** floating voters

éléphant nm Pol **les éléphants du parti** = the old guard of the Socialist party

"

Accusé d'"apathie" par les députés Julien Dray et Arnaud Montebourg, et le porte-parole du PS Vincent Peillon, qui ont appelé à la naissance d'un "nouveau parti socialiste" dans une tribune publiée mercredi par Libération, secoué par des patrons de fédérations départementales qui reprochent aux **éléphants du parti** de "confisquer" le débat militant, le premier secrétaire du PS entend se préserver jusqu'au conseil national du 19 octobre.

77

élevé, -e *adj (prix, taux)* high

éligibilité *nf Pol* eligibility

éligible *adj Pol* eligible

élire *vt Pol (candidat)* to elect; **élire un député** to elect a deputy; **élire un nouveau président** to elect *or* to vote in a new president; **élire qn président** to elect sb president, to vote sb in as president; **se faire élire** to be elected

ELSJ *nm UE (abrév* **Espace de liberté, de sécurité et de justice)** AFSJ

élu, -e *Pol* **1** *adj* elected
2 *nm,f (député)* elected representative; *(conseiller)* elected representative, councillor; **les élus locaux** local councillors

Élysée *nm Pol* **(le palais de) l'Élysée** the Élysée Palace *(the official residence of the French President)*; **on attend la réaction de l'Élysée sur cette question** we're waiting for the President's reaction on this subject

44

L'**Élysée** a annoncé, le 7 mai au début de la soirée, la composition du gouvernement de Jean-Pierre Raffarin. S'il fait la part belle au rajeunissement et à la société civile, dont émanent cinq ministres, il est dominé par le RPR qui détiendra les postes clefs.

77

élyséen, -enne *adj Pol* from the Élysée Palace, presidential; **une décision élyséenne** a decision made by the President

émasculation *nf (d'une politique, d'une directive)* castration

émasculer *vt (politique, directive)* to castrate

embargo *nm Écon & Pol* embargo; **mettre un embargo sur qch** to place *or* impose an embargo on sth; **lever l'embargo sur qch** to lift *or* to raise the embargo on sth
◇ **embargo commercial** trade embargo
◇ **embargo économique** economic embargo

émergent, -e *adj Écon (pays, économie)* emerging

émirat *nm Pol* emirate

émission *nf* **(a)** *(d'actions)* issue; *(d'un emprunt)* flotation; *(d'une lettre de crédit)* opening **(b)** *(programme)* programme
◇ **émission d'expression directe** *(de parti politique)* party political broadcast

emparer s'emparer *vpr* **s'emparer de** *(territoire)* to take over, to seize; *(pouvoir)* to seize

empire *nm (régime, territoire)* empire

emploi *nm* **(a)** *(situation)* job; *(embauche)* employment, work; **être sans emploi** to be out of work *or* unemployed; **chercher un emploi, être à la recherche d'un emploi** to be looking for work *or* a job **(b)** *(usage)* use
◇ *Écon* **emploi optimum des ressources** optimum employment of resources

employé, -e *nm,f* employee

employeur, -euse *nm,f* employer

emporter *vt Pol (victoire)* to win, to carry off; **emporter la victoire (contre)** to be victorious (over), to be the victor (over); **emporter tous les suffrages** to get all the votes

emprunt *nm (procédé)* borrowing; *(argent)* loan
◇ **emprunt d'État** government loan
◇ **emprunt forcé** forced loan

◇ **emprunt or** gold loan

◇ **emprunt public** government loan

emprunter 1 *vt* to borrow (**à** from) **2** *vi* to take out a loan, to borrow

ENA *nf* (*abrév* **École nationale d'administration**) = prestigious university-level college preparing students for senior posts in the civil service and in public management

énarchie *nf* = network of graduates of the "ENA"

énarque *nmf* = student or former student of the "ENA"

encadrement *nm Écon (du prix, des crédits)* control

encadrer *vt Écon (prix, crédits)* to control

enchère *nf (vente)* auction; **vendre qch aux enchères** to sell sth by *or* at auction

endettement *nm Écon (état)* debt

◇ **endettement des consommateurs** consumer debt

◇ **endettement extérieur** foreign debt

◇ **endettement intérieur** internal debt

◇ **endettement public** public debt

endiguement *nm* **(a)** *(du chômage, de dettes)* checking, curbing; **tenter l'endiguement de la hausse des prix** to attempt to contain price increases **(b)** *Pol (d'un mouvement, d'une révolte)* containment

endiguer *vt* **(a)** *(chômage, dettes)* to check, to curb **(b)** *Pol (mouvement, révolte)* to contain

enjeu *nm* **(a)** *(d'une guerre)* stake, stakes; **quel est l'enjeu de cette élection?** what is at stake in this election? **(b)** *(problème)* issue; *(défi)* challenge; **l'environnement est un enjeu primordial dans ces élections** the environment is a key issue in this election; **l'énergie est un enjeu planétaire** energy is a worldwide concern

enlever *vt Pol* **enlever les suffrages** to win *or* to capture votes

enquête d'opinion *nf Pol* opinion poll

entente *nf* agreement, understanding; **arriver à une entente (sur qch)** to come to an understanding *or* agreement (over sth); **une entente entre producteurs** an agreement between producers

◇ **entente industrielle** cartel, combine

entrant, -e *adj* incoming; *(fonctionnaire)* newly appointed; *(représentant parlementaire)* newly elected

entreprise *nf* **(a)** *(société)* company, business **(b)** *(régime économique)* enterprise

◇ **entreprise citoyenne** socially responsible company

◇ **entreprise d'État** state-owned *or Br* public company

◇ **entreprise exportatrice** export company

◇ **entreprise multinationale** multinational company

◇ **entreprise privée** private enterprise

◇ **entreprise publique** public enterprise

entrer *vi* **(a)** *Écon (devises)* to enter; *(marchandises)* to enter, to be imported; **entrer dans un marché** to enter a market; **pour faire entrer plus de devises étrangères** to attract more foreign currencies

(b) **entrer en pourparlers** to start *or* to enter negotiations; **entrer en concurrence** to enter into competition

(c) **entrer dans** *(association, parti)* to join, to become a member of; *(entreprise)* to join; **entrer dans l'Union européenne** to enter *or* to join *or* to become a member of the European Union

entretien *nm (colloque)* discussion, talk

entrisme *nm Pol* entryism, entrism

entriste *Pol* **1** *adj* entryist **2** *nmf* entryist

envahissement nm Écon crowding-in

enveloppe nf (a) (don) sum of money, gratuity; (illégal) bribe (b) (crédits) budget; **l'enveloppe du ministère de la Culture** the arts budget

◇ **enveloppe budgétaire** budget allocation

> **"**
>
> Par ailleurs, les Quinze doivent s'entendre sur le montant des aides structurelles et régionales ; La Commission propose une **enveloppe** de 25,5 milliards d'euros, mais les Allemands voudraient réduire cette somme de 4 milliards.
>
> **"**

environnement nm Écon & Pol environment

environnemental, -e adj Écon & Pol environmental

envolée nf Écon sudden rise, soar; **l'envolée du dollar** the sudden rise of the dollar

envoler s'envoler vpr Écon (prix, inflation) to soar, to spiral; Pol **s'envoler dans les sondages** to rise rapidly in the opinion polls

envoyé, -e nm,f Pol envoy

épargne nf Écon (a) (économies) **l'épargne** savings (b) (fait d'économiser) saving; **encourager l'épargne** to encourage saving

◇ **épargne forcée** forced saving
◇ **épargne institutionnelle** institutional savings
◇ **épargne investie** investments
◇ **épargne privée** private investors

épargner vi Écon to save (money)

épuration nf Pol (élimination d'éléments indésirables) purge

épurer vt Pol (administration, parti) to purge

équilibre nm (rapport de force) balance, equilibrium

◇ Écon **équilibre budgétaire** balanced budget

◇ **équilibre du compte courant** current account equilibrium
◇ **équilibre économique** economic equilibrium
◇ **équilibre fiscal** fiscal balance
◇ **équilibre des forces** balance of power
◇ **équilibre instable** unstable equilibrium
◇ **équilibre des pouvoirs** balance of power
◇ **l'équilibre de la terreur** the balance of terror

équipe nf

◇ **équipe gouvernementale** Government, Br ≃ Cabinet, Am ≃ Administration
◇ **équipe ministérielle** ministerial team

érosion fiscale nf Écon fiscal drag

espace nm

◇ UE **Espace économique européen** European Economic Area
◇ UE **espace judiciaire européen** common European legal framework
◇ UE **espace social européen** common European social legislation
◇ Pol **espace vital** lebensraum

espèces nfpl (argent) cash

esprit de parti nm Pol party spirit

essor nm (d'une entreprise, d'une industrie) rise, rapid growth; **une industrie en plein essor** a booming or fast-growing industry; **la sidérurgie connaît un nouvel essor** the steel industry is booming again; **prendre son essor** to take off

◇ **essor économique** (rapid) economic expansion, boom

Est nm Pol **l'Est** Eastern Europe, Eastern European countries

établi, -e adj (ordre, relation, système de gouvernement) established

établir vt (règlement) to introduce; (pouvoir) to implement; (ordre, relation, système de gouvernement) to establish

étalon *nm Écon (référence)* standard
◊ *étalon de change-or* gold exchange standard

étalon-or *nm Écon* gold standard
◊ *étalon-or lingot* gold bullion standard

État *nm* (a) *Pol (nation)* state; **un État dans l'État** a state within a state (b) *Écon (administration)* state; **géré par l'État** state-run, publicly run
◊ *État croupion* rump state
◊ *État fédéral* federal state
◊ *l'État français* the French state *or* nation
◊ *État membre* member state
◊ *État neutre* neutral state
◊ *État paria* rogue state
◊ *État paternaliste* nanny state
◊ *État providence* Welfare State
◊ *État tampon* buffer state
◊ *État voyou* rogue state

état *nm* state, condition
◊ *état de droit* legitimate state
◊ *état d'exception* state of emergency
◊ *Pol état de grâce* honeymoon period; **le président est en état de grâce** the President is enjoying a honeymoon period
◊ *état de siège* state of siege
◊ *état d'urgence* state of emergency

"

L'**état d'exception** ne doit être décrété qu'en dernier recours pour faire face à des situations d'extrême gravité … Si la gouvernabilité du pays était en jeu, nous pourrions être contraints de décréter l'**état d'exception**, mais nous n'en sommes pas encore là.

"

étatique *adj Écon & Pol* under state control, state-controlled

étatisation *nf Écon & Pol* (a) *(gestion par l'État) (de l'économie, d'un secteur d'activité)* establishment of state control (**de** over) (b) *(nationalisation)* nationalization (**de** of) (c) *(dirigisme étatique)* state control

étatisé, -e *adj Écon & Pol (secteur, économie)* state-controlled, state-run; **une société étatisée** a state-owned company

étatiser *vt Écon & Pol* to bring under state control

étatisme *nm Écon & Pol* state control, statism

étatiste *Écon & Pol* **1** *adj* state-control, statist; **un système étatiste** a system of state control
2 *nmf* supporter of state control, statist

état-major *nm (d'un parti politique)* leadership; **le président et son état-major** the president and his advisers

"

La carrière politique de Rios Montt risque cependant d'être fortement perturbée, en mai prochain, lorsqu'il sera accusé "de génocide et de crimes contre l'humanité" par un groupe d'indigènes du nord du pays. Selon eux, l'ancien président et son **état-major** ont orchestré, entre les mois de mars et décembre 1982, au moins treize massacres qui ont fait plus de 1200 morts dans 600 villages des hauts plateaux.

"

État-nation *nm* nation-state

État-patron *nm* **l'État-patron** the State as an employer

étiquette politique *nf* political affiliation; **sans étiquette politique** *(candidat, journal)* independent

ethniciser *vt Pol* to ethnicize

ethnicité *nf Pol* ethnicity

ethnie *nf* ethnic group

ethnique *adj* ethnic

ethnocentrique *adj Pol* ethnocentric

ethnocentrisme *nm Pol* ethnocentrism

ethnocide *nm Pol* ethnocide

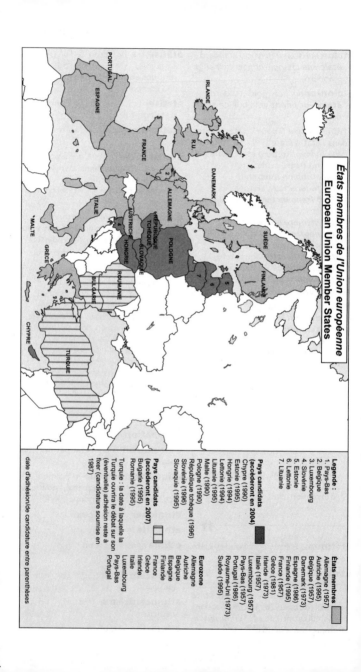

États membres de l'Union européenne
European Union Member States

étranger, -ère *adj* foreign

Euratom *nm UE* (*abrév* **European Atomic Energy Commission**) Euratom

euro *nm UE* (*monnaie*) euro; **en euros** in euro

eurobanque *nf* Eurobank

eurocentrique *adj* Eurocentric

eurocentrisme *nm* Eurocentrism

eurocommunisme *nm* Eurocommunism

eurocommuniste 1 *adj* Eurocommunist
   2 *nmf* Eurocommunist

Eurocorps *nm* Eurocorps

eurocrate *nmf* Eurocrat

eurocratie *nf* Eurocracy

eurocratique *adj* Eurocratic

eurodéputé, -e *nm,f Pol* Euro-MP, MEP

eurodevise *nf* eurocurrency

eurodollar *nm* eurodollar

Eurolande *nf Pol* Euroland

euromarché *nm* Euromarket

euromonnaie *nf* eurocurrency

Europe *nf* **l'Europe** Europe
◊ ***l'Europe centrale*** Central Europe
◊ ***l'Europe continentale*** mainland Europe
◊ ***Europe à deux vitesses*** two-speed Europe
◊ ***l'Europe de l'Est*** East *or* Eastern Europe
◊ ***l'Europe du Nord*** Northern Europe
◊ ***l'Europe des quinze*** = the fifteen member states of the European Union
◊ ***l'Europe sociale*** social Europe (*a united Europe committed to a progressive social and welfare policy*)
◊ ***l'Europe du Sud*** Southern Europe
◊ ***l'Europe Verte*** European Union agriculture *or* farming; **ils ont parlé de l'Europe Verte** they discussed agriculture in the EU

> **❝**
>
> Parallèlement, l'Europe doit se retrouver une politique économique commune. Le pacte de stabilité budgétaire doit être redéfini, le chantier de l'harmonisation fiscale enfin relancé, et l'**Europe sociale** abordée de façon empirique en trouvant des solutions à des problèmes tels que la "transférabilité" effective des retraites.
>
> **❞**

européanisation, européisation *nf* Europeanization, Europeanizing

européaniser 1 *vt* to Europeanize, to make European
   2 s'européaniser *vpr* to become Europeanized

européanisme, européisme *nm* Europeanism

européaniste 1 *adj* Europeanist
   2 *nmf* Europeanist

Européen, -enne *nm,f* European

européen, -enne *adj* European

européocentrisme *nm* Eurocentrism

europhile *nmf* Europhile

europhobe *nmf* Europhobe

euroscepticisme *nm* Euroscepticism

eurosceptique 1 *adj* Eurosceptic
   2 *nmf* Eurosceptic

Eurostat *nm UE* Eurostat

eurosterling *nm* Eurosterling

eurozone *nf* Euro zone

évaluation *nf* (*estimation*) evaluation, appraisal
◊ ***évaluation contingente*** contingent valuation
◊ ***évaluation économique*** economic appraisal

évaluer *vt* (*estimer*) to evaluate, to appraise

évasion des capitaux *nf Écon* flight of capital

éviction financière *nf Écon* crowding-out

évincer *vt (concurrent, rival)* to oust, to supplant (**de** from); **se faire évincer** to be ousted

excédent *nm Écon* (a) *(surplus)* surplus, excess; **un excédent de blé/main-d'œuvre** a wheat/labour surplus (b) *(d'un budget)* surplus; **dégager un excédent** to show a surplus; **il y a un excédent des exportations sur les importations** there is an excess of exports over imports
◇ **excédent de la balance commerciale** balance of trade surplus
◇ **excédent budgétaire** budget surplus
◇ **excédent commercial** trade surplus
◇ **excédent de dépenses** deficit

excédentaire *adj Écon (production)* excess, surplus; *(budget)* surplus

exceptionnel, -elle *adj Pol (assemblée, conseil, mesures)* special, emergency

exclus *nmpl* **les exclus** the underprivileged

exclusion *nf (dans la société)* marginalization of the underprivileged
◇ **l'exclusion sociale** social exclusion

exécutif, -ive *Pol* **1** *adj* executive
2 *nm* **l'exécutif** the executive

exemption *nf* (a) *(dispense)* exemption (**de** from) (b) *UE* opting out
◇ **exemption fiscale** tax exemption
◇ **exemption d'impôts** tax exemption

> “
>
> Le Danemark, pays européen atypique avec ses trois **exemptions** (opting out), sur l'euro, la défense européenne et la coopération judiciaire, aura-t-il l'autorité nécessaire pour relever un tel défi ?
>
> ”

exercice *nm Br* financial year, *Am* fiscal year
◇ **exercice budgétaire** budgetary year

◇ **exercice financier** *Br* financial year, *Am* fiscal year
◇ **exercice fiscal** tax year

exil *nm* exile

exilé, -e **1** *adj* exiled
2 *nm,f* exile

exonération *nf* exemption (**de** from), exempting
◇ **exonération fiscale** tax exemption
◇ **exonération d'impôt** tax exemption
◇ **exonération de TVA** exemption from VAT

exonérer *vt (contribuable, revenus)* to exempt; **exonérer qn d'impôts** to exempt sb from income tax; **être exonéré d'impôts** to be exempt from tax; **exonérer des marchandises de taxes** to exempt goods from import duty

expansion *nf Écon* **en expansion** expanding, booming
◇ **expansion économique** economic growth
◇ **expansion monétaire** currency expansion

export *nm* exportation

exportable *adj* exportable, which can be exported

exportateur, -trice **1** *adj (pays)* exporting; *(secteur)* export; **être exportateur de qch** to be an exporter of sth, to export sth; **les pays exportateurs de pétrole/céréales** oil-/grain-exporting countries
2 *nm,f* exporter

exportation *nf* (a) *(action)* export, exportation; **faire de l'exportation** to export (b) **exportations** *(marchandises)* exports
◇ **exportation de capitaux** export of capital
◇ **exportations invisibles** invisible exports
◇ **exportations visibles** visible exports

exporter *vt* to export (**vers** to); **exporter des marchandises des États-Unis en France** to export goods from the United States into France

ex post *adj Écon* ex post

expulser *vt Pol (d'un parti, d'un pays)* to expel (**de** from)

expulsion *nf Pol (d'un parti, d'un pays)* expulsion

extérieur, -e *Écon & Pol* **1** *adj (étranger) (dette, commerce)* foreign, external; *(politique)* foreign
2 *nm* **l'extérieur** abroad, foreign countries; **à l'extérieur** abroad; **les relations avec l'extérieur** foreign relations

externalisation *nf Écon* outsourcing

externaliser *vt Écon* to outsource

externalité *nf Écon* externality

extraordinaire *adj Pol (mesures, impôt)* special; *(pouvoirs)* special, emergency

extraparlementaire *adj Pol* extra-parliamentary

extrême *adj Pol*
◇ **extrême droite** extreme *or* far right
◇ **extrême gauche** extreme *or* far left

extrémisme *nm Pol* extremism
◇ **extrémisme de droite** right-wing extremism
◇ **extrémisme de gauche** left-wing extremism

extrémiste *Pol* **1** *adj* extremist
2 *nmf* extremist
◇ **extrémistes de droite** right-wing extremists
◇ **extrémistes de gauche** left-wing extremists

facho *Fam Péj Pol* **1** *adj* fascist
2 *nmf* fascist

facteur *nm Écon* factor
◇ **facteur de consommation** demand factor
◇ **facteur coût** cost factor
◇ **facteur de croissance** growth factor
◇ **facteur de demande** demand factor
◇ **facteur de déséquilibre** destabilizing factor
◇ **facteur déterminant** controlling factor
◇ **facteur économique** economic factor
◇ **facteur de production** production factor

faction *nf* faction

facture *nf* invoice, bill; *Écon* **la facture pétrolière de la France** France's oil bill

faible *adj (économie, monnaie, marché)* weak

faiblesse *nf (d'une économie, d'une monnaie, d'un marché)* weakness

faiblissant, -e *adj (économie, monnaie, marché)* weakening

fanatique *Pol* **1** *adj* fanatical, zealous
2 *nmf* fanatic, zealot

fanatisme *nm Pol* fanaticism, zealotry

fantôme *nm* **un fantôme de parti politique** a phantom political party

FAO *nf (abrév* **Food and Agriculture Organization of the United Nations)** FAO

fardeau *nm (contrainte)* burden
◇ **fardeau de la dette** debt burden
◇ **fardeau fiscal** tax burden

fascisant, -e *adj Pol* fascist, fascistic, pro-fascist

fascisation *nf Pol* **la fascisation d'une politique** the increasingly fascistic *or* fascist tendencies of a policy; **on assiste à la fascisation du régime** the regime is becoming more fascist

fasciser *vt Pol* **fasciser un État** to take a state towards fascism; **fasciser un régime/une politique** to make a regime/policy increasingly pro-fascist

fascisme *nm Pol* fascism

fasciste *Pol* **1** *adj* fascist
2 *nmf* fascist

faucon *nm Pol* hawk

fauteur, -trice *nm,f*
◇ **fauteur de guerre** warmonger
◇ **fauteur de troubles** incendiary

FECOM *nm (abrév* **Fonds européen de coopération monétaire)** EMCF

FED *nm (abrév* **Fonds européen de développement)** EDF

FEDER *nm (abrév* **Fonds européen de développement régional)** ERDF

fédéral, -e *adj* **(a)** *(État, structure, dépenses)* federal **(b)** *Suisse* federal *(relative to the Swiss Confederation)*

fédéraliser *vt* to federalize, to turn into a federation

fédéralisme *nm* **(a)** *(forme de gouvernement)* federalism **(b)** *Suisse* = political tendency defending the independence of the Swiss cantons from federal authority (**c**) *Can* = political ideology favouring a strong central government

fédéraliste 1 *adj* federalist, federalistic

    2 *nmf* federalist, federal

fédération *nf* federation; *(au Canada)* confederation

◇ **Fédération de la gauche démocrate et socialiste** = former French socialist party

◇ **fédération syndicale** trade union

◇ **Fédération syndicale mondiale** World Federation of Trade Unions

◇ **fédération de syndicats (ouvriers)** amalgamated (trade) unions

fédéré, -e *adj* federate

fédérer 1 *vt* to federate, to form into a federation

    2 se fédérer *vpr* to federate

FEI *nm* (*abrév* **Fonds européen d'investissement**) EIF

femme *nf*

◇ **femme député** *(en France)* (female) deputy; *(en Grande-Bretagne)* (woman) MP; *(aux États-Unis)* Congresswoman

◇ **femme politique** (female) politician

FEN *nf* (*abrév* **Fédération de l'Éducation nationale**) = French teachers' trade union

féodal, -e *adj Pol* feudal

féodalisme *nm Pol* feudalism

féodalité *nf Pol* (**a**) *(système)* feudal system (**b**) *Péj (puissance)* feudal power

FEOGA *nm* (*abrév* **Fonds européen d'orientation et de garantie agricole**) EAGGF

ferme *adj Écon* steady, firm; **le dollar est resté ferme** the dollar stayed firm

fermeté *nf Écon* steadiness, firmness

Fgaf *nf Pol* (*abrév* **Fédération générale autonome des fonctionnaires**) = French civil servants' trade union

FGDS *nf Pol* (*abrév* **Fédération de la gauche démocrate et socialiste**) = former French socialist party

FGEN *nf* (*abrév* **Fédération générale de l'Éducation nationale**) = French teachers' trade union

fief *nm* stronghold, heartland; **un fief du parti socialiste** a socialist stronghold; **un fief électoral** a politician's fief

finance *nf* (**a**) *(domaine)* finance; **la finance, le monde de la finance** *(profession)* (the world of) finance; **entrer dans la finance** to enter the world of finance; **la haute finance** *(milieu)* high finance; *(personnes)* the financiers, the bankers

    (**b**) *Pol* **les Finances** *Br* ≃ the Exchequer, *Am* ≃ the Treasury Department

◇ **finance d'entreprise** corporate finance

◇ **finance internationale** global finance

◇ **finances publiques** public funds

financement *nm* financing, funding

◇ **financement d'entreprise** corporate financing

financer *vt* to finance, to fund

financier, -ère 1 *adj (crise, politique)* financial

    2 *nm* financier

finlandisation *nf Pol* Finlandization

firme *nf* firm, company

◇ **firme multinationale** multinational company

fiscal, -e *adj* fiscal, tax

fiscaliser *vt* to tax

fiscalité *nf* taxation (system)

◇ **fiscalité directe** direct taxation

◇ **fiscalité écologique** green taxation

◇ **fiscalité excessive** excessive taxation

◇ **fiscalité indirecte** indirect taxation

◇ **fiscalité locale** local taxation

❝

Derrière la volonté affichée de protéger l'environnement à travers une **fiscalité écologique**, les mesures sont maigres … l'idée de taxer les activités polluantes, nuisibles au développement durable, pour alléger en revanche les charges sociales qui pèsent sur l'emploi, restera encore l'an prochain assez théorique.

99

fixation nf Écon (de prix, de revenu, de salaire) fixing

◇ **fixation concertée des prix** common pricing, common price fixing

◇ **fixation de l'impôt** tax assessment; **être chargé de la fixation de l'impôt** to be responsible for setting tax levels

fixe adj Écon (prix, revenu, salaire) fixed; **à prix fixe** at fixed prices

fixer vt Écon (prix, revenu, salaire) to fix

flexibilité nm Écon (de la main-d'œuvre) flexibility

flexible nf Écon (main-d'œuvre) flexible

flottant nm Écon float

flottement nm Écon (d'une monnaie) flotation

flotter vi Écon (monnaie) to float; **faire flotter qch** (monnaie) to float sth

fluctuant, -e adj fluctuating

fluctuation nf fluctuation

◇ **fluctuation des prix** price fluctuation

◇ **fluctuation saisonnière** seasonal fluctuation

fluctuer vi to fluctuate; **la production de pétrole fait fluctuer les cours mondiaux** oil production affects trading prices all over the world

fluide adj Écon (main-d'œuvre) fluid, flexible

fluidité nf Écon (de la main-d'œuvre) fluidity, flexibility

flux circulaire des revenus nm Écon circular flow of income

FME nm (abrév **Fonds monétaire européen**) EMF

FMI nm (abrév **Fonds monétaire international**) IMF

FN nm (abrév **Front national**) = French political party of the extreme right

FNA nf (abrév **Fédération nationale de l'artisanat automobile**) = French car mechanics' trade union

Fnap nf (abrév **Fédération nationale autonome de la police**) = French police trade union

FNSEA nf (abrév **Fédération nationale des syndicats d'exploitants agricoles**) = French farmers' trade union

FO nf (abrév **Force ouvrière**) = large French trade union (formed out of the split with Communist CGT in 1948)

fonction nf (a) (emploi) office; **entrer en fonction** ou **fonctions** (président, ministre) to take up office; **être en fonction** to be in office (b) (rôle) function

◇ Écon **fonction de la demande** demand function, market demand function

◇ **fonction publique** ≃ civil or public service

fonctionnaire nmf ≃ civil servant, government official

◇ **fonctionnaire détaché** ≃ civil servant Br on secondment or Am on a temporary assignment

◇ **fonctionnaire municipal** ≃ local government official

fonctionnalisme nm Écon functionalism

fonctionnaliste Écon **1** adj functionalist, functionalistic **2** nmf functionalist

fonctionnariat nm ≃ civil servant status

fonctionnariser vt ≃ to make part of the civil service

fonctionnarisme nm officialdom, bureaucracy

fondamentalisme *nm* fundamentalism

fondamentaliste 1 *adj* fundamentalist
　2 *nmf* fundamentalist

fonds 1 *nm (organisme)* fund
　2 *nmpl (ressources)* funds, capital
◇ *fonds d'État* government stocks
◇ *Fonds européen de cohésion* European cohesion fund
◇ *Fonds européen de coopération monétaire* European Monetary Cooperation Fund
◇ *Fonds européen de développement* European Development Fund
◇ *Fonds européen de développement régional* European Regional Development Fund
◇ *Fonds européen d'investissement* European Investment Fund
◇ *Fonds européen d'orientation et de garantie agricole* European Agricultural Guidance and Guarantee Fund
◇ *Fonds monétaire européen* European Monetary Fund
◇ *Fonds monétaire international* International Monetary Fund
◇ *fonds propres* capital stock
◇ *fonds publics* public funds
◇ *fonds de secours* relief fund
◇ *Fonds social européen* European Social Fund
◇ *fonds de stabilisation* stabilization fund
◇ *fonds structurels* structural funds
◇ *fonds structurels et de cohésion* structural and cohesion funds

force *nf*
◇ *force de dissuasion* deterrent
◇ *force de frappe* strike force
◇ *force d'interposition* interposition force
◇ *Écon* *forces du marché* market forces
◇ *Pol* *Force ouvrière* = French trade union
◇ *force de paix* peacekeeping force
◇ *force politique (parti)* political force
◇ *forces productives* productive forces

formation *nf* **(a)** *(groupe)* group **(b)** *(d'un gouvernement, d'une association)* formation, forming
◇ *formation paramilitaire* paramilitary group
◇ *formation politique* political group
◇ *formation syndicale* (trade) union

former *vt (gouvernement, association)* to form

formulaire de recensement *nm* census return

formule *nf* **(a)** *(méthode)* way **(b)** *Suisse Pol* = name given to the coalition that forms the executive body of the Swiss government
◇ *formule de paix* peace formula

Forum social mondial *nm* World Social Forum

fraction *nf Pol* **(a)** *(sous-groupe)* splinter group, fraction **(b)** *Suisse* = parliamentary committee

fractionnel, -elle *adj Pol* divisive

fractionner 1 *vt (diviser)* to divide, to split up
　2 se fractionner *vpr* to split (up); **le groupe s'est fractionné en deux** the group split *or* divided in two

fractionnisme *nm Pol (tactique)* divisive tactics; *(caractère)* factionalism

fractionniste *Pol* **1** *adj* factionalist
　2 *nmf* factionalist

fracture *nf (cassure)* split
◇ *fracture Nord-Sud* North-South divide
◇ *fracture numérique* digital divide
◇ *fracture sociale* social divide

❝

L'Europe doit aussi contribuer à réduire la **fracture Nord-Sud**. Il ne s'agit pas seulement de "développement durable" mais d'articuler de manière originale la croissance économique, la justice sociale et l'équilibre écologique.

❞

fragile *adj (économie)* weak, shaky

fragilité *nf (de l'économie)* weakness, shakiness

fraude *nf (tromperie)* fraud, malpractice
◊ *fraude électorale* electoral fraud, vote *or* ballot rigging
◊ *fraude fiscale* tax evasion

freinage *nm (de l'inflation)* curbing; *(de production)* cutting back; *(des importations, des salaires)* reduction

freiner *vt (inflation)* to curb; *(production)* to cut back; *(importations, salaires)* to reduce

frein fiscal *nm Écon* fiscal drag

front *nm Pol* front
◊ *Front national* National Front *(extreme right-wing French politcal party)*
◊ *Front populaire* Popular Front

frontalier, -ère 1 *adj* border
2 *nm,f (travailleur)* cross-border commuter

frontière *nf Pol* border; **dans nos frontières** within our borders

fructifier *vi Écon* to yield a profit

FSE *nm (abrév* **Fonds social européen)** ESF

FSM *nf (abrév* **Fédération syndicale mondiale)** WFTU

FSU *nf (abrév* **Fédération syndicale unitaire)** = French association of teachers' and lecturers' trade unions

fuite *nf Pol (d'un secret, d'une information)* leak; **il y a eu des fuites sur le budget** the budget details were leaked
◊ *Écon* **fuite de capitaux** flight of capital
◊ *Écon* **fuite des cerveaux** brain drain

> ❝
> La lutte de la banque centrale de Russie contre les **fuites de capitaux** porte ses fruits – ces fuites ont été réduites de moitié – et devrait se concrétiser par l'adoption d'une réglementation bancaire cohérente et efficace.
> ❞

fusion *nf Écon* merger
◊ *fusion horizontale* horizontal merger
◊ *fusion verticale* vertical merger

fusionnement *nm Écon* merger, amalgamation

fusionner *vi Écon* to merge, to amalgamate

fusions-acquisitions *nfpl Écon* mergers and acquisitions

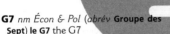

G7 *nm Écon & Pol (abrév* **Groupe des Sept**) **le G7** the G7

G8 *nm Écon & Pol (abrév* **Groupe des Huit**) **le G8** the G8

gagner *Pol* **1** *vt (élection)* to win
2 *vi (l'emporter)* to win; **gagner aux élections** to win the election

gain *nm* (**a**) *Pol* gain; **un gain de 30 sièges aux élections** a gain of 30 seats in the elections (**b**) *Écon (bénéfice financier)* profit, gain; *(rémunération)* earnings
◇ *Écon* **gain de change** exchange gain
◇ *Écon* **gains invisibles** invisible earnings
◇ *Écon* **gains visibles** visible earnings

garantie *nf* guarantee
◇ *Écon* **garantie de crédit à l'exportation** export credit guarantee
◇ *Pol* **garantie individuelle** guarantee of individual liberties

garde des Sceaux *nm* (French) Minister of Justice, *Br* ≃ Lord Chancellor, *Am* ≃ Attorney General

GATT *nm Écon (abrév* **General Agreement on Tariffs and Trade**) GATT

gauche *nf Pol* (**a**) **la gauche** the left (wing); **être à gauche** to be left-wing; **être très à gauche** to be very left-wing; **quand la gauche est arrivée au pouvoir** when the left came to power; **voter à gauche** to vote (for the) left
(**b**) **de gauche** left-wing; **être de gauche** to be left-wing *or* a left-winger; **idées/parti de gauche** left-wing ideas/party

◇ *Fam* **la gauche caviar** champagne socialism
◇ **la gauche dure** the hard left
◇ **la gauche modérée** the soft left
◇ **la gauche plurielle** = the rainbow coalition of socialists, communists and ecologists in the government of Lionel Jospin (elected in 1997)

> On fait attention à la **gauche caviar**, qui s'embourgeoise. Jospin va vers la droite, alors qu'il devrait réaffirmer les valeurs de gauche, celles du dialogue, du partage des richesses, plus vers la masse moyenne que vers les couches favorisées.

gauchisant, -e *Pol* **1** *adj* **être gauchisant** to have left-wing tendencies, to be a left-winger
2 *nm,f* **c'est un gauchisant** he's a left-winger, he's got left-wing tendencies

gauchisme *nm Pol* leftism; *(depuis 1968)* New Leftism

gauchiste *Pol* **1** *adj* left; *(depuis 1968)* (New) Leftist
2 *nmf* leftist; *(depuis 1968)* (New) Leftist

gaucho *Fam Péj Pol* **1** *adj* pinko, *Br* lefty
2 *nmf* pinko, *Br* lefty

gaullisme *nm Pol* Gaullism

gaulliste *Pol* **1** *adj* Gaullist
2 *nmf* Gaullist

GEIE *nm (abrév* **Groupement européen d'intérêt économique**) EEIG

gel *nm Écon* freeze
◊ *gel des crédits* credit freeze
◊ *gel des salaires* wage freeze
◊ *UE gel des terres* setaside

gelé, -e *adj Écon* frozen

geler *vt Écon* to freeze ; **tous les crédits sont gelés jusqu'à nouvel ordre** all funding has been frozen until further notice

général, -e *adj Pol (assemblée, direction)* general

Génération Écologie *nf Pol* **la Génération Écologie** = one of the two green parties in France

génocidaire **1** *adj* genocidal
2 *nmf* genocidaire

génocide *nm* genocide

géographie politique *nf* political geography

géopolitique **1** *adj* geopolitical
2 *nf* geopolitics

gérer *vt* **(a)** *(budget, ville)* to administer, to manage ; *(finances, conflit)* to manage **(b)** *(entreprise)* to manage, to run

gestion *nf* management
◊ *gestion budgétaire* budgetary control
◊ *gestion de portefeuille* portfolio management

gestionnaire *nmf* manager
◊ *gestionnaire de portefeuille* portfolio manager

GIEC *nm (abrév Groupement Intergouvernemental de l'étude du climat)* IPCC

glasnost *nf Pol* glasnost

glissement *nm Écon (d'une monnaie, des salaires)* slide ; **une progression annuelle de quatre pour cent en glissement** a yearly four percent slide

glisser *vi Écon (monnaie, salaires)* to slide

globalisation *nf* globalization

globaliser *vt* to globalize

gouvernable *adj Pol* governable

gouvernance *nf Pol* **(a)** *(action de gouverner)* government **(b)** *(manière de gérer)* governance, government
◊ *gouvernance mondiale* global governance

gouvernant, -e *Pol* **1** *adj* ruling, governing
2 *nm,f* ruler ; **les gouvernants** those in power, the Government

gouvernement *nm Pol* **(a)** *(régime)* government ; **un gouvernement démocratique/monarchique** a democratic/monarchic government ; **sous le gouvernement socialiste** under the Socialist government
(b) *(ensemble des ministres)* government ; **le Premier ministre a formé son gouvernement** the Prime Minister has formed his government *or* cabinet ; **le gouvernement a démissionné** the government has resigned ; **il est au gouvernement depuis 15 ans** he has been in government *or* in power for 15 years ; **sous le gouvernement Jospin** during Jospin's term of office, during Jospin's administration
◊ *gouvernement central* central government
◊ *gouvernement de coalition* coalition government
◊ *gouvernement de cohabitation* = government in which the President and the parliamentary majority are from different parties
◊ *gouvernement d'État* state government
◊ *gouvernement fantoche* puppet government
◊ *gouvernement fédéral* federal government
◊ *gouvernement majoritaire* majority government
◊ *gouvernement minoritaire* minority government
◊ *gouvernement provisoire* provisional government
◊ *gouvernement représentatif* representative government
◊ *gouvernement de transition* interim government

> Les résultats du premier tour des élections législatives, dimanche 9 juin, ont été très favorables à la droite. Jacques Chirac, Président de la République depuis 1995, peut espérer avoir une majorité de députés de son camp politique à l'Assemblée nationale. Pour les cinq années à venir, la France ne devrait plus connaître un **gouvernement de cohabitation**, avec un président de droite et un premier ministre de gauche. L'effondrement de la gauche se confirme. Les résultats ont aussi montré une chute radicale du vote en faveur du Front National, le parti d'extrême droite de Jean-Marie Le Pen : entre le 21 avril et le 9 juin, il a perdu 40 % de ses électeurs !

gouvernemental, -e *Pol adj (parti)* ruling, governing; *(presse)* pro-government; *(politique, décision, crise)* government, governmental; **des dispositions gouvernementales** measures taken by the government

gouverner *Pol* **1** *vt* to rule, to govern; **le pays n'était plus gouverné** the country no longer had a government

2 *vi* to govern; **un parti qui gouverne depuis des années** a party which has governed *or* has been in government for years

3 se gouverner *vpr* to govern oneself; **le droit des peuples à se gouverner eux-mêmes** the right of peoples to self-government

gouverneur *nm Pol* governor; **le Gouverneur de la Banque de France** the Governor of the Bank of France

grâce présidentielle *nf Pol* presidential pardon

grands 1 *nm* **les deux Grands** the two superpowers

2 *adj*

◇ **grand corps de l'État** = senior civil servants recruited through the "École nationale d'administration"

◇ **grands électeurs** = body electing members of the (French) Senate

◇ **le Grand Marché (européen)** the European Market

grille *nf*

◇ *Écon* **grille indiciaire** salary structure *or* scale; *(de la fonction publique)* wage index

◇ *Écon* **grille de rémunération** salary scale

◇ *Écon* **grille des salaires** salary scale

groupe *nm* group

◇ **groupe de consommateurs** consumer group

◇ *Pol* **groupe de contact** contact group

◇ **groupe dissident** splinter *or* dissident group

◇ **Groupe des États d'Afrique, des Caraïbes et du Pacifique** African, Caribbean and Pacific Group of States

◇ *Écon & Pol* **le Groupe des Huit** the Group of Eight

◇ **groupe industriel** industrial group

◇ **groupe d'intérêt** interest group

◇ **Groupe interministériel de contrôle** interdepartmental regulatory committee

◇ **groupe d'intervention** task force

◇ *Pol* **groupe marginal** fringe group

◇ **groupe parlementaire** parliamentary group

◇ **groupe de pression** pressure group, lobby

◇ **groupe de réflexion** think tank

◇ **groupe scissionniste** splinter group

◇ *Écon & Pol* **le Groupe des Sept** the Group of Seven

◇ **groupe socio-économique** socio-economic group

◇ **groupe témoin** focus group

◇ **groupe de travail** working group *or* party

groupement *nm (association)* group

◇ *Écon* **Groupement européen d'intérêt économique** European Economic Interest Group

◇ *Écon* **groupement d'intérêt économique** economic interest group

◇ *Groupement intergouvernemental de l'étude du climat* Intergovernmental Panel on Climate Change

groupuscule *nm Pol* small group; **les groupuscules gauchistes** tiny ultra-left splinter groups

guérilla *nf Pol (guerre)* guerrilla warfare; *(soldats)* group of guerrillas, guerrilla unit; **la guérilla parlementaire de l'opposition** the guerrilla tactics employed by the opposition in parliament

guérillero *nm Pol* guerrilla

guerre *nf* war

◇ *guerre atomique* nuclear war

◇ *guerre civile* civil war

◇ *Écon guerre commerciale* trade war

◇ *guerre froide* cold war

◇ *guerre larvée* undeclared war

◇ *guerre préventive* preemptive *or* preventive war

◇ *Écon guerre des prix* price war

harmonisation *nf (mise en accord)* harmonization; **ils ont réclamé l'harmonisation des salaires du public et du privé** they have demanded that public sector salaries be brought into parity *or* line with those in the private sector
◇ *harmonisation fiscale* tax harmonization

harmoniser *vt (mettre en accord)* to harmonize; **harmoniser les salaires du public et du privé** to bring public and private sector salaries into line

hausse *nf* rise, increase (**de** in); **la hausse du coût de la vie** the rise in the cost of living; **les prix ont subi une forte hausse** prices have increased sharply, prices have shot up; **une hausse de quatre pour cent** a four percent rise; **une hausse des prix** a price increase; **pousser qch à la hausse** to have an inflationary effect on sth

hausser *vt* to raise, to increase, to put up; **le prix a été haussé de dix pour cent** the price has been increased *or* has gone up by ten percent

haut, -e *adj*
◇ *Haute Assemblée* (French) Senate
◇ *Haute cour* High Court *(for impeachment of president or ministers)*
◇ *haut fonctionnaire* ≃ senior civil servant, senior government official
◇ *haute trahison* high treason

hégémonie *nf* hegemony

Hémicycle *nm Parl* **l'Hémicycle** *(salle)* = the benches or chamber of the French National Assembly; *(Assemblée)* the French National Assembly

> Les travaux pratiques ont commencé deux heures plus tard, lors de l'audition publique de M. Fillon par la commission des affaires sociales à l'Assemblée. Un premier "tour de chauffe" plutôt contenu, chacun promettant de se réserver pour le débat dans l'**Hémicycle**, à partir du 2 octobre.

homme *nm*
◇ *homme économique* economic man
◇ *homme d'État* statesman
◇ *homme de parti* party man
◇ *homme politique* politician

horizontal, -e *adj Écon (concentration, intégration)* horizontal

hôtel *nm*
◇ *l'hôtel de Brienne* = building in Paris where the French Ministry of Defence is situated
◇ *hôtel de ville* *Br* town hall, *Am* city hall

hyperinflation *nf Écon* hyperinflation

hypothèse du cycle de vie *nf Écon* life-cycle hypothesis

idéologie *nf Pol* ideology

IDH *nm Écon* (*abrév* **indicateur de développement humain**) HDI

IED *nm* (*abrév* **investissement étranger direct**) FDI

IEP *nm* (*abrév* **Institut d'études politiques**) = "grande école" for political sciences in Paris, commonly known as "Sciences-Po"

IFOP *nm UE* (*abrév* **instrument financier d'orientation de la pêche**) FIFG

IME *nm* (*abrév* **Institut monétaire européen**) EMI

immigrant, -e 1 *adj* immigrant
  2 *nm,f* immigrant

immigration *nf* immigration

immigré, -e 1 *adj* immigrant
  2 *nm,f* immigrant
◇ *immigré clandestin* illegal immigrant

immigrer *vi* to immigrate; **immigrer en France/aux États-Unis** to immigrate to France/to the (United) States

immobilisme *nm Pol* immobilism

immobiliste *Pol* **1** *adj* conservative; **la politique immobiliste du gouvernement** the government's conservative policies
  2 *nmf* conservative, upholder of the status quo

immunité *nf* immunity
◇ *immunité diplomatique* diplomatic immunity
◇ *immunité fiscale* immunity from taxation
◇ *immunité parlementaire* parliamentary privilege

impartition *nf Écon* subcontracting

impeachment *nm Pol* impeachment

impérialisme *nm* imperialism

impérialiste 1 *adj* imperialist
  2 *nmf* imperialist

implantation *nf* (**a**) *Écon* (*d'une entreprise, d'une activité*) establishment, setting up (**b**) *Pol* (*d'un parti politique*) establishment

implanter 1 *vt* (**a**) *Écon* (*entreprise, activité*) to establish, to set up (**b**) *Pol* (*parti politique*) to establish
  2 s'implanter *vpr* (**a**) *Écon* (*entreprise, activité*) to be established *or* set up (**b**) *Pol* (*parti politique*) to become established

import *nm* import

importable *adj* importable, which can be imported

importateur, -trice 1 *adj* importing; **les pays importateurs de pétrole** the oil-importing countries
  2 *nm,f* importer; **c'est l'importateur exclusif de cette marque pour la France** they are the sole French importers of this brand

importation *nf* (**a**) (*activité*) importing (**b**) (*produit*) import, importation; **importations** imports; **nos importations dépassent nos exportations** we import more than we export
◇ *importation en franchise* duty-free importation
◇ *importations invisibles* invisible imports
◇ *importations parallèles* parallel imports

◇ *importation temporaire* temporary importation

◇ *importations visibles* visible imports

importer *vt (marchandises)* to import; **importer des marchandises des États-Unis en France** to import goods from the United States into France

import-export *nf* import-export

imposable *adj (personne, marchandises)* taxable, liable to tax; *(revenu)* taxable

imposer *vt (personne, marchandises)* to tax; **imposer des droits sur qch** to tax sth

imposition *nf* taxation

◇ *imposition en cascade* cascade taxation

◇ *imposition des entreprises* business taxation

◇ *imposition forfaitaire* basic-rate taxation

◇ *imposition progressive* progressive taxation

◇ *imposition régressive* regressive taxation

◇ *imposition à la source* taxation at source

impôt *nm* tax; **avant impôt** before tax; **après impôt** after tax; **frapper qch d'un impôt** to tax sth; **payer 5000 euros d'impôts** to pay 5,000 euro in tax(es)

◇ *impôt sur le chiffre d'affaires* turnover tax

◇ *impôt déguisé* hidden tax

◇ *impôt direct* direct tax

◇ *impôt indirect* indirect tax

◇ *impôt local* local tax

◇ *impôt négatif sur le revenu* negative income tax

◇ *impôt à la production* input tax

◇ *impôt progressif* progressive tax; *(sur le revenu)* graduated income tax

◇ *impôt proportionnel* proportional tax

◇ *impôt régressif* regressive tax

◇ *impôt retenu à la source* withholding tax

◇ *impôt sur le revenu* income tax

◇ *impôt sur les sociétés* *Br* corporation tax, *Am* corporation income tax

improductif, -ive *adj Écon* non-productive

inactif, -ive *Écon* **1** *adj* **(a)** *(personne)* non-working; *(population)* non-working, inactive **(b)** *(marché)* sluggish, dull

2 *nm,f (personne)* person without paid employment; **les inactifs** the non-working population

inamovible *adj (fonctionnaire)* permanent, irremovable

incidence fiscale *nf Écon* fiscal effect, tax impact

incitation fiscale *nf Écon* tax incentive

incompétent, -e *Pol* **1** *adj* incompetent

2 *nm,f* incompetent

incontesté, -e *adj Pol (siège)* uncontested, undisputed

indécis, -e *nm,f Pol* floating voter

indemnité *nf (allocation)* allowance

◇ *indemnité parlementaire* = salary paid to French "députés"

indépendance *nf Pol (d'un pays, d'une personne)* independence

indépendant, -e *Pol* **1** *adj* independent

2 *nm,f* independent

indépendantisme *nm Pol* **l'indépendantisme** the independence *or* separatist movement

indépendantiste *Pol* **1** *adj* separatist

2 *nmf* separatist

index *nm Belg Écon* index **(des prix)** price index

indexation *nf Écon (des prix, des salaires)* indexation, index-linking **(sur** to); **l'indexation des salaires sur les prix** the index-linking of salaries to prices

indexé, -e *adj Écon (prix, salaires)* indexed, index-linked **(sur** to)

indexer vt Écon (prix, salaires) to index, to index-link (**sur** to)

indicateur nm (indice) indicator, pointer

◇ **indicateur d'activité économique** economic indicator

◇ **indicateurs d'alerte** economic indicators, business indicators

◇ **indicateur de développement humain** human development index

◇ **indicateur économique** economic indicator

◇ **indicateur de marché** market indicator

◇ **indicateur statistique** statistical indicator

◇ **indicateur de tendance** market indicator

indice nm Écon (chiffre indicateur) index

◇ **indice d'activité industrielle** industrial activity index

◇ **indice boursier** exchange index

◇ **indice de confiance** consumer confidence index

◇ **indice corrigé des variations saisonnières** seasonally adjusted index

◇ **indice du coût de la vie** cost of living index

◇ **indice de croissance** growth index

◇ **indice non-corrigé des variations saisonnières** non-seasonally adjusted index

◇ **indice pondéré** weighted index

◇ **indice pondéré par le commerce extérieur** trade-weighted index

◇ **indice des prix** price index

◇ **indice des prix à la consommation** consumer price index

◇ **indice des prix de détail** retail price index

◇ **indice des prix de gros** wholesale price index

◇ **indice des prix à la production** producer price index

◇ **indice des prix et des salaires** wage and price index

◇ **indice de rémunération** salary grading

◇ **indice de traitement** salary grading

❝

Les commandes de biens durables et la consommation augmentent, tout comme les dépenses de construction et, plus important encore, le moral des ménages. L'**indice de confiance** était tombé, en octobre, à son plus bas niveau depuis neuf ans.

❞

---

indiciaire adj Écon index-based

indiciel, -elle adj Écon index

indirect, -e adj (coûts) indirect

individualisme nm Pol individualism

individualiste Pol **1** adj individualistic

2 nmf individualist

industrialisation nf industrialization; **une économie en voie d'industrialisation** an industrializing economy

industrialisé, -e adj industrialized

industrialiser 1 vt to industrialize

2 s'industrialiser vpr to industrialize, to become industrialized

industrialisme nm industrialism

industrie nf industry, manufacturing; **travailler dans l'industrie** to work in industry or in manufacturing

◇ **industrie de base** basic industry

◇ **industrie clé** key industry

◇ **industrie de consommation** consumer (goods) industry

◇ **industrie en croissance rapide** growth industry

◇ **industrie manufacturière** manufacturing industry

◇ **industrie nationalisée** nationalized or state-owned industry

◇ **industrie de pointe** high-tech industry

◇ **industrie primaire** primary industry

◇ **industrie secondaire** secondary industry

◇ **industrie de services** service industry

◇ *industrie subventionnée* subsidized industry

industriel, -elle 1 *adj* industrial
2 *nm,f* industrialist

INED, Ined *nm* (*abrév* **Institut national d'études démographiques**) = French national institute of population studies

inégalité *nf* inequality

inféodation *nf Pol* subservience, subjection (**à** to)

inféodé, -e *adj Pol* subservient (**à** to); **un pays inféodé à une grande puissance** a country subjugated by a great power

inféoder s'inféoder *vpr Pol* **s'inféoder à** to become subservient to

inflation *nf Écon* inflation; **à l'abri de l'inflation** inflation-proof

◇ *inflation par les coûts* cost-push inflation
◇ *inflation par la demande* demand-pull inflation
◇ *inflation fiduciaire* inflation of the currency
◇ *inflation galopante* galloping inflation
◇ *inflation larvée* creeping inflation
◇ *inflation monétaire* monetary inflation
◇ *inflation des prix* price inflation
◇ *inflation des salaires* wage inflation

inflationnisme *nm Écon* inflationism

inflationniste *Écon* **1** *adj (tendance)* inflationary; *(politique)* inflationist
2 *nmf* inflationist

inflatoire *adj Belg Écon (tendance)* inflationary; *(politique)* inflationist

infraction politique *nf* ≃ offence/ offences against the state

infraétatique *adj* infrastate

infrastructure *nf* infrastructure

ingérence *nf Pol* interference, intervention

initiative *nf (idée)* initiative
◇ *initiative gouvernementale* = governmental prerogative to propose legislation; *(idée)* government initiative
◇ *Pol* **initiative de paix** peace initiative *or* overture
◇ *initiative parlementaire* = parliamentary prerogative to legislate
◇ *initiative populaire* citizen's initiative

injecter *vt (argent, capitaux)* to inject (**dans** into)

injection *nf (d'argent, de capitaux)* injection (**dans** into)

input *nm Écon* input

inscription *nf (d'électeur, de membre)* registration, enrolment; **son inscription sur les listes électorales** *Br* his/ her registration on the electoral roll, *Am* his/her voter registration

inscrire 1 *vt (électeur, membre)* to register
2 s'inscrire *vpr* **s'inscrire à** *(parti)* to join, to enrol as a member of; **s'inscrire sur une liste électorale** to register to vote, *Br* to have one's name put on the electoral roll

inscrit, -e *Pol* **1** *adj (électeur, membre)* registered
2 *nm,f (à un parti)* registered member; *(électeur)* registered elector; *Pol* **les inscrits au prochain débat** the scheduled speakers for the next debate

INSEE, Insee *nm* (*abrév* **Institut national de la statistique et des études économiques**) = French national institute of statistics and information about the economy, *Br* ≃ ONS

insertion sociale *nf* social integration

insolvabilité *nf Écon* insolvency

insolvable *Écon* **1** *adj* insolvent
2 *nmf* insolvent

instabilité *nf (d'un régime politique, du marché, des prix)* instability

instable *adj (régime politique, marché, prix)* unstable

instance *nf (organisme)* authority; **les instances économiques/communautaires** the economic/EU authorities; **les plus hautes instances du parti** the leading bodies of the party
◊ *instance de contrôle* regulatory body
◊ *instances dirigeantes* ruling body
◊ *instance législative* legislative body

institut *nm (organisme)* institute
◊ *Institut d'Études politiques* = "grande école" for political sciences in Paris, commonly known as "Sciences-Po"
◊ *Institut européen d'administration* = European business school in Fontainebleau
◊ *Institut monétaire européen* European Monetary Institute
◊ *Institut national d'études démographiques* = French national institute of population studies
◊ *Institut national de la statistique et des études économiques* = French national institute of statistics and information about the economy, *Br* ≃ Office for National Statistics
◊ *institut de sondage* polling company

institution *nf* (a) *(établissement)* institution (b) *(mise en place)* institution, establishment; *(d'une loi)* introduction; *(d'une règle)* laying down
◊ *institution financière* financial institution
◊ *institution politique* political institution

instruction *nf* directive

instrument *nm*
◊ *instrument dérivé* derivative
◊ *instrument financier* financial instrument
◊ *UE instrument financier d'orientation de la pêche* Financial Instrument for Fisheries Guidance

insurgé, -e *Pol* 1 *adj* insurgent
2 *nm,f* insurgent

insurger s'**insurger** *vpr Pol* s'**insurger contre qn** to rise up *or* to rebel against sb; s'**insurger contre qch** to rebel against sth

insurrection *nf Pol* insurrection, insurgency

intégration *nf Écon* integration
◊ *intégration en amont* backward integration
◊ *intégration ascendante* backward integration
◊ *intégration en aval* forward integration
◊ *intégration descendante* forward integration
◊ *intégration économique* economic integration
◊ *intégration européenne* European integration
◊ *intégration financière* financial integration
◊ *intégration horizontale* horizontal integration
◊ *intégration latérale* lateral integration
◊ *intégration sociale* social integration
◊ *intégration verticale* vertical integration

intégrer 1 *vt (inclure)* to integrate (**à** *ou* **dans** in)
2 s'**intégrer** *vpr (personne)* to become integrated *or* assimilated (**à** *ou* **dans** in)

intégrisme *nm Pol* fundamentalism

intégriste *Pol* 1 *adj* fundamentalist
2 *nmf* fundamentalist

intensif, -ive *adj Écon* intensive

intentions de vote *nfpl* voting intentions; **ils enregistrent 28 pour cent des intentions de vote** 28 percent of those polled said that they would vote for them

❝

Largement en tête dans les sondages, le candidat du Parti des Travailleurs (PT), Luis Inacio Lula da Silva, pourrait être élu dès le premier tour de l'élection présidentielle au Brésil, dimanche 6 octobre. A défaut, il devrait affronter, le 27 octobre, au second tour, José Serra, le dauphin du président sortant, Fernando Henrique Cardoso, crédité de 21% des **intentions de vote**.

"

interafricain, -e *adj* Pan-African

interaméricain, -e *adj* Pan-American, Inter-American

interarabe *adj* Pan-Arab, Pan-Arabic

intercommunalité *nf Pol* cooperation between neighbouring "communes"

interdépartemental, -e *adj (accord, comité, coordination)* between "départements"

interdépendance *nf Pol* interdependence

interdépendant, -e *adj Pol* interdependent

interdiction *nf* ban
◇ **interdiction d'exportation** export ban
◇ **interdiction d'importation** import ban

interdire *vt* to ban; **le gouvernement a fait interdire toute manifestation de rue** the government issued a ban on all street demonstrations; **interdire qch d'exportation/d'importation** to impose an export/import ban on sth

intérêt *nm (financier)* interest
◇ *Écon* **intérêt personnel** self-interest

interétatique *adj* interstate

intereuropéen, -enne *adj* Pan-European

interfinancement *nm* cross-subsidization

intergouvernemental, -e *adj* intergovernmental

intergroupe *nm Pol* joint committee

intérieur, -e 1 *adj* (a) *(national) (marché)* domestic, home; *(politique)* domestic; **le gouvernement est aux prises avec des difficultés intérieures** the government is battling against difficulties at home *or* domestic problems
(b) *(interne)* internal; **les problèmes intérieurs du parti** the party's internal problems
2 *nm Fam* **l'Intérieur** *Br* ≃ the Home Office, *Am* ≃ the Department of the Interior

intérim *nm Pol (remplacement)* **assurer l'intérim** to take over on a caretaker basis; **j'assure l'intérim de la secrétaire en chef** I'm deputizing *or* covering for the chief secretary; **par intérim** *(président, ministre)* acting; *(gouvernement, cabinet)* caretaker; **gouverner par intérim** to govern in the interim *or* for an interim period

"

Le nouveau gouvernement **par intérim** du président Adolfo Rodriguez Saa doit encore dévoiler les détails de son plan de sauvetage de l'économie, qui s'articule déjà autour d'un moratoire sur le remboursement de la dette extérieure du pays et sur l'introduction d'une nouvelle monnaie, l'argentino, qui devrait permettre de réinjecter des liquidités dans une économie qui en manque cruellement.

"

intérimaire 1 *adj* (a) *(président, ministre)* acting; *(gouvernement, cabinet)* caretaker (b) *(non durable) (fonction)* interim; *(commission)* provisional, temporary
2 *nmf (cadre)* deputy

interministériel, -elle *adj Pol Br* ≃ joint ministerial; *Am* ≃ joint Congressional

internalisation *nf Écon* internalization

internaliser *vt Écon* to internalize

international, -e *adj* international
  2 *nm Écon* **l'international** world markets; **ces entreprises réalisent près de la moitié de leur chiffre d'affaires à l'international** these companies make almost half their profits in international trade *or* on the international market

internationalisation *nf* internationalization

internationaliser 1 *vt* to internationalize
  2 s'internationaliser *vpr* to take on an international dimension; **le conflit s'est internationalisé** the conflict took on an international dimension

internationalisme *nm* internationalism

internationaliste 1 *adj* internationalist
  2 *nmf* internationalist

interne *adj Pol (conflit, politique)* internal

interner *vt Pol* to intern

interparlementaire *adj* interparliamentary

interpellateur, -trice *nm,f Parl* questioner, interpellator

interpellation *nf Parl* question, interpellation

interpeller *vt Parl* to put a question to, to interpellate

intersession *nf Parl* recess

intersyndical, -e 1 *adj* interunion, joint union
  2 *nf* **intersyndicale** interunion committee

intervenant, -e *nm,f (dans un débat, un congrès)* participant, speaker
  ◇ **intervenant principal** keynote speaker

intervenir *vi* (a) *Écon & Pol* to intervene; **l'État a dû intervenir pour renflouer la société** the state had to intervene to keep the company afloat (b) *(dans un débat, un congrès)* to speak

intervention *nf Écon & Pol* intervention
  ◇ **intervention de l'État** state intervention
  ◇ **intervention gouvernementale** government intervention

interventionnisme *nm Écon & Pol* interventionism

interventionniste *Écon & Pol* **1** *adj* interventionist
  2 *nmf* interventionist

intifada *nf* intifada

intolérance *nf* intolerance
  ◇ **intolérance politique** political intolerance

intolérant, -e *adj* intolerant

intracommunautaire *adj UE* intra-Community, within the EU

intrant *nm Écon* input

intrigues politiques *nfpl* political intrigues

introduction *nf (d'un projet de loi, d'une règle)* introduction

introduire *vt (projet de loi, règle)* to introduce, to bring in

intronisation *nf* (a) *(d'un monarque)* enthronement (b) *(mise en place)* establishment; *Pol* **l'intronisation du nouveau gouvernement** the establishment of the new government

introniser *vt* (a) *(monarque)* to enthrone; **il s'est fait introniser à l'âge de 60 ans** he came to the throne when he was 60 (b) *(établir)* to establish

investir *vt* (a) *(somme)* to invest (b) *Pol (personne)* **investir qn d'une dignité** to invest sb with a function

investissement *nm (action)* investing, investment; *(somme)* investment
  ◇ **investissement direct** direct investment
  ◇ **investissement à l'étranger** outward *or* foreign investment
  ◇ **investissement de l'étranger** inward investment
  ◇ **investissement étranger direct** foreign direct investment

◊ *investissement indirect* indirect investment

investiture *nf Pol (d'un candidat)* nomination, selection; *(d'un gouvernement)* vote of confidence

inviolabilité *nf Pol* immunity
◊ *inviolabilité diplomatique* diplomatic immunity
◊ *inviolabilité parlementaire* Br ≃ Parliamentary privilege, *Am* ≃ congressional immunity

inviolable *adj Pol* untouchable, immune

invisible *Écon* 1 *adj (exportations, importations)* invisible
   2 *nmpl* **invisibles** *(échanges)* invisibles, invisible trade; *(exportations)* invisibles, invisible exports; **la balance des invisibles** the balance of invisible trade

invocation *nf Pol* invocation

invoquer *vt* to invoke, to cite

IPC *nm Écon (abrév* **indice des prix à la consommation)** CPI

IPP *nm Écon (abrév* **indice des prix à la production)** PPI

irrédentisme *nm Pol* irredentism

irrédentiste *Pol* 1 *adj* irredentist
   2 *nmf* irredentist

irresponsabilité *nf (du chef de l'État)* non-accountability
◊ *irresponsabilité parlementaire* Br parliamentary privilege, *Am* congressional immunity

islamique *adj* Islamic

islamisme *nm* Islamism

islamiste 1 *adj* Islamic
   2 *nmf* Islamic fundamentalist

isolationnisme *nm Pol* isolationism

isolationniste *Pol* 1 *adj* isolationist
   2 *nmf* isolationist

isolé, -e *Pol* 1 *adj (personne)* isolated
   2 *nm,f* maverick, isolated activist; **ce sont les revendications de quelques isolés** only a few isolated people are putting forward these demands

isolement *nm Pol* isolation

isoloir *nm Pol* voting booth, polling booth

jachère nf UE setaside; **mettre la terre en jachère** to set land aside

jacobin, -e Pol **1** adj Jacobin
2 nm,f Jacobin

jacobinisme nm Pol Jacobinism

jargon nm
◇ *jargon administratif* officialese
◇ *jargon communautaire* Eurospeak

jeune-turc, jeune-turque nm,f Pol Young Turk

jour nm
◇ *jour des élections* election or polling day
◇ *jour du scrutin* election or polling day

journal nm (publication) paper, newspaper; (spécialisé) journal
◇ Pol *le Journal officiel de la République Française* = French government publication giving information to the public about new laws, parliamentary debates, government business and new companies, Br ≃ Hansard, Am ≃ Federal Register
◇ *journal d'opinion* quality newspaper

journaliste nmf journalist
◇ *journaliste économique* economics correspondent or journalist
◇ *journaliste parlementaire* parliamentary correspondent, lobby correspondent
◇ *journaliste politique* political correspondent or journalist

journée nf Pol
◇ *journée d'action* day of action
◇ *les journées (parlementaires) du parti* Br ≃ the Party Conference, Am ≃ the Party Convention

juge nm judge

junte nf Pol junta

jusqu'au-boutisme nm Pol hardline policy

jusqu'au-boutiste Pol **1** nmf hardliner
2 adj hardline

> Toujours sur le plan diplomatique de cette crise, l'UE hausse quelque peu le ton, face à un Sharon **jusqu'au-boutiste** qui, malgré toutes les manifestations qui ont eu lieu un peu partout dans le monde contre son action néfaste et sa désastreuse campagne et les appels multiples émanant de toutes les capitales, persiste dans son action.

justice sociale nf social justice

keiretsu nm Écon keiretsu

kern nm Belg Pol inner cabinet

keynésianisme nm Écon Keynesianism, Keynesian economics

keynésien, -enne adj Écon Keynesian

know-how nm inv Écon know-how

Komintern nm Comintern

krach nm (financial) crash
◇ *krach boursier* Stock Exchange crash

laissez-faire *nm Écon* laissez-faire

lancer *se lancer vpr* **se lancer dans la politique** to enter politics, to go into politics

LCR *nf Pol* (*abrév* **ligue communiste révolutionnaire**) = militant Trotskyist organization

leader *nm Pol* (*chef*) leader; **le leader du parti socialiste** the leader of the socialist party
◊ *leader de la majorité* majority leader

lecture *nf Pol* reading; **le texte a été adopté en première/dernière lecture** the bill was passed on its first/last reading

légalisme *nm* legalism

légaliste 1 *adj* legalistic, legalist
2 *nmf* legalist

légiférer *vi* to legislate

législateur, -trice 1 *adj* lawmaking
2 *nm,f* lawmaker, legislator
3 *nm* **le législateur** the legislature

législatif, -ive 1 *adj* (a) (*qui fait les lois*) legislative; **des réformes législatives** legislative reforms (b) (*de l'Assemblée*) *Br* ≃ parliamentary, *Am* ≃ Congressional
2 *nm* **le législatif** the legislature
3 *nfpl* **législatives** *Br* ≃ general election, *Am* ≃ Congressional election

législation *nf* legislation; **la législation en vigueur** current legislation; **la législation française/anglaise** French/English legislation *or* laws
◊ *législation antitrust* antitrust *or Br* anti-monopoly legislation
◊ *législation européenne* EU legislation
◊ *législation fiscale* tax laws
◊ *législation du travail* labour laws, labour legislation

législativement *adv* legislatively

législature *nf* (a) (*durée du mandat*) term (of office); **les crises qui ont agité la précédente législature** the crises in the previous administration (b) (*corps*) legislature, legislative body

légitime *adj* lawful, legitimate; **le gouvernement légitime de la France** the legitimate government of France

légitimité *nf Pol* legitimacy

lepeniste *Pol* **1** *adj* = relating to supporters of Jean-Marie Le Pen
2 *nmf* = supporter of Jean-Marie Le Pen

> "
>
> Invoquer l'instrumentalisation de l'insécurité pour expliquer le score du leader du FN est une analyse à courte vue, de même que dénoncer la fracture (réelle) entre la France d'en haut et la France d'en bas pour tenter de comprendre la poussée des extrêmes, de droite comme de gauche, demeure insuffisant même si l'électorat **lepeniste** compte nombre de "petits" et de "sans grade".
>
> "

lettres de récréance *nfpl* (ambassador's) letters of recall

levée nf (a) (de sanctions, d'un embargo) lifting; **il a demandé la levée des sanctions/de l'embargo** he asked for the sanctions/the embargo to be lifted

(b) (d'une séance) adjournment; **demander la levée de la séance** to ask for an adjournment; **cela nécessiterait la levée de son immunité parlementaire** this would involve withdrawing his parliamentary immunity

lever vt (a) (sanctions, embargo) to lift (b) (séance) to adjourn

levier nm Écon leverage

libéral, -e 1 adj (a) Écon free-market, free-enterprise (b) Pol (en Grande-Bretagne, au Canada) Liberal
2 nm,f (a) Écon (en France) free-marketeer (b) Pol (en Grande-Bretagne, au Canada) Liberal

libéralisation nf (a) Pol liberalization (b) Écon deregulation, easing of restrictions; **la libéralisation du commerce** the deregulation of trade, the easing of trade restrictions; **la libéralisation complète de l'économie** the application of free-market principles throughout the economy; **la libéralisation des télécommunications** the deregulation of the telecommunications market

> ❝
>
> Elle court le risque, en outre, de voir affluer sur son marché plusieurs dizaines de millions de tonnes d'acier produites au Japon, en Corée du Sud, en Australie ou au Brésil. Plus grave, cette poussée de fièvre protectionniste américaine menace les fragiles accords sur la **libéralisation** des échanges récemment conclus à Doha.
>
> ❞

libéraliser vt (a) Pol to liberalize (b) Écon (commerce) to deregulate, to ease restrictions on; **libéraliser l'économie** to reduce state intervention in the economy

libéralisme nm (a) Pol liberalism (b) Écon free-market economics, free enterprise

libérateur, -trice Pol **1** adj liberating
2 nm,f liberator

libération nf Écon easing of restrictions, deregulation, decontrol; **la libération des changes** the relaxing of foreign exchange controls; **la libération des échanges commerciaux** the deregulation of trade; **la libération des prix** the deregulation of prices, the removal of price controls

libérer vt Écon to lift restrictions on, to deregulate, to decontrol

libertaire Pol **1** adj libertarian, anarchist
2 nmf libertarian, anarchist

liberté nf (a) (droit) freedom (b) libertés (droits légaux) liberties, freedom; **atteinte aux/défense des libertés** attack on/defence of civil liberties

◇ **liberté d'association** freedom of association
◇ **libertés du citoyen** civil liberties
◇ **libertés civiques** civil liberties
◇ **liberté du commerce** freedom of trade
◇ **liberté de conscience** freedom of conscience
◇ **liberté du culte** freedom of worship
◇ **liberté d'entreprise** freedom of enterprise
◇ **liberté d'expression** freedom of speech
◇ **liberté d'information** freedom of information
◇ **liberté des prix** freedom from price controls; **instaurer la liberté des prix** to end or to abolish price controls
◇ **libertés publiques** civil liberties
◇ **liberté de réunion** freedom of association
◇ **liberté syndicale** freedom to join a union, union rights
◇ **liberté du travail** right to work

libre adj Pol (personne, pays) free; **le monde libre** the free world
◇ **libre circulation** free movement

◇ *libre entreprise* free enterprise

libre-échange *nm Écon* free trade

libre-échangisme *nm Écon* (doctrine of) free trade

libre-échangiste *Écon* **1** *adj (politique, économie)* free-trade; *(idée, personne)* in favour of free trade
   2 *nmf* free trader

licence *nf*
◇ *licence d'exportation* export licence
◇ *licence d'importation* import licence

licenciement *nm (structurel)* layoff, *Br* redundancy
◇ *licenciements boursiers* = redundancies made to improve the stock market valuation of a company
◇ *licenciement collectif* mass redundancies
◇ *licenciement économique* redundancy

licencier *vt (pour raison économique)* to lay off, *Br* to make redundant; **se faire licencier** to get laid off, *Br* to be made redundant

LICRA *nf Pol (abrév* **Ligue internationale contre le racisme et l'antisémitisme)** = anti-racist movement

ligne du parti *nf Pol* party line; **suivre la ligne du parti, être dans la ligne du parti** to follow *or* to toe the party line

ligue *nf* league, pressure group
◇ *Ligue Arabe* Arab League
◇ *Ligue Communiste Révolutionnaire* = militant Trotskyist organization
◇ *Ligue des droits de l'homme* League of Human Rights

ligueur, -euse *nm,f Pol* member *(of a league)*

limitation *nf*
◇ *Pol* **limitation des armements** arms control *or* limitation
◇ *Écon* **limitation des prix** price restrictions *or* controls

limogeage *nm (d'un fonctionnaire, d'un ministre)* dismissal

> **❝**
>
> Même l'expert de plus basé du régime de Saddam Hussein doit être déconcerté par le brutal **limogeage**, par décret présidentiel, du ministre irakien du pétrole, Amer Mohammed Rachid. Officiellement démis de ses fonctions "pour avoir atteint l'âge de la retraite", ce général a été remplacé, mardi 7 janvier, par Samil Abdel Aziz Al-Najm.
>
> **❞**

limoger *vt (fonctionnaire, ministre)* to dismiss

liquide 1 *adj Écon* liquid
   2 *nm (espèces)* cash

liquidité *nf Écon* liquidity

lire *vt Pol (projet de loi)* to read

lissage *nm Écon* smoothing (out)

lisser *vt Écon* to smooth (out)

liste *nf Pol* list
◇ *liste bloquée* set list of candidates *(which electors cannot modify)*
◇ *liste civile* civil list
◇ *liste commune* joint list (of candidates)
◇ *liste électorale* electoral roll; **être inscrit sur les listes électorales** to be on the electoral roll
◇ *liste des exportations* export list
◇ *liste des importations* import list
◇ *liste d'opposition* list of opposition candidates
◇ *liste panachée* = ballot paper in which a voter votes for candidates from different lists rather than for a list as a whole

livre¹ *nf (unité monétaire)* pound
◇ *livre sterling* (pound) sterling
◇ *livre verte* green pound

livre² *nm*
◇ *Pol* **livre blanc** white paper

lobby *nm* lobby, pressure group

lobbying *nm* lobbying

"

Pourquoi n'a-t-on jamais eu un ministre de l'Industrie issu du monde de l'entreprise ? Le problème, c'est que les chefs d'entreprise n'ont pas le temps de se consacrer au **lobbying** de réseau qui leur permettrait d'être décideurs à la fois politique et économique.

"

lobbyiste *nmf* lobbyist

lobbysme *nm* lobbying

local, -e *adj (économie, entreprises, producteurs)* local

locomotive *nf Fam (d'un parti, d'une économie)* pacemaker, pacesetter

loi *nf* **(a)** *(règles publiques)* law ; **les lois de notre pays** the law of the land **(b)** *(législation)* act, law ; **la loi Dupont a été votée la nuit dernière** the Dupont Act was passed last night **(c)** *(domination)* law, rule ; **tenir qn/un pays sous sa loi** to rule sb/a country

◇ *loi antitrust* antitrust *or Br* antimonopoly law

◇ *lois de l'apartheid* apartheid laws

◇ *Écon loi des avantages comparés* comparative cost

◇ *loi électorale* electoral law

◇ *loi d'exception* emergency legislation

◇ *Pol loi de Finances* Finance Act

◇ *loi fondamentale* fundamental law

◇ *loi martiale* martial law

◇ *loi organique* organic law

◇ *loi d'orientation* = act laying down the basic principles for government action in a given field

◇ *loi de prescription* statute of limitations

◇ *lois tarifaires* tariff laws

lord *nm* lord

◇ *lord Chancelier* Lord Chancellor

lord-maire *nm* Lord Mayor

loyalisme *nm Pol* loyalism, Loyalism

loyaliste *Pol* **1** *adj* loyalist, Loyalist **2** *nmf* loyalist, Loyalist

loyer de l'argent *nm* **le loyer de l'argent** the interest rate, the cost of money

"

La Réserve fédérale a abaissé le **loyer de l'argent** à son plus bas niveau depuis quarante-deux ans. Cela a permis aux entreprises et aux ménages de supporter plus facilement un endettement record, mais l'activité tarde à repartir.

"

lutte *nf Pol* struggle ; **la lutte pour l'indépendance/pour la liberté** the struggle for independence/for freedom ; **la lutte menée par les intellectuels/syndicats** the struggle led by the intellectuals/unions

◇ *lutte des classes* class struggle *or* war

◇ *Lutte Ouvrière* = militant Trotskyist organization

◇ *lutte politique* political struggle

lutter *vi Pol* to fight, to struggle (**pour/contre** for/against) ; **ils luttent contre le gouvernement** they are struggling against *or* fighting the government ; **ils luttent pour leurs droits** they are fighting for their rights ; **toute sa vie elle a lutté pour que soient reconnus les droits de la femme** she struggled all her life for the recognition of women's rights

maccarthysme, maccarthyste = maccartisme, maccartiste

maccartisme *nm Pol* McCarthyism

maccartiste *Pol* **1** *adj* McCarthyist **2** *nmf* McCarthyist

machination *nf* plot, conspiracy; **des machinations** plotting, machinations

machine *nf (organisation)* machine, machinery; **les lourdeurs de la machine judiciaire** the cumbersome machinery of the law
◇ *machine du parti* party machine

machinisme *nm Écon* mechanization

macroéconomie *nf* **(a)** *(discipline)* macroeconomics **(b)** *(système)* macroeconomy

macroéconomique *adj* macroeconomic

magistrat *nm Pol* = any high-ranking civil servant with judicial authority
◇ *magistrat municipal Br* town councillor, *Am* city councillor

magistrature *nf* **(a)** *(personnes)* **la magistrature** the judicial authorities **(b)** *(fonction)* office; **pendant sa magistrature** during his/her period in office
◇ *la magistrature suprême* the presidency

main-d'œuvre *nf Écon* labour
◇ *main-d'œuvre directe* direct labour
◇ *main-d'œuvre indirecte* indirect labour
◇ *main-d'œuvre peu qualifiée* unskilled labour
◇ *main-d'œuvre productive* productive labour
◇ *main-d'œuvre qualifiée* skilled labour
◇ *main-d'œuvre syndiquée* organized labour

main invisible *nf Écon* invisible hand

maïoral, -e *adj Belg* mayoral

maïorat *nm Belg* office of mayor

maire *nm (d'une commune, d'un arrondissement)* ≃ mayor; *(d'une grande ville) Br* ≃ (lord) mayor, *Am* ≃ mayor
◇ *maire adjoint* deputy mayor

mairesse *nf* **(a)** *(femme maire)* (lady) mayor **(b)** *(épouse du maire)* mayoress

mairie *nf* **(a)** *(fonction)* office of mayor, mayoralty; **il brigue la mairie de Paris** he's running for the office of mayor of Paris; **la mairie l'occupe beaucoup** his/her duties as mayor keep him/her very busy
   (b) *(administration)* town council; *(d'une grande ville)* city council; **organisé par la mairie de Lyon** sponsored by Lyons city council
   (c) *(édifice) Br* town hall, *Am* city hall
◇ *mairie d'arrondissement* district council

maison *nf (entreprise)* firm, company, business

Maison-Blanche *nf* **la Maison-Blanche** the White House

majoritaire 1 *adj* **(a)** *(plus nombreux)* majority; **être majoritaire** to be in the *or* a majority; **quel est le parti majori-**

taire au Parlement? which party has the majority or which is the majority party in Parliament? (**b**) Écon *(participation)* majority

2 *nmf* member of a majority group

majorité *nf Pol* (**a**) *(à l'issue d'élection)* majority; **avoir la majorité** to have the majority; **remporter la majorité des suffrages** to win a or the majority of the votes, to win a majority; **élu avec dix voix de majorité** elected by a majority of ten; **ils ont gagné avec une faible/écrasante majorité** they won by a narrow/overwhelming margin

(**b**) *(parti)* majority party; **la majorité** the majority, the party in power, the governing party; **être dans la majorité** to be a member of the majority party

◇ *majorité absolue* absolute majority; **être élu à la majorité absolue** to be elected with an absolute majority

◇ *majorité gouvernementale* parliamentary majority

◇ *majorité parlementaire* legislative majority

◇ *majorité plurielle* plural majority

◇ *majorité qualifiée* qualified majority

◇ *majorité relative* plurality

◇ *majorité sénatoriale* Senate majority

◇ *majorité simple* simple majority

malaise *nm Pol (mécontentement)* discontent, anger; **il y a un malaise croissant chez les enseignants** there is mounting tension or discontent among teachers

◇ *malaise social* social unrest

malthusianisme *nm* Malthusianism

malthusien, -enne 1 *adj* Malthusian **2** *nm,f* Malthusian

mandant, -e *nm,f Pol* voter; *(d'un député)* constituent

mandarin *nm Péj Pol (personnage influent)* mandarin

> **❝**
>
> Sous un gouvernement dirigé par l'ADQ, les nominations des **manda-**

rins du pouvoir, tels les sous-ministres et les présidents de sociétés d'État, cesseraient d'être la prérogative du conseil des ministres. Elles seraient toutes soumises à l'approbation de l'Assemblée nationale. Aux Etats-Unis, toutes les nominations importantes doivent être filtrées par les parlementaires.
>
> **❞**

mandarinat politique *nm* political establishment

mandat *nm* (**a**) *Pol (fonction)* mandate; *(durée)* term of office; **mandat de député** member's (electoral) mandate; **l'homme à qui vous avez donné votre mandat** the man you have elected; **tel est mon mandat** that is what I was elected to do; **ces prérogatives n'entrent pas dans son mandat** he does not have a mandate to exercise these prerogatives; **solliciter le renouvellement de son mandat** to seek re-election; **elle a rempli son mandat** she's fulfilled her mandate

(**b**) *(autorité)* mandate; **les pays sous mandat (international)** mandated countries, mandates

◇ *mandat international* international mandate

◇ *mandat de maire* mayoralty

◇ *mandat parlementaire* parliamentary mandate

◇ *mandat présidentiel* president's or presidential term of office

mandataire *nmf Pol* representative

mandater *vt Pol* **mandater qn** to elect sb, to give sb a mandate; **mandater des délégués pour un congrès** to mandate delegates to a conference

manifestant, -e *nm,f* demonstrator

manifestation *nf* demonstration; **une manifestation contre la guerre** an anti-war demonstration; **participer** *ou* **prendre part à une manifestation** to take part in a demonstration

manifeste *nm Pol* manifesto

manifester *vi* to demonstrate; **mani-**

fester contre qch to demonstrate against sth

manipulateur, -trice *nm,f* manipulator; **le comité est la proie de manipulateurs** the committee has fallen prey to a group of manipulators

manipulation *nf* manipulation; **le nouvel organisme risque d'être victime des pires manipulations** the new organization risks falling victim to the worst kinds of manipulation; **nous craignons la manipulation des statistiques de l'emploi** we are afraid the employment figures might be interfered with *or* massaged; **à travers son journal, il orchestre la manipulation de l'opinion publique** he manipulates public opinion through his newspaper

◇ **manipulations électorales** vote-rigging

manipuler *vt (personne, électeurs)* to manipulate; *(scrutin)* to rig; *(statistiques)* to massage; **l'opinion publique est plus difficile à manipuler qu'ils ne le croient** public opinion is not as easily swayed *or* manipulated as they think

marasme *nm Écon* slump, stagnation; **le marasme des affaires** the slump in business; **l'économie des pays d'Asie traverse actuellement une période de marasme** Asian economies are currently going through a period of stagnation; **dans le marasme économique actuel** in the present economic slump; **nous sommes en plein marasme** we're going through a slump, our economy's in the doldrums

“

La visite de la délégation était d'autant plus intéressante que le Japon est à un tournant de son histoire. Elle est en effet intervenue dans le contexte de la grave récession économique et financière à laquelle le pays est confronté depuis 1997, aggravée par la crise qui touche le reste de l'Asie orientale. Ce **marasme** économique se double

d'une crise politique et d'une perte de confiance généralisée dans l'avenir, tant de la part des ménages que des investisseurs.

”

marathon **1** *adj (discussion, séance)* marathon
   2 *nm*
◇ **marathon diplomatique** diplomatic marathon
◇ **marathon électoral** electoral marathon

marchandise *nf Écon (produit)* commodity; **marchandises** goods, merchandise
◇ **marchandises à l'export** export goods
◇ **marchandises à l'import** import goods

marché *nm* (a) *Écon* market; **marché des matières premières/du sucre/du café** raw materials/sugar/coffee market; **conquérir un marché** to break into a market; **arriver sur le marché** to come onto the market; **mettre** *ou* **lancer qch sur le marché** to put *or* to launch sth on the market

(b) *(accord)* deal, bargain; *(plus officiel)* contract; **faire** *ou* **passer un marché (avec qn)** to strike a deal *or* bargain (with sb), to clinch a deal (with sb)

◇ **marché à la baisse** buyers' market
◇ **marché boursier** stock market
◇ **marché des capitaux** capital market, investment market
◇ **marché des changes** currency (exchange) market
◇ *UE* **Marché commun** Common Market
◇ *UE* **Marché commun européen** European Common Market
◇ **Marché commun des pays du cône sud** Mercosur
◇ **marché demandeur** buyers' market
◇ **marché des devises étrangères** foreign exchange market
◇ **marché disputable** contestable market
◇ **marché efficient** efficient market

◇ *marché à l'export* export market

◇ *marché extérieur* foreign or overseas market

◇ *marché financier* money or financial market

◇ *marché global* global market

◇ *marché imparfait* imperfect market

◇ *marché intérieur* home or domestic market

◇ *marché international* international market

◇ *marché libre* free market

◇ *marché libre des capitaux* open money market

◇ *marché des matières premières* commodity market

◇ *marché mondial* world market

◇ *marché monétaire* money market

◇ *marché monopolistique* monopoly market

◇ *marché national* national market, home market

◇ *marché noir* black market

◇ *marché de l'or* gold market

◇ *marché ouvert* open market

◇ *marché parallèle* parallel market, black market

◇ *marché porteur* growth market

◇ *marché de produit* product market

◇ *marchés publics* public procurement

◇ *marché à terme* forward market

◇ *marché du travail* labour market

◇ *Marché unique* Single Market

◇ *Marché unique européen* Single European Market

marchéisation *nf* marketization

marge de fluctuation *nf Écon* fluctuation margin

marginal, -e *adj Écon* marginal

marginalisme *nm Écon* marginalism

marginaliste *Écon* **1** *adj* marginalist
2 *nmf* marginalist

martial, -e *adj (guerrier)* martial, warlike

marxien, -enne *adj* Marxian

marxisant, -e *adj* Marxist-influenced

marxisme *nm* Marxism

marxisme-léninisme *nm* Marxism-Leninism

marxiste 1 *adj* Marxist
2 *nmf* Marxist

marxiste-léniniste 1 *adj* Marxist-Leninist
2 *nmf* Marxist-Leninist

masse *nf Écon & Pol* **les masses** the masses

◇ *Écon masse monétaire* money supply

◇ *Écon & Pol les masses populaires* the masses, the mass of ordinary people

matériel humain *nm Écon* le **matériel humain** the workforce, human material

Matignon *nm* (l'hôtel) **Matignon** = building in Paris which houses the offices of the Prime Minister; **les accords (de) Matignon** the Matignon Agreements; *Fam* **le locataire de Matignon** the (French) Prime Minister; **Matignon a décidé que...** the Prime Minister's office has decided that...

> **"**
>
> L'incertitude porte notamment sur l'Irak, où le déclenchement d'une guerre pourrait provoquer une envolée des prix du pétrole, et sur l'évolution des marchés boursiers, en proie à une "crise grave". Pour 2002, **Matignon** a abaissé toutefois sa prévision de croissance de 1,4% à 1,2%.
>
> **"**

MCAC *nm* (*abrév* **Marché commun d'Amérique centrale**) CACM

MCCA *nm* (*abrév* **Marché commun centraméricain**) CACM

mécanisme *nm* (*processus*) mechanism

◇ *mécanisme budgétaire* budgetary mechanism

◇ *UE mécanisme de change* Exchange Rate Mechanism

◇ *UE mécanisme de change euro-péen* European Exchange Rate Mechanism

◇ *mecanismes économiques* economic machinery

◇ *mécanisme du marché* market mechanism

◇ *mécanisme de l'offre et de la demande* supply and demand mechanism

◇ *mécanisme des prix* price mechanism

◇ *UE mécanisme des taux de change* Exchange Rate Mechanism

mécontent, -e *nm,f Pol* **les mécontents** the discontented, the disgruntled; **cette politique va faire des mécontents** this measure is going to displease quite a few people

mécontentement *nm Pol* discontent, unrest; **il y a un mécontentement croissant chez les étudiants** there is growing discontent *or* unrest amongst students; **cela risque de provoquer le mécontentement des agriculteurs** that might anger the farmers

◇ *mécontentement populaire* popular unrest

Medef *nm* (*abrév* **Mouvement des Entreprises de France**) French employers' association, *Br* ≃ CBI

médiane *nf (en statistique)* median

médiateur, -trice **1** *adj* mediating, mediatory

2 *nm,f* intermediary, go-between, mediator; **servir de médiateur** to act as a go-between; **le président sert de médiateur entre les deux factions** the president is mediating *or* arbitrating between the two factions

3 *nm Pol* mediator, ombudsman; **le Médiateur** ≃ the Parliamentary Commissioner, *Br* ≃ the Ombudsman

◇ *le Médiateur européen* the European Ombudsman

◇ *le Médiateur de la République* ≃ the Parliamentary Commissioner, *Br* ≃ the Ombudsman

médiation *nf Pol* mediation

médiatisation *nf Pol* mediatization

médiatiser *vt Pol* to mediatize

membre *nm* member; **les membres de l'ONU** the members of the UN

◇ *Can Membre de l'Assemblée nationale* Member of the National Assembly

◇ *membre du Parlement* member of Parliament

◇ *membre du Parlement européen* Member of the European Parliament, MEP, Euro-MP

◇ *membre du parti* party member

mémorandum *nm (communication)* memorandum

mémorial *nm Pol* memorial

ménage *nm Écon* household

> **❝**
>
> Car, outre le climat social alourdi par la remontée du chômage, c'est la hausse du pétrole, plus importante que prévu mais peut-être provisoire, qui motive une baisse de forme de la consommation des **ménages**.
>
> **❞**

mercantile *adj Écon* mercantile

mercantilisme *nm Écon (théorie)* mercantilism; *(système)* mercantile system

mercantiliste *Écon* **1** *adj* mercantilist

2 *nmf* mercantilist

Mercosur *nm* (*abrév* **Marché commun du cône sud**) Mercosur

méritocratie *nf* meritocracy

mesure *nf* measure, step; **prendre des mesures** to take measures *or* steps *or* action; **prendre des mesures contre qch** to take action against sth

◇ *mesures d'austérité* austerity measures

◇ *mesure conservatoire* protective measure

◇ *mesures déflationnistes* deflationary measures

⬦ *mesure fiscale* fiscal measure

⬦ *mesure incitative* initiative

⬦ *mesures protectionnistes* protectionist measures

⬦ *mesures protectrices* protective measures

⬦ *mesures provisoires* temporary measures

⬦ *mesure de rétorsion* retaliatory measure, reprisal

⬦ *mesure d'urgence* emergency measure

méthode *nf Pol* strategy; **la méthode Raffarin** Raffarin's strategy

⬦ *UE* **méthode communautaire** Community method

“

En fin de compte, l'ouverture du capital de GDF, qui devait être discutée à l'Assemblée Nationale en juin, a été repoussée au minimum d'un an. Cette décision du gouvernement de renoncer (c'est un des nouveaux exemples de la **méthode** Jospin : beaucoup d'annonces mais également beaucoup de reculades) résulte de la pression exercée par le PC et une partie des députés socialistes.

”

microéconomie *nf* (a) *(discipline)* microeconomics (b) *(système)* microeconomy

microéconomique *adj* microeconomic

micro-État *nm Pol* statelet, microstate

microfinance *nf* microfinance

migrant, -e 1 *adj* migrant

2 *nm,f* migrant

⬦ *migrant économique* economic refugee

migration *nf* migration

migrer *vi* to migrate (**vers** to)

milieu *nm (entourage)* environment, milieu; **dans les milieux financiers** in financial circles

militaire 1 *adj* military

2 *nm* **les militaires** the military, the armed forces, the services

militant, -e *Pol* **1** *adj* militant

2 *nm,f* militant, activist; **les militants de base sont d'accord** the grassroots militants agree

⬦ *militant syndical* trade union militant *or* activist

militarisation *nf* militarization

militariser *vt* to militarize

militer *vi Pol* to be a militant *or* an activist; **militer au** *ou* **dans le parti socialiste** to be a socialist party activist; **militer pour/contre qch** to fight for/against sth

Mines *nfpl* **les Mines** = government department responsible for supervising all construction projects involving tunnelling

ministère *nm Pol* (a) *(charge) Br* ministry, *Am* administration; **elle a refusé le ministère qu'on lui proposait** she turned down the government position she was offered; **sous le ministère de Thiers** when Mr Thiers was (the) minister, under Mr Thiers' *Br* ministry *or Am* administration

(b) *(cabinet)* government, ministry; **former un ministère** to form a government; **entrer au ministère** to take over as a minister, *Am* to take a position in the administration

(c) *(bâtiment) Br* ministry, *Am* department (offices); *(département) Br* ministry, *Am* department

⬦ *ministère des Affaires étrangères* Ministry of Foreign Affairs, *Br* ≃ Foreign Office, *Am* ≃ State Department

⬦ *ministère des affaires sociales, du travail et de la solidarité* Ministry of Social Affairs, Employment and Solidarity

⬦ *ministère de l'Agriculture et de la Pêche* Ministry of Agriculture and Fisheries

⬦ *ministère de l'Aménagement du territoire et de l'Environnement*

Ministry for the Environment

◇ *ministère du Commerce* Ministry of Trade, *Br* ≃ Department of Trade and Industry, *Am* ≃ Department of Commerce

◇ *ministère de la Culture et de la Communication* Ministry of Culture and Communication

◇ *ministère de la Défense Br* ≃ Ministry of Defence, *Am* ≃ Department of Defense

◇ *ministère de l'Économie, des Finances et de l'Industrie* Ministry of the Economy, Finance and Industry

◇ *ministère de l'Éducation nationale, de la Recherche et de la Technologie* Ministry of Education, Research and Technology

◇ *ministère de l'Équipement, des Transports, du Logement, du Tourisme et de la Mer* Ministry of Road Maintenance, Transport, Housing, Tourism and Maritime Affairs

◇ *ministère de la Fonction publique, de la Réforme de l'État et de la Décentralisation* = ministry responsible for public sector workers, state reform and decentralization

◇ *ministère de l'Intérieur* Ministry of the Interior, *Br* ≃ Home Office, *Am* ≃ Department of Interior

◇ *ministère de la Justice Br* ≃ Lord Chancellor's Department, *Am* ≃ Department of Justice

◇ *ministère des Relations extérieures* Ministry of Foreign Affairs, *Br* ≃ Foreign Office, *Am* ≃ State Department

◇ *ministère des Relations avec le Parlement* Ministry of Parliametary Affairs

◇ *ministère de la Santé et de la Sécurité Sociale Br* ≃ Department of Health, *Am* ≃ Department of Health and Human Services

◇ *ministère des Sports* Ministry of Sport

◇ *ministère des Transports* Ministry of Transport

◇ *ministère du Travail Br* ≃ Department for Work and Pensions, *Am* ≃ Department of Labor

ministériel, -elle *adj Pol* (a) *(émanant d'un ministre)* Br ministerial, *Am* departmental (b) *(concernant le gouvernement)* cabinet, *Br* ministerial, *Am* departmental

ministre *nm Pol Br* minister, *Am* secretary

◇ *ministre des Affaires étrangères* Foreign Minister, *Br* ≃ Foreign Secretary, *Am* ≃ Secretary of State

◇ *ministre des affaires sociales, du travail et de la solidarité* Minister for Social Affairs, Employment and Solidarity

◇ *ministre de l'Agriculture et de la Pêche* Agriculture and Fisheries Minister, Minister for Agriculture and Fisheries

◇ *ministre de l'Aménagement du territoire et de l'Environnement* Minister for the Environment

◇ *ministre du Commerce Br* ≃ Secretary of State for Trade and Industry, *Am* ≃ Secretary of Commerce

◇ *ministre de la Culture* ≃ Minister for the Arts

◇ *ministre de la Culture et de la Communication* Minister of Culture and Communication

◇ *ministre de la Défense (nationale)* Minister of Defence, *Br* ≃ Secretary of State for Defence, *Am* ≃ Secretary of Defense

◇ *ministre de l'Économie, des Finances et de l'Industrie* Minister for the Economy, Finance and Industry

◇ *ministre de l'Éducation nationale, de la Recherche et de la Technologie* Minister for Education, Research and Technology

◇ *ministre de l'Équipement, des Transports, du Logement, du Tourisme et de la Mer* Minister for Road Maintenance, Transport, Housing, Tourism and Maritime Affairs

◇ *ministre d'État* = honorary title given to certain French ministers responsible for a specific office or duty

◇ *ministre de l'Intérieur* ≃ Minister of the Interior, *Br* ≃ Home Secretary, *Am* ≃ Secretary of Interior

◇ *ministre de la Justice* ≃ Justice Minister, *Br* ≃ Lord (High) Chancellor, *Am* ≃ Attorney General

◇ *ministre plénipotentiaire* Minister Plenipotentiary

◇ *ministre de la Fonction publique, de la Réforme de l'État et de la Décentralisation* = minister responsible for public sector workers, state reform and decentralization

◇ *ministre des Relations extérieures* ≃ Minister of Foreign Affairs, *Br* ≃ Foreign Secretary, *Am* ≃ Secretary of State

◇ *ministre des Relations avec le Parlement* Minister for Parliamentary Affairs

◇ *ministre sans portefeuille* Minister without portfolio

◇ *ministre de la Santé et de la Sécurité Sociale Br* ≃ Health Secretary, *Am* ≃ Secretary of Health and Human Services

◇ *ministre des Sports Br* Minister for Sport

◇ *ministre des Transports Br* ≃ Secretary of State for Transport, *Am* ≃ Secretary of Transportation

◇ *ministre du Travail Br* ≃ Secretary of State for Work and Pensions, *Am* ≃ Secretary of Labor

minoritaire 1 *adj (moins nombreux)* minority; **ils sont minoritaires à l'Assemblée** they are in the minority in the Assembly; **les femmes sont minoritaires dans cette profession** women are a minority in this profession

2 *nmf* member of a minority (group)

minorité *nf* (a) *(groupe)* minority (group) (b) **en minorité** in a or the minority; **mettre le gouvernement en minorité** to defeat the government; **la gauche a été mise en minorité lors des dernières élections** the left became the minority party at the last elections

◇ *minorité agissante* active minority

◇ *Écon minorité de blocage* blocking minority

◇ *minorité ethnique* ethnic minority

◇ *minorité nationale* national minority

miracle économique *nm* economic miracle

mise de fonds *nf* capital investment

mission *nf* (a) *(charge)* mission, assignment; *(dans le cadre d'une entreprise)* assignment; *(dossier)* brief; **un ministre en mission spéciale à Paris** a minister on a special mission to Paris (b) *(groupe)* mission

◇ *mission de bons offices* goodwill mission

◇ *mission commerciale (gouvernementale)* trade mission

◇ *mission diplomatique* diplomatic mission

> Il a demandé à M. Annan l'envoi d'un représentant pour une **mission de bons offices** auprès de la guérilla et des paramilitaires avec pour objectif d'obtenir un cessez-le-feu.

MNR *nm (abrév* **Mouvement National Républicain)** = right-wing French political party

mobilisation *nf* (a) *Pol* mobilization; **il appelle à la mobilisation de tous les syndicats** he is calling on all the unions to mobilize; **les syndicats comptent beaucoup sur la mobilisation des enseignants contre ce projet de réforme** the unions are relying heavily on the teachers rallying to fight this proposed reform (b) *Écon (des capitaux, des fonds)* mobilization

mobiliser 1 *vt* (a) *Pol (syndicalistes, électorat)* to mobilize; **ils ont mobilisé l'opinion en faveur des réfugiés politiques** they rallied public opinion for the cause of the political refugees; **mobiliser les forces vives d'une nation** to call upon the full resources of a nation (b) *Écon (capitaux, fonds)* to mobilize

2 se mobiliser *vpr Pol* to mobilize (**contre** against; **en faveur de** in support of)

mobilité *nf (du capital, des travailleurs)* mobility
◇ **mobilité sociale** upward mobility

> **"**
> On a souvent l'impression que les gens à faible revenu sont très nombreux et que pour la majorité d'entre eux, c'est une condition de vie permanente. Cette perception est, en fait, contraire à la réalité. La permanence de la pauvreté est une des questions auxquelles les recherches sur la mobilité sociale permettent de répondre. Une grande **mobilité sociale** rend possible une meilleure adaptation aux changements constants de la vie économique.
> **"**

modalité *nf* (a) *(d'application, d'une loi)* mode (b) *(circonstances)* **les modalités de l'accord** the terms of the agreement

mode *nm (en statistique)* mode

modèle *nf (représentation schématique)* model
◇ **modèle économique** economic model
◇ **modèle d'évaluation des actifs** capital asset pricing model

modéré, -e *Pol* **1** *adj* moderate
2 *nm,f* moderate

moderniser 1 *vt* to modernize
2 se moderniser *vpr* to modernize

modification *nf (à une loi)* amendment; *(à une politique)* modification, change, alteration; **apporter une modification à la loi** to amend *or* change the law

modifier *vt (loi)* to amend, to change; *(politique)* to modify, to change, to alter

modulation *nf UE* modulation

modus vivendi *nm inv Pol* modus vivendi, working arrangement

monarchie *nf* monarchy
◇ **monarchie absolue** absolute monarchy
◇ **monarchie constitutionnelle** constitutional monarchy
◇ **monarchie parlementaire** parliamentary monarchy

monarchisme *nm* monarchism

monarchiste 1 *adj* monarchist
2 *nmf* monarchist

monarque *nm* monarch

monde *nm* world
◇ **le monde libre** the Free World

mondial, -e *adj* worldwide, global, world

mondialisation *nf* globalization; **on assiste à la mondialisation de la reprise économique** a worldwide economic revival is taking place
◇ **la mondialisation libérale** liberal globalization

mondialiser 1 *vt* to globalize
2 se mondialiser *vpr* to become globalized; **la crise s'est rapidement mondialisée** the crisis has rapidly taken on an international dimension

monétaire *adj Écon* monetary

monétarisme *nm Écon* monetarism

monétariste *Écon* **1** *adj* monetarist
2 *nmf* monetarist

monétisation *nf Écon* monetization

monétiser *vt Écon* to monetize

monnaie *nf (d'un pays)* currency; *Écon* **la mauvaise monnaie chasse la bonne** bad currency drives out good
◇ *UE* **monnaie commune** common currency
◇ **monnaie faible** soft currency
◇ **monnaie forte** hard currency
◇ **monnaie d'or** gold currency
◇ **monnaie de réserve** reserve currency
◇ **monnaie unique** single currency
◇ **monnaie verte** green currency

monocaméral, -e *adj Pol* unicameral

monocaméralisme *nm Pol* unicameralism

monocolore *adj Pol* one-party

monolithique *adj (État, gouvernement)* monolithic

monométallisme *nm Écon* monometallism

monopole *nm Écon* monopoly; **avoir
le monopole de qch** to have a monopoly on sth; **exercer un monopole sur
un secteur** to monopolize a sector
◇ *monopole d'achat* buyer's monopoly
◇ *monopole bilatéral* bilateral monopoly
◇ *monopole d'embauche* closed shop
◇ *monopole d'État* state monopoly,
government monopoly
◇ *monopole d'exploitation* operating
monopoly
◇ *monopole de fabrication* manufacturing monopoly
◇ *monopole naturel* natural monopoly
◇ *monopole des prix* price monopoly,
price ring
◇ *monopole de vente* sales monopoly

monopoleur, -euse *nm,f* monopolist

monopolisation *nf* monopolization

monopoliser *vt* (a) *Écon* to monopolize, to have a monopoly on (b) **monopoliser l'antenne** *(parti politique,
groupe de pression)* to rule *or* to monopolize the airwaves; **il a monopolisé
l'antenne pendant la majeure partie
du débat** he dominated the discussion
for most of the programme

monopoliste 1 *adj* monopolistic
 2 *nmf* monopolist

monopolistique *adj* monopolistic

monopsone *nm Écon* monopsony

montage financier *nm Écon* financial arrangement

montagne *nf*
◇ *UE montagne de beurre* butter
mountain

◇ *UE montagne de bœuf* beef mountain

montant compensatoire *nm UE*
compensatory amount
◇ *montants compensatoires monétaires* monetary compensatory
amounts

moral des ménages *nm Écon* consumer morale

Le **moral des ménages** français est
resté stable en novembre par rapport
à octobre, qui s'était caractérisé par le
premier redressement après quatre
mois de baisse, indique mardi l'INSEE.

moratoire *nm* moratorium; **décréter
ou déclarer un moratoire** to declare a
moratorium

Les manifestations de ces épar-
gnants avaient déjà fait chuter le
président Fernando de la Rua et son
éphémère successeur qui avait **déclaré un moratoire** unilatéral sur la
dette publique du pays (141 milliards
de dollars).

moratorium *nm* moratorium; **décréter *ou* déclarer un moratorium** to declare a moratorium

morose *adj (économie)* sluggish, slack

morosité *nf (de l'économie)* sluggishness, slackness

mot d'ordre *nm Pol* slogan, catchword

motion *nf* motion; **voter une motion**
to pass a motion; **la motion a été adoptée** the motion was carried
◇ *motion de censure* vote of no
confidence

mouvance *nf Pol (domaine d'influence)* circle of influence; **ils se situ-
ent dans la mouvance socialiste** they
belong to the socialist camp

> L'AKP, qui rejette l'étiquette d'isla-
> miste, est profondément enraciné en
> Anatolie et dans les grandes villes,
> où il semble avoir attiré non seule-
> ment les électeurs issus de la **mou-
> vance** islamiste, mais également
> ceux des partis conservateurs du
> centre et de la droite nationaliste.

mouvement nm (a) Pol (action collective) movement (b) Écon (déplacement) movement; (tendance) trend
◇ Écon **mouvement ascensionnel** upward trend
◇ Écon **mouvement de baisse** downward trend
◇ Écon **mouvement des capitaux**
movement or flow of capital
◇ Pol **mouvement clandestin** underground movement
◇ Pol **mouvement de contestation**
protest movement
◇ Écon **mouvement de hausse** upward trend
◇ Pol **mouvement indépendantiste**
independence or separatist movement
◇ **Mouvement National Républicain**
= right-wing French political party
◇ Pol **mouvement ouvrier** labour movement
◇ Pol **mouvement pacifiste** peace
movement
◇ Pol **mouvement pour la paix** peace
movement
◇ Pol **mouvement de protestation**
protest rally
◇ Pol **mouvement séparatiste** separatist or independence movement
◇ Pol **mouvement social** industrial
action

◇ Pol **mouvement syndical** Br trade-
union or Am labor-union movement

moyen¹, -enne¹ adj (prix, salaire,
consommation) average

moyen² nm (façon, possibilité)
means; **avoir les moyens de sa politique** to be able to deliver (on a policy)
◇ Écon **moyen d'échange** medium of
exchange
◇ Écon **moyen de production** means
of production

moyenne² nf average, mean; **établir
la moyenne de qch** to average sth
◇ **moyenne mobile** moving average
◇ **moyenne pondérée** weighted average

multilatéral, -e adj multilateral

multilatéralisme nm multilateralism

multinational, -e 1 adj multinational
2 nf **multinationale** multinational

multipartisme nm multiparty system

multipartite adj multiparty, multipartite

multiplicateur nm Écon multiplier
◇ **multiplicateur du commerce extérieur** foreign trade multiplier

municipal, -e Pol **1** adj (élection,
conseil) local, municipal
2 nfpl **municipales** local or Br council
elections

mutation nf (a) (d'une entreprise, d'un
marché) change (b) (d'un employé,
d'un fonctionnaire) transfer

muter vt (employé, fonctionnaire) to
transfer

nation *nf* nation
- *nation commerçante* mercantile nation
- *nation la plus favorisée* most favoured nation
- *les Nations Unies* the United Nations
- *nation en voie de développement* developing nation

national, -e 1 *adj (de la nation)* national; *(économie, monnaie)* domestic; *(parti, politique)* nationalist
  2 *nmpl* **nationaux** nationals

nationalisation *nf* nationalization

nationalisé, -e *adj* nationalized

nationaliser *vt* to nationalize

nationalisme *nm* Pol nationalism

nationaliste *Pol* **1** *adj* nationalist, nationalistic
  2 *nmf* nationalist

national-populisme *nm* Pol national populism

national-socialisme *Pol nm* National Socialism

national-socialiste *Pol* **1** *adj* National Socialist
  2 *nmf* National Socialist

navette parlementaire *nf Parl* = successive readings of bills by the "Assemblée nationale" and the "Sénat"

> Les députés ont adopté à l'unanimité la proposition de loi visant à moderniser le statut des SEM dans sa version issue de la commission mixte paritaire. La **navette parlementaire** s'achèvera, le 20 décembre, par l'adoption définitive de cette réforme par le Sénat.

négoce *nm (commerce)* trade; **faire le négoce de qch** to trade in sth; **faire du négoce avec un pays** to trade with a country
- *le négoce international* international trade *or* trading

négociateur, -trice *nm,f Pol* negotiator

négociation *nf Pol* negotiation; **entamer des négociations (sur qch)** to enter into negotiations (on sth); **les deux pays ont engagé des négociations** the two countries have begun negotiations
- *négociations d'adhésion* accession negotiations
- *négociations collectives* joint negotiations
- *négociations commerciales* trade negotiations
- *négociations commerciales multilatérales* multilateral trade negotiations
- *négociations pour la paix* peace negotiations

négocier *Pol* **1** *vt* to negotiate (**avec** with)
  2 *vi (discuter)* to negotiate (**avec** with)

NEI *nm (abrév* **Nouvel État Indépendant)** newly independent state, NIS

néocapitalisme *nm* neo-capitalism

néocapitaliste 1 *adj* neo-capitalist
  2 *nmf* neo-capitalist

néocolonial, -e *adj* neocolonial

néocolonialisme *nm* neocolonialism

néocolonialiste 1 *adj* neocolonial,
neocolonialist
  2 *nmf* neocolonialist

néofascisme *nm* neofascism

néofasciste 1 *adj* neofascist
  2 *nmf* neofascist

néolibéral, -e 1 *adj* neo-liberal
  2 *nm,f* neo-liberal

néolibéralisme *nm* neo-liberalism

néomercantilisme *nm* Écon neomercantilism

néonazi, -e 1 *adj* neo-Nazi
  2 *nm,f* neo-Nazi

néonazisme *nm* neo-Nazism, neo-
Naziism

net, nette *adj* *(revenu, salaire, augmentation)* net

netéconomie *nf* Écon Internet economy

nettoyage ethnique *nm* Pol ethnic
cleansing

neutraliser Pol **1** *vt* *(déclarer neutre)*
to neutralize; **neutraliser un État** to
neutralize a state
  2 se neutraliser *vpr* to neutralize

neutralisme *nm* Pol neutralism

neutraliste Pol **1** *adj* neutralist, neu-
tralistic
  2 *nmf* neutralist

neutralité *nf* Pol neutrality; **observer
la neutralité** to remain neutral; **sortir
de sa neutralité** to abandon one's neutrality *or* one's neutral position; **violer
la neutralité d'un État** to violate a state's neutrality

neutre Pol **1** *adj* neutral
  2 *nmf* **les neutres** the neutral countries

New Deal *nm* Pol **le New Deal** the
New Deal

niveau *nm* *(degré)* level; **maintenir les**

prix à un niveau élevé to maintain prices at a high level
◇ *niveau de prix* price level

niveleur, -euse *nm,f* Pol leveller

nomenklatura *nf* **(a)** Pol nomenklatura **(b)** *(élite)* elite; **faire partie de la
nomenklatura** to be part of the Establishment

nomination *nf* *(désignation)* appointment, nomination (**à** to)

nommer *vt* *(désigner)* to appoint (**à**
to); **le président a nommé son gouvernement** the President appointed the
government

non *nm* Parl no; **les non de la majorité**
the noes of the majority

non-agression *nf* non-aggression

non-aligné, -e Pol **1** *adj* nonaligned
  2 *nm,f* nonaligned country

non-alignement *nm* Pol nonalignment

non-cumul *nm* Pol **les règles de non-
cumul des mandats** the laws prohibit-
ing politicians from holding more
than one post at a time

non-intervention *nf* nonintervention; **une politique de non-intervention** a noninterventionist policy

non-interventionniste 1 *adj* noninterventionist
  2 *nmf* non-interventionist

non-marchand, -e *adj* Écon non-
market

non-prolifération *nf* non-proliferation

non-violence *nf* nonviolence

non-violent, -e 1 *adj* nonviolent
  2 *nm,f* non-violent protester

nouveau, -elle *adj* new
◇ Pol **la nouvelle droite** the New
Right
◇ *nouvelle économie* new economy
◇ *nouvel État indépendant* newly in-
dependent state
◇ Pol **la nouvelle gauche** the New
Left

◇ *nouveau pays industrialisé* newly industrialized country

noyau dur *nm Pol* hard core

> **"**
>
> "Mais la salle de la Convention, là où les décisions sont prises, sera remplie du **noyau dur** du parti : de riches hommes blancs," indique le Chicago Tribune qui ajoute : " Les délégués présents aujourd'hui ressemblent à ceux des précédentes Conventions.
>
> **"**

noyautage *nm Pol* infiltration, entryism

noyauter *vt Pol* to infiltrate; **le syndicat a été noyauté** the union has been infiltrated

NPF *nf* (*abrév* **nation plus favorisée**) MFN

NPI *nf* (*abrév* **nouveau pays industrialisé**) NIC

nucléaire *adj* nuclear

nucléarisation *nf* nuclearization

nucléariser *vt* to supply with nuclear weapons, to nuclearize

objecteur de conscience *nm Pol* conscientious objector

obligation *nf* bond
◇ *obligation assimilable du Trésor* = French government bond
◇ *obligation d'État* government bond

observateur, -trice *nm,f Pol* observer; **un observateur de l'ONU** a UN observer

observatoire *nm Écon*
◇ *Observatoire français des conjonctures économiques* = economic research institute
◇ *observatoire des prix* price-monitoring watchdog

obstruction *nf Pol* **faire de l'obstruction** to obstruct (legislation)

obstructionnisme *nm Pol* obstructionism

obstructionniste *Pol* **1** *adj* obstructionist
2 *nmf* obstructionist

Occident *nm Pol* **l'Occident** the West, the Occident

Occidental, -e *nm,f Pol* Westerner, Occidental

occidental, -e *adj Pol* Western, Occidental; **les pays occidentaux, le monde occidental** Western countries, the West

occupation *nf Pol (d'un pays, d'un territoire)* occupation

occupé, -e *adj Pol (pays, territoire)* occupied

occuper *vt Pol (envahir)* to occupy, to take over; **les rebelles occupent tout le Nord** the rebels have occupied the entire northern area

OCDE *nf (abrév* **Organisation de coopération et de développement économique)** OECD

ochlocrate *nmf* ochlocrat

ochlocratie *nf* ochlocracy

ochlocratique *adj* ochlocratic

OECE *nf (abrév* **Organisation européenne de coopération économique)** OEEC

offensive de paix *nf* peace offensive

office *nm* **(a)** *(fonction)* office **(b)** *(agence)* office, bureau
◇ *Office du commerce extérieur* Foreign Trade Office
◇ *office ministériel* ministerial office

officiel, -elle **1** *adj (public)* official; **il a rendu officielle sa décision de démissionner** he made public *or* he officially announced his decision to resign
2 *nm (représentant)* official; **les officiels du Parti** the Party officials

officier de renseignements *nm Pol* intelligence officer

offre *nf Écon* supply; **l'offre et la demande** supply and demand; **lorsque l'offre excède la demande, les prix ont tendance à baisser** when supply exceeds demand, prices have a tendency to fall
◇ *offre de devises* currency supply
◇ *offre excédentaire* excess supply
◇ *offre globale* aggregate supply
◇ *offre de monnaie* money supply

offreur, -euse *nm,f Écon* seller

ogive *nf* warhead
◇ *ogive nucléaire* nuclear warhead

OIT *nf (abrév* **Organisation internationale du travail)** ILO

oligarchie *nf* oligarchy

oligarchique *adj* oligarchic, oligarchical

oligarque *nm* oligarch

oligopole *nm Écon* oligopoly

oligopolistique *adj Écon* oligopolistic

oligopsone *nm Écon* oligopsony

oligopsonique *adj Écon* oligopsonistic

ombudsman *nm* ombudsman

OMC *nf (abrév* **Organisation mondiale du commerce)** WTO

omnium *nm Écon* combine

Oncle Sam *nm (gouvernement des USA)* Uncle Sam

ONG *nf (abrév* **organisation non gouvernementale)** NGO

ONU *nf (abrév* **Organisation des Nations unies)** UN, UNO

ONUDI, Onudi *nf (abrév* **Organisation des Nations unies pour le développement industriel)** UNIDO

onusien, -enne *adj* UN; **projet/expert onusien** UN project/expert

"

Le ministère des affaires étrangères n'a pas caché son "inquiétude" quand au sort des troupes américaines, qui sont également déployées – sous la bannière de l'OTAN – en vertu d'un mandat **onusien**.

"

open-market *nm* open market

OPEP *nf (abrév* **Organisation des pays exportateurs de pétrole)** OPEC

opération *nf (transaction)* operation, transaction

◇ *opération de change* exchange transaction
◇ *opération mercantile* mercantile operation

opinion *nf (point de vue)* opinion (**de** of; **sur** about *or* on); **opinions politiques/subversives** political/subversive views; **informer l'opinion** to inform the public
◇ *opinion publique* public opinion

opposant, -e 1 *adj (adverse)* opposing
2 *nm,f (adversaire)* opponent (**à** of); *Br Pol* member of the Opposition; **les opposants au régime** the opponents of the regime; **les opposants à la politique actuelle** those who oppose current policy

opposer s'opposer *vpr* **s'opposer à** *(être contre)* to object to, to oppose; **le premier ministre s'est opposé au projet de loi** the prime minister opposed the bill

opposition *nf* (a) *(résistance)* opposition; **le ministre a fait** *ou* **mis opposition au projet** the minister opposed the plan; **nous avons rencontré une forte opposition** we encountered strong opposition; **la loi est passée sans opposition** the bill went through unopposed (b) *Br Pol* **l'opposition** the Opposition; **les dirigeants/partis de l'opposition** the Opposition leaders/parties

oppositionnel, -elle *Pol* **1** *adj* oppositional, opposition
2 *nm,f* oppositionist

oppresseur *nm* oppressor

oppressif, -ive *adj* oppressive

oppression *nf (d'un peuple, d'une nation)* oppression

opprimer *vt* (a) *(peuple, nation)* to oppress (b) *(la presse)* to gag

optimal, -e *adj* optimal, optimum

optimalité de Pareto *nf Écon* Pareto optimality

optimum 1 *adj* optimum, optimal

2 *nm* optimum; **optimum second** second best

opting-out *nm UE* opting out

option zéro *nf Pol* zero option

opt-out *nm Pol* opt-out

orange *Belg Pol* **1** *adj* Christian Socialist
2 *nmf* Christian Socialist

orangisme *nm Pol* Orangeism

orangiste *Pol* **1** *adj (en Irlande du Nord)* Orange
2 *nmf* Orangeman, *f* Orangewoman

ordonnance *nf Pol (loi)* ordinance, statutory instrument; **gouverner par ordonnances** to govern by decree

ordinaire *adj Pol (session)* ordinary

ordre du jour *nm* agenda; *Parl* order of the day

organe *nm* **(a)** *(institution)* organ; **les organes de l'État** the apparatus of the state **(b)** *(porte-parole, publication)* mouthpiece, organ; **l'organe officiel du parti** the official organ *or* mouthpiece of the party

organisation *nf* organization

◇ *Organisation de coopération et de développement économiques* Organization for Economic Cooperation and Development

◇ *Organisation européenne de coopération économique* Organization for European Economic Cooperation

◇ *organisation gouvernementale* governmental organization

◇ *organisation humanitaire* aid agency

◇ *organisation internationale* international organization *or* agency

◇ *Organisation internationale de normalisation* International Standards Organization

◇ *Organisation internationale du travail* International Labour Organization

◇ *Organisation mondiale du commerce* World Trade Organization

◇ *Organisation des Nations unies* United Nations Organization

◇ *Organisation des Nations unies pour le développement industriel* United Nations Industrial Development Organization

◇ *organisation non gouvernementale* non-governmental organization

◇ *organisation patronale* employers' organization *or* association

◇ *Organisation des pays exportateurs de pétrole* Organization of Petroleum Exporting Countries

◇ *organisation politique* political organization

◇ *organisation de solidarité* aid organization

◇ *organisation de solidarité internationale* international aid organization

◇ *organisation syndicale* trade union

◇ *Organisation du traité de l'Atlantique Nord* North Atlantic Treaty Organization

◇ *organisation de travailleurs* workers' organization

organisme *nm (organisation)* organization, body, institution

◇ *organisme d'aide* aid organization

◇ *organisme de contrôle* watchdog

◇ *organisme international* international organization

◇ *organisme de normalisation* standards committee

◇ *organisme professionnel* professional body

◇ *organisme de surveillance* watchdog

orientation *nf (d'un mouvement)* orientation; *(d'une politique)* thrust

◇ *orientation politique (d'un journal, d'une personne)* political leanings *or* tendencies; *(d'un parti)* political direction

OSI *nf (abrév* **organisation de solidarité internationale***)* international aid organization

OTAN, Otan *nf (abrév* **Organisation du traité de l'Atlantique Nord***)* NATO

oui *nm Parl* aye, yes; **un oui franc et massif** a solid yes vote; **les oui et les non** the yesses *or* ayes and the noes; **il y a eu cinq oui** there were five votes for *or* five ayes

outre-mer *adv* overseas; **la France d'outre-mer** France's overseas territories and departments

ouverture *nf Pol* **(a)** *(d'une session, d'un débat)* opening **(b)** **l'ouverture vers la gauche/droite** broadening the base of government to the left/right

ouvriérisme *nm Pol (autogestion)* worker control; *(syndicalisme) Br* trade unionism, *Am* labor unionism

ouvrir *vt (session, débat, négociations)* to open

PAC, Pac *nf UE* (*abrév* **politique agricole commune**) CAP

pacificateur, -trice *Pol* **1** *adj* peacemaking

2 *nm,f* peacemaker

pacification *nf Pol* pacification

pacifique *adj Pol* peace-loving

pacifiquement *adv Pol* peacefully, pacifically; **le changement de régime s'est fait pacifiquement** the change of regime was achieved by peaceful means

pacte *nm Pol* pact, treaty, agreement
◇ *pacte de non-agression* non-aggression pact
◇ *UE pacte de stabilité* stability pact
◇ *UE pacte de stabilité et de croissance* stability and growth pact

pair *nm* peer
◇ *pair à vie* life peer

pairie *nf* peerage
◇ *pairie à vie* life peerage

paix *nf Pol* peace; **demander la paix** to sue for peace; **une menace pour la paix mondiale** a threat to world peace; **négocier la paix** to negotiate peace; **en temps de paix** in peacetime; **faire la paix** to make peace; **signer/ratifier un traité de paix** to sign/to ratify a peace treaty
◇ *paix armée* armed peace
◇ *paix séparée* separate peace

palais *nm* palace
◇ *le Palais Brongniart* = the Paris Stock Exchange
◇ *le Palais du Luxembourg* = the seat of the French Senate

Palais-Bourbon *nm* **le Palais-Bourbon** = the seat of the French National Assembly

PAM *nm* (*abrév* **programme alimentaire mondial**) WFP

pamphlet *nm Pol* pamphlet

pamphlétaire *nmf Pol* pamphleteer

panachage *nm Pol* panachage, = voting for candidates from different parties rather than from the set list of one party

> Par ailleurs, pour les élections municipales dans les communes de moins de 3 500 habitants, les électeurs peuvent pratiquer le **panachage**. Ils peuvent composer euxmêmes la liste pour laquelle ils votent, en changeant et en ajoutant des noms.

panacher *vt Pol* **panacher une liste électorale** = to vote for candidates from different parties rather than from the set list of one party

panafricain, -e *adj* Pan-African

panafricanisme *nm* Pan-Africanism

panaméricain, -e *adj* Pan-American

panaméricanisme *nm* Pan-Americanism

panarabe *adj* Pan-Arab

panarabisme *nm* Pan-Arabism

paneuropéen, -enne *adj* Pan-European

paneuropéanisme *nm* Pan-Europeanism

panier *nm Écon*
◇ *panier de devises* basket of currencies
◇ *le panier de la ménagère* the shopping basket
◇ *panier de monnaies* basket of currencies

Panthère noires *nfpl Pol* les Panthères noires the Black Panthers

papier *nm* papiers (official) papers
◇ *Pol papier ministre* official paper

paquet fiscal *nm* tax package

❝

Cependant, M. Bush, accusé d'avoir passé, au printemps 2001, des réductions d'impôts avantageant les plus aisés, souhaite des dispositions favorables, cette fois, aux revenus modestes et moyens … Le **paquet fiscal** 2003 ne comprendrait donc pas seulement des mesures dénoncées d'avance par la gauche … Il comprendrait aussi des aides pour les foyers plus modestes, comme l'augmentation du crédit d'impôt pour enfants à charge.

❞

paradigme économique *nm* economic paradigm

paradis fiscal *nm* tax haven

paradoxe de l'épargne *nm Écon* paradox of thrift

parallèle *adj (marché, transaction)* unofficial

parapluie atomique, parapluie nucléaire *nm* nuclear umbrella

parité *nf Écon* parity
◇ *parité de change* parity of exchange
◇ *parité euro-dollar* euro-dollar parity
◇ *parité des monnaies* monetary parity
◇ *parité hommes-femmes* sexual equality

◇ *parité du pouvoir d'achat* purchasing power parity
◇ *parité rampante* crawling peg

parlement *nm* parliament; le Parlement Parliament; au Parlement in Parliament
◇ *Parlement bicaméral* bicameral *or* two-chamber parliament
◇ *Parlement européen* European Parliament

parlementaire 1 *adj (débat, habitude, régime)* parliamentary
2 *nmf (député) (en France)* deputy; *(en Grande-Bretagne)* Member of Parliament; *(aux États-Unis)* Congressman, *f* Congresswoman
◇ *parlementaire européen* member of the European Parliament, Euro-MP, MEP

parlementarisme *nm* parliamentarism, parliamentary government

parlementer *vi* to negotiate; *Pol* **parlementer avec** to parley with

parler-vrai *nm Pol* straight talking

❝

Le nouveau président est appuyé cette fois par un très large spectre de forces politiques et ses premiers discours ont été marqués du sceau du **parler-vrai**. L'Argentine est en faillite a-t-il déclaré sans détour … Pour les Argentins, ce **parler-vrai** est bienvenu mais il représente aussi un saut dans l'inconnu.

❞

parole *nf* prendre la parole *(au parlement, au tribunal)* to take the floor; **vous avez la parole** you have the floor

parrain *nm Pol (d'un candidat, d'un postulant)* proposer, *Am* sponsor

parrainage *nm Pol (d'un candidat, d'un postulant)* proposing, *Am* sponsoring

parrainer *vt Pol (candidat, postulant)* to propose, *Am* to sponsor

parraineur nm Pol (d'un candidat, d'un postulant) proposer, Am sponsor

part nf Écon share
◊ **part de marché** market share

partage du pouvoir nm power sharing

partenaire nmf Écon (business) partner
◊ **partenaires commerciaux** trading partners
◊ **les partenaires sociaux** the two sides of industry, unions and management

partenariat nm (trading) partnership
◊ **partenariat public-privé** Public-Private Partnership, private finance initiative

parti nm Pol party; **les partis de droite** the parties of the right, the right-wing parties; **les partis de gauche** the parties of the left, the left-wing parties; **à parti unique** one-party
◊ **le Parti communiste** the Communist Party
◊ **le Parti communiste français** the French Communist Party
◊ **le Parti conservateur** (en Grande-Bretagne) the Conservative Party, the Tory Party; (au Canada) the Progressive Conservative Party
◊ **parti croupion** rump party
◊ **le Parti démocrate** the Democratic Party
◊ **parti majoritaire** majority party
◊ **parti minoritaire** minority party
◊ **parti politique** political party
◊ **le Parti radical** = right-of-centre French political party
◊ **le Parti radical de gauche** = left-of-centre French political party
◊ **le Parti républicain** the Republican Party
◊ **le Parti socialiste** = left-of-centre French political party
◊ **le Parti travailliste** (en Grande-Bretagne) the Labour Party

participation nf (a) Pol turnout; **un faible taux de** ou **une faible participation aux élections** a poor or low turn-

nout at the polls (**b**) Écon (détention de capital) interest, share
◊ **participation aux bénéfices** profit-sharing
◊ **participation croisée** crossholding
◊ **participation électorale** voter turnout
◊ **participation aux frais** cost sharing
◊ **participation majoritaire** majority interest
◊ **participation minoritaire** minority interest
◊ **participation ouvrière** worker participation
◊ **participation des salariés aux bénéfices** profit-sharing scheme

participer participer à vt ind Écon (profits, pertes) to share (in); **participer aux bénéfices** to share in the profits

partielle nf Pol by-election

partisan, -e 1 adj (querelles) sectarian; (esprit) partisan
2 nm,f (**a**) (adepte, défenseur) supporter (**b**) (dans une guerre) partisan

partition nf Pol partition, partitioning; **lors de la partition de l'Inde** when India was partitioned

passation des pouvoirs nf Pol transfer of power

> François Bayrou l'a nommé, en 1993, à la fois président du Conseil national des Programmes (CNP) et parrain d'une de ses filles, Claude Allègre l'a reconduit dans ses fonctions (mais ne lui a confié aucun de ses enfants) et Jack Lang, qui ne tarit pas d'éloges sur cet autre séducteur, l'a gardé comme conseiller pour les programmes. Le jour de la **passation de pouvoirs**, on eût dit que l'ancien ministre partait quelques semaines en vacances et laissait la maison à son homme de confiance.

passer vi Pol (projet de loi, amende-

ment) to pass, to be passed; *(député)* to be elected, to get in; **la loi est passée** the law was passed; **si les socialistes passent** if the socialists get in *or* are elected

paternalisme *nm Pol* paternalism

paternaliste *adj Pol* paternalist, paternalistic

patronage *nm Pol (soutien officiel)* patronage; **sous le haut patronage du président de la République** under the patronage of the President of the Republic

patronat *nm* employers; **le patronat et les syndicats** employers and unions

paupérisation *nf Écon* pauperization

paupériser *Écon* **1** *vt* to pauperize
2 se paupériser *vpr* to become pauperized

pauvre 1 *adj* poor; **il recrute ses partisans dans les milieux pauvres** his supporters come from the poorer sections of the population
2 *nmf* poor person; **les pauvres** the poor

pauvreté *nf (manque d'argent)* poverty; **pauvreté relative** relative poverty

pays *nm* country
◇ *UE* **pays candidat** applicant country
◇ **pays créditeur** creditor country, creditor nation
◇ **pays débiteur** debtor country, debtor nation
◇ **pays développé** developed country
◇ **pays émergent** newly industrialized country
◇ **pays d'Europe centrale et orientale** Central and East European Countries
◇ **pays d'Europe de l'Est** Eastern European countries, countries of Eastern Europe
◇ **pays exportateur** exporting country
◇ **pays importateur** importing country

◇ *UE* **pays in** = EU member state that has adopted the euro
◇ **pays industrialisé** industrialized country
◇ **pays membre** member state
◇ *UE* **pays out** = EU member state that has not adopted the euro
◇ **pays pétrolier** oil-producing country
◇ *UE* **pays pré-in** = EU member state that has not yet adopted the euro
◇ **pays signataire** *(d'un accord)* signatory country
◇ **pays sous-développé** developing country
◇ *UE* **pays tiers** third *or* non-EU country
◇ **pays en voie de développement** developing country

paysage politique *nm* political landscape

"

Le raz-de-marée populaire qui a porté au pouvoir, dimanche 3 novembre, le Parti de la justice et du développement (AKP), issu de la mouvance islamiste, remodèle totalement le **paysage politique** turc en balayant 16 des 18 partis en lice pour ces législatives, dont les trois membres de la coalition sortante.

"

PC *nm (abrév* **Parti Communiste***)* CP

PCF *nm (abrév* **Parti Communiste français***)* French Communist Party

PECO *nm (abrév* **pays d'Europe centrale et orientale***)* CEEC

pénurie *nf (manque)* **pénurie de** lack *or* shortage of
◇ *Écon* **pénurie de main-d'œuvre** labour shortage

percée *nf Écon* breakthrough; **faire une percée dans un marché** to break into a market

perchoir *nm Parl* = raised platform for the seat of the President of the French National Assembly; **obtenir**

le perchoir to become President of the (French) National Assembly

> **"**
>
> Mercredi matin, sur RTL, M. Leroy a indiqué qu'il soutiendrait M. Morin : "Quand on est 31, il faut quelqu'un qui connaisse bien les arcanes parlementaires", a-t-il expliqué, avant d'ajouter quels centristes soutiendraient "évidemment" la candidature de M. Balladur au **perchoir**.
>
> **"**

péréquation *nf Écon (d'impôts, de salaires)* equalization

période de double circulation *nf UE (de la monnaie nationale et de l'euro)* double circulation period

permanence *nf Pol* ≃ surgery

permis *nm* permit
◇ **permis d'exportation** export permit
◇ **permis d'importation** import permit

personnel *nm (d'une entreprise)* staff, workforce; *(d'un service)* staff, personnel
◇ **personnel d'ambassade** embassy staff
◇ **personnel titulaire** permanent staff

PESC *nf UE (abrév* **politique étrangère et de sécurité commune***)* CFSP

petit, -e *adj*
◇ *Pol* **petit fonctionnaire** minor official
◇ **petite et moyenne entreprise** small business, SME
◇ **petite et moyenne entreprise industrielle** small industrial firm, SMI
◇ **petite phrase** *(énoncé)* soundbite

pétition *nf (texte)* petition; **adresser une pétition à qn** to petition sb

pétitionner *vi* to petition

pétrole *nm* oil, petroleum
◇ **pétrole brut** crude oil

pétrolier, -ère *adj (industrie, compagnie, choc)* oil; *(pays)* oil-producing

pétromonarchie *nf* oil kingdom

phalangiste *Pol* **1** *adj* Falangist
2 *nmf* Falangist

PHARE *nm UE (abrév* **Pologne Hongrie Aide à la Reconstruction Économique***)* PHARE

physiocrate *nm Écon* physiocrat

physiocratie *nf Écon* physiocracy

PIB *nm Écon (abrév* **produit intérieur brut***)* GDP
◇ **PIB nominal** nominal income
◇ **PIB potentiel** potential GDP

piétinement *nm Écon (stagnation)* stagnation

> **"**
>
> Mais avant même le krach des Bourses mondiales, les chefs d'entreprise s'inquiètent du **piétinement** de l'économie.
>
> **"**

piétiner *vi Écon (stagner)* to stagnate

pilier *nm UE* pillar

PIN *nm Écon (abrév* **produit intérieur net***)* NDP

piquet *nm* picket
◇ **piquet de grève** picket
◇ **piquets de grève volants** flying pickets

placement *nm (investissement)* investment

placer *vt (investir)* to invest

plafond *nm (limite)* ceiling; **le dollar a atteint son plafond** the dollar has reached its ceiling *or* upper limit; **crever le plafond** to exceed the limit, to break the ceiling; **fixer un plafond à un budget** to put a ceiling on a budget, to cap a budget
◇ **plafond des charges budgétaires** spending limit, budgetary limit
◇ **plafond de crédit** credit ceiling *or* limit
◇ **plafond de l'impôt** tax ceiling

plan *nm* **(a)** *Écon* plan **(b)** **sur le plan économique/politique** on the economic/political front

◇ *plan d'assainissement* stabilization plan

◇ *plan d'austérité* austerity programme

◇ *plan de campagne* campaign plan

◇ *plan quinquennal* Five Year plan

◇ *plan de redressement* recovery plan

◇ *plan social (du gouvernement)* = corporate restructuring plan, usually involving job losses

planétaire *adj (mondial)* worldwide, global

planétarisation *nf* globalization

planifiable *adj Écon* plannable

planificateur, -trice *nm,f Écon* planner

planification *nf Écon* planning

◇ *planification budgétaire* budget planning

◇ *planification à court terme* short-term planning

◇ *planification économique* economic planning

◇ *planification à long terme* long-term planning

◇ *planification nationale* state planning

◇ *planification stratégique* strategic planning

planifié, -e *adj Écon (économie)* planned

planifier *vt Écon* to plan

plate-forme *nf Pol* platform

◇ *plate-forme électorale* election platform

plébiscite *nm* plebiscite

plébisciter *vt* **(a)** *(élire) (par plébiscite)* to elect by (a) plebiscite; *(à une large majorité)* to elect by a large majority **(b)** *(approuver)* to approve (by a large majority)

plein-emploi *nm Écon* full employment

> **"**
>
> Avec un taux de chômage à 9,5 %, la France connaît le **plein-emploi**, pensent certains. Pour le faire baisser, il faudrait s'attaquer aux "causes structurelles". C'est-à-dire aux deux boulets qui entravent la création d'emplois : le montant des charges et la complexité administrative. Seul problème : chaque fois que les politiques réduisent les charges, ils accroissent la complexité. Donc, on stagne.
>
> **"**

plénier, -ère *adj* plenary

plénipotentiaire 1 *adj* plenipotentiary

2 *nmf* plenipotentiary

plénum *nm Pol* plenum

plural, -e *adj Pol* plural

pluralisme *nm Pol* pluralism

pluraliste *Pol* **1** *adj* pluralist, pluralistic

2 *nmf* pluralist

pluralité *nf Pol* plurality

pluripartisme *nm* pluralist (party) *or* multi-party system

pluripartite *adj* pluralist, multiparty

plus-value *nf Écon (bénéfice)* capital gain, profit; *(augmentation de la valeur)* appreciation, increase in value

PmaC *nf Écon (abrév* **propension marginale à consommer)** APC

PmaE *nf Écon (abrév* **propension marginale à épargner)** APS

PME *nf (abrév* **petite et moyenne entreprise)** small business, SME

PMI *nf (abrév* **petite et moyenne entreprise industrielle)** small industrial firm, SMI

PmoC *nf Écon (abrév* **propension moyenne à consommer)** APC

PmoE *nf Écon (abrév* **propension moyenne à épargner)** APS

PNB *nm Écon (abrév* **produit national brut)** GNP

PNN *nm Écon (abrév* **produit national net)** NNP

PNUD nm (abrév **programme des Nations unies pour le développement**) UNDP

pointage nm (de votes) counting

pointer vt (votes) to count

pôle nm
◊ Écon **pôle de conversion** special economic zone
◊ Écon **pôles de croissance** main centres of economic growth
◊ Écon **pôle économique** economic hub
◊ Écon **pôle de reconversion** development or reconversion zone
◊ Pol **Pôle Républicain** = French political party created in 2002 by Jean-Pierre Chevènement with a republican and anti-EU agenda

Politburo nm Politburo

politicaillerie nf Fam Péj backroom politics

politicard, -e nm,f Fam Péj careerist politician

politicien, -enne 1 adj (d'habile politique) political; **une manœuvre politicienne** a successful political move
2 nm,f politician

politico-économique adj politico-economic

politique 1 adj political; **quelles sont ses opinions politiques?** what are his politics?; **une carrière politique** a career in politics; **dans les milieux politiques** in political circles
2 nf (a) (activité) politics; **faire de la politique** to be involved in politics (b) (stratégie) policy; **suivre** ou **adopter une nouvelle politique** to follow or adopt a new policy; **une politique de gauche** a left-wing policy; **c'est de bonne politique** it's good political practice
3 nmf (a) (politicien) politician (b) (prisonnier) political prisoner
4 nm politics; **faire passer le politique avant le social** to accord more importance to politics than to welfare
◊ **politique d'accommodement** give-and-take policy

◊ UE **politique agricole commune** Common Agricultural Policy
◊ **politique antichômage** policy that aims to reduce unemployment
◊ **politique antiprotectionniste** free-trade policy
◊ **politique d'apaisement** policy of appeasement
◊ **politique d'austérité** austerity policy
◊ **politique budgétaire** budgetary or fiscal policy
◊ **politique commerciale** trade policy
◊ UE **politique communautaire** EU policy
◊ **politique commune de la pêche** Common Fisheries Policy
◊ **politique conjoncturelle** economic policy (responding to changes in the business cycle)
◊ **la politique consensuelle** consensus politics
◊ **politique conventionnelle** = policy relating to union-management agreements
◊ **politique de la corde raide** political brinkmanship
◊ **politique à court terme** short-termism
◊ **politique du crédit** credit policy
◊ **politique de déflation** deflationary policy
◊ **politique déflationniste** deflationary policy
◊ **politique économique** economic policy
◊ **politique d'élargissement européenne** policy of enlarging the European Union
◊ **politique électoraliste** vote-catcher
◊ **politique d'endiguement** policy of containment
◊ **politique étrangère** foreign policy
◊ UE **politique étrangère et de sécurité commune** Common Foreign and Security Policy
◊ **politique extérieure** foreign policy
◊ **politique fiscale** fiscal policy
◊ **politique d'indexation des salaires sur les prix** threshold wage policy

◇ *politique industrielle* industrial policy

◇ *politique d'inflation* inflationary policy

◇ *politique inflationniste* inflationary policy

◇ *politique intérieure* domestic policy

◇ *politique d'investissement* investment policy

◇ *politique de juste milieu* middle-of-the-road politics

◇ *politique de laisser-faire* laissez-faire policy

◇ *politique de libre-échange* free-trade policy

◇ *politique locale* local politics

◇ *politique à long terme* long-term policy

◇ *politique de la main tendue* policy of the outstretched hand; **pratiquer la politique de la main tendue** to make friendly overtures, to be conciliatory

◇ *politique minoritaire* minority politics

◇ *politique monétaire* monetary policy

◇ *politique d'open-market* open-market policy

◇ *politique d'ouverture* consensus politics

◇ *politique de parti* party politics

◇ *politique partisane* partisan politics

◇ *la politique du pire* = deliberately worsening the situation to further one's ends

◇ *politique politicienne* party politics

◇ *politique de la porte ouverte* open-door policy

◇ *politique des prix* price policy

◇ *politique des prix et des salaires* prices and incomes policy

◇ *politique régionale* regional policy

◇ *politique de relance* reflationary policy

◇ *politique des revenus* incomes policy

◇ *politique de rigueur* policy of austerity

◇ *politique sécuritaire* repressive law-and-order policy

◇ *politique de stabilité* stabilizing policy

politiquement *adv Pol* politically

politisation *nf* (a) *(d'un débat, d'une question, d'un conflit)* politicization (b) *(d'une personne)* political awareness

politiser 1 *vt* (a) *(débat, question, conflit)* to politicize, to bring politics into; **politiser une grève** to give a strike a political dimension (b) *(personne)* to make politically aware; **ils sont moins/plus politisés** they are less/more politically aware
2 se politiser *vpr* (a) *(débat, question, conflit)* to become political (b) *(personne)* to become politically aware

polycentrisme *nm Pol* polycentrism

polycentriste *adj Pol* polycentrist

pondérateur, -trice *adj Écon* balancing, stabilizing; **les éléments pondérateurs du marché** the stablizing factors of the market

pondération *nf* (a) *Écon (d'un indice, d'une moyenne)* weighting (b) *Pol (de pouvoirs)* balance, equilibrium

pondéré, -e *adj* (a) *Écon (indice, moyenne)* weighted (b) *Pol (pouvoirs)* balanced (out), counterbalanced

pondérer *vt* (a) *Écon (indice, moyenne)* to weight (b) *Pol (pouvoirs)* to balance (out), to counterbalance

pool *nm Écon* pool
◇ *pool de l'or* gold pool

populaire *adj* (a) *(ouvrier)* working-class (b) *Pol (gouvernement)* popular; *(démocratie, tribunal)* people's; *(soulèvement)* mass; **la volonté populaire** the will of the people

popularité *nf* popularity; **le président a perdu de sa popularité** there's been a decline in the president's popularity

population *nf* population
◇ *population active* working population

◇ *population **excédentaire*** surplus population

◇ *population **inactive*** non-working population

◇ *population **mère*** basic population

>
> En Finlande, plus on part tôt, plus la pension est maigre. Au début des années 90, en Finlande, le chômage approchait 20% de la **population active**, et les préretraites étaient massivement accordées.
>

populisme *nm* populism

populiste 1 *adj* populist
2 *nmf* populist

portefeuille *nm Pol* portfolio; **on lui a confié le portefeuille des Affaires étrangères** he has been given *or* he holds the foreign affairs portfolio

porte-parole *nm inv (personne)* spokesperson, spokesman, *f* spokeswoman; **se faire le porte-parole de qn** to speak on sb's behalf

position *nf Pol (opinion)* position, stance, standpoint; **prendre position (sur qch)** to take a stand *or* to take up a position (on sth); **prendre position contre qch** to come out against sth; **quelle est la position de la France dans ce conflit?** what's France's position on this conflict?

◇ *position **commune*** common stance

◇ *position **de principe*** policy position

poste *nm (métier)* post, job, position

potentat *nm Pol* potentate

potentiel, -elle 1 *adj Écon (croissance)* potential
2 *nm*

◇ *potentiel **électoral*** chances of electoral success

poujadisme *nm Péj Pol* **le poujadisme** Poujadism

poujadiste *nmf Péj Pol* Poujadist

pourparlers *nmpl* negotiations, talks; **être/entrer en pourparlers avec**

qn to have/to enter into talks *or* negotiations with sb; **les pourparlers vont reprendre** negotiations will be resumed

◇ *UE **pourparlers d'adhésion*** entry talks

◇ *pourparlers **bilatéraux*** bilateral talks

◇ *pourparlers **de paix*** peace talks

poussée *nf* upsurge, rise

◇ *poussée **de l'inflation*** rise in inflation

◇ *poussée **inflationniste*** rise in inflation

>
> L'économie batave a non seulement suivi la chute de sa voisine allemande, mais elle l'a même précédée. Après quatre années à un rythme de 4%, le plus élevé des pays moyens européens, la croissance du PIB est tombée à 1,1% en 2001. Raisons principales: la réforme fiscale de janvier 2001 générant une hausse de la TVA, et une **poussée inflationniste** mal contrôlée sur un marché du travail artificiellement étroit.
>

pouvoir *Pol* **1** *nm* **le pouvoir** *(exercice)* power; *(gouvernants)* government; **arriver au pouvoir** to come to power; **être au pouvoir** *(parti élu)* to be in power *or* office; *(junte)* to be in power; **prendre le pouvoir** *(élus)* to take office; *(dictateur)* to seize power; **exercer le pouvoir** to exercise power, to govern, to rule; **partager le pouvoir** to share power; **elle est trop proche du pouvoir pour comprendre** she's too close to the seat of power to understand; **les gens au pouvoir ne connaissent pas nos problèmes** those in power *or* the powers that be don't understand our difficulties

2 *nmpl* **pouvoirs** *(fonctions)* powers, authority; **outrepasser ses pouvoirs** to overstep *or* to exceed one's authority; **avoir tous pouvoirs pour faire qch**

(administrateur) to have full powers to do sth

◇ *pouvoir absolu* absolute power

◇ *pouvoir d'achat* purchasing power, spending power

◇ *le pouvoir central* central government

◇ *pouvoir constituant* constituent power

◇ *les pouvoirs constitués* the legally constituted government

◇ *pouvoirs exceptionnels* special powers

◇ *le pouvoir exécutif* executive power, the executive

◇ *pouvoirs extraordinaires* special powers

◇ *le pouvoir législatif* legislative power, the legislature

◇ *le pouvoir local* local government, the local authorities

◇ *pouvoirs partagés* shared powers

◇ *le pouvoir personnel* (absolute) personal power

◇ *les pouvoirs publics* the authorities

❝

Ils perdent sur tous les tableaux: l'emploi (160 000 cadres inscrits au chômage en 1994), le salaire (leur **pouvoir d'achat** évolue moins vite que celui de l'ensemble des salariés depuis 1992) ou les avantages acquis (la prime d'ancienneté, par example) qui disparaissent à vue d'œil.

❞

PPE *nf* (*abrév* **prime pour l'emploi**) = tax credit awarded to low wage-earners, as an incentive to continue working and not claim benefit instead

PR *nm* (*abrév* **Parti radical**) = right-of-centre French political party

pragmatique *adj Pol* pragmatic

pragmatisme *nm Pol* pragmatism

pragmatiste *Pol* **1** *adj* pragmatist
2 *nmf* pragmatist

pratiques restrictives *nfpl UE* restrictive practices

préadhésion *nf UE* pre-accession

précarité *nf* **la précarité de l'emploi** the lack of job security

prédominance *nf* (*d'un parti politique*) predominance

prédominant, -e *adj* (*parti politique*) predominant

préfectoral, -e *adj* prefectoral, prefectural

préfecture *nf* (*chef-lieu*) prefecture; (*édifice*) prefecture building; (*services*) prefectural office; (*emploi*) post of "préfet"

préférence *nf Écon*

◇ *préférence douanière* preferential duty

◇ *préférence pour la liquidité* liquidity preference

préfet *nm* préfet, prefect; **elle était préfet du Lot** she used to be a prefect *or* préfet of the Lot department; **le préfet de Paris** the prefect of Paris

prélèvement *nm* deduction, levy

◇ *UE prélèvements agricoles* agricultural levies

◇ *UE prélèvement compensatoire* compensatory levy

◇ *prélèvement à l'exportation* export levy

◇ *prélèvements fiscaux* taxes

◇ *prélèvement à l'importation* import levy

◇ *prélèvement de l'impôt à la source* taxation at source

◇ *prélèvements obligatoires* tax and social security contributions

◇ *prélèvement salarial* deduction from wages

◇ *prélèvements sociaux* social security contributions

premier, -ère **1** *adj* (*haut placé*) (*commis*) chief; **le premier personnage de l'État** the country's Head of State; **premier secrétaire (du parti)** first secretary (of the party)

2 *nm,f Pol* **le Premier (britannique)** the (British) Prime Minister *or* Premier

◇ *premier ministrable* potential Prime Minister
◇ *Premier ministre* Prime Minister

prescription légale *nf* statute of limitations

présentation *nf Pol (d'une pétition)* submission; *(d'un projet de loi)* tabling, introduction, sponsorship

présenter *Pol* **1** *vt (pétition)* to put in, to submit; *(projet de loi)* to table, to introduce, to sponsor
2 se présenter *vpr (être candidat) Br* to stand, *Am* to run; **se présenter aux présidentielles** *Br* to stand for president, *Am* to run for president

présidence *nf* **(a)** *(fonction)* presidency
(b) *(durée) (prévue)* term of office; *(effectuée)* period in office; **sa présidence aura duré un an** he'll/she'll have been in office for a year
(c) *(lieu)* presidential residence *or* palace
(d) *(services)* presidential office; **vous avez la présidence en ligne** you're through to the President's *or* the Presidential office; **à la présidence, on ne dit rien** presidential aides are keeping silent
◇ *UE présidence tournante* rotating presidency

président, -e *nm,f* president
◇ *président de l'Assemblée nationale* President of the National Assembly
◇ *président de la Commission européenne* President of the European Commission
◇ *président de la Confédération helvétique* President of the Swiss Confederation
◇ *président élu* president elect
◇ *président fantoche* puppet president
◇ *le président du Parlement européen* the President of the European Parliament
◇ *le président de la République française* the French President
◇ *président du Sénat* President of the Senate

◇ *président à vie* life president

présidentiable *nmf* potential president

> **"**
> En France, un parti sans **présidentiable** est un parti en crise, mais un **présidentiable** sans le soutien d'un parti n'a guère d'avenir. Bref, les partis politiques comptent toujours sous la Vᵉ République.
> **"**

présidentialisme *nm* presidential (government) system

présidentiel, -elle **1** *adj* **(a)** *(du président)* presidential, president's; *(élection)* presidential; **dans l'entourage présidentiel** among the president's close associates **(b)** *(régime)* presidential
2 *nf* **présidentielle** presidential election

présider *vt (séance)* to preside at *or* over; *(commission)* to preside over, to be the president of

presse *nf (journaux, magazines)* **la presse (écrite)** the press, the papers

pression *nf (influence)* pressure; **faire pression sur** to pressurize, to lobby
◇ *Écon pression fiscale* tax burden
◇ *Écon pression inflationniste* inflationary pressure

prestation *nf (allocation)* allowance, benefit
◇ *prestations sociales* social security benefits

prêt *nm* loan
◇ *prêt avantageux* soft loan
◇ *prêt à la consommation* consumer loan
◇ *prêt à des conditions avantageuses* soft loan
◇ *prêt aux conditions du marché* hard loan
◇ *prêt en devises étrangères* foreign currency loan
◇ *prêt garanti par l'État* sovereign loan

prêt-bail *nm Écon* lend-lease

prêter *vt Pol* **prêter serment** to be sworn in

prévision *nf (résultat)* forecast; *(activité)* forecasting

◇ **prévision boursière** *(résultat)* stock market forecast; *(activité)* stock market forecasting

◇ **prévision budgétaire** *(résultat)* budget forecast; *(activité)* budget forecasting

◇ **prévision conjoncturelle** *(résultat)* economic forecast; *(activité)* economic forecasting

◇ **prévision économique** *(résultat)* economic forecast; *(activité)* economic forecasting

◇ **prévision de l'industrie** *(résultat)* industry forecast; *(activité)* industry forecasting

◇ **prévision du marché** *(résultat)* market forecast; *(activité)* market forecasting

prévisionniste *nmf* forecaster

prévoir *vt* to forecast

PRG *nm* (*abrév* **Parti radical de gauche**) = left-of-centre French political party

primaire 1 *adj Écon (secteur)* primary
2 *nm Écon* primary sector
3 *nf Pol* primary (election); **les primaires** the primaries

prime *nf Écon* subsidy

◇ **prime de développement industriel** industrial development subsidy

◇ **prime de développement régional** regional development subsidy

◇ **prime pour l'emploi** = tax credit awarded to low wage-earners, as an incentive to continue working and not claim benefit instead

◇ **prime à l'exportation** export subsidy, export incentive

◇ **prime à l'investissement** investment subsidy

principauté *nf* principality

principe *nm*

◇ **principe d'accélération** acceleration principle

◇ **principe d'efficacité économique** economic efficiency principle

◇ **principe de précaution** precautionary principle

◇ **principe de préférence communautaire** Community preference principle

◇ **principe de solidarité** solidarity principle

◇ **principe de subsidiarité** subsidiarity principle

prise *nf*

◇ *Écon* **prise de bénéfice** profit-taking

◇ *Écon* **prise de contrôle** takeover

◇ **prise de position** opinion, stand

◇ **prise de pouvoir** *(légale)* (political) takeover; *(illégale)* seizure of power

prisonnier, -ère *nm,f* prisoner

◇ **prisonnier de guerre** prisoner of war

◇ **prisonnier d'opinion** prisoner of conscience

◇ **prisonnier politique** political prisoner

privatisation *nf* privatization

privatiser *vt* to privatize

privé, -e *adj (non géré par l'État)* private

privilège fiscal *nm* tax privilege

prix *nm (tarif fixe)* price, cost

◇ **prix de déséquilibre** disequilibrium price

◇ **prix d'équilibre** equilibrium price

◇ **prix d'équilibre concurrentiel** competitive equilibrium price

◇ **prix à l'export** export price

◇ **prix fixe** fixed price

◇ **prix hors taxe(s)** price net of tax, price before tax

◇ **prix à l'import** import price

◇ **prix imposé** fixed price, administered price

◇ **prix d'intervention** intervention price

◇ **prix libre** deregulated price

◊ *prix plafond* ceiling price
◊ *prix plancher* floor price
◊ *prix pratiqué* current price
◊ *prix préférentiel* preferential price
◊ *prix de seuil* threshold price
◊ *prix de soutien* support price

probabilité *nf* probability

procédure *nf*
◊ UE *procédure de l'avis conforme* assent procedure
◊ *procédure de codécision* codecision procedure
◊ *procédure législative* legislative procedure
◊ *procédure parlementaire* parliamentary procedure
◊ *procédure d'urgence* emergency or special powers

processus *nm* process; **le processus de démocratisation est en marche** the democratization process is under way
◊ UE *processus de convergence* convergence process
◊ *processus de paix* peace process

66

"L'importance des écarts de revenus ainsi que la faiblesse des différentiels de croissance augurent d'un **processus de convergence** réelle très graduel et susceptible de s'étendre bien au-delà des dates envisagées pour l'adhésion", selon un récent rapport de la Banque centrale européenne (BCE).

99

procès-verbal *nm (d'une assemblée, d'un débat)* minutes

producteur, -trice **1** *adj* producing; **les pays producteurs de pétrole** oil-producing countries
2 *nm* producer; **ce pays est le premier producteur de composants électroniques du monde** this country is the world's largest producer of electronic components

productif, -ive *adj* productive

production *nf* (a) *(activité économique)* **la production** production; **la production ne suit plus la consommation** supply is failing to keep up with demand (b) *(rendement)* output; **la production a augmenté/diminué** output has risen/dropped
◊ *production excédentaire* surplus production
◊ *production globale* aggregate production or output

productivité *nf* productivity, productive capacity
◊ *productivité marginale* marginal productivity

produire **1** *vt* to produce, to manufacture
2 *vi* to produce, to be productive

produit *nm* product
◊ *produits de consommation* consumable goods
◊ *produit d'exportation* exported product, export
◊ *produits de grande consommation* consumer products
◊ *produit homogène* homogeneous product
◊ *produit d'importation* imported product, import
◊ *le produit industriel* industrial earnings
◊ *produit intérieur brut* gross domestic product
◊ *produit intérieur net* net domestic product
◊ *produit marginal décroissant* diminishing marginal product
◊ *produit national* national product
◊ *produit national brut* gross national product
◊ *produit national net* net national product
◊ Écon *produit principal* main product

66

Le **produit intérieur brut** (PIB) irlandais, qui mesure la totalité de la richesse créée, est supérieur de 30% au **produit national brut**

(PNB), mesure de la richesse créée par les entreprises nationales. Cela s'explique simplement par le poids des multinationales américaines, dont la valeur ajoutée en Irlande est comptabilisée dans le PNB des Etats-Unis.

"

profil démographique *nm* demographic profile

profit *nm Écon (bénéfice)* profit; **faire ou réaliser des profits** to make a profit; **vendre à profit** to sell at a profit; **profits et pertes** profit and loss
◇ *profit brut* gross profit
◇ *profits exceptionnels* windfall profits
◇ *profits de l'exercice* year's profits
◇ *profit d'exploitation* operating profit
◇ *profits fictifs* paper profits
◇ *profit minimal* minimum trading profit
◇ *profit net* net profit
◇ *profits non matérialisés* paper profits
◇ *profit pur* pure profit
◇ *profit réel* real profit

programmation *nf Écon* programming

programme *nm* **(a)** *Pol (plate-forme)* programme, *Br* manifesto, *Am* ticket **(b)** *(projet)* programme
◇ *programme alimentaire mondial* world food programme
◇ *programme commun* common *or* joint programme, *Br* common *or* joint manifesto, *Am* common *or* joint platform
◇ *programme économique* economic programme *or* plan
◇ *programme électoral Br* (election) programme, *Am* (electoral) platform
◇ *programme de gouvernement Br* government manifesto, *Am* government platform
◇ *programme des Nations unies pour le développement* United

Nations Development Programme

progressif, -ive *adj (croissance, déclin)* steady

progression *nf* **(a)** *(d'un parti politique)* progression, progress **(b)** *(d'un secteur économique)* expansion; *(du chômage)* rise **(de** in)

progressiste **1** *adj (politique, parti)* progressive
2 *nmf* progressive

projet *nm Pol*
◇ *projet d'acte législatif* draft legislation
◇ *projet de budget* draft budget
◇ *projet de convention* draft treaty
◇ *projet de loi* bill; **mettre un projet de loi au vote** to vote on a bill; **adopter/repousser un projet de loi** to pass/reject a bill

prolifération *nf* proliferation
◇ *prolifération des armes* arms proliferation

promesse électorale *nf Pol* electoral promise

promoteur, -trice *nm,f Écon* developer

promulgation *nf (d'un projet de loi)* enactment, promulgation

promulguer *vt (projet de loi)* to enact, to promulgate

prononcer *vt (parole)* to say, to utter; *(discours)* to make, to deliver; **il a prononcé quelques mots sur la situation en Chine** he said a few words about the situation in China

pronostic *nm Écon* forecast

pronostiquer *vt Écon* to forecast

pronostiqueur, -euse *nm,f Écon* forecaster

propagande *nf (politique)* propaganda
◇ *propagande électorale* electioneering

propagandisme *nm* propagandism

propagandiste **1** *adj* propagandist
2 *nmf* propagandist

propension *nf Écon* propensity

◊ *propension à consommer* propensity to consume

◊ *propension à épargner* propensity to save

◊ *propension à importer* propensity to import

◊ *propension marginale à consommer* marginal propensity to consume

◊ *propension marginale à épargner* marginal propensity to save

◊ *propension moyenne à consommer* average propensity to consume

◊ *propension moyenne à épargner* average propensity to save

proportionnalité *nf (répartition)* equal distribution

◊ *Écon* **proportionnalité de l'impôt** fixed-rate system of taxation

proportionnel, -elle 1 *adj* (a) *Écon (droits, impôt)* ad valorem (b) *Pol* proportional

2 *nf Pol* **proportionnelle** *(processus)* proportional system; *(résultat)* proportional representation, PR; **être élu à la proportionnelle** to be elected by proportional representation

◊ *proportionnelle intégrale* list system

proportionnellement *adv Écon* proportionally, in direct ratio (**à** to)

proposer *vt* **proposer une loi** to introduce a bill; **proposer un ordre du jour** to move an agenda; **proposer la suspension de la séance** to move that the session be suspended

proposition *nf Parl* motion; **mettre une proposition aux voix** to put a motion to the vote; **la proposition est votée** the motion is passed

◊ *proposition européenne* proposed European legislation

◊ *proposition de loi* *Br* private member's bill, *Am* private bill

◊ *proposition de paix* peace proposal

◊ *proposition de réforme* reform proposal

propriété *nf* property

◊ *propriété collective* social ownership

◊ *propriété de l'État* government or state property

prorogation *nf Parl (d'une assemblée)* adjournment, prorogation

proroger *vt Parl (assemblée)* to adjourn, to prorogue

prospective *nf (dans l'administration)* long-term planning; *Écon* (long-term) forecasting

prospectiviste 1 *adj Écon (analyse, approche)* that forecasts future or long-term trends

2 *nmf (dans l'administration)* long-term planner; *Écon* (economic) forecaster

prostration *nf Écon* collapse, crash

protecteur, -trice *adj Écon* protectionist; *(droits, tarif)* protective

protection *nf Écon* protection

protectionnisme *nm Écon* protectionism

protectionniste *Écon* 1 *adj* protectionist

2 *nmf* protectionist

protectorat *nm* protectorate

protéger *vt Écon (industrie)* to protect

protestataire 1 *adj (délégué)* protesting; *(mesure)* protest

2 *nmf* protester, protestor

protestation *nf* (a) *(mécontentement)* protest, discontent (b) *(opposition)* protest; **en signe de protestation** as a protest

protester *vi* to protest (**contre** against or about)

protocole *nm Pol* protocol

◊ *protocole d'accord* draft agreement

◊ *protocole d'intention* statement of intent

province *nf Belg & Can* = administrative district similar to the French "département"

provisoire *adj (gouvernement)* provisional, interim

provocateur, -trice *Pol* **1** *adj (discours, propagande)* incendiary
2 *nm,f* agitator

PS *nm (abrév* **Parti socialiste**) = left-of-centre French political party

PSC *nm (abrév* **Pacte de stabilité et de croissance**) GSP

public, -ique **1** *adj (de l'État)* public, state
2 *nm (secteur)* **le public** the public sector

publiquement *adv* publicly

puissance *nf* **(a)** *(pouvoir, autorité)* power; **un État au sommet de sa puissance** a state at the height of its power **(b)** *(pays puissant)* power; **les grandes puissances** the great powers
◇ *puissance économique* economic power
◇ *puissance industrielle* industrial power
◇ *puissance mondiale* world power

◇ *puissance nucléaire* nuclear power

puissant, -e *adj (pouvoir, autorité)* powerful; *(mouvement)* strong, powerful

pur, -e *nm,f Pol (fidèle)* loyal member; *(intransigeant)* hardliner

purge *nf Pol (au sein d'un groupe)* purge

purger *vt Pol (débarrasser)* to purge; **le parti a été purgé de ses contestataires** the party has been purged of disloyal elements

putsch *nm* military coup, putsch

putschiste **1** *adj (officier)* involved in the putsch
2 *nmf* putschist, author of a military coup

PVD *nm (abrév* **pays en voie de développement**) developing country

pyramidal, -e *adj Écon* pyramidal

pyramide *nf Écon* pyramid

Quai *nm* **le Quai (d'Orsay)** the (French) Foreign Office

quantité d'équilibre *nf* equilibrium quantity

quartile *nm* quartile

questeur *nm Pol* parliamentary administrator

question *nf* question; *Parl* **poser une question** to table a question; **poser la question de confiance** to ask for a vote of confidence
◇ *question écrite* written question
◇ *question orale* oral question

questure *nf Pol* = treasury and administrative department of the French Parliament

quinquennat *nm Pol* (five-year) term of office; **pendant son premier quinquennat** during his first term of office

Quinze *nm* **les Quinze** = the fifteen member states of the European Union

> **"**
>
> Dans leur communiqué, les **Quinze** ont prévu de faire figurer une clause sur la gestion des flux migratoire dans les futurs accords de coopération.
>
> **"**

quorum *nm Parl* quorum

quota *nm* quota
◇ *quota à l'exportation* export quota
◇ *quota d'exportation* export quota
◇ *quota à l'importation* import quota
◇ *quota d'importation* import quota
◇ *quotas volontaires à l'export* voluntary export restraint

quote-part *nf* share; **une quote-part des bénéfices** a share in the profits

rabatteur, -euse *nm,f Pol* canvasser

rachat *nm (d'une entreprise)* buy-out

racheter *vt (entreprise)* to buy out

racoler *vt Pol* to canvass

racoleur, -euse *Pol* **1** *adj (campagne électorale)* vote-catching
2 *nm,f (politicien)* canvasser

radiation *nf Pol (d'un candidat, d'un parti)* removal, deregistration

radical, -e *Pol* **1** *adj* radical
2 *nm,f* radical; *(membre du parti radical)* member of the "Parti radical"
◇ *radical de gauche* member of the "Parti radical de gauche"

radicalisation *nf Pol* radicalization; **il est pour la radicalisation des revendications** he wants the demands to be made more radical; **la radicalisation du conflit** the heightening of the conflict

radicaliser *Pol* **1** *vt* to radicalize, to make more radical
2 se radicaliser *vpr* **le mouvement étudiant s'est radicalisé** the student movement has become more radical

radicalisme *nm Pol* radicalism

radier *vt Pol (candidat, parti)* to remove, to deregister

raison d'État *nf* **la raison d'État** reasons of State, raison d'état; **le gouvernement a invoqué la raison d'État pour justifier cette mesure** the government said that it had done this for reasons of State

> 66
>
> Longtemps, même dans les démocraties, **la raison d'État** l'a emporté sur la morale et sur le droit. Quand un gouvernement estimait, à tort ou à raison, que l'intérêt collectif exigeait de fermer les yeux sur des actes répréhensibles, la justice laissait ses dossiers au placard et les militants des droits de l'homme se contentaient de manifestations symboliques.
>
> 99

rajustement *nm Écon* adjustment
◇ *rajustement des prix* price adjustment
◇ *rajustement des salaires* wage adjustment

rajuster *vt Écon (prix, salaires)* to adjust

ralentir **1** *vt (croissance économique)* to slow down
2 *vi* to slow down

ralentissement *nm* reduction; **un ralentissement de l'économie** economic slowdown

ralliement *nm* **(a)** *(adhésion)* **lors de son ralliement à notre parti/notre cause** when he came over to our party/cause **(b)** *(rassemblement)* rally, gathering

rallier **1** *vt* **(a)** *(adhérer à)* to join; **c'est pour cela que j'ai fini par rallier ce parti** that's why I ended up joining this party **(b)** *(rassembler)* to rally, to gather together

2 se rallier *vpr (se joindre)* **se rallier à une cause** to rally to a cause

ramification *nf (d'une organisation, d'un parti, d'un mouvement)* branch, offshoot

rappel *nm (d'un ambassadeur, d'un ministre, du Parlement)* recall
◇ *Parl* **rappel à l'ordre** call to order, *Br* ≃ naming; **il a fallu trois rappels à l'ordre pour qu'il se taise** he had to be called to order three times before he stopped talking

rappeler *vt (ambassadeur, ministre, Parlement)* to recall

rapport *nm* (a) *(compte rendu)* report (b) *Écon (proportion)* ratio
◇ *Écon* **rapport de parité** parity ratio

rapporter *vt (faire le compte rendu de)* to report (on); **rapporter les décisions d'une commission** to report on the decisions of a committee

rapporteur, -euse *nm,f Pol (porte-parole)* reporter, recorder
◇ *rapporteur de la commission* = committee member who acts as spokesman
◇ *rapporteur officiel* official recorder

rassemblement *nm* (a) *(en politique)* rally; **disperser un rassemblement** to break up *or* to disperse a rally (b) *(dans un nom de parti)* party, union, alliance (c) *(union)* union; **œuvrer au rassemblement de la gauche** to work towards the union of the left
◇ *rassemblement électoral* campaign rally
◇ *rassemblement pour la paix* peace rally
◇ *Rassemblement pour la République* = right-wing French political party

rassembler *Pol* 1 *vt* to rally
2 se rassembler *vpr* to rally

ratification *nf Pol* ratification, confirmation

ratifier *vt Pol* to ratify, to confirm; **ils ont fait ratifier le traité par le gouvernement** they put the treaty before Parliament for ratification

rating *nm Écon* rating
◇ *rating de la dette* debt rating

ratio *nm Écon* ratio
◇ *ratio de capitalisation* price-earnings ratio, p/e ratio
◇ *ratio capital-travail* capital-labour ratio
◇ *ratio cours-bénéfices* price-earnings ratio
◇ *ratio d'endettement* debt ratio
◇ *ratio d'intensité de capital* capital-output ratio
◇ *ratio de levier* leverage
◇ *ratio de liquidité* liquidity ratio
◇ *ratio de trésorerie* cash ratio

rationalisation *nf Écon (d'une industrie)* rationalization, streamlining

rationaliser *vt Écon (industrie)* to rationalize, to streamline

rationnel, -elle *adj Écon* **l'organisation rationnelle de l'industrie** the rationalization *or* streamlining of industry

rattachement *nm Pol* **le rattachement de la Savoie à la France** the incorporation of Savoy into France; **opérer le rattachement de territoires à la métropole** to bring territories under the jurisdiction of the home country

rattacher *vt Pol* **rattacher un territoire à un pays** to bring a territory under the jurisdiction of a country

rattachiste *Belg Pol* **1** *adj (personne, politique)* = advocating the integration of French-speaking regions of Belgium into France
2 *nmf* = advocate of the integration of French-speaking regions of Belgium into France

rattrapage *nm Écon* adjustment; **après le blocage des prix, il y a eu un effet de rattrapage** prices have adjusted following the end of the freeze
◇ *rattrapage des salaires* wage adjustment

rattraper *vt Écon* to catch up with

réaction *nf Pol* **la réaction** reaction,

reactionary attitudes; *(personnes)* reactionaries

réactionnaire *Pol* **1** *adj* reactionary **2** *nmf* reactionary

réalignement *nm* realignment
◇ **réalignement monétaire** realignment of currencies

réaligner *vt* to realign

réalisme politique *nm* political realism *or* pragmatism

realpolitik *nf Pol* realpolitik

réaménagement *nm (d'une politique)* reshaping

réaménager *vt (politique)* to reshape

réarmement *nm Pol* rearmament

réarmer *Pol* **1** *vt (pays)* to rearm **2** *vi (pays)* to rearm

rebelle *Pol* **1** *adj* rebel **2** *nmf* rebel

rebond *nm (d'un marché, de l'économie)* recovery

rebondir *vi (marché, économie)* to recover, to pick up again

recensement *nm (de population)* census; *(de votes)* registering, counting; **faire le recensement de la population** to take a census of the population; **faire le recensement des votes** to register *or* count the votes

recenser *vt (population)* to take *or* to make a census of

recenseur, -euse *nm,f* census taker

recentrage *nm* **(a)** *Écon* streamlining, rationalization **(b)** *Pol* refocusing, redefinition

recentrer *vt* **(a)** *Écon* to streamline **(b)** *Pol* to refocus, to redefine

récessif, -ive *adj Écon* recessionary

récession *nf Écon* recession
◇ **récession économique** economic recession

recettes *nfpl (sommes touchées)* income, revenue
◇ **recettes en devises** foreign currency earnings

◇ **recettes de l'État** public revenue, state revenue
◇ **recettes publiques** public revenue, state revenue

rechute *nf Écon* slump; **on craint une rechute de l'activité économique** there are fears of a further slump in economic activity

réciprocité *nf (d'un accord)* reciprocity

réciproque *adj (accord)* reciprocal

reclassement *nm* **(a)** *(d'un fonctionnaire)* regrading; **le reclassement de la fonction publique** the restructuring of the state sector **(b)** *(d'un employé)* placing

reclasser *vt* **(a)** *(fonctionnaire)* to regrade **(b)** *(employé)* to place

recommandation *nf Pol* recommendation; **une recommandation de l'ONU** a UN recommendation

recompter *vt Pol (voix)* to count again

reconduction *nf (de mandat)* renewal; *(de mesures, d'une politique, d'une grève)* continuation; **voter la reconduction de la grève** to vote for the continuation of the strike *or* for continued strike action

reconduire *vt (mandat)* to renew; *(mesures, politique, grève)* to continue

reconnaissance *nf Pol (d'un gouvernement, d'un État)* recognition

reconnaître *vt Pol (gouvernement, État)* to recognize

reconstituer *vt (gouvernement)* to reconstitute; *(parti)* to revive

reconstitution *nf (d'un gouvernement)* reconstitution; *(d'un parti)* revival

reconversion *nf*
◇ **reconversion économique** economic restructuring
◇ **reconversion industrielle** industrial redeployment

reconvocation *nf (du Parlement, d'un ministre)* recall

reconvoquer vt *(Parlement, ministre)* to recall

recouvrer vt *(électeurs, sièges)* to win back

reculade nf Péj *(d'une prise de position)* climbdown; **Jospin prépare une reculade sur la Corse** Jospin is preparing to climb down over Corsica

reculer vi Péj *(d'une prise de position)* to climb down

récupération nf Pol hijacking, takeover; **il y a eu récupération du mouvement par les extrémistes** the movement has been hijacked *or* taken over by extremists

récupérer vt Pol to hijack, to take over; **le mouvement a été récupéré par le gouvernement** the movement has been taken over by the government for its own ends

redécoupage électoral nm Pol redrawing of electoral boundaries; **procéder à** ou **effectuer un redécoupage électoral** to redraw the electoral boundaries

> ❝
>
> De son côté, le ministre de l'intérieur devrait procéder à un **redécoupage électoral**. M. Sarkozy prévoit de ne se livrer qu'à quelques "ajustements cantonaux", tenant compte des résultats du recensement de 1999. Il n'envisage une véritable refonte des cantons, ainsi que des circonscriptions législatives, que pour les scrutins de 2007.
>
> ❞

redémarrage nm Écon recovery, upturn

redémarrer vi Écon to recover

redéploiement nm Écon *(d'une entreprise, de ressources)* reorganization, restructuring

redéployer vt Écon *(entreprise, ressources)* to reorganize, to restructure

rédiger vt *(manifeste, projet de loi)* to draw up

redistribuer vt *(revenus, terres, richesses)* to redistribute

redistribution nf *(des revenus, des terres, des richesses)* redistribution

redressement nm *(d'une économie)* recovery

redresser 1 vt *(économie)* to put back on its feet; **pour redresser l'économie** in order to bring about an economic recovery, in order to put the economy back on its feet

  2 se redresser vpr *(économie)* to recover; **l'économie se redresse depuis mai** the economy has been looking up *or* has been recovering since May

réduction nf *(baisse)* reduction, cut **(de** in); **la réduction du temps de travail** = reduction of the working week in France from 39 to 35 hours, introduced by the government of Lionel Jospin in 1998 and phased in from 2000 onwards

réduire vt to reduce, to cut

rééchelonnement nm Écon *(d'une dette)* restructuring

> ❝
>
> Comme une lueur au bout du tunnel, l'Argentine est parvenue, jeudi 16 janvier, à un accord intérimaire de principe avec le Fonds monétaire international (FMI) portant sur le **rééchelonnement** de 6,6 milliards de dettes multilatérales dues par Buenos Aires entre janvier et août 2003.
>
> ❞

rééchelonner vt Écon *(dette)* to restructure

réélection nf re-election

rééligible adj re-eligible; **ils sont/ne sont pas rééligibles** they are/aren't entitled to stand for election again

réélire vt to re-elect; **elle compte bien**

se faire réélire she's quite sure she'll be re-elected

réévaluation nf Écon (de monnaie) revaluation

réévaluer vt Écon (monnaie) to revalue

réexamen nm (d'une politique) re-examination, reassessment

réexaminer vt (politique) to re-examine, to reassess

réexportation nf (activité) re-exportation, re-exporting; (produit) re-export

réexporter vt to re-export

référendaire adj referendum; **par voie référendaire** by means of a referendum

référendum nm referendum; **organiser un référendum** to hold a referendum; **les Norvégiens ont décidé par référendum de ne pas entrer dans l'Union européenne** the Norwegians have decided in a referendum or by referendum not to join the European Union

◇ **référendum révocatoire** = referendum in which voters decide whether or not to dismiss an elected representative (who may be a member of Parliament, civil servant, head of state etc)

> **"**
>
> La Constitution vénézuélienne est une des rares Constitutions au monde à permettre aux électeurs de révoquer un élu s'ils ne sont pas satisfaits de lui. C'est une décision grave : la Constitution a donc fixé des règles pour assurer la stabilité des institutions. Je respecte ces règles et j'accepte le principe d'un **référendum révocatoire** à partir d'août 2003.
>
> **"**

refluer vi Écon **faire refluer le dollar/yen** to keep down the value of the dollar/yen

> **"**
>
> Les interventions massives, sur le marché des changes, de la Banque du Japon se sont révélées totalement inefficaces. De surcroît, la banque centrale nippone, soucieuse d'empêcher l'apparition de tensions inflationnistes dans l'archipel, a résisté aux pressions gouvernementales qui lui demandaient, pour faire **refluer le yen**, d'assouplir sa politique monétaire.
>
> **"**

refondation nf (d'un parti politique) radical reform; **les militants ont réclamé une refondation du parti** the militants have called for radical reform of the party

refonder vt (parti politique) to radically reform

réformateur, -trice nm,f reformer

réforme nf (de loi, de système) reform
◇ **réforme constitutionnelle** constitutional reform
◇ **réforme électorale** electoral reform
◇ **réforme monétaire** monetary reform
◇ **réformes sociales** social reforms

réformer vt (loi, système) to reform

réformisme nm Pol reformism

réformiste Pol **1** adj reformist **2** nmf reformist

réfugié, -e nm,f refugee

régent, -e nm,f Pol regent

régie nf (d'une entreprise publique) (par l'Etat) state control; (par le département) local government control; (par la commune) local authority control

régime nm Pol (système) regime, (system of) government; (gouvernement) regime; **la chute du régime** the fall of the regime or the government; **sous le régime de Pompidou/Thatcher** during the Pompidou/Thatcher administration; **sous le régime actuel** under the present regime

◇ *régime électoral* electoral system

Écon *régime de faveur* preference

◇ *régime fiscal* tax system

◇ *régime d'imposition* tax system

◇ *régime militaire* military regime

◇ *régime parlementaire* parliamentary regime

Écon *régime préférentiel* special arrangements

◇ *régime de protection sociale* social welfare system

◇ *régime totalitaire* totalitarian regime

Région *nf* region *(French administrative area made up of several "départements")*

région *nf* region, area
◇ Pol *région tampon* buffer zone

régional, -e *adj* (**a**) *(de la région)* regional; *(de la localité)* local (**b**) *(sur le plan international)* local, regional; **un conflit régional** a regional conflict

régionalisation *nf* Pol regionalization

régionaliser *vt* Pol to regionalize

régionalisme *nm* Pol regionalism

régionaliste Pol **1** *adj* regionalist **2** *nmf* regionalist

règle *nf (principe, code)* rule
◇ Écon *règle 80/20* Pareto's rule

règlement *nm* regulation, rules
◇ *règlement d'administration publique* ≃ statutory decree or declaration
◇ *règlement européen* piece of European legislation
◇ *règlement municipal* ≃ by-law
◇ *règlement de police municipale* ≃ by-law

réglementaire *adj* regulatory

réglementation *nf* (**a**) *(mesures)* regulations (**b**) *(limitation)* control, regulation
◇ *réglementation des changes* exchange control
◇ *réglementation des prix* price regulation
◇ *réglementation du travail* labour regulations or legislation

réglementer *vt* to regulate

règne *nm* reign

régner *vi* to reign, to rule (**sur** over)

régression sociale *nf* downward mobility

regroupement *nm* Pol realignment

regrouper Pol **1** *vt* to realign **2** *se regrouper* *vpr* to realign

régulateur, -trice *adj (mécanisme)* regulating, regulative

régulation *nf (de l'économie)* control

réguler *vt (économie)* to control

régulier, -ère *adj (croissance, déclin)* steady

reine *nf* queen

réintégration *nf (d'un fonctionnaire)* reinstatement; *(dans un parti)* readmission

réintégrer *vt (fonctionnaire)* to reinstate; *(membre d'un parti)* to readmit; **réintégrer qn (dans ses fonctions)** to reinstate sb (in their job), to restore sb to their former position

rejet *nm (d'un projet de loi)* rejection, throwing out

rejeter *vt (projet de loi)* to reject, to throw out

rejoindre *vt* Pol *(adhérer à)* to join; **elle a fini par rejoindre le parti socialiste** she ended up joining the Socialist Party

relance *nf* Écon revival, boost; **il y a une relance de la production sidérurgique** steel production is being boosted or increased
◇ *relance économique* reflation

relancer *vt* Écon to revive, to boost; **relancer l'économie d'un pays** to give a boost to or to boost or to reflate a country's economy

relation *nf* relations; **les relations sino-japonaises** relations between China and Japan, Sino-Japanese relations; **les deux pays ont cessé**

toute relation the two countries have broken off all relations

◇ *relations diplomatiques* diplomatic relations or links

◇ *relations extérieures* foreign affairs

◇ *relations industrielles* industrial relations

◇ *relations internationales* international relations

◇ *relations sociales* labour relations

relèvement nm (a) *(rétablissement)* recovery, restoring; **contribuer au relèvement d'un pays/d'une économie** to help a country/an economy recover; **ces mesures ont été prises pour favoriser le relèvement de la société** these measures were adopted to help put the company back on its feet or to help a company recover (b) *(de prix, de salaires)* increase, rise; **le relèvement des impôts** tax increase

relever vt (a) *(rétablir)* to recover, to restore (b) *(prix, salaires)* to increase, to raise, to put up

remaniement nm (a) *(d'un projet de loi)* revision, amendment; **procéder au remaniement d'un projet de loi** to revise or amend a bill (b) *(d'un gouvernement, d'un ministère)* reshuffle

◇ *remaniement ministériel* cabinet reshuffle

remanier vt (a) *(projet de loi)* to amend, to revise (b) *(gouvernement, ministère)* to reshuffle; **le cabinet a été complètement remanié** the cabinet was completely reshuffled

remboursement des droits de douane nm customs drawback

renaissant, -e adj *(économie)* reviving

renaître vi *(économie)* to revive, to recover

rencontre nf meeting, conference; **une rencontre internationale sur l'énergie nucléaire** an international meeting or conference on nuclear energy

◇ *rencontre au sommet* summit (meeting or conference)

rendement nm (a) *(production)* output (b) *(sur un investissement)* yield, return

◇ *rendements décroissants* diminishing returns

renflouage, renflouement nm Écon bailing out, refloating

renflouer vt Écon to bail out; **renflouer les caisses de l'État** to swell the government's coffers·

renforcer vt *(loi, contrôle, règlement)* to tighten up

renouvelable adj Pol **le comité est renouvelable tous les ans** the committee must Br stand or Am run for office each year; **mon mandat est renouvelable** I am eligible to Br stand or Am run (for office) again

renouveler vt Pol *(groupe, assemblée)* to re-elect

renseignements nmpl Pol *(espionnage)* intelligence; **elle travaille pour les services de renseignements** she works in intelligence

◇ *Renseignements généraux* = secret intelligence branch of the French police force, Br ≃ Special Branch, Am ≃ FBI

rente nf Écon rent

◇ *rentes sur l'État* government stock or funds

rentrée nf *(au Parlement)* reopening (of Parliament), new (parliamentary) session; **les députés vont devoir avancer leur rentrée** Parliament will have to start the new session earlier than usual; **à la prochaine rentrée parlementaire** at the beginning of the new parliamentary session; **faire sa rentrée politique** *(après les vacances)* to start the new political season *(after the summer)*; *(après une absence)* to make a (political) comeback

◇ *rentrée sociale* = return to work after the summer holidays

> **"**
>
> A défaut de son grand rendez-vous parisien, annulé pour cause d'an-

> née du cirque, qui a vu la pelouse de Reuilly réquisitionnée pour accueillir les chapiteaux, le leader de l'extrême droite s'est replié à Aix-en-Provence pour **faire sa rentrée politique**. Une région où, à la présidentielle, Le Pen est arrivé en tête dans quatre départements sur six. Il devrait lui-même y conduire la prochaine liste aux régionales de 2004.
>
> **"**

renversement *nm (d'un régime, d'un gouvernement)* overthrow

renverser *vt (régime)* to overthrow, to topple; **le président a été renversé** the President was thrown out of *or* removed from office; **renverser un gouvernement** *(par la force)* to overthrow *or* to topple a government; *(par un vote)* to bring down *or* to topple a government

réorientation *nf Pol* reorientation

réorienter *vt Pol* to reorientate

répartir *vt* (a) *(d'argent)* to divide, to distribute; *(responsabilités)* to allocate (b) *(impôts)* to assess

répartition *nf* (a) *(d'argent)* division, distribution; *(de responsabilités)* allocation; **la répartition des richesses est très inégale** the distribution of wealth is very unequal; **la répartition des portefeuilles ministériels** the distribution of ministerial posts (b) *(des impôts)* assessment

◇ *répartition optimale des ressources* optimal resource allocation

◇ *répartition des votes* voting pattern

repositionnement *nm Pol (d'un parti politique)* repositioning

repositionner *vt Pol (parti politique)* to reposition

repreneur *nm Écon* buyer

représailles *nfpl Pol* reprisals, retaliation; **user de représailles contre un pays** to take retaliatory measures *or* to retaliate against a country; **exercer** des représailles contre *ou* envers qn to take reprisals against sb; **en (guise de)** *ou* **par représailles contre** in retaliation for, as a reprisal for; **nos représailles seront militaires et économiques** we shall retaliate both militarily and economically

représentant, -e *nm,f* (a) *Pol* (elected) representative; **les représentants du peuple** the people's representatives (b) *(porte-parole)* representative (c) *(délégué)* delegate, representative; **le représentant de la France à l'ONU** France's *or* the French representative at the UN

◇ *représentant syndical* union representative, *Br* shop steward

représentatif, -ive *adj Pol* representative; **vous ne pouvez prétendre être représentatif** you cannot claim to represent anybody

représentation *nf Pol* representation; **assurer la représentation d'un pays** to represent a country, to act as a country's representative; **réduire sa représentation diplomatique dans un pays** to cut down on *or* to reduce one's diplomatic representation in a country

◇ *représentation proportionnelle* proportional representation

représenter 1 *vt* (a) *Pol (électeurs, membres)* to represent (b) *(remplacer)* to represent; **le maire s'est fait représenter par son adjoint** the mayor was represented by his deputy, the mayor sent his deputy to represent him

2 **se représenter** *vpr Pol (à une élection)* to *Br* stand *or* *Am* run (for election) again

reprise *nf (des affaires)* recovery, upturn; **une reprise des affaires** an upturn *or* a recovery in business activity

◇ *reprise économique* economic recovery

◇ *reprise de travail* return to work; **les grévistes ont voté la reprise de travail** the strikers have voted to return to work

républicain, -e *Pol* **1** *adj (esprit, système)* republican; *(aux États-Unis)* Republican

2 *nm,f* republican; *(aux États-Unis)* Republican

républicanisme *nm Pol* republicanism

république *nf* **(a)** *(régime politique)* republic; **vivre en république** to live in a republic **(b)** *(État)* Republic

◇ *Fam* **république bananière** banana republic

réserve *nf (d'argent, de fonds)* reserve, stock

◇ *réserves bancaires* bank reserves
◇ *réserves de change* monetary reserves
◇ *réserves de devises* currency reserves
◇ *Écon réserve légale* reserve assets
◇ *réserves mondiales (de matières premières)* world reserves
◇ *réserves monétaires* monetary reserves
◇ *réserves monétaires internationales* international monetary reserves
◇ *réserve d'or* gold reserve

résolution *nf Pol* resolution; **prendre une résolution** to pass a resolution; **la résolution a été votée à l'unanimité par l'Assemblée** the resolution was unanimously adopted by the "Assemblée générale"

responsabilité *nf* **(a)** *(charge administrative)* function, position; **des responsabilités gouvernementales/ministérielles** a post in the government/cabinet

(b) *(fait de répondre de ses actes)* accountability; **le Premier ministre a engagé la responsabilité du gouvernement sur cette question** the Prime Minister has accepted that the government is accountable on this matter; **ceci relève de la responsabilité du ministère de la Défense** this is a matter for which the Ministry of Defence is accountable

responsable *Pol* **1** *adj* **le ministre est responsable devant le parlement** the Minister is responsible *or* answerable *or* accountable to Parliament

2 *nmf* leader

◇ *responsable politique* political leader
◇ *responsable syndical* union representative *or* official

resserrement *nm Écon (du marché)* stringency

◇ *resserrement du crédit* credit control

ressortissant, -e *nm,f* national; **un ressortissant d'un pays de l'Union européenne** an EU national

restreindre *vt Écon* to restrict

restrictif, -ive *adj (pratiques, mesures)* restrictive

restriction *nf Écon* restriction, limitation; **imposer des restrictions sur qch** to place restrictions on sth

◇ *restrictions budgétaires* budget restrictions
◇ *restriction de concurrence* trade restraint
◇ *restrictions à l'exportation* export restrictions
◇ *restrictions gouvernementales* government restrictions
◇ *restrictions à l'importation* import restrictions
◇ *restrictions salariales* wage restraint
◇ *restriction volontaire des exportations* voluntary export restraint

restructuration *nf* **(a)** *(d'une industrie, d'une entreprise)* restructuring **(b)** *(de dette)* rescheduling

restructurer *vt* **(a)** *(industrie, entreprise)* to restructure **(b)** *(dette)* to reschedule

"

Dans l'impossibilité de rembourser les obligations qui arrivent à échéance, l'État a donc décidé de **restructurer** sa dette et de transformer les bons du Trésor à court terme en bons à long terme.

"

résultat nm Pol result
◇ **résultat partiel** by-election result; **le résultat partiel pour la Corse et les Alpes-Maritimes** the by-election result for Corsica and the Alpes-Maritimes

rétablir vt (fonctionnaire) to reinstate

rétablissement nm (d'un fonctionnaire) reinstatement

retour de manivelle nm Pol backlash

rétrograde adj (mesure, politique) reactionary, backward-looking

rétrograder vt (fonctionnaire) to downgrade, to demote

réunification nf reunification

réunifier vt to reunify

réunion nf (a) (séance) session, sitting; **réunion du Parlement** Br ≃ Parliamentary session, Am ≃ Congressional session (b) (regroupement) (d'États) union; **la réunion de ces territoires à la France a eu lieu en 1823** these territories were united with France in 1823
◇ **réunion au sommet** summit (meeting or conference)

revalorisation nf (a) (d'une monnaie) revaluation (b) (des salaires, des retraites) raising, increase

revaloriser vt (a) (monnaie) to revaluate (b) (salaires, retraites) to raise, to increase

revenu nm revenue, income; **à faible revenu** low-income; **à haut revenu** high-income
◇ **revenus disponibles** disposable income
◇ **revenus de l'État** public revenue
◇ **revenus de l'exportation** export revenue, export earnings
◇ **revenu imposable** taxable income
◇ **revenu marginal** marginal revenue
◇ **revenu national** national income
◇ **revenu national brut** gross national income
◇ **revenu national net** net national income
◇ **revenu nominal** nominal income
◇ **revenu par habitant** per capita income
◇ **revenu public** public revenue
◇ **revenu réel** effective income
◇ **revenus du secteur public** public sector earnings
◇ **revenu de transfert** transfer income

revers nm Écon setback

revigorer vt (économie) to boost, to give a boost to; **les subventions ont revigoré l'entreprise** the subsidies gave the company a new lease of life

revirement nm (changement d'avis) about-turn, about-face; (de situation) turnaround; **un revirement dans l'opinion publique** a complete swing or turnaround in public opinion

révisionnisme nm revisionism

révisionniste 1 adj revisionist **2** nmf revisionist

revitalisation nf (de l'économie) revitalization

revitaliser vt (économie) to revitalize; **ce nouveau plan économique est destiné à revitaliser la région** this new economic programme is designed to revitalize or bring new life to the area

révocabilité nf (a) (d'un fonctionnaire) dismissibility (b) Pol (d'un élu) recallability

révocable adj (a) (fonctionnaire) dismissible (b) Pol (élu) recallable, subject to recall

révocation nf (a) (d'un fonctionnaire) dismissal (b) Pol (d'un élu) recall

révolution nf Pol revolution; **faire la révolution** to have a revolution
◇ **révolution verte** green revolution

révolutionnaire Pol **1** adj revolutionary **2** nmf Br revolutionary, Am revolutionist

révolutionnarisme nm Pol revolutionism

révoquer vt (a) (fonctionnaire) to dismiss (b) Pol (élu) to recall

riche 1 *adj* rich, wealthy
  2 *nmf* wealthy person; **les impôts indirects touchent davantage les pauvres que les riches** indirect taxes penalize the poor more than the rich

richesse *nf* (a) *(d'une personne, d'un pays)* wealth (b) **richesses** *(ressources)* resources

rideau de fer *nm Pol* Iron Curtain

risque de change *nm* exchange rate risk

risque-pays *nm* country risk

rival, -e 1 *adj* rival
  2 *nm,f* rival
◊ *rival politique* political rival or opponent

RMI *nm (abrév* **revenu minimum d'insertion***)* = minimum welfare payment paid to people with no other source of income

RN *nm Écon (abrév* **revenu national***)* national income

roi *nm* king

romain, -e *Belg Pol* **1** *adj* Christian Socialist
  2 *nm,f* Christian Socialist

rompre *vt (négociations, relations diplomatiques)* to break off

rose *adj Pol* left-wing *(relating to the French Socialist Party)*; **il a des idées de gauche, mais il est plutôt rose que rouge** he has left-wing ideas, but he's more left-of-centre than really socialist

rotation du personnel *nf Écon* labour turnover

rouge 1 *adj Péj Pol (communiste)* red
  2 *adv Péj Pol* **voter rouge** to vote communist
  3 *nmf Péj Pol (communiste)* red
  4 *nm Écon* **être dans le rouge** to be in the red; **sortir du rouge** to get out of the red

royal, -e *adj Pol (puissance)* royal, regal

royaume *nm Pol* kingdom

RP *nf Pol (abrév* **représentation proportionnelle***)* PR

RPR *nm Anciennement Pol (abrév* **Rassemblement pour la République***)* = right-wing French political party

RTGS *nm (abrév* **Real-Time Gross Settlement***)* RTGS

RTT *nf (abrév* **réduction du temps de travail***)* = reduction of the working week in France from 39 to 35 hours, introduced by the government of Lionel Jospin in 1998 and phased in from 2000 onwards

ruine *nf (d'une institution)* downfall, ruin; **le scandale fut la ruine de sa carrière politique** the scandal ruined his political career

rupture *nf (de négociations)* breaking off; *(de relations diplomatiques)* severance, breaking off; **la rupture des pourparlers était inévitable** the talks were bound to break down; **être en rupture avec le parti** to be at odds with the party

RVE *nf Écon (abrév* **restriction volontaire des exportations***)* VER

SADC nf (abrév **Southern African Development Community**) SADC

sain, -e adj (économie, entreprise) healthy, sound

saisonnier, -ère adj (demande, variations) seasonal

sanction nf (a) (mesure répressive) sanction; **imposer des sanctions à** to impose sanctions on; **lever des sanctions (prises) contre** to raise (the) sanctions against; **prendre des sanctions contre** to take sanctions against (b) (approbation) sanction, ratification

◇ *sanctions diplomatiques* diplomatic sanctions

◇ *sanctions économiques* economic sanctions

sanctionner vt (a) (pays) to impose sanctions on (b) (loi) to sanction, to ratify

sanctuaire nm Pol territory under the nuclear umbrella

sans-parti nmf inv Pol independent member (of an assembly or a Parliament); (dans un système de parti unique) non-party member

santé nf (d'une économie, d'une entreprise) health, soundness

satellite nm Pol (pays) satellite; **les satellites du bloc socialiste** the satellite countries of the socialist bloc

saupoudrage nm Pol = allocation of small amounts of funding to various beneficiaries

"

La politique commerciale a parfois été sensible aux arguments des industriels (accord nippo-européen sur l'automobile). Mais la politique technologique, au nom de la cohésion économique et sociale, s'est enlisée dans un **saupoudrage** de fonds au demeurant très faibles (2 % du budget communautaire, soit 0,02 % du PIB communautaire).

"

saupoudrer vt Pol **saupoudrer des crédits** ou **des fonds** = to allocate small amounts of funding to various beneficiaries

sauter vi Fam (être renvoyé) to fall; **le gouvernement a sauté** the government has fallen; **le ministre a sauté** the minister was fired or Br got the sack

SCI nf (abrév **société de commerce international**) international trading corporation

science nf

◇ *sciences économiques* economics

◇ *sciences politiques* politics, political science

scinder Pol **1** vt to divide, to split (up) (en into)
2 se scinder vpr to split (en into); **le parti s'est scindé en deux tendances** the party split into two

scission nf Pol split, rift; **faire scission** to split off, to secede

scissionniste *Pol* **1** *adj* secessionist
2 *nmf* secessionist

scrutateur, -trice *nm,f Pol Br* scrutineer, *Am* teller

scrutin *nm Pol* **(a)** *(façon d'élire)* vote,
voting, poll; **procéder au scrutin** to take a vote; **dépouiller le scrutin** to
count the votes
   (b) *(fait de voter)* ballot; **par (voie de)
scrutin** by ballot
   (c) *(consultation électorale)* election;
**le dernier scrutin a été favorable à la
gauche** the last election showed a
swing to the left

◇ *scrutin d'arrondissement* district
   election system
◇ *scrutin de ballottage* second ballot, *Am* run-off election
◇ *scrutin à deux tours* second ballot,
◇ *scrutin de liste* list system
◇ *scrutin majoritaire* election on a
   majority basis, first-past-the-post
   system
◇ *scrutin majoritaire plurinominal*
   first-past-the-post system *(voting
   for as many candidates/parties as
   there are seats)*
◇ *scrutin majoritaire uninominal*
   first-past-the-post system *(voting
   for a single candidate)*
◇ *scrutin plurinominal* = voting for
   more than one candidate
◇ *scrutin proportionnel* (voting using
   the system of) proportional representation
◇ *scrutin à la proportionnelle* (voting
   using the system of) proportional
   representation
◇ *scrutin secret* secret ballot; **voter
   au scrutin secret** to have a secret
   ballot
◇ *scrutin uninominal* = voting for a
   single candidate
◇ *scrutin uninominal préférentiel
   avec report de voix* single transferable vote system

séance *nf* session, sitting; **être en
séance** *(comité, Parlement)* to be sitting *or* in session; **lever la séance** *(au
Parlement)* to adjourn; **suspendre la**

séance *(au Parlement)* to adjourn
◇ *séance de concertation* policy
   meeting
◇ *séance plénière* plenary (session)
◇ *séance publique* public sitting

SEBC *nm* (*abrév* **Système Européen de
Banques Centrales**) ESCB

sécession *nf Pol* secession; **faire sécession** to secede

sécessionniste *Pol* **1** *adj* secessionist
2 *nmf* secessionist

secondaire *Écon* **1** *adj* *(secteur)* secondary
2 *nm* **le secondaire** secondary production

secrétaire *nmf*
◇ *Pol* **secrétaire d'ambassade** embassy secretary
◇ *secrétaire d'État* *(en France)* ≃ Junior Minister; *(en Grande-Bretagne)*
   Secretary of State; *(aux États-
   Unis)* State Secretary
◇ *secrétaire général* *(auprès d'un ministre) Br* ≃ permanent secretary;
   (dans un parti) general secretary
◇ *secrétaire général de l'Assemblée
   Br* ≃ Clerk of the House
◇ *secrétaire général de l'ONU* UN
   Secretary-General
◇ *secrétaire général du Sénat Br* ≃
   Clerk of the Parliaments
◇ *secrétaire particulier* private secretary

secrétariat *nm (fonction)* secretaryship; *(bureau)* secretariat
◇ *Pol* **secrétariat d'État** *(fonction en
   France)* post of Junior Minister;
   (ministère français) Junior Minister's Office; *(fonction en Grande-
   Bretagne)* post of Secretary of
   State; *(ministère britannique)* Secretary of State's Office; *(fonction
   aux États-Unis)* post of State Secretary
◇ *secrétariat général de l'ONU* UN
   Secretary-Generalship

secteur *nm Écon* sector
◇ *secteur d'activité* area of activity
◇ *secteur d'affaires* business sector

◇ *secteur de croissance* growth sector

◇ *secteur économique* economic sector

◇ *secteur en expansion* growth sector

◇ *secteur industriel* industrial sector

◇ *secteur primaire* primary sector

◇ *secteur privé* private sector *or* enterprise

◇ *secteur public* public sector

◇ *secteur secondaire* secondary sector

◇ *secteur des services* service sector

◇ *secteur tertiaire* tertiary sector

section *nf* (a) *(d'un service)* branch, division, department (b) *(d'un parti)* local branch

◇ *Pol* **section électorale** ward

◇ *section syndicale* = local branch of a union

sécurité *nf* security

◇ *sécurité intérieure* national security

◇ *sécurité internationale* international security

◇ *sécurité nationale* national security

Sécurité sociale *nf* = French social security system providing public health benefits, pensions, maternity leave etc

séditieux, -euse 1 *adj* (a) *(propos, écrit)* seditious (b) *(troupe, armée)* insurrectionary, insurgent
2 *nm,f* insurgent, rebel

sédition *nf* rebellion, revolt, sedition

segment *nm (en statistique)* segment

◇ *segment démographique* demographic segment

segmentation *nf (en statistique)* segmentation

◇ *segmentation démographique* demographic segmentation

ségrégation *nf* segregation; **soumettre à la ségrégation** to segregate

ségrégationniste 1 *adj (personne)* segregationist; *(politique)* segregationist, segregational, discriminatory
2 *nmf* segregationist

seigneurage *nm* *Écon* seignorage

SEM *nf* *Écon (abrév* **société d'économie mixte)** = company financed by state and private capital

semi-fini, -e *adj* *Écon (produit)* semi-finished

semi-ouvré, -e *adj* *Écon (produit)* semi-finished

semi-présidentiel, -elle *adj* *Pol* semi-presidential

sénat *nm* (a) *(assemblée)* senate ; **le Sénat** the (French) Senate (b) *(lieu)* senate (house)

sénateur *nm* senator

sénatorial, -e 1 *adj* senatorial, senate
2 *nfpl* **sénatoriales** senatorial elections

séparation des pouvoirs *nf* *Pol* **la séparation des pouvoirs** the separation of powers

séparatisme *nm* separatism

séparatiste 1 *adj* separatist
2 *nmf* separatist

séparer *vt* to separate, to divide

septennat *nm* *Anciennement Pol* (seven-year) term of office

serment d'allégeance *nm* oath of allegiance

série *nf (de discussions, de négociations)* series

serpent *nm* *UE* snake

◇ *serpent monétaire* currency snake

◇ *serpent monétaire européen* European currency snake

service *nm* (a) *(pour la collectivité)* service, servicing (b) *(département) (d'un ministère)* department (c) *Écon (secteur)* **services** services, service industries; **biens et services** goods and services

◇ *service diplomatique* diplomatic service

◇ *service des douanes* customs service

◇ *service de presse* press office

◇ *service public* *Br* public utility, *Am* utility

◇ *Pol* **services de renseignements** intelligence service

◇ *services de santé* health services

◇ *Pol* **services secrets** secret service

◇ *Pol* **services spéciaux** secret service

servir *Pol* **1** *vt (pays, parti, cause)* to serve; **servir l'intérêt public** *(loi, mesure)* to be in the public interest; *(personne)* to serve the public interest; **servir l'État** to serve the state; *(être fonctionnaire)* to be employed by the state

2 *vi (travailler)* **il a servi sous MacArthur** he served under MacArthur

session *nf* session, sitting; **pendant la session de printemps du Parlement** during Parliament's spring session

seuil *nm* threshold; **la dette a atteint le seuil critique des deux milliards** debt has reached the critical level *or* threshold of two billion

◇ *Écon* **seuil de pauvreté** poverty line

SGDG *(abrév* **sans garantie du gouvernement***)* without government guarantee

SGEN *nm (abrév* **Syndicat général de l'Éducation nationale***)* = French teachers' union

siège *nm* *Pol* **(a)** *(au Parlement)* seat; **perdre/gagner des sièges** to lose/to win seats; **disputer un siège** to contest a seat **(b)** *(centre)* seat; *(d'un parti)* headquarters; **le siège du gouvernement** the seat of government; **au siège du PS** at (the) PS headquarters

◇ *siège administratif* administrative headquarters

◇ *siège parlementaire* seat in Parliament

◇ *siège à pourvoir* vacant seat

◇ *siège vacant* vacant seat

siéger *vi* **(a)** *(député)* to sit; **siéger au Parlement** to have a seat *or* to sit in Parliament; **siéger à un comité/au conseil d'administration** to sit on a committee/on the board **(b)** *(assemblée)* to be in session

signal du marché *nm* *Écon* market indicator

Sur un plan stratégique, l'OPEP aurait intérêt à agir le plus rapidement possible, car une réaction immédiate au **signal du marché** lui permettrait de préserver durablement son pouvoir d'influence. Plus les décisions tarderont et plus le coût – en termes de réduction de production – sera élevé.

signature *nf (sur document)* signature; **la signature de la France doit être honorée** France must honour the agreement it made

signer *vt (document)* to sign

slogan *nm* *Pol* slogan, catchword

SMCT *nm* *UE (abrév* **soutien monétaire à court terme***)* STMS

SME *nm* *Écon (abrév* **Système monétaire européen***)* EMS

SMI *nm* *Écon (abrév* **Système monétaire international***)* IMS

SNALC *nm (abrév* **Syndicat national des lycées et collèges***)* = French teachers' union

SNC *nf* *Écon (abrév* **société en nom collectif***)* general partnership

SNES *nm (abrév* **Syndicat national de l'enseignement secondaire***)* = French secondary school teachers' union

Sne-sup *nm (abrév* **Syndicat national de l'enseignement supérieur***)* = French university teachers' union

SNJ *nm (abrév* **Syndicat national des journalistes***)* = French journalists' union

social, -e 1 *adj (réformes, ordre, politique)* social

2 *nm* **le social** social issues

social-chrétien, sociale-chréti-

enne *Belg* **1** *adj* Christian Socialist
2 *nm,f* Christian Socialist

social-démocrate, sociale-démocrate 1 *adj* social democratic
2 *nm,f* social democrat; *(adhérent d'un parti)* Social Democrat

social-démocratie *nf* social democracy

socialisant, -e *Pol* **1** *adj* left-leaning, with left-wing tendencies
2 *nm,f* socialist sympathizer

socialisation *nf* *Écon* collectivization; *(du capital, des industries)* socialization, collectivization

socialiser *vt* *Écon* to collectivize; *(capital, industries)* to socialize, to collectivize

socialisme *nm* socialism
◇ **socialisme chrétien** Christian Socialism
◇ **socialisme d'État** State socialism

socialiste 1 *adj* socialist
2 *nmf* socialist

socialo *Fam* (*abrév* **socialiste**) **1** *adj* lefty
2 *nmf* lefty

social-révolutionnaire, sociale-révolutionnaire 1 *adj* social-revolutionary
2 *nmf* social-revolutionary

société *nf* **(a)** *(communauté)* society; **la société** society **(b)** *(entreprise)* company
◇ **société d'abondance** affluent society
◇ **société d'affacturage** factoring company, factor
◇ **société civile** civil society
◇ **société de commerce international** international trading corporation
◇ **société de consommation** consumer society
◇ **société de crédit** credit union
◇ **société de crédit immobilier** *Br* ≃ building society, *Am* ≃ savings and loan association
◇ **société d'économie mixte** semi-public company

◇ **société d'État** public company
◇ **société d'exportation** export company
◇ **société d'importation** import company
◇ **société d'import-export** import-export company
◇ **société multinationale** multinational company
◇ **société plurielle** plural society
◇ **société privée** private company
◇ **société d'utilité publique** *Br* public utility company, *Am* utility company

socio-économique *adj* socio-economic

solde *nm* *(financier)* balance
◇ **solde commercial** balance of trade
◇ **soldes en sterling** sterling balances

sommet *nm* *Pol* summit

somnolence *nf* *(d'une économie)* lethargy, sluggishness

somnolent, -e *adj* *(économie)* lethargic, sluggish

somnoler *vi* *(économie)* to be lethargic *or* sluggish

sondage *nm* *(enquête)* poll, survey; **faire un sondage (sur qch)** to carry out a poll *or* survey (on sth); **faire un sondage auprès d'un groupe** to poll a group, to carry out a survey among a group
◇ **sondage Gallup** Gallup poll
◇ **sondage d'opinion** opinion poll

sonder *vt* *(personne)* to poll; **sonder l'opinion** to carry out or conduct an opinion poll; **dix pour cent de la population sondée** ten percent of those polled

sondeur, -euse *nm,f* pollster

sortant, -e *Pol* **1** *adj* outgoing; **le maire sortant** the outgoing mayor
2 *nm,f* incumbent; **tous les sortants ont été réélus au premier tour** all the incumbents were re-elected in the first round

sortie *nf* *Écon* *(de produits, de devises)* export; *(de capital)* outflow; *(sujet de* *dépense)* item of expenditure; *(dépense)* outgoing; **la sortie de devises est limitée à 5000 euros par personne** currency export is limited to 5,000 euro per person

sous-capitalisation *nf Écon* undercapitalization, underfunding

sous-capitalisé, -e *adj Écon* undercapitalized, underfunded

sous-consommation *nf Écon* under-consumption

sous-développé, -e *adj Écon (pays, économie)* underdeveloped

sous-développement *nm Écon* underdevelopment

sous-emploi *nm Écon* underemployment

sous-employé, -e *adj Écon* underemployed

sous-équipé, -e *adj Écon* underequipped

sous-équipement *nm Écon* underequipment

sous-préfet, -ète *nm,f (fonctionnaire)* subprefect

sous-production *nf Écon* underproduction

sous-représentation *nf Pol* underrepresentation

sous-représenté, -e *adj Pol* underrepresented

sous-secrétaire *nmf Pol* undersecretary

◇ **sous-secrétaire d'État** junior minister

soutenir *vt* **(a)** *(candidat, gouvernement, politique)* to support, to back **(b)** *(monnaie, économie)* to prop up, to bolster

"

La banque centrale russe dépensait un milliard de dollars par semaine, dans la dernière période, pour **soutenir** le rouble. L'équipe au pouvoir a donc décidé d'élargir la bande de fluctuation de la monnaie, qui pourra désormais flotter entre 6 et 9,5 roubles pour un dollar.

"

soutien *nm* **(a)** *(d'un candidat, d'un gouvernement, d'une politique)* support; **apporter son soutien à qn** to support sb, to back sb up **(b)** *(de l'économie)* propping up, bolstering; **des mesures de soutien à l'économie** measures to bolster the economy

◇ *UE* **soutien monétaire à court terme** short-term monetary support

◇ *Écon* **soutien des prix** price pegging

souverain, -e **1** *adj Pol (pouvoir, peuple)* sovereign; **la Chambre est souveraine** the House is a sovereign authority

2 *nm,f* monarch, sovereign; **notre souveraine** our Sovereign

◇ **souverain absolu** absolute monarch

◇ **souverain fantoche** puppet monarch

souverainement *adv* with sovereign power

souveraineté *nf* sovereignty

◇ **souveraineté populaire** popular sovereignty

souverainiste **1** *adj* separatist **2** *nmf* separatist

soviet *nm (assemblée)* soviet

Soviétique *nmf* Soviet

soviétique *adj* Soviet

soviétisation *nf* sovietization, sovietizing

soviétiser *vt* to sovietize

speaker *nm Parl (en Grande-Bretagne, aux États-Unis)* Speaker

spécial, -e *adj Pol (extraordinaire)* special, extraordinary, exceptional

SPI *nmpl (abrév* **Secrétariats professionnels internationaux)** ITS

spirale *nf (hausse rapide)* spiral

◇ **spirale inflationniste** inflationary spiral

◇ *spirale des prix et des salaires* wage-price spiral

spontanéisme *nm Pol* = belief in spontaneous political action

spontanéiste *nmf Pol* = believer in spontaneous political action

stabilisateur, -trice *Écon* **1** *adj* stabilizing
  2 *nm* stabilizer
◇ *stabilisateur automatique* automatic stabilizer

stabilisation *nf (d'une monnaie, des prix, du marché, de situation politique)* stabilization

stabiliser 1 *vt (monnaie, prix, marché, situation politique)* to stabilize
  2 se stabiliser *vpr (monnaie, prix, marché, situation politique)* to stabilize

stabilité *nf (d'une monnaie, des prix, d'un marché)* stability, steadiness; *(de situation politique)* stability

stable *adj (monnaie, prix, marché)* stable, steady; *(situation politique)* stable

stagflation *nf Écon* stagflation

stagnant, -e *adj (économie, affaires)* stagnant, sluggish

stagnation *nf (d'économie, d'affaires)* stagnation, sluggishness

stagner *vi (économie, affaires)* to stagnate, to be sluggish; **l'industrie du textile stagne** the textile industry is stagnating

stalinien, -enne *Pol* **1** *adj* Stalinist
  2 *nm,f* Stalinist

stalinisme *nm Pol* Stalinism

standardisation *nf Écon* standardization

standardiser *vt Écon* to standardize

statisticien, -enne *nm,f* statistician

statistique 1 *adj* statistical
  2 *nf* **(a)** *(étude)* statistics **(b)** *(donnée)* statistic; **des statistiques** statistics
◇ *statistiques corrigées des variations saisonnières* seasonally adjusted statistics

◇ *statistiques démographiques* demographics
◇ *statistiques désaisonnalisées* seasonally adjusted statistics

statistiquement *adv* statistically

statut *nm (état)* status; **avoir le statut de cadre/de fonctionnaire** to have executive/civil servant status; **il réclame le statut de réfugié politique** he is asking for political refugee status

statuts *nmpl (règlements)* statutes, articles of association, *Am* bylaws

sténographe *nmf Parl* reporter

sterling 1 *adj inv* sterling
  2 *nm inv* sterling

stimuler *vt (activité, industries, économie, demande)* to stimulate

stock *nm Écon* stock, supply
◇ *stocks excédentaires* surplus stock
◇ *stock tampon* buffer stock

stop-and-go *nm Écon* stop-and-go policy

stratège *nmf* strategist

stratégie *nf* strategy
◇ *stratégie de campagne* campaign strategy

stratification sociale *nf* social stratification

structure *nf* **(a)** *(d'un service, d'une société)* structure **(b)** *(institution)* system, organization
◇ *structures administratives* administrative structures
◇ *structures politiques* political structures

structurel, -elle *adj Écon* structural

subside *nm* subsidy, grant
◇ *subside de l'État* state subsidy

subsidiation *nf Belg* subsidization

subsidier *vt Belg* to subsidize

subvention *nf* subsidy, grant
◇ *subvention d'État* government subsidy
◇ *subvention à l'exportation* export subsidy

◇ *subvention de fonctionnement* operational subsidy

◇ *subvention d'investissement* investment grant

subventionné, -e *adj* subsidized; **subventionné par l'État** government-funded

subventionner *vt* to subsidize, to grant financial aid to

SUD–PTT *nm* (*abrév* **solidaires, unitaires et démocratiques–postes, télécommunications et télédiffusion**) = French post office and telecommunications trade union

suffrage *nm Pol* (a) *(système)* suffrage (b) *(voix)* vote; **obtenir beaucoup/peu de suffrages** to poll heavily/badly; **décrocher 60 pour cent des suffrages** to get 60 percent of the votes; **c'est leur parti qui a eu le plus de suffrages** their party headed the poll

◇ *suffrage direct* direct suffrage; **être élu au suffrage direct** to be elected by direct suffrage

◇ *suffrage indirect* indirect suffrage; **être élu au suffrage indirect** to be elected by indirect suffrage

◇ *suffrage restreint* restricted suffrage

◇ *suffrage universel* universal suffrage

◇ *suffrage universel direct* direct universal suffrage

◇ *suffrage universel indirect* indirect universal suffrage

suffragette *nf Pol* suffragette

suicide politique *nf* political suicide

sujétion *nf Pol* (*d'un peuple*) subjection, enslavement (**à** to)

superétatique *adj* suprastate

superpuissance *nf* superpower

suppléance *nf Pol* deputy

suppléant, -e *Pol* 1 *adj* deputy 2 *nm,f* deputy

suppléer *vt Pol* to deputize for

suppression *nf* (*d'une loi*) annulment

◇ *suppressions d'emploi* job losses; **il**

y a eu beaucoup de suppressions d'emploi dans la région there were many job losses in the area

supprimer *vt* (a) *(loi)* to annul, to repeal (b) **supprimer des emplois** to cut *or* axe jobs

surcapacité *nf Écon* overcapacity, excess capacity

surchauffe *nf Écon* overheating

surchauffer *vt Écon* to overheat

surconsommation *nf Écon* overconsumption

surdéveloppé, -e *adj Écon* highly developed; *(excessivement)* overdeveloped

surdéveloppement *nm Écon* high state of development; *(excessif)* overdevelopment

surdévelopper *vt Écon* to develop to a high degree; *(excessivement)* to overdevelop

suremploi *nm Écon* overemployment

surendetté, -e *adj Écon* overindebted

surendettement *nm Écon* excessive debt

sûreté *nf* (*sécurité*) safety

◇ *sûreté de l'État* state security

suroffre *nf Écon* oversupply

surplus *nm Écon* (*stock excédentaire*) surplus (stock); *(gain)* surplus

◇ *surplus d'importation* import surplus

surproduction *nf Écon* overproduction

surproduire *Écon* 1 *vt* to overproduce 2 *vi* to overproduce

surprofit *nm Écon* excessive profit

surréaction *nf Écon* overshooting

sursaturation *nf Écon* oversaturation

sursaturer *vt Écon* to oversaturate

surtaxe *nf (taxe supplémentaire)* surcharge; *(taxe excessive)* excessive tax
◇ **surtaxe à l'importation** import surcharge

surtaxer *vt (frapper d'une taxe supplémentaire)* to surcharge; *(frapper d'une taxe excessive)* to overcharge

suspendre *vt (négociations)* to suspend, to break off; *(séance)* to adjourn

suspension *nf (de négociations)* suspension, breaking off; *(de séance)* adjournment

suzerain, -e 1 *adj* suzerain
2 *nm* suzerain lord

sympathisant, -e *nm,f* sympathizer

syndical, -e *adj Pol (Br* trade *or Am* labor) union

syndicalisation *nf* unionization; **le taux de syndicalisation dans l'industrie est en chute libre depuis 20 ans** union membership has been plummeting for the last 20 years; **ils ont monté une campagne de choc pour essayer de relancer la syndicalisation dans les grandes entreprises** they launched a hard-hitting campaign to try to boost union membership in large companies

Le **taux de syndicalisation** en Belgique tourne autour de 60 %; sur 100 travailleurs actifs, on en trouve donc 60 qui sont affiliés à un syndicat. Plus de la moitié de ces 60 travailleurs affiliés le sont à la CSC. Par rapport à d'autres pays industrialisés, la Belgique connaît un **taux de syndicalisation** très élevé. Seuls les pays scandinaves font mieux, avec des **taux de syndicalisation** oscillant entre 60 et 85 %.

syndicaliser *vt* to unionize, to organize

syndicalisme *nm* **(a)** *(mouvement)*

(Br trade *or Am* labor) unionism **(b)** *(ensemble des syndicats) (Br* trade *or Am* labor) unions **(c)** *(action)* union activities; **faire du syndicalisme** to be active in a union **(d)** *(doctrine)* syndicalism, unionism

syndicaliste 1 *adj* **(a)** *(mouvement)* *(Br* trade *or Am* labor) union **(b)** *(doctrine)* unionist
2 *nmf (Br* trade *or Am* labor) unionist

syndicat *nm* **(a)** *Pol (travailleurs) (Br* trade *or Am* labor) union; **se former** *ou* **se regrouper en syndicat** to form a union **(b)** *(association)* association
◇ **syndicat de communes** association of communes
◇ **Syndicat intercommunal à vocation multiple** = group of local authorities pooling public services
◇ **syndicat interdépartemental** association of regional administrators
◇ **syndicat ouvrier** *(Br* trade *or Am* labor) union
◇ **syndicat patronal** employers' confederation *or* association
◇ **syndicat professionnel** trade *or* professional association, trade body

syndiqué, -e 1 *adj* belonging to a *(Br* trade *or Am* labor) union; **être syndiqué** to be a member of a *(Br* trade *or Am* labor) union
2 *nm,f (Br* trade *or Am* labor) union member

syndiquer 1 *vt* to unionize, to organize; **syndiquer les travailleurs d'un atelier** to organize the workers in a workshop
2 se syndiquer *vpr* **(a)** *(se constituer en syndicat)* to form a *(Br* trade *or Am* labor) union **(b)** *(adhérer à un syndicat)* to join a *(Br* trade *or Am* labor) union

synergie *nf Écon* synergy

système *nm (structure)* system
◇ *Pol* **système bicaméral** two-chamber system
◇ **système bipartite** two-party system
◇ **système des dépouilles** spoils system

◇ *système économique* economic system

◇ *système électoral* electoral system

◇ *système européen de banques centrales* European System of Central Banks

◇ *système généralisé de préférences* Generalized System of Preferences

◇ *système marchand* mercantile system

◇ *Écon système monétaire* monetary system

◇ *Système monétaire européen* European Monetary System

◇ *Système monétaire international* International Monetary System

◇ *système du parti unique* one-party system

◇ *système de protection sociale* social welfare system

◇ *système de Réserve fédérale* Federal Reserve System

◇ *système RTGS* RTGS system

table *nf (liste, recueil)* table
- *table des négociations* negotiating table ; *s'asseoir à la table des négociations* to sit round the negotiating table
- *Écon* *table des parités* parity table

> Le porte-parole de la SRC, Marc Sévigny, estime plutôt que c'est le syndicat qui s'absente trop souvent de la **table des négociations**. "On n'a aucun intérêt à retarder ça ... On voudrait aller plus vite, mais il y a eu plusieurs délais causés non pas par la partie patronale mais par la partie syndicale", dit-il. M. Sévigny précise également que le conseil d'administration soutient les représentants de Radio-Canada à la **table des négociations**.

tableau *nm (diagramme)* table ; *(graphique)* chart
- *Écon* *tableaux d'activité économique* economic activity tables
- *Écon* *tableau de bord* (list of) indicators

take-off *nm Écon* take-off

tarif *nm (barème)* rate, rates, tariff
- *tarif discriminatoire* price discrimination
- *tarif douanier* customs rate
- *tarif douanier commun* common customs or external tariff
- *tarif douanier fiscal* revenue tariff
- *tarif d'entrée* import list
- *tarif export* export tariff
- *tarif externe commun* common external tariff
- *Écon* *tarif de faveur* preference
- *tarif import* import tariff
- *tarif de sortie* export list
- *tarif syndical* union tariff

tarifaire *adj (disposition, réforme)* tarif

taux *nm* rate
- *taux d'accroissement* rate of growth
- *taux d'activité* participation rate
- *taux annuel effectif* effective annual rate
- *taux de base* base rate
- *taux de change* exchange rate
- *taux de change concerté* dirty float
- *taux de change fixe* fixed exchange rate
- *taux de change flottant* floating exchange rate
- *taux de change libre* floating exchange rate
- *taux de chômage* unemployment rate
- *taux de chômage naturel* natural unemployment rate
- *taux de crédit* credit rate
- *taux de crédit export* export credit rate
- *taux de croissance* growth rate
- *taux de croissance économique* economic growth rate
- *taux effectif global* annual or annualized percentage rate
- *taux d'épargne* savings rate
- *taux d'expansion économique* economic growth rate

◇ *taux d'imposition* rate of taxation

◇ *taux d'imposition effectif* effective tax rate

◇ *taux d'inflation* rate of inflation

◇ *taux d'intérêt* interest rate

◇ *taux d'intérêt réel* real interest rate

◇ *taux d'intervention* intervention rate

◇ *Pol taux de participation* turnout

◇ *Pol taux de participation électorale* voter turnout

◇ *taux pivot* designated rate

◇ *taux de rendement* rate of return

◇ *taux de rendement réel* real rate of return

◇ *taux de rentabilité économique* economic rate of return

◇ *taux de rotation des stocks* rate of turnover

◇ *taux des salaires* wage rate

◇ *taux standard* standard rate

◇ *taux usuraire* usurious rate

◇ *taux de l'usure* usurious rate

◇ *taux vert* green rate

taxable *adj Écon* taxable, liable to duty

taxation *nf Écon* taxation

taxe *nf Écon* tax; *(prix fixé)* controlled price; **vendre des marchandises à la taxe** to sell goods at the controlled price

◇ *taxe sur le chiffre d'affaires* turnover tax

◇ *taxe de douane* customs duty

◇ *taxe écologique* ecotax

◇ *taxe à l'exportation* export tax

◇ *taxe d'habitation* = tax paid on residence, *Br* ≃ council tax

◇ *taxe à l'importation* import tax

◇ *taxe de port* harbour dues

◇ *taxe professionnelle* = tax paid by businesses and self-employed people

◇ *taxe sur la valeur ajoutée* value-added tax

taxer *vt Écon* to tax; **taxer les disques à dix pour cent** to tax records at ten percent, to put a ten percent tax on records

taylorisme *nm Écon* Taylorism, time and motion studies

TEG *nm Écon* (*abrév* **taux effectif global**) APR

tendance *nf* (a) *(position, opinion)* allegiance, leaning, sympathy; **un parti de tendance libérale** a party with liberal tendencies; **la tendance centriste au sein du parti** the middle-of-the-road tendency within the party; **des partis de toutes tendances étaient représentés** the whole spectrum of political opinion was represented; **le groupe a décidé, toutes tendances réunies** *ou* **confondues, de voter l'amendement** all the factions within the group voted in favour of supporting the amendment; **à quelle tendance appartiens-tu?** what are your political leanings?, where do your (political) sympathies lie?

(b) *Écon* trend

◇ *tendance à la baisse* downward trend, downswing

◇ *tendance baissière* downward trend, downswing

◇ *tendance conjoncturelle* economic trend

◇ *tendance de croissance* growth trend

◇ *tendance économique* economic trend

◇ *tendance à la hausse* upward trend, upswing

◇ *tendance haussière* upward trend, upswing

◇ *tendance inflationniste* inflationary trend

◇ *tendance du marché* market trend

termaillage *nm Écon* leads and lags

terme *nm* (a) *(dans le temps)* end, term; **quel est le terme de son mandat?** when does his mandate end? (b) **termes** *(conditions)* terms (c) **à court/moyen/long terme** *(prêt, prévision)* short-/medium-/long-term

◇ *termes de l'échange* (commodity) terms of trade

◇ *termes factoriels de l'échange* factorial terms of trade

territoire *nm* area, territory

◇ *Pol* **territoires occupés** occupied territories

◇ **territoires d'outre-mer** (French) overseas territories

◇ **territoire sous mandat** mandate

terrorisme *nm* terrorism

◇ **terrorisme d'État** government-sponsored terrorism

terroriste 1 *adj* terrorist
  2 *nmf* terrorist

tertiaire *Écon* **1** *adj* (*secteur*) tertiary
  2 *nm* **le tertiaire** the tertiary sector

tertiarisation *nf Écon* expansion of the tertiary sector, tertiarization; **la tertiarisation de l'économie** the tertiarization of the economy

test conjoncturel *nm* economic test

tête *nf* (**a**) (*meneur, leader*) head, leader; **il est la tête du mouvement** he's the leader of the movement (**b**) *Écon* **par tête** per capita

◇ *Pol* **tête de liste** *Br* leading candidate, *Am* head of the ticket

> **"**
>
> Le procureur général Rahoui Kheï-reddine, **tête de liste** indé-pendante, semble intéresser les populations des communes d'El Gor et de Sebdou. Ce candidat issu d'une famille aisée, et selon ses sympathisants, n'est pas prêt à avancer des promesses.
>
> **"**

texte *nm* (*teneur d'une loi, d'un traité*) terms; (*loi*) law, act; (*traité*) treaty; **selon le texte de la loi/du traité** according to the terms of the law/treaty

thatchérien, -enne 1 *adj* Thatcherite
  2 *nm,f* Thatcherite

thatchérisme *nm* Thatcherism

théorie *nf* theory

◇ *Écon* **théorie de la dépendance** dependency theory

◇ **théorie des jeux** game theory

◇ **théorie des prix** price theory

◇ **théorie quantitative** quantity theory

thésaurisation *nf Écon* hoarding

thésauriser *Écon* **1** *vt* to hoard (up)
  2 *vi* to hoard money

ticket *nm* *Pol* (*aux États-Unis*) ticket

tiers-monde *nm* **le tiers-monde** the Third World

tiers-mondisme *nm* = support for the Third World

tiers-mondiste 1 *adj* (**a**) (*du tiers-mondisme*) pro-Third World (**b**) (*du tiers-monde*) (*population, réfugié*) Third World
  2 *nmf* (**a**) (*spécialiste du tiers-monde*) Third World expert (**b**) (*idéologue du tiers-mondisme*) Third Worldist

tolérance *nf* tolerance; **le gouvernement doit faire preuve de tolérance envers les réfugiés politiques** the government must show tolerance towards political refugees

◇ *Pol* **tolérance zéro** zero tolerance

TOM *nm inv* (*abrév* **territoire d'outre-mer**) = French overseas territory

tomber *vi* (*dictature, gouvernement, empire*) to fall, to be brought down; **les candidats de droite sont tombés au premier tour** the right-wing candidates were eliminated in the first round; **faire tomber** (*dictature, gouvernement, empire*) to bring down, to topple

tombeur *nm* *Fam Pol* **le tombeur des conservateurs** the man who defeated the Conservatives

tory *Pol* **1** *adj* Tory
  2 *nmf* Tory

torysme *nm* *Pol* toryism

totalitaire *Pol* **1** *adj* totalitarian
  2 *nmf* totalitarian

totalitarisme *nm* *Pol* totalitarianism

tour *nm* **au premier/second tour** in the first/second ballot *or* round

◇ *Pol* **tour de scrutin** ballot

◇ *Écon* **tour de table** = meeting of

shareholders or investors to decide a course of action

tournée électorale *nf* faire une tournée électorale *(candidat député)* to canvass one's constituency; *(dans une élection présidentielle)* to go on the campaign trail

tract *nm Pol* leaflet, pamphlet

traditionaliste *Pol* **1** *adj* traditionalist

2 *nmf* traditionalist

trafic d'influence *nm* influence peddling

trahison *nf Pol* treason

traité *nm (accord)* treaty
◇ *traité d'adhésion* membership treaty
◇ *traité d'alliance* treaty of alliance
◇ *traité de Maastricht* Maastricht Treaty
◇ *traité de non-prolifération nucléaire* Nuclear Non-Proliferation Treaty
◇ *traité de paix* peace treaty
◇ *traité sur l'Union européenne* Treaty on European Union

tranche *nf Écon (subdivision)* bracket
◇ *tranche d'imposition* tax bracket
◇ *tranche de revenu* income bracket
◇ *tranche de salaire* salary bracket

transaction *nf Écon* transaction, deal
◇ *transactions invisibles* invisible trade

transférer *vt (employé, fonctionnaire)* to transfer

transfrontalier, -ère *adj* cross-border

transfuge *nmf Pol* renegade, turncoat; *(qui change de camp)* defector

transition *nf (entre deux gouvernements)* interim

transitionnel, -elle *adj* transitional, interim

transmettre *vt (pouvoir, autorité)* to hand over

transparence *nf (d'un parti politique, des négociations)* transparency, openness

transparent, -e *adj (parti politique, négociations)* transparent, open

travail *nm (activité)* work; *(emploi)* employment, job; **être sans travail** to be out of work, to be unemployed
◇ *travail au noir* black economy

travailleur, -euse *nm,f* worker
◇ *travailleur immigré* immigrant worker
◇ *travailleur au noir* = worker in the black economy
◇ *travailleurs pauvres* working poor

travaillisme *nm* Labour doctrine *or* philosophy

travailliste **1** *adj* Labour; **être travailliste** to be a member of the Labour Party
2 *nmf* member of the Labour Party; **les travaillistes se sont opposés à cette mesure** Labour opposed the move

treizième mois *nm* = extra month's salary paid as an annual bonus

trend *nm Écon* trend

trésor *nm* treasury; **le Trésor (public)** *(institution)* = department dealing with the State budget, *Br* ≃ the Treasury, *Am* ≃ the Treasury Department; *(finances publiques)* public funds *or* finances

trésorerie *nf* **(a)** *(bureaux)* public revenue office **(b)** *(fonction)* treasurership; *(d'un trésorier-payeur)* paymastership
◇ *Trésorerie générale* paymaster's office

trésorier-payeur général *nm* paymaster *(for a "département" or "région")*

trêve *nf* truce
◇ *la trêve des confiseurs* = the lull in political activities between Christmas and New Year in France

> **"**
> Près de soixante personnes – adhérents du Parti communiste ou non

– ont participé à cette réception conviviale qui marquait la fin de la traditionnelle **trêve des confiseurs**. Joë Triché a rappelé le bilan de l'action politique de la section au cours de l'année écoulée ; une année fortement marquée par les élections municipales.

"

triangulaire *nf Pol* three-cornered contest *or* fight

Tribunal de première instance *nm UE* European Court of First Instance

tribune *nf (estrade)* rostrum, platform; *Parl* **monter à la tribune** to address the House
◇ *tribune de la presse* press gallery
◇ *Parl tribune du public* public gallery, *Br* strangers' gallery

troc *nm Écon* barter, countertrade; **faire du troc** to barter

troïka *nf* troika
◇ *troïka européenne* European troika

troisième voie *nf Pol* **la troisième voie** the Third Way

trotskisme *nm Pol* Trotskyism

trotskiste *Pol* **1** *adj* Trotskyist
2 *nmf* Trotskyist

troubles *nmpl (agitation sociale)* unrest, disturbances; **les troubles s'étendent** the rioting is spreading

trust *nm* **(a)** *(cartel)* trust **(b)** *(entreprise)* corporation
◇ *trust commercial* commercial monopoly
◇ *trust industriel* industrial monopoly
◇ *trust de placement* investment trust
◇ *trust de valeurs* holding company

TUE *nm (abrév* **traité sur l'Union européenne**) TEU

tutelle *nf Pol* trusteeship; **un territoire sous tutelle** a trust territory

TVA *nf (abrév* **taxe sur la valeur ajoutée**) *Br* VAT, *Am* sales tax

UDF *nf Pol* (*abrév* **Union pour la démocratie française**) = right-of-centre French political party

UE *nf* (*abrév* **Union européenne**) EU

UEAPME *nf* (*abrév* **Union européenne de l'artisanat et des petites et moyennes entreprises**) UEAPME, European Association of Craft, Small and Medium-sized Entreprises

UEM *nf Écon* (*abrév* **Union économique et monétaire**) EMU

UEMOA *nf* (*abrév* **Union économique et monétaire ouest-africaine**) WAEMU

UEO *nf* (*abrév* **Union de l'Europe occidentale**) WEU

UFT *nf* (*abrév* **Union française du travail**) = French association of independent trade unions

UMA *nf* (*abrév* **Union du Maghreb arabe**) AMU

UME *nf* (*abrév* **union monétaire européenne**) EMU

UMP *nf Pol* (**a**) (*abrév* **Union pour un Mouvement Populaire**) = centre-right French political party, formed mainly from members of the former RPR party (**b**) *Anciennement* (*abrév* **Union pour la Majorité Présidentielle**) = former centre-right coalition, now renamed "Union pour un Mouvement Populaire"

unanime *adj* unanimous

unanimement *adv* unanimously

unanimité *nf* unanimity; **voter à l'unanimité pour qn** to vote unanimously for sb; **élu à l'unanimité moins une voix** elected with only one dissenting vote; **faire l'unanimité** to win unanimous support; **un candidat qui fait l'unanimité contre lui** a candidate who has no support from anyone; **sa politique n'a pas fait l'unanimité** his/her policy failed to win unanimous support

unicaméral, -e *adj Pol* unicameral

unicaméralisme *nm Pol* unicameralism

unification *nf* unification

unifié, -e *adj* unified

unifier *vt* to unify

unilatéral, -e *adj* unilateral

unilatéralisme *nm* unilateralism

union *nf* (**a**) (*fait de mélanger*) union; (*mélange*) union, integration (**b**) (*solidarité*) union, unity; **réaliser l'union européenne** to make European union a reality (**c**) (*regroupement*) union, association

⬦ *Pol* **Union pour la démocratie française** = right-of-centre French political party

⬦ **union douanière** customs union

⬦ **Union douanière européenne** European Customs Union

⬦ **Union économique et monétaire** Economic and Monetary Union

⬦ **Union européenne** European Union

⬦ **Union de l'Europe occidentale** Western European Union

⬦ *Anciennement* **Union pour la Majorité Présidentielle** = former centre-right coalition, now renamed "Union pour un Mouvement Populaire"

◇ **Union monétaire européenne** European Monetary Union

◇ **Union pour un Mouvement Populaire** = centre-right French political party

◇ **union nationale** national coalition

unionisme *nm Pol* Unionism

unioniste *Pol* **1** *adj* Unionist **2** *nmf* Unionist

unir 1 *vt (lier)* to unite, to ally; **unir deux pays** to unite two countries; **unir une province à un pays** to unite a province with a country **2 s'unir** *vpr (se regrouper)* to unite; **s'unir à qn** to join forces with sb; **s'unir contre un ennemi commun** to unite against a common enemy

unitaire *adj (principe, slogan)* uniting; *(politique)* unitarian; *(système)* unitary

unité *nf* **(a)** *Pol* unity; **l'unité et la pluralité** unity and plurality **(b)** *(étalon)* unit, measure

◇ *Écon* **unité de compte** unit of account

◇ **unité de compte européenne** European unit of account

◇ **unité de compte monétaire** money of account

◇ **unité monétaire** monetary unit

◇ *Anciennement* **Unité monétaire européenne** European currency unit

◇ **l'unité nationale** national unity

université *nf Pol* **les universités d'été du parti socialiste** = the Socialist party summer school during which party leaders meet younger members

Unsa *nf (abrév* **Union nationale des**

syndicats autonomes) = French trade union representing civil servants and other workers

UPA *nf (abrév* **Union professionnelle artisanale)** = French employers' organization for craft industries

urne *nf Pol* ballot box; **se rendre aux urnes** to go to the polls

Les électeurs étaient appelés à **se rendre aux urnes** dimanche en Hongrie pour participer au scrutin législatif, à l'occasion des quatrièmes élections libres organisées dans le pays depuis le retour de la démocratie en 1990.

utilisation *nf Écon* utilization

◇ **utilisation du potentiel de production** capacity utilization

utilitarisme *nm* utilitarianism

utilitariste 1 *adj* utilitarian **2** *nmf* utilitarian

utilité *nf Écon* utility

◇ **utilité collective** collective utility

◇ **utilité marginale** marginal utility

◇ **utilité marginale décroissante** diminishing marginal utility

utopie *nf* utopia, Utopia; **votre programme politique relève de l'utopie** your political programme is rather utopian

utopique *adj* utopian, Utopian

utopisme *nm* utopianism, Utopianism

utopiste 1 *adj* utopian, Utopian **2** *nmf* utopian, Utopian

Historique de l'Union européenne

History of the European Union

Avril 1951	Le traité de Paris institue la Communauté européenne du charbon et de l'acier (CECA) qui comprend la France, l'Allemagne, l'Italie, la Belgique, les Pays-Bas et le Luxembourg
Oct 1954	Les six pays membres de la CECA et le Royaume-Uni fondent l'Union de l'Europe occidentale (UEO) pour un renforcement de la coopération en matière de sécurité entre les pays européens
Mars 1957	Les traités de Rome établissent la Communauté économique européenne (CEE) et la Communauté européenne de l'énergie atomique (Euratom)
Mai 1960	Création de l'Association européenne de libre-échange (AELE) par l'Autriche, le Danemark, la Norvège, le Portugal, le Royaume-Uni, la Suède et la Suisse
Janv 1962	La politique agricole commune est acceptée par les Six
1963	La Turquie signe un accord d'association
Juil 1968	Établissement de l'Union douanière européenne
Oct 1970	Le Conseil européen crée de nouvelles procédures pour une coopération en matière de politique étrangère
1971	Le rapport Werner présente un projet en trois étapes devant aboutir à l'UEM
Janv 1973	Adhésion du Royaume-Uni, de l'Irlande et du Danemark à la CEE
Mars 1975	Établissement du Fonds européen de développement régional
Mars 1979	Création du SME : le système monétaire européen (accord sur le rétrécissement des marges) avec huit monnaies et introduction de l'ECU, la moyenne pondérée de toutes les monnaies européennes
Janv 1981	Adhésion de la Grèce à la CEE
Fév 1984	Le projet de traité sur l'Union européenne est adopté par une large majorité au Parlement européen
Juin 1985	Ratification de l'accord de Schengen par l'Allemagne, la Belgique, la France, le Luxembourg et les Pays-Bas : suppression des contrôles aux frontières
1986	Adhésion du Portugal et de l'Espagne à la CEE
1987	Candidature de la Turquie à la CEE
1986-87	L'Acte unique européen fixe les modalités du Marché unique européen
1989	Publication du rapport Delors sur l'union économique et monétaire : il définit les étapes concrètes de la mise en œuvre de l'UEM
Mai 1990	Signature de l'accord établissant la Banque européenne pour la reconstruction et le développement
Juin 1990	Signature du deuxième accord de Schengen qui concerne maintenant tous les pays membres, excepté l'Irlande, le Royaume-Uni et, dans une certaine mesure, le Danemark
Juil 1990	1ère étape de l'UEM : abolition de la réglementation des changes en Europe, ainsi que celle des contrôles des capitaux. Candidature de Chypre et Malte à la CEE
Déc 1991	Signature d'accords européens avec la Pologne et la Hongrie ; d'autres pays d'Europe centrale suivront
Fév 1992	Traité de Maastricht : il précise les modalités de l'union monétaire et prescrit les

	critères de convergence pour les états membres candidats à la monnaie unique ; il renforce les pouvoirs du Parlement européen, instaure la citoyenneté européenne et met en place deux nouveaux piliers intergouvernementaux : politique étrangère et de sécurité commune, et coopération en matière de justice et d'affaires intérieures
Mai 1992	Signature d'un pacte entre les pays de l'AELE et les pays de la CEE : institution de l'Espace économique européen (EEE)
Janv 1993	La CEE devient l'Union européenne (UE)
Nov 1993	Le traité de Maastricht entre en vigueur ; la composition du panier de devises est gelée
Janv 1994	2ème étape de l'UEM : l'Institut monétaire européen (IME) est fondé en précurseur de la Banque centrale européenne
1995	Adhésion de l'Autriche, de la Finlande et de la Suède à l'UE
Déc 1995	La nouvelle monnaie est officiellement baptisée l'euro lors de la réunion du Conseil européen à Madrid. Entrée en vigueur de l'Union douanière entre l'UE et la Turquie
Mars 1996	Début de la Conférence intergouvernementale (CIG) à Turin : discussion des réformes institutionnelles de l'UE et préparations à un élargissement de l'UE
Déc 1996	Pacte de stabilité et de croissance pour assurer le maintien d'une discipline économique au sein des États membres de l'UE
1997	Signature du traité d'Amsterdam : résolution sur le SME II incluse ; extension de la codécision et réformes des piliers concernant la politique étrangère et la justice et les affaires intérieures
Mars 1998	Négociations d'adhésion avec Chypre, l'Estonie, la Hongrie, la Pologne, la République tchèque et la Slovénie ; mise en œuvre d'une stratégie européenne pour la Turquie
Mai 1998	Début officiel de l'UEM : les chefs d'État de l'UE décident quels États peuvent prétendre à l'adhésion à la monnaie unique, fixent le taux de conversion entre les devises et s'accordent à maintenir leurs économies respectives en conformité avec les critères de convergence
Juin 1998	Inauguration de la Banque centrale européenne (BCE)
Oct 1998	Le Conseil européen adopte des mesures de coopération en matière de défense
Janv 1999	L'euro devient la monnaie officielle des États de l'UEM : le taux de conversion de leur monnaie est figé par rapport à l'euro
Mars 1999	Adoption des propositions de l'Agenda 2000 visant à modifier les politiques de l'UE en prévision de l'élargissement
Janv 2000	Ouverture des négociations d'adhésion avec la Bulgarie, la Lettonie, la Lituanie, Malte, la Roumanie et la Slovaquie
· Déc 2000	Traité de Nice : il prépare les institutions en vue de l'élargissement et favorise une coopération renforcée entre les nations. Établissement de la Charte des droits fondamentaux
Fév 2001	Ratification du traité de Nice
Janv 2002	Introduction des billets et pièces en euros
Juil 2002	3ème étape de l'UEM : les billets et pièces des pays participant à l'UEM sont retirés de la circulation
Déc 2002	Sommet de Copenhague : 10 nouveaux pays (Chypre, l'Estonie, la Hongrie, la Lettonie, la Lituanie, Malte, la Pologne, la République tchèque, la Slovénie, la Slovaquie) accèderont à l'UE en 2004

vacance *nf (d'une fonction politique)* **pendant la vacance du siège** while the seat is empty; **une élection provoquée par la vacance du siège** an election made necessary because the seat became vacant; **pendant la vacance du pouvoir** while there is no one officially in power; **dû à la vacance du pouvoir** because there is no one officially in power; **il n'y aura pas de vacance du pouvoir** there will be a smooth transition of control

◇ *vacances parlementaires* Br Parliamentary recess, Am Congressional recess

vague de prospérité *nf Écon* boom

valeur *nf* (a) *Écon* value; **créer de la valeur pour l'actionnaire** to create shareholder value (b) **valeurs** *(actions, titres)* shares, Am stock

◇ *valeur ajoutée* added value, value added
◇ *valeur d'échange* exchange value
◇ *valeur marginale* marginal value
◇ *valeur au pair* parity value

valise diplomatique *nf* diplomatic bag, diplomatic pouch

valorisation *nf Écon (mise en valeur)* economic development; *(valeur)* enhanced value

valoriser *Écon* **1** *vt (région)* to develop the economy of; *(bien, monnaie)* to increase the value of

2 se valoriser *vpr* to increase in value; **un région/secteur qui se valorise** a region/an industry which is going through a period of growth, an up-and-coming region/industry

vaquer *vi (parlement)* to be on vacation

variable 1 *adj (taux)* variable
2 *nf Écon* variable

◇ *variable endogène* endogenous variable

variation *nf (fluctuation)* variation, change **(de** in**)**

◇ *Écon* **variations saisonnières** seasonal variations; **corrigé des variations saisonnières** seasonally adjusted

va-t-en-guerre 1 *adj inv* warmongering
2 *nmf inv* warmonger

> Les Etats-Unis disposent de l'appui des Philippines, les plus **va-t-en-guerre** de leurs alliés asiatiques. Depuis le début de l'année, Manille a accueilli des milliers de soldats américains, dont plus de mille ont assuré pendant six mois, dans le sud islamisé de l'archipel, la formation, l'équipement et la logistique des unités philippines qui y traquaient les extrémistes d'Abu Sayyaf.

vélocité *nf Écon* velocity

vendre *vt* to sell

vente *nf (opération)* sale; *(activité)* selling

◇ *Pol* **ventes d'armes** arms sales
◇ *ventes à l'exportation* export sales
◇ *vente à perte* dumping
◇ *Pol* **vente de voix** vote-selling

vert, -e 1 adj **(a)** (agricole, rural) agricultural, rural **(b)** (écologiste) green; **les candidats verts** the green candidates
2 nmpl Pol **les Verts** = the French Green Party

vertical, -e adj Écon (concentration, intégration) vertical

veto nm Pol veto; **mettre** ou **opposer son veto à une mesure** to veto a measure
◇ **veto formel** absolute veto

viabilité nf Écon (d'une entreprise, de l'économie, d'un État) viability

viable adj Écon (entreprise, économie, État) viable

vice-présidence nf (d'un État) vice-presidency; (d'un congrès, d'une entreprise) vice-chairmanship

vice-président, -e nm,f (d'un État) vice-president; (d'un congrès, d'une entreprise) vice-chairman, f vice-chairwoman, vice-chairperson

victoire nf Pol victory

vie nf **(a)** (conditions économiques) (cost of) living; **dans ce pays, la vie n'est pas chère** prices are very low in this country **(b)** Pol **à vie** for life, life

village planétaire nm Écon global village

ville nf town; (plus grande) city; **la ville** (administration) the local authority; (représentants) the (town) council; **financé par la ville** financed by the local authorities
◇ **ville ouverte** open city

virage nm Pol shift, change; **le parti prend un virage** the party is shifting ground or changing direction; **un virage net dans la vie politique du pays** a U-turn in the political life of the country
◇ **virage à droite** shift to the right
◇ **virage à gauche** shift to the left

virer virer à vt ind Pol **cette région a viré à gauche** this region has swung to the left

visite nf visit
◇ **visite officielle** official visit
◇ **visite privée** private visit

visiter vt to visit

vital, -e adj (économie) vital

vitalité nf (d'une économie) vitality

vitesse nf **à deux vitesses** two-tier, two-speed; **médecine/sécurité sociale à deux vitesses** two-tier medical/social security system; **une Europe à deux vitesses** a two-speed Europe
◇ Écon **vitesse de circulation de la monnaie** velocity of circulation of money
◇ Écon **vitesse de transformation des capitaux** income velocity of capital

voix nf Pol vote (pour/contre for/against); **un homme, une voix** one man one vote; **obtenir 1500 voix** to win or to get 1,500 votes; **donner sa voix à** to give one's vote to, to vote for; **recueillir** ou **remporter 57 pour cent des voix** to win 57 percent of the vote or votes; **le parti qui a le plus grand nombre de voix** the party which heads the poll or with the largest number of votes; **élu à la majorité des voix** elected by a majority; **mettre qch aux voix** to put sth to the vote; **où iront les voix du parti radical?** how will the Radical Party vote?; **avoir voix délibérative** to have the right to vote; **avoir voix prépondérante** to have the casting vote

volant nm
◇ Écon **volant de main-d'œuvre** labour reserve
◇ Écon **volant de sécurité** reserve fund
◇ Écon **volant de trésorerie** cash reserve

volet nm (d'une politique, d'un projet de loi) point, part; **une politique sociale en trois volets** a social policy in three points or parts
◇ UE **le volet social** the social chapter

volte-face nf inv (d'opinion, d'attitude) U-turn, about-turn, about-face; **le parti a fait une volte-face** the party did a U-turn

votant, -e *nm,f* voter

vote *nm* (a) *(voix)* vote (b) *(élection)* vote; *(action)* voting; **prendre part au vote** to go to the polls, to vote; **procédons** *ou* **passons au vote** let's have *or* take a vote (c) *(d'une loi)* passing; *(d'un projet de loi)* vote

◇ **vote par acclamation** voice vote
◇ **vote blanc** blank ballot paper
◇ **vote bloqué** = enforced vote on a text containing only government amendments
◇ **vote à bulletin secret** secret ballot
◇ **vote de confiance** vote of confidence
◇ **vote par correspondance** *Br* postal vote *or* ballot, *Am* absentee ballot vote défavorable "no" vote
◇ **vote de défiance** vote of no confidence
◇ **vote direct** direct vote
◇ **le vote des femmes** the women's vote
◇ **vote indirect** indirect vote
◇ **vote libre** free vote
◇ **vote à main levée** vote by show of hands
◇ **vote majoritaire** majority vote
◇ **vote nul** spoilt ballot paper
◇ **vote obligatoire** compulsory vote
◇ **vote pondéré** weighted vote
◇ **vote préférentiel** preferential voting
◇ **vote par procuration** proxy vote
◇ **vote de protestation** protest vote
◇ **vote réactionnaire** reactionary vote
◇ **vote secret** secret ballot
◇ **vote unique transférable** single transferable vote
◇ **vote utile** tactical vote

voter **1** *vt (loi)* to pass; *(projet de loi)* to vote for; *(budget)* to approve; **être voté** *(projet de loi)* to go through; **voter la peine de mort** to pass a vote in favour of capital punishment
  2 *vi* to vote; **voter à droite/à gauche/ au centre** to vote for the right/left/ centre; **voter pour qn** to vote for sb; **voter (pour les) conservateurs** to vote Conservative; **voter à main levée** to vote by show of hands; **voter par procuration** to vote by proxy; **voter contre/pour qch** to vote against/for sth; **on leur a demandé de voter pour ou contre la grève** they were balloted about the strike; **voter utile** to vote tactically; **votons sur la dernière motion présentée** let's (take a) vote on the last motion before us

ZLEA *nf* (*abrév* **Zone de libre-échange des Amériques**) FTAA

zone *nf* zone, area
◊ *zone démilitarisée* demilitarized zone
◊ *zone euro* euro area
◊ *zone franche* free zone
◊ *zone frontière* border area
◊ *zone de libre-échange* free-trade area
◊ *Zone de libre-échange des Amériques* Free-Trade Area of the Americas
◊ *zone monétaire* monetary area
◊ *zone sterling* sterling area

◊ *zone tampon* buffer zone

> Dix des treize pays candidats à l'Union vont se voir confirmer ... leur feuille de route pour terminer les négociations d'ici décembre en vue d'une adhésion en 2004. A Francfort, les dirigeants de la Banque centrale européenne ne tablent cependant pas sur un élargissement de la **zone euro** avant l'horizon 2006, dans l'hypothèse la plus favorable.

Sources of English Quotes
Sources de citations anglaises

ABOUT-FACE *The Guardian* 2001
ADVANCE MAN *Goizueta Magazine* 2001
AFFIRMATIVE ACTION *The Guardian* 2001
AGENDA *Foreign Policy* 2000
ALLEGIANCE www.wsws.org 1998
ALL-PARTY *The Washington Post* 1996
ANNOUNCE www.mediaresearch.org 2000
APPROVAL *USA Today* 2001
BACKBENCH *The Guardian* 2001
BALKANIZE www.bbc.co.uk 2001
BANANA REPUBLIC *Asian Economic News* 2000
BELTWAY *The Chief Executive* 2001
BIG *USA Today* 2002
BLAIR BABE *The Independent* 2001
BOOM *The Guardian* 2002
BUBBLE www.bbc.co.uk 2001
BUSHITE *The Seattle News* 2002
CARPETBAGGER *The Washington Post* 1999
CHAMPAGNE *The Guardian* 2002
CHILTERN HUNDREDS www.bbc.co.uk 1997/2000
CLIENT *The Chicago Tribune* 2001
COATTAIL EFFECT www.thisnation.com 2002
COLLECTIVE *The Guardian* 2002
COMPASSIONATE CONSER-VATISM *The Guardian* 2002
CONSENSUS POLITICS *New Statesman* 1998
CONVICTION POLITICS *The Guardian* 2002
CRONY www.cnn.com 2002
DARK HORSE www.outreach.psu.edu 2000
DEFICIT www.worldgameofeconomics.com 2002
DEPENDENCY *The Guardian* 2002
DESELECT *The Guardian* 2002
DIEHARD *The Guardian* 1999
DIRTY www.worldsocialism.org 2002

DISPATCH www.telegraph.co.uk 2001
DOUGHNUT *The Daily Telegraph* 2002
DRY www.worldsocialism.org 2002
EARLY DAY MOTION www.emfguru.org 2000
ECONOMIC www.bbc.co.uk 2002
E-ECONOMY *The Scotland Office* 2002
ELECTED www.bbc.co.uk 2001
ENTERPRISE *The Guardian* 2002
ESTABLISHMENT www.bbc.co.uk 2002
EUROBABBLE *The Guardian* 2002
EURO-REBEL *The Guardian* 2002
EXIT www.freep.com 2002
FAVORITE SON *The Hill* 2002
FED www.wired.com 2000
FIRESIDE CHAT *The New York Observer* 2000
FIRST www.bbc.co.uk 2001
FRONTBENCH *The Guardian* 2002
GANGWAY *The Guardian* 2001
GERRYMANDERING www.insideonline.com 2002
GOP *The Guardian* 2002
GRASS ROOTS www.bbc.co.uk 2002
GUILLOTINE *The Guardian* 2001
HAWK www.bbc.co.uk 2002
HONEYMOON PERIOD www.bbc.co.uk 2002
HOT www.washblade.com 2002
IMPEACHMENT *The Observer* 2002
INAUGURAL www.newsmax.com 2001
INDUSTRIALIZED *The Guardian* 2002
INFANT INDUSTRY *Corporation for Enterprise Development* 2000
INFLUENCE PEDDLING *Insight* 2001
INNER CIRCLE *The Guardian* 2002
INWARD INVESTMENT www.bbc.co.uk 2001
JUST WAR *Daily Southtown* 2002

KITCHEN CABINET *The Guardian* 2002

LAME-DUCK PRESIDENT *Christian Science Monitor* 1999

LANDSLIDE *The Guardian* 2002

LEFTY *The Washington Times* 2002

LOBBY www.bbc.co.uk 2002

LOGROLLING *Le Québécois libre* 2001

MAIDEN SPEECH www.andrewduffmep.org 1999

MANDARIN www.alba.org.uk 2000

MARGINAL *The Guardian* 2002

MAVERICK www.bbc.co.uk 1999

MISERY INDEX www.worldbank.org 2000

MORAL HAZARD *British Medical Journal* 2000

NANNY STATE *Freedom Today* 2002

NATIVIST *The Guardian* 2000

NEGOTIATING TABLE *The Guardian* 2002

NEW www.spiked-online.com 2001

NUMBER *The Observer* 2002

OFFICIAL www.bbc.co.uk 2002

OFF-MESSAGE www.bbc.co.uk 1998

ON-MESSAGE www.sourceuk.net 1999

OVAL OFFICE *The Observer* 2002

OVERTIME *Newsbytes News Network* 2000

PARACHUTED CANDIDATE www.nsnews.com 2002

PARTY *News Tribune* 2001

PLACE *The Guardian* 2002

PMQS *The Guardian* 2002

POCKET *Newsbytes News Network* 2000

POLITICAL *The Guardian* 2002

POLLING *St Petersburg Times* 2000

PORK-BARREL www.deanesmay.com 2002

POVERTY *The Guardian* 2000

PRESIDENTIAL *Roll Call* 2001

PRIVY www.bbc.co.uk 1999

PROROGUE *People's Daily* 2001

PUMP-PRIMING www.newaus.com.au 2001

QUESTION *The Guardian* 2002

RATCHET EFFECT *The Minimum Wage and Poverty: A Critical Evaluation* 2000

REBEL *New Statesman* 2001

REGISTER *The Guardian* 1999

RESHUFFLE *The Guardian* 2001

RING-FENCE *The Guardian* 2002

RUBBER www.cnn.com 2002

RUNNING MATE www.wsws.org 2000

SAFE SEAT *The Guardian* 2001

SECTION 28 www.bbc.co.uk 2000

SHUTTLE DIPLOMACY *The Guardian* 2002

SHYSTER *The Guardian* 2002

SIN TAX *The Guardian* 2000

SLEAZE www.bbc.co.uk 2002

SLUMPFLATION *Finance and Development* 1999

SOUNDBITE www.bbc.co.uk 2002

SPECIAL *The Guardian* 2002

SPIN *The Times* 2002

STAGFLATION *Finance and Development* 1999

STALKING HORSE *New Statesman* 2002

STEALTH TAX *The Guardian* 2002

STEAMROLLER www.bbc.co.uk 2002

STUMP www.oweb.com 2002

SWING www.news-record.com 2002

TAX www.bbc.co.uk 2002

THIRD *New Statesman* 2001

THREE-LINE WHIP *The Guardian* 2002

TOUCHSTONE ISSUE *The Guardian* 2002

TRICKLE-DOWN ECONOMICS *The Guardian* 2002

TRUSTBUSTER www.bloomberg.com 2002

UNION-BASHING www.bbc.co.uk 2002

VISIBLE www.bbc.co.uk 2002

VOODOO ECONOMICS *Dollar & Sense* 2001

VOTER www.bbc.co.uk 2001

WATCHDOG *New Statesman* 2001

WHISPERING CAMPAIGN *The Guardian* 2002

WOOLSACK *The Guardian* 2002

WRECKING AMENDMENT *The Guardian* 2002

ZERO www.bbc.co.uk 2002